International Cooking
A CULINARY JOURNEY

Patricia A. Heyman

Upper Saddle River, NJ 07458

Library of Congress Cataloging-in-Publication Data

Heyman, Patricia A., date
   International cooking : a culinary journey / Patricia A. Heyman.
      p.   cm.
   Includes bibliographical references and index.
   ISBN 0-13-032659-3
   1. Cookery, International.   I. Title.

TX725.A1 H48 2002
641 .59—dc21
                                        2002020573

Editor-in-Chief: Stephen Helba
Executive Assistant: Nancy Kesterson
Executive Acquisitions Editor: Vern Anthony
Director of Manufacturing and Production: Bruce Johnson
Assistant Editor: Marion Gottlieb
Editorial Assistant: Ann Brunner
Managing Editor: Mary Carnis
Production Liaison: Adele M. Kupchik
Marketing Manager: Ryan DeGrote
Production Management: Karen Berry/Pine Tree Composition, Inc.
Manufacturing Manager: Ilene Sanford
Manufacturing Buyer: Cathleen Petersen
Creative Director: Cheryl Asherman
Senior Design Coordinator: Miguel Ortiz
Design Coordinator: Christopher Weigand
Formatting: Pine Tree Composition, Inc.
Copyeditor: Diane D. Burke
Printer/Binder: Courier Kendallville
Cover Designer: Kevin Kall
Cover Illustration: Larry Moore/Stock Illustration Source
Cover Printer: Coral Graphics

Pearson Education LTD.
Pearson Education Australia PTY, Limited
Pearson Education Singapore, Pte. Ltd
Pearson Education North Asia Ltd
Pearson Education Canada, Ltd.
Pearson Educación de Mexico, S.A. de C.V.
Pearson Education—Japan
Pearson Education Malaysia, Pte. Ltd

10 9 8 7 6 5 4
ISBN 0-13-032659-3

Dedicated to four who are in my heart forever—

For limitless love and support:
Lisa Heyman, my mom
and
Alan Roer, my husband

I wish you could see this book:
Julius Heyman, my dad
and
Emma Frank, my Oma

CONTENTS

PREFACE

People say the world is becoming smaller. Of course, the world is not shrinking, but more accessible travel, familiarity with people from foreign lands, and efficient communication make faraway destinations seem not so remote.

No longer reserved for the wealthy, travel to foreign lands is obtainable for many people. The price of an airline ticket to Europe often costs less than flying from New York to California, and myriad flights travel overseas every day. So even though college spring break used to mean a trip to Florida for the lucky, now a week in Paris or scuba diving in Belize fits into the realm of spring break possibilities.

With the help of telephones, computers, wireless technology, satellites, and planes, business and pleasure truly span the globe. As a result, more and more people are familiar with foods from foreign lands, and dishes from all corners of the world penetrate the menus of other cuisines.

Although culinary schools used to teach continental cookery primarily covering the cuisines found in Europe, this no longer suffices. Now, international cookery is the necessary course. As travel to Asia, Latin America, and destinations throughout the world has increased, so has the interest and knowledge of cuisines spanning the globe.

Demographic changes also have altered our perspective of the world. Great increases in the number of immigrants play a significant part in the composition of cities, schools, and neighborhoods. Of course, ethnic restaurants thrive in areas with substantial ethnic population, leading to these cuisines becoming more mainstream throughout the United States. According to the last census, the fastest growing ethnic groups in the United States are Hispanics and Asians. Mexican and Asian restaurants proliferate. No wonder salsa replaced ketchup as the leading condiment in the United States. Today, many businesses operate globally. Companies from around the world relocate employees to other countries for varied periods of time. The influx of people from foreign lands leads to familiarity with other cultures and cuisines, as well as adding to the ethnic diversity of neighborhoods.

Immigration and birthrates continue to change the demographics throughout the world. Predictions released from the United Nations estimate that about 87 percent of the world's population will consist of people from Asia, Africa, and Latin America by 2050. The remaining 13 percent will reside in other regions, including North America and Europe. People from densely populated, developing countries continue to seek opportunities in more prosperous nations. As a result, many immigrate to the more affluent countries. So although the world is not shrinking, it certainly is changing, and that change results in people being exposed to more countries, more cultures, and more cuisines.

GOAL OF THE BOOK

The goal of this book is to provide a comprehensive picture of cuisines found throughout the world by presenting information about the food and culture as well as recipes. Explanation focuses on the development of each cuisine, therefore making the evolution seem both logical and natural. This is accomplished through an understanding of many issues that molded the cuisine.

PREMISE OF THE BOOK

What makes each cuisine unique? This book shows that neither random selection nor chance caused a cuisine to develop as it did. First, many of a cuisine's culinary traits result from conditions that naturally exist in the region or country—factors such as the geography, topography, climate, what grows/is raised there, and historical influences from settlers, invaders, and bordering countries.

Second, although often determined by the factors listed earlier, many food issues create the differences that distinguish one cuisine from another. The preferred carbohydrate, whether rice, pasta, bread, or corn, makes a significant impact on the cuisine. How can one think of the Asian cuisines without thinking of rice? The herbs, spices, and other flavorings utilized in the cooking create the taste associated with each country. For example, chili peppers are identified with Mexican cookery. Finally, the variety of protein consumed in the region further defines the cuisine. A preference for lamb in the Middle East, the absence of beef in India, and the abundance of seafood and fish in areas near water characterize the cuisine. All these issues clearly affected the cookery in each region and country, causing it to evolve into the cuisine it is today.

ORGANIZATION OF THE BOOK

Each chapter is divided into six sections: history, topography, common food ingredients and flavorings, cooking methods, regions, and general characteristics of the cuisine. The development and the evolution of each cuisine are apparent through an understanding of the issues discussed in these sections. Following this, each chapter contains a glossary (a master glossary is located in the back of the book), a chart summarizing the material covered in the chapter, and a selection of recipes characteristic of the cuisine and its heritage with dishes representing all segments of the menu. The collection of recipes contains at least one first course, soup, salad, vegetable, starch, and dessert. When appropriate, the choice of entrées includes a selection of meat, poultry, and seafood to offer sufficient variety. Hopefully, the group of recipes is well rounded enough to prepare a successful buffet representing the country(ies) in the chapter.

Throughout history and today, wine has been valued for enhancing food, as well as the whole dining experience. Food and wine pairing is an important aspect of dining today and should be included in a book of this type. Beringer Blass Winery has provided wine recommendations for each first course, soup, and entrée. Also, Jerry Comfort, executive chef at Beringer Blass Winery, wrote an introduction for this book that explains their philosophy and guidelines for food and wine pairing.

The cooking method(s) involved appear at the top of each recipe. My colleague, Bob Chapman, always told his students that there are only six ways to cook—no matter what you're cooking. Whether the cuisine is American, French, or Chinese, the six cooking methods remain bake/roast, grill/broil, braise, boil/simmer/poach/steam, sauté, and deep-fry. Braising is braising, regardless of what spices and flavorings surround the foods. Please let that thought help to demystify the journey through cookery from around the world.

Some chapters cover one country, others include two or more countries, and still others contain a whole continent. Choosing to group countries together or exclude them from this book occurred for two reasons: the time limitations of a course and the magnitude of the task of covering every country in the world. As a result, I tried to include countries that are culinary representatives of the world.

Many of the European countries covered in a continental cookery course are individually discussed. They remain the most familiar cuisines to many of the dining customers, and they still guide many of the cookery principles and standards in the western world. This does not lessen the profound, significant, and growing influence from a myriad of other "lesser known" cuisines that are included in this book. Realize that the popularity and influence of any particular cuisine continually changes. Triggered by a limitless number of factors, trends come and go, leaving today's hottest cuisines passé tomorrow.

Although this book probably contains too many chapters for a one-semester course, I included countries knowing that the instructor might need to omit some. Rather than write a textbook that fits into a semester, I opted to offer a valuable book for one's personal library covering cuisines from around the world.

WHY I WROTE THIS BOOK

The idea for this book began when I was the program coordinator for the culinary arts program at Jefferson Community College in Louisville, Kentucky. Searching in vain for a book on international cuisine for our students, I called colleagues across the country only to find that they did just what we did—lectured on the cuisine and distributed lots of handouts. So, finally, here is the book I wanted to find!

MY HOPE

Writing this book has been a joy on many levels. For more than two years, I submerged myself into researching and learning about the cultures and cuisines of other lands and testing over 250 recipes. Although I have barely scratched the surface of knowledge about the world's cuisines, it's been a fascinating culinary journey!

I always tell my students before espousing strong personal opinions, "This is from the world according to Patsy." So here are some thoughts from my world—I strongly believe that knowledge of a cuisine is an important part in understanding the culture and the people who live there. Armed with knowledge, we can understand and appreciate others for both their similarities and differences to us. It is my sincere hope that this book will open some doors to knowledge of other cuisines and cultures, which will lead to greater tolerance for others.

INTRODUCTION TO FOOD AND WINE PAIRING

When Patricia asked me to recommend the food and wine pairings for the recipes in this book, I told her that I view food and wine pairing in an unconventional way. Instead of the traditional manner of my suggesting a single wine for each dish, I want people to understand why they are pairing a particular wine or wine style with a recipe. Through that understanding, people can select a wine that they would enjoy with the dish.

Let me start by giving a little background on me and explaining my philosophy of food and wine pairing. I have been cooking for over twenty-five years and became very serious about food and wine in the late 1970s while living in San Francisco. At the time, I was working as a *sous* chef at the Stanford Court Hotel, one of eight 5-star hotels in the United States. One of my mentors, the general manager of the hotel, Jim Nassikas, was passionate about food and wine. Here I first tasted different varietals of wines in their proper glasses—now Riedel makes a different glass for just about every type of wine.

After leaving the Stanford Court Hotel, I opened the restaurant Masa's, my first French three-star restaurant experience. At Masa's, we often ended the evening with John Cunin bringing in a different wine from the wine list concealed in a brown bag. The goal was to taste the wine and guess what it was.

I left Masa's to open Star's with Jeremiah Tower. Although many think of Tower as the king of California cuisine, he was passionately tied to the classics. He had a recommended reading list for the staff composed of Escoffier's *Le Guide Culinaire* for technique and Richard Olney and Elizabeth David for philosophy.

My next move took me to Napa Valley to become *chef de cuisine* at Moet Chandon's California winery, Domaine Chandon. At this winery restaurant, we paired food with wine daily, using the traditional manner of food and wine pairing. It was at Domaine Chandon that a great friend of mine, General Manager Daniel Shanks, taught me how to make wine. I've been an avid home winemaker for over fifteen years.

I then moved to Los Angeles to open Campton Place's sister hotel "Checkers" which was named one of the top ten new restaurants by *Esquire* that year. After that, I returned to Napa Valley both as executive chef of Beringer Vineyards and to raise my children in the wine country.

This is when food and wine pairing became more interesting for me. At about the same time I was hired, Beringer hired the first American "Master of Wine," Tim Hanni, truly my mentor when it comes to food and wine pairing. I like to call Tim the "Dr. Frankenstein of Wine Gurus," and I'm the monster he created. As I worked with Tim, I realized I had been pairing food and wine in the traditional methods that almost everyone used. Typically, food and wine pairing is based upon a few methods or theories.

One method is to copy the food and wine pairing of a wine-producing region such as Italy, France (Bordeaux, Burgundy, Alsace), Spain, Germany, and so on. The problem with this method is that when we say Riesling, Chardonnay, Cabernet Sauvignon, or Sangiovese, the wine varieties and clone types grown in different countries, terrains, and climates vary greatly from each other. As a result, wines produced from the same type of grape but grown in different regions might vary significantly. The same principle applies to the food ingredients used in a recipe. For example, the beef available in Chile is quite different from the beef in Iowa, so the same beef dish prepared in those two places will differ in taste and/or texture.

Second, the mirroring method imitates the color, flavors, and the so-called weight of the wine with the ingredients of the food. One example is a light Chardonnay with tropical fruit bouquet and a buttery finish paired with delicate white fish or poultry with tropical fruit chutney and a butter sauce. Or a heavy red wine with blackberry fruit aromas and spicy black pepper flavors becomes paired with a peppered venison roast (also heavy and red) served with a blackberry port sauce. In a few cases, we mirror the dominant taste of the food to that of the wine, such as sweet food with sweet wine (*foie gras* with aspic and Sauterne) or acidic food with acidic wine (oysters mignonette with Muscadet/Sancerre). These examples are extremes and not universally applied; however, although most recipes fall somewhere in between these two examples, they generally do have a dominant taste. Unfortunately, we still don't know why either the copying or mirroring methods work or do not work.

The third method is the "real world" food and wine pairing. This occurs when four people go out to eat and order one bottle of wine to accompany four different entrées. Or each person orders a different wine by the glass and then everyone orders the same special of the day. Who has successfully paired the food and wine?

To deal with all these variations, we developed the Beringer Food and Wine in Balance philosophy. Madeleine Kamman, a legendary chef, teacher, and the creator of the Beringer School for American Chefs, asked Tim to teach the food and wine pairing segment in her school. Tim isolated foods that created specific reactions with wine and showed which wines should not be served with those foods. Tim called this the "cause and effect." He then began to evolve this theory into menu form so we could show which wines tasted best with specific foods.

Traditionally, wine selection focused on the center of the plate item, but we realized that the meat usually had the least reaction with the wine. Instead, it seemed that the sauces, vegetables, and seasonings played the larger role. We created a menu that had a sweet sauce and a sour sauce to illustrate the point that the chicken breast or meat had little effect on the wine, but the sauces played a major part. It was here, I observed, that seasoning each sauce properly created a balance that reduced the reaction with the wine. Tim and I played with many elements from salt, sweet, sour, to spicy. At about this time, Tim changed the direction of the seminar. Instead of concentrating on which wine not to serve with certain foods, the main issue became the idea that you could balance these dominant tastes in foods to taste delicious with any wine. Now we focused on the dominant taste in a dish: salty, sour, sweet, or a new taste, *umami*, which is also called the protein taste.

On a business trip to Nestle, Beringer's owner at that time, Tim did some research in the food data bank and found several articles on the Asian discovery of *umami*, the fifth taste sensation. *Umami* is the taste of the amino acid, glutamic acid, and/or the taste of two ribonucleotides. Basically, glutamic acid is found in virtually anything that grows (meats, fish, poultry, dairy products, fruits, vegetables, grains, and legumes). Remember we are talking about tastes, not the complexities of flavor. Good examples of the *umami* taste are the insides of an unseasoned baked potato, a cooked but unseasoned mushroom, tofu, or very fresh unseasoned sushi.

The four most dominant tastes are salty, sour, sweet, and protein. Bitter is also a recognized taste sensation, but its perception is too inconsistent to apply evenly. Although spice is not classified as a "taste," it does affect the flavor of the wine. The acknowledgment of these tastes helps explain certain reactions with wines. Here is how we apply this understanding to the balance of a dish.

A wine maker intentionally makes each wine to taste the way it does. You select a wine because you like its taste. Now the variable: food changes the way a wine tastes. The dominant taste in food will change all wines (all varietals from all countries) in the same way but in varying degrees. When the food changes the flavor of the wine only minimally, we call it a good or seamless food and wine pairing or marriage.

Sweet, protein, or spice dominant foods should be paired to the softer, lighter styles of wines. To illustrate this, taste a wine, and then eat a recipe predominately sweet or high in *umami* (the protein taste). Follow that food with another taste of wine, and the perception of the wine's acidity and/or astringency will rise. If there is bitterness or tannins, they will become more pronounced. We describe this as the wine getting stronger. A lighter style of wine will not react as much as a stronger style. For an example of poor balance or a beverage getting stronger, just think of the last time you brushed your teeth (toothpaste is sweet) and then drank a glass of orange juice (acid balanced).

Salty and acidic foods lower our perception of a wine's acidity and soften the astringency/bitterness/tannins. We describe this as making the wine milder or softer. Salty and acidic foods can be enjoyed with a wide variety of wines, including the strongest styles. To select lighter or stronger styles of wine, an understanding of the taste profile of each wine is necessary. Tim was asked to categorize the wines of Beringer Wine Estates, which includes six different wineries: Beringer Vineyards, Château St. Jean, Château Souverain, Stags' Leap Winery, St. Clement, and Meridian. Tim realized that without tasting the wines together, it was difficult to convey the different tastes and styles of each winery's wines. As a result, he decided to categorize them based on their flavor profile from the lightest, fruitiest, and least oak to the strongest and most astringent or tannic. He called this Beringer's Progressive Wine List. It is essential to understand that this list relates to how each wine will react or taste with food. The following information is a shortened version of Beringer's Progressive Wine List. When categorizing wines, these characteristics can be applied to all wines in general, by varietal, by country, or by region.

1. Soft and fruity, no oak, and listed from the sweetest to least sweet. These include Johannisberg Riesling, Gewürztraminer, Chenin Blanc, Semillion, Marsanne, Blush wines, and so on.
2. Light and fruity, white wine, dry (without sweetness), and no oak. Can include the above and champagne/sparkling wines, Sauvignon Blanc, Pinot Gris, Chardonnay, Pinot Grigio, Pinot Blanc, Viognier, and so on.
3. Strong white wines from the least amount of oak to the most. Can include all the above and other varietals, including Pinot Blanc, Sauvignon Blanc, and Chardonnay.
4. Soft and fruity red wines (not much oak or tannins). Can include Beaujolais, Dolcetto, Rosé, Pinot Noir, Shiraz, Sangiovese, Nebbiolo, Merlot, and Tempranillo.

5. Light red wines with light oak, astringency, and soft tannins. Can include the above and some Zinfandels, Cabernet Sauvignon, Mouvedre, Syrah, Petite Syrah, and Amarone.

6. Strong red wines with firmer tannins to strong tannins. Can include the above and many Cabernet Sauvignons, Barolo, Merlot, Super Tuscans, and so on.

For a simple exercise to illustrate this at home, take a medium-bodied red wine, a slice of lemon, a wedge of sweet red apple, and a salt shaker. Taste the wine first to see how the wine maker intended it to taste, then take a bite of the apple. The wine becomes more sour, bitter and tannic. Now suck on the lemon, and try the wine again. Now the wine becomes milder because the lemon has more acidity than the wine. Next, do what we call the tequila shot—put a few drops of lemon on your hand and sprinkle it with salt. Lick this and try the wine; the wine becomes very mild. Salt reduces our perception of the bitterness and tannins. This experiment reflects what happens when a dish is balanced like the apple (sweet). Protein makes the wine's astringency stronger so we say it makes the wine stronger, too. If the dish has an acid/salt balance, the wine tastes milder. Spice is also reactive to stronger styles of wines, so, unless there is a lot of acidity, the lighter styles of wine change less.

There are two ways to apply this knowledge. The first involves defining the balance of the dish, identifying the dominant tastes, and then selecting a wine from the Progressive Wine List that will change the least. A recipe can be very complex with a wide variety of flavors and aromas, but, when you reduce each recipe to its basic taste, it will have a dominant taste. In order to utilize this system, we need to identify the basic tastes, such as sweet, sour, salty, protein, and the sensation of hot spices.

The second way to apply this knowledge is to adjust the balance of the dish so most wines taste good. This is accomplished by slightly adjusting the seasonings and acid balance that is often already in the dish, thereby creating a less reactive dish. Generally, most food is dominant in either the protein taste or the sweetness. This includes ripe vegetables, fruits, and the addition of sweet sauces or glazes.

So how should the wine suggestions for each recipe in this book be used? First, I identified the dominant taste in each dish. Then I suggested a wine style along with some recommendations that illustrate that style. There will be others that fit that style so don't hesitate to substitute other wines. I have given a specific recommendation or example for those who want to try a direct suggestion. As you read through the book and begin to experiment with the wine suggestions, try a wine that you think might fit that category or try a wine from another category to see its reaction with the food. Will it be like the apple or the lemon and salt? Who knows what you might like? That's the last idea to remember. Wine pairing is very subjective and personal. So relax, enjoy these great recipes and some wonderful wines.

Jerry Comfort, Executive Chef
Beringer Blass Winery

NOTES ON USING THIS BOOK

Always read the entire recipe before beginning. Reading through the recipe makes it easy to understand the preparation, assembly, and overview of what the recipe involves. Then gather all the needed ingredients.

Another topic, the homemade stock versus stock prepared from bases, must be addressed. For better or worse, because of labor and money issues, the majority of cooks and chefs use prepared bases for stocks. Of course, the recipes in this book do not designate homemade or stock prepared from bases; however, most bases are quite salty. As a result, recipes containing stock include little or no salt in the ingredients. Toward the end of every recipe, instructions call for correcting the seasonings. At that point, the recipe should be tasted and then salt or any other needed seasonings should be added. Remember that it is easier to add more salt at the end of the recipe than to remove salt from the dish!

Every recipe in this book includes both weight and volume measurements. Although all the culinary schools I have visited use scales, that might not be the case in every restaurant or catering kitchen. Certainly, I have worked in restaurants without scales or with only one digital scale. With both measurements available, anyone can prepare the recipes in this book.

Finally, this international cookery book obviously contains many ingredients not commonly used in North American cookery. Throughout this book, my goal was to keep the unusual ingredients to a minimum so that the recipes can be prepared in areas that do not have large ethnic communities. Don't let the foreign-sounding ingredients intimidate you! Most of the ingredients listed in this book can be obtained from a large supermarket. An Asian market will carry many of the ingredients needed for India, as well as the Oriental and Middle Eastern cuisines. I even bought a few of the dried peppers needed for the Mexican recipes from a Mexican restaurant in town. A natural foods store or co-op might also sell some of the herbs, spices, or other items needed for the recipes. If an ingredient cannot be found, substitute. Many foreign cheeses are similar to ones easily obtained in the United States. Although the taste or melting quality might not be exactly as it is in the native country, it should be close enough to prepare the dish and enjoy it. Substitute freely if necessary, but try to use the listed ingredients, if at all possible, to create the most authentic dish.

WEB SITES

A world of information exists on the Web, but obtaining that information often presents a formidable challenge. After much searching, I have compiled a list of Web sites that contain information about some of the countries discussed in this book, food products, and recipes. There are literally thousands of Web sites with information and/or recipes on international cuisines. This list represents just a small portion of the sites available in "cyberland."

Web sites for embassies, consulates, and national tourism agencies often contain worthwhile information about the history, customs, foods, and food traditions of the country. Food companies and organizations feature particular products and recipes utilizing their products.

A disclaimer—Web sites come and go, so realize that this list is constantly changing and some of these sites may disappear. I view this merely as a start for further research...

COUNTRIES:

www.gksoft.com	lists Web sites of country's tourism agencies
www.totaltravel.com	lists many countries' ministry and tourism agencies
www.chef2chef.com	many countries
www.soar.berkley.edu/recipes	many countries
www.kitchenlink.com	many countries
www.globalgourmet.com	many countries
www.ethnicgrocer.com	many countries
www.about.com	many countries
www.sallys-place.com	many countries
www.abica.com	many countries
www.goyafoods.com	Latin America, Caribbean
www.latinsynergy.org	Central and South America—look under countries' references
www.mexico-travel.com	Mexico
www.cocinamexicana.com.mx/ingles.html	Mexico
www.jamaicatravel.com	Jamaica
www.brazil.org.uk	Brazil
www.mincom.gov.ma	Morocco
www.ziyad.com	Middle East
www.touregypt.net	Egypt
www.turizm.gov.tr	Turkey
www.kultur.gov.tr	Turkey
www.syriatourism.org	Syria
www.kulturdanmark.dk	Denmark
www.denmarkemb.org	Denmark
www.norway.org	Norway
http://italianfood.about.com	Italy
www.italianmade.com	Italy
www.mangiarebene.net	Italy

www.italiantourism.com	Italy
www.agferrari.com	Italy
www.portugal-insite.pt	Portugal
www.portugal.org	Portugal
www.portugal-live.net/essential/food	Portugal
www.russianfoods.com	Russia and Eastern Europe
www.gotohungary.com	Hungary
www.fsz.bme.hu	Hungary
www.orientalfood.com	Asian countries
www.bitesofasia.com	Asian countries
www.thaitrade.com	Thailand
www.tourismthailand.org	Thailand
http://expo.nectec.or.th	Thailand
www.tat.or.th	Thailand—contains section on food
www.visitkorea.or.kr	Korea (click on restaurants)
www.bento.com/tokyofood.html	Japan
www.jnto.go.jp/interests/eating	Japan
www.jin.jcic.or.jp	Japan
www.discoverhongkong.com/usa	Hong Kong
www.visit-china-97.com	China
www.cnta.com	China
www.cnto.com	China
www.indiagov.org	India
www.tourismofindia.com	India
http://india-tourism.de	India—check links
www.fhraindia.com/home/state	India—history
www.itihaas.com	India—history
www.australia.com	Australia—click on about Australia

MEAT:

www.mla.com.au	Australia—beef and lamb
www.nzbeeflamb.co.nz	New Zealand—beef and lamb information and recipes
www.veal.org	veal
www.beeftips.org	beef and veal—Wisconsin Beef Council
www.beef.org	beef
www.angusbeef.com	beef
www.beeffoodservice.com	beef
www.otherwhitemeat.com	pork
www.lambchef.com	lamb

POULTRY:

www.mapleleaffarms.com	duck
www.turkeyfed.org	turkey
www.eatchicken.com	chicken
www.tyson.com	chicken

SEAFOOD:

www.seafood.no/worldwide	Norwegian Seafood Export Council
www.ca-seafood.com	California seafood
www.fl-seafood.com	Florida seafood
www.nfi.org	National Fisheries Institute
www.seafood.is	Icelandic Seafood

www.horizonfoods.com	seafood
www.alaskaseafood.org	Alaska seafood
www.seafood.com	seafood

CHEESE:

www.polliofs.com	cheese company
www.cheesefromspain.com	Spanish cheeses
www.cheese.com	cheeses from many countries
www.cheese-online.com	French cheeses
www.aco-igp.com	Designation of Origin (DO) cheeses

BEANS:

www.americanbeans.org	American Dry Bean Board
www.pea-lentil.com	USA Dry Pea and Lentil Council

FRUITS AND VEGETABLES:

www.avocado.org	avocado
www.idahopotato.com	potatoes
www.mainepotatoes.com	potatoes
www.aboutproduce.com	produce
www.caltreefruit.com	peaches, plums, nectarines

OLIVE OIL:

www.bertolli.com	
www.colavita.com	
www.asoliva.com	Spanish olive oil

SEASONINGS:

www.astaspice.org	information on spices
www.monafederzoni.com	balsamic vinegar
www.kikkoman.com	Kikkoman soy sauce and other products

MISCELLANEOUS:

www.abika.com	various countries and food products (click on "How To" Guides on side menu bar, then click on Food and Recipes)
www.foodgalaxy.com	check industry links
www.vino.eunet.es	Spanish products—olive oil, Serrano ham, wine
www.riceusa.com	rice
www.riceweb.org	rice history, production, and recipes
www.macsoc.com.au	macadamia nuts
www.almondsarein.com	almonds
www.dececco.it	pasta
www.pasta.com	pasta
www.pastalabella.com	pasta
www.ilovepasta.org	pasta
www.professionalpasta.it	pasta
www.landolakes.com	butter
www.cuisinenet.com	various ingredients
www.unlv.edu/tourism	links to many food-related sites
www.aeb.org	American Egg Board
www.goya.com	Goya Foods—Latin American and Caribbean recipes

ACKNOWLEDGMENTS

So many people have helped and supported me with this endeavor. First and foremost, my husband, Alan Roer, and my mom, Lisa Heyman. They have listened, offered advice, encouraged me, and given as much help, support, and love as possible. Many friends, including Holly, Judy, Laraine, Patti, and more, cared about this project and me. I thank all the people who tasted over 250 recipes that I tested for this book—two years of dinner parties and get-togethers that Alan and I will never forget. More thanks to my entire family, including my stepchildren who can finally quit wondering when I'll finish this book, and to my father-in-law, Irving Roer, who really wanted to see this book in print—I wish he could have.

Wine has become an intrinsic part of the dining experience, and I think all culinary textbooks should include wine pairings with the recipes. I am thrilled for the collaboration with Beringer Blass Winery and Jerry Comfort, executive chef at Beringer Blass Winery. When I first spoke with Jerry about the idea of including a wine pairing suggestion with each recipe, his initial response was "What a great idea!" His enthusiasm for this project never wavered. Jerry, I appreciate your hard work and know that your input increases the value of this book as a reference tool for the student/cook/chef/manager in the future. I hope we have started a trend so that future textbooks will include this valuable asset, too. Thank you, Jerry.

Much gratitude to Jim Tedesco and the people at Alliant Foodservice in Clifton Park, New York, for generously allowing me to use their test kitchen for the sequential photography shots. Another thanks to Carl Petrone at Buffalo Hotel Supply Company for loaning me dishes to use for the photography.

I also want to thank the many individuals representing organizations around the world that provided photographs for use in this book or helped me track down someone who had the "right" photograph. Through countless e-mails sent, I encountered many, many helpful individuals who went out of their way to help me (a stranger) find photographs for this book. Often, it made me pause and think how many kind people are out there.

Thank you to the reviewers of this book: David Wasson, North Seattle Community College, and Rick Swartz, Harford Community College.

Finally, thanks to all the people at Prentice Hall for their help, guidance, and for making it possible for this idea of mine to become a reality. In addition, thanks to the reviewer who suggested that I list Web sites. I immediately knew that was a great idea and would be a valuable tool for anyone wanting to explore international cookery. Constantly changing, the Internet contains a wealth of information for anyone wishing to learn more. Like with wine pairings, Web site references need to be part of every textbook.

Unfortunately, I cannot name everyone, but many more are in my heart. Thank you all—I realize what a lucky woman I am.

CHAPTER 1
British Isles

By the end of this chapter, you will be able to

- Name foods that are available in the British Isles and explain why those particular foods are prevalent
- Identify similarities and differences between the cuisines of the various countries of the British Isles
- Identify cooking methods commonly used in the British Isles
- Name some foods typically served at tea and in a pub
- Prepare a variety of dishes from the British Isles

HISTORY

The British Isles consists of the islands of Great Britain, Ireland, several larger islands, and about 5,500 small islands. The countries of England, Scotland, and Wales make up the island of Great Britain while Ireland contains two countries, Northern Ireland and Ireland. Protected by the surrounding water, the British Isles endured relatively few invasions throughout history.

Evidence found in caves confirms the existence of Old Stone Age people more than 10,000 years ago in Britain. By 3000 B.C., inhabitants of this land were raising cattle, pigs, sheep, and crops.

Julius Caesar discovered Britain in 55 B.C. Soon after, the Romans gained control of most of the land. Leaving numerous contributions throughout these countries, the Romans built many cities, as well as roads that were used for transportation and trading.

Following the rule of the Romans, Germanic tribes and Danes invaded at various times before the Norman Invasion took place in 1066. At that time, a group of Vikings, the Normans, sailed across the English Channel and conquered England. Simple and hearty characterizes the food of the British Isles, with the most profound culinary influences coming from the Celtics, Germans, and Normans.

In 1536, Wales and England united. Scotland remained independent until the 1700s when it joined England and Wales. From the 1700s to the 1900s, Britain built a huge empire that covered one-quarter of the world. Their colonies stretched around the globe, including islands in the Caribbean, parts of North and South America, Africa, the Middle East, India, the Orient, Australia, and islands in the Pacific. This far-reaching colonization resulted in a strong British influence around the world and significant influences from faraway lands on Britain. Influences on cooking techniques and food ingredients, as well as dishes from these worldwide colonies, greatly impacted the culinary scene of the British Isles.

Introduced to Ireland from the New World in the 1600s, potatoes quickly became a staple and major part of the diet in this poor country. In the 1840s, Ireland was hit with a potato blight. A fungus destroyed the potato crop, and starvation raged throughout the country. A million people died and more than a million fled Ireland and emigrated to other countries during that time. The population of Ireland today remains just a bit over half of what it was before the potato blight.

Today, Ireland remains torn by religious strife, as it has been for many, many years. The Protestants of Northern Ireland wished to align with predominately Protestant Great Britain; however, the people living in the south of Ireland, who are mostly Catholic, did not wish to become the religious minority of Britain. In 1920, the British Parliament passed the Government of Ireland Act that allowed the people of Ireland to choose many aspects of self-government. As a result, the northeastern corner of Ireland became Northern Ireland and united with Britain. The remaining section of Ireland chose not to join Britain and, in 1921, became the independent country of Ireland. Still experiencing ongoing political troubles with Britain, in 1949, Ireland declared independence from anything to do with the British.

TOPOGRAPHY

Situated to the northwest of Europe, the English Channel, Strait of Dover, North Sea, and Atlantic Ocean border the British Isles. The English Channel lies to the south and separates Britain from France. The North Sea is to the east, and the Atlantic lies to the west.

Scotland comprises approximately one-third of Great Britain and lies in the northern part of the island. Wales is situated in the southwest corner, and England covers the southern two-thirds of Great Britain.

The topography of Great Britain is quite varied, ranging from the windswept land of Northern Scotland to the rugged mountains and deep valleys of Wales, to the gently rolling plains and meadows of England. The coastline also differs greatly, with parts being rocky, some consisting of steep cliffs, and others sandy beaches.

Although the British Isles lies at quite a northern latitude, they experience temperate weather. This mild climate results from the ocean currents that moderate the temperature and cause mild summers and cool, damp winters with almost no snow.

England consists of three regions. The Pennines lies in the northern half and contains coast, mountains, hills, and lakes. The Southwest Peninsula, obviously in the southwest, is comprised of low plateaus, highlands, and coast. The rest of England is known as the English Lowlands and consists of fertile farmland, plains, hills, valleys, coast, and the Thames River.

Numerous lakes and rivers are found throughout England. More than 2,000 miles of waterways flow through this land. The River Tweed and the Cheviot Hills form the border between England and Scotland.

Rugged Scotland contains many mountains, valleys, and lakes. The northern two-thirds consists of barren and mountainous highlands, conducive to raising sheep and cattle. The only fertile land in Scotland is found in the lowlands of the central section. Rivers, valleys, rolling hills, and fertile farmland make up this central area. In addition to the staple potato, grains for feeding both livestock and people grow well in this region. These include oats, barley, and wheat. The south contains rugged highlands, rolling treeless moors, and pastureland for grazing sheep and cattle. Known for milk production, many dairy products come from this area.

Wales is situated on the western coast of Great Britain. With England to its east, the Atlantic Ocean surrounds the rest of the land. Wales consists of low broad mountains and deep valleys. The northern section contains rugged mountains, which provide a good place for raising sheep and cattle for beef. In the central section, the mountains become more rounded, and, again, lots of sheep and cattle graze. The southern area consists of plateaus and valleys. Besides raising cattle for dairy production, most of the crops produced in Wales grow in the south.

A separate island about the size of Maine, Ireland lies to the west of Great Britain. The Irish Sea separates Ireland from Great Britain, and the Atlantic Ocean borders the north and west of Ireland. Northern Ireland occupies the northeast corner, while the country of Ireland comprises the remaining five-sixths of the island. Composed of low mountains and rolling hills, Ireland is dotted with lakes and rivers. The central portion contains lowlands and rolling green pastures, and mountains lie near the coasts.

Ingredients and Foods Commonly Used Throughout the Cuisines of the British Isles Include:

- lamb and mutton
- beef
- seafood including cod, haddock, salmon, herring, mackerel, shrimp, and oysters
- ham and bacon
- potatoes
- winter vegetables including kale, cabbage, cauliflower, Brussels sprouts, rutabagas, carrots, and peas
- cucumber and celery
- oats
- scones and crumpets

COOKING METHODS

Roasting, braising, and frying remain the most common cooking methods used in meat preparation. The ample amounts of mutton (old sheep) and tough cuts of meat often appear braised in stews. Pies, puddings, and larger cuts of meat are usually baked or roasted. Whether deep-frying or sautéing, the British often fry foods. Fish and chips is a popular example of deep-frying served throughout the British Isles.

Surrounded by seas, very fresh, high-quality seafood abounds, so poaching is often the preferred cooking method. With the bounty of fish, fish and seafood are smoked frequently, providing a method of preserving seafood for times when less is available.

Many identify boiling and blandness with British cookery. Indeed, boiled foods appear frequently, including all sorts of vegetables and meats.

REGIONS

Several dishes are associated with the cuisine of England. Fish and chips, deep-fried fish and thickly cut French fries, is served accompanied by malt vinegar. Steak and kidney pie consists of a stewlike combination of kidneys and steak topped with a pastry crust. Bangers and mash translates into sausages and mashed potatoes. Another dish made with those ubiquitous mashed potatoes, Shepherd's pie, combines ground or minced beef with a topping of those favorite potatoes.

With lots of coastline, lakes, and rivers, abundant fish and seafood are available. Favorites include cod, haddock, Dover sole, and plaice. Shellfish also appears often, particularly prawns (large shrimp) and oysters.

Condiments rank high in the English cuisine. Horseradish sauce accompanies roast beef; strong mustards, chutneys, vinegars, and Worcestershire sauce appear frequently.

Scottish cooking includes plentiful seafood, especially cod, haddock, salmon, and mackerel. Salmon from the waters of Scotland is considered some of the finest in the world. Most commonly, the salmon is served grilled, smoked, or poached. Other popular fish include herring and *kippers*, smoked herring, which are eaten throughout the British Isles. Because abundant sheep thrive in this mountainous land, lamb remains the most often consumed meat. All parts of the animal are used, as demonstrated with the famous dish, *haggis*. A Scotch delicacy, *haggis* consists of sheep's offal mixed with oatmeal, stuffed in a sheep's stomach and boiled. Oatmeal appears often, both as a filler combined with other ingredients and eaten alone as porridge (cooked cereal).

With lots of sheep and cattle grazing in the hills and mountains throughout the British Isles, lamb, mutton, and beef remain the most popular meats. Mint sauce often accompanies lamb. Ample dairy products are produced, and high cheese consumption exists all through the British Isles. *Welsh rarebit*, a melted cheese dish served on toast, originated in Wales.

Known as the Emerald Isle, Ireland contains rolling farmland and lush, green lands because of the high annual rainfall. Potatoes rank as *the* dietary staple, whereas seafood, mutton, lamb, and beef are consumed regularly. Irish stew, a stew containing mutton or lamb cooked with potatoes and onions, remains a favorite. Cabbage also appears often. With plentiful pastureland in the interior portions of this country, sheep, cattle for meat and dairy, and hogs thrive. The staggering range of available seafood includes cod, herring, mackerel, whiting, shrimp, lobster, salmon, and trout. With so much access to oceans, seaweed functions as an important ingredient in the diet on this small island, as it does on the island of Japan.

CUISINE

Simple cooking prevails throughout the British Isles. On Sunday, the typical main meal consists of roast beef (or perhaps mutton, lamb, or pork) with potatoes and one or two vegetables. Yorkshire pudding, a savory battercake cooked in the fat drippings from the roast, usually accompanies the meat. The remainders from Sunday's roast often form the basis for several meals later in the week. Two popular dishes, Shepherd's pie and bubble and squeak, begin with leftover meats.

The British use few spices in their cooking, resulting in a reputation for serving bland dishes. With lots of cool, damp weather, soups play a substantial role in the diet in these countries. *Cawl*, clear broth with vegetables, is a creation from Wales. *Cockaleekie* hails from Scotland and is their version of very thick chicken soup containing leeks and barley.

With miles and miles of shoreline surrounding this large island, seafood remains a staple. Cod and haddock appear everywhere; fish and chips are widely consumed. In addition, many varieties of game thrive and remain an important part of the cuisine.

As a result of the short growing season, winter vegetables, including cabbage, cauliflower, Brussels sprouts, carrots, and peas, are most available and frequently served. The British prepare most vegetables simply by boiling and seasoning with salt, pepper, and butter.

Puddings and pies remain popular fare throughout the British Isles. Unlike the American version of these two foods, in the British Isles, puddings and pies can be sweet or savory. Pies and puddings can contain all sorts of meats and/or vegetables. The sweet varieties often are prepared with dried fruits and/or treacle (sweet syrup on the order of maple syrup or molasses). The main difference between a pie and a pudding depends on the dish in which it is baked. A pie comes in a dish about 2- or 3-inches high, whereas a pudding is prepared in a bowl or basin-type dish. Either way, they appear frequently in the cuisines found in all of these countries. A variation of the pie, the *pasty*, resembles a turnover. Cornish pasties, filled with meat, potatoes, and sometimes vegetables, remain a popular snack, first course, or light entrée. Schoolchildren frequently eat a Cornish pasty after school.

The pub, short for public house, is the British name for a bar. Truly a British/Irish institution, people gather together to meet friends, watch sports on television, listen to music, eat, and, of course, drink. Typically, one can order food to accompany the drink. Pub food includes such favorites as fish and chips, bangers and mash, sandwiches, cheese plates, and many other dishes.

The most popular alcoholic beverages include beer, ale, lager, and stout; however, the British Isles have certainly made a mark on the world of hard liquor. Commonly known as Scotch, Scottish whiskey was first produced in Scotland in the 1400s. Irish whiskey is also quite well known. Gin originated in England. The most popular nonalcoholic beverage, tea, is brewed until quite strong and served with cream and sugar as we serve coffee in the United States.

Steak and Kidney Pie; photo courtesy of Dorling Kindersley

Hearty breakfasts are customary throughout the British Isles. Eggs, breakfast meat (bacon, sausage, and/or ham), toast, marmalade, oatmeal or porridge, fruit, and kippers frequent breakfast plates. Like the United States, lunch consists of a sandwich, cold meats, or cheese. Around four or five o'clock in the afternoon, many still consume tea, which is served with assorted sweet and savory foods. Many types of sandwiches, fish, cold meats, cheeses, pickled vegetables, scones, crumpets, breads, cookies (known as biscuits throughout the British Isles), and/or cakes may accompany the tea. The selection of foods served can be quite simple or very elaborate. Therefore, the size of the evening meal depends on whether tea was served and how much food was consumed.

REGION	AREA	WEATHER	TOPOGRAPHY	FOODS
England	Pennines (northern half)	Mild, damp winters, mild summers	Coast, mountains, hills, lakes	Seafood, cattle, sheep, chicken, eggs, milk
	Southwest Peninsula (southwest)	Mild, damp winters, mild summers	Coast, low plateaus, highlands	Seafood, barley, beets, wheat, potatoes, fruit
	English Lowlands (remaining southern half)	Mild, damp winters, mild summers	Coast, valleys, fertile farmland, plains, hills, Thames River	Seafood, vegetables, fruits
Scotland	Northern two-thirds	Mild, damp winters, mild summers	Coast, mountains, treeless moors, valleys, lakes	Seafood, sheep, cattle
	Central	Mild, damp winters, mild summers	Rivers, valleys, fertile farmland, rolling hills	Seafood, wheat, oats, barley, potatoes
	South	Mild, damp winters, mild summers	Rolling treeless moors, pastures, highlands	Seafood, sheep, cattle, milk, dairy products
Wales	North	Mild, damp winters, mild summers	Mountains, coast, valleys	Seafood, sheep, cattle
	Central	Mild, damp winters, mild summers	Rounded mountains, coast, valleys, lakes, plateaus	Seafood, sheep, cattle, dairy
	South	Mild, damp winters, mild summers	Plateaus, valleys, coast, forests, lakes, pasture, plains	Seafood, cattle, dairy, oats, potatoes, barley, cauliflower, cabbage
Northern Ireland	North	Mild, damp winters, mild summers	Low mountains, coast, lakes, rolling hills	Seafood, sheep, cattle, potatoes
	Central	Mild, damp winters, mild summers	Plains, fertile farmland	Seafood, sheep, cattle, chicken, eggs, dairy, potatoes, cabbage, turnips, pears, plums, apples, mushrooms
Ireland	Coasts	Mild, damp winters, mild summers	Mountains, coast	Seafood, sheep, cattle, potatoes, seaweed
	Central	Mild, damp winters, mild summers	Pastureland, rolling hills	Sheep, cattle, fruits, winter vegetables, potatoes

---

CHEESES FROM THE BRITISH ISLES

England

Cheddar Made from cow's milk, sharp deep flavor, firm texture

Cheshire Made from cow's milk, the oldest variety of English cheese from the twelfth century, tangy yet mild flavor, firm crumbly texture, a tall cheese

Derby From Derbyshire, made from cow's milk, mild flavor, firm yet flaky texture, often mixed with sage

Gloucester Made from cow's milk, mild with a little sharpness in flavor, firm texture

Lancashire Made from cow's milk, tangy yet mild flavor, firm crumbly texture

Leicester Made from cow's milk, sweet yet sharp flavor, creamy texture

Stilton Made from cow's milk, a blue cheese, creamy texture

Wensleydale Made from sheep's milk in the early days but now made from cow's milk, from Yorkshire, mild with buttermilklike taste, crumbly firm texture

Scotland

Crowdie Made from cow's milk, hails from the time of the Vikings, fresh cheese, slightly tart flavor, creamy yet crumbly texture

Orkney Extra Mature Cheddar Made from cow's milk, aged at least one year, firm texture

Seriously Strong Cheddar Made from cow's milk, aged one and one-half to two years, strong flavor, firm texture

Wales

Caerphilly Made from cow's milk, mild flavor, creamy, semifirm texture

Ireland

Cashel Blue Made from cow's milk, a blue cheese, soft texture

---

Review Questions

1. Discuss the geographic factors of the British Isles as they relate to the cuisines of the various countries.
2. How does the weather influence the cuisines of these countries?
3. Name four food ingredients that are prevalent in the British Isles.
4. Name beverages (alcoholic and nonalcoholic) that are favored in the countries of the British Isles.
5. What is tea and what foods are served there?
6. What is a pub and what foods are typically served there?
7. Name and describe four dishes served in the British Isles. Tell whether they are regional dishes or are served throughout the British Isles.

Glossary

bangers and mash Sausages and mashed potatoes

biscuits British word for cookies

cawl Clear broth containing vegetables served in Wales

chips Thickly cut French fries served throughout the British Isles

cockaleekie A thick chicken soup containing leeks and barley from Scotland

colcannon An Irish dish containing potatoes mixed with kale or cabbage

fish and chips Deep-fried fish and thickly cut French fries, served with malt vinegar

haggis Scottish dish consisting of sheep's heart, liver, and lung mixed with oatmeal, stuffed in a sheep's stomach and boiled

kippers Smoked herring, frequently served at breakfast or tea

mutton Old lamb, which contains a stronger flavor and tougher texture than younger lamb

pasty A turnover usually filled with meat, potatoes, and vegetables

porridge Cooked cereal, usually oatmeal

potato crisps British for the American version of potato chips

prawns Large shrimp

scone A slightly sweetened bread product (like an American biscuit) containing dried currants

shepherd's pie A dish containing cooked beef topped with a crust of mashed potatoes

steak and kidney pie A stewlike combination of kidneys and steak topped with a pastry crust

treacle A sweet syrup like maple syrup or molasses

Yorkshire pudding A savory battercake cooked in meat fat, usually served with roast beef

PICKLED ONIONS (England)

Total Yield: 1 pint   Cooking Method: Boil

Food Balance: Sweet/sour
Wine Style: Light and fruity Riesling, Pinot Blanc, Dolcetto, soft-style Reds
Example: Beringer Vineyards Johannisberg Rielsing

INGREDIENTS	WEIGHT	VOLUME
white boiling onions, small	1 lb	
kosher salt	2¼ oz	¼ cup
malt vinegar	1 lb	2 cups
sugar	3¾ oz	¼ cup
pickling spices	¼ oz	1 tablespoon
cloves, whole		3 each
black peppercorns, whole		5 each

1. Place onions in pot of boiling water, boil one minute, drain, rinse with cold water.
2. Peel onions, place in bowl, sprinkle with salt, stir to coat evenly.
3. Cover bowl, set in cool place for 12 hours.
4. Drain onions, rinse well with cold water, let drain.
5. Combine vinegar, sugar, pickling spices, cloves, and peppercorns in nonreactive pan.
6. Bring to boil, stir to dissolve sugar, boil for 5 minutes.
7. Add onions, adding water if liquid does not cover onions.
8. Return to boil for 10 minutes, uncovered, until onions show slight resistance when pierced with sharp knife.
9. Remove onions from heat, cool.
10. Process onions in canning jars or store in nonreactive container in refrigerator at least 2 weeks before serving.

CORNISH PASTY (England)

Beef, Onion, and Potato Turnover

Number of Servings: 12 or 24   Cooking Method: Bake
Serving Size: 1 or 2 per serving
Total Yield: 24 turnovers

Food Balance: Balanced protein
Wine Style: Wide variety of wines—Sauvignon Blanc, Chardonnay,
    Pinot Noir, Merlot, Shiraz
Example: Beringer Founders' Estate Pinot Noir

INGREDIENTS	WEIGHT	VOLUME
PASTRY:		
flour, all-purpose	1 lb, 4 oz	4½ cups
salt		¼ teaspoon
butter, shortening, or combination, chilled, cut into ¾-inch pieces	12 oz	3 sticks or 1½ cups
water, cold	6 to 8 oz	¾ to 1 cup
FILLING:		
beef, top round, trimmed, minced	1 lb	
potatoes, peeled, small dice	10½ oz	3 medium
onions, medium dice	8 oz	2 medium
salt	¾ oz	1 tablespoon
pepper	¼ oz	2 teaspoons
parsley, fresh, minced	½ oz	¼ cup
ASSEMBLY:		
egg, lightly beaten	1¾ oz	1 each

> Cornish pasties make a good snack, first course, luncheon entrée, or item to serve at tea.

PASTRY:

1. Place flour and salt in bowl of food processor. Pulse to mix.
2. Add butter, shortening, or combination, pulse to mix until size of peas.
3. With machine running, add water through feed tube until dough comes together into ball. Pulse, if needed.
4. Wrap ball in film wrap, refrigerate until well chilled, several hours or overnight.

Cornish Pasty (Beef, Onion, and Potato Turnover); photo courtesy of Dorling Kindersley

FILLING:

1. Combine all filling ingredients in bowl, mix well.
2. Cover and refrigerate until ready to use.

ASSEMBLY:

1. Preheat oven to 400 degrees.
2. On lightly floured surface, roll pastry thin, ⅛- to ³⁄₁₆-inch thick.
3. Cut 5- to 5½-inch circles, place 1½ oz (3 tablespoons) filling just under center of dough.
4. Brush edges of dough with cold water, fold dough over filling until edges meet to form half-circle, crimp edges to seal well.
5. Place on baking sheet, brush with egg.
6. Place in center of oven for 12 minutes, reduce heat to 325 degrees, bake another 45 minutes.
7. Serve immediately or slightly cooled.

COCKALEEKIE (Scotland)

Chicken and Leek Soup

Number of Servings: 23   Cooking Method: Braise
Serving Size: 8 oz
Total Yield: 11 lbs, 10 oz

Food Balance: Protein
Wine Style: Light- to medium-bodied Viognier, Chardonnay, soft Reds Merlot, Shiraz
Example: Château Souverain Chardonnay or Stone Cellars Merlot

INGREDIENTS	WEIGHT	VOLUME
chicken, stewing, washed	about 6 lbs	
water, cold	10 lbs	5 qt
leeks, thoroughly washed, sliced ½-inch thick, including 2 inches of the green stems	1 lb, 7 oz	6 each
barley	4 oz	½ cup
salt	¾ oz	1 tablespoon
pepper	to taste	
nutmeg, grated	to taste	

Cockaleekie Soup (Chicken and Leek Soup)

INGREDIENTS	WEIGHT	VOLUME
GARNISH:		
parsley, fresh, minced	¼ oz	2 tablespoons

1. Remove excess fat from cavity of chicken.
2. Place water and chicken in pot.
3. Bring to boil over high heat, skimming when necessary.
4. Add leeks, barley, and salt, reduce heat to low, simmer about 3 hours, until chicken is well done.
5. Remove chicken, set aside to cool slightly. Remove and discard skin and bones, cut meat into pieces no larger than 2 inches.
6. Cool soup in cold water bath, refrigerate overnight to solidify fat. Remove fat and discard.
7. Return meat to soup, heat thoroughly.
8. Add pepper and nutmeg. Correct seasonings.
9. Serve, garnished with parsley.

WATERCRESS AND ORANGE SALAD (Ireland)

Number of Servings: 15
Serving Size: 3 oz
Total Yield: 2 lbs, 13 oz

INGREDIENTS	WEIGHT	VOLUME
watercress, washed, tough stems removed, dried	8½ oz	2 bunches
celery, thinly sliced	12½ oz	6 stalks
onion, minced	4 oz	1 small
oranges, peeled, pith removed, sliced thinly	1 lb, 2 oz	4 each
DRESSING:		
lemon juice, fresh	2 oz	¼ cup
salt		½ teaspoon
white pepper		⅛ teaspoon
olive oil	2 oz	¼ cup

1. Mix all dressing ingredients in a jar or bowl of food processor, beat until mixture thickens.
2. Place watercress, onion, and celery in bowl, top with oranges.
3. Pour dressing over salad, mix gently to distribute dressing. Correct seasonings.
4. Serve immediately, make sure at least one orange slice tops each serving.

WELSH RAREBIT (Wales)

Cheddar Cheese Sauce over Toast

Number of Servings: 8   Cooking Method: Simmer
Serving Size: 2½ oz cheese sauce
  on toast
Total Yield: 1 lb, 5 oz

Food Balance: Protein
Wine Style: Soft and fruity wines—Blush wines, Pinot Blanc, Chenin
    Blanc, Merlot, Shiraz, Zinfandel
Example: Château Souverain or Beringer Vineyards Zinfandel

INGREDIENTS	WEIGHT	VOLUME
Cheddar cheese, sharp, grated	1 lb	6 cups
flour	½ oz	2 tablespoons
beer	4 oz	½ cup
butter	1 oz	2 tablespoons
Worcestershire sauce		2 teaspoons
mustard, dry		½ teaspoon
cayenne pepper		pinch
egg yolk	1½ oz	2 each
toast, crusts removed		8 each

1. Place toast in individual shallow ovenproof dishes, set aside. Pre-heat broiler.
2. In pan, mix cheese with flour, then add beer, butter, Worcestershire sauce, mustard, and cayenne pepper.
3. Stirring constantly, melt in top of double boiler or over medium low heat. Do not let mixture boil.
4. Place yolk in small bowl, whisk briefly.
5. Stirring constantly, slowly add some cheese to temper yolk.
6. Off heat, stir yolk mixture into cheese. Correct seasonings.
7. Pour cheese evenly over toast.
8. Place cheese dishes under broiler until lightly brown, about 1 or 2 minutes. Serve immediately.

BEEF STEW BRAISED IN GUINNESS (Ireland)

Number of Servings: 11   Cooking Method: Sauté, braise
Serving Size: 8 oz
Total Yield: 5 lbs, 14 oz

Food Balance: Protein
Wine Style: Light- to medium-bodied, fruity Sauvignon Blanc, Merlot,
    Shiraz, Cabernet
Example: Château Souverain Cabernet Sauvignon

INGREDIENTS	WEIGHT	VOLUME
oil	2 oz	4 tablespoons
bay leaves		6 each
beef, chuck or round, trimmed, cut into 2-inch chunks	4 to 4½ lb	
onion, sliced ¼ inch thick	1 lb, 2 oz	2 large
carrots, peeled, cut into 1-inch slices	1 lb	5 each
flour	1 oz	4 tablespoons
Guinness	12 oz	1½ cups
water	1 lb	2 cups
parsley, fresh, minced	¼ oz	2 tablespoons
salt	¼ oz	1 teaspoon
pepper		½ teaspoon
prunes	12 oz	2 cups

Beef Stew Braised in Guinness; photo courtesy of Dorling Kindersley

1. Preheat oven to 300 degrees. Cover prunes with hot water, set aside.
2. Heat oil in pan, add bay leaves and sauté.
3. Add beef, sauté until seared on all sides.
4. Add onion, sauté until lightly browned.
5. Sprinkle flour over mixture in pan, mix until browned.
6. Add Guinness and water. If necessary, add more water to cover meat.
7. Add salt, pepper, parsley, and carrots; stir to distribute seasonings.
8. Place in oven and braise for 2 to 2½ hours. Stir occasionally.
9. Add soaked prunes 30 minutes before serving.
10. Correct seasonings and serve.

COD CAKES (Scotland)

Number of Servings: 9
Serving Size: Two 3-oz patties
Total Yield: 3 lbs, 7 oz

Cooking Method: Sauté

Food Balance: Protein
Wine Style: Soft and fruity Viognier, Marsanne, Chardonnay, Dolcetto, Beaujolais
Example: Greg Norman Chardonnay

INGREDIENTS	WEIGHT	VOLUME
cod or haddock, poached, flaked	1 lb, 1 oz	3 cups
onion, finely minced	2 oz	4 tablespoons
potatoes, cooked, mashed	1 lb, 8 oz	3 cups
salt		¾ teaspoon

> Like many recipes from the British Isles, this recipe is a bit bland. If you want to spice it up, add some nutmeg and cayenne pepper. Be careful not to overdo it.

Cod Cakes; photo courtesy of The Norwegian Seafood Export Council—www.seafood.no. Photography by Russel French

INGREDIENTS	WEIGHT	VOLUME
pepper		½ teaspoon
thyme, dried, crushed		½ teaspoon
parsley, fresh, minced	½ oz	3 tablespoons
mustard, prepared		1½ teaspoons
egg	5 oz	3 each
Béchamel sauce, thick	8¼ oz	¾ cup
BÉCHAMEL SAUCE:		
butter	1 oz	2 tablespoons
flour	1 oz	2 tablespoons
milk, hot	8 oz	1 cup
salt	to taste	
pepper	to taste	

frying oil

GARNISH:

lemon, minced parsley, and/or tartar sauce

BÉCHAMEL SAUCE:

1. Melt butter in pan over medium heat, add flour, and whisk until blond *roux* (very lightly colored).
2. Reduce heat to low, add milk slowly, whisking constantly until thickened to medium consistency.
3. Season with salt and pepper.
4. Correct seasonings. Strain through China cap or *chinois* to remove any lumps. Cover and refrigerate if not using immediately.

ASSEMBLY:

1. In bowl, mix first 10 ingredients, stir gently until blended.
2. Prepare 3-oz patties with floured hands. Refrigerate until ready to sauté.
3. Heat ¼- to ½-inch oil in skillet.
4. Sauté cakes on medium heat until golden brown on both sides.
5. Drain on absorbent paper.
6. Serve, garnished with lemon, parsley, and/or tartar sauce.

SHEPHERD'S PIE (England)

Beef Topped with Mashed Potatoes

Number of Servings: 12
Serving Size: 5 oz, ⅙ pie
Total Yield: Two 9-inch pies

Cooking Method: **Boil, bake**

Food Balance: Protein
Wine Style: Light- to medium-bodied—Chardonnay, Merlot, Shiraz,
  Zinfandel, Cabernet Sauvignon
Example: Beringer Founders' Estate Merlot

INGREDIENTS	WEIGHT	VOLUME
cooked beef, minced or ground beef, cooked	1 lb, 8 oz	
onion, diced	14 oz	2 large
butter or meat drippings	1 oz	2 tablespoons
flour	1 oz	3 tablespoons
beef stock, hot	1 lb, 8 oz	3 cups
salt	to taste	
pepper		¾ to 1 teaspoon, to taste
potatoes, peeled, quartered	3 lbs	

TOPPING:

butter, melted		for top of mashed potatoes

1. While preparing meat, boil potatoes in water until done, process into mashed potatoes. Season potatoes with salt and pepper, to taste.
2. Preheat oven to 425 degrees.
3. Melt butter or meat drippings in skillet, add onions, sauté over medium low heat until soft, about 4 minutes.
4. Add flour and cook until light brown in color.

Shepherd's Pie (Beef Topped with Mashed Potatoes);
photo courtesy of Dorling Kindersley

5. Slowly whisk in stock, add meat, salt, and pepper, and simmer at least 10 minutes. Add more stock if too thick. Correct seasonings.
6. Place meat mixture into pie pans, steam table pan, or individual ovenproof dishes. Top with mashed potatoes, which can be spread or decoratively piped over meat. Dot or brush with melted butter.
7. Bake for 25 to 30 minutes. Brown under broiler if not golden. Serve immediately, accompanied by your choice of vegetable.

IRISH STEW (Ireland)

Number of Servings: 9   Cooking Method: Braise
Serving Size: 8 oz
Total Yield: 4 lbs, 10 oz

Food Balance: Balanced protein
Wine Style: Wide variety—Sauvignon Blanc, Pinot Blanc, Pinot Noir, Merlot
Example: Château St. Jean Pinot Noir

INGREDIENTS	WEIGHT	VOLUME
lamb, boneless, lean, neck or shoulder, cut into 1½-inch cubes	2 lbs	
potatoes, peeled, ¼-inch slices	1½ lbs	
onions, peeled, ¼-inch slices	1 lb	4 each
salt	½ oz	2 teaspoons
pepper		½ teaspoon
thyme		1 teaspoon
parsley, fresh, minced	¼ oz	2 tablespoons
stock or water	8 oz	1 cup

1. Preheat oven to 300 degrees.
2. Place half of potatoes (12 oz) in ovenproof pan.

Idaho Potato Irish Stew; photo courtesy of the Idaho Potato Commission

3. Top with half of onions (8 oz), then lamb.
4. Sprinkle half of seasonings over lamb.
5. Place remaining onions over lamb.
6. Arrange remaining potatoes on top.
7. Sprinkle with remaining seasonings.
8. Pour in stock or water.
9. Cover pan, place in oven on lower shelf. Bake for 2 to 2½ hours, until lamb is tender. Add more water if becoming too dry; remove lid if too soupy. Correct seasonings. Serve.

YORKSHIRE PUDDING (England)

Number of Servings: 8
Serving Size: 3- by 4½-inch piece
Total Yield: 9- by 13-inch pan

Cooking Method: Bake

INGREDIENTS	WEIGHT	VOLUME
flour, all-purpose	4½ oz	1 cup
salt		½ teaspoon
eggs	3½ oz	2 each
milk	8 oz	1 cup
pan drippings or butter	1 oz	2 tablespoons

> Yorkshire pudding typically accompanies roast beef or other large pieces (joints) of meat. Note: To prepare Yorkshire pudding in individual servings, pour the batter into small dishes or muffin tins instead of baking pan.

1. Place flour and salt in bowl of food processor, pulse to mix.
2. With processor running, add eggs and milk through tube, pulse to mix well.
3. Remove batter to bowl, refrigerate at least 1 hour.
4. Meanwhile, preheat oven to 400 degrees.

Yorkshire Pudding; photo courtesy of Dorling Kindersley

5. Place pan drippings or butter in 9- by 13-inch pan or ½-steam table pan; heat until hot.
6. Stir batter, pour batter into pan, bake for 15 minutes.
7. Reduce heat to 350 degrees, bake another 10 to 15 minutes, until puffy, crisp, and golden.
8. Remove from oven, cut into squares, serve immediately.

COLCANNON (Ireland)

Mashed Potatoes with Kale or Cabbage

Number of Servings: 13   Cooking Method: Boil, sauté
Serving Size: 4 oz
Total Yield: 3 lbs, 6 oz

INGREDIENTS	WEIGHT	VOLUME
potatoes, peeled, quartered	2 lbs	
kale or green cabbage, washed, cut finely or shredded	1 lb	
butter	1 oz	2 tablespoons
scallions, with 3-inches green, sliced	2½ oz	1 bunch
milk	8 oz	1 cup
salt	¼ oz	1 teaspoon
pepper		¼ teaspoon
mace		¼ teaspoon

GARNISH:

parsley, minced

1. Place milk and scallions in small pan, heat.
2. Boil potatoes in water until tender, drain well.
3. While potatoes boil, sauté kale in butter until tender or boil cabbage until tender, then sauté in butter.
4. Mash potatoes using milk and scallions for liquid.
5. Stir cooked kale or cabbage and seasonings into potatoes.
6. Correct seasonings, serve, garnished with minced parsley if desired.

BOXTY (Ireland)

Potato Pancakes

Number of Servings: 11 pancakes   Cooking Method: Sauté
Serving Size: 3-oz pancake
Total Yield: 2 lbs, 1 oz

INGREDIENTS	WEIGHT	VOLUME
potatoes, peeled, grated	2 lbs	6 each
flour	4 oz	1 cup
salt	¼ oz	1 teaspoon
pepper		½ teaspoon
caraway seeds		1 teaspoon

Boxty (Potato Pancakes); photo courtesy of Dorling Kindersley

INGREDIENTS	WEIGHT	VOLUME
milk	4 oz	½ cup
butter, for frying	2 to 4 oz	4 to 8 tablespoons or ½ to 1 stick

1. Mix flour, salt, pepper, caraway seeds, and milk in bowl.
2. In colander, squeeze excess moisture from potatoes.
3. Add potatoes to milk-flour mixture, correct seasonings, form into 3-oz patties (flour hands, if necessary).
4. Heat 1½ oz (3 tablespoons) butter, or enough for sautéing, in skillet.
5. Sauté pancakes until golden and crisp on edges, about 3 minutes on each side.
6. Serve.

SCONES (England)

Rich Biscuits with Currants

Total Yield: 12 biscuits　　　　Cooking Method: Bake

INGREDIENTS	WEIGHT	VOLUME
flour, all purpose	9½ oz	2 cups
baking powder	¼ oz	2 teaspoons
sugar	1 oz	2 tablespoons
salt		½ teaspoon
butter, unsalted, cold, cut into 12 equal pieces	3 oz	6 tablespoons
egg	1¾ oz	1 each
milk	4 oz	½ cup
currants, dried	1¾ oz	⅓ cup

> Served warm with butter and jam, honey, or lemon curd, scones appear regularly accompanied by tea.

1. Preheat oven to 400 degrees, grease or place parchment paper on baking sheet.
2. Place flour, baking powder, sugar, and salt in bowl of food processor, pulse to mix.
3. Place butter pieces on top of flour mixture, pulse until butter is size of peas.

Scones; photo courtesy of Dorling Kindersley

4. Mix egg and milk. With processor running, pour egg and milk through feed tube, pulse until dough forms ball, add currants, and pulse once or twice.
5. Remove from bowl to lightly floured counter, mix gently, if necessary, to mix in currants.
6. Divide dough into three even parts, pat each part into 4- to 5-inch circle.
7. Cut each circle into quarters, place pieces on prepared baking sheet.
8. Bake in center of oven for about 15 minutes, until lightly brown. Serve immediately with butter and jam, honey, or lemon curd.

TRIFLE (England)

Sherry-Flavored Cake Layered with Vanilla Custard, Raspberry Preserves, and Whipped Cream

Number of Servings: 10
Serving Size: 5 oz
Total Yield: 3 lbs, 4 oz

> *Trifle looks beautiful layered in a glass bowl or oversized brandy snifter; however, it may be prepared in individual bowls or glasses for easy service. Many use pound cake instead of sponge cake when preparing trifle.*

INGREDIENTS	WEIGHT	VOLUME
sponge cake, cut in 1-inch cubes, homemade or purchased	15 oz	6½ cups
sherry, dry	6 oz or to taste	¾ cup or to taste
vanilla pastry cream or custard *(recipe follows)*	1 lb	2 cups

INGREDIENTS	WEIGHT	VOLUME
raspberry preserves	4 to 8 oz, to taste	4 to 8 tablespoons, to taste
heavy cream	12 oz	1½ cups
confectioners' sugar	¾ oz	2 tablespoons
vanilla	¼ oz	1½ teaspoons

1. Place cake pieces in bowl, sprinkle with sherry to taste. Do not add more sherry than the cake can absorb without collapsing.
2. Whip heavy cream until half thickened and barely holds peak. Scrape down sides of bowl with spatula.
3. Add confectioners' sugar and vanilla, whip until thickened and holds peak.
4. Place whipped cream in pastry bag.
5. Place ⅓ of cake pieces in bowl (use ½ of cake if the bowl is wide and shallow, the cake needs to cover bottom).
6. Top with ⅓ (or ½) of raspberry preserves (drop bits of preserves on top of cake pieces).
7. Using pastry bag or spoon, cover with layer of pastry cream, about ¼ inch thick (use ⅓ or ½).
8. Pipe layer of whipped cream over pastry cream (use about ⅓ or ½).
9. Repeat layers (if using thirds, repeat all layers twice; with ½, repeat layers once).
10. Decoratively pipe whipped cream on top. Garnish with a dollop of raspberry preserves. Cover and refrigerate until serving time.
11. Spoon onto plates to serve.

Sprinkling sherry on cake pieces

Assembling the trifle—placing preserves over cake pieces

PASTRY CREAM

Custard

Total Yield: 1 lb, 8 oz or 3 cups

INGREDIENTS	WEIGHT	VOLUME
milk	1 lb, 2 oz	2¼ cups
sugar	5½ oz	⅔ cup
cornstarch	1¼ oz	¼ cup
egg yolks	4 oz	6 each
butter, unsalted	1 oz	2 tablespoons
vanilla		2 teaspoons

1. Combine sugar and 12 oz (1½ cups) milk in nonreactive pan, stir, bring to boil over medium heat.
2. Whisk cornstarch and remaining milk together in bowl, add yolks, whisk well.
3. While whisking, very slowly pour hot milk into yolk mixture to temper eggs.
4. Return mixture to pan, whisk constantly over medium low heat until mixture boils. Make sure to whisk into corners of pan to prevent sticking and burning.
5. Cook for 1 minute, remove to nonreactive bowl.
6. Add butter and vanilla, stir well.
7. Stirring frequently, chill in ice water bath until cool, then cover with film wrap and refrigerate until needed.

Trifle for a crowd and an individual serving

Use a stainless steel saucepan since the constant whisking against aluminum can cause the custard to become gray in color. Pastry cream should be used in 24 hours.

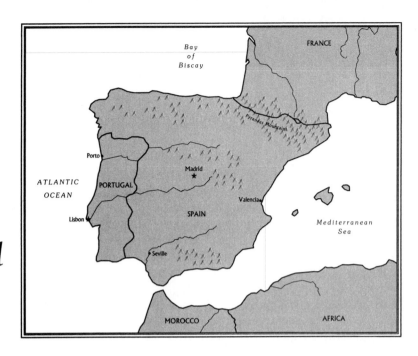

CHAPTER 2
Spain and Portugal

By the end of this chapter, you will be able to

- Identify differences and similarities in the regional cuisines of Spain and Portugal
- Explain how the topography and climate influence the cuisines found on the Iberian peninsula
- Know which food products are prevalent in various regions of Spain and Portugal
- Prepare several Iberian dishes

HISTORY

Lying in southeastern Europe, the Iberian Peninsula contains the countries of Spain and Portugal. Archeologists believe people first inhabited this peninsula about 100,000 years ago. The Iberians settled there 5,000 years ago and built the first cities in Spain. Throughout history, many invading countries left a great impact on the cuisines of Iberia. Around 200 B.C., the Romans entered Spain from the south bringing grapes for wine, garlic, wheat, and olives to this new land.

The Moors, who were Arabs from North Africa, invaded the south of Spain in 711 A.D. Eventually they conquered most of Spain and ruled the country for hundreds of years, until the late fifteenth century. The Moors introduced oranges, lemons, almonds, herbs, fruits, vegetables, and a variety of spices, including nutmeg, saffron, and pepper. The Spanish adopted combining sweet with savory, as well as the use of honey from the Moors. In addition to many new foods, these Arabs acquainted the Spanish with cooking techniques such as marinating and frying foods in olive oil. With a particularly strong presence felt in the region of Andalusia that lies in southern Spain, the Arab influence still prevails in that region's cooking, architecture, and religion.

Finally, another major influence on the Iberian cuisines came in the late 1400s when Christopher Columbus and other explorers returned from the

New World. Along with their triumphs of discovering new lands and claiming them for Spain or Portugal, these explorers returned to their homeland with tomatoes, corn, potatoes, sweet peppers, and chocolate from the New World.

At the end of the fifteenth century, when all of the invaders were gone, Spain finally became a unified country. At that time, Spain began to build its own empire. The Spaniards gained control of lands in South America, North America, Asia, Africa, and Europe. They ruled their empire for about 100 years, until the late sixteenth century.

The Portuguese also built an empire in the late 1400s, which lasted about a century. Like the Spanish, their empire began with explorers discovering foreign lands around the world and claiming these new territories for Portugal.

TOPOGRAPHY

Spain makes up five-sixths of the Iberian Peninsula. The Atlantic Ocean borders Spain on the northwest, the Bay of Biscay on the north, and the Mediterranean Sea lies to the east and south. Only eight miles of water separate Africa from the south of Spain. France neighbors Spain on the northeast; Portugal joins on the west.

Great diversity in topography exists within Spain and Portugal, including mountains, coastlines, plateaus, hills, rivers, and streams. The majority of Spain consists of poor soil, a dry climate, and *meseta*—high, dry plateaus. Not very fertile, this land is used primarily for the grazing of sheep and goats. The coastal areas receive more rainfall than the interior where dry conditions prevail. More precipitation occurs in the north of Spain than in the south. Hot, sunny summers and cold winters dominate Spain's climate; however, the southern areas near the Mediterranean Sea enjoy a warmer climate, and the mountainous regions are colder.

Situated in the northwest of Spain, the dramatic landscape in Galacia contains beaches, mountains, and valleys. The Pyrenees Mountains lie in the northeast forming the border with France. Significant isolation exists here because of the barrier created by this rugged mountain range.

The central portion of Spain is a large, open expanse of land. With poor soil and a fairly dry climate, this area produces thin cattle that yield tough meat.

The southwest of Spain consists of dry basin; however, any of the land in this area that is supplied with water—whether by rivers, streams, or irrigation—transforms into fertile farmland. The area along the Mediterranean in the south contains fertile plains.

Because of moderation from the ocean breezes, Portugal's climate remains more temperate than Spain's with cooler summers and warmer winters. The entire west and south side of Portugal borders the Atlantic Ocean, so lots of coastline and plentiful seafood exist. Spain joins Portugal on its east. Generally, this country consists of two regions—the mountainous, humid north and the drier, more temperate south. Actually, the mountains lie in the northeastern, central, and southwestern areas, whereas most of the remainder of the country consists of flat land. Coastal plains line the coasts on the south and west.

Ingredients Commonly Used Throughout the Cuisines of Spain and Portugal Include:

- seafood
- pork and lamb
- *Serrano* ham and chorizo sausage

- blood sausage
- dried beans
- olive oil and olives
- garlic
- saffron and Spanish paprika
- parsley
- citrus fruits
- honey
- almonds

COOKING METHODS

The Spanish began using one-pot cookery in the Middle Ages when shepherds and nomads roamed the countryside, cooking any available ingredients in one pot over a fire. Because most of the flocks were sheep, lamb became the most prevalent meat. As a result, braising remains a common cooking method.

Grilling and frying initially occurred in the southern region of Andalusia where the Moors first entered Spain. Actually Arabs from North Africa, the Moors used cooking methods that came from the Arabians traveling through the desert cooking over an open fire. As the Moors extended their rule throughout Spain, their cooking techniques permeated into the cuisine.

With the introduction of the olive by the Romans hundreds of years before the Moors entered Spain, olive oil became a popular cooking fat. The Moors subsequently popularized frying and chose olive oil as the preferred cooking fat. Today Spain produces an enormous quantity of olive oil, and the export of olive oil is a major industry for Spain.

REGIONS

The various regions of Spain and Portugal exhibit huge diversity in topography, climate, and influences from the many invaders throughout history. Differences in the foods that grow, the selection of herbs and spices, and the cultural aspects of each area cause vast variations in the regional cuisines found in these two countries. Although many of the same dishes are prepared

---

OLIVE OIL

Many claim that Spain produces more olive oil than any other country in the world, which it exports to many countries around the world. In fact, the Spanish claim Italy imports lots of bulk olive oil from Spain, then labels it as Italian olive oil. Countries producing olive oil include Spain, Italy, Greece, Israel, France, Portugal, Morocco, Tunisia, and Turkey. Olive oil production also occurs in California and South America. Generally, olive trees thrive in a dry climate without low temperatures. The Mediterranean climate is ideal—mild winters and long, hot, dry summers, rainy springs and falls. Many of the countries with high olive production border the Mediterranean Sea.

Of course, numerous varieties of olives grow. The variety determines many of the characteristics of the oil, including the color and some of the flavor traits. In addition to the type of olive, the weather and soil conditions, as well as other factors determine the characteristics of the olive oil. This explains why olive oil differs so greatly from region to region. With so much difference between oils, sometimes varieties of oils are mixed; other times one varietal is used alone.

in most of the regions of Spain and Portugal, the recipes vary significantly from area to area, creating regional adaptations.

Known for simple, fresh food based on their bounty of fine produce and proximity to the sea, Galicia lies in the northwest corner of Spain. Galicia is the home of the *empanada*, traditionally a meat pie or turnover with a soft, flaky crust that appears as a first course or entrée throughout Spain and Latin America. Fillings range from pork to seafood to vegetable mixtures. Galicia remains lush because it receives a large amount of rainfall. Hearty food compliments the harsh climate found in this region.

Situated in the north of Spain, the Basque region contains a rugged terrain that resulted in significant isolation. Many think the finest and most simple food in Spain comes from this region. The Basque cuisine exhibits strong influence from its neighbor, France. The Basque region and its neighbor, Catalonia, are known for their use of many sauces. Because of the terrain, game and many types of mushrooms abound.

With a sparse population and large, open expanse of land, much of the central portion of Spain is known as the land of "the hunt." To the south of Madrid lies La Mancha, an area with many windmills and sheep. *Olla podrida*, a casserole containing almost anything that can be stewed, originated in this region. Literally translated *rotten pot*, every region has its own version of this national dish. Meat is the protein of choice in the central part of Spain, although the inhabitants of the coastal areas consume ample amounts of seafood.

Valencia is situated on the eastern coast bordering the Mediterranean Sea. Rice, oranges and other citrus fruits, olives, and grapes thrive here as well as in the south of Spain. A profusion of rice-based dishes come from this eastern part of Spain. Probably the most well-known Spanish dish, *paella*, originated in this region. *Paella*, named for the pot in which it is cooked, is a casserole of saffron-flavored rice with a variety of meats, chicken, seafood, and vegetables. Countless variations of *paella* flourish throughout Spain, but the constant ingredients include saffron, rice, a variety of seafood, sausage, chicken, and peas.

Lying in the south of Spain, Andalusia remains known for fried foods and the home of *gazpacho*, the famous cold tomato vegetable soup. Recipes from this region often contain cloves, cumin, cinnamon, and other spices exhibiting the Moorish influence.

Extremadura in the west consists primarily of farmland. Pigs thrive in this region, and a myriad of pork dishes originated here. The profusion of sausages and cured meats found throughout Iberia hails from the western part of Spain from the times when the rich people kept all the "good parts" of the hogs and gave the peasants the "insides" and less desirable parts. To make these parts palatable, the peasants ground them into sausages or created sauces from these undesirable scraps.

Portugal experiences a milder climate than Spain because of the ocean breezes. The south is warmer and drier than the northern portion. Grapes for wine and port thrive in the river valleys. Many crops, including potatoes, tomatoes, and corn, flourish here. The ocean lying on Portugal's west and south yields abundant seafood, the major protein consumed here.

CUISINE

Culinary similarities among the regions of Spain and Portugal include the simplicity of the food and a strong emphasis on fresh ingredients. Although Spain was a trade center for spices in the fifteenth century, Spanish cooking remained very simple. Fresh parsley and garlic appear in many recipes, but an overabundance of spices does not appear in Iberian dishes. Contrary to what many believe, the dishes served in Spain and Portugal are *not* hot and spicy. Many people confuse the Iberian cuisines with those found in Mexico and other Spanish-speaking countries.

Spain currently produces and exports most of the world's saffron. Saffron remains a very expensive, labor-intensive spice that is harvested by hand from the crocus flower. A major flavoring ingredient in the famous Spanish dish, *paella*, the flavor of saffron permeates the rice and tints it saffron's characteristic golden color.

As is true in many countries, the people who live near the oceans, seas, rivers, and lakes consume lots of seafood. Both Spain and Portugal have miles and miles of coastline where fishing provides plenty of fine-quality seafood. The many varieties of seafood form the basis of the diet in all of the coastal areas. Cod, sardines, and tuna are particularly popular in Portugal. Both fresh and dried (salted) cod are widely consumed in the north. In fact, according to Portuguese folklore, a bride must know at least ten different recipes for cod before she can marry. Anchovies, cod, squid, and many types of shellfish are among the fish that abound in Spain. In the central interior regions, lamb, mutton, goat, and pork prevail as the main source of protein.

Many high-quality cheeses are produced in Spain from cow's, sheep's, and goat's milk, or a combination of all three. Like most countries that produce cheese, different regions specialize in making certain types of cheeses. The governments of many European countries, including Spain, regulate production of some of the cheeses. There are currently twelve Designation of Origin (DO) cheeses in Spain.

The Portuguese use more herbs and spices than the Spanish. Fresh cilantro appears in many recipes. The addition of cream and butter makes Portuguese cooking richer than the cuisines found in Spain. Besides providing fruits and nuts, the numerous orange, lemon, and almond trees lead to significant honey production in Portugal.

In Madrid and throughout Spain, people typically go to bars in the early evening for sherry and *tapas*, small snacks or appetizers. Often, *tapas* are eaten in the late morning or early afternoon as a snack before the main meal. Similar to the Chinese *dim sum*, *tapas* have gained much popularity outside of Spain in recent years.

Endless varieties of *tapas* exist—seafood in various sauces, olives in all sorts of herbs and brines, fillings wrapped in pastry dough, and on and on. Many *tapas* are just small portions of popular Iberian dishes; for example, small turnovers become the *tapas* version of *empanadas*. A slice of *tortilla*, the

---

PDO STATUS

The governments in most European countries have instituted PDO (Protected Designation of Origin) for some agricultural and food products. Simply stated, this is a government-controlled quality program. This designation (often called DO) means that the government guarantees the origin of the product, preparation methods, its production within a certain location in the country, and the quality.

Currently, twelve countries regulate cheese. They are France, Italy, Spain, Portugal, Greece, Switzerland, the British Isles, Ireland, Austria, Germany, Holland, and Belgium. The number of DO cheeses changes as new cheeses obtain this status. Government control is not limited to cheeses. Many countries control wine and all sorts of other products. For example, Spain controls *Serrano* ham, Italy controls balsamic vinegar and *prosciutto di Parma* ham, and the list goes on and on.

SPANISH DO CHEESES

Cabrales Made from cow's milk mixed with goat's or sheep's milk, a type of blue cheese, semifirm texture, from northern Spain

Cantabria Made from cow's milk, mild flavor, soft creamy texture, from Cantabrian

Idiazábal Made from sheep's milk, smoked cheese with sharp flavor, dry crumbly firm texture, from Basque region

La Serena Made from sheep's milk, nutty pungent flavor, soft texture, from Extremadura

Mahon Made from cow's milk, slightly acidic and salty taste, smooth firm texture, from island of Minorca in Mediterranean, used for grating

Majorero Made from goat's milk, aged cheese, buttery texture, from Canary Islands

Manchego Made from sheep's milk, aged, tangy taste, crumbly texture, from La Mancha in central Spain

Picón Made from cow's, goat's, and sheep's milk, aged, robust full flavor, a type of blue cheese, from northern Spain

Quesucos de Liebana A group of several cheeses from northern Spain, made from cow's milk or mixed with sheep's and goat's milk, fresh or aged, smoked or unsmoked

Roncal Made from sheep's milk, nutty flavor, firm smooth texture, from northern Spain

Tetilla Made from cow's milk, aged, mild flavor, soft creamy texture, from Galicia

Zamorano Made from sheep's milk, aged, intense sharp flavor, firm yet crumbly texture, from northwest Spain

---

popular egg dish that is like an unfolded omelet, is served as *tapas*. Usually eaten at room temperature, *tortillas* can be filled with almost anything. Potatoes and onion make the classic *tortilla* filling.

Although Portugal produces excellent port, Spain is known for sherry, most of which comes from a small, hot, flat area in Andalusia. Both sherry and port are fortified wines. In addition, much wine production exists throughout Iberia, with each region producing its own varieties. Wine usually accompanies both the afternoon and evening meals. Another popular drink, *sangria*, consists of red wine with brandy, soda water, and fresh fruits. Favorite non-alcoholic beverages include strong coffee and hot chocolate.

Throughout Spain and Portugal breakfast usually is eaten at a coffee shop, rather than at home. People often buy *churros*, *choux* pastry dough deep-fried in olive oil, from a street vendor. Coffee or hot chocolate accompanies the *churros*. In the late morning, *tapas* or a snack may be consumed to hold the diner until *comida*, the main meal of the day. Served after two in the afternoon, *comida* begins with a course of soup or salad, followed by a fish or *tortilla* course, then meat, and finally dessert which is usually fruit. A *siesta* or rest follows this large meal which occurs during the hottest part of the day. After the *siesta*, people return to work. In the early evening, around six or seven, people go to a *tapas* bar for sherry and *tapas*. *Cena*, a light supper, is consumed after nine in the evening.

Review Questions

1. What ingredients were brought to Spain and Portugal from the explorers who returned from the New World?
2. What is *paella* and in which region did this dish originate?
3. Give examples of the Moorish influence on the cuisine of Spain.

REGION	AREA	WEATHER	TOPOGRAPHY	FOODS
Galica	Northwest	Lush and green, harsh climate	Borders Atlantic, coast, mountains, valleys	Seafood, empanadas
Basque	North	Cool	Mountains, coast	Seafood, trout, game, sheep's cheese, mushrooms, sauces
Castile	Central	Flat and arid	Plateau, *meseta*	Livestock, sheep, goats, *tapas*
La Mancha	South of Madrid	Arid, cold winters and hot summers	Mountainous plateau, *meseta*	Lamb, mutton, goats, sheep's cheese, *olla podrida*
Valencia	East	Warm summers, mild winters	Borders Mediterranean Sea, coast	Seafood, *paella*, rice, olives, citrus fruit, oranges, grapes, wine
Andalusia	South	Hot summers, mild winters	Coast, flat land	Seafood, gazpacho, olives, citrus fruit, oranges, grapes, wine, sherry
Extremadura	West	Warm summers, mild winters	Farmland	Pigs, sausages, cured hams
Northern Portugal		Temperate; spring and summer: warm and dry; winter and fall: cool and rainy	Coast, forests, mountains, plains, *meseta*	Seafood, cod, grapes, wine, port
Southern Portugal		Temperate; spring and summer: warm and dry; winter and fall: cool and rainy	Coast, forests, rolling, mountains, *meseta*, plains	Seafood, sardines, lemons, oranges, melons, almonds, grapes, wine, port

4. What are *tapas*? Give at least three examples.
5. How do the weather and topography influence the cuisines of Spain and Portugal?
6. Name at least four regions in Spain and tell what types of foods are most common in each region.
7. Discuss differences and similarities between the cuisines of Spain and Portugal.

Glossary

aioli Mayonnaise flavored with garlic

chorizo A sausage flavored with garlic and paprika

churros *Choux* pastry dough deep-fried in olive oil and eaten at breakfast; sold by street vendors

empanada A meat pie with a soft, flaky crust that is served throughout Spain

gazpacho Cold tomato vegetable soup; originated in Andalusia

jambon Serrano Cured ham with a sweet-salty taste similar to the *prosciutto* of Italy

meseta High, dry plateaus

olla podrida A casserole containing almost anything that can be stewed; literally translated, "rotten pot"; originated in central Spain

paella A casserole of saffron rice with a variety of meats, chicken, seafood, and vegetables named for the pot in which it is cooked; originated in Valencia; every region has its own variation on this national dish

tapas Small snacks or appetizers

EMPANADA DE CERDO Y PIMIENTOS (Spain)

Pork and Pepper Pie

Number of Servings: 12 to 16 tapas   Cooking Method: Bake
Total Yield: Two 10-inch pies

Food Balance: Protein
Wine Style: Light- to medium-bodied Chenin Blanc, Pinot Grigio, soft Chardonnay, Pinot Noir, Chianti
Example: Castello di Gabbiano Pinot Grigio or Chianti

> *Start preparation of dough and meat several hours in advance or the day before. This dish may be served as tapas or an entrée.*

INGREDIENTS	WEIGHT	VOLUME
DOUGH:		
flour	12½ oz	3 cups
salt		1½ teaspoons
water, cold	6 oz	¾ cup
vinegar	¾ oz	1½ tablespoons
egg, lightly beaten	1¼ oz	1 each
lard, shortening, or butter	8 oz	1 cup or 2 sticks
FILLING:		
pork shoulder or loin, cut in strips ⅛- by 2½-inches	12 oz	
paprika	¼ oz	1 tablespoon
parsley, fresh, minced		1 tablespoon
thyme		½ teaspoon
oregano		½ teaspoon
garlic, minced		1 large clove
salt		½ teaspoon
olive oil	2½ oz	5 tablespoons
peppers, green or mixture of green and red, cut in thin strips	12 oz	2 each
onions, thinly sliced	10 oz	2 medium
white wine, dry	1 oz	2 tablespoons
GLAZE:		
egg	1¼ oz	1 each
water		1 teaspoon

Folding Empanada dough into thirds

Empanada dough folded into thirds

Placing filling ingredients on rolled out dough

DOUGH:

1. Mix flour and salt in large bowl, form a well in center and add water, vinegar, and egg.
2. Stir until stiff, then work by hand until dough forms smooth ball.
3. Cover, let sit for 30 minutes.
4. Roll dough into 10- by 15-inch rectangle.

Crimping edge of dough

Cutting slits in Empanada so steam can escape

Baked Empanada (Pork and Pepper Pie)

5. Spread two-thirds of dough with ⅓-cup lard, shortening, or butter. Fold in thirds business-letter style, folding uncovered dough over half of buttered dough. Fold last third over folded dough. (This folding alternates layers of fatted dough with plain dough.)
6. Wrap in plastic wrap and refrigerate at least 15 minutes.
7. Repeat from step 4, using another ⅓ cup lard, shortening, or butter. Refrigerate again.
8. Repeat with remaining fat, refrigerate at least one hour, preferably overnight.

FILLING:
1. Combine paprika, 1½ oz (3 tablespoons) oil, parsley, garlic, other spices, and salt in small bowl.
2. Add meat and stir to coat well.
3. Marinate for several hours or overnight.
4. Heat ½ oz (1 tablespoon) oil in skillet. Add peppers and sauté for one minute.
5. Add 1 tablespoon water, lower heat, cover, and cook about 15 minutes, until peppers are tender. Remove peppers from skillet.
6. Heat remaining tablespoon of oil in same skillet and sauté onions over low heat until tender but not brown. Remove onions from skillet.
7. Turn heat to high, add marinated meat mixture, fry until it loses its color.
8. Add wine and cook another minute.

9. Add peppers and onions to meat, mix well. Correct seasonings, making sure it's well seasoned because it will be surrounded by dough.

ASSEMBLY:

1. Preheat oven to 350 degrees.
2. Roll dough into 10- by 15-inch rectangle, fold in thirds as before.
3. Cut dough in half, roll each half of dough into 10- by 20-inch rectangle and cut each into two 10-inch squares.
4. Trim square into 10-inch circle. Place one circle on parchment lined half-sheet pan.
5. Cover with filling, not quite reaching to edges. Dip finger into water, moisten edges of dough with wet finger. Cover with remaining dough circle.
6. Roll edges and press firmly to seal.
7. Lightly beat egg with water for glaze, brush over dough.
8. Make several slits in top of dough.
9. Bake about 35 minutes, until golden.
10. Cool slightly before serving or serve at room temperature. Cut into wedges.

TORTILLA A LA ESPAÑOLA (Spain)

Potato and Onion Omelet

Number of Servings: 8 to 10   Cooking Method: Sauté
Total Yield: 1 lb, 14 oz, 9- or 10-inch round
   cut into small wedges

Food Balance: Protein
Wine Style: Light- to medium-bodied Riesling, Pinot Blanc, Sauvignon
   Blanc, mild Chardonnay, Pinot Noir
Example: Beringer Founders' Estate Chardonnay or Pinot Noir

INGREDIENTS	WEIGHT	VOLUME
olive oil	6 oz	¾ cup
potatoes, baking, peeled, cut into ⅛-inch slices	1 lb, 5 oz	4 large
onion, thinly sliced	6 oz	1 large
salt	to taste	
eggs	8½ oz	5 each

1. Heat oil in 9- or 10-inch skillet over medium heat.
2. Add potato slices, one at a time, to form layer.
3. Top with layer of onion slices. Sprinkle lightly with salt.
4. Continue layering, using all potatoes and onions. Turn occasionally with spatula so all potatoes and onions cook evenly. Cook until potatoes are tender, remain separate, and not browned, about 10 minutes.
5. Drain potatoes and onions in colander, reserve oil.
6. In bowl, beat eggs with fork until slightly foamy. Salt to taste.
7. Add potatoes and onions to eggs, making certain potatoes and onions are covered with egg. Let mixture rest for 15 minutes.

Tortilla a la Española (Potato and Onion Omelet); courtesy of Olive Oil from Spain (ASOLIVA)

8. Heat ½ to 1 oz (1 to 2 tablespoons) reserved oil in skillet until smoking point.
9. Add potato and egg mixture, tilting and shaking pan to level.
10. Lower heat to medium high, shake pan often to prevent sticking.
11. When brown on bottom, invert plate over skillet and flip omelet onto plate. Slide omelet back into skillet to cook other side.
12. Lower heat to medium, cook until browned yet juicy inside.
13. Place on serving platter, cut into small wedges. Serve warm or at room temperature.

ESPINACAS A LA CATALANA (Spain)

Catalan Spinach

Number of Servings: 11   Cooking Method: Sauté
Serving Size: 4 oz
Total Yield: 2 lbs, 15 oz

Food Balance: Protein/sweet
Wine Style: Soft and fruity Riesling, Pinot Blanc, Blush, soft Syrah
Example: Meridian Vineyards Syrah

> *This may be served as a tapas, first course, or vegetable.*

INGREDIENTS	WEIGHT	VOLUME
raisins	3¾ oz	9 tablespoons
spinach, fresh, washed, tough stalks removed	4½ lbs	
olive oil	2½ oz	5 tablespoons
garlic, minced, mashed		3 cloves
pine nuts	3¾ oz	9 tablespoons
salt		1½ teaspoons
pepper		¾ teaspoon

1. Soak raisins in warm water. Set aside.
2. Boil spinach, covered, with a few drops of water.

Espinacas a la Catalana (Catalan Spinach); photo courtesy of Dorling Kindersley

3. Drain and press spinach to remove excess water. Chop roughly.
4. Roughly chop raisins.
5. Heat oil in skillet, add garlic and sauté about one minute.
6. Add spinach, pine nuts, and raisins, sauté another minute.
7. Season with salt and pepper, sauté about 5 minutes. Correct seasonings.
8. Serve immediately.

CHAMPINOÑES AL AJILLO

Mushrooms in Garlic Sauce

Number of Servings: 7
Serving Size: 3 oz tapas
Total Yield: 1 lb, 6 oz

Cooking Method: Sauté

Food Balance: Protein/acid balanced
Wine Style: Light- to medium-bodied Pinot Gris, dry Sherry, Gewürztraminer, Beaujolais
Example: Beringer Vineyards Gewürztraminer or Gamay Beaujolais

INGREDIENTS	WEIGHT	VOLUME
olive oil	1½ oz	3 tablespoons
mushrooms, wild or cultivated, cleaned, left whole if small or cut if larger	1 lb	
garlic, minced, mashed	1 oz	8 cloves
stock, mushroom, veal, or beef	4 oz	½ cup

Champinoñes al Ajillo (Mushrooms in Garlic Sauce);
photo courtesy of Dorling Kindersley

INGREDIENTS	WEIGHT	VOLUME
sherry, dry	2 oz	¼ cup
lemon juice, fresh	½ to ¾ oz	4 teaspoons
red pepper flakes		½ teaspoon
salt		½ teaspoon
pepper		¼ teaspoon
parsley, minced	½ oz	¼ cup

1. Heat oil in skillet over high heat until hot.
2. Add mushrooms and garlic, sauté for about 3 or 4 minutes.
3. Add remaining ingredients except for parsley, cook 3 minutes.
4. Add parsley and cook another 2 minutes. Correct seasonings. Serve.

GAZPACHO (Spain)

Cold Tomato Vegetable Soup

Number of Servings: 9
Serving Size: 6 oz
Total Yield: 3 lbs, 6 oz

Food Balance: Protein/sweet/acid
Wine Style: Light-bodied Pinot Gris, Pinot Grigio, Sauvignon Blanc,
  Chablis-style Chardonnay, Blush, Rosé
Example: Beringer Vineyards Rosé de Saignee

Gazpacho (Cold Tomato Vegetable Soup); photo courtesy of Olive Oil from Spain (ASOLIVA)

INGREDIENTS	WEIGHT	VOLUME
tomatoes, peeled, coarsely chopped, fresh or canned	1 lb, 12 oz	5 medium or 1 can
cucumbers, peeled, diced	9½ oz	1 large
onion, diced	7 oz	1 large
green pepper, deribbed, seeded, diced	6 oz	1 each
garlic, peeled, minced	¼ oz	2 cloves
red wine vinegar	2 oz	¼ cup
olive oil	½ oz	1 tablespoon
bread, white, stale, crumbled	¾ oz	1 slice
salt	¼ oz	1 teaspoon
tomato juice	12 oz	1½ cups

GARNISH:

bread cubes, ¼-inch
onions, finely chopped
cucumbers, peeled, finely chopped
green peppers, finely chopped

1. Combine all ingredients in bowl, stir.
2. Purée in food processor in batches.
3. Strain mixture through sieve or China cap.
4. Chill thoroughly for several hours or overnight. Correct seasonings.
5. Serve in chilled soup bowls. Pass bowls of garnishes for guests to add to soup.

CALDO VERDE (Portugal)

Potato and Kale Soup

Number of Servings: 8   Cooking Method: Boil
Serving Size: 7 oz
Total Yield: 3 lbs, 13 oz

Food Balance: Protein
Wine Style: Light- to medium-bodied Riesling, Pinot Blanc, Sauvignon
   Blanc, Pinot Grigio, Pinot Noir
Example: Château Souverain Sauvignon Blanc

INGREDIENTS	WEIGHT	VOLUME
potatoes, peeled, cubed	1 lb	3 large
water	3 lb	6 cups
salt	½ oz	2 teaspoons
garlic, minced, mashed	¼ oz	2 cloves
pepper, ground		¼ teaspoon
olive oil	1 oz	2 tablespoons
kale, fresh, washed, deribbed, finely shredded	8 oz	

1. Combine potatoes, water, and salt in saucepan. Bring to boil.
2. Cover and simmer for 25 minutes.
3. Add garlic, purée in food processor until almost smooth. Some potato chunks remaining are fine.
4. Return to saucepan. Add oil and pepper, bring to boil over high heat.
5. Add kale and boil uncovered for about 5 minutes. Correct seasonings. Serve.

ENSALADA DE ARROZ (Spain)

Rice Salad

Number of Servings: 8   Cooking Method: Sauté, boil
Serving Size: 4 oz
Total Yield: 2 lbs

> Prepare this dish several hours in advance so the flavors marry.

INGREDIENTS	WEIGHT	VOLUME
RICE:		
olive oil	½ oz	1 tablespoon
onion, small dice	½ oz	1 tablespoon
rice, short or medium grain	8 oz	1 cup
chicken stock	8 oz	1 cup
water, boiling	8 oz	1 cup
parsley		1 sprig
thyme		¼ teaspoon
tarragon		⅛ teaspoon
SALAD:		
mushrooms, chopped	4 oz	1⅓ cups
lemon juice, fresh	½ oz	1 tablespoon
olive oil	1½ oz	3 tablespoons

INGREDIENTS	WEIGHT	VOLUME
red wine vinegar	½ oz	1 tablespoon
sugar		¼ teaspoon
garlic, minced, mashed		1 clove
mustard, Dijon		¼ teaspoon
thyme		¼ teaspoon
salt		¼ teaspoon
pepper		⅛ teaspoon
parsley, minced		1 tablespoon
anchovy, finely chopped		1 each
anchovy oil (from anchovy can)		½ teaspoon
roasted red pepper or pimento, diced	1½ oz	1 each

RICE:

1. Preheat oven to 400 degrees. Heat oil in ovenproof pan.
2. Add onion and sauté until wilted. Add rice, stir to coat.
3. Add liquids and seasonings to rice, cover and bake for 15 minutes.
4. Remove from oven, discard parsley, let sit covered for 10 minutes.
5. Cool completely.

SALAD:

1. Combine mushrooms with lemon juice, set aside.
2. Mix oil, vinegar, sugar, salt, pepper, mustard, thyme, garlic, parsley, anchovy, and anchovy oil in small bowl.
3. Place rice in bowl, pour dressing over rice.
4. Fold in red pepper and mushrooms and lemon juice.
5. Let salad sit several hours before serving. Correct seasonings. Serve cold or at room temperature.

PAELLA A LA VALENCIANA (Spain)

Chicken and Seafood Rice

Number of Servings: 13
Serving Size: 13 oz
Total Yield: 10 lbs, 13 oz

Cooking Method: Sauté, braise

Food Balance: Protein/spicy
Wine Style: Light- to medium-bodied Riesling, Pinot Blanc, light Chardonnay, Pinot Grigio, Beaujolais
Example: Beringer Vineyards Riesling or Founders' Estate Chardonnay

INGREDIENTS	WEIGHT	VOLUME	
chicken stock, strong	3 lbs	6 cups	
shrimp	1 lb		
lobsters, live, split, divided into tail sections and claws	3 to 4 lbs	2 each	
saffron thread, crumbled		½ teaspoon	→ use turmeric in place
white wine, dry	4 oz	½ cup	
chorizo sausage, ¼-inch slices	4 oz		
cured ham, *Serrano*, diced	4 oz		
pork, lean, ½-inch cubes	4 oz		
chicken, cut into small pieces, breast into 4, thigh into 2 pieces	2½ to 3 lbs	1 each	

INGREDIENTS	WEIGHT	VOLUME
olive oil	3 oz	6 tablespoons
red pepper, finely diced	7 oz	1 each
onion, diced	5 oz	1 medium
garlic, minced	½ oz	4 cloves
mussels, cleaned	12 oz to 1 lb	12 each
clams, cleaned	about 1 lb	12 each
rice, short or medium grain	1 lb, 6½ oz	3 cups
parsley, fresh, minced	¾ oz	5 tablespoons
salt	to taste	
peas, fresh or frozen	4 oz	1 cup
roasted red pepper, pimento, sliced	1½ oz	1 each

GARNISH:

lemon wedges
parsley, fresh, minced

1. Peel and devein shrimp, reserve shells for stock.
2. Separate tail section and claws from lobster. Cut each tail in half. Reserve small feelers and head for stock. Crack lobster claws.
3. Cook stock with shrimp and lobster shells for one hour. Strain, reserve 5½ cups.
4. Add wine and saffron to stock.
5. Heat oil in *paella* pan, braising pan, or ovenproof dish.
6. Add chicken pieces, fry over high heat until golden. Remove.
7. Sauté chorizo, ham, pork, shrimp, and lobster about 3 minutes.

Paella a la Valenciana (Chicken and Seafood Rice); photo courtesy of The Norwegian Seafood Export Council—www.seafood.no. Photography by Per Alfsen

8. Remove shrimp and lobster.
9. Add red peppers, onions, and garlic to pan, sauté over medium heat about 5 minutes.
10. Add rice and parsley, coating well. *Can be prepared in advance to this point.*
11. Meanwhile, bring broth to boil. Add to rice. Stir, salt to taste.
12. Preheat oven to 325 degrees.
13. Bring to boil, cook uncovered, stirring occasionally, over medium-high heat, about 10 minutes.
14. Mix peas into rice, bury shrimp and chicken in rice. Place clams and mussels in rice so side that will open faces up.
15. Arrange pepper strips and lobster pieces over rice.
16. Bake uncovered for 20 minutes. Remove from oven, tent with foil, let rest about 10 minutes.
17. Garnish with lemon wedges and parsley, serve from pan.

SCALLOPS IN GREEN SAUCE (Spain)

Number of Servings: 8
Serving Size: 7 oz
Total Yield: 3 lbs, 12 oz

Cooking Method: Braise

Food Balance: Protein
Wine Style: Light- to medium-bodied Riesling, Sauvignon Blanc, Pinot Grigio, Blush, Rosé
Example: Château Souverain Sauvignon Blanc

INGREDIENTS	WEIGHT	VOLUME
olive oil	1½ oz	3 tablespoons
garlic, minced	1½ oz	8 teaspoons or 10 to 12 cloves

This versatile dish may be prepared with any variety of seafood or a combination. Try shrimp, clams, mussels, lobster, or a combination of fish and shellfish.

Scallops in Green Sauce

INGREDIENTS	WEIGHT	VOLUME
onion, finely chopped	7 oz	1½ cups
parsley, finely chopped	4½ oz	2½ cups
flour, all purpose	2½ oz	8 tablespoons
chicken stock, strong	1 lb, 4 oz	2½ cups
dry sherry	5 oz	⅔ cup
scallops	3 lb	
salt	to taste	

1. Heat oil in skillet or braising pan over medium heat.
2. Sauté onion for 1 or 2 minutes.
3. Add garlic, parsley, and seafood, sauté for another 4 or 5 minutes.
4. Add flour and stir for one minute.
5. Add stock, stir constantly for 5 minutes.
6. Add sherry and cook for another 3 minutes.
7. Correct seasonings. Serve over rice.

POLLO AL AJILLO (Spain)

Garlic Chicken

Number of Servings: 8   Cooking Method: Sauté
Serving Size: ¼ chicken
Total Yield: 3 lbs, 14 oz

Food Balance: Protein/salt
Wine Style: Light and fruity Riesling, White Merlot, Rosé, Dolcetto, Beaujolais
Example: Beringer Vineyards Johannisberg Riesling, White Merlot, or Gamay Beaujolais

INGREDIENTS	WEIGHT	VOLUME
chicken	5 to 6 lbs	2 each
garlic, peeled, minced	5 oz	2 heads
olive oil	2 oz	4 tablespoons
pepper		¼ teaspoon
brandy or cognac	4 oz	½ cup
Kosher salt	to taste	

1. Cut chicken into small serving pieces, each thigh, split breast, and wing into 2 parts. Dry well.
2. Mince garlic in food processor, reserve 2 tablespoons for later use.
3. Heat oil in pan or skillet over moderate heat.
4. Sauté chicken until pieces are well browned.
5. Add garlic (except reserved portion), pepper, and brandy. Be careful, it may flame.
6. Cover and cook over low heat about 15 minutes.
7. Sprinkle with the remaining garlic and salt. Serve topped with sauce and garlic from pan.

CHULETA DE TERNERA HORTELANA (Spain)

Veal Chops with Ham, Mushrooms, and Pimiento

Number of Servings: 8   Cooking Method: Sauté
Serving Size: 1 chop, 1¼ oz sauce
Total Yield: 10½ oz sauce

Food Balance: Protein/acid balanced
Wine Style: Wide variety—very balanced dish, enjoy the wine of your choice such as Pinot Blanc, Chardonnay, Pinot Noir, Merlot, Cabernet Sauvignon, Rioja
Example: Château Souverain Chardonnay or Cabernet Sauvignon

INGREDIENTS	WEIGHT	VOLUME
olive oil	2 oz	4 tablespoons
veal chops, rib, about 1-inch thick	about 9 oz each	8 each
onion, minced	4½ oz	1 cup
garlic, minced	¼ oz	2 cloves
cured ham, *serrano*, minced	2 oz	4 tablespoons
mushrooms, finely chopped	7 oz	2 cups
pimentos or roasted red pepper, finely chopped	5 oz	4 each
salt		½ teaspoon
pepper, ground		¼ teaspoon
thyme		½ teaspoon
white wine, dry	4 oz	½ cup
bay leaf		1 each
parsley, fresh, minced		2 tablespoons

1. Heat 1 oz (2 tablespoons) oil in skillet, sauté onion for 2 minutes, add garlic and sauté until onion is wilted.
2. Add ham, mushrooms, red pepper, salt, pepper, and thyme. Cook 5 minutes more. Remove from skillet.
3. Meanwhile, sprinkle chops with salt and pepper.
4. Heat remaining oil in skillet.
5. Sauté chops slowly until they are cooked, about 10 to 15 minutes. Remove them to warm platter.

Chuleta de Ternera Hortelana (Veal Chops with Ham, Mushrooms, and Pimento)

6. Deglaze pan juices with wine, season with salt and pepper, add bay leaf. Stir constantly, scraping pan drippings from bottom of pan.
7. Cook slowly 2 or 3 minutes, adding water or veal or chicken broth if necessary. Add ham and vegetable mixture and heat thoroughly. Correct seasonings.
8. To serve, top chops with ham and vegetable mixture, then coat center two-thirds of chop with sauce. Sprinkle with parsley.

BATATAS À PORTUGUÊSA (Portugal)

Fried Potatoes

Number of Servings: 9
Serving Size: 4 oz
Total Yield: 2 lbs, 4 oz

Cooking Method: Sauté

INGREDIENTS	WEIGHT	VOLUME
butter	2½ oz	5 tablespoons
olive oil	2½ oz	5 tablespoons
new potatoes, peeled, sliced ¼-inch thick	4½ lbs	15 to 18 each
salt		1¼ teaspoon
black pepper, ground		½ teaspoon
parsley, fresh, minced	¼ oz	2 to 3 tablespoons

1. Melt butter and olive oil until hot in heavy skillet over medium high heat.
2. Add potatoes. Turning often with spatula, cook until tender and golden brown, about 20 minutes. Lower heat if burning.
3. Season with salt and pepper, correct seasonings, and sprinkle with parsley just before serving.

GUISANTES A LA ESPAÑOLA (Spain)

Peas with Cured Ham

Number of Servings: 11
Serving Size: 4 oz
Total Yield: 2 lbs, 15 oz

Cooking Method: Sauté

INGREDIENTS	WEIGHT	VOLUME
olive oil	2 oz	4 tablespoons
carrot, minced	5 oz	1 cup
onion, minced	5½ oz	1 cup
cured ham, *serrano*, minced	6 oz	1 cup
salt	to taste	
pepper		½ teaspoon
peas, fresh or frozen	2 lbs	

1. Heat oil in pan, sauté onion and carrot until onion is wilted, about 3 minutes.
2. Add ham and cook one minute.
3. Add peas, salt, and pepper. Be careful with salt if ham is salty.
4. Cover tightly, and cook on low heat about 15 minutes, or until peas are tender.

PORTO PUDIM FLAN (Portugal)

Portugese Baked Caramel Custard

Number of Servings: 8 to 12
Total Yield: One 8-inch or
  10 to 12 individual

Cooking Method: Bake

INGREDIENTS	WEIGHT	VOLUME
CARAMEL:		
sugar	7¼ oz	1 cup
water	2 oz	¼ cup
CUSTARD:		
sugar	4¾ oz	¾ cup
milk	12 oz	1½ cups
heavy cream	11½ oz	1½ cups
egg yolks	4 oz	6 each
port	½ oz	1 tablespoon

CARAMEL:

1. Combine sugar and water in small pan, mixing so all sugar is wet.
2. Bring to boil over high heat. Do not stir. Use pastry brush dipped in cold water to wash any sugar crystals from sides of pan.
3. Reduce heat to medium high, cook without stirring until golden brown color.
4. Immediately pour into flan dish, tip dish to coat bottom and up part of sides. Set dish aside.

CUSTARD:

1. Preheat oven to 350 degrees.
2. Heat milk and heavy cream in pan until small bubbles appear around the edge of the pan. Set aside.
3. Place sugar in small heavy pan over medium heat and caramelize. Stir until it melts and turns golden brown. Remove from heat.
4. Pour hot cream mixture very slowly into caramel, stirring with large spoon. Be careful, it will bubble and splatter. Stir until caramel has dissolved. Return to heat if needed to dissolve caramel.
5. Beat egg yolks until well blended with mixer or whisk.
6. Slowly pour in cream mixture, stirring constantly.
7. Stir in port, strain mixture through fine sieve, pour into prepared dish(es).

Coating dish with caramelized sugar; photo courtesy of Dorling Kindersley

Pouring custard into prepared dish; photo courtesy of Dorling Kindersley

Porto Pudim Flan (Portugese Baked Caramel Custard); photo courtesy of Dorling Kindersley

8. Place dish(es) in roasting pan on middle shelf of oven. Pour boiling water into pan to come halfway up sides of molds.
9. Bake until knife inserted in center of custard comes out clean, about 1 hour, 10 minutes for large dish or 40 minutes for individual molds.
10. Cool, then refrigerate until chilled, at least 3 hours or overnight.
11. To unmold, run sharp knife around inside edge of mold, invert on chilled serving plate.

CHAPTER 3
France

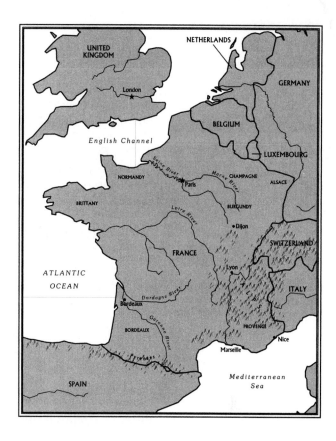

By the end of this chapter, you will be able to

- Explain the origins of classical French cookery
- Understand and explain differences in classical and regional French cookery
- Name dishes from various regions of France and explain why they originated there
- Name countries and cultures that influenced French cuisine and describe how their impact affected the cuisine of France
- Name food items that flourish in various areas of France
- Prepare a variety of regional and classical French dishes

HISTORY

Drawings discovered on the walls of caves in southwest France confirm the presence of prehistoric man. Researchers believe Cro-Magnon men lived in this area as early as 25,000 B.C.

Because of its geographic location, France was subjected to invasions on all sides by many different groups of people throughout history. In about 125 B.C., the Romans conquered Provence in the south of France from the Gauls. Roman rule existed until the late fifth century A.D., when the Roman Empire declined. At that time, France came under the power of the Franks and Germans.

Sharing a border with Germany, the northeastern areas of Alsace and Lorraine exhibit strong German culinary influence. A rich, fertile land, this area exchanged nationalities numerous times throughout history, sometimes won by the Germans, other times under the rule of France.

Fifteen hundred years ago, the Celtics came to Brittany from England. The Vikings from Scandinavia landed in Normandy around 1000 A.D. Meanwhile, the Arabs entered the south of France, and their influence is apparent in dishes from that area such as *cassoulet*, a one-pot dish containing meats and beans. One-pot dishes characterize the cooking of the Arabs who wandered the desert and cooked any available ingredients in one pot over an open fire.

In 1533, Catherine de' Medici of Italy came to France to marry the future king, Henry II. She brought fine Italian chefs with her, introducing the French aristocracy to the Italian splendor in table setting, as well as numerous new foods including broccoli, peas, artichokes, sauces, and fine pastries. The course of dining in France changed forever.

The French Revolution began in 1789, resulting in the end of the ruling aristocracy, and France became an independent nation. In 1804, Bonaparte Napoleon became the ruler and conquered much of Europe. The French Revolution brought an important culinary change to France and to the world—the proliferation of the restaurant. After the revolution, the cooks who had worked for the aristocracy found themselves without jobs, so they found work in the restaurants of France. These chefs and cooks transformed many French restaurants into world-renowned eating establishments, a reputation that still exists today.

TOPOGRAPHY

Two major mountain chains are found in France. Situated on the east and southeastern side of France, the Alps forms the border between France, Italy, and Switzerland. The highest peak in the Alps, Mont Blanc, actually lies in France. Bordering Spain on the southwest, the Pyrenees Mountains created a difficult, rugged terrain which resulted in significant isolation.

Two bodies of water form miles and miles of coastline in France. On the southern side lies the Mediterranean Sea; the Atlantic Ocean borders the west and northwest.

Several rivers transect France, resulting in fertile farmlands and valleys where vineyards flourish and world-famous wines are produced. The longest river, the Loire, runs through central and western France; the Seine and the Marne lie in the central area; the Dordogne transects the southwest; and the Rhine and Rhone are in the east.

With the exception of the central highlands in the central portion, most of the land in France consists of fertile farmland used for the production of grains, fruits, and vegetables or cattle and sheep raised for meat and dairy. In the northwest, Normandy contains coast, rolling hills, and forests. Just south in Brittany, the landscape changes to rugged coast, rocky terrain, and forests.

Ingredients and Foods Commonly Used Throughout the Cuisine of France Include:

- lamb
- pork
- duck, chicken, and goose
- beef
- fish and seafood
- *foie gras*
- butter
- cream
- cheese
- apples, pears, and cherries
- truffles and all types of mushrooms
- numerous vegetables, including peas and *haricots*

- shallots, leeks, onions, and garlic
- wine and brandy

COOKING METHODS

The cooks and chefs of France use virtually all preparation methods. From *bouillabaisse* to *cassoulet* to *confit*, braising and one-pot cookery appear often in regional cookery. The famous French fries are among the deep-fried food items; the list of dishes prepared by sautéing goes on and on. Poaching is commonly used for fish. Baking, roasting, and broiling appear frequently.

REGIONS

The north and northwest receive ample rainfall, resulting in a fertile soil that produces abundant crops. Many orchards thrive in this area, which is particularly known for apples. Although temperatures on the coasts remain more moderate, inland areas experience cold winters and hot summers.

Located in the northwest, Normandy consists of coast, dairy country, and farmland. This region yields very high quality butter, cream, cheese, and eggs. Apple orchards thrive in Normandy, where *calvados*, apple brandy, originated. Cream sauces, Camembert cheese, fresh seafood (especially sole), sheep, lamb, and apple desserts are trademarks of this region. Butter is the cooking fat of choice here.

Just to the south of Normandy, the people of Brittany prefer heavy, simple food—quite a contrast to the cuisine of Normandy. Buckwheat, whole grains, pork, and seafood remain staples. Excellent shellfish, particularly oysters, are bred here. *Crêpes*, thin, delicate pancakes that are rolled around a filling, originated in Brittany. Situated just across the channel from Great Britain, the Welsh influence appears prominently here. *Beurre blanc*, butter sauce, accompanies many dishes in Brittany.

Known as Ile de France, the north central region includes Paris and the surrounding countryside. Surprisingly, most of this region remains quite rural. All types of soups are appreciated here, from consommés to cream soups and from thick purées to the classic French onion soup with its topping of cheese and bread. Pâtés are widely consumed; Brie cheese hails from this region. Finally, Ile de France is the home of the very popular *pomme frittes*, better known as French fries.

In the northeast, the valleys around the Rhine River create fertile farmland suitable for lots of crops. Bordering Germany and Belgium, the culinary influence of those countries is strongly felt. Alsace contains very fertile farmland and produces a bounty of fruits and vegetables. Known for onion tart and *choucroute*, a dish containing sauerkraut cooked with sausages and meats and accompanied by boiled potatoes, this region serves some of the hearty foods of its neighbor, Germany. Noodles, dumplings, and *spaetzel* (a German specialty that is a cross between a noodle and dumpling) are regular menu items here; pork ranks as the favorite meat, and *charcuterie* is prevalent. In addition to the fondness for wine so prevalent throughout France, beer is served often in this region.

The Jura Mountains and French Alps lie in the southeast. Potatoes, milk, cream, cheese, freshwater fish, and beef dominate the cuisine here. Gruyère cheese, a type of Swiss cheese, comes from the French Juras while several creamy cheeses including Reblochon are produced in the French Alps.

The region of Burgundy in central France boasts excellent wines and the birthplace of the famous culinarian, Jean Brillat-Savarin. This area contains rivers supplying fish, forests abounding with mushrooms and game, and the city of Dijon, which is famous for its mustards. The cooking in Burgundy often incorporates wine and cream; pork fat is the fat of choice here. *Boeuf bourguignon* and *coq au vin*, both dishes braised in wine, originated in this area. *Escargot*, snails prepared with garlic butter, are another famous specialty from this region. Chalky caves found in Burgundy and in the Champagne district to its north provide excellent storage for the aging of fine wines.

To the south of Burgundy lies the city of Lyon, reputed to be the gastronomical capital of France, and perhaps the world. Pork, all sorts of sausages, onions, and potatoes are popular in this area. *Quenelles*, a dumpling of puréed fish, originated here. Much of the gastronomical splendor of this area comes from its proximity to other areas in France that produce the finest food products. For example, beef from Charlois, poultry from Bresse, lamb from Auvergne, forests providing a variety of mushrooms, abundant rivers and streams yielding freshwater seafood, and some of the best wines in the world come from areas lying close to Lyon.

Much of the central region contains poor soil and highlands. This land is good for grazing livestock and sheep, but not great for crops. As a result, this area yields a lot of meat and dairy products. In addition, wild mushrooms and much game thrive in the central to west-central area. This region claims the invention of *Tarte Tatin*, apple pie that is baked with a top crust only and then inverted on a plate immediately after baking.

The Mediterranean Sea borders the south of France in the area called the Riviera. The mild winters and hot, dry summers result in a proliferation of crops, including olive trees and grapevines. Olive oil replaces butter as the fat of choice here. Provence, a southern province, displays food products typical of the Mediterranean cuisines. Tomatoes, olives, olive oil, garlic, peppers, anchovies, and a variety of herbs are widely used and characteristic of dishes called *provençal*. Goat cheeses, which often appear seasoned with herbs, come from this southern region.

The southwestern border with Spain contains the high, rugged Pyrenees Mountains creating incredibly difficult terrain. These mountains are so rugged that the French used to travel by sea to reach Spain rather than crossing this mountainous barrier. Known as the Basque region, seafood, pork, tomatoes, and both mild and spicy red peppers frequent many dishes in this region.

South central France contains the region called Languedoc. From this region comes oysters and other shellfish; *confit*, a method of slow cooking goose or duck in its own fat; *foie gras*, the highly prized goose liver; and *cassoulet*, a one-pot dish containing various meats, white beans, and herbs. Famous for the sheep's cheese of the same name, the town of Roquefort lies in Languedoc. Lots of caves exist in this area, providing an excellent place for aging cheeses.

In the southwest of France lies Perigord, an area known for black truffles, cheeses, mushrooms, walnuts, red wine, cognac, game, pork, goose, duck, *foie gras*, *pâté*, and *confit*. As in Languedoc, the many caves existing here are used for aging cheeses.

The Loire Valley in the west produces an abundance of fruits and vegetables from the rich soil, grapes for wine, and many types of goat cheeses. Shallots flavor many of the dishes here. Throughout French history, kings chose this beautiful area to the west of Paris to build *châteaux*, country homes.

CUISINE

Throughout history, the people of France displayed extraordinary interest in food and dining. As a result, the French embraced all types of culinary influences from other groups, adapting ones that improved their dining experience. In addition, France has had many talented chefs whose goal was to improve and refine the foods and the culinary experience.

Two distinctly different cuisines are associated with the cooking of France. The first—classical cookery—initially existed only for the upper class and aristocracy. Definite rules governed classical cooking in its early days, as well as today. In classical preparations, the marriage of sauces with dishes held the utmost importance with the goal of achieving gastronomical perfection.

The second type of cuisine—regional cookery—involves much simpler preparations than classical cooking in addition to utilizing the foods available in each region. Although quite different from each other, both classical and regional cuisines remain very important components of the cookery of France. First, French classical cookery is addressed.

The Greeks treated dining with sophistication and felt dining should be a relaxing and enjoyable time. Music, dancing, and dinner conversation accompanied the food. The Greeks taught two momentous lessons about eating and drinking: the first was moderation and balance in both eating and drinking; the second was an association of these two tasks with great joy and pleasure.

After the Romans entered France's culinary world, the French learned overindulgence of eating. The rich partook in huge banquets featuring hundreds of varieties of fish, meat, and other dishes. In the meantime, the poor subsisted on a diet of porridge and gruel.

Throughout the Middle Ages until the fourteenth century, the food was heavily spiced and without a lot of variety. In those days before refrigeration, the heavy spices hid the taste and smell of rancid food.

Culinary issues changed during the Renaissance in the fifteenth century. An emphasis on fine cuisine, tableware, and service began in Italy. This trend toward culinary opulence spread to France, helped along when Italian Catherine de' Medici married the future king of France in 1533. The Italian chefs who accompanied her to France introduced sweetbreads, truffles, the Italian tradition for splendid foods and table settings, in addition to the Italian pastries that became the basis for French pastries. The French nobility embraced the lavish banquets with many courses, extravagant centerpieces, and carvings made from foods.

Since the 1700s, the *haute cuisine* of France has set the standard for excellence. The French have made remarkable contributions to the culinary world, especially with their repertoire of sauces. From growing to selling to cooking, the French treat food with great respect. Food and wine rank as some of life's greatest pleasures throughout France. By the 1700s, the heavy spices had disappeared, and the emphasis became the flavors found in natural foods. The nobility continued their grandiose banquets, until the execution in 1793 of King Louis XVI and his wife Queen Marie Antoinette, which marked the French Revolution. Not realizing that the poor people were starving while the

---

Stocks form the foundation of classical cooking; sauces are prepared from stocks. The five mother sauces are béchamel, velouté, tomato, espagnole, and hollandaise. All the other sauces are derived from these five sauces.

RULES FOR CLASSICAL COOKERY

- Offer a variety of textures in the different foods—soft, puréed, firm, crunchy, and so on.
- Food items should not be repeated within a meal—for example, if potato soup is served, potatoes should not accompany the entrée.
- Offer an interesting array of colors on the plate to stimulate the appetite.

---

aristocracy consumed lavish banquets, Marie Antoinette made the famous "let them eat cake" statement when told that the people had no bread to eat.

During the rule of Napoleon following the French Revolution, food became even more elegant. Considered the father of French classical cuisine, Marie-Antoine Carême (1784–1833) trained as a cook and then as a pastry chef around 1800. He made several significant contributions in the culinary world, one being the introduction of symmetry and order to French cooking. Carême also initiated the concept of balancing the flavors and textures of the foods both within individual courses and throughout the meal. This led to the belief that the entire meal must unite to form a pleasing, whole experience. Later Carême wrote several cookbooks that were the first books to contain actual recipes and menus in addition to defining the French cooking methods. Carême's recipes included precise amounts of ingredients, exacting directions, and the feeling of artistic execution for each dish.

Always interested in architecture, Carême created centerpieces from pastry materials that were replicas of the architectural masterpieces found throughout the world. These pastry feats adorned opulent tables of food, some of these tables holding dozens of different cold or hot dishes. Among the well-known dishes invented by Carême is *charlotte russe*, a confection featuring a core of vanilla Bavarian cream folded with whipped cream surrounded by ladyfinger biscuits. Considered "the queen of all entrées" by Carême, *chartreuse* consists of a molded dish with a decorative outside of colorful vegetables around a center containing vegetables, game, and/or poultry.

Another prominent chef who left a significant legacy on culinary history was Georges Auguste Escoffier (1846–1935). Known as "the king of chefs and the chef of kings," he is credited with adapting classical cooking for the modern world.

Among his many contributions, Escoffier reorganized the kitchen, developing stations for the kitchen personnel that are still used today in many kitchens. Instead of having one cook responsible for each dish, cooks were assigned to *brigades* or teams that prepared items according to the type of cooking techniques. For example, the *saucier* was responsible for preparing the sauces; the *garde manger* prepared cold foods and garnishes; the *rôtisseur* handled the foods requiring roasting.

Prior to Escoffier's time, all the foods in a meal were presented at the same time in an elaborate display on one or more tables. Escoffier and another French chef, Urbain Dubois, initiated serving the meal in courses. This resulted in hot food being served hot, and cold foods served cold. Also, the *brigade* system in the kitchen greatly expedited the delivery of food to the diner after an order was placed.

Escoffier established several changes that affected the presentation of food; many of these changes are still followed today. He said all garnishes and centerpieces should be edible and that food and its presentation should reflect simplicity. He greatly reduced the size of the menus, making them more man-

---

FAMOUS CHEFS AND GASTRONOMES

- Jean Anthelme Brillat-Savarin (1755–1826)—great gastronome
- Marie-Antoine Carême (1784–1833)—father of classical cuisine; created ornate and elaborate table decorations as well as beautifully presented foods
- Urbain Dubois (1818–1901)—promoted Russian table service which resulted in meals being served by courses
- Auguste Escoffier (1846–1935)—father of modern cooking; reorganized setup of kitchen personnel by initiating cooking stations in the kitchen to expedite food preparation
- Prosper Montagné (1865–1948)—wrote *Larousse Gastronomique*; simplified classical cuisine by eliminating many garnishes
- Maurice Edmond Sailland (1872–1956)—gastronome, professional food critic, wrote forerunner for *Guide Michelin* (which rates restaurants and hotels)
- Fernand Point (1897–1955)—excellent restaurateur who owned the restaurant, Pyramid in Vienne, France; developed many recipes and trained many chefs; instrumental in the *nouvelle cuisine* movement which emphasized creating lighter versions of traditional French dishes

---

ageable for the kitchen staff. A lasting legacy, Escoffier wrote several cookbooks, leaving more than 5,000 recipes for future generations of cooks.

Escoffier became associated with Cesar Ritz and ran the kitchens in elite hotels in many cities in Europe, Canada, and the United States. In this position, he cooked for many prominent patrons, including nobility, actors and actresses, and many of the most wealthy people of the time. Escoffier invented numerous dishes that were named for the event or the patron for whom it was created. Peche Melba and Melba toast were named after Nellie Melba, a famous soprano. The actress, Sarah Bernhardt, had several dishes named in her honor, too.

Although Carême's legacy depicts him as the father of classical cuisine, Escoffier is remembered as the father of modern classical cooking. He made numerous profound contributions to the culinary world; many of these form the foundation of today's culinary ideas.

The second type of cooking, regional cookery, developed as a result of strong variations existing between the cuisines of the different regions. Like most countries, the creation of dishes is based on what grows best and what is raised in each area. A number of factors, including the topography, climate,

---

MAJOR COOKBOOKS IN FRENCH HISTORY

1300s—Taillevent—demonstrates the heavily spiced foods of that time which used lots of cinnamon, ginger, clove, and nutmeg; sauces were thickened with bread rather than *roux*; emphasis on soups, meats, and poultry; exhibited little variety in the foods

1600s—La Varenne—first cookbook that moved toward classical cuisine; first cookbook with alphabetized recipes; included vegetable cookery; moved away from heavily spiced foods; used *roux* instead of bread to thicken sauces; emphasis on the natural flavors of foods

1800s—Brillat-Savarin—*The Physiology of Taste*—this book took twenty-five years to write; it chronicles the food of the time

1800s—Carême—described classical cookery in great detail; wrote precise recipes

1800 to 1900s—Montagné—wrote *Larousse Gastronomique*, the basic French cooking encyclopedia

1900s—Escoffier—wrote more than 5,000 recipes documenting classical cuisine

and the neighboring countries, influence the cuisine found in each region. Availability and selection of wines, cheeses, produce, cooking fat, meats, fish, and poultry as well as the preparation methods vary with the different regions. Sauces found in regional cookery are often derived from liquids added to the ingredients in the pot, rather than preparing a separate sauce as is customary in classical cookery. Regional specialties are frequently prepared in other areas; however, they often appear with great differences. Originating in the Mediterranean area, variations on *bouillabaisse*, the traditional fish stew, show up in many coastal areas. The same is true for *cassoulet*, which is served throughout France.

As a country, France has a rich bounty of crops. Abundant apples, cherries, peaches, pears, and grapes grow. Many vegetables, including sugar beets, beans, peas, carrots, potatoes, cauliflower, and tomatoes, thrive in various regions of France. Besides plentiful produce, all sorts of seafood, fish, and animals for meat flourish here. Sheep, cattle, poultry, game, as well as freshwater fish and saltwater seafood from the Atlantic, Mediterranean, and the many rivers, provide a wide variety of animal protein products.

With an abundance of dairy products available, France produces more than 500 varieties of cheeses, reputed by most to be some of the world's best cheeses. Most regions make cheeses that are known as specialties from that particular area. Cow, goat, and sheep milk are used for cheese making. Many think the exceptionally high quality of French cream and butter accounts for recipes not tasting the same when prepared outside of France. Generally, olive oil is the cooking fat used in the south while the rest of France prefers butter or pork fat.

Charcuterie shops selling all sorts of sausages and cured meats are found throughout the various regions of France. Like with the cheeses, regional specialties exist, and they often are available only in that particular region.

Known throughout the world for their fine breads and pastries, French pastries actually evolved from Italian pastries. With bread served at every meal, the French consume a tremendous amount of bread daily. People walking down the street with a baguette or two is a common sight in both large cities and small towns throughout France. To ensure high quality, the government regulates bread standards. Most French bakers prepare bread twice each day so that only very fresh bread is sold.

Second only to Italy in wine production, France is renowned for creating some of the finest wines and other spirits in the world. Excellent quality grapes flourish in a number of regions throughout France. Each area specializes in grapes that grow best in that region, and, based on the type of grape and the growing conditions, a specific type of wine is produced there. By government regulation, a sparkling wine can be called champagne only if it is produced in the Champagne district of France. Brandy and cognac come from the southwest, while Burgundy, Bordeaux, Alsace, Champagne, and the Loire Valley are known for fine wines.

Typically, breakfast in France consists of bread and coffee. The bread may be *croissant*, *brioche*, or a crusty hard roll. *Café au lait*, strong coffee mixed with warmed milk, remains the morning beverage of choice.

The main meal includes several courses and is eaten midday. People return home and take two hours for this meal. A first course of soup or appetizer precedes the entrée. A salad and then a fruit or cheese course follow the entrée. Depending on the area of France, wine or beer accompanies the meal. For a special occasion, a fish course is added before the entrée and a dessert follows the cheese. The evening meal, which is much lighter than the midday meal, is not eaten until eight or nine at night. Often, two hot meals are consumed daily.

REGION	AREA	WEATHER	TOPOGRAPHY	FOODS
North and northwest north	Normandy, Brittany	Coast: cool winters, mild summers; inland: cold winters, hot summers	Coast, rolling hills, plains, Seine River	Seafood, pork, beef, butter, cream, cheeses, wheat, buckwheat, apples, sugar beets, *calvados*
Northeast	Rhine Valley	Cold winters, hot summers	Mountains, valleys, flat bottom lands, plateaus, forests, Rhine River	Cattle, sheep, pork, *choucroute*, *charcuterie*, noodles, *spaetzel*, grapes, various crops, fruit orchards
Central	Burgundy, Champagne	Cool winters, hot summers	Hills, rivers, valleys	Fish, game, beef, pork, snails, cheeses, mushrooms, mustards, vegetables, fruits, wine
Central	Central highlands	Cold winters, hot summers	Hills, mountains, grasslands, forest, Loire River	Cattle, sheep, game, cream, milk, cheeses, rye, mushrooms
Southwest	Bordeaux, Perigord	Coast: cool winters, mild summers; inland: cold winters, hot summers	Coast, forests, rolling plains, Garonne River	Seafood, pork, goose, duck, game, *confit*, *foie gras*, *pâté*, cheeses, truffles, mushrooms, walnuts, grapes
Southwest	Pyrenees	Cold winters, mild summers	Mountains	Seafood, pork, red peppers, tomatoes
Southeast	Riviera	Mild winters, hot, dry summers	Mountains, hills, valleys, lowlands, Rhone River	Seafood, anchovies, goats, goat cheese, vegetables, olives, olive oil, herbs, peppers, tomatoes, fruits, grapes
East	French Alps, Jura Mountains	Cold winters, mild summers	Mountains, valleys	Beef, fish, cheeses, cream, butter, potatoes
Corsica (island)	100 miles southeast of France	Mild	Hills, mountains	Seafood, sheep, goats, cheeses, grains, vegetables, olives, fruits, grapes

Review Questions

1. Who were Carême and Escoffier? What contributions did each make to the culinary profession?
2. What is the difference between classical and regional French cookery? Give examples of each.
3. How did the Greeks and Romans influence classical cookery? What were some later influences on the development of the classical cuisine?
4. Name four regions, explain the type of dishes prepared in each region, and discuss why those dishes are prepared there.

SOME FRENCH CHEESES

Brie Made from cow's milk, full flavored yet mild flavored, buttery soft texture that oozes, rind-ripened cheese from Ile-de-France

Brillat-Savarin Made from cow's milk, mild rich savory flavor, soft buttery texture, a triple cream cheese from Normandy

Camembert Made from cow's milk, full flavored yet mild, buttery soft texture that oozes, rind-ripened cheese from Normandy

Crottin de Chavignol Made from goat's milk, becomes stronger flavored and more firm as it ages, natural rind cheese from Loire

Epoisses de Bourgogne Made from cow's milk, mild to pungent flavor depending on age; heady, yeasty aroma; smooth, semisoft texture, from Burgundy

Munster Made from sheep's milk, full flavored and aromatic, heady aroma, creamy semisoft texture, from Alsace

Neufchâtel Made from sheep's milk; bitter, salty flavor; creamy and soft yet grainy texture; similar to cream cheese; from Normandy

Port-Salut Made from cow's milk, mild, smoky flavor, buttery, semisoft texture, from Loire

Reblochen Made from sheep's milk, fresh flower taste, creamy oozing texture like Brie, from mountainous area in the east

Roquefort Made from sheep's milk, blue cheese, crumbly yet soft texture with holes and cracks, from Rouergue

Tomme de Savoie Made from cow's milk, complex flavor with several levels, semisoft texture, from mountainous area in the east

Vacherin du Haut-Doubs Made from cow's milk, woody flavor, heady aroma, creamy runny semisoft texture, like the Swiss Vacherin Mont d'Or, from mountainous area in the east

5. What is the cooking fat of choice in the south of France and the rest of France? Why are they different?

6. How did the Italian influence come to the French culinary scene? What culinary influences did the French learn from the Italians?

Glossary

beurre blanc Butter sauce

brigades Teams of people working in the kitchen who prepare food items according to the type of cooking techniques involved in their preparation

café au lait Strong coffee mixed with warmed milk

calvados Apple brandy made in Normandy in the northwest of France

cassoulet A one-pot dish containing various meats, white beans, and herbs; originated in Languedoc

charcuterie Refers to all sorts of sausages and cured meats

charlotte russe A molded dessert consisting of a core of Bavarian cream folded with whipped cream surrounded by ladyfinger biscuits

chartreuse A molded dish with a decorative outside of colorful vegetables and an inside containing vegetables, game, and/or poultry

choucroute A dish served in Alsace containing sauerkraut cooked with sausages, meats, and served accompanied by boiled potatoes

confit A method of slow cooking goose or duck in fat

crêpes Thin, delicate pancakes, served rolled around a savory or sweet filling; originated in Brittany

foie gras The highly prized goose liver, produced by force-feeding geese so they develop large livers for this delicacy

garde manger Preparation of cold foods and garnishes

haricots Thin, tender green beans

rôtisseur Person in kitchen responsible for foods that require roasting

saucier Person in kitchen responsible for preparation of sauces

spaetzel A homemade noodle/dumpling that is popular in Germany and areas in France near the German border

tarte Tatin An upside-down apple pie; apples, butter, and sugar are caramelized, then topped with pie dough and baked; the cooked tart is inverted on a plate after baking

COQUILLES ST. JACQUES À LA PARISIENNE
(Classic)

Scallops and Mushrooms in White Wine Sauce

Number of Servings: 12   Cooking Method: Poach
Serving Size: 5 oz
Total Yield: 4 lbs

Food Balance: Protein/acid balance
Wine Style: Light- to medium-bodied Pinot Blanc, Pinot Grigio, Chardonnay, Viognier, Pinot Noir, light Reds
Example: Beringer Vineyards Napa Valley Chardonnay or North Coast Pinot Noir

INGREDIENTS	WEIGHT	VOLUME
scallops, bay or sea, washed	2 lbs	
mushrooms, fresh, sliced	1 lb	
dry white wine	1 lb	2 cups
salt	¼ oz	1 teaspoon
white pepper		¼ teaspoon
bay leaf		2 each
shallots, minced	1½ oz	4 tablespoons
water	4 to 8 oz	½ to 1 cup
SAUCE:		
butter	3 oz	6 tablespoons
flour	2½ oz	8 tablespoons
heavy cream	8 oz	1 cup
egg yolks	2¾ oz	4 each
milk, heated	12 oz	1½ cups
salt	to taste	

Coquilles St. Jacques à la Parisienne (Scallops and Mushrooms in White Wine Sauce); photo courtesy of The Norwegian Seafood Export Council—<u>www. seafood.no</u>. Photography by Per Alfsen

INGREDIENTS	WEIGHT	VOLUME
white pepper	to taste	
lemon juice		¼ teaspoon
Swiss cheese, grated	4 oz	12 tablespoons
parsley, fresh, minced		

1. Place wine, salt, white pepper, bay leaf, shallots, and water in pan. Simmer for 5 minutes.
2. Add scallops and mushrooms to pan, cover and simmer gently for another 5 minutes.
3. Remove scallops and mushrooms with slotted spoon, refrigerate until ready to use.
4. Reduce cooking liquid to 1 lb (2 cups).

SAUCE:
1. Slowly cook butter and flour until white to blonde roux, about 2 minutes.
2. Remove from heat, whisk in hot reduced liquid, then milk.
3. Boil 1 minute.
4. Blend egg yolks and heavy cream together, add hot liquid very slowly while whisking, to temper eggs.
5. Return mixture to pan, boil, stirring constantly, for 1 minute.
6. Season to taste with salt, white pepper, and lemon juice. Strain.

ASSEMBLY:
1. Butter scallop shells or serving dishes.
2. Blend two-thirds of sauce with scallops and mushrooms, correct seasonings.
3. Place scallop mixture into prepared dishes, cover with remaining sauce.

4. Sprinkle with Swiss cheese, broil about 8 or 10 inches from broiler, until golden brown.
5. Place hot dish on serving plate, serve immediately, sprinkled with minced parsley, if desired.

GRATINÉE LYONNAISE (Lyonnais)

Onion Soup

Number of Servings: 13 Cooking Method: Braise
Serving Size: 12 oz
Total Yield: 10 lbs, 2 oz

Food Balance: Sweet/protein
Wine Style: Soft and fruity Johannisberg Riesling, fruity mild Chardonnay or Viognier, Blush, rich mild Reds, Syrah
Example: Meridian Vineyards Santa Barbara Chardonnay or Syrah

INGREDIENTS	WEIGHT	VOLUME
onions, thinly sliced	4 lbs	
butter	4 oz	8 tablespoons
oil	1 oz	2 tablespoons
flour	1½ oz	6 tablespoons
beef stock, rich, hot	8 lbs	1 gallon
pepper		½ teaspoon
salt	to taste	
port	5 oz	⅔ cup

TOPPING:

French bread, 1-inch thick slices	1 per bowl	
olive oil	2 oz	4 tablespoons
garlic, peeled, cut in half	½ oz	4 cloves
Gruyère cheese, grated or sliced, about 1½ to 2 oz per bowl	1 lb, 10 oz	

1. Heat butter and oil in large saucepan, add onions and cook slowly over medium low heat about 30 minutes, until rich golden color from carmelization. Stir occasionally.
2. Sprinkle with flour, stir well.
3. Slowly add beef stock, stirring constantly, add pepper and simmer for 40 minutes.
4. Add port, and salt, if needed. Correct seasonings.
5. Meanwhile, prepare *croûtons*: place oil and garlic in small bowl, set aside. Preheat oven to 325 degrees.
6. Place bread slices on sheet pan, bake for 15 minutes, turn over and bake another 5 or 10 minutes, until dry. Remove from oven.
7. Brush both sides of bread with oil, rub with garlic.

ASSEMBLY:

1. Pour soup into heated bowl, float *croûton* on top, sprinkle generously with cheese.
2. Place bowl under broiler until cheese is melted and golden brown. Serve immediately.

Adding onions to pan for sweating; photo courtesy of Dorling Kindersley

Brushing bread with butter to make croûtons; photo courtesy of Dorling Kindersley

Assembling the soup—sprinkling cheese over croûtons; photo courtesy of Dorling Kindersley

Gratinée Lyonnaise (Onion Soup); photo courtesy of Dorling Kindersley

POTAGE CRÉCY

Carrot Cream Soup

Number of Servings: 14   Cooking Method: Sauté, boil
Serving Size: 7 oz
Total Yield: 6 lbs, 2 oz

Food Balance: Sweet/protein
Wine Style: Soft and fruity Johannisberg Riesling, Gewürztraminer,
    Pinot Blanc, Blush, Grenache
Example: Wolf Blass Gold Label Riesling or Grenache

INGREDIENTS	WEIGHT	VOLUME
butter	2½ oz	5 tablespoons
onion, diced	12 oz	2 large
carrots, peeled, diced	2 lbs	
flour	1½ oz	¼ cup
stock, chicken or vegetable, hot	4 lbs	2 qts or 8 cups
sugar		2 teaspoons
pepper		½ teaspoon
nutmeg	few grindings, to taste	
heavy cream	1 lb	2 cups

GARNISH:

parsley, minced

1. Heat butter in pan over medium low heat, add onions, sauté a couple of minutes.
2. Add carrots, sauté to sweat them, about 10 minutes.
3. Sprinkle flour, stirring constantly, continue to cook a few minutes to cook flour.
4. Slowly whisk stock into carrots, add sugar, pepper, and nutmeg, simmer for 30 minutes, until vegetables are soft.
5. Purée mixture in food processor or strain through food mill or China cap. Refrigerate until serving time or return to pan.
6. Before serving, reheat soup, add heavy cream, simmer gently to heat thoroughly. Correct seasonings.
7. Serve in warmed bowls, garnished with parsley.

Potage Crécy (Carrot Cream Soup); photo courtesy of
Dorling Kindersley

SALADE DE BETTERAVES AUX NOIX (North)

Beet Salad with Walnuts

Number of Servings: 8
Serving Size: 3 oz
Total Yield: 1 lb, 8 oz

INGREDIENTS	WEIGHT	VOLUME
Belgian endive, washed, cut into ¾-inch slices	8 oz	2 each
mesculin mix lettuce or other greens	4 oz	
beets, cooked and diced or canned	15 oz	2 fresh or 15-oz can
salt	to taste	
pepper	to taste	
walnuts, coarsely chopped, toasted	2¼ oz	½ cup
VINAIGRETTE:		
red wine vinegar	½ oz	1 tablespoon
Dijon mustard	¼ oz	1 teaspoon
salt	to taste	
pepper	to taste	
oil	1½ oz	3 tablespoons

1. Mix vinaigrette ingredients together in bowl, set aside.
2. Place endive and lettuce in bowl.
3. Add beets to lettuce, toss with vinaigrette.
4. Correct seasonings. Serve, sprinkled with walnuts.

BOEUF BOURGUIGNON (Burgundy and Lyonnaise)

Beef Burgundy Stew

Number of Servings: 13   Cooking Method: Braise
Serving Size: 10 oz
Total Yield: 8 lbs, 2 oz

Food Balance: Balanced-acid/protein
Wine Style: Wide variety—very balanced dish, enjoy with the wine of your choice
Example: Beringer Chenin Blanc to Chardonnay, North Coast Pinot Noir to Private Reserve Cabernet Sauvignon

INGREDIENTS	WEIGHT	VOLUME
beef, rump, trimmed, cut into 2-inch cubes	4 to 5 lbs	
MARINADE:		
red wine	3 lbs	6 cups
onion, sliced	10 oz	2 medium to large
carrot, sliced	5 oz	2 each
garlic, minced	¼ oz	2 cloves
peppercorns, black		12 each
cloves, whole		4 each

INGREDIENTS	WEIGHT	VOLUME
bay leaves		2 each
thyme		1 teaspoon
bacon, chopped	12 oz	
mushrooms, sliced	1 lb	28 medium
pearl or small boiling onions, peeled	1 lb, 6 oz	32 each
oil	1½ oz	3 tablespoons
flour	1½ oz	6 tablespoons
beef stock	1 lb, 8 oz	3 cups
red wine	8 oz	1 cup
salt		¼ teaspoon
pepper		½ teaspoon

1. Place marinade herbs in cheesecloth bag, mix with remaining marinade ingredients in nonreactive bowl.
2. Add meat, cover, and marinate in refrigerator for 1 to 2 days.
3. Drain meat well, reserve marinade liquid, discard cheesecloth bag, reserve vegetables.
4. Preheat oven to 300 degrees.
5. Sauté bacon until well done, remove from skillet.
6. Sauté onions in same pan until browned, remove from skillet.
7. Sauté mushrooms in same pan until tender, remove from skillet. Refrigerate bacon, onions, and mushrooms until needed.
8. Add well-drained meat pieces in one layer, sauté until sealed on all sides, remove from skillet and place in ovenproof pan.
9. Pour red wine 8 oz (1 cup) in pan and deglaze, pour over meat.
10. Wash and dry skillet if necessary, then add oil and heat.
11. Sauté marinade vegetables slowly until soft, add flour and cook, stirring, until mixture is rich brown color.
12. Whisk in hot stock, then liquid marinade and seasoning.
13. Add to meat mixture, cover pan, place in oven, and braise, stirring occasionally, for about 3 to 4 hours, until tender.
14. Add reserved bacon, onions, and mushrooms for last 15 to 20 minutes of cooking. Correct seasonings.
15. Serve with wide noodles or boiled potatoes. Garnish with minced parsley, if desired.

Boeuf Bourguignon (Beef Burgundy Stew); photo courtesy of The National Cattlemen's Beef Association

GIGOT À LA BRETONNE (Brittany)

Leg of Lamb with Haricot (White) Beans

Number of Servings: 12   Cooking Method: Bake
Serving Size: 4 oz meat, 4 oz beans,
    1 oz sauce
Total Yield: 3 lbs, 3 oz meat,
            3 lbs, 5 oz beans,
            12 oz sauce

Food Balance: Protein/acid balanced
Wide Style: Wide variety—very balanced dish, enjoy with the wine of
    your choice
Example: Château Souverain Sauvignon Blanc, Chardonnay, Zinfandel or Cabernet Sauvignon

INGREDIENTS	WEIGHT	VOLUME
leg of lamb, boned, trimmed of all but thin layer of fat	4 lb, 6 oz	
garlic, slivered	½ oz	4 cloves
carrots, peeled, cut in thick chunks	8 oz	4 each
onions, ⅜-inch slice	14 oz	4 each
rosemary	½ oz	4 teaspoons
pepper	to taste	
thyme	to taste	
SAUCE:		
white wine	8 oz	1 cup
stock, lamb or beef	1 lb	2 cups
BEANS:		
white beans, dried	1 lb	
onion, stuck with 4 cloves	4 oz	1 small
carrot, diced	2 oz	1 each
onions, diced	7 oz	2 small
garlic, minced		1 clove
bay leaf		½ each
thyme		½ teaspoon
pepper		¼ teaspoon
salt	¼ oz	1 teaspoon
GARNISH:		
parsley, minced	¼ oz	2 tablespoons

TO PREPARE BEANS:

1. Wash beans well, cover with water, soak overnight.
2. Add vegetables and seasonings except salt, cover with water, cook until beans are tender, about one hour.
3. Add salt, discard onion stuck with cloves.
4. Correct seasonings, sprinkle with parsley, serve with lamb.

TO PREPARE MEAT:

1. Preheat the oven to 450 degrees. Rinse meat under cold water.
2. With point of knife, make incisions in meat and push garlic slivers into them.
3. Place onions and carrots in roasting pan, place lamb on top of the vegetables.

4. Season with pepper and thyme.
5. Place in middle of oven for 10 minutes, reduce heat to 400 degrees, cook for about 1 hour, basting occasionally, until meat tests done with thermometer.
6. Remove from oven, move lamb to plate, let rest for 10 minutes before carving.
7. Meanwhile, remove excess fat from roasting pan.
8. Pour white wine and stock in pan, cook, scraping bits from bottom of pan to deglaze, simmer 5 to 10 minutes, correct seasonings.
9. Strain sauce, serve with sliced lamb.

COQ AU VIN (Burgundy)

Chicken in Red Wine

Number of Servings: 8 each ¼-chicken or
   10 each ½-chicken breast
Serving Size: about 11 oz chicken and sauce
Total Yield: about 12 lbs

Cooking Method:
   Sauté, braise

Food Balance: Balanced acid/protein
Wine Style: Wide variety—very balanced dish, enjoy this with the wine of your choice (try the unexpected).
Example: Château St. Jean Gewürztraminer, Chardonnay, Pinot Noir, or Merlot

INGREDIENTS	WEIGHT	VOLUME
butter	2 oz or as needed	4 tablespoons or as needed
slab bacon, lean or salt pork, diced	5 oz	
chicken, cut into quarters *or* breasts cut in half (10 each)	6 to 8 lbs	2 each
button mushrooms, cut into halves or quarters if large	1 lb	
celery, minced	7 oz	4 stalks
onions, small, white, peeled	2 lbs	
garlic, minced, crushed	½ oz	4 cloves
flour	2½ oz	¼ cup
chicken stock, hot	1 lb	2 cups
cognac	2 oz	¼ cup
red Burgundy wine	3 lbs	6 cups
bay leaf		2 each
thyme	¼ oz	1½ teaspoons
salt	¼ oz	1 teaspoon
pepper		½ teaspoon

GARNISH:

parsley, minced

> The total weight and serving size numbers look odd, but the number of servings is limited to the amount of chicken, not amount of sauce. Also, this recipe can be prepared with bone-in chicken breasts instead of whole chickens.

1. Simmer bacon or salt pork in water for 10 minutes, drain thoroughly, dry.
2. Melt 1 oz (2 tablespoons) butter in pan, sauté bacon or salt pork several minutes, until golden, remove from pan.

Coq au Vin (Chicken in Red Wine); photo courtesy of Dorling Kindersley

3. Sauté chicken in same pan until brown on all sides, remove from pan.
4. Add remaining butter when needed. Stirring often, sauté mushrooms several minutes, remove from pan and refrigerate until last 30 minutes of cooking.
5. Stir and sauté onions and celery for 3 minutes until brown, add garlic and sauté another couple of minutes.
6. Sprinkle flour over vegetables, stir constantly a couple of minutes, until beginning to color.
7. Slowly whisk in hot stock, then add cognac, wine, and seasonings.
8. Stirring constantly, bring to boil, add chicken and bacon, reduce heat, cover and simmer 30 minutes.
9. Add mushrooms, cover and continue simmering another 30 minutes. Correct seasonings.
10. Skim excess fat from sauce, remove bay leaves, serve immediately accompanied by boiled, mashed, or potatoes of choice. Garnish with parsley.

CANARD MONTMORENCY (Classic)

Roast Duck with Cherry Sauce

Number of Servings: 4 or 8   Cooking Method: Bake
Serving Size: ½ or ¼ duck

Food Balance: Sweet/sour
Wine Style: Light- to medium-bodied Riesling, Gewürztraminer, Blush, Grenache, Pinot Noir, mild Shiraz, or Zinfandel

Example: Meridian Vineyards Gewürztraminer, Pinot Noir, Syrah or
  Zinfandel

INGREDIENTS	WEIGHT	VOLUME
duck, washed, giblets removed from neck cavity	11 to 12 lbs	2 each
salt	to taste	
pepper	to taste	
onion, sliced	6 oz	2 small
carrot, peeled, sliced	4 oz	2 small to medium
onion, sliced	10 oz	2 medium
SAUCE:		
sugar	3 oz	6 tablespoons
red wine vinegar	4 oz	½ cup
strong duck stock	2 lbs	1 qt
arrowroot	1 oz	4 tablespoons
port	3 oz	6 tablespoons
CHERRIES:		
cherries, red or black, pitted	1 lb, 2½ oz	Two #2 cans, drained
lemon juice, fresh	1 oz	2 tablespoons
sugar	2 oz	¼ cup
port	3 oz	6 tablespoons
DEGLAZING:		
port	8 oz	1 cup
optional: butter	1 to 2 oz	2 to 4 tablespoons

> *For crisp duck, place duck in broiler while deglazing the pan. Broil until crisp and golden on both sides.*

1. Preheat oven to 425 degrees.
2. Season inside cavity of duck with salt and pepper, place sliced small onion (3 oz) inside cavity.
3. Place duck on rack in roasting pan, breast side up. Place vegetables in pan, bake in middle of oven for 20 minutes.
4. Reduce oven temperature to 350 degrees, drain fat from pan, turn duck over on breast.
5. Cook another 30 minutes, drain fat, and turn duck breast side up.
6. Continue baking, draining fat occasionally, until duck reaches proper temperature, about 2 to 2½ hours total.

SAUCE:

1. While duck cooks, prepare sauce. Blend arrowroot with port, set aside.
2. Boil sugar and vinegar over moderately high heat for several minutes until mixture turns into brown syrup.
3. Remove from heat, pour in 1 cup duck stock. Be careful pouring, it might splatter.
4. Return to heat, simmer one minute, stirring to dissolve caramel.
5. Add remaining stock, mix in arrowroot mixture, and simmer about 3 to 4 minutes, just bringing to boil, until sauce is clear and lightly thickened. Correct seasonings.
6. Set aside.

> *Unlike a roux, once an arrowroot sauce boils and thickens, it is as thick as it will become. Continuing to boil the sauce will cause it to become thin.*

CHERRIES:

1. Mix all ingredients in bowl.
2. Soak for at least 30 minutes.

Canard Montmorency (Roast Duck with Cherry Sauce);
photo courtesy of Dorling Kindersley

DEGLAZING:

1. Remove as much fat as possible from roasting pan.
2. Add port and boil rapidly, until reduced to couple of tablespoons.
3. Strain deglazing liquids and add to sauce. Do not boil.
4. Add cherries and marinade to sauce, simmer for 3 to 4 minutes. Correct seasonings.
5. Remove from heat. If desired, add butter to sauce, swirl to melt.
6. Serve over duck.

CÔTES DE PORC NORMANDE (Normandy)

Pork Chops with Apples and Cream

Number of Servings: 8   Cooking Method: Bake
Serving Size: 9 oz (2 pork chops, apple, and sauce)
Total Yield: 4 lbs, 9 oz

Food Balance: Protein/sweet
Wine Style: Soft and fruity Riesling, Viognier, mild Chardonnay, Blush, Amarone, mild Reds, Shiraz, Merlot
Example: Beringer Founders' Estate Chardonnay, Shiraz, or Merlot

INGREDIENTS	WEIGHT	VOLUME
butter	2 oz	4 tablespoons
pork chops	about 4 oz each, total about 4 lbs	16 each
salt	to taste	
pepper	to taste	
bread crumbs	2 oz	½ cup

INGREDIENTS	WEIGHT	VOLUME
apples, firm, tart like Granny Smith, peeled, cored, sliced ½-inch rings	1lb, 12 oz	4 each
heavy cream	15 oz	2 cups

1. Melt butter in skillet, butter ovenproof pan. Preheat oven to 450 degrees.
2. Season pork chops with salt and pepper, sauté quickly over medium high to high heat, until lightly brown.
3. Remove chops, place in prepared pan, top with bread crumbs.
4. Add apple rings to skillet, sauté until beginning to soften and brown lightly, place on top of pork chops.
5. Add heavy cream to skillet, scrape bits at bottom of pan to deglaze while it comes to boil.
6. Pour immediately over pork, place in oven for 10 to 15 minutes, being careful not to overcook.
7. Add a bit more cream to sauce if necessary to thin; correct seasonings. Serve immediately.

RATATOUILLE (Provence)

Vegetable Stew

Number of Servings: 11 Cooking Method: Braise
Serving Size: 5 oz
Total Yield: 3 lbs, 8 oz

Food Balance: Protein/sweet
Wine Style: Light- to medium-bodied Riesling, Pinot Blanc, Sauvignon Blanc, White Zinfandel, mild Reds like Grenache, Beaujolais, Shiraz
Example: Wolf Blass Riesling, Grenache, or Shiraz

INGREDIENTS	WEIGHT	VOLUME
eggplant	1 lb, 9 oz	1 medium
salt	as needed	
olive oil	1 oz	2 tablespoons
onions, sliced thin	15 oz	3 medium
zucchini, cut in ¾-inch pieces	1 lb, 7 oz	3 medium
peppers, red, yellow, or green, cored, sliced into 2- to 3-inch strips	1 lb	2 large
garlic, minced, mashed	½ oz	4 cloves
tomatoes, fresh, peeled, chopped or canned plum tomatoes	1 lb	4 medium
anise seed, ground		⅛ teaspoon
basil, dried		1 teaspoon
thyme, dried		1 teaspoon
black pepper		½ teaspoon
salt		½ teaspoon
bay leaf		1 each
coriander, ground		½ teaspoon

This vegetable can be prepared ahead and partially cooked, then reheated gently at service. The flavors marry well for the second day.

Ratatouille (Vegetable Stew); photo courtesy of Dorling Kindersley

INGREDIENTS	WEIGHT	VOLUME
GARNISH:		
parsley, fresh, finely chopped	½ oz	2 tablespoons

1. Cut eggplant into ½- to ¾-inch cubes. Place in colander in sink or on a plate, sprinkle with salt. Let stand for 30 minutes, then rinse and dry with paper towels.
2. Heat oil in large skillet or braising pan. Add onions, cook about 3 minutes.
3. Add eggplant, cook another 3 minutes.
4. Add garlic, zucchini, peppers, tomatoes, and seasonings.
5. Simmer, uncovered, for about 40 minutes, until vegetables are tender but not mushy.
6. Remove bay leaf, correct seasonings.
7. Serve, hot or at room temperature, garnished with fresh parsley.

PETITS POIS FRAIS À LA FRANCAISE (Classical)

Peas Braised with Lettuce and Onions

Number of Servings: 12   Cooking Method: Braise
Serving Size: 4 oz
Total Yield: 3 lbs

INGREDIENTS	WEIGHT	VOLUME
peas, shelled, fresh or frozen	2 lbs	
scallions, bottom 2-inches with bulb, cut into 1-inch sections	5 oz	24 each
lettuce, Boston bibb	15 oz	2 heads
butter	3 oz	6 tablespoons
water, boiling	2½ oz	⅓ cup
sugar	1½ oz	3 tablespoons

INGREDIENTS	WEIGHT	VOLUME
salt	¼ oz	1 teaspoon
pepper		¼ teaspoon
thyme or chervil		1 teaspoon
parsley		5 sprigs
butter, optional	½ oz	1 tablespoon

1. Wash lettuce, cut into strips, discarding core.
2. Place thyme or chervil and parsley in cheesecloth bag.
3. Melt 3 oz (6 tablespoons) butter in pan, add scallions, lettuce, and peas; stir to coat with butter.
4. Add water, sugar, salt, pepper, and spice bag to pan.
5. Cover, cook over low fire until peas are tender, about 10 minutes (for frozen).
6. Add more water if necessary.
7. Discard cheesecloth bag, correct seasonings.
8. Mix ½ oz (1 tablespoon) butter into peas, if desired. Serve.

EPINARDS À LA BASQUAISE (Basque)

Gratin of Spinach and Potatoes with Anchovies

Number of Servings: 9
Serving Size: 4 oz
Total Yield: 2 lbs, 5 oz

Cooking Method: Bake

INGREDIENTS	WEIGHT	VOLUME
spinach, washed	1 lb, 4 oz	Two 10-oz bags
Swiss cheese, grated	2 oz	½ cup
potatoes, peeled, sliced ⅛-inch thick	1 lb, 2 oz	3 each
anchovies	1¼ oz	2 tablespoons
butter, softened	1 oz	2 tablespoons
pepper		⅛ teaspoon
Swiss cheese, grated	1½ oz	⅓ cup
bread crumbs, dry	¾ oz	3 tablespoons
butter, melted	1 oz	2 tablespoons

1. Remove stems and coarsely chop spinach leaves. Wash well.
2. Braise spinach in sauté pan until cooked, about 5 minutes. Water clinging to leaves should provide enough moisture.
3. Stir 2 oz (½ cup) cheese into the braised spinach. Set aside.
4. Cook potatoes in boiling water until just tender, about 5 minutes. Drain.
5. Mash anchovies with 1 oz (2 tablespoons) softened butter. Set aside.
6. Mix 1½ oz (⅓ cup) cheese with bread crumbs.
7. Butter baking dish. Preheat oven to 375 degrees.
8. Place half of potatoes in bottom of baking dish.
9. Cover with half of anchovy mixture.
10. Place half of spinach over potatoes.
11. Repeat layering with remaining ingredients.
12. Spread cheese and bread crumbs mixture over spinach, pour melted butter over top.
13. Bake 30 minutes, until golden brown. Serve immediately.

GRATIN SAVOYARD (Provence)

Scalloped Potatoes

Number of Servings: 14   Cooking Method: Bake
Serving Size: 4 oz
Total Yield: 3 lbs, 10 oz

> Countless variations of scalloped potatoes appear all over France. Many replace the stock and olive oil used in this recipe from the south of France with cream and butter. This potato makes a fine accompaniment for a chop or roast chicken.

INGREDIENTS	WEIGHT	VOLUME
olive oil	½ oz	1 tablespoon
potatoes, peeled, sliced very thin, about ¹⁄₁₆-inch thick	2 lbs, 8 oz	about 6 medium
onion, cut in half through root end, then sliced thinly	6 oz	1 large
cheese, Swiss, or other strong variety, grated	5 oz	1½ cups
stock, strong beef or chicken, hot	14 oz	1¾ cups
pepper		¼ to ½ teaspoon

1. Spread oil in shallow ovenproof dish. Preheat oven to 350 degrees.
2. Mix potatoes, onion, and pepper in bowl, layer half in prepared dish.
3. Top with half of cheese, layer remaining potatoes over cheese.
4. Sprinkle with salt if stock is not salty, then pour stock over potatoes.
5. Cover tightly, bake for 30 minutes, remove cover, top with remaining cheese.

Pouring stock over Potatoes Savoyard; photo courtesy of Dorling Kindersley

Gratin Savoyard (Scalloped Potatoes); photo courtesy of the Idaho Potato Commission

6. Bake another 30 to 40 minutes, uncovered, until potatoes are done and top is golden brown.
7. Serve immediately.

TARTE DES DEMOISELLES TATIN (Central)

Upside-down Caramelized Apple Tart

Number of Servings: 8
Serving Size: ⅛ tart
Total Yield: One 10-inch tart

Cooking Method: Bake

INGREDIENTS	WEIGHT	VOLUME
butter, unsalted	2 oz	4 tablespoons
sugar	5½ oz	¾ cup
apples, peeled, cored, sliced ¼- to ⅜-inch thick	2 lb, 3 oz	about 5 large
cinnamon		1 teaspoon

DOUGH:

pâte brisée, well chilled, *recipe follows*	7 to 7½ oz	

GARNISH:

crème frâiche or whipped cream, optional

Arranging apple slices on top of caramelized sugar

Reversing direction of apples forming second ring of apples

Cutting slits in top of tart

Baked Tarte Tatin in Skillet

Unmolded Tarte des Demoiselles Tatin (Upside-down Caramelized Apple Tart)

Slice of Tarte des Demoiselles Tatin (Upside-down Caramelized Apple Tart)

1. Preheat oven to 350 degrees.
2. Melt butter in heavy ovenproof 10-inch skillet over medium heat, add sugar.
3. Cook, stirring, until sugar caramelizes to golden brown, remove from heat.
4. Place apples in overlapping concentric circles over sugar.
5. Sprinkle cinnamon over first layer of apples, repeat layering.
6. Roll out pâte brisée ³⁄₁₆- or ⅛-inch thick, at least 10 inches in diameter, to cover pan.
7. Cover apples with dough, trimming edges if necessary. Make 2 or 3 slits 2-inches in length in crust so steam can escape.
8. Bake on middle rack until golden, about 40 to 45 minutes.
9. Remove from oven, let cool a couple of minutes, invert pan on serving dish.
10. Serve immediately, accompanied by crème frâiche or whipped cream, if desired.

This pastry dough is a recipe from French Pastry Chef Gaston LeNôtre. This recipe works well for both sweet or savory purposes. Pâte brisée freezes very well either baked or unbaked. Excess balls of dough or rolled out unbaked dough fitted into the pie tin store well in the freezer if properly wrapped. If freezing baked dough, be careful to wrap securely so it does not break when jostled in the freezer. Eliminating contact with air prevents freezer burn.

PÂTE BRISÉE (Classic)

All Butter Pastry (Pie) Dough

Serving Size: 11 oz ball of dough for 9-inch tart pan,
2½ balls for ½-sheet pan, 5 balls for full sheet pan
Total Yield: 3 balls of dough, 2 lbs, 3 oz

INGREDIENTS	WEIGHT	VOLUME
flour, all purpose	1 lb, ½ oz	3¾ cups
salt	½ oz	2 teaspoons
sugar	¾ oz	1½ tablespoons
butter, unsalted, cold	13½ oz	1⅔ cups
eggs	3½ oz	2 each
milk	1 oz	2 tablespoons

PREPARATION IN FOOD PROCESSOR:

1. Place all dry ingredients in bowl of food processor, pulse a couple of times to mix.
2. Cut cold butter into small pieces, about half-tablespoon size. Place on top of dry ingredients, pulse several times, until butter is pea size.
3. Mix eggs and milk. With processor running, pour through feed tube. Pulse until dough comes together into ball.
4. Remove from processor, divide into three equal balls. Wrap in plastic wrap and refrigerate until well chilled, several hours or overnight.

PREPARATION IN MIXER:

1. With flat beater, mix salt and sugar in mixing bowl. Add butter cut in small pieces, about half-tablespoon size, then add eggs and milk.
2. Beat for a few seconds, then add flour all at once.
3. Beat ingredients just long enough to blend. Small pieces of butter visible in dough are fine. Do not overwork dough.
4. Remove from mixer, divide into three equal balls. Wrap in plastic wrap and refrigerate until well chilled, several hours or overnight.

PREPARATION BY HAND:

1. Place flour on table in mound, make well in center. Sprinkle sugar and salt around edges, place butter pieces, milk, and eggs in well.
2. Mix together until crumbly, working very quickly with tips of your fingers. Knead dough gently by pushing it away from you against table with your palm (called *fraiser*).
3. Gather dough into ball and *fraiser* once more, working quickly and gently.
4. Form dough into three equal balls; wrap in plastic wrap, and refrigerate until well chilled, several hours or overnight.

TO ROLL DOUGH:

1. Place chilled ball on table. With rolling pan, hit ball to flatten into disk about one-inch thick. Lightly flour table and rolling pin, if needed.
2. Roll dough, from middle to sides, releasing dough from table with icing spatula every few rolls. Turn dough one-quarter turn to keep dough even and roll into circle until desired thickness.
3. Release from table with spatula. Fold gently in half. Lift and move dough to pan. Position dough over pan so it covers pan when unfolded.
4. Press dough into all corners of pan. Either flute edges or cut flush with top of pan.
5. Chill for one hour before baking.

SOUFFLÉ AU CITRON (Classic)

Lemon Soufflé

Number of Servings: 6　　　　Cooking Method: Bake
Total Yield: One 1½-quart soufflé dish

Soufflés make excellent desserts or savory (like cheese) first courses. Whether sweet or savory, the preparation and techniques involved remain the same.

INGREDIENTS	WEIGHT	VOLUME
butter, unsalted	¼ oz	½ tablespoon
sugar	½ oz	1 tablespoon
yolks	3½ oz	5 each
sugar	3¾ oz	½ cup
lemon zest, grated	½ oz	2 tablespoons
lemon juice	2 oz	¼ cup
egg whites	7 oz	7 each
cream of tartar		½ teaspoon
confectioners' sugar for dusting		

1. Butter bottom and sides of soufflé dish, dust with ½ oz (½ tablespoon) sugar.
2. Place collar on soufflé dish by folding parchment paper to make double thickness sheet 6 or 8 inches wide, then wrap around dish and tie with string (you may need to overlap two pieces of parchment paper so it is long enough to wrap dish). Butter or pan spray parchment paper.
3. Preheat oven to 425 degrees.
4. With whisk attachment on mixer, beat yolks and sugar until thick and pale yellow.
5. Place over pan of barely simmering water, vigorously whisk until mixture is almost too hot to touch and ribbons (mixture drops from whisk to write an "M" and the beginning line of "M" remains on top of mixture when the whole letter is formed).

Placing collar on soufflé dish; photo courtesy of Dorling Kindersley

Soufflé au Citron (Lemon Soufflé); photo courtesy of Dorling Kindersley

6. Whisk in lemon zest and lemon juice, cool pan in ice water bath, refrigerate until ready to use.
7. With whisk attachment on mixer, beat egg whites and cream of tartar until stiff peaks.
8. With rubber spatula, stir large spoonful of whites into yolk mixture to lighten, fold remaining whites into mixture in two parts.
9. Transfer mixture to prepared dish, gently smooth top.
10. Bake on middle to upper rack for 2 minutes, reduce heat to 400 degrees, bake another 20 or 30 minutes, until lightly browned.
11. Remove from oven, sift confectioners' sugar over top, serve immediately.

CHAPTER 4
Italy

By the end of this chapter, you will be able to

- Identify differences and similarities in the regional cuisines of Italy
- Explain how the topography of the various regions in Italy affect their cuisine
- Know what food products are prevalent in various regions of Italy
- Identify and explain the courses served at a typical Italian meal
- Prepare a northern and southern Italian meal

HISTORY

Throughout history, Italy's geographic location made it an ideal stopping place for traders and sailors traveling between Europe and the Middle or Far East. The travelers stopped or docked in Italy, replenished their supplies, and traded goods. Venice, a port city in northeastern Italy, and Naples in the south became trading centers for spices and other goods on this well-traveled route between the east and west.

One country after another occupied Sicily, an Italian island in the Mediterranean. Many of these countries left their culinary mark, but the Arabs, who ruled during the Middle Ages, left a huge impact. They introduced pastries, ice cream, many spices, pasta, rice, raisins, honey, almonds, and pine nuts, as well as many types of stuffed vegetable dishes that still remain popular today. Every nationality of traders, sailors, invaders, and conquerors that entered Italy left some of their culinary influences behind.

From 200 B.C. to 100 A.D., the Roman Empire flourished and grew. With the city of Rome as the center of the Empire, the Romans conquered and ruled many nations until their fall in 400 A.D. Much of the foundation for the Italian cuisine came from the Roman Empire with significant influence from the foods of Greece and Asia Minor, which included the area from the Black Sea to the Mediterranean. Leaving a legacy that still lives today, the Greeks planted olive trees, grapevines, and wheat in Italy. Pungent, full-flavored

Although no one knows for sure, many believe the origins for ice cream and sherbet came from the Roman emperor, Nero. He had snow brought from the mountains to chill his drinks, and he combined the snow with fruits and honey, creating the forerunner of sherbet.

sauces reflected the Middle Eastern influence. The Italians added their own rich bounty of local ingredients such as cheeses, seafood, olives, nuts, assorted pastas, and native fruits and vegetables to the foreign recipes. Those adapted recipes became a permanent part of the Italian cuisine.

Many consider the cuisine of Italy to be the most imaginative of the European cuisines. According to *Larousse Gastronomique*, Italy is the mother of all European cuisines. In fact, Italian cooking played a major role in the development of the French cuisine. In 1533, Catherine de' Medici married future King Henri II of France. Taking Italian cooks with her to France, the French learned and adopted much from the Italian cuisine. The Italians introduced broccoli, peas, artichokes, sauces, fine pastries, and much more to the French during this time.

Another major culinary impact on the cuisine of Italy occurred in the sixteenth century when explorers returned from the New World bearing vegetables previously unknown in Italy. These vegetables, including corn, bell peppers, hot peppers, tomatoes, and beans, quickly became an intrinsic part of the Italian cuisine.

In the 1800s, Napoleon conquered Italy and it became part of the French Empire. That rule lasted until the latter part of the nineteenth century. At that time, the regions of Italy finally unified into a nation.

TOPOGRAPHY

Situated in the southern part of Europe, Italy is a boot-shaped peninsula jutting out into the Mediterranean Sea. Two large islands lying to the south and west, Sicily and Sardinia, as well as some smaller islands, comprise the nation of Italy. Because of the long, narrow shape of this peninsula, most regions contain both seashore and mountains. Obviously, plentiful seafood exists near the coasts, and meats from herding and hunting are prevalent in the mountainous areas.

Italy contains two mountain ranges. The Alps lies across the northern part bordering France, Switzerland, and Austria. The Apennine Mountains run from the north to the south through the middle of the country. The resulting topography provides hilly terrain for herding, fertile valleys for agriculture, and caves for aging cheese. Similar to Scandinavia, the mountains in Italy exerted a profound effect on the cookery, causing considerable differences among the regional cuisines because of two factors: First, difficult travel through the mountainous areas led to significant isolation. That isolation resulted in limited sharing of both food products and recipes. Second, growing conditions changed with the varied terrain, and those conditions determined the products produced in each area. As a result, the available food items differed from region to region.

In addition, Italy contains diverse climates. Of course, cooler conditions exist in the mountainous areas, whereas the coastal regions have warmer weather. The north experiences cool winters, warm summers, and average rainfall; the south has mild winters and hot, dry summers with very limited rainfall in parts of the south.

Ingredients Commonly Used Throughout the Cuisine of Italy Include:

- seafood
- cured hams, sausages, and other pork products
- veal
- game
- pasta
- olives and olive oil
- garlic and onions
- anchovies
- dried beans
- fresh herbs—including parsley, basil, oregano, rosemary, fennel, marjoram, mint, and thyme
- cheeses—used in a number of ways: grated over finished dishes from salad to pasta to entrées, used as an ingredient in dishes before cooking, and for eating
- tomatoes, eggplant, and peppers
- all sorts of mushrooms and truffles
- wine

COOKING METHODS

The Italian cuisine uses virtually all of the cooking methods. Sautéing, deep-frying, braising, roasting, grilling, or spit roasting are commonly used meat preparations. A well-known dish, *ossobuco*, is braised veal shanks. Preparation of veal scaloppini involves pounding the meat until thin, then sautéing it. Pizza, calzone, and focaccia, as well as a number of pasta dishes, are just a few of the baked dishes. Even deep-frying appears, like *fritto misto di pesce*, deep-fried mixed seafood items.

The most usual cooking methods for vegetables include boiling, sautéing, or baking. Generally, vegetables and pastas are cooked until *al dente*, literally meaning "to the tooth." This term refers to foods cooked until done but still crisp or maintaining a little "bite."

REGIONS

Often the cuisines of Italy are classified into two large regions with distinct culinary differences—the more affluent, industrial north and the poorer, hotter, more sparsely populated south. Generally butter is used in the north whereas olive oil prevails in the south. The north is known for vegetables, creamy sauces, red meats, fresh pastas, rice, and polenta; dried pastas, pizza, white meats, garden spices, red sauces, and more highly seasoned foods typify dishes from the south. People from the north tend to cook with wine, but the southern cooks incorporate tomatoes into many dishes. All Italian cooks use pepper, but those in the north prefer black pepper to the spicy, hot peppers of the south. Although these generalizations apply to the cookery of the north and south, it is a bit of an oversimplification, as distinct regional cuisines flourish throughout Italy.

Many independent regions form the country of Italy, and each of these regions claims their own history, culture, and culinary traditions. Depending on the source, Italy is divided into anywhere from fourteen to twenty regions. Great diversity exists among the cuisines of these regions based on what is grown/raised in the area, the methods of food preparation, the topography, the affluence of the region, cultural differences, and historical influences by other countries. Prior to World War II, the regions maintained separate and distinct identities. In the aftermath of World War II, however, a weakening of culinary boundaries occurred between the various regions.

Strong influence from neighboring countries affected the cuisines of several regions in the north. The Piedmont region shares a border with France; Austria and Switzerland lie next to Trentino-Alto Adige, Veneto, and Lombardy; and Yugoslavia borders Venezia Giulia. Each of these regions exhibits culinary influences from their neighboring countries.

Very fresh seafood is available throughout the northeastern region of Veneto, including the city of Venice, the famous port city with canals and boats instead of paved streets and cars. Delicately cooked with an absence of strong or overpowering sauces describes the seafood served throughout this region. Veneto also produces a bounty of high-quality fruits and vegetables comparable to any other region in Italy. Peas, asparagus, many varieties of mushrooms, pumpkin, zucchini, and radicchio are just a few of the vegetables grown here. The Arabs introduced rice to Veneto, and many rice dishes, including their own variation on risotto, prevail in this region. A major trade center linking Europe and the Middle East, Venice and the other ports of Italy experienced culinary influences from countries around the world.

The city of Milan lies in Lombardy, Italy's richest region. Nestled between the Po Valley and the Alpine area, Milan is known for several dishes including *ossobucco*, braised veal shanks, and *risotto*, a creamy dish made from arborio rice prepared by constantly stirring the rice while it cooks. Flavored with any variety of ingredients, many types of risotto are served. One of the best known, *risotto alla milanese*, takes its golden color from saffron.

Although many think of pasta as Italy's only starch, rice thrives in the fertile Po Valley lying in the regions of Lombardy and Piedmont. As a result, lots of rice is consumed throughout the north of Italy. In fact, rice production in Italy ranks higher than any other country in Europe, and the 530-bushel per acre yield of rice found in Italy is greater than any in the world. Corn also grows well, providing cornmeal for polenta, which is a thick cornmeal mixture eaten by the spoonful or chilled and sliced, then sautéed.

From the Emilia region comes Parma ham, Parmesan cheese, high-quality pork, and balsamic vinegar. Called the culinary capital of Italy since the 1100s, Bologna lies in this region. Famous for bologna, sausages, tomato sauce containing meat (*Bolognese*), and many other dishes, the town of Bologna produces the robust, rich, Italian food that characterizes the cooking of Emilia.

Florence, lying in the region of Tuscany, reached its peak during the Renaissance in the fifteenth century when some of the greatest artists and architects of the period resided there. Some say the cooking of Tuscany represents the simplest of all the regional cooking, with an emphasis on the flavors found in the fresh, high-quality ingredients.

Located in the center of Italy, Umbria remains a poor area with simple, straightforward food. Black truffles, many varieties of mushrooms, and olives proliferate in this region and appear in all sorts of dishes. Pork and cured pork products, including salami, sausage, and cured ham, dominate the menu. Meat is often grilled or spit roasted, giving it the characteristic flavor of wood.

People in Marche, a region in the east, eat pasta every day. More truffles come from this region than any other area in Italy.

Moving toward the south, Naples in Campania claims to be the home of pizza. Incredible vegetables grow in this region. Lots of seafood and cheese are consumed, but little meat.

Sicily, an island just off the toe of the boot of Italy, shows culinary influences from the series of invaders who occupied the island throughout history. Some of those include the Greeks, Romans, Arabs, Spanish, Turks, French, Germans, English, and Austrians. Seafood and fresh vegetables remain cherished foods in the Sicilian diet. Besides supplying high-quality tuna and swordfish from the seas around the island, Sicily made several contributions to the cuisine of Italy, including a sweet and sour sauce called *agrodolce*, ice cream, and *zabaglione*, a dessert sauce containing eggs, sugar, and Marsala wine. Further west, the island of Sardinia yields very large lobsters from the sea while sheep graze in the mountainous interior.

Each region in Italy produces its own wine based on the type of grapes that grow best there. With varying climates and topography as well as diverse soil conditions including volcanic ash in the central section, a wide range of wines come from Italy. The wines produced in each region influence the cooking of that area.

CUISINE

Many attribute the excellence of Italian cooking to the fact that high-quality, fresh ingredients are combined simply. Italy was a country of hardworking farmers who toiled long hours on their land. As a result, much of the cuisine consisted of the freshest ingredients growing on the farm, which were prepared simply and quickly. Even now, the sauce accompanying the meat course is often served on pasta as the first course. The heavy sauces so prominent in the cooking of France are not found in Italy, allowing the natural flavors of the foods to dominate the dish.

Very high-quality Italian fruits and vegetables thrive throughout Italy, and fresh produce plays an important part in each region's cuisine. Some attribute the exceptional quality of the fruits and vegetables, including the grapes for wine, to the high volume of volcanic ash found in the soil. Many of the most popular varieties of fresh vegetables such as tomatoes, eggplant, zucchini, and artichokes appear in dishes from antipasto and salads to pasta and pizza. As stated earlier, Italians cook vegetables, pasta, and rice *al dente*, meaning done yet still a bit crunchy, never overcooked and mushy.

With many miles of coastline, all types of seafood play an important role in the Italian cuisine. A variety of fish soups and chowders are served along the coasts. Many types of fish are available, including tuna, red mullet, sardines, sole, sea bass, anchovies, and eel. Shellfish, octopus, and squid are widely consumed. Anchovies function as a flavoring in sauces, as well as appearing on pizza and in a myriad of other dishes.

In terms of meat, veal and pork remain the most popular. Some of the many veal dishes include *ossobuco* (braised veal shanks), *saltimbocca* (veal with a slice of *proscuitto* braised in white wine), veal *piccata* (veal in a lemon and white wine sauce), and veal *marsala* (veal in a sherry sauce). Used alone or as a flavoring for other dishes, pork products, cured hams, and a variety of sausages made from pork, wild game, and/or veal are widely available. *Proscuitto*, a well-known, cured, air-dried ham, flavors many dishes or is served as part of antipasto (appetizer). A typical meal that a farmer or shepherd might take to the fields or mountains consists of sausage, cheese, bread, and wine.

Pasta spread through Italy after the Arabs introduced it in Sicily. Of course, it still remains a staple throughout the country. The size and shape of pasta varies from *acini di pepe*, tiny bead-shaped pasta used in soups, to *lasagna*, three inch wide sheets of pasta used to layer with meats and/or vegetables,

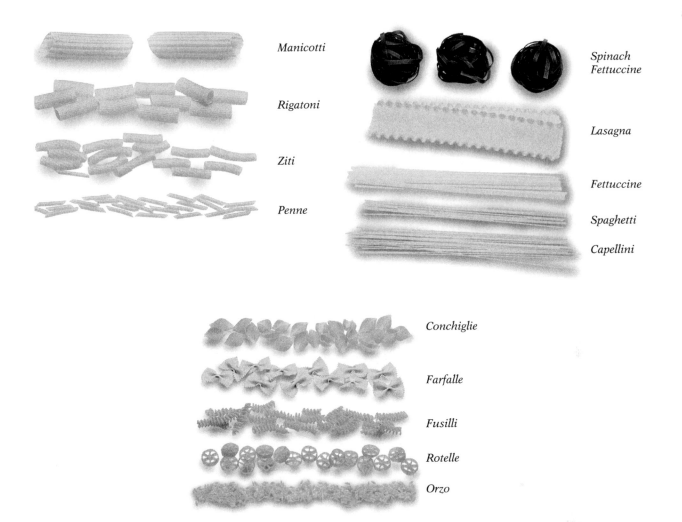

Pasta Shapes

cheeses, and sauce in a casserole. The myriad of other pasta shapes include large tubes such as manicotti for stuffing with cheese and/or meat and many sizes of small tubes so the sauce coats the pasta on the inside and outside. Sometimes pasta dough is shaped to enclose a filling (e.g., ravioli and tortellini). Many shapes for pasta acquired their names from literal translations of Italian: *farfelle*, butterflies (sometimes called bowties); *fusilli*, spindles (sometimes called corkscrews); *ditalini*, little thimbles; and *conchiglie*, conch shells. Obviously, pasta comes in a huge assortment of sizes and shapes to fit any need.

GUIDELINES FOR MATCHING PASTA AND SAUCES

- Thin sauces pair best with thin pastas
- Thick sauces pair best with thick pastas
- Chunky sauces pair best with pastas containing holes or ridges in order for the sauce to cling

SOME CHEESES OF ITALY

Asiago Made from cow's milk, sharp flavor, hard granular texture

Bel Paese Made from cow's milk, yellow tender cheese with mild, slightly salty flavor, soft creamy texture

Caviocavallo A delicate, creamy cheese for the first two or three months, after that it becomes sharp and spicy; provolone is a variety of Caviocavallo

Fontina Made from cow's milk, sweet, creamy mild, delicate flavor; semihard texture with a few holes; fontina melts well

Gorgonzola Type of blue cheese

Mascarpone Made from cow's milk, fresh cheese, white cream cheese made from fresh cream with buttery, delicate flavor

Mozzarella Made from the milk of cows or buffaloes, mild flavor, rubbery texture

Parmesan Made from cow's milk, sharp full flavor, hard granular texture, found throughout Italy, eaten as is or grated and used as a condiment

Pecorini Made from sheep's milk, sharp flavor, hard texture, found throughout much of Italy

Provolone Made from cow's milk, aromatic, aging sharpens the flavor and firms the texture

Ricotta Made from sheep and buffalo's milk, fresh cheese, mild flavor, moist, unsalted cooking cheese similar to cottage cheese in texture

Robiole Made from goat's, sheep's, cow's milk, or a mixture of milks, can be mild or strong in flavor, smooth, soft and delicate texture

Stracchino Made from cow's milk, strong and tart full flavor, soft creamy texture that oozes from rind

Taleggio Made from cow's milk, full flavor; smooth, soft, creamy, even textured, melt-in-your-mouth

Region	Cheese
Piedmont	Fontina, Robiole, Parmesan, Gorgonzola
Lombardy	Gorgonzola, Taleggio, Stracchino, Bel Paese, Mascarpone, Parmesan, Reggiano
Veneto	Asiago, Grana Padano
Liguria	Fiore Sardo
Emilia-Romagna	Parmesan Reggiano, Grana Padano
Tuscany	Fiore Sardo
Rome-Lazio	Pecorino Romano, Fiore Molle
Naples-Campagna	Fiore Sardo
Apulia	Provole di Bufala, mozzarella, Ricotta
Sicily	Pecorino Siciliano
Sardinia	Pecorino Romano, Fiore Sardo

In the north, pasta recipes contain egg although pasta made in the south omits the egg. Pasta can be dried and stored, or it can be cooked fresh after rolling out the dough into the desired shape. Although people in northern Italy often replace pasta with other starches such as polenta or rice, people in the south consume pasta at least once each day.

Many, many types of cheeses are produced throughout Italy, and they play an important part of each region's cuisine. Grated cheese is frequently served as a condiment and functions as an important flavoring. Parmesan, Gorgonzola, and Bel Paesa are just a few of the many cheeses found in the north whereas mozzarella and sharp sheep cheeses like Pecorini are prevalent in the south.

An inexpensive item, beans appear on the Italian menu in every category, including antipasto, soups, pasta dishes, and entrées. Some of the many varieties consumed are white kidney beans (*cannellini*), red kidney beans, garbanzo beans (chickpeas), and navy beans.

Italian cooking features an abundance of herbs, creating variety in the flavors. Some of the herbs found in the Italian kitchen include basil, parsley, oregano, rosemary, fennel, juniper, marjoram, mint, bay, and thyme. Pesto, a basil garlic sauce that originated in Genoa, is used as a sauce for pasta, as well as a flavoring in other dishes. In addition to herbs, liberal amounts of garlic and onion flavor most dishes.

Olive trees grow well in poor soil and on hillsides, so they thrive in Italy. An important crop, olives are valued for both the fruit and the oil that is pressed from them. Black and green olives as well as capers appear on antipasto plates and as flavoring for many Italian dishes and sauces.

Like wines, olive oils all taste differently. Numerous grades of olive oil are available, and the type selected depends on its intended use. The most common olive oil and the least expensive is marketed as "olive oil." If heating the oil, this olive oil is usually the choice. However, if the oil is intended for use in a cold dish, an extra virgin or virgin olive oil is preferred. Considered the finest, extra virgin olive oil has an excellent, delicate flavor. Virgin olive oil is the next best type.

As explained in the chapter on Spain, various growing conditions, weather, and soil conditions yield olive oils with different characteristics. Because olive trees grow in many regions of Italy, a wide range of olive oils with varying flavors is available throughout the country.

SOUPS

- Soup remains an important part of the diet in Italy. *Minestrone,* Italian vegetable soup, and *pasta e fagioli,* a tomato-based soup containing pasta and beans, appear on menus throughout the country. *Zuppa alla pavese,* Pavia soup, comes form the region of Lombard. The story goes that in the mid-sixteenth century, Francis I, the king of France, was losing the battle of Pavia. Retreating before the surrender, he stopped at a peasant's cottage and asked for a meal. A pot of *minestrone* was on the stove, but the peasant thought that was not good enough for a king. So the peasant placed slices of toasted and buttered stale bread in a bowl, placed some eggs over the bread, and topped it with Parmesan cheese. When the boiling soup was poured over this concoction, *zuppa alla pavese* was created.
- Each town on the coast has its own version of a fish chowder or soup. *Brodetto,* an assortment of seafood in broth similar to the French *bouillabaisse,* is well known in the Marches region.
- Broth, another popular soup, appears frequently, too. Pasta, bread, vegetables, or meats are sometimes added to the clear broth.

PIZZA

A popular snack or meal throughout Italy, a whole pizza or a slice can be purchased from open-air shops or in restaurants. There are countless flavor combinations. Some of the most well-known ones are as follows:

- Margherita pizza—named for the first queen of Italy; the pizza is topped with basil, tomato, and mozzarella, representing the green, red, and white of the Italian flag
- Neapolitan—contains tomatoes, mozzarella, and anchovies

DESSERTS

Amaretti The Italian version of macaroons, an almond cookie

Biscotti A twice-baked cookie; many like to dip them in sweet wine or coffee

Panforte Christmas cake, which comes from the city of Siena, containing almonds, hazelnuts, cocoa, spices, and fruits

Pannettone Spiced Christmas cake containing citron and raisins, which the Milanese claim they invented

Tiramisu Layered confection consisting of espresso and/or liquor soaked ladyfinger biscuits and a marscapone cheese mixture

Zabaglione Custard sauce flavored with marsala; usually served over fresh fruits; the same sauce in France is flavored with white wine instead of marsala and called *Sabayon*

REGION	AREA	WEATHER	TOPOGRAPHY	FOODS
Piedmont	Northwest	Cool winters, warm summers	Mountains, hills, plains	Trout, *fontina* cheese, butter, corn, barley, rye, wheat, rice, polenta, vegetables, garlic, white truffles, mushrooms, nuts, fruits, grapes, *zabaglione*
Lombardy	North central	Cool winters, warm summers	Rivers, lakes, plateaus, mountains, hills, fertile farmland	Livestock, diary, *ossobuco*, pork products, game, salami, butter, *gorgonzola*, polenta, rice, corn, risotto, saffron, *zuppa alla pavese*, *panettone*
Veneto	Northeast	Cool winters, warm summers	Coast	Fish, seafood, cows, pigs, *bacala*, cheese, rice, polenta, vegetables, radicchio, peas, asparagus, mushrooms, fruits, grapes, grappa, wine, tiramisu
Liguria	Northwest	Cool winters, warm summers	Coast, mountains	Shellfish, olives, olive oil, pesto, herbs, vegetables, fruits, grapes

(continued)

REGION	AREA	WEATHER	TOPOGRAPHY	FOODS
Emilia-Romagna	North central	Cool winters, warm summers	Mountains, valleys, plains	Pork products, sausages, cured hams, ragu, pasta, Parmesan cheese, white truffles, mushrooms, balsamic vinegar
Tuscany	East central	Mild winters, dry, hot summers	Mountains, coast, hills, plains	Grilled meats, seafood, polenta, olive oil, spinach, vegetables, pine nuts, chestnuts, fruits, grapes
Umbria	Midcentral	Mild winters, hot, dry summers	Mountains, hills	Pork, lamb, spit roasted meats, game, seafood, fish soups, wheat, black truffles, mushrooms, beets, olive oil
Marches	Mideast	Mild winters, hot, dry summers	Coast, mountains	Seafood, cattle, sheep, pigs, wheat, corn, vegetables, truffles, mushrooms, *brodetto*
Rome-Lazio	Midwest	Mild winters, hot, dry summers	Mountains, coast, forests, lakes	Sheep, lamb, pork, seafood, *saltimbocca*, Pecorino cheese, spicy red sauces, pasta, artichokes
Abruzzo-Molise	Mideast	Mild winters, hot, dry summers	Mountains, coast, lakes, forests, hills, valleys	Lamb, pork, ham, salami, game, Pecorino cheese, pasta, wheat, mushrooms, hot peppers
Naples-Campagna	Midsouthwest	Mild winters, hot, dry summers	Volcanoes, mountains	Seafood, mozzarella, cheeses, pizza, wheat, pasta, olives, vegetables, tomatoes, fruits, grapes, wine
Calabria-Lucania	South	Mild winters, hot, dry summers	Coast, mountains, forests, plateaus, plains	Seafood, swordfish, pork, lamb, sausage, sheep, cheese, bread, chili peppers, eggplant, black pepper
Apulia	Southeast	Mild winters, hot, dry summers	Coast, plains, mountains, fertile farmland	Fish, seafood, mozzarella, cheeses, pasta, olives, olive oil, vegetables, tomatoes, almonds, grapes, wine
Sicily	South island	Mild winters, hot, dry summers	Mountains, coast, hills, volcanoes	Seafood, swordfish, tuna, sardines, sheep, goats, pigs, cheese, wheat, pasta, olives, olive oil, tomatoes, eggplant, artichokes, citrus fruit, nuts, almonds, ice cream, grapes, wine
Sardinia	Midwest island	Mild winters, hot, dry summers	Barren, rocky mountains, hills, plains, coast	Sheep, game, fish, seafood, lobster, sheep's cheese, bread, artichokes, grapes

---

CULINARY CAPITALS

- Many believe the city of Bologna has the richest and best cooking in all of Italy, certainly in the north.
- Tuscany and the city of Florence are reputed to have the purist cooking in the country.
- Naples is known as the culinary capital of the south.

Numerous street vendors and shops selling *gelato* (ice cream) and *granita* (ices) are prevalent all over Italy. In fact, some think Italian ice creams and ices rank as the best in the world. For sure, Italians consume a lot of frozen confections! Sicily is known for a variety of fine desserts. *Cannoli*, a fried pastry tube filled with a mixture of creamed cheeses, candied fruits, nuts, and chocolate, originated on this island.

A typical Italian breakfast consists of cappuccino (a coffee drink combining espresso and steamed milk) and bread. Served at the end of a meal or in the late afternoon with a pastry or ice cream, many Italians drink espresso, very strong coffee served in a small cup called *demitasse*.

The largest meal of the day is served midday. Shops close for part of the afternoon, and people usually dine at home. Several small courses make up this main meal, yet the incorrect generalization (outside of Italy) is that the main meal consists of a huge plate of pasta. In fact, if pasta is served, it is the course served before the entrée.

When the meal begins with *antipasto*, it precedes the pasta course. Most likely, *antipasto* appears with a Sunday or holiday meal, or it may be served alone as the light evening meal. Examples of *antipasto* include cheese, salami, sausage, marinated vegetables, fresh fruit wrapped with *prosciutto* (cured ham), or other simple foods. The typical first course, *primo piatto*, consists of soup, pasta, rice, or polenta. Next comes the meat, seafood, or egg course accompanied by vegetables and perhaps salad. Fruit and/or cheese for dessert follow the main course. Wine, the beverage of choice, accompanies the midday and evening meals. Each region produces its own local wine, which is served with meals in that area.

Review Questions

1. Name four foods associated with the north of Italy and four foods associated with the south of Italy.
2. Name four food products and flavorings that are prevalent throughout Italy.
3. What two topographical features are found in most regions of Italy?
4. According to Larousse, how does the cuisine of Italy compare with that of other European countries?
5. Describe polenta, risotto, and pasta, including from which grain each is made and in which areas of Italy each of these is commonly served.
6. Explain the courses served at a typical Italian midday meal and give examples of dishes for each course.

Glossary

al dente Literally, "to the tooth," meaning cooked until done but still crisp

antipasto An assorted appetizer platter usually containing salami, cheese, olives, and grilled vegetables

bacala Salted cod fish

brodetto Fish soup resembling the French *bouillabaise*

Campari Bitter red liquor served as an aperitif from the region of Lombard

cannellini White kidney beans

frito misto di mare Assorted deep-fried fish and seafood

grappa Clear-colored, sharp-tasting brandy

gremolada Aromatic ingredients, including lemon zest, parsley, rosemary, sage, and garlic, which are added to braised veal shanks (*ossobuco*) a few minutes before serving

marinara A tomato-based sauce containing no meat

minestrone Italian vegetable soup

ossobuco Braised veal shanks

pancetta Unsmoked pork used for flavoring

pasta e fagioli Tomato-based soup containing pasta and beans

pesto Basil garlic sauce served with pasta and other dishes, originated in the city of Genoa

polenta Starch made of cornmeal that sometimes replaces pasta in the north of Italy

primo piatto Literally first course, this usually consists of soup, pasta, rice, or polenta and is followed by the meat course

prosciutto Salted, air-cured ham

ragu A tomato-based sauce containing meat

risotto Creamy rice dish popular in the north of Italy

saltimbocca Dish consisting of pounded veal with a thin slice of *prosciutto*, seasoned and braised in white wine

Sambuca Clear, anise-flavored liqueur served as an after-dinner cordial

zabaglione Dessert sauce containing eggs, sugar, and Marsala wine

BEANS AND ESCAROLE GREENS

Number of Servings: 10   Cooking Method: Braise
Serving Size: 7 oz
Total Yield: 4 lbs, 9 oz

Food Balance: Protein
Wine Style: Light- to medium-bodied Pinot Grigio, Sauvignon Blanc, Grenache, Pinot Noir, mild Chianti
Example: Castello di Gabbiano Pinot Grigio or Chianti, Meridian Vineyards Sauvignon Blanc or Pinot Noir

INGREDIENTS	WEIGHT	VOLUME
escarole	2 lbs, 10 oz	2 large heads
garlic, pulverized	2½ oz	12 cloves
olive oil	1 oz	2 tablespoons
salt	¼ oz	1 teaspoon
pepper		½ teaspoon
white beans, *cannellini*, cooked	1 lb, 14 oz	4 cups
Parmesan cheese, grated		to taste

> Note: Escarole can be quite sandy, so wash the leaves well.

Beans and Escarole Greens

1. Cut off bottom of escarole and remove leaves. Wash well, removing dirt from ribs.
2. Slice in pieces across ribs, add to pot containing a few inches of boiling water.
3. Parboil until tender, a few minutes, stirring often.
4. Meanwhile, heat oil in large skillet or braising pan. Sauté garlic, do not let it brown.
5. Remove greens from pot using spoon so some cooking liquid comes with it, add greens to skillet.
6. Sauté a few minutes, add salt and pepper. Sauté a few minutes more.
7. Add beans and cook until hot.
8. Correct seasonings. Serve sprinkled generously with grated Parmesan cheese.

PASTA E FAGIOLI

Pasta and Bean Soup

Number of Servings: 15   Cooking Method: Boil
Serving Size: 8 oz
Total Yield: 7 lbs, 15 oz

Food Balance: Protein
Wine Style: Light- to medium-bodied Pinto Blanc, mild Chardonnay, Pinot Noir, mild Shiraz
Example: Stone Cellars Chardonnay or Shiraz

> This soup appears in countless variations all over Italy. Some recipes use no tomato; others add cut up tomatoes or tomao paste. A very thick soup, some people mash a few of the beans to thicken it while others cook the pasta in the soup so the starch from the pasta acts as a thickener.

INGREDIENTS	WEIGHT	VOLUME
white kidney beans, *cannellini*, dried	15 oz	2 cups
prosciutto, minced	6 oz	
onion, small diced	8 oz	2 medium
celery, small diced	4½ oz	2 stalks
carrot, small diced	6 oz	2 large
garlic, minced	½ oz	4 cloves

INGREDIENTS	WEIGHT	VOLUME
potato, peeled, small dice	8 oz	2 small
tomato paste	1½ oz	2 tablespoons
bay leaf		1 each
salt (omit if using salty stock)		1½ teaspoons or to taste
pepper		1 teaspoon
pasta, small like ditalini, dry	10 oz	2 cups
chicken or beef stock or water	as needed	

Parmesan cheese, grated

1. Wash beans well, soak overnight or add beans to pot of boiling water, turn off heat and let beans soak 1 or 2 hours.
2. Cover beans with water, add *prosciutto*, onion, celery, carrot, garlic, potato, tomato paste, and bay leaf. Simmer until tender, about 2 hours.
3. Add salt, pepper, and stock or water, adding enough liquid to cook pasta.
4. Bring to boil, add pasta, cook until pasta is *al dente*. Correct seasonings and add more liquid if too thick.
5. Serve accompanied by Parmesan cheese.

PANZANELLA

Bread Salad

Number of Servings: 11
Serving Size: 5 oz
Total Yield: 3 lbs, 10 oz

Panzanella (Bread Salad); photo courtesy of Dorling Kindersley

INGREDIENTS	WEIGHT	VOLUME
white bread, crusty, medium dice	8 oz	
red wine vinegar	2½ oz	5 tablespoons
cold water, as needed	1 oz	2 tablespoons
tomatoes, ripe, large dice	1 lb	6 small
red onion, minced	4 oz	1 small
cucumber, peeled, diced	6 oz	½ each
celery, diced	4½ oz	2 stalks
basil leaves, shredded	¼ oz	10 leaves
salt	¼ oz	1 teaspoon
pepper		½ teaspoon
olive oil	3 oz	6 tablespoons

1. Place bread in bowl, mix vinegar and water, sprinkle over bread.
2. Sprinkle more water, if needed, to moisten lightly, set aside for 30 minutes.
3. Add vegetables, basil, salt, and pepper to bread, mix gently.
4. Sprinkle oil throughout, mix well, correct seasonings, refrigerate for at least 30 minutes before serving.

RAVIOLI DI MELANZANE E POMODORI

Ravioli Filled with Eggplant and Tomato

Number of Servings: 9
Serving Size: Four 2-inch raviolis
Total Yield: 1 lb, 9 oz pasta dough
           1 lb, 11 oz filling

Cooking Method: Boil

Food Balance: Protein
Wine Style: Light- to medium-bodied Pinot Gris, Viognier, Gewürz-traminer, Blush, fruity Reds, Grenache, Dolcetto, Pinot Noir, Zinfandel
Example: Beringer Vineyards Gewürztraminer or Viognier, Founders' Estate Zinfandel

> Serve as an appetizer or an entrée.

INGREDIENTS	WEIGHT	VOLUME
PASTA:		
flour, all-purpose	13 oz	2¾ cups
flour, semolina	3 oz	½ cup
eggs	8½ to 10 oz	5 or 6 each
FILLING:		
eggplant, peeled, diced	1 lb, 1 oz	1 each
salt	½ oz	2 teaspoons
sun-dried tomatoes, diced	1¼ oz	½ cup
onions, finely diced	6 oz	1 large
garlic, minced	½ oz	4 cloves
tomatoes, peeled, ripe or canned, diced	8 oz	4 plum
black pepper, ground		⅛ teaspoon
parsley, minced	½ oz	¼ cup
basil, minced	½ oz	¼ cup

INGREDIENTS	WEIGHT	VOLUME
olive oil	1½ oz	3 tablespoons
Parmesan cheese, grated	2¼ oz	½ cup

GARNISH:

sauce of choice—light tomato sauce or garlic-herb olive oil
Parmesan cheese, grated

PREPARATION:

1. Place eggplant in colander, sprinkle with salt, let sit 30 to 60 minutes.
2. Place sun-dried tomatoes in bowl, cover with warm water, let sit at least 30 minutes.

PASTA:

1. Place flours in bowl, form a well in center, add eggs.
2. Mix with fork until well combined.
3. Knead on table until smooth, add more flour if too wet or water if too dry.
4. Cover with plastic wrap, let rest 30 minutes.

FILLING:

1. Rinse eggplant with water, dry. Drain sun-dried tomatoes, chop.
2. Heat olive oil in skillet, add onions, sauté until lightly browned.
3. Add garlic and eggplant, sauté over high heat for about 5 minutes.
4. Add both types of tomatoes, cook over low heat until mixture breaks down, about 5 minutes.
5. Remove from skillet, add pepper, parsley, basil and Parmesan, stir to combine, correct seasonings.

TO ASSEMBLE:

1. Divide pasta dough into 6 pieces.
2. Roll one piece at a time through pasta machine to form thin sheet, place on lightly floured table.

Stirring egg into dry ingredients; photo courtesy of Dorling Kindersley

Kneading pasta dough; photo courtesy of Dorling Kindersley

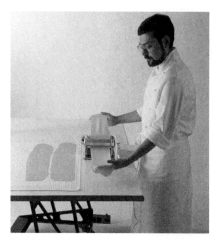

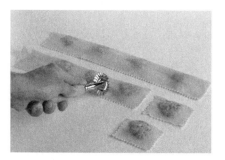

Rolling pasta dough with pasta machine; photo courtesy of Dorling Kindersley

Cutting ravioli squares; photo courtesy of Dorling Kindersley

Ravioli with Tomato Sauce—finished plate; photo courtesy of Dorling Kindersley

Ravioli with Herb and Oil—finished plate; photo courtesy of Dorling Kindersley

3. Place ½ to ¾ oz (1 teaspoon) filling on dough spacing at regular intervals to form raviolis.
4. Wet finger and make line of water around edges and between mounds (wherever dough will meet dough), cover with second sheet of dough, press between mounds of filling with handle of dough cutter or hand to seal well and mark squares.
5. Cut out squares, seal edges with tines of fork or crimper.
6. Place prepared ravioli on lightly floured pan.
7. Refrigerate or freeze until ready to cook for service.

COOKING RAVIOLI:

1. Add ravioli to pot of boiling water.
2. Cook until *al dente*, about 10 minutes. Serve immediately or shock (rinse with cold water to stop cooking) for later use.
3. Serve accompanied by sauce of choice and grated Parmesan cheese.

PIZZA DOUGH

Total Yield: 6 lbs, 6 oz
Scaling: about 1 lb, 7 oz for half sheet-pan

INGREDIENTS	WEIGHT	VOLUME
water, warm	1 lb, 8 oz + 6 oz	3 cups + ¾ cup
sugar	1¼ oz	3 tablespoons
yeast, granulated	1 oz	2 tablespoons + 1 teaspoon
flour, all purpose	3 lbs, 3½ oz	12 cups
semolina flour	8¾ oz	1½ cups
salt	2 oz	3 tablespoons
olive oil	3 oz	6 tablespoons

Can be prepared 1 day ahead and refrigerated. Also, this dough freezes well. Freeze in balls of an appropriate size.

1. Place 6 oz (¾ cup) warm water in bowl. Add sugar and yeast; stir to dissolve. Let stand until foamy, about 5 minutes.
2. In large bowl, mix 1 lb, 15½ oz (7½ cups) flour, semolina, and salt.
3. Gradually mix in remaining 1 lb, 8 oz (3 cups) water. Add oil, stir until well blended, about 2 minutes.
4. Fold in yeast mixture with rubber spatula.
5. Mix in 1 lb, 4 oz (4½ cups) flour.
6. Knead on lightly floured surface until smooth and elastic, about 10 minutes. Add more flour if necessary.
7. Place dough in bowl, smooth side up. Cover with plastic wrap, allowing room to double. Let rise in warm area until doubled, about 1 hour.
8. Punch dough down.
9. Refrigerate, well covered with plastic wrap, until ready to use. Allow to rest 20 minutes at room temperature before punching down dough and proceeding.
10. Roll into pizza crust.

PESTO

Basil and Garlic Sauce

Traditionally, pesto is stirred into hot pasta and served with additional Parmesan cheese. Many now incorporate pesto into many dishes using it as a flavoring for chicken, a spread on canapés, or whatever the imagination creates.

Serving Size: 8 oz or 1 cup pesto
    for 1 lb (dry) pasta
Total Yield: 10 oz or 1¼ cups

Food Balance: Protein
Wine Style: Light- to medium-bodied Orvieto or Verdicchio, Sauvignon Blanc, Chenin Blanc, Blush, mild Reds, Beaujolais, Grenache, Shiraz, Merlot
Example: Meridian Vineyards Sauvignon Blanc or Syrah

INGREDIENTS	WEIGHT	VOLUME
basil leaves	3¼ oz	2 cups, firmly packed
salt	¼ oz	1 teaspoon
garlic, minced, mashed	¼ oz	2 cloves
pine nuts	¾ oz	2 tablespoons
olive oil	3¾ oz	½ cup
Parmesan cheese	2½ oz	½ cup

1. Wash basil, dry, pick leaves from stems.
2. Place all ingredients in bowl of food processor, process until smooth paste, stopping to scrape sides, if necessary.
3. Add Parmesan cheese and pulse just to mix.

Adding oil to basil mixture; photo courtesy of Dorling Kindersley

Mixing pesto into pasta; photo courtesy of Dorling Kindersley

Pesto (Basil and Garlic Sauce) on Pasta; photo courtesy of Dorling Kindersley

PASTA ALLE OLIVE

Pasta with Olive and Mushroom Sauce

Serving Size: need 11 oz sauce   Cooking Method: Sauté
   for 1 lb pasta
Total Yield: 11 oz sauce

Food Balance: Protein/salt balanced
Wine Style: Light- to medium-bodied Johannisberg Riesling, Sauvignon
   Blanc, Pinot Grigio, mild Chardonnay, Pinot Noir, Merlot
Example: Beringer Vineyards Sauvignon Blanc or Red Alluvium (rich
   Merlot)

INGREDIENTS	WEIGHT	VOLUME
mushrooms, any variety, thinly sliced	8 oz	
olive oil	½ oz	1 tablespoon
garlic, minced, mashed		1 clove
black olives, pitted, Greek or Italian variety, chopped	6 oz	1¼ cups
parsley, minced	½ oz	3 tablespoons
red pepper, hot, ground		¼ teaspoon
water or mushroom stock, to thin	as needed	
pasta, dry	1 lb	

GARNISH:
Parmesan cheese, grated
heavy cream, whipped

1. Heat oil in skillet, add mushrooms, sauté until tender.
2. Place mushrooms, garlic, olives, parsley, and red pepper in bowl of food processor, process until paste.
3. Cook pasta until *al dente*.
4. Heat sauce adding water or stock to thin until coating consistency.
5. Mix sauce with pasta, toss well, correct seasonings.
6. Serve accompanied by Parmesan cheese and whipped cream.

TONNO IN AGRODOLCE

Sweet and Sour Tuna

Number of Servings: 9   Cooking Method: Sauté
Serving Size: 5 oz
Total Yield: 3 lbs

Food Balance: Acid/spicy
Wine Style: Wide variety—Gewürztraminer, Pinot Gris, Pinot Grigio,
   Grenache, Chianti
Example: Castello Di Gabbiano Pinot Grigio or Chianti

INGREDIENTS	WEIGHT	VOLUME
tuna steaks, fresh, cut 1-inch thick	3 lbs	
onion, sliced thinly	12 oz	3 medium
olive oil	1 oz	2 tablespoons

This dish originated in Sicily.

INGREDIENTS	WEIGHT	VOLUME
salt	to taste	
black pepper	to taste	
hot red pepper flakes		⅛ teaspoon
sugar	½ oz	1 tablespoon
red wine vinegar	3 oz	6 tablespoons
white wine	4 oz	½ cup
mint leaves, fresh, coarsely chopped	1½ oz	6 tablespoons

1. Heat oil in large skillet over medium high heat, wash tuna, dry it, and sprinkle with salt and black pepper.
2. Place fish, onion, and hot red pepper flakes in skillet, sear (sauté until light brown to seal in juices) on both sides.
3. Reduce heat to medium low, cover, cook until desired doneness, turning fish after 3 minutes (8 minutes total cooking time for no pink flesh, which is typical where this dish originates).
4. Remove tuna from skillet, keep warm.
5. Turn heat to high, add half the sugar and vinegar and all the wine to skillet, deglaze the pan, stirring constantly, until liquid is syrupy.
6. Add remaining sugar and vinegar, simmer for a few seconds.
7. Correct seasonings, stir mint leaves into sauce, pour sauce over tuna. Serve immediately.

POLLO ALLA CACCIATORA

Hunter Style Chicken

Number of Servings: 8 Cooking Method: Braise
Serving Size: ¼ chicken
Total Yield: 9 lbs, 12 oz

Food Balance: Protein/acid
Wine Style: Light- to medium-bodied Johannisberg Riesling, Blush, Sauvignon Blanc, mild Red Grenache, Shiraz, or Zinfandel
Example: Beringer Founders' Estate Sauvignon Blanc or Zinfandel

INGREDIENTS	WEIGHT	VOLUME
olive oil	2 oz	4 tablespoons
pancetta, diced	6 oz	
chicken, cut in quarters	about 6 lbs	2 each
flour, for dredging	3 oz	⅔ cup
onion, diced	14 oz	2 large
garlic, minced	1 oz	8 cloves
mushrooms, button or any variety, sliced	1 lb	
rosemary	¼ oz	2 teaspoons
marjoram	¼ oz	2 teaspoons
sage		1 teaspoon
bay leaves		4 each
salt	½ oz	2 teaspoons

Pollo alla Cacciatora (Hunter Style Chicken); photo courtesy of Dorling Kindersley

INGREDIENTS	WEIGHT	VOLUME
pepper		1 teaspoon
tomatoes, peeled, chopped	2 lbs	
white wine, dry	10 oz	1¼ cups

1. Wash chicken, dredge with flour.
2. Heat oil in large pot, sauté pancetta, then add chicken pieces, sauté until brown.
3. Add onion and garlic, sauté another couple minutes, until softened.
4. Add mushrooms, herbs, salt, pepper, tomatoes, and wine.
5. Bring to gentle boil, turn down heat, cover, and simmer until done, about 50 to 60 minutes. Turn chicken over after 25 minutes.
6. If desired, remove cover last 10 or 15 minutes for thicker sauce. Correct seasonings.
7. Serve immediately over rice or pasta.

OSSOBUCO ALLA MILANESE

Braised Veal Shanks

Number of Servings: 8   Cooking Method: Braise
Serving Size: 1 shank piece
Total Yield: 8 lbs, 4 oz

Food Balance: Protein/acid balanced
Wine Style: Wide variety, very balanced, enjoy the wine of your choice
Example: Château Souverain Sauvignon Blanc or Zinfandel

Traditional recipes for ossobuco call for the addition of gremolada at the end of cooking the shanks. The aromatic ingredients that make up gremolada are the same as those used in this recipe as "Seasoning." The gremolada is added at the end, and the dish continues to cook until just heated.

INGREDIENTS	WEIGHT	VOLUME
GREMOLADA SEASONINGS:		
parsley, minced	1 oz	6 tablespoons
rosemary	¼ oz	2 teaspoons
sage		2 teaspoons
garlic, minced, mashed	¼ oz	2 cloves
lemon zest, grated	½ oz	2 tablespoons
veal shanks, about 2-inches thick	about 8 lbs	8 each
flour, for dredging	as needed	
butter	3 oz	6 tablespoons
white wine	12 oz	1½ cups
tomatoes, peeled, diced, fresh or canned Italian plum	1 lb	2 cups
stock, veal or mixture of beef and chicken, to cover meat	about 5 lbs	10 cups or 2½ qts
pepper		½ teaspoon

1. Mix *gremolada* seasoning ingredients together in small bowl, set aside.
2. Coat veal shanks with flour.
3. Heat butter in pan large enough to hold all shanks (or divide into 2 pans), then brown meat in butter on both sides over medium heat.
4. Add wine, simmer until almost evaporated, about 10 minutes.
5. Add tomatoes, pepper, seasoning mixture, and just enough stock to almost cover meat.
6. Cover and simmer for about 2 hours, stirring occasionally, until very tender (meat comes away from bone).

Browning veal shanks; photo courtesy of Dorling Kindersley

Adding stock to browned veal shanks; photo courtesy of Dorling Kindersley

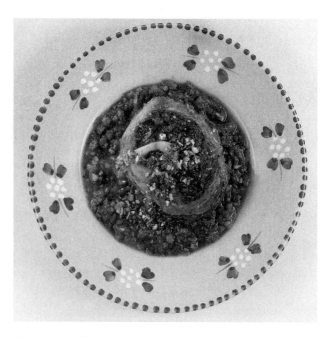

Ossobuco alla Milanese (Braised Veal Shanks); photo courtesy of Dorling Kindersley

7. If sauce is not thick, remove meat and cook sauce over medium high heat to reduce, skim impurities and scum from surface, if necessary. Correct seasonings.
8. Serve hot, accompanied by risotto or plain rice.

RISOTTO AI FUNGI

Saffron Mushroom Risotto

Number of Servings: 21 side dish   Cooking Method: Braise
               9 entrée
Serving Size: 4 oz side dish
         9 oz entrée
Total Yield: 5 lbs, 4 oz

Food Balance: Protein
Wine Style: Light- to medium-bodied Johannisberg Riesling, Pinot Blanc, Viognier, Chardonnay, light Pinot Noir, or Chianti
Example: Meridian Vineyards Santa Barbara Chardonnay or Pinot Noir

INGREDIENTS	WEIGHT	VOLUME
butter	4 oz	8 tablespoons or 1 stick
onion, diced small	10 oz	2 medium
Arborio rice	1 lb, 4 oz	2⅔ cups
stock, chicken, mushroom, or combination, hot	4 lbs	2 qts or 8 cups
white wine	8 oz	1 cup
saffron threads soaked in couple tablespoons of stock		¾ to 1 teaspoon
mushrooms, assorted wild, sliced	14 oz	
Parmesan cheese, grated	2½ oz	⅔ cup

> This dish usually appears as a first course on Italian menus; however, it is the traditional accompaniment for ossobuco.

1. Melt half butter (2 oz or 4 tablespoons) in large pan or skillet, add onion, sauté until soft.
2. Add wine to pan, boil until almost evaporated, add rice, stir to coat grains well.
3. Stirring constantly over medium heat, add boiling stock gradually, 4 oz (½ cup) at a time.
4. When almost absorbed, add another 4 oz stock, still stirring.
5. Continue this process of stirring and adding stock as it is absorbed.
6. After about 15 minutes, add saffron to risotto.
7. Meanwhile, in separate pan sauté mushrooms in remaining butter until mushrooms release liquid, then add to risotto and continue cooking risotto.
8. Continue stirring and adding stock until all stock is almost absorbed.
9. Cook until rice is *al dente*, but sauce is creamy. Add extra stock if needed.
10. Correct seasonings, stir cheese into risotto.
11. Serve immediately, accompanied by extra Parmesan cheese.

PARMIGIANA DI MELANZANE

Eggplant Parmigiana

Number of Servings: 27 side dish   Cooking Method: Sauté, bake
11 entrée
Serving Size: 4 oz side dish
10 oz entrée
Total Yield: 6 lbs, 14 oz

Food Balance: Protein/sweet
Wine Style: Soft and fruity Gewürztraminer, Pinot Blanc or Grigio, Blush, mild Reds, Grenache, Dolcetto, Merlot, Shiraz
Example: Château St. Jean Gewürztraminer, Pinot Blanc, or Merlot

> Although many recipes for eggplant Parmigiana prepare the eggplant slices with a standard breading procedure before frying, this recipe calls for sautéing the eggplant in olive oil without breading.

INGREDIENTS	WEIGHT	VOLUME
eggplant, thickly sliced, about ½-inch thick	4 lbs, 4 oz	4 each
salt	as needed	
olive oil, for frying	as needed	
TOMATO SAUCE:		
tomatoes, peeled, diced, fresh ripe or canned Italian plum	2 lbs, 10 oz	5 cups
garlic, minced, mashed	¼ oz	2 cloves
onion, diced small	9 oz	2 medium
olive oil	1 oz	2 tablespoons
sugar		2 teaspoons
basil or mint leaves, minced	1 oz	½ cup
pepper		¼ teaspoon or to taste
salt		¼ teaspoon or to taste

Parmigiana di Melanzane (Eggplant Parmigiana); photo courtesy of Dorling Kindersley

PASTA ALLE OLIVE

Pasta with Olive and Mushroom Sauce

Serving Size: need 11 oz sauce   Cooking Method: Sauté
   for 1 lb pasta
Total Yield: 11 oz sauce

Food Balance: Protein/salt balanced
Wine Style: Light- to medium-bodied Johannisberg Riesling, Sauvignon
   Blanc, Pinot Grigio, mild Chardonnay, Pinot Noir, Merlot
Example: Beringer Vineyards Sauvignon Blanc or Red Alluvium (rich
   Merlot)

INGREDIENTS	WEIGHT	VOLUME
mushrooms, any variety, thinly sliced	8 oz	
olive oil	½ oz	1 tablespoon
garlic, minced, mashed		1 clove
black olives, pitted, Greek or Italian variety, chopped	6 oz	1¼ cups
parsley, minced	½ oz	3 tablespoons
red pepper, hot, ground		¼ teaspoon
water or mushroom stock, to thin	as needed	
pasta, dry	1 lb	

GARNISH:
Parmesan cheese, grated
heavy cream, whipped

1. Heat oil in skillet, add mushrooms, sauté until tender.
2. Place mushrooms, garlic, olives, parsley, and red pepper in bowl of food processor, process until paste.
3. Cook pasta until *al dente*.
4. Heat sauce adding water or stock to thin until coating consistency.
5. Mix sauce with pasta, toss well, correct seasonings.
6. Serve accompanied by Parmesan cheese and whipped cream.

TONNO IN AGRODOLCE

Sweet and Sour Tuna

Number of Servings: 9   Cooking Method: Sauté
Serving Size: 5 oz
Total Yield: 3 lbs

Food Balance: Acid/spicy
Wine Style: Wide variety—Gewürztraminer, Pinot Gris, Pinot Grigio,
   Grenache, Chianti
Example: Castello Di Gabbiano Pinot Grigio or Chianti

INGREDIENTS	WEIGHT	VOLUME
tuna steaks, fresh, cut 1-inch thick	3 lbs	
onion, sliced thinly	12 oz	3 medium
olive oil	1 oz	2 tablespoons

This dish originated in Sicily.

INGREDIENTS	WEIGHT	VOLUME
salt	to taste	
black pepper	to taste	
hot red pepper flakes		⅛ teaspoon
sugar	½ oz	1 tablespoon
red wine vinegar	3 oz	6 tablespoons
white wine	4 oz	½ cup
mint leaves, fresh, coarsely chopped	1½ oz	6 tablespoons

1. Heat oil in large skillet over medium high heat, wash tuna, dry it, and sprinkle with salt and black pepper.
2. Place fish, onion, and hot red pepper flakes in skillet, sear (sauté until light brown to seal in juices) on both sides.
3. Reduce heat to medium low, cover, cook until desired doneness, turning fish after 3 minutes (8 minutes total cooking time for no pink flesh, which is typical where this dish originates).
4. Remove tuna from skillet, keep warm.
5. Turn heat to high, add half the sugar and vinegar and all the wine to skillet, deglaze the pan, stirring constantly, until liquid is syrupy.
6. Add remaining sugar and vinegar, simmer for a few seconds.
7. Correct seasonings, stir mint leaves into sauce, pour sauce over tuna. Serve immediately.

POLLO ALLA CACCIATORA

Hunter Style Chicken

Number of Servings: 8   Cooking Method: Braise
Serving Size: ¼ chicken
Total Yield: 9 lbs, 12 oz

Food Balance: Protein/acid
Wine Style: Light- to medium-bodied Johannisberg Riesling, Blush, Sauvignon Blanc, mild Red Grenache, Shiraz, or Zinfandel
Example: Beringer Founders' Estate Sauvignon Blanc or Zinfandel

INGREDIENTS	WEIGHT	VOLUME
olive oil	2 oz	4 tablespoons
pancetta, diced	6 oz	
chicken, cut in quarters	about 6 lbs	2 each
flour, for dredging	3 oz	⅔ cup
onion, diced	14 oz	2 large
garlic, minced	1 oz	8 cloves
mushrooms, button or any variety, sliced	1 lb	
rosemary	¼ oz	2 teaspoons
marjoram	¼ oz	2 teaspoons
sage		1 teaspoon
bay leaves		4 each
salt	½ oz	2 teaspoons

Spinaci in Tegame (Sautéed Spinach); photo courtesy of Dorling Kindersley

Food Balance: Protein
Wine Style: Light- to medium-bodied Pinot Gris, Pinot Grigio, Sauvignon Blanc, Grenache, Beaujolais
Example: Campanile Pinot Grigio

INGREDIENTS	WEIGHT	VOLUME
olive oil	3 oz	6 tablespoons
spinach, washed, stems removed, coarsely cut	2 lbs, 5 oz	Four 10-oz bags
garlic, minced	1¼ oz	8 cloves
salt	¼ oz	1 teaspoon
pepper		½ teaspoon

1. Heat olive oil in large sauté pan until hot, add garlic, sauté about a minute.
2. Add spinach, stirring constantly, sauté until wilted and tender, about 4 or 5 minutes. Enough water should cling to leaves from washing, but, if necessary, add a teaspoon of water to prevent burning.
3. Add salt and pepper, correct seasonings.
4. Serve immediately.

ZABAGLIONE

Marsala Flavored Dessert Sauce

Number of Servings: 12   Cooking Method: Boil (Bain-Marie)
Serving Size: 1 oz
Total Yield: 14 oz

> Traditionally, zabaglione is served over fresh fruit. After cooking, serve this sauce immediately; it does not hold well. If it becomes too thick, thin with a little Marsala.

Whisking ingredients for Zabaglione; photo courtesy of Dorling Kindersley

Whisked ingredients forming a ribbon; photo courtesy of Dorling Kindersley

Pouring Zabaglione from ladle; photo courtesy of Dorling Kindersley

Pouring Zabaglione (Marsala Flavored Dessert Sauce) over fruit; photo courtesy of Dorling Kindersley

Zabaglione (Marsala Flavored Dessert Sauce); photo courtesy of the American Egg Board

This same sauce appears in France with white wine replacing the Marsala. In France the sauce is called Sabayon.

INGREDIENTS	WEIGHT	VOLUME
egg yolks, room temperature	8 oz	12 each
sugar	3½ oz	½ cup
Marsala wine, dry	5 oz	⅔ cup

1. Place all ingredients in heatproof bowl, place bowl over pan of barely simmering water (Bain-Marie), whisk constantly.
2. Continue whisking until mixture is pale yellow, thick, and 185 degrees, about 8 minutes. If water becomes too hot, the eggs will cook, so immediately remove pan from heat if water starts to boil so it cools a bit.
3. Serve immediately over fresh fruit.

CHAPTER 5
Germany

By the end of this chapter, you will be able to

- Identify food products prevalent in Germany and discuss why those particular foods thrive
- Understand the effects of climate on the cuisine of Germany
- Describe how the geographic location and the bordering countries affected Germany's cuisine
- Identify differences and similarities between the cuisines of the various regions in Germany
- Prepare a variety of German dishes

HISTORY

As early as 1000 B.C., tribes from northern Europe inhabited the area of central Europe that is now called Germany. By 100 B.C., they had moved south into the middle and southern sections of Germany, where the Romans ruled. In fact, the Romans planted the first grapes for wine along the steep banks of the Rhine and Mosel rivers about 2,000 years ago. At that time, most Germans were hunters, farmers, and nomads with a simple diet consisting of grains, wild fruits and berries, milk and cheeses, and game that they hunted. These early Germans learned much from the Romans about both food and civilization. They learned of gardens, orchards, and gold and silver dining implements. The Roman rule lasted until 9 A.D., when the Romans lost the battle, and the Germanic tribes continued moving southward. By 400 A.D., the Germans had conquered Rome and ruled much of the former Roman Empire.

Charlemagne conquered Germany in 800 A.D. He restored the vineyards, which had fallen into disrepair. He also imparted knowledge about many foods, planting herbs, and meal planning.

Germany was divided into five regions by the early 900s. By the Middle Ages, the German diet included lots of fish, goose, and game. As was true in many other countries during this time period, heavily spiced foods prevailed, partially to cover the spoiled or rancid taste in foods so prevalent in these times before refrigeration. During the Middle Ages, banquets contained many courses, and, for the first time, the visual aspects of food became an important consideration.

The Renaissance brought awareness of luxury and opulence in all sorts of things, including food and dining. Table settings and food decoration acquired new importance. Silver and porcelain became prized serving pieces. French influence on the food and customs dominated during the seventeenth and eighteenth centuries, but the lavish food of this period was only enjoyed by the upper class, not the peasants. They still subsisted on grains, gruel, sauerkraut, dumplings, and bacon.

From 1806 until 1813, Napoleon ruled western Germany. The nation of Germany did not become united under one sovereign until 1871. As a result, great differences exist between the various regions.

Prior to World War I, many individuals enjoyed an affluent lifestyle. People entertained frequently and indulged in lavish food. The aftermath of World Wars I and II left the country and people of Germany shattered, both physically and emotionally.

At the end of World War I in 1918, Germany was a devastated country. Between the effects of losing the war and the Treaty of Versailles, Germany lost its colonies and much of its territory. By 1923, the German economy collapsed. The worldwide economic depression of 1929 further eroded their economy and morale, making the climate ripe for political extremism. The Nazis became a strong political force by 1933. The leader of the Nazi Party, Adolf Hitler planned to conquer Europe, beginning with the east.

After World War II, Germany was shattered again. This time, the country was divided into East and West Germany. Isolated from the west, East Germany was under the Communist rule of Russia until 1992, when the country was united.

Throughout history, many battles and different rulers ensued. Borders changed, and the various European countries fought and gained control over each other, which accounts for a lot of the overlap in foods and cuisine with Belgium, France (Alsace-Lorraine), Austria, Czechoslovakia (Czech Republic), and Poland.

TOPOGRAPHY

Surrounded by nine countries, the only coastline in Germany lies to the north at the North and Baltic seas. Denmark borders on the north; Belgium, the Netherlands, Luxembourg, and France lie to the west; Switzerland and Austria are on the south; and Poland and the Czech Republic are situated to the east.

The northern part of Germany consists of flat terrain, the central section is hilly, and the south contains hills and mountains. The Alps lies in the southern section and forms the border with Austria.

Two large forests lie in Germany—the Black Forest in the southwest and the Bohemian Forest in the east. Many smaller forests are scattered throughout the country. From the forests comes a bounty of game, many varieties of mushrooms, and berries.

Several rivers transect the countryside, providing fertile land for crops, as well as hills and valleys where grapes used for wine thrive. The Rhine and Mosel rivers lie in the west, the Danube in the south, the Oder in the east, and the Elbe and Weser in the north.

Ingredients and Foods Commonly Used Throughout the Cuisine of Germany Include:

- sausages
- pork and veal
- goose
- lentils and split peas
- rye bread
- potatoes
- red and white cabbage, sauerkraut
- turnips, kohlrabi, cauliflower, Brussels sprouts, beets, and carrots
- white asparagus
- vinegar
- juniper berries and caraway seeds
- onions
- fruits including apples, cherries, and plums
- nuts
- honey

COOKING METHODS

Boiling, a popular cookery method used in Germany, applies to all sorts of foods, including vegetables, potatoes, meats, and even fresh fish. *Forellen blau*, literally blue trout, is prepared by dropping a live trout in boiling water that contains a little vinegar. The vinegar causes the skin of the fish to take on a blue cast, therefore the name. Often, a tank of swimming fish stands in the lobby of restaurants, and the customer can choose the desired fish. Although lobster receives this same treatment in the United States, trout or salmon are the usual fish swimming in the fish tanks in Germany. Of course, this is especially prevalent in mountainous areas containing the freshwater streams where these fish live.

Germans broil, sauté, or braise smaller pieces of meat. Large pieces of meat are either braised or roasted. Often, meats are marinated in buttermilk, wine, beer, or vinegar, and then braised in the acidic marinade. *Sauerbraten* uses this cooking method. Roasting is the usual cooking method for game as well as other meats.

Smoking and pickling appear frequently with meats, fish, and vegetables. These preparations preserve the foods, providing sustenance for the long winters. Germans prepare and can sauerkraut, fermented cabbage, and all sorts of other pickled vegetables for the cold winter months.

REGIONS

Distinct differences exist between the foods of the northern, central, and southern areas of Germany. Foods in the north resemble those of Denmark and Scotland, although the cuisine of southern Germany is more like that of Austria. All the regions bordering other nations exhibit significant culinary influences from those neighboring countries.

In the regions of the north, typical cold climate cooking prevails, and the cookery in the north reflects the cuisines of Denmark and Sweden. The eastern section demonstrates influence from Poland, Russia, and Lithuania; the west shows the effect of Holland; and the cookery in the south resembles that of Austria.

Major cities of northern Germany include Berlin and Hamburg. Pork, beef, goose, game, and lamb come from this area, with the game served primarily in the fall. Often, meats are cooked with fruits and vegetables. Sweet and sour dishes enjoy much popularity in the north, and bacon and bacon grease flavor dishes in all courses, including appetizers, soups, salads, and entrées. People throughout Germany consume numerous types of sausages and cold cuts; in fact, many consider this a staple in the German diet. *Braunschweiger*, a liverwurst or liver sausage, hails from the town of Braunschweig in the north. The North and Baltic seas provide abundant seafood with eel and herring being favorites. Both pickled and smoked fish and meats appear often. Typical cold weather crops such as potatoes, beets, cabbage, barley, hops, and rye grow well in the north and remain an important part of the diet.

From the eastern European influence, the Germans adopted the use of both sweet and soured cream into the cuisine found in the north. As a result, cream sauces and soups appear often. All types of soups, from hearty soups to fruit soups, are favored in this northern region. Beer and *Schnaps*, a strong liquor resembling gin flavored with juniper berries, accompany many meals.

Famous for Westphalian ham and pumpernickel bread, central Germany thrives on hearty foods, including pork, dumplings, sauerkraut, beer, rye bread, cheese, and butter. Sausages and stews such as *Pfefferpotthast*, a stew of beef short ribs containing lots of pepper, remain popular. This portion of Germany includes the cities of Dresden, Westphalia, and Frankfurt, for which the hot dog or frankfurter sausage is named.

Whether sautéed as an accompaniment to meat or in *Zwiebelkuchen*, a quichelike pie consisting of a pastry shell with a filling of bacon, eggs, cream, and onions, onions receive special prominence in the western part of the central region. Another much-loved food, the ubiquitous dumpling can be made from potatoes, bread, flour, or oats. Dumplings appear often and in a number of varieties, as a side dish as well as in soup.

Fruits grow in orchards throughout this region, and the forests provide abundant berries that often become part of pastries. The traditional Christmas bread, *Stollen*, which originated in Dresden, comes from this region.

Vineyards thrive on the banks rising from the Rhine and Mosel rivers. Much wine is produced in this area. After the harvest in the fall, many towns throughout the grape-growing region celebrate with wine festivals.

The southern regions claim many specialties. Here, as in the rest of Germany, potatoes, dumplings, sausage, and beer are consumed in great quantities, but some of the preparations are a bit lighter than those from regions to the north. Four states lie in the south—Bavaria, Swabia, Baden, and Alsace-Lorraine. Bavaria, lying in the southeast, borders Austria. Swabia lies to its west, and Baden is west of Swabia. Alsace-Lorraine is tucked in the southwest corner sharing a border with France. This region shows strong French culinary influence mixed into the German cuisine. Likewise, the area bordering Austria exhibits lots of Austrian characteristics in the cuisine. These borders have changed through the years as one country gained control over the other. Alsace-Lorraine is a perfect example, having belonged to France or Germany at many different times throughout its history.

Lush fields and meadows make up the southern part of Bavaria. This is beer country, with stringent government-controlled standards to ensure the high quality of the beer produced in the many breweries. Besides generating fine wines from the vineyards along the Rhine and Mosel rivers, the northern part of Bavaria's fertile countryside yields many vegetables.

Radishes, white asparagus, and cabbage rank supreme as vegetables here. Most meals include at least one type of salad, which might consist of lettuces or any variety of vegetables tossed with vinegar and oil dressing. Myriad varieties of plums, cherries, apples, and berries grow well in this area and appear in many desserts.

Every region boasts its own sauerkraut recipes. Although pig's feet and snout in sauerkraut continues as a northern treat, sauerkraut in Swabia is cooked with apples, onions, and white wine. Hunting and fishing remain popular throughout the south. As a result, game and freshwater fish from the mountain streams are served often. *Spaetzel*, a cross between a dumpling and a noodle, accompanies many plates. Served as a light meal, *Käsespaetzel* is *Spaetzel* combined with *Emmentaler* (a type of Swiss cheese) and sometimes onions. Several fine cheeses come from Bavaria, including *Emmentaler* and beer cheese.

The Black Forest area in the southwest is known for several specialties. Besides yielding many varieties of mushrooms, the forest produces ample berries and game. Famous for *Schwartzwälder Kirschtorte*, Black Forest cherry cake, this torte features cake layers flavored with *Kirschwasser*, a cherry liquor, filled with whipped cream and a cherry filling. Although this specialty comes from the Black Forest region, variations are served throughout Germany.

CUISINE

Basically, the German diet consists of many soups, salads, vegetables, meat, and potatoes. Their hearty cooking includes plenty of starches—dumplings, *Spaetzel*, and, of course, potatoes. Potatoes were brought to Germany from South America in the seventeenth century. Considering how important they are to the German cuisine, it's hard to believe they were not widely grown until about the nineteenth century. However, once they started growing potatoes, the Germans embraced them heartily, and potatoes became the starch of choice. Today, they are consumed daily and prepared in a myriad of ways—fried, boiled, mashed, puréed, pancakes, soup, salad, dumplings, stews, and on and on. Potatoes appear in every part of the menu from appetizers, salads, entrées, side dishes, to desserts.

Meat plays a large role in the German diet with pork ranking as the most popular meat, followed by veal. Dating from the times of the Romans, the Germanic tribes consumed pork (wild boar), deer, and rabbit. Today as in the past, all parts of the pig are used. Bacon and other cured pork products flavor many German dishes, including soups and salads. Westphalian ham, a delicate, smoked ham similar to Italian *prosciutto*, is sliced very thinly and served with buttered rye or pumpernickel bread.

Of course, both pork and veal are frequent ingredients in the endless varieties of *wurst*, German sausages. Every region has its own specialty, but *wurst* certainly ranks as a German national food. Prepared in any imaginable way, *wurst* appears in *choucroute*, the popular sauerkraut, various meats, and sausage casserole of Alsace-Lorraine, or *wurst* can be purchased from a street vendor, served on a roll accompanied by mustard.

Schnitzel, veal cutlets that are pounded thin and sautéed, appear on menus with a variety of toppings. These cutlets are sometimes breaded as in *Wiener Schnitzel* or sautéed plain as with *Schnitzel Natur*. Goose, the traditional Christmas meal, is prepared in several ways. Some stuff goose with fruit while others smoke the bird. Germany's most famous beef dish, *Sauerbraten*, starts with a beef roast that is marinated for at least three days in an acidic liquid (usually vinegar) and spices. The acid from the vinegar tenderizes the tough meat. Like many dishes, the preparation of *Sauerbraten* varies with the region. In the north, the beef is marinated in buttermilk instead of vinegar,

Assortment of Favorite German Foods—clockwise from top: assorted breads, cheeses, sausage, hams, white asparagus, and cabbage; photo courtesy of CMA, The German Agricultural Marketing Board

while vinegar and red wine are used in the south. Some even marinate with beer. After marinating, the beef is braised until tender. Variations on the recipes involve more than the choice of marinating liquid. *Sauerbraten* from the Rhineland contains raisins; other areas thicken the gravy with broken gingersnap cookies in addition to flour.

Often German meat recipes incorporate fruit with the meats, either in the cooking process or as an accompaniment. Dried fruits appear frequently in stuffing. *Rouladen*, another popular beef dish, consists of beef pounded thin, spread with mustard, rolled around a dill pickle spear or sauerkraut, and then braised.

Since the Middle Ages, hunting has remained a strong tradition in Germany. In the fall of the year, menus found both in restaurants and homes prominently feature all sorts of game. Variety meats, including liver, tongue, heart, kidneys, brains, and sweetbreads, are frequently eaten. Germans waste none of the animal.

Much fish is consumed. In the southern regions, freshwater fish such as trout and salmon from the mountain streams reigns supreme, while ocean fish from the Baltic and North Sea remains most popular in the north. Prevalent in all regions, the ever-popular herring is prepared in a number of manners, including *rollmops*, where the pickled herring is rolled around a dill pickle. Many Germans choose herring marinated in vinegar instead of the milder wine marinade preferred in most countries.

Because of the cold, northern climate, winter vegetables thrive. This includes many varieties of cabbage, turnips, carrots, cauliflower, Brussels sprouts, kohlrabi, and spinach. One exception to the winter vegetables is a German passion—white asparagus. Available in the spring, restaurants often display banners announcing their arrival. Unlike the American preference for thin asparagus, Germans prize thick ones. Wasting none of the vegetable, the tough bottom of stalks becomes the basis for cream of asparagus soup.

Heartier fruits such as apples grow extremely well here, but all sorts of fruits, including cherries, apricots, plums, grapes, and many berries, thrive in different areas of Germany. While some of these are paired with meats, many become part of the dessert repertoire.

Many dishes were created as a method of preserving foods and preventing spoilage. Because they extended the freshness of many food products in this cold climate with a short growing season, pickling, marinating, smoking, and sausage making were popular. Some examples of these preparations include sauerkraut, pickled cabbage, and sauerbraten. Sausages use many leftover or unused parts of the animal.

The Tartars, who learned of fermented cabbage when they invaded China, introduced sauerkraut in the 1200s. Bringing it with them to Hungary and then to Austria, sauerkraut finally made its way to Germany, where it became a staple in the diet.

The forests provide many varieties of mushrooms, berries, and game. Germany is also known for fine cheeses with specialties produced in the various regions.

Open markets selling fruits and vegetables are found in all but the smallest towns. Supermarkets now exist, but many people still prefer to shop at individual markets for their food items. These include *konditorei*, bakeries for pastries; *backerei*, bakeries for breads; butcher shops carrying raw meats; *metzgerei* carrying cold cuts and sausages; *molkerien* for milk, cheeses, and other dairy products; stores for fresh produce; and other stores for grocery items. Clustered close together, the shoppers go from one store to the next for their purchases.

With a preference for sour tastes, vinegar flavors numerous foods, including lentil soup and countless varieties of salads. Vinegar and/or lemon juice is added to many entrées, often forming the basis for the sauce.

Butter, lard, and bacon grease remain the cooking fats of choice. Bacon or other cured or smoked pork imparts flavor to many dishes.

From clear soups to thick bean or pea soups to cream soups, the Germans usually include some variety of soup in any major meal. In past times, soup was actually served three times a day. Clear soups may contain dumplings, *Spaetzel*, noodles, or thin slices of crêpelike pancakes. Thick soups use flour, cream, or egg to achieve the desired thickeness.

Famous for their breads, entire shops called *backerei* are devoted to preparing and selling the many types and varieties of breads. Ranging from light to dense, rye breads abound. Excellent fine white breads, many varieties

Assortment of German Breads; photo courtesy of CMA,
The German Agricultural Marketing Board

TYPES OF *SCHNITZEL* (FRIED VEAL CUTLET)

- *Jaeger Schnitzel*—served with a sauce containing mushrooms, onions, white wine, and cooked tomatoes
- *Paprika Schnitzel*—served with a paprika and sour cream sauce
- *Rahmschnitzel*—served with a cream sauce that often contains mushrooms
- *Schnitzel a la Holstein*—topped with a fried egg, garnished with anchovy and capers
- *Schnitzel a la Oscar*—topped with asparagus tips and crab meat, then napped with Bernaise sauce
- *Schnitzel Natur*—plain, fried cutlet; pan deglazed with water or stock and lemon juice
- *Wiener Schnitzel*—breaded with standard breading procedure using flour, egg, and bread crumbs, then pan fried; garnished with lemon, caper, and anchovy

---

of rolls, and large, soft pretzels sprinkled with coarse salt are also quite popular.

World known, German pastries include *torten* (cakes), *kuchen* (pie or single layer cake), and a number of pastries from puff pastry, *choux* pastry, and yeast dough. *Lebkuchen*, honey cookies, become the foundation of the gingerbread houses made around Christmastime.

Many pastries include nuts. Quite popular in Germany, *marzipan*, almond paste is dyed with food coloring and formed into miniature fruits, vegetables, animals, and other whimsical shapes. Most *konditorei* have a counter filled with homemade truffles, candies, and marzipan pieces.

Austrian and German pastries are very similar, as opposed to French pastries which remain quite different. Many of the same pastries are served in *konditorei* in both countries, particularly in southern Germany, which borders Austria.

A simple breakfast of coffee and bread with butter and jam is standard fare, sometimes accompanied by a soft-boiled egg. Another snack or "second breakfast" used to be eaten in the late morning. For school children or farmers, this consisted of a sandwich. Most no longer have this meal, as *mittagessen*, the main meal of the day is served around twelve or one o'clock. Soup followed by meat with vegetables and a starch makes up this hearty main meal. In the late afternoon, people meet at a *konditorei* or at home for *kaffeestunde*, literally translated coffee hour. Similar to the English tea, people consume a pastry and coffee. This remains a popular time for entertaining friends, particularly on the weekends. The light evening meal consists of sausage, cold cuts, cheese, bread, and often salad.

GERMAN CHEESES

Butterkäse Made from cow's milk, buttery flavor, semisoft texture

Cambozola Made from cow's milk, cross between Brie and Gorgonzola, flavor of blue cheese, smooth soft texture

Emmentaler Made from cow's milk, type of Swiss cheese, flavor of Swiss cheese, contains holes, from Bavaria in southern Germany

Limburger Made from cow's milk, very sharp pungent flavor, soft creamy texture

Muenster Made from cow's milk, mild flavor, semisoft texture

Tilsiter Made from cow's milk, full-bodied strong flavor, tiny holes

Quark Made from cow's milk, fresh cheese with mild fresh flavor, smooth soft texture

REGION	AREA	WEATHER	TOPOGRAPHY	FOODS
North	Baltic Sea and North Sea	Cold winters, mild summers	Coast, sand dunes	Seafood, eel, herring, turbot, plaice
	Inland	Cold winters, mild summers	Lowlands, plains, sandy soil, rich farmland, lakes, forest in northeast	Cattle, sheep, geese, pigs, *wurst*, game, fish, rye, barley, wheat, hops, potatoes, winter vegetables, cabbage, sugar beets, mushrooms, fruits, apples, berries
Central	Rhine and Mosel rivers	Cold winters, mild summers	Hills, forests, valleys, plateaus, rivers, vineyards	Sheep, pigs, *wurst*, Westphalian ham, rye, wheat, dumplings, potatoes, turnips, sugar beets, cabbage, onions, fruits, berries, grapes, wine
South	Bavaria, Swabia, Baden, Alsace-Lorraine	Cold winters, mild summers	Hills, mountains, forests, fertile farmland, orchards, vineyards	Cattle, *wurst*, fish, trout, salmon, game, *Emmentaler* cheese, dairy, barley, wheat, *spaetzel*, vegetables, white asparagus, cabbage, radishes, mushrooms, fruits, cherries, plums, grapes, wine, beer

Consumption of both beer and wine remain high. Beer is often brewed using natural fermentation, a brewing method employed since the Middle Ages. The Germans invented the lagering process for making beer. An excellent pairing with the hearty German foods, many types of German beer are produced in breweries throughout the countryside. The northern Germans generally prefer a lighter beer served well chilled, whereas the southerners like darker beer at room temperature.

Most of the wine production occurs around the Rhine and Mosel rivers and primarily consists of varieties of white wine. *Kirschwasser* is a cherry liqueur produced in the Black Forest where many cherry trees thrive. Brandies also come from Germany.

Review Questions

1. Name countries that border Germany and give examples of their influence on Germany's cuisine.
2. How has the climate and topography in Germany affected the cuisine?
3. Name at least five food products and/or flavorings that appear commonly in Germany.
4. Discuss the prevalence and types of starches in the German diet.
5. Discuss the meals eaten in the normal German's day, including the types of foods that would be served at each meal.

Glossary

Backerei Bakeries that sell all sorts of breads and rolls

Braunschweiger Liverwurst or liver sausage that originated from the town of Braunschweig in the north

Choucroute Popular casserole containing sauerkraut, various meats, and sausage served in Alsace-Lorraine

Emmentaler Type of Swiss cheese from Bavaria

Forellen blau Literally meaning blue trout, this fish is prepared by dropping a live trout in boiling water containing a little vinegar; the vinegar causes the skin of the fish to take on a blue cast, therefore the name

Kaffeestunde Literally translated, coffee hour, a late afternoon snack consisting of pastry and coffee or other beverage

Kirschwasser A strong cherry liqueur produced in the Black Forest

Konditorei Bakeries that sell pastries; they usually contain tables and chairs where customers can sit and order a slice of pastry or ice cream, and coffee or other beverages

Lebkuchen A spiced honey cookie eaten alone or baked in large pieces and used as the base for gingerbread houses

Metzgerie Shops carrying cold cuts and sausages

Mittagessen The main meal of the day, served in the afternoon around twelve or one o'clock

Molkerien Shops selling milk, cheeses, and other dairy products

Pfefferpotthast A stew of beef short ribs containing lots of pepper

Sauerbraten Beef marinated in an acidic liquid (often vinegar, but it depends on the region), then braised

Schnitzel Veal cutlets that are pounded thin, sometimes breaded, and then pan-fried

Schwartzwälder Kirschtorte Black Forest cherry cake, a torte featuring cake layers flavored with *Kirschwasser*, a cherry liquor, filled with whipped cream and a cherry filling; originated in the Black Forest region

Spaetzel A starch that is a cross between a dumpling and a noodle

Stollen Traditional Christmas bread that originated in Dresden

Westphalian ham A delicate, smoked ham similar to Italian *prosciutto*, served sliced very thinly on buttered rye or pumpernickel bread

Wurst Any of the countless varieties of sausages

Zwiebelkuchen Quichelike pie consisting of a pastry shell with a filling of bacon, eggs, cream, and onions

---

Note: A good German beer makes an excellent accompaniment with any of the entrées.

Traditionally, this is served throughout Germany with the new wine in the fall. This tart may be prepared as one large pie (which is traditional) or as individual tarts.

ZWIEBELKUCHEN

Onion Tart

Number of Servings: 8 to 10   Cooking Method: Bake
Total Yield: 9-inch tart

Food Balance: Sweet/protein
Wine Style: Soft and fruity Alsatian Riesling or Liebfraumilch, Viognier, Rosé, Pinot Noir
Example: Beringer Viognier or Rosé de Saignee

Zwiebelkuchen (Onion Tart); photo courtesy of Dorling Kindersley

INGREDIENTS	WEIGHT	VOLUME
pie shell, partially baked		
bacon, diced	4 oz	5 slices
onion, finely chopped	1 lb, 2 oz	3½ cups, about 4 medium
caraway seeds		1 teaspoon
pepper		⅛ teaspoon
eggs	3½ oz	2 each
egg yolk	¾ oz	1 each
sour cream	6 oz	¾ cup

1. Prepare pie shell. Do not dock (make small holes in bottom crust), but weight shell and bake until halfway done.
2. Fry bacon until translucent, then add onions. Sauté, stirring frequently, until onions are clear yellow in color.
3. Add pepper and caraway seeds. Remove from heat and cool.
4. Preheat oven to 400 degrees.
5. Beat eggs and yolk into sour cream. Spread onion mixture in bottom of pie crust, pour in sour cream mixture slowly so that it penetrates through onion mixture.
6. Bake for 15 minutes, then reduce temperature to 350 and bake another 20 minutes, until golden brown.
7. Cut into wedges, serve warm.

BLUMENKOHLSUPPE

Cream of Cauliflower Soup

Number of Servings: 9   Cooking Method: Boil
Serving Size: 6 oz
Total Yield: 3 lbs, 7 oz

Food Balance: Sweet and protein
Wine Style: Light and fruity Sauvignon Blanc, fruity Chardonnay, Beaujolais
Example: Château Souverain Sauvignon Blanc

INGREDIENTS	WEIGHT	VOLUME
cauliflower	approx 2 lb, 3 oz	1 large
chicken stock	2 lbs	1 quart or 4 cups
butter	2 oz	4 tablespoons or ½ stick
flour	1¼ oz	5 tablespoons
water	8 oz to 1 lb	1 to 2 cups
milk	8 oz	1 cup
white pepper		½ teaspoon
nutmeg, ground		¼ teaspoon
egg yolk	¾ oz	1 each

GARNISH:

paprika

1. Remove core and outer green leaves from cauliflower. Separate flowerets, wash well. Reserve some small flowerets to add to puréed soup at end. Chop remaining cauliflower.
2. Bring stock to boil, add chopped cauliflower, cook until almost soft. Add 8 oz (1 cup) water.
3. Melt butter over moderate heat, add flour and whisk briefly over low heat until white roux.
4. Slowly whisk hot stock into roux, a ladle-full at a time, cook until smooth and thick. If needed, add remaining 8 oz (1 cup) water to cauliflower.
5. Whisk roux into cauliflower. Add milk, white pepper, and nutmeg, cook about 10 to 15 minutes, until cauliflower is soft. Add remaining 8 oz (1 cup) water if too thick.
6. Purée mixture, using food processor or ricer.
7. Return to saucepan, add reserved cauliflower flowerets, cook until almost soft.
8. Place yolk in separate bowl. Add hot soup by tablespoons, whisking continually, to temper yolk. Add yolk to soup, cook another

Blumenkohlsuppe (Cream of Cauliflower Soup)

few minutes, stirring occasionally. Be careful not to boil or soup could curdle.

9. Correct seasonings. Serve immediately in warmed bowls. If desired, garnish with sprinkling of paprika.

KALTER KARTOFFELSALAT

Cold Potato Salad

Number of Servings: 8
Serving Size: 4 oz
Total Yield: 2 lbs, 3 oz

Cooking Method: Boil

INGREDIENTS	WEIGHT	VOLUME
potatoes, red, unpeeled	2 lb	6 medium to large
onion, finely minced	3 oz	1 small
oil	1½ oz	3 tablespoons
vinegar	2 oz	4 tablespoons
pepper, ground		¾ teaspoon
salt	¼ oz	1 teaspoon
parsley or dill, minced (optional)	½ to 1 oz	2 to 4 tablespoons

1. Wash potatoes well, place in pan, cover with cold water. Cook potatoes until tender.
2. Drain, saving ⅓ cup cooking liquid. Let potatoes cool slightly until able to handle, then peel potatoes, slice thinly into bowl.
3. Add onion, oil, and reserved cooking liquid, mix gently.
4. Add vinegar, salt, and pepper, mix gently.
5. Let sit at room temperature for several hours.
6. Add parsley or dill, if desired. Correct seasonings. Serve.

WARMER KARTOFFELSALAT MIT SPECK

Warm Potato Salad with Bacon

Number of Servings: 13
Serving Size: 4 oz
Total Yield: 3 lbs, 5 oz

Cooking Method: Boil, sauté

INGREDIENTS	WEIGHT	VOLUME
potatoes, red, scrubbed, unpeeled	3 lb	9 medium
bacon, finely diced	½ lb	
onions, minced	3 oz	1 small
cider vinegar	5 oz	⅔ cup
water	2 oz	¼ cup
salt	¼ oz	1 teaspoon
black pepper		¾ teaspoon
parsley, finely chopped	½ oz	2 tablespoons

Warmer Kartoffelsalat mit Speck (Warm Potato Salad with Bacon)

1. Place unpeeled potatoes in pot and cover with water. Bring to boil and cook until potatoes are three-quarters done. Do not overcook.
2. Drain potatoes, peel while still quite warm. Cut into ⅛- to ¼-inch slices. Cover bowl of potatoes to keep warm.
3. Cook bacon in skillet over moderate heat until brown and crisp, drain well on paper towels.
4. Add onions to bacon fat and cook, stirring frequently, for 5 minutes, until onions are soft and transparent.
5. Stir in vinegar, water, salt, and pepper, and cook, stirring constantly, for a minute or so.
6. Pour hot sauce over potatoes, turning gently with spatula to coat evenly.
7. Gently stir reserved bacon pieces into salad. Correct seasonings.
8. Serve at once or cover and store at room temperature until service. For longer storage, refrigerate, then serve at room temperature.
9. At service, stir salad gently and sprinkle top with parsley.

SCHWEINE-FILET

Pork Tenderloin (in a Lemon Sauce)

Number of Servings: 6 to 8   Cooking Method: Braise
Serving Size: 4 to 5 oz
Total Yield: 1 lb, 10 oz to 2 lb, 2 oz meat
    (depending on size of tenderloins)

Food Balance: Acid balanced
Wine Style: Wide variety—Pinot Grigio, Chardonnay, Merlot, Cabernet Sauvignon
Example: Beringer Knights Valley Cabernet Sauvignon

INGREDIENTS	WEIGHT	VOLUME
pork tenderloin, trimmed of fat	¾ to 1 lb each	3 each
onions, sliced in 1/8-inch rings	9 oz	1 to 1½ large
flour, all purpose or bread	2 oz	½ cup minus 1 tablespoon

Schweine-Filet (Pork Tenderloin [in a Lemon Sauce])

INGREDIENTS	WEIGHT	VOLUME
oil	1½ oz	3 tablespoons
hot water	about 2 lb	about 4 cups or 1 quart
lemon	2 to 2¼ oz, to taste	1 or 1½ each, to taste
salt and pepper	to taste	

1. Dredge pork in flour. Heat oil in skillet or braising pan until hot. Sear pork on all sides, then add onions. Sauté until brown.
2. Add remaining flour to pan, brown lightly.
3. Whisk in water very slowly to make medium-thin sauce. Add more water as necessary, if sauce becomes too thick.
4. Add lemon juice, salt, and pepper. Cover and braise about 45 minutes, until pork is done. Stir occasionally to keep meat from sticking. Add water, as necessary to make medium-thin sauce. Correct seasonings.
5. Slice and serve with *Spaetzel*, fried potatoes, or pasta.

SAUERBRATEN

Marinated Beef Roast

Number of Servings: 8
Serving Size: 4 oz meat
　　　　　　2 oz sauce
Total Yield: 2 lbs, 1 oz meat
　　　　　　1 lb, 1 oz sauce

Cooking Method: Braise

Food Balance: Acid/balanced

Wine Style: Wide variety—Sauvignon Blanc, Pinot Grigio, Pinot Noir, Shiraz, Chianti, or Barbera
Example: Castello di Gabbiano Chianti

> *Begin marinating the meat 2 to 3 days before cooking.*

INGREDIENTS	WEIGHT	VOLUME
MARINADE:		
red wine	4 oz	½ cup
red wine vinegar	4 oz	½ cup
water	1 lb	2 cups
onion, peeled, sliced thin	5 oz	1 medium
peppercorns, whole		6 each
cloves, whole		6 each
bay leaves		2 each
salt, kosher	¼ oz	1 teaspoon
beef roast, bottom round, chuck, rump, or shoulder	4 lb	
oil	1 oz	2 tablespoons
onion, finely diced	3 oz	1 small onion or ½ cup
celery, finely diced	2¾ oz	½ cup
carrot, finely diced	2½ oz	½ cup
flour	½ oz	2 tablespoons
gingersnap crumbs	2¼ oz	½ cup
water	4 oz	½ cup

TO MARINATE:

1. Place marinade ingredients (first eight) in saucepan. Bring to boil, remove from heat. Cool.
2. Trim meat of excess fat, wash well. Place in nonreactive bowl. Pour cooled marinade over meat. Add more wine, if needed, to cover meat half way.
3. Refrigerate for 2 to 3 days, turning two or three times daily.

TO COOK:

1. Remove meat from marinade, pat dry. Strain marinade and reserve liquid.
2. Place oil in braising or roasting pan and heat until hot. Sear meat on all sides, browning lightly. Remove meat from pan.
3. Add vegetables, sauté until soft and lightly browned, about 5 to 7 minutes. Sprinkle flour on vegetables and cook, stirring about 2 to 3 minutes.
4. Slowly whisk in 1 lb (2 cups) marinade and water (if not enough marinade). Return meat to pan and cover tightly.
5. Braise on top of stove, simmering until meat is tender, about 2 to 2½ hours or cook in 300-degree oven for 2 to 3 hours.
6. Remove meat and keep warm.
7. Strain liquid, discard vegetables. There should be about 1 lb, 4 oz (2½ cups) liquid. If not, add more reserved marinade to make that amount. Skim excess fat. Add gingersnap crumbs and cook about 10 minutes over medium heat. Strain, if lumpy. If sauce is too thick, add more marinade or water. Bring to boil.
8. Correct seasonings. To serve, slice meat in thin slices against grain. Nap with sauce. Serve with *Spaetzel*, mashed potatoes, boiled potatoes, or potato pancakes.

WIENER SCHNITZEL

Veal Cutlet Viennese Style

Number of Servings: 2   Cooking Method: Sauté
Serving Size: 4 oz
Total Yield: 8¼ oz

Food Balance: Balanced
Wine Style: Wide variety Riesling, Chardonnay, Pinot Noir, Merlot
Example: Château Souverain Merlot

INGREDIENTS	WEIGHT	VOLUME
veal cutlets, boneless, (scaloppine)	6 to 7 oz	2 each
salt	to taste	
pepper	to taste	

Dredging veal in flour; photo courtesy of Dorling Kindersley

Dipping veal in egg; photo courtesy of Dorling Kindersley

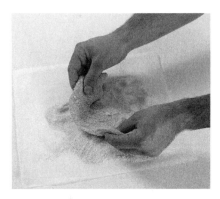

Dredging veal in bread crumbs; photo courtesy of Dorling Kindersley

Frying veal cutlet; photo courtesy of Dorling Kindersley

Wiener Schnitzel (Veal Cutlet Viennese Style); photo courtesy of Dorling Kindersley

INGREDIENTS	WEIGHT	VOLUME
BREADING:		
egg	1 oz	½ each
milk	1 oz	2 tablespoons
flour	1 oz	4 tablespoons
bread crumbs	1¼ oz	5 tablespoons
oil and/or clarified butter	1 oz	2 tablespoons

GARNISH:

lemon wedge
rolled anchovy

1. Lightly flatten each piece of veal with meat mallet. Be careful not to tear meat.
2. Season with salt and pepper.
3. Set up breading ingredients, as for standard breading. Mix egg and milk in shallow dish. Place flour in flat dish. Place bread crumbs in flat dish.
4. Bread meat by coating with flour, then egg, then bread crumbs. Make sure meat is thoroughly coated with each ingredient.
5. Heat about ¼-inch fat in skillet until hot. Sauté cutlets until golden brown on both sides.
6. Garnish with lemon and anchovy, serve immediately.

SCHWEINE FLEISCH MIT SAUERKRAUT

Pork with Sauerkraut

Number of Servings: 12   Cooking Method: Braise
Serving Size: 1 chop and ½ sausage
  with kraut
Total Yield: 9 lbs, 10 oz

Food Balance: Acidic protein
Wine Style: Acid balanced to strong dry Riesling to Pinot Grigio, Chianti to strong Cabernet
Example: Castello De Gabbiano Chianti Classico or Reserva

INGREDIENTS	WEIGHT	VOLUME
sauerkraut, drain and rinsed	3 lbs, 6 oz	2 each 27–oz cans
red potato, peeled and grated	11½ oz	2 medium
apple, tart, peeled and grated	11 oz	2 medium
onion, peeled and grated	8 oz	2 medium
caraway seeds	½ oz	4 teaspoons
country style ribs, pork chops, sausage, or any combination	6 lbs	

1. Preheat oven to 325 degrees.
2. Combine sauerkraut, red potato, apple, onion, and caraway seeds in ovenproof casserole.
3. Top with ribs or chops, bury sausages in sauerkraut.
4. Bake, uncovered, for about 1½ hours, until done.

Schweine Fleisch mit Sauerkraut (Pork with Sauerkraut)

SPAETZEL

Small Noodlelike Dumplings

Number of Servings: 14
Serving Size: 3 oz
Total Yield: 2 lb, 10 oz

Cooking Method: Boil, sauté

INGREDIENTS	WEIGHT	VOLUME
flour, all purpose	13 oz	3 cups
salt		½ teaspoon
nutmeg		⅛ teaspoon
eggs	6¾ oz	4 each
water	8 oz, approximately	1 cup, approximately

TO SERVE:
butter
salt
pepper
dill, finely chopped (optional)

1. Place dry ingredients in bowl, form a well.
2. Beat eggs to blend, place in well in dry ingredients. Add about half the water, beat well.
3. Add water, a little at a time, and beat mixture until bubbles start to appear and smooth batter no longer adheres to the spoon. Batter will be thick but wet.
4. Fill large pot with water, bring to boil.
5. Use small board and icing spatula (or dull side of chef's knife). Moisten board with a little boiling water, take a little bit of dough, and press it flat on board with spatula.

Pushing spaetzel dough into boiling water; photo courtesy of Dorling Kindersley

Removing cooked spaetzel from boiling water; photo courtesy of Dorling Kindersley

Spaetzel (Small Noodlelike Dumplings); photo courtesy of CMA, The German Agricultural Marketing Board

6. Cut off fine strips of dough, push them off edge of board into boiling water with spatula. Dip spatula into boiling water if sticking to dough.
7. Remove *Spaetzle* with skimmer when they float to surface. Place in bowl of cold water to remove excess starch and hold until service.
8. To serve, sauté in butter to reheat. Season with salt, pepper, and finely chopped dill, if desired.

KAESESPAETZEL

Cheese Noodlelike Dumplings

Number of Servings: 8   Cooking Method: Sauté
Serving Size: 7 oz entrée
                4 oz side dish
Total Yield: 1 lb, 14 oz

Food Balance: Protein
Wine Style: Light- to medium-bodied Pinot Blanc, Chardonnay, Merlot, Zinfandel
Example: Château St. Jean Pinot Blanc

INGREDIENTS	WEIGHT	VOLUME
Spaetzel (recipe above)	1 lb, 4 oz	5 cups
Emmentaler or other Swiss cheese, grated	10 oz	2 cups
butter	1 oz	2 tablespoons
salt	¼ oz	1 teaspoon
pepper		½ teaspoon

> This is served in Germany as a light entrée accompanied by a salad. We term this a luncheon entrée.

1. Melt butter in skillet.
2. Spread single layer of *Spaetzel* in ovenproof skillet. (Do not use thick layer of *Spaetzel*.) Sprinkle with salt and pepper.
3. Sauté lightly, sprinkle cheese on top.
4. Broil until lightly brown.

BLAUKRAUT

Sweet and Sour Red Cabbage

Number of Servings: 8
Serving Size: 4 oz
Total Yield: 2 lbs, 2 oz

Cooking Method: Braise

INGREDIENTS	WEIGHT	VOLUME
red cabbage, cored, sliced thin across the grain	2 lb	1 medium head, about 10 cups
apple, cored, cut in 12 pieces	about 6 oz	1 medium or large
water	about 12 oz	1½ cups, as needed
sugar	2¾ oz	⅓ cup
red wine vinegar	10 to 12 oz	1¼ to 1½ cups

> This cabbage may be cooked a day ahead. Some say the flavors actually marry better when reheated.

Blaukraut (Sweet and Sour Red Cabbage); photo courtesy of CMA, The German Agricultural Marketing Board

INGREDIENTS	WEIGHT	VOLUME
salt	¼ to ½ oz	1½ teaspoons
pepper		¼ teaspoon
cloves, ground		⅛ teaspoon

1. Place cabbage, apple, and 8 oz (1 cup) water in large pan over medium heat until starting to cook.
2. Add three-quarters of the sugar and vinegar. Add cloves.
3. Cook, covered, for about one hour over low heat, adding more water if needed, to prevent scorching.
4. Add salt and pepper. Taste and add more vinegar and sugar to balance sweet and sour.
5. Continue cooking until cabbage is soft.
6. Correct seasonings and serve.

SÜSS UND SAURE GRUENE BOHNEN

Sweet and Sour Green Beans

Number of Servings: 10   Cooking Method: Boil
Serving Size: 4 oz
Total Yield: 2 lbs, 10 oz

INGREDIENTS	WEIGHT	VOLUME
green beans, stems and strings removed, broken, if desired	2 lb	
butter	1 oz	2 tablespoons
flour	1 oz	4 tablespoons
water, hot	12 oz	1½ cup
sugar	2 oz	4 tablespoons
cider vinegar	5 oz	10 tablespoons
salt	¼ oz	1 teaspoon
pepper		½ teaspoon

1. Make white roux: melt butter over medium heat, add flour and mix with whisk. Cook briefly so it does not color. Add water slowly, whisking constantly.
2. Add sugar, vinegar, and seasonings to sauce. Add green beans.
3. Cook until beans reach desired doneness, about 15 minutes. If necessary add more water.
4. Correct seasonings and serve.

LINZERTORTE

Spiced Dough Filled with Raspberry Preserves

Number of Servings: 10 to 12   Cooking Method: Bake
Yield: 9- or 10-inch tart in French tart pan
   with removable bottom or springform pan
Total Yield: 1 lb, 10 oz dough
Scaling: 9-inch French tart pan with
   removable bottom needs 1 lb, 5 oz dough

INGREDIENTS	WEIGHT	VOLUME
butter, unsalted	8 oz	1 cup or 2 sticks
sugar	7½ oz	1 cup
lemon peel, grated		1½ teaspoons
orange peel, grated		1 tablespoon
egg yolks	1½ oz	2 each
white flour, all purpose, sifted	6½ oz	1½ cups
baking powder		1 teaspoon
cinnamon	¼ oz	2 teaspoons
cloves, ground		¼ teaspoon
nutmeg, ground		½ teaspoon
salt		¼ teaspoon
almonds, blanched, ground	4 oz	1 cup
raspberry preserves	13½ oz	1 cup plus 2 tablespoons

> *Served often in Germany, this pastry is actually of Austrian origin.*

GARNISH:

confectioners' sugar, sifted
whipped cream, slightly sweetened

1. Sift together flour, baking powder, salt, and spices.
2. Cream butter, sugar, and grated peels in mixer with flat beater. Add egg yolks, one at a time, mixing well after each one.
3. Add sifted dry ingredients to creamed mixture.
4. Add nuts. Mix well, by hand if necessary, until smooth.
5. Wrap dough and chill thoroughly for several hours or overnight.
6. Preheat oven to 350 degrees.
7. Press dough into pan about ¼- to ⅜-inch thick. If using springform, press dough about 1-inch up sides; if using French tart pan or pie pan, press dough to top of pan.
8. Spread preserves over dough to depth of about ⅜- to ½-inch.
9. Roll out remaining dough, form long strips, about ⅜ to ½ inch across, and place them on cake in lattice pattern.
10. Bake in middle of oven for 45 to 55 minutes, until golden brown.
11. Cool thoroughly on rack, sift lightly with confectioners' sugar.
12. Serve, garnished with slightly sweetened whipped cream.

Linzertorte (Spiced Dough Filled with Raspberry Preserves); photo courtesy of Dorling Kindersley

ZWETSCHGEN KUCHEN

Plum Pie

Number of Servings: 8
Total Yield: 9-inch pie

Cooking Method: Bake

> Muerbe Teig is sweet butter dough
> similar to the French pâte
> sucrée or a sugar cookie.

INGREDIENTS	WEIGHT	VOLUME
MUERBE TEIG:		
butter, unsalted, cut into pieces	2 oz	½ stick or 4 tablespoons
sugar	3¾ oz	½ cup
flour, all purpose	4½ oz	1 cup
egg	1¾ oz	1 each
FILLING:		
plums, prune-type	2 lb	
sugar		1 to 3 tablespoons, to taste
cinnamon		½ teaspoon

GARNISH:

whipped cream, slightly sweetened

DOUGH:

1. Lightly pan spray 9-inch pie pan with sloped sides.
2. Soften butter until a little colder than room temperature. Cut in sugar with fingertips.
3. Add flour, mix with fingertips, then add egg.
4. Mix until well blended and dough forms ball. Do not overmix.
5. Pat into prepared pie pan. Refrigerate while preparing filling.

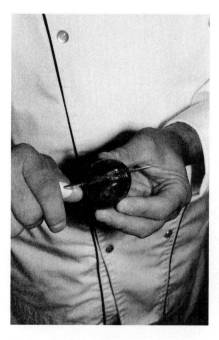

First cut in plum along crease; photo courtesy of Patricia Heyman

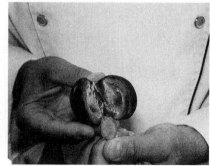

Removing pit from plum; photo courtesy of Patricia Heyman

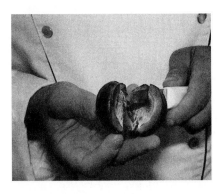

Cutting slit in top of plum half; photo courtesy of Patricia Heyman

Cut plum ready for placing in pie; photo courtesy of Patricia Heyman

FILLING:

1. Wash plums. Preheat oven to 350 degrees.
2. Hold plum in hand, cut through half of plum along crease line on one side, do not cut plum in half.
3. Open plum and remove pit. Parallel to first cut, slice halfway down each half. Plum can be opened like a book with two cuts splaying top.
4. Repeat with remaining plums.
5. Starting at edge of pie shell, place plums, upright, in tight concentric circle around pie until center is filled.
6. Sprinkle with cinnamon and sugar.
7. Bake for 25 minutes. If desired, sprinkle another tablespoon sugar over tart, return to oven.
8. Bake another 5 to 15 minutes, until crust is golden. Cool to room temperature.
9. Serve, garnished with slightly sweetened whipped cream.

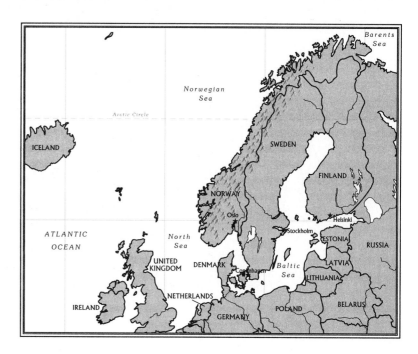

CHAPTER 6
Scandinavia

By the end of this chapter, you will be able to

- Know which foods are prevalent in Scandinavia, why those foods are available, and how they are used in various dishes
- Identify similarities in the cooking methods and cuisines of the countries of Scandinavia
- Understand the concept of a *smörgåsbord*
- Prepare a variety of Scandinavian dishes

HISTORY

Situated at the far northern end of Europe, the area known as Scandinavia consists of four countries: Denmark, Norway, Sweden, and Finland. (Some sources include Iceland as the fifth Scandinavian country.) Throughout history, these four countries politically united with each other in various combinations in attempts to rule one another. Today, each of the countries is an independent nation, yet people often group them together because of their many similarities and close geographic proximity.

Because they are situated so far north, the Scandinavian countries experience daylight most of the day in the summer and almost full days of darkness in the winter. As a result of this phenomenon, Scandinavia is called the "Land of the Midnight Sun." During the long, cold, dark winter, food and drink play a prominent role in the lives of Scandinavians. Using techniques that they learned from the Vikings more than a thousand years ago, the Scandinavians became very proficient at preserving meats, fish, fruits, and vegetables. This helped them survive the long, severe winters.

From about 800 A.D. to 1050 A.D., the Vikings from Scandinavia sailed the seas fortified with all sorts of smoked meats and dried, salted fish. Many customs and traditions still exist from those Viking days, including methods for preserving foods and a fondness for wine that still remains throughout Scandinavia.

Sharing a border with Denmark, Germany became a significant influence. Around the 1600s and 1700s, the nobility of Denmark started imitating the royalty of France, resulting in a strong French effect on the foods throughout Denmark. French influence became even more pronounced when one of Napoleon's generals joined the nobility of Norway and Sweden in the nineteenth century. With the Scandinavian countries being as close as they are both politically and in geographic proximity, soon the French and German influence appeared throughout all the Scandinavian countries.

In the sixteenth century, the Dutch settled in Denmark bringing all sorts of fruits and vegetables with them to plant in their new land. Meanwhile, at different times in their history, Finland came under the rule of Russia and Sweden, so both of these countries exerted a large impact on the cuisine of Finland. Again, with the great influence of these nations on each other, the effect of each country was felt throughout Scandinavia.

TOPOGRAPHY

Glaciers played a significant role in sculpting the land and forming the topography that exists throughout the Scandinavian countries. Interestingly, the melting glaciers left different features on the land in each country. Although in one country they created mountains, in another the glaciers scraped the surface of the land leaving it all around sea level.

The most southern of the Scandinavian countries, Denmark is a peninsula with Germany situated on its southern border. Denmark also includes over 480 islands. The country consists of coasts, rolling hills, many lakes, and fertile farmland that formed when the glaciers melted. The retreating glaciers left most of the land being just about sea level.

Norway, the most barren of the Scandinavian countries, contains mostly high, mountainous plateaus, mountains, fjords (inlets), forests, and rocky shores. Counting the fjords and peninsulas along the coast, this country contains over 13,000 miles of coastline! The melting glaciers formed deep valleys and many lakes. When the glaciers left, the soil was gone and bare rock remained covering the mountainous plateaus, leaving the northern half of Norway with a terrain of mountains. Sweden joins the eastern side of Norway.

Remnants of the glaciers, Sweden and Finland contain thousands of lakes. Large areas of forest exist in both countries. With the Baltic Sea on the east, Sweden is comprised of lots of coastline, as well as mountains, rivers, rocky islands, forests, and lakes. Glaciers still remain in the mountains in the north of Sweden, a cold, barren land where it is even too cold for trees to grow.

Finland shares a border with Russia on the east. Forest covers two-thirds of Finland, and over 60,000 lakes dot the countryside. Plateaus with gentle hills and valleys describe most of the land. There are some mountains, but most of the land is fairly low.

Ingredients and Foods Commonly Used Throughout the Cuisine of Scandinavia Include:

- all sorts of seafood including herring, cod, and salmon
- game including elk, hare, and reindeer
- cheese, cream, sour cream, and butter
- dill, fennel, anise, and horseradish
- cardamom, allspice, caraway, nutmeg, and cinnamon

- winter vegetables, including cabbage, beets, winter squash, rutabagas, and carrots
- apples and berries
- potatoes
- cucumbers
- rye bread

COOKING METHODS

To survive the long, hard, cold winters, the Scandinavians preserved all sorts of foods to provide sustenance through the winter. Meats and seafood were salted, smoked, and pickled. On the other hand, the high quality and incredible freshness of seafood lent itself to simple preparations such as grilling, sautéing, poaching, or cooking on a spear or plank over an open fire.

Because meat was not abundant, the Scandinavians used all parts of the animal, and braising (in the popular stews) functioned as a method of using the tougher cuts of meat, as well as extending the meager meat supplies. Baking and slow one-pot cookery remain common as plentiful wood for fuel comes from the many forests, and the heat from a long-burning oven also helps combat the cold weather.

REGIONS

Denmark contains the most fertile land of the four Scandinavian countries. The countryside consists of green and rolling land, conducive to raising cattle that produce both top-quality meat as well as milk for butter and cheese. The animals most often raised are cows and pigs. With miles of coastline and many lakes, fishing remains a big industry here.

The Danish people are known for their love of food, and raising much livestock for both dairy and meat. Sweet cream appears in many dishes, including soups, salads, sauces, and desserts. Breakfast in Denmark consists of coffee with either "Danish" (a sweet roll) or rye bread and cheese. Typically, the afternoon meal is *smørrebrød*, literally meaning "buttered bread." Actually a canapé, a base of thin bread or cracker, is spread with butter, then topped with meat, seafood, or cheese. An eye-catching garnish tops these beautiful, opened-faced sandwiches. Accompanied by cold beer, *smørrebrød* is truly a Danish institution. Shops serving these beautiful canapés are found all over the larger cities such as Copenhagen. As early as the eighteenth century, *smørrebrød* became unique in Denmark because it was eaten with a knife and fork rather than the diner picking up the bread with their hands and eating it like a sandwich. Endless varieties of *smørrebrød* exist; the only constant is that the base consists of thinly sliced bread or cracker spread evenly with butter.

Meat and potatoes remain staples with pork reigning as the most popular meat. The Danes export significant quantities of both pork and beef, so, although ample meat is produced, it remains rather expensive. As a result, the Danes prepare and serve meat conservatively. Every household possesses their favorite recipe for *frikadeller*, a ground meat mixture formed into meatballs, patties, or used as forcemeat. Quite popular, dessert might simply consist of fresh fruits and cheeses or a more involved confection such as cake, mousse, pudding, or crêpelike pancakes filled with lingonberries, a native berry often used in desserts and on the famous pancakes served throughout Scandinavia.

The hearty evening meal served in Denmark usually consists of roasted meat or fish accompanied by potatoes and vegetables. Later in the evening, people often partake in dessert and coffee.

Although comprised of very beautiful countryside, only about 4 percent of the land in Norway is suitable for cultivation. As a result, Norwegians rely on the sea for much of their food. Because of the rugged, mountainous terrain, severe isolation within the country became a significant factor, even making it difficult to share recipes. Therefore, each family has its own recipes for many common dishes, and those recipes vary widely from one family to the next.

Because so little of the land in Norway can be cultivated, the mainstays of the Norwegian cuisine remain fish and potatoes. With miles and miles of fjords, long coastal channels, mountain streams, and coastline, many varieties of fresh fish and seafood abound. Although the seas yield herring, cod, turbot, plaice, and sole, the streams are abundant with trout and salmon. Because the freshness of the fish dominates, preparations remain quite simple, usually poached or boiled. Smoked and salted fish are prevalent to make it through the long winter. Salted cod, *klippfisk,* remains a popular food item.

Goats and sheep survive in this mountainous land, which accounts for the popularity of goat cheeses. Available meat is usually mutton, lamb, or game. In the northern region, reindeer are hunted. Sour cream appears in all sorts of dishes from appetizers to desserts. As in the other Scandinavian countries, cabbage cookery is omnipresent.

In Norway, breakfast continues as a large, hearty meal consisting of cold meat and fish, cheese, eggs, a variety of breads and jams. Herring remains a breakfast staple. Lunch is light, usually a sandwich. Consumed early when the children arrive home from school and the adults return from work, the evening meal is usually the only warm meal of the day. This meal often consists of fish accompanied by boiled potatoes, vegetables, and dessert. Served in the late evening, supper is usually a sandwich.

Norway claims several national dishes. *Rømmegrøt,* a porridge made with sour cream, is served at all important functions, including weddings and harvest celebrations. Salt-cured meats called *spekemat* are dried, cured, and/or salted mutton or pork.

Only about 10 percent of Sweden's land can be farmed, and most of that farmland lies in the southern portion. Pigs are raised in addition to cows for both meat and dairy. Main crops include oats, potatoes, sugar beets, and wheat. Of course, seafood continues as a staple, both for consumption and export.

Forests of fir trees and thousands of lakes dot the landscape of Sweden and Finland. In addition to ample access to the sea and seafood, the myriad lakes provide fish, and the forests yield many varieties of berries, mushrooms, and game.

The most lavish *smörgåsbord* of any of the Scandinavian countries is found in Sweden. The *smörgåsbord* consists of a buffet laden with all sorts of meats, seafood, vegetables, salads, cheeses, and breads. No one actually knows when the tradition of the *smörgåsbord* began. Many believe it hails from the time of the Vikings a thousand years ago; others think it first appeared in the sixteenth century. But by the eighteenth century, the *smörgåsbord* had become a tradition in Swedish homes. Served in both homes and restaurants, the *smörgåsbord* contains as many as sixty food items. Guests serve themselves and usually begin with a herring course that offers a choice of several preparations of herring. Another fish course follows, then a cold meat course, consisting of pâté, smoked meat, or pork accompanied by salads. After that, the hot dishes are served, followed by cheeses with dessert or fruit.

Buffet table of fish; photo courtesy of The Swedish Institute

Buffet table of cold meats; photo courtesy of The Swedish Institute

Buffet table of hot foods; photo courtesy of The Swedish Institute

Although the Swedes are the most affluent of the Scandinavians, simplicity describes the everyday cooking of Sweden. A tradition continuing from the Middle Ages, many homes have very thick, hearty yellow pea soup every Thursday night for dinner followed by Swedish pancakes.

A light breakfast of cereal or pastry with coffee starts the day. Lunch consists of an open-faced sandwich. The only hot meal of the day, dinner is comprised of meat or fish accompanied by boiled potatoes. A Swedish staple, the potato is frequently eaten at both lunch and dinner.

Like the rest of Scandinavia, Finland experiences relatively mild winters along the coasts. The average winter temperature might be around 30 degrees; however, very long winters and quite short summers are normal. The inland portions of all of these countries experience extremely cold temperatures. As a result, most people live in the southern coastal areas. The northern end of Norway, Sweden, and Finland lie in the Arctic Circle and endure extremely cold weather. People in the north, the Lapps, mostly herd reindeer.

Finland's cookery reflects culinary influences from both Sweden and neighboring Russia, both of whom ruled them in the past. The cuisine of Finland remains simple, straightforward, and plentiful. Salmon is smoked on a plank over a fire, abundant caviar exists, and a myriad of game, mushrooms, and berries come from the forests. Soups prevail in every variety; porridge and gruel remain favorites. The Finns consume lots of seafood, particularly herring, pike, salmon, and perch. Boiled potatoes topped with butter accompany most dinners.

In August, the crayfish season arrives, and the crayfish and vodka parties begin. The people of Finland are known for high consumption of beer and cognac. In addition, more milk is used per capita here than in any other nation.

In Finland, an early morning light breakfast of coffee and bread with butter and cheese is followed by a hearty breakfast in the late morning or even at noon. The hearty breakfast consists of two courses—meat or fish and porridge. The other substantial meal of the day is dinner at seven or eight o'clock.

CUISINE

Water, rough terrain, and long, harsh winters of snow and ice created the isolation that cut off these four countries from the rest of the world. This isolation, an overwhelming factor affecting the cuisine of the Scandinavian countries, resulted in the preservation of culinary traditions within Scandinavia while keeping much of the rest of the world's culinary traits out of these countries.

The common thread in the cuisines of Scandinavia is the simplicity of the dishes and the connection to the seasons. With such long, harsh winters and short, mild, lush summers, the garden and the preservation of meats, seafood, fruits, and vegetables remains integral to the Scandinavian diet. In fact, the preservation of foods was a major determinant for survival in the past. Short summers mean a short growing season, so the profusion of hardy "winter" vegetables, including potatoes, carrots, turnips, parsnips, winter squashes, rutabagas, cabbage, cauliflower, and spinach, become mainstays. They store great amounts of these root and cold weather vegetables for use during the winter. The Scandinavians heartily feast on the bounty of fruits and vegetables that grow in the summer, then they preserve all that is left. Dried, smoked, pickled, and salted meats and seafood help extend the food supplies throughout the winter. The Scandinavians even ferment fish and milk. Soured milk and cream are used extensively in Norway, Sweden, and Finland. Yet pure, natural, simple, plain, and fresh are all words that describe the cuisine of Scandinavia.

Surrounded by ocean and filled with rivers and inlets, both saltwater seafood and freshwater fish play a major role in the Scandinavian diet. *Gravlax*, salmon cured in salt, sugar, and dill, remains a famous Scandinavian dish. As needed for the preserving of meats and seafood, salt is a very important commodity. Even though sea surrounds Scandinavia, in the past adequate salt was rare for all but the rich people in these countries.

The Scandinavian fondness for herring dates back to the time when the Europeans were still nomads. Greatly prized in all of the countries of Scandinavia, herring appears in several different preparations on every smörgåsbord. This fatty fish commands much respect throughout these countries. Surely, if there were a national fish, the ubiquitous herring would win the title.

Hearty winter vegetables, including beets, cabbage, rutabagas (often called "Swedes" in England), and potatoes, thrive in this rich soil with a short growing season. From the many forests come all sorts of mushrooms and berries, including the famous Scandinavian lingonberries. Because of the high production of dairy cattle, butter and cheese are consumed in substantial quantity throughout Scandinavia.

When meat is available, every bit of the animal is used, from the blood to the organs. Blood is used both in soups and sausages throughout Scandinavia. Containing the blood of pig and goose, the Vikings originated *svartsoppa*, known as black soup, over 1,000 years ago. Blood sausage remains popular in Scandinavia, as well as Germany.

Soup continues as a staple in the diet of the Scandinavians and is served daily in many homes. Hot soups appear often in the winter; cold soups from

---

SCANDINAVIAN CHEESES

Denmark

Blue Castello Made from cow's milk, a cross between blue cheese and brie similar to Saga cheese, soft, creamy texture

Danbo Made from cow's milk, mild flavor, semisoft texture

Esrom Made from cow's milk, mild but full flavor, semifirm texture, called Danish Port-Salut

Havarti Made from cow's milk, mild flavor, creamy, semisoft texture containing tiny holes, sometimes with added ingredients such as dill or caraway seeds

Saga Cross between blue and brie cheeses, flavor of mild blue cheese, soft creamy texture

Sweden

Gradost Made from cow's milk, mild, similar to Gruyere in flavor, creamy, semihard texture

Hushallsost Made from cow's milk, mild with fresh flavor, smooth texture with some holes

Norway

Gjetost Made from mixture of cow's and goat's milk, fresh cheese, sweet caramel-like flavor, semihard texture

Jarlsberg Made from cow's milk, similar to "baby Swiss," firm texture

Finland

Juustoleipa Made from cow and reindeer's milk, mild flavor, creamy smooth semifirm texture

Turunmaa Made from cow's milk, aromatic tangy flavor, smooth, creamy semifirm texture

fruits or vegetables are popular in the summer. Sometimes the cold soups function as a dessert instead of a soup course. The hot soups consumed during the winter often use dried and preserved vegetables, fish, and meats.

The alcoholic beverages of choice in Scandinavia remain beer and aquavit. Many varieties of each of these appear within each country. First made in the 1400s, aquavit literally means "water of life." A strong liquor made from potatoes or grains, its flavoring comes from caraway, anise, fennel, coriander, star anise, or any combination of these herbs. Excellent with the hearty Scandinavian foods, both beer and aquavit accompany meals. Traditionally, the shot of aquavit is drunk in one gulp. Although imported, wine is greatly appreciated and widely consumed.

Scandinavians love coffee, often drinking it at all three meals, as well as between meals. Strong coffee accompanies pastry, particularly cookies, pound cakes, and yeast breads. Well known for desserts, Scandinavians enjoy their sweets. Served daily in many homes, dessert and coffee either follows the meal, is served as a separate course in the afternoon, or a few hours after the evening meal. Many, many varieties of cookies come from the Scandinavian kitchen; people keep cookies on hand to serve unexpected guests along with a cup of coffee. A type of rich, sweet roll or coffeecake dough with folded-in butter like puff pastry, Danish pastry was actually invented by the Viennese but improved by Danish bakers. This ranks as a Scandinavian specialty and appears with endless variations in shape and flavor. Desserts can be as complex as Danish pastry or as simple as the apple cake that appears frequently in many homes throughout Scandinavia. This very simple dessert consists of

REGION	AREA	WEATHER	TOPOGRAPHY	FOODS
Denmark	North of Germany	Mild and damp, moderated by surrounding seas	Coast on three sides, lakes, flat land, rolling hills (central), granite in the north	Seafood, beef, game, pork, bacon, ham, cream, butter, cheese, potatoes, apples, cherries
Norway		Moderate on coasts; inland: extremely cold winters and short summers	Coast on three sides, high, mountainous plateau, fjords, lakes, mountains, streams	Seafood, sheep, goats, livestock, goat cheese, smoked meats, salted cod, game, rye bread, potatoes, sour cream
Sweden	North	Cold winters, short, cool summers	Coast, lakes, mountains, hills	Seafood, herring
	Central and south	Somewhat milder winters, short, cool summers	Coast, forests, lakes, plains, highlands, fertile farmland	Seafood, herring, game, beef, dairy, pork, cream, oats, wheat, dill, potatoes, sweet and sour dishes, sugar beets
Finland	North	Very, cold winters, short, cool summers	Many lakes and forests	Seafood
	Central and south	Moderately cold winters, short, cool summers	Many lakes, forests, plateau, small hills and valleys	Seafood, caviar, trout, salmon, crayfish, game, livestock, dairy, oats, rye, barley, wheat, beets, potatoes, mushrooms, berries

sautéed bread crumbs or zweiback layered with applesauce and then baked. Almonds, almond paste, fresh fruits, and berries appear in many desserts, and no scrimping of butter or cream occurs in Scandinavian pastries.

Scandinavians produce a bounty of yeast breads, flatbreads, and crackers for which they are well known. Light and dark rye breads as well as limpa rye, pumpernickel, and wheat serve both as the base for sandwiches and an accompaniment to meals. Many breads are aromatic due to the addition of fennel, anise, caraway, cardamom, and/or orange peel. Crackers and hard breads remain popular because they store well in the cooler temperatures of Scandinavia.

Review Questions

1. Discuss geographic and topographical factors that created the isolation in Scandinavia.
2. How has the weather in Scandinavia affected the cuisines?
3. What did the Vikings contribute to the cuisines of Scandinavia?
4. Name at least five food products and flavorings that are prevalent throughout Scandinavia.
5. Discuss which animal proteins are consumed in various areas of Scandinavia and why.

Glossary

aquavit Literally, "water of life," a strong liquor made from potatoes or grains, its flavoring comes from caraway, anise, fennel, coriander, star anise, or any combination of these herbs; first made in the 1400s

fjords Inlets

frikadeller Ground meat mixture that is made into meatballs, patties, or used as forcemeat

gravlax Salmon cured with salt, sugar, and dill

klippfisk Popular dish containing salted cod served in Norway

rømmegrøt Porridge made with sour cream that is popular in Norway

smörgåsbord A buffet laden with all sorts of meats, seafood, vegetables, salads, cheeses, and breads; contains as many as sixty food items

smørrebrød Literally, "buttered bread," an open-faced sandwich with a base of thin bread or cracker that is spread with butter, then topped with meat, seafood, or cheese and crowned with an eye-catching garnish; the Danes are known for these sandwiches, which resembles a canapé

GRAVLAX (Scandinavia)

Sugar and Salt Cured, Marinated Salmon

Total Yield: 2½ to 3 lbs

Food Balance: Protein
Wine Style: Light- to medium-bodied Champagne or Sparkling Wine, Gewürztraminer, Pinot Blanc, Viognier, White Zinfandel, or Rosé
Example: Greg Norman Sparkling Chardonnay

INGREDIENTS	WEIGHT	VOLUME
salmon, fresh, center-cut, skin left on	2½ to 3 lbs	

Cod Cakes; photo courtesy of The Norwegian Seafood Export Council—www.seafood.no. Photography by Russel French

Cockaleekie Soup (Chicken and Leek Soup)

Beef Stew Braised in Guinness; photo courtesy of Dorling Kindersley

Shepherd's Pie (Beef Topped with Mashed Potatoes); photo courtesy of Dorling Kindersley

Cornish Pasty (Beef, Onion, and Potato Turnover); photo courtesy of Dorling Kindersley

Idaho Potato Irish Stew; photo courtesy of the Idaho Potato Commission

Yorkshire Pudding; photo courtesy of Dorling Kindersley

Boxty (Potato Pancakes); photo courtesy of Dorling Kindersley

Scones; photo courtesy of Dorling Kindersley

Trifle for a crowd and an individual serving

Espinacas a la Catalana (Catalan Spinach); photo courtesy of Dorling Kindersley

Tortilla a la Española (Potato and Onion Omelet); courtesy of Olive Oil from Spain (ASOLIVA)

Baked Empanada (Pork and Pepper Pie)

Champinoñes al Ajillo (Mushrooms in Garlic Sauce); photo courtesy of Dorling Kindersley

Gazpacho (Cold Tomato Vegetable Soup); photo courtesy of Olive Oil from Spain (ASOLIVA)

Paella a la Valenciana (Chicken and Seafood Rice); photo courtesy of The Norwegian Seafood Export Council—www.seafood.no. Photography by Per Alfsen

Scallops in Green Sauce

Porto Pudim Flan (Portugese Baked Caramel Custard); photo courtesy of Dorling Kindersley

Coquilles St. Jacques à la Parisienne (Scallops and Mushrooms in White Wine Sauce); photo courtesy of The Norwegian Seafood Export Council—www.seafood.no. Photography by Russel French

Chuleta de Ternera Hortelana (Veal Chops with Ham, Mushrooms, and Pimiento)

Gratinée Lyonnaise (Onion Soup); photo courtesy of Dorling Kindersley

Potage Crécy (Carrot Cream Soup); photo courtesy of Dorling Kindersley

Canard Montmorency (Roast Duck with Cherry Sauce);
photo courtesy of Dorling Kindersley

Coq au Vin (Chicken in Red Wine); photo courtesy of
Dorling Kindersley

Boeuf Bourguignon (Beef Burgundy Stew); photo courtesy of The National Cattlemen's Beef Association

Ratatouille (Vegetable Stew); photo courtesy of Dorling
Kindersley

Gratin Savoyard (Scalloped Potatoes); photo courtesy of
the Idaho Potato Commission

Unmolded Tarte des Demoiselles Tatin (Upside-down Caramelized Apple Tart)

Slice of Tarte des Demoiselles Tatin (Upside-down Caramelized Apple Tart)

Soufflé au Citron (Lemon Soufflé); photo courtesy of Dorling Kindersley

Panzanella (Bread Salad); photo courtesy of Dorling Kindersley

Beans and Escarole Greens

Ravioli with Tomato Sauce—finished plate; photo courtesy of Dorling Kindersley

Ravioli with Herb and Oil—finished plate; photo courtesy of Dorling Kindersley

Pesto (Basil and Garlic Sauce) on Pasta; photo courtesy of Dorling Kindersley

Pollo alla Cacciatora (Hunter Style Chicken); photo courtesy of Dorling Kindersley

Ossobuco alla Milanese (Braised Veal Shanks); photo courtesy of Dorling Kindersley

Parmigiana di Melanzane (Eggplant Parmigiana); photo courtesy of Dorling Kindersley

Salsa Verde (Green Sauce for Asparagus); photo courtesy of Dorling Kindersley

Spinaci in Tegame (Sautéed Spinach); photo courtesy of Dorling Kindersley

Pouring Zabaglione (Marsala Flavored Dessert Sauce) over fruit; photo courtesy of Dorling Kindersley

Zwiebelkuchen (Onion Tart); photo courtesy of Dorling Kindersley

Blumenkohlsuppe (Cream of Cauliflower Soup)

Zabaglione (Marsala Flavored Dessert Sauce); photo courtesy of the American Egg Board

Schweine Fleisch mit Sauerkraut (Pork with Sauerkraut)

Schweine-Filet (Pork Tenderloin [in a Lemon Sauce])

Warmer Kartoffelsalat mit Speck (Warm Potato Salad with Bacon)

Spaetzel (Small Noodlelike Dumplings); photo courtesy of CMA, The German Agricultural Marketing Board

Wiener Schnitzel (Veal Cutlet Viennese Style); photo courtesy of Dorling Kindersley

Blaukraut (Sweet and Sour Red Cabbage); photo courtesy of CMA, The German Agricultural Marketing Board

Linzertorte (Spiced Dough Filled with Raspberry Preserves); photo courtesy of Dorling Kindersley

Gravlax (Sugar and Salt Cured, Marinated Salmon); photo courtesy of The Norwegian Seafood Export Council—www.seafood.no. Photography by Foto—Eff

Sillsallad (Herring and Apple Salad); photo courtesy of Dorling Kindersley

Agurkesalat (Pickled Cucumber Salad)

Frikadeller (Meat Patties or Meatballs); photo courtesy
of the National Cattleman's Beef Association

Lanttulaatikko (Rutabaga Pudding); photo courtesy of Dorling Kindersley

Fiskepudding (Fish Mousse); photo courtesy of The
Norwegian Seafood Export Council—www.seafood.no.
Photography by Per Børjessen

Jansson's Frestelse (Jansson's Temptation); photo
courtesy of Dorling Kindersley

Mørbrad Med Svedsker Og Aebler (Pork Loin Stuffed
with Prunes and Apples)

Mazarintårta (Swedish Almond Raspberry Torte)

Mazarintårta (Swedish Almond Raspberry Torte)

Borshch Ukraïnsky (Ukrainian Beet Soup); photo courtesy of Dorling Kindersley

Salat Iz Krasnoi Kapusty (Red Cabbage Salad); photo courtesy of Dorling Kindersley

Bef Stroganov (Beef Stroganoff); photo courtesy of Dorling Kindersley

Csirke Paprikás (Chicken Paprika) and Galuska (Small Dumplings); photo courtesy of Hemzö Károly/Gust-Art Studio, Budapest-Hungary

Kasha (Buckwheat Groats with Mushrooms and Onions)

Bramborové Knedlíky (Bohemian Potato Dumplings); photo courtesy of Dorling Kindersley

Gulyás (Hungarian Goulash)

Slice of Jablkový Závin (Apple Strudel) on plate decorated with caramelized sugar

Moroccan Olives; photo courtesy of Dorling Kindersley

Harira (Vegetable and Meat Soup); photo courtesy of Dorling Kindersley

Mafe (Chicken Peanut Stew)

Chicken and Apricot Tagine; photo courtesy of the New Zealand Beef and Lamb Marketing Bureau

Gravlax (Sugar and Salt Cured, Marinated Salmon); photo courtesy of The Norwegian Seafood Export Council—www.seafood.no. Photography by Foto—Eff

INGREDIENTS	WEIGHT	VOLUME
dill, fresh	1 large bunch	
kosher salt	1¾ oz	¼ cup
sugar	1¾ oz	¼ cup
peppercorns, crushed	¾ oz	2 tablespoons

GARNISH:

fresh dill

lemon wedges

1. Wash salmon thoroughly. Cut in half lengthways through center (like fillet) and remove all bones.
2. Place one piece fish, skin side down, in deep glass dish. Spread dill over fish. Sprinkle salt, sugar, and crushed peppercorns over dill. Top with other fish fillet, skin side up.
3. Cover with foil and weight with 5-lb weight on a board. Refrigerate for 48 to 72 hours, turning the salmon and basting every 12 hours with juices from pan.
4. Color and texture of fish change when cured. Texture is more firm and color is darker orange.
5. To serve, remove fish from marinade, scrape away dill and spices, pat dry. Slice salmon thinly on the diagonal. Arrange on platter or plate, garnish with lemon wedges and fresh dill. Serve with thin rye bread or crackers. May be accompanied by mustard sauce (laxås) and pickled cucumbers (*recipes follow*).

LAXÅS (Scandinavia)

Mustard Dill Mayonnaise

Total Yield: 7½ oz

INGREDIENTS	WEIGHT	VOLUME
mustard, Dijon-style	2¼ oz	¼ cup

INGREDIENTS	WEIGHT	VOLUME
dry mustard		1 teaspoon
white vinegar	1 oz	2 tablespoons
sugar	1¼ oz	3 tablespoons
cardamom		⅛ teaspoon
vegetable oil	4 oz	½ cup
dill, fresh, minced	¾ oz	3 tablespoons

1. Combine both mustards in small bowl, blend in sugar, cardamom, and vinegar to make a paste. Transfer to bowl of food processor, if desired.
2. Whisk in oil by hand or if using food processor, drop oil very slowly into running processor through feed tube. Mixture should emulsify to become thick mayonnaise. Stir in dill.
3. Let sauce stand at room temperature 25 minutes before serving.
4. Refrigerate to store.

SILLSALLAD (Norway)

Herring and Apple Salad

Number of Servings: 6 (4 oz) or 9 (3 oz)
Serving Size: 4 oz or 3 oz
Total Yield: 1 lb, 11 oz

INGREDIENTS	WEIGHT	VOLUME
pickled herring pieces, cut about ½-inch wide	7½ oz	1 cup
onion, finely diced	6 oz	1 large

Sillsallad (Herring and Apple Salad); photo courtesy of Dorling Kindersley

INGREDIENTS	WEIGHT	VOLUME
celery, diced	3 oz	½ cup
apple, peeled, cored, large dice	10 oz	1 large
lemon juice	1 oz	½ lemon or 2 tablespoons
sugar		1 teaspoon
vinegar, apple cider	1 oz	2 tablespoons
heavy cream	4 oz	½ cup
white pepper	to taste	

1. Combine herring, onions, apples, and celery in bowl. Sprinkle with lemon juice.
2. Dissolve sugar in vinegar. Whip cream until stiff peaks. Fold in vinegar, season with white pepper. Fold cream dressing into herring salad.
3. Cover and chill for several hours before serving. Correct seasonings. Serve on bed of lettuce or as part of *smörgåsbord*.

CABBAGE SOUP (Sweden, Denmark)

Number of Servings: 8
Serving Size: 8 oz
Total Yield: 4 lbs, 7 oz

Cooking Method: Sauté, boil

Food Balance: Protein/sweet
Wine Style: Soft and fruity Johannisberg Riesling, Gewürztraminer, Blush, Grenache
Example: Château St. Jean Gewürztraminer or Wolf Blass Grenache

INGREDIENTS	WEIGHT	VOLUME
cabbage, cored, cut thin or shredded	2 lbs, 9 oz	1 large head
butter	2 oz	4 tablespoons
brown sugar	1 oz	2 tablespoons
beef stock	3 lbs	6 cups or 1½ qt
pepper		½ teaspoon
allspice, ground		½ teaspoon

1. Melt butter in pan. Add cabbage, sauté until lightly brown.
2. Add sugar, cook a few minutes, stirring often.
3. Add stock and seasoning, simmer, covered for one hour. Correct seasonings.
4. Serve with dumplings, if desired.

AGURKESALAT (Denmark)

Pickled Cucumber Salad

Number of Servings: 10
Serving Size: 2½ oz
Total Yield: 1 lb, 10 oz

Agurkesalat (Pickled Cucumber Salad)

INGREDIENTS	WEIGHT	VOLUME
cucumbers	3 lb, 3 oz	4 large
salt	1 oz	2 tablespoons
white vinegar	8 oz	1 cup
sugar	2 oz	4 tablespoons
white pepper		½ teaspoon
dill, fresh, finely chopped	1 oz	4 tablespoons

1. Peel cucumbers, slice very thin. Layer with salt in colander, drain a couple of hours to eliminate water and bitterness (place colander in bowl or sink to catch liquid).
2. Press cucumbers lightly to expel liquid, blot with towel. Place them in a bowl.
3. Combine vinegar, sugar, and white pepper in small bowl. Pour over cucumbers and mix well. Mix in dill. Chill for 2 or 3 hours. Correct seasonings. Drain before serving.

FRIKADELLER (Denmark)

Meat Patties or Meatballs

Number of Servings: 10 patties or 56 meatballs   Cooking Method: Sauté
Serving Size: 5 oz patties, 1 oz meatballs
Total Yield: 3 lbs, 8 oz

Food Balance: Protein/salt balance
Wine Style: Wide variety—Pinot Blanc, Chardonnay, Blush, Beaujolais, Merlot, Cabernet Sauvignon
Example: Beringer Vineyards Knights Valley Cabernet Sauvignon

Frikadeller (Meat Patties or Meatballs); photo courtesy of The National Cattleman's Beef Association

INGREDIENTS	WEIGHT	VOLUME
ground beef	1 lb	
ground pork	1 lb	
salt	¼ oz	1 teaspoon
pepper		1 teaspoon
flour, all purpose	3 oz	⅔ cup
onion, finely diced	8 oz	2 medium
egg	3½ oz	2 each
water	12 oz	1½ cup
butter, for frying		

> Serve as an hors d'oeuvres or entrée. An equal amount of ground veal may be substituted for either one of the ground meats.

1. Combine all ingredients except butter, blend thoroughly. Let stand for 15 minutes so flour absorbs water. Shape into patties or meatballs.
2. Heat butter in skillet until very hot. Reduce heat to medium and fry meat until golden brown, about 5 minutes per side.
3. Serve.

MØRBRAD MED SVEDSKER OG AEBLER (Denmark)

Pork Loin Stuffed with Prunes and Apples

Number of Servings: 10   Cooking Method: Bake
Serving Size: 6 oz
Total Yield: 3 lbs, 12 oz

Food Balance: Sweet and sour
Wine Style: Light- to medium-bodied, rich Chenin Blanc, Blush, Chardonnay, Zinfandel, and rich Merlot
Example: Beringer Vineyards Alluvium (rich Merlot)

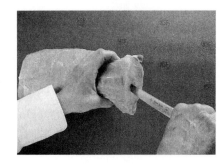

Inserting point of knife in pork to start hole for filling

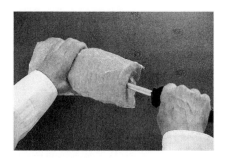

Pushing sharpening steel through pork to create cavity

Filling cavity of pork with fruit

INGREDIENTS	WEIGHT	VOLUME
pork loin, center cut, boned, fat trimmed	4½ to 5 lb	
prunes, pitted	5 oz	18 each
apple, tart, peeled, cored, diced into 1-inch cubes	7 oz	1 large
lemon juice	as needed	
butter	¾ oz	1½ tablespoons
oil	¾ oz	1½ tablespoons
dry white wine	5 oz	⅔ cup
heavy cream	5 oz	⅔ cup
red currant jelly	1½ oz	1½ tablespoons
salt	to taste	
black pepper, ground	to taste	

1. Place prunes in saucepan, cover with cold water, bring to a boil. Remove from heat, let prunes soak in water for 30 minutes. Drain well, cut prunes in half.
2. Sprinkle apple with a little lemon juice to prevent discoloring, mix apples with prunes.
3. With knife, make opening about ½- to 1-inch in diameter through center of pork. Either make whole opening with knife or start with knife and then use sharpening steel to push through meat to form cavity. Be careful not to break through meat.
4. Stuff fruits tightly into cavity. If meat must be held together, tie pork with string at 1-inch intervals to keep shape while cooking.
5. Preheat oven to 350 degrees.
6. Melt butter and oil over moderate heat in pan just large enough to hold pork. Sauté pork until brown on all sides. Remove pork from pan.
7. Remove fat from pan. Deglaze with wine, then whisk in heavy cream, bring to simmer, then add pork.
8. Cover pan, cook in center of the oven for 1 to 1¼ hours, until meat is correct internal temperature with meat thermometer.
9. Remove pork from pan, rest on warm plate. Skim fat from liquid in pan, place pan over heat, reduce liquid by half.
10. Stir in red currant jelly, simmer until sauce is smooth. Add salt and pepper to taste. Correct seasonings.
11. Remove strings from pork, slice. Arrange pork slices on plate. Nap with sauce or place sauce under slices.

Searing meat

Removing meat from oven

Mørbrad Med Svedsker Og Aebler (Pork Loin Stuffed with Prunes and Apples)

FISKEPUDDING (Norway)

Fish Mousse

Number of Servings: 12
Serving Size: 6 oz
Total Yield: 3 lbs, 2 oz

Cooking Method: Bake

Food Balance: Protein
Wine Style: Light- to medium-bodied Chenin Blanc, Sauvignon Blanc, soft Chardonnay, Blush, Rosé
Example: Meridian Vineyards Santa Barbara Chardonnay

INGREDIENTS	WEIGHT	VOLUME
butter, for greasing pan		
bread crumbs, for dusting pan	¾ to 1 oz	3 to 4 tablespoons
cod, skinned and boned	3 lbs	
salt		1½ teaspoons
pepper		½ teaspoon
cardamom, ground		½ teaspoon
mace		½ teaspoon
cornstarch	1 oz	3 tablespoons
milk	4 oz	½ cup
heavy cream	1 lb, 4 oz	2½ cups

> This common Norwegian dish is made with very fresh fish. It may be served as an entrée or first course. Leftovers are served either cold or hot. Cold slices are used as a sandwich filling or the cold slices are breaded and sautéed.

1. Butter 2- to 3-quart pan, ring mold, or terrine pan; dust with bread crumbs. Remove excess crumbs.
2. Preheat oven to 350 degrees. Boil a couple of quarts water for bain marie.
3. Cut fish into pieces and place in food processor fitted with steel blade. Add seasonings and cornstarch.
4. Mix milk and cream together. Turn on processor, add cream slowly through feed tube while processing until mixture is smooth and fluffy.
5. Pour purée into prepared mold. Tap it once or twice on counter to remove air bubbles. Smooth surface with spatula. Cover pan tightly with aluminum foil, seal well.

Fiskepudding (Fish Mousse); photo courtesy of The Norwegian Seafood Export Council—www.seafood.no. Photography by Per Børjessen

6. Place pan inside larger pan (for bain marie) and place in middle of oven. Pour boiling water in larger pan to depth of about ¾-inch.
7. Bake for 50 to 60 minutes, until knife comes out clean. The water should not boil while baking or mousse will have holes in it.
8. Remove pan from bain marie. Let stand about 5 minutes.
9. Drain any liquid from pan containing mousse. Unmold mousse. Invert on warm serving platter. Remove any excess liquid from platter.
10. Serve with melted butter flavored with lemon and finely chopped fresh dill or a shrimp sauce.

PAISTETUT SIENET (Finland)

Mushrooms with Sour Cream

Number of Servings: 6   Cooking Method: Sauté
Serving Size: 3 oz
Total Yield: 1 lb, 2 oz

INGREDIENTS	WEIGHT	VOLUME
butter	1 oz	2 tablespoons
onions, finely diced	1¼ oz	¼ cup
mushrooms, fresh, button or any variety, thinly sliced	1 lb	
bread crumbs, fine, dry	1 oz	¼ cup
sour cream	4½ oz	½ cup

GARNISH:

herbs, fresh, minced

paprika

1. Melt butter over moderate heat. Sauté onions until soft and transparent but not brown.
2. Add mushrooms and cook another 3 to 5 minutes, until light brown.
3. Sprinkle in bread crumbs, mix. Turn heat to low.
4. Add sour cream and mix until evenly coated. Correct seasonings.
5. Serve as a vegetable accompaniment to meat or fish dishes. If desired, garnish with minced fresh herbs or paprika.

LANTTULAATIKKO (Finland)

Rutabaga Pudding

Number of Servings: 9
Serving Size: 4 oz
Total Yield: 2 lbs, 4 oz

Cooking Method: Boil, bake

INGREDIENTS	WEIGHT	VOLUME
rutabagas, peeled, ¼-inch dice	2 lbs, 7 oz	2 medium
heavy cream	2 oz	¼ cup
bread crumbs	1 oz	¼ cup
salt	¼ oz or to taste	1 teaspoon or to taste

Lanttulaatikko (Rutabaga Pudding); photo courtesy of Dorling Kindersley

INGREDIENTS	WEIGHT	VOLUME
pepper		¼ teaspoon
nutmeg		½ teaspoon
sugar (optional)		2 teaspoons
eggs, lightly beaten	3½ oz	2 each
butter	1¾ oz	3½ tablespoons

1. Place rutabagas in pan, cover with cold water, partially cover and cook until tender.
2. Combine bread crumbs and cream, let sit a few minutes. Add seasonings, sugar, and eggs.
3. Preheat oven to 350 degrees, grease baking dish.
4. Drain liquid from rutabagas and mash as for mashed potatoes using some reserved liquid, if needed. Add bread crumb mixture and 1 oz (2 tablespoons) butter to rutabagas. Correct seasonings.
5. Place rutabaga mix in prepared dish. Dot with remaining ¾ oz (1½ tablespoons) butter.
6. Bake uncovered for 1 hour, until lightly browned. Serve.

BRUNEDE KARTOFLER (Denmark)

Caramelized Potatoes

Number of Servings: 8
Serving Size: 4 oz

Cooking Method: Boil, sauté

> *Good served with pork roasts, ham, braised or sautéed pork chops, roast beef, and poultry.*

INGREDIENTS	WEIGHT	VOLUME
new potatoes, small	2 lbs	10 to 12 each
sugar	2¼ oz	5 tablespoons
butter, unsalted	1½ oz	3 tablespoons
dill, fresh, chopped fine	¼ oz	1 tablespoon

1. Place unpeeled potatoes in pot, cover with cold water, bring to boil, simmer until potatoes are tender.
2. Drain potatoes. Peel as soon as cool enough to handle.
3. In heavy skillet over medium heat, stir sugar until melted and light brown.
4. Add butter and stir until thoroughly blended into sugar.
5. Add potatoes (do not crowd the pan). Coat them with caramelized mixture by shaking pan or rolling potatoes with wooden spoon.
6. Remove glazed potatoes and keep them warm while glazing next batch(es).
7. To serve, sprinkle potatoes with dill.

JANSSON'S FRESTELSE (Sweden)

Jansson's Temptation (Potato Casserole)

Number of Servings: 9
Serving Size: 4 oz
Total Yield: 2 lbs, 6 oz

Cooking Method: Bake

INGREDIENTS	WEIGHT	VOLUME
potatoes, peeled and cut into ¼-inch strips	2 lbs, 15 oz	7 medium
onions, cut in thin rings	13 oz	3 medium

Jansson's Frestelse (Jansson's Temptation); photo courtesy of Dorling Kindersley

INGREDIENTS	WEIGHT	VOLUME
butter	1 oz	2 tablespoons
anchovy fillets	2 oz	1 small can
white pepper	to taste	
heavy cream	8 oz	1 cup
milk	4 oz	½ cup
bread crumbs	1½ oz	1 cup
butter (optional for top)	1 oz	2 tablespoons

1. Preheat oven to 350 degrees, butter 2-quart pan.
2. Place potatoes in cold water to prevent discoloring.
3. Sauté onion rings in butter over medium heat until soft but not brown, about 5 to 10 minutes.
4. Place alternate layers of potatoes, onion rings, and anchovies, ending with layer of potatoes. Sprinkle a little white pepper on potato layers.
5. Mix cream and milk. Pour over potatoes. Top with bread crumbs. If desired, dot with butter.
6. Bake for 45 to 60 minutes or until potatoes are tender and most liquid is absorbed.

MAZARINTÅRTA (Sweden)

Swedish Almond Raspberry Torte

Number of Servings: 12 to 16   Cooking Method: Bake
Total Yield: 9-inch fluted tart or 9-inch
   springform pan

INGREDIENTS	WEIGHT	VOLUME
DOUGH:		
flour, all purpose, sifted	5¼ oz	1⅓ cups
baking powder		1 teaspoon
sugar	2¾ oz	⅓ cup
butter, unsalted, cold	4 oz	1 stick or ½ cup
egg	1¾ oz	1 each

Best prepared a day ahead.

INGREDIENTS	WEIGHT	VOLUME
FILLING:		
butter, unsalted	4 oz	1 stick or ½ cup
sugar	5½ oz	⅔ cup
almonds, blanched, ground	3½ oz	1 cup
vanilla		½ teaspoon
eggs	3½ oz	2 each
raspberry preserves	7½ oz	⅔ cup
TOPPING:		
confectioners' sugar, sifted	4 oz	1 cup
lemon juice, fresh	½ oz	1 tablespoon
water		about 1 teaspoon

TO PREPARE DOUGH:

1. Sift flour, sugar, and baking powder together. Place in bowl of food processor and pulse to mix.
2. Cut butter into 8 or 10 pieces. Place on top of dry ingredients. Pulse to cut in butter until size of peas. Add egg and mix until dough comes together.
3. Remove from bowl, knead, if necessary, to form ball. Wrap in film and refrigerate until needed.

TO PREPARE FILLING:

1. Cream butter and sugar with flat paddle of mixer, beat until fluffy.
2. Add almonds and vanilla.
3. Add eggs, one at a time, beating well after each addition.

TO ASSEMBLE:

1. Preheat oven to 350 degrees.
2. Roll chilled dough between sheets of parchment or waxed paper. Remove top paper, invert into springform pan or tart pan. Re-

Mazarintårta (Swedish Almond Raspberry Torte)

Mazarintårta (Swedish Almond Raspberry Torte)

lease dough from paper, press evenly on bottom and about an inch or so up sides of pan. Make sure any holes are covered so filling doesn't leak out while baking.

3. Spread half of raspberry preserves over bottom of dough. Top with filling.
4. Bake about 40 minutes or until torte tests done. Cool torte 10 minutes. Remove sides of pan, cool completely.

FOR TOPPING:

1. Mix confectioners' sugar and lemon juice. Add water, a few drops at a time, until spreading consistency.
2. Let topping rest 5 to 10 minutes.
3. Spread remaining raspberry preserves over cooled torte. Drizzle topping over torte.

TOSKAKAKE (Norway)

Almond Caramel Cake

Number of Servings: 12 to 16   Cooking Method: Bake
Total Yield: 11-inch tart pan with removable
  bottom or 10-inch springform pan

INGREDIENTS	WEIGHT	VOLUME
CAKE:		
heavy cream	8 oz	1 cup
eggs	3½ oz	2 each
vanilla		1 teaspoon
flour, all purpose	7½ oz	1½ cups
sugar	7½ oz	1 cup
baking powder	¼ oz	2 teaspoons
salt		½ teaspoon
TOPPING:		
butter, unsalted	2½ oz	⅓ cup
sugar	2¾ oz	⅓ cup
almonds, chopped	4¼ oz	¾ cup
flour, all purpose	¼ oz	1 tablespoon
heavy cream	½ oz	1 tablespoon

1. Preheat oven to 350 degrees. Butter tart or springform pan.
2. Sift together flour, sugar, baking powder, and salt.
3. Whip cream until stiff peaks, add eggs and vanilla and mix. Add flour mixture, mix just to combine.
4. Pour into prepared pan.
5. Bake 30 to 35 minutes or until cake pulls away from side of pan and knife comes out clean.
6. Meanwhile, melt butter in small saucepan over medium heat. Add remaining ingredients, bring to boil, stirring constantly.
7. Cook about 2 to 3 minutes, until slightly thickened.
8. Pour hot topping over hot cake. Spread with icing spatula to cover top. Return to oven and bake about 15 minutes, until golden brown.
9. Serve warm or cold.

CHAPTER 7
Russia and Eastern Europe

By the end of this chapter, you will be able to

- Identify similarities and differences among the cuisines of the Eastern European countries and Russia
- Understand the historical, geographic, and climatic influences on the cuisines of these countries
- Identify food products prevalent in the cuisines of Russia and Eastern Europe and explain why they appear so frequently
- Prepare a variety of dishes from Russia and Eastern Europe

Although this chapter covers a lot of area spanning portions of both Europe and Asia, the similarities among the cuisines of Russia and Eastern Europe facilitate discussing these countries together.

HISTORY

The Eastern European countries lie east of Germany, Austria, and Italy. Some of these countries include Poland, Hungary, the Czech Republic, Yugoslavia, Romania, Albania, Lithuania, Bulgaria, Ukraine, and the part of Russia that lies in Europe. Throughout history, Russia and the countries of Eastern Europe have intertwined, conquering one another and then losing control. Boundaries in Eastern Europe continue to change. Some countries previously found in Eastern Europe no longer exist, having been annexed by more powerful nations. On the other hand, new nations form, such as Czechoslovakia becoming the Czech Republic and Slovakia.

One common thread among these countries is their Slavic ancestry. Evidence exists of Slavic tribes in Poland as early as 2000 B.C. These tribes migrated from Poland and Russia, settling in Yugoslavia during the sixth century. By the 800s A.D., tribes of Slavic origin inhabited most of the lands covered in this chapter. Around that time, Polane tribes settled in Poland, Magyars came to Hungary, and East Slavs inhabited Ukraine.

Named for the Romans who ruled the land in the first two centuries A.D., Romania was conquered and controlled by numerous tribes and countries until the middle of the nineteenth century. At that time, Romania finally became an independent country. Unfortunately, those numerous ruling countries did little to develop Romania into an independent or economic power. As a result, Romania remains the Eastern European country with the lowest standard of living.

Being such a large country, Russia felt the effects of diverse groups of invaders from both Asia and Europe; however, the long, bitter winters stopped many aggressors throughout Russia's history. Iranians conquered around 700 B.C., and Germanic tribes entered about 500 years later. During medieval times, trade with the Byzantine Empire brought buckwheat, rice, and spices to Russia. Because of their location on the trade route between China and Europe, Russians became acquainted with many new foods and spices.

Czars ruled Russia from the middle 1500s until the Bolshevik Revolution in 1917. Frequent battles and exchanges of power with Eastern European countries, particularly with Ukraine and Poland, took place under the leadership of the czars. During his rule in the late 1600s, Peter the Great established ties with Europe, resulting in strong influences between the various European countries and Russia. The infatuation with Europe continued, and, during the time of Napoleon's conquests in the early nineteenth century, France and all things French were almost idolized. Although the peasants subsisted on grains, cereals, and some vegetables, the wealthy enjoyed dining on the classical cuisine of the French aristocracy.

In 1922, the Communists in Russia created the USSR, United Soviet Socialist Republic. The USSR extended the arm of its control to include many Eastern European countries during the 1940s, after World War II ended. This control lasted until the late 1980s when these countries began to regain their freedom and the Communist Empire dissolved.

TOPOGRAPHY

The largest country in the world, Russia, encompasses part of the continents of Europe and Asia. Running through Russia, the Ural Mountains forms the boundary that divides Europe and Asia. Almost twice the size of Canada, this mammoth country contains eight time zones. Bordered by four bodies of water, Russia spans from the Arctic Ocean on the north to the Black Sea on the south. The Baltic Sea lies to the east and the Pacific Ocean to the west. In addition to oceans or seas in each direction, Russia contains many major rivers.

The second largest country in Europe, Ukraine ranks second in size only to Russia. The Black Sea borders Ukraine on the south, Russia lies to the east, and Romania and Poland are to the west.

Although mountains fill the landscape in the southern part of Poland, the rest of the country consists of flat plains, rolling hills, and lakes. The Baltic Sea lies on its northern side.

Miles of coastline along the Adriatic Sea form the western side of Yugoslavia. The interior section of the country contains a more rugged terrain with mountains, hills, and plains.

The Czech Republic lies south of Poland, north of Hungary, and to the east of Germany and Austria. The countryside consists of forests, mountains, plains, plateaus, and rivers.

Nestled between the Czech Republic, Romania, Yugoslavia, and Austria; Hungary consists of low-lying land. Most of the land in the eastern part of this small country is flat while rolling hills and low mountains describe the terrain found in the west.

To the east of Romania lie Moldova and the Baltic Sea. Yugoslavia and Hungary are situated to the west, Bulgaria to the south, and Ukraine to the north. A range of mountains runs through the north and central portions of the country, with fertile land found at the base of the mountains. Forests abound in Romania, producing mushrooms, berries, and game. Many rivers and lakes transect the land, providing fish.

Ingredients and Foods Commonly Used Throughout the Cuisines of Russia and Eastern Europe Include:

- beef
- pork
- potatoes
- dumplings
- winter vegetables including cabbage, beets, carrots, cauliflower, kohlrabi, and turnips
- grains including rye, buckwheat, barley, and millet
- dairy products, frequent use of sour cream
- mushrooms
- dill and caraway seeds
- pickled and brined vegetables and fruits
- smoked and pickled fish

COOKING METHODS

Stews braised in a pot over an open flame remain from the nomadic tribes who inhabited these lands in the early days. Braising allowed the tough cuts of meat to become tender and extended the small amount of available meat.

As a result, the popularity of stews continues throughout Russia and all of Eastern Europe. Grilling, another carryover from the nomadic tribes cooking over an open fire, still flourishes.

In the early days, Russian homes used stoves for both heating and cooking. These early stoves contained a large oven but no burners. As a result, braising and baking were the most prevalent cooking methods; even preparation of the ever-popular soups took place in the oven. In the 1700s, the rich acquired stoves with burners. Peasants did not obtain burners until about 150 years ago; however, with plenty of lard and oils available, frying was common.

Making preserves and the pickling of fruits and vegetables continues as a mainstay for the people in Russia and Eastern Europe to survive the long winters. Cabbage becomes sauerkraut; cucumbers and mushrooms change into some of the many pickled vegetables; apples, watermelons, and other fruits enter brines for winter consumption. Many fruits are processed into preserves for use during the many cold months. Also common, pickled fish and sausage are popular foods originating from the necessity of preserving seafood and meat for use during the long winter. Another method of preservation—drying—still prevails with both fruits and vegetables.

REGIONS

Influences on the cuisines in this area depended heavily on geographic area. The countries lying in the southern part of this block, Bulgaria and Albania, show strong Turkish and Middle Eastern overtones. Although the countries situated near the Baltic Sea in the north exhibit pronounced Scandinavian influences, those located near Austria resemble the Germanic cuisines. Eastern Poland and Romania trace strong Russian influence. Although similar recipes appear in all these countries, each adds special touches and variations, creating recipes unique to their own region.

Because of the very short growing season and the lack of rainfall, only a small percentage of the land in Russia is suitable for agriculture. Russia experiences a harsh, cold climate with long, bitter winters and short, cool summers. Most of the population resides in the western portion of Russia, which lies within Europe. The Asian section remains quite remote due to the extremely rugged terrain.

Straddling Europe and Asia, Russia exhibits influences from both continents. Scandinavians taught the Russians about drying, smoking, and pickling all sorts of foods, including fish, meat, vegetables, and fruits. They adopted pilafs and many other dishes from their Middle Eastern neighbors, and influences are apparent from both China and India. Now staples in the Russian diet, the Turks and the Chinese introduced noodles, dumplings, and tea. German, Dutch, and French effects on Russian cuisine arrived during the 1700s, when contact with Europe intensified.

The Russian Orthodox Church, which still flourishes, had a great impact on the cuisine of Russia. With more than 200 fast days throughout the year, fish entrées and hearty vegetable dishes play an important role.

Of course, Russia's history of territorial expansion heavily affected the cuisine. As borders changed, so did the cuisines of both Russia and the invaded country. The foods of Eastern Europe penetrated into the cuisine of Russia, and the foods of Russia entered the cuisines of the other Eastern European countries.

Zakuska, assorted hors d'oeuvres or bite-size morsels of food, were traditionally served with vodka before dinner. Reminiscent of the Scandinavian *smörgåsbord*, this custom developed into the *zakuska* table, an elaborate table laden with salads, cold and hot smoked fish, caviar, pâtés, aspics, galantines, and pastries.

Much of the land in Ukraine consists of fertile, flat plains, yielding some of the best farmland in Eastern Europe. Abundant grains grow in this region, including rye, wheat, buckwheat, millet, and oats. As a result of the bounty of grain, the people of Ukraine are known for making many wonderful varieties of breads.

Poland's climate varies from mild, temperate weather in the coastal areas to very cold in the mountains. The diverse climate creates better conditions for growing a variety of crops and raising livestock.

Like Poland, mild weather exists along the coast of Yugoslavia while a harsh climate with very cold winters prevails in the interior areas. About half of the land in Yugoslavia is farmland; one-quarter of the country remains as forest. Several ethnic groups comprise the population of Yugoslavia, which contributes to the diversity of the cuisine. For example, Serbian cooking uses many spices, and the grilling of meats is common. Having ruled Yugoslavia for five centuries, the Turks left a strong mark on the cuisine. As a result, many dishes incorporate ingredients commonly used in the Middle East such as rice, eggplant, tomatoes, and lamb. *Moussaka, pilaf,* and *mezze* (Middle Eastern appetizers) appear here, particularly in the southern portions of the country. The northern part follows the typical Slavic cooking pattern, including the stews, soups, and hearty cooking commonly seen throughout most of Eastern Europe.

The climate in the Czech Republic consists of warm summers and cold winters. Good agricultural conditions exist for the production of barley, rye, corn, hops, wheat, potatoes, beets, vegetables, and fruits. Hogs, cattle, poultry, and sheep thrive here.

Landlocked, Hungary experiences cold winters and hot summers. Fertile soil and a good climate for agriculture create a favorable situation for growing crops. Lots of hogs and chickens are raised, followed by cattle and sheep. Grapes become excellent Hungarian wines. As with much of Eastern Europe and Russia, beets and potatoes thrive in this area.

Fertile land, which is suitable for crops, comprises the plains and plateaus in Romania. Corn, wheat, beets, potatoes, grapes, and other fruits flourish. Sheep, cattle, pigs, and poultry are raised here.

CUISINE

Hearty cuisine best describes the foods prepared and consumed in Russia and Eastern Europe. Much of the cuisine results from the harsh winters and short growing season, which makes root vegetables, winter vegetables, pickled fruits and vegetables, dried fruits and vegetables, and grains mainstays in the diet of people from these countries. Some of the winter and root vegetables include cabbage, cauliflower, potatoes, beets, carrots, and turnips. Forests provide ample mushrooms and game for cooking in Ukraine, Russia, and many of the Eastern European countries. A wide variety of grains play a prominent role in the diets of Eastern Europe because many grains grow quickly and tolerate the cold climate.

Heavy foods dominate the meals, frequently featuring meats, stews, and vegetables in sour cream sauces. The cuisines in these countries include lots of soup, as well as abundant use of dairy products and sugar.

Multiple starches often accompany the entrée with dumplings, potatoes, and noodles appearing regularly. With a strong liking for foods wrapped in dough, both large and small savory pies are widely consumed for appetizers,

According to folklore, Ukrainian guests are offered bread and salt as a greeting. The bread symbolizes hospitality and health (as the staff of life), and the salt represents friendship since salt maintains its same quality, does not become stale, and retains its same taste in spite of its age.

to accompany soup, or as an entrée. Noodles and pancakes of all sorts abound. Many of these countries serve thin, crêpelike pancakes rolled around a savory filling for an entrée or around sweetened cheese or fruit purée for dessert. When filled with slightly sweetened cheese and sautéed, this becomes the popular *blintz* from Israeli cookery. A well-known hors d'oeuvre or appetizer, *blinis* from Russia are a thicker, small pancake served with a garnish of sour cream and salmon, caviar, or other topping.

A staple, dumplings come in a myriad of sizes, shapes, and varieties. Whether served unfilled as a solid dumpling or filled with meat, grain, or cheese, this ubiquitous starch shows up everywhere on the menu. Made from potatoes, flour, bread, cottage cheese, or a combination of these ingredients, dumplings appear floating in soup, as a side dish, entrée, or dessert.

Heavy bread, usually made of rye, oat, buckwheat, or barley, accompanies every meal. Bread products differ based on the type of flour used and the cooking method. Baking produces bread, frying results in fritters, and boiling yields the ever-popular dumplings. Quite important in all the Slavic cuisines, bread and salt are long considered symbols of hospitality.

In many recipes and guises, sauerkraut and cabbage appear regularly in all of these countries. Sauerkraut soup, cabbage soup, sauerkraut salad, stuffed cabbage rolls, as well as all sorts of sauerkraut and meat dishes, emerge as just a few of the diverse cabbage creations. *Bigos*, the national dish of Poland, consists of sauerkraut cooked with a variety of meats and sausages. Often referred to as "hunter's stew," this sweet and sour dish is flavored with apples, mushrooms, prunes, tomatoes, or other ingredients. *Bigos* resembles the French dish, *cassoulet*.

Even though each of the countries creates its own version of stuffed cabbage rolls, a cabbage roll by any other name is still a cabbage roll. Usually filled with rice and pork or a mixture of beef and pork, a sweet and sour tomato–based sauce surrounds the Polish *golabki*. The Russian *golubtsi* is served in a sour cream sauce, and the spicy Yugolslav *sarma* contains cayenne and garlic. The Hungarians call them *töltött kaposzta*, the Romania version is *sarmale*, and *holubtsi* are served in Ukraine. Grains sometimes fill these popular items, particularly on fast days or in times of meager meat supplies. Some prefer wrapping the filling with pickled cabbage leaves, others use boiled fresh leaves of cabbage. When using fresh leaves, some cook the cabbage rolls on a bed of sauerkraut. Obviously, endless variations of cabbage rolls exist, depending on the country and the region within the country.

People of Eastern Europe and Russia share a liking for sour foods. Vinegar, sour cream, and horseradish appear often in both the sauces and the many pickled foods.

Some well-known Russian dishes include beef stroganoff, a stewlike dish consisting of pieces of beef cooked with mushrooms, onions, and sour cream; *blinis*; *borscht*, a soup made from beets; and *piroshki*, baked or fried dumplings filled with meat and cabbage. An often-consumed grain, *kasha* (buckwheat groats) shows up as a side dish, an entrée, or as stuffing for meat (roast chicken or veal breast) or vegetables (cabbage leaves). Many varieties of mushrooms appear regularly in soups, meat dishes, vegetables, and pickled and served as a condiment. Favorite beverages include tea, vodka, beer, and wine.

CHEESES

Abertam   Made from sheep's milk, robust flavor, firm texture

Daralagjazsky   Made from sheep's or cow's milk, salty with added garlic and thyme, soft texture

Feta   Made from sheep's milk but sometimes made from goat's milk, fresh cheese stored in brine, salty flavor, crumbly soft texture, used in cooking, as well as eaten as an appetizer

Kaskaval   Made from sheep's milk, a stretched curd cheese, which refers to the process of handling the curds when making the cheese, resulting in cheese with a springy texture that resembles cooked chicken

Liptauer   Made from sheep's milk or a combination of sheep's and cow's milk, spicy flavor often with added caraway, onion, capers, and paprika, soft texture

Oszczypek   Made from sheep's milk, salty flavor, semifirm texture, traditional cheese made by shepherds in the mountains of Poland

Sirene   Made from sheep's and cow's milk, fresh clean flavor, soft slightly grainy texture

Urdu   A fresh cheese produced from the whey remaining after making feta cheese, nutty flavor, flavor and texture similar to ricotta cheese, used in cooking sweet and savory foods as well as eaten plain

The same hearty foods reign in Poland as in Russia. Meat stews, beet or cabbage soups, potatoes, mushrooms, and rich desserts appear regularly. Favorite meats include pork and sausages. As with Russia, frequent use of sour cream and flavoring with dill and horseradish prevail. Both the Russians and the Poles have a fondness for sweet and sour dishes.

The diet in Ukraine includes pork products, fish, chicken, potatoes, kasha, and rye or oat breads. Again, hearty soups, stews, and breads are favored; mushroom and potato dishes remain very popular. Some of the traditional dishes include *varenyky*, boiled dumplings filled with potatoes, sauerkraut, cheese, or fruits, garnished with sour cream, fried onions, or bacon bits; *borscht*; and *holubtsi*, stuffed cabbage rolls filled with meat, kasha, and rice.

The cuisine of northern Yugoslavia contains great similarity to that of Germany and Austria, but the southern areas exhibit Middle Eastern, Mediterranean, and Italian influences. Pork reigns as the most popular meat in most of the country with seafood prevalent in the coastal areas. Dumplings, sauerkraut, potatoes, pickled herring, and desserts such as apple strudel appear often, but unlike most of Eastern Europe, the Yugoslavian cuisine contains hot peppers and some highly seasoned dishes. Ample amounts of onions and garlic flavor the cooking of Yugoslavia. Excellent beers are produced here; wine is also consumed.

Like the Yugoslavs, the Hungarians also prefer highly seasoned foods, which is characterized by their liberal use of paprika. Hungarian paprika ranges from sweet to hot in flavor, and the spiciness of the food varies according to the type of paprika chosen. Tomatoes appear in many dishes. As with the rest of this area, the diet includes daily soup and abundant starches, including noodles, dumplings, and potatoes. Pork remains the most popular meat, but Hungarians also eat poultry and beef. Well-known Hungarian dishes include *goulash*, a beef stew containing onions, tomatoes, and potatoes and *paprikash*, another stew-type dish containing plenty of paprika. Famous for their pastries, Hungarian strudel remains a trademark dessert.

The rich, heavy Czech cuisine uses lots of bacon and caraway for flavoring. Both sweet and savory, in soup or as a side dish to meat, *knedliky*, dumplings, appear everywhere. Soups of all types abound, and they may be consumed for any meal, including breakfast. The beverage of choice remains beer in much of the Czech Republic, which is the home of Pilsen beer. This cuisine also includes a variety of fine pastries.

Grilled meats remain popular in Romania, where pork ranks as the favorite meat. Grilled *mititei*, garlic-infused meatballs, are a national favorite. Cornmeal mush, *mamaliga*, resembles the Italian polenta and continues as a staple in Romania. Favorite beverages include wine and plum brandy.

Russians and most Eastern Europeans typically begin the day with a hearty breakfast which might consist of eggs, porridge, cheese and/or sausage accompanied by bread, butter, and jam. The main meal occurs around mid-

REGION	AREA	WEATHER	TOPOGRAPHY	FOODS
Russia	Northwestern Europe, northern Asia	Long, bitter winters, short summers	Tundra, forests, plains, mountains, semidesert, four seas on borders, numerous rivers	Cattle, sheep, hogs, game, cod, haddock, herring, salmon, sturgeon, caviar, flax, barley, oats, wheat, rye, buckwheat, potatoes, vegetables, beets, mushrooms, fruits, vodka
Poland	West of Russia	Warmer at coast, very cold in mountains	Plains, hills, lakes, Baltic Sea in north, mountains in south	Hogs, cattle, sheep, potatoes, rye, barley, beets
Ukraine	Southeast of Poland, southwest of Russia	Cold winters, warm summers	Fertile, flat plains, forests, Black Sea to south	Beef, dairy cattle, hogs, mackerel, tuna, carp, trout, perch, pike, game, wheat, barley, beets, corn, potatoes, mushrooms, rye, berries
Yugoslavia	West of Hungary, Romania, and Bulgaria, south of Austria	Temperate coast, harsh interior	Hills and plains on coast, mountains in interior	Cattle, hogs, sheep, wheat, potatoes, corn, grapes, olives, fruits, beer
Czech Republic	South of Poland, north of Hungary, east of Germany and Austria	Cold winters, warm summers	Forests, mountains, plains, plateaus, rivers	Hogs, cattle, poultry, sheep, game, wheat, rye, corn, barley, oats, potatoes, hops, beets, mushrooms, berries, vegetables, fruits, beer
Hungary	Yugoslavia to southwest, Czech Republic to north, Romania to east	Cold winters, warm summers	Flat in east, hills and low mountains in west, fertile soil	Hogs, poultry, cattle, sheep, wheat, corn, potatoes, beets, fruits, apricots, grapes
Romania	Baltic Sea and Ukraine to east, Bulgaria to south, Yugoslavia and Hungary to west, Moldova to north	Hot summers, cold winters	Mountains in north and central, plateaus, plains, forests, lakes, rivers	Sheep, pigs, cattle, poultry, game, wheat, corn, potatoes, beets, mushrooms, fruits, grapes, berries

day and starts with salad or appetizer followed by soup, then meat or fish with potatoes and/or another grain, and dessert. The evening meal is light.

Review Questions

1. Name five foods or ingredients that frequently appear in the cuisines of Russia and Eastern Europe.
2. Name three methods of food preservation. Explain why these methods are so important in these countries.
3. How has the weather affected the cuisines of Russia and Eastern Europe?
4. Discuss countries that have influenced these cuisines from an historical or geographic standpoint and why they became an influence.

Glossary

bigos The national dish of Poland, consists of sauerkraut cooked with a variety of meats and sausages

beef *stroganoff* A stewlike dish consisting of pieces of beef cooked with mushrooms, onions, and sour cream

blinis Small, buckwheat pancakes traditionally topped with sour cream, smoked salmon, caviar, or other toppings

borscht Soup made from beets and other ingredients

golabki Polish stuffed cabbage roll in a tomato-based sweet and sour sauce

golubtsi Russian stuffed cabbage roll surrounded by a sour cream sauce

goulash Hungarian beef stew containing onions, tomatoes, and potatoes

holubtsi Ukrainian stuffed cabbage rolls filled with meat, kasha, and rice

kasha Buckwheat groats, which is a grain

knedliky Dumplings served frequently in the Czech Republic

mamaliga Cornmeal mush served in Romania, resembles the Italian polenta

mititei Garlic-infused meat balls from Romania

paprikash Hungarian stew-type dish containing plenty of paprika

piroshki Baked or fried dumplings filled with meat and cabbage popular in Russia

sarma Spicy stuffed cabbage roll containing cayenne and garlic prepared in Yugoslavia

sarmale Romanian stuffed cabbage roll

töltött kaposzta Hungarian stuffed cabbage roll

varenyky Boiled dumplings with potatoes, sauerkraut, cheese, or fruits, garnished with sour cream, fried onions, or bacon bits, served in the Ukraine

zakuska Assorted hors d'oeuvres or bite-size morsels of food

PIEROGI (Poland)

Filled Dumplings

Total Yield: 1 lb, 4 oz filling   Cooking Method: Boil, sauté
1 lb, 15 oz dough
50 dumplings with
3½-inch cutter

Food Balance: Protein
Wine Style: Light- to medium-bodied Chenin Blanc, Sauvignon Blanc, Blush,
   Pinot Noir, mild Merlot
Example: Château Souverin Sauvignon Blanc or Merlot

INGREDIENTS	WEIGHT	VOLUME
DOUGH:		
flour	1 lb, 1 oz	4 cups
eggs	6¾ oz	4 each
water, cold	5 oz	⅔ cup
salt		½ teaspoon
FILLING:		
mushrooms, button or any variety, washed, minced	1 lb	
onions, minced	8 oz	1 cup or 2 small
butter	1 oz	2 tablespoons
salt		½ teaspoon
pepper		¼ teaspoon
nutmeg		⅛ teaspoon
dill, fresh, minced	1½ oz	6 tablespoons
sour cream	4½ oz	½ cup
COOKING:		
butter		as needed for sautéing
GARNISH:		
dill		
sour cream		

DOUGH:

1. Place flour in mixing bowl, form a well in center.
2. Place eggs, water, and salt in well, mix thoroughly with wooden spoon.
3. Knead for several minutes on lightly floured table. Cover until ready to use.

FILLING:

1. Sauté onions in butter until tender.
2. Add mushrooms, sauté about 4 minutes, until soft and almost dry.
3. Season with salt, pepper, and nutmeg.
4. Remove from heat and stir in dill and sour cream. Correct seasonings. Let cool.

ASSEMBLY:

1. Using ¼ of dough, roll out on lightly floured table until thin, about ⅛-inch thick.
2. Cut out circles with 3- or 3½-inch cutter.
3. Moisten edge of each disk with water.
4. Place rounded teaspoonful of filling just off center on each disk. Fold disk in half to cover filling.
5. Seal well, crimping edges with fork.
6. Repeat with remaining dough. Reroll scraps.
7. Place on floured, parchment lined sheet pan until ready to cook. Seal sheet well if not using immediately and refrigerate.

TO COOK:

1. Boil large pot of water.

2. Place pierogi in boiling water. Do not crowd in pot.
3. When pierogi rise to the surface, they are cooked. Remove to plate with slotted spoon.
4. Melt butter in skillet over moderate heat.
5. Sauté pierogi until lightly brown, couple of minutes.
6. Serve immediately, garnished with a sprig of dill and dollop of sour cream.

BORSHCH UKRAÏNSKY (Ukraine)

Ukrainian Beet Soup

Number of Servings: 13   Cooking Method: Braise
Serving Size: 10 oz (full bowl)
Total Yield: 8 lbs, 2 oz

Food Balance: Protein/acid balanced
Wine Style: Light- to medium-bodied Riesling, Pinot Gris, Blush, Rosé, soft Reds, Shiraz, Zinfandel
Example: Meridian Vineyards Syrah or Zinfandel

> *Unlike most borscht served in the United States, Ukrainian borscht resembles thick vegetable soup. Apparently, the sign of a good pot of borscht is one thick enough so that a spoon will stand up in the pot.*

INGREDIENTS	WEIGHT	VOLUME
water or light beef stock	4 lbs	2 quarts
beef short ribs, chuck, or brisket	1 lb	
ham bone	8 oz	1 each
butter	½ oz	1 tablespoon
onions, diced	6 oz	1 large
garlic, smashed	½ oz	4 cloves
tomatoes, peeled, chopped or canned plum chopped	1 lb	2 cups
beets, peeled, coarsely grated	1 lb, 3 oz	5 each
celery bunch, bottom 3-inches, coarsely grated	3 oz	1 each
parsnip, peeled, coarsely grated	4 oz	1 each
carrot, peeled, coarsely grated	4 oz	1 each
sugar		½ teaspoon
red wine vinegar	2 oz	¼ cup
potatoes, peeled, cut into 1½-inch chunks	1 lb	3 to 4 large
cabbage, cored, coarsely shredded	1 lb	½ small head
salt	to taste	
ham, cut into 1-inch cubes	8 oz	

GARNISH:

sour cream
dill or parsley, fresh, minced

1. Wash beef and ham bone, place in pot with about 4 lbs (2 quarts) water or light beef stock, to cover.
2. Simmer about 1½ hours, until meat is tender; skim stock occasionally to remove scum.
3. Strain, reserve stock and meat. Remove meat from bones and cut into 1-inch cubes.
4. Melt butter in pan. Add onions, sauté a few minutes.

Borshch Ukraïnsky (Ukrainian Beet Soup); photo courtesy of Dorling Kindersley

5. Add garlic, sauté, stirring frequently, until soft and lightly colored, a few minutes.
6. Stir in grated vegetables, tomatoes, sugar, vinegar, and 2 lb (1 quart) stock.
7. Bring to boil, reduce heat, partially cover, and simmer 40 minutes.
8. Meanwhile, place remaining stock (1 to 1½ lbs or 2 to 3 cups) into pot with potatoes and cabbage.
9. Bring to boil, lower heat, simmer partially covered about 20 minutes, until potatoes are tender but not falling apart.
10. Combine vegetables and potatoes, add meat, and simmer about 10 or 15 minutes.
11. Correct seasonings, serve with sour cream and sprinkling of parsley or dill.

SALAT IZ KRASNOI KAPUSTY (Russia)

Red Cabbage Salad

Number of Servings: 13 or 9   Cooking Method: Boil
Serving Size: 3 or 4 oz
Total Yield: 2 lbs, 7 oz

INGREDIENTS	WEIGHT	VOLUME
red cabbage, cored, julienned	2 to 2½ lb	2 small heads
vinegar, cider	12 oz	1½ cups
water	1 lb	2 cups
bay leaf		2 each
allspice		¼ teaspoon
peppercorns		8 each
cloves, whole		4 each

May be used as an hors d'oeuvre or a side dish.

Salat Iz Krasnoi Kapusty (Red Cabbage Salad); photo courtesy of Dorling Kindersley

INGREDIENTS	WEIGHT	VOLUME
sugar	2¾ oz	6 tablespoons
salt		1½ teaspoons
olive oil	1 oz	2 tablespoons

1. Place whole spices in cheesecloth bag for marinade.
2. Combine all ingredients except cabbage and olive oil in pan. Bring to boil.
3. Add cabbage, return to boil, lower heat, and simmer until cabbage is tender but not mushy, about 15 minutes.
4. Chill well. Correct seasonings.
5. Before serving, discard marinade. If desired, sprinkle with olive oil immediately before serving.

SALATA MIZERJA (Poland)

Cucumber Salad

Number of Servings: 14
Serving Size: 4 oz
Total Yield: 3 lbs

> This may be served as a salad or an item for a zakuska table.

INGREDIENTS	WEIGHT	VOLUME
cucumbers	3 lb, 3 oz	4 large
salt	as needed	
cider vinegar	2 oz	¼ cup
white pepper		½ teaspoon
dill, fresh, finely chopped	1½ oz	6 tablespoons
sour cream	8½ oz	1 cup

1. Peel cucumbers, slice very thin. Layer with salt in colander, drain at least one hour to eliminate water and bitterness (place colander in bowl to catch liquid).
2. Press cucumbers lightly to expel liquid, blot with towel.
3. Combine remaining ingredients with cucumbers in small bowl, mix gently.
4. Chill. Correct seasonings. Serve.

GOLABKI (Poland)

Stuffed Cabbage Rolls

Number of Servings: 14   Cooking Method: Braise
Serving Size: 9 oz or 2 rolls
Total Yield: 8 lbs, 5 oz, about 30 rolls

Food Balance: Protein/sweet
Wine Style: Soft and fruity Riesling, Pinot Blanc, soft Chardonnay, Blush, soft Merlot, Shiraz, Zinfandel
Example: Beringer Founders' Estate Chardonnay or Shiraz

INGREDIENTS	WEIGHT	VOLUME
cabbage	2 to 3 lbs	1 or 2 heads
FILLING:		
onion, diced	1 lb, 4 oz	4 medium
oil or butter	1 oz	2 tablespoons
ground beef	1 lb	
ground pork	1 lb	
rice	7 oz	1 cup
water	8 oz	1 cup
salt	¼ oz	1 teaspoon
pepper		¼ to ½ teaspoon
dill, fresh, minced	1 oz	4 tablespoons
SAUCE:		
tomatoes, peeled, chopped, fresh or canned plum tomatoes	4 lbs	
apple, peeled, chopped	12 oz	2 each
vinegar, cider	2 oz	4 tablespoons
sugar	3½ oz	½ cup
honey	1½ oz	2 tablespoons
raisins	3½ oz	½ cup
salt		½ teaspoon
pepper		¼ teaspoon
GARNISH:		
dill, minced		
sour cream		

CABBAGE LEAVES:

1. Place detached cabbage leaves in boiling water for about 5 minutes, until pliable. If leaves tear when detaching, place cabbage head in boiling water for couple of minutes, until leaves can be

removed. Then boil leaves until pliable. Do not use small inner leaves.
2. Drain and set aside to cool.

FILLING:

1. Heat fat in skillet, add onions and sauté until soft. Transfer to bowl.
2. Add remaining filling ingredients with onions, mix well.
3. Refrigerate until ready to use.

SAUCE:

1. Combine all ingredients in saucepan.
2. Heat briefly, to combine well.

ASSEMBLING:

1. Preheat oven to 325 degrees.
2. Trim core by cutting thick part even with leaf. (This is necessary to roll leaf around filling.) *Note: If uniform-size rolls are desired, use cabbage leaves of the same size. Trim large ones and use two overlapping leaves for small ones. Also, overlap two leaves to cover a torn leaf.*
3. Place about 2 oz filling (depending on size of leaf—more for large leaves, less for small) on lower third of cabbage leaf.
4. Fold bottom of leaf over filling, fold in sides, then roll leaf to top. Place seam side down, in baking pan.
5. Continue, until all filling is encased.
6. Pour sauce over cabbage rolls.
7. Bake, covered for 1 to 1½ hours, until meat tests almost cooked with meat thermometer.
8. Uncover and bake for another 30 minutes. Baste, if rolls seem too dry. Correct seasonings.
9. Serve 2 or 3 rolls, depending on size, napped with sauce. If desired, serve with sprinkling of minced fresh dill and/or dollop of sour cream.

SERBIAN DUCK WITH SAUERKRAUT (Yugoslavia)

Number of Servings: 8   Cooking Method: Bake
Serving Size: ¼ duck with about
  5 oz sauerkraut
Total Yield: 8 lbs, 5 oz

Food Balance: Protein/acid balanced
Wine Style: Wide variety—very balanced, enjoy the wine of your choice.
Example: Beringer Vineyards Riesling, Chardonnay, Pinot Noir, or Cabernet Sauvignon

INGREDIENTS	WEIGHT	VOLUME
duck, cleaned, excess fat removed	8 to 10 lbs	2 each
oil	¼ oz	½ tablespoon
onions, diced	1 lb, 2 oz	3 large
paprika	¾ oz	3 tablespoons
sauerkraut, drained, rinsed	3 lbs	
dill, fresh, minced	¾ oz	3 tablespoons

1. Preheat oven to 425 degrees.
2. Place duck on rack in roasting pan. Prick with fork all over. Place about ¼-inch water in bottom of pan.
3. Bake for 30 minutes. Remove from oven. Drain fat and water. Prick duck with fork. Put ¼-inch water in pan. Return to oven for another 30 minutes.
4. Drain again. Lower temperature to 325 degrees, return to oven.
5. Meanwhile, sauté onions in oil in saucepan.
6. Add paprika; cook 1 minute. Stir in sauerkraut; add 3 cups water.
7. Cook slowly, covered, for 30 minutes.
8. When duck is done, about 1½ hours, remove from oven. Cut ducks into quarters.
9. Pour off all fat from roasting pan. Place sauerkraut in pan. Top with duck pieces. Return to oven.
10. Bake about 30 to 45 minutes.
11. Serve sprinkled with dill, on bed of sauerkraut. Accompany with boiled potatoes or dumplings.

BEF STROGANOV (Russia)

Beef Stroganoff

Number of Servings: 9
Serving Size: 7 oz
Total Yield: 4 lbs, 3 oz

Cooking Method: Braise

Food Balance: Protein/acid balanced
Wine Style: Light- to medium-balance Chenin Blanc, Pinot Blanc, Chardonnay, Pinot Noir
Example: Château St. Jean Pinot Blanc, Chardonnay, or Pinot Noir

INGREDIENTS	WEIGHT	VOLUME
beef, sirloin or tenderloin	3 lbs	
onion, diced	12 oz	2 large
mushrooms, button or any variety, cleaned, sliced	1½ lbs	
butter	2 oz	4 tablespoons or ½ stick
mustard, Dijon	¾ oz	1½ tablespoons
flour		1½ tablespoons
beef stock, hot	12 oz	1½ cups
pepper		¼ teaspoon
sugar		1½ teaspoons
sour cream	13½ oz	1½ cups
salt	to taste	

1. Trim meat of all fat, cut into strips ¼- to ½-inch thick.
2. Heat half butter in skillet over high heat.
3. Sauté meat to sear and remove to plate. If meat gives off too much liquid, drain and save for sauce.
4. Add remaining butter, sauté onions until soft, about 4 minutes.
5. Add mushrooms, sauté until almost dry, about 5 to 10 minutes.
6. Lower heat, add flour, and sauté a couple of minutes.
7. Whisk in stock and any reserved juice from meat.

Bef Stroganov (Beef Stroganoff); photo courtesy of Dorling Kindersley

8. Add mustard, sugar, and pepper, bring to boil, lower heat, cover, and simmer for 10 minutes, adding more liquid, if needed.
9. Stir in sour cream, simmer another 3 to 5 minutes. Correct seasonings, adding salt if needed.
10. Serve over wide noodles.

CSIRKE PAPRIKÁS (Hungary)

Chicken Paprika

Number of Servings: 8 or 10 Cooking Method: Braise
Serving Size: ¼ chicken or
  one bone-in split breast
Total Yield: 7 lbs, 14 oz

Food Balance: Protein
Wine Style: Light- to medium-bodied Chenin Blanc, Pinot Gris, Sauvignon Blanc, Blush, Dolcetto, Shiraz
Example: Stone Cellars Shiraz

INGREDIENTS	WEIGHT	VOLUME
chicken, fryers, cut into quarters	5 to 6 lb	2 each
or		
bone-in split chicken breasts	5 to 6 lb	10 each
oil	1 oz	2 tablespoons
onions, diced	12 oz	2 large
bell pepper, green or red, diced	12 oz	2 small
garlic cloves, crushed	½ oz	4 cloves
tomato, peeled, chopped	10 oz	2 medium
paprika, Hungarian	¾ oz	3 tablespoons
pepper		½ teaspoon

Csirke Paprikás (Chicken Paprika) and Galuska (Small Dumplings); photo courtesy of Hemzö Károly/Gust-Art Studio, Budapest-Hungary

INGREDIENTS	WEIGHT	VOLUME
chicken stock	10 oz	1¼ cups
sour cream	1 lb, 2 oz	2 cups
flour	½ oz	2 tablespoons

GARNISH:

parsley, minced
paprika

1. Wash chicken pieces, wipe dry.
2. Heat oil in pan, sauté chicken pieces on both sides until golden.
3. Add onions and bell peppers, cook until soft.
4. Add garlic, tomatoes, pepper, and paprika, sauté another minute or two.
5. Mix in chicken stock; bring to a boil. Return chicken to pan.
6. Lower heat, cover, and simmer until chicken is done, about 45 minutes.
7. Remove chicken and keep warm.
8. Combine flour and sour cream, add to pan. Cook slowly, stirring, until thickened and smooth. Correct seasonings.
9. Return chicken to sauce for a few minutes.
10. Serve chicken on a bed of dumplings, wide noodles, or rice, napped with sauce. Sprinkle with parsley and paprika, if desired.

GULYÁS (Hungary)

Hungarian Goulash

Number of Servings: 8   Cooking Method: Braise
Serving Size: 8 oz
Total Yield: 4 lbs, 3 oz

Food Balance: Protein
Wine Style: Light- to medium-bodied Riesling, Gewürztraminer,
  White Zinfandel, rich Merlot, Zinfandel
Example: Beringer Vineyards White Zinfandel or Alluvium (Merlot)

INGREDIENTS	WEIGHT	VOLUME
lean beef, cubed, boneless chuck or stew meat	2 lbs	
oil	1 oz	2 tablespoons
paprika, Hungarian	½ oz	2 tablespoons
onions, diced	12 oz	2 large
water	12 oz	1½ cups
garlic, smashed	¼ oz	2 cloves
caraway seeds		1 teaspoon
tomatoes, peeled and diced	10 oz	2 medium
salt	¼ oz	1 teaspoon
pepper		½ teaspoon
potatoes, peeled and diced	2 lbs	8 medium

1. Wash meat and dry.
2. Heat oil in pan, brown meat on all sides, add onions and sauté
   until tender.
3. Add paprika, garlic, and caraway seeds, cook for 1 minute.
4. Add water just to cover; simmer, tightly covered, for 1 hour.

Gulyás (Hungarian Goulash)

5. Add tomatoes, salt and pepper; continue cooking until almost tender.
6. Add potatoes, cook another 30 minutes, until tender. If necessary, add more water, but not too much. Final gravy should be thick and no thickeners are added.
7. Correct seasonings. Serve over *galuska* (dumplings) or wide noodles.

GALUSKA (Hungary)

Small Dumplings

Number of Servings: 11   Cooking Method: Boil
Serving Size: 5½ oz
Total Yield: 3 lbs, 15 oz

INGREDIENTS	WEIGHT	VOLUME
flour, unsifted	1 lb, 8 oz	5⅔ cups
salt		1½ teaspoons
water	12 oz	1½ cups
butter, melted	1½ oz	3 tablespoons
egg	5 oz	3 each

1. Sift flour and salt together.
2. In bowl, mix butter and egg. Add water.
3. Stir dry ingredients into wet ingredients, mix just until combined. Let rest in cool place for one hour.
4. With floured hands, drop small pieces of dough (about size of dime to quarter) into pot of boiling salted water.
5. Cook until done, about 10 to 15 minutes. Dumplings will rise to surface and not look floury.
6. Serve like pasta, to accompany stew or any dish with sauce.

BRAMBOROVÉ KNEDLÍKY (Czech Republic)

Bohemian Potato Dumplings

Number of Servings: 7 or 14   Cooking Method: Boil
Serving Size: 1 or 2 dumplings
Total Yield: 14 dumplings at 1¾ oz
              1 lb, 9 oz dough

INGREDIENTS	WEIGHT	VOLUME
potatoes, cooked, cooled, riced	1 lb, 1½ oz	2 cups, about 4 or 5 each
eggs	3½ oz	2 each
salt	¼ oz	1 teaspoon
flour	2 oz	½ cup
semolina	3 oz	½ cup

GARNISH:
melted butter
fine dry bread crumbs

> This fluffy dumpling may be prepared with half semolina and half flour or all flour.

Bramborové Knedlíky (Bohemian Potato Dumplings); photo courtesy of Dorling Kindersley

1. Combine riced potatoes, eggs, and salt in bowl; beat thoroughly with wooden spoon.
2. Add flour and semolina, mix well. Dough should be stiff.
3. With floured hands, shape dough into 1½-inch balls.
4. Drop into large kettle of boiling water; bring water to slow boil again.
5. Cook about 12 to 15 minutes, until dumplings rise to top. Test by tearing dumpling apart with two forks.
6. Remove with slotted spoon and drain.
7. Serve with melted butter and sprinkling of bread crumbs, if desired.

MORAVSKÉ ZELÍ (Czech Republic)

Moravian Cabbage

Number of Servings: 10
Serving Size: 4 oz
Total Yield: 2 lbs, 10 oz

Cooking Method: Boil, sauté

INGREDIENTS	WEIGHT	VOLUME
cabbage, shredded	3 lbs	2 small heads
water	1 lb	2 cups
onion, diced	10 oz	2 medium
oil	1½ oz	3 tablespoons
flour	2 oz	4 tablespoons
caraway seeds		1 teaspoon
sugar	1½ oz	3 tablespoons

INGREDIENTS	WEIGHT	VOLUME
salt	¼ oz	1 teaspoon
vinegar	5½ oz	⅔ cup

1. Simmer cabbage in water for 5 minutes.
2. Sauté onion in oil until soft, about 3 minutes, add flour and stir for a minute or so.
3. Slowly whisk in liquid from cabbage, whisk until smooth. Add more water, if necessary.
4. Add cabbage and remaining ingredients.
5. Simmer for 20 minutes, adding more water, if needed. Correct seasonings. Serve.

KASHA (Russia)

Buckwheat Groats with Mushrooms and Onions

Number of Servings: 11 or 8   Cooking Method: Braise
Serving Size: 3 or 4 oz
Total Yield: 2 lbs, 2 oz

Food Balance: Protein
Wine Style: Light- to medium-bodied Pinot Blanc, Sauvignon Blanc, Blush, rich Cabernet Sauvignon
Example: Château Souverain Sauvignon Blanc or Cabernet Sauvignon

INGREDIENTS	WEIGHT	VOLUME
kasha, coarse	6 oz	1 cup
egg	1¾ oz	1 each

Kasha (Buckwheat Groats with Mushrooms and Onions)

INGREDIENTS	WEIGHT	VOLUME
salt		1¼ teaspoons
pepper		¼ teaspoon
water, boiling	1 lb to 1 lb, 8 oz	2 to 3 cups
butter	1½ oz	3 tablespoons
onions, diced	9½ oz	2 cups or 2 medium
mushrooms, button or any variety, diced	½ lb	2½ cups

1. Place *kasha* and egg in bowl, mix until grains are thoroughly coated.
2. Cook in ungreased skillet, stirring constantly, until *kasha* is lightly toasted and dry.
3. Add salt, pepper, and 2 cups boiling water. Stir well.
4. Cover pan, reduce the heat to low, and simmer for 20 minutes.
5. If *kasha* is not yet tender and seems dry, stir in additional cup of boiling water and cook covered 10 minutes, or until water is absorbed and grains are separate and fluffy.
6. Remove pan from heat, let sit undisturbed for 10 minutes.
7. Meanwhile, melt butter in skillet.
8. Add onions and sauté over medium heat until soft, about 3 minutes.
9. Add mushrooms and sauté over high heat until liquid evaporates, about 3 minutes.
10. Add to cooked kasha. Correct seasonings. Serve.

POTATOES AND MUSHROOMS IN SOUR CREAM
(Poland)

Number of Servings: 17
Serving Size: 4 oz
Total Yield: 4 lbs, 5 oz

Cooking Method: Braise

INGREDIENTS	WEIGHT	VOLUME
potatoes, peeled	3 lbs	6 to 8 large
onions, diced	15 oz	3 medium to large
butter	1½ oz	3 tablespoons
mushrooms, button or any variety, diced	1½ lbs	
salt		1 to 1½ teaspoons
pepper		½ to ¾ teaspoon
sour cream	13½ oz	1½ cups
dill, fresh, minced	1½ oz	6 tablespoons

1. Place potatoes in saucepan, cover with cold water. Bring to boil, continue boiling for 5 minutes. Drain well, slice into ¼-inch rounds. Place aside.
2. Sauté onions in butter until tender, about 4 minutes.
3. Add mushrooms, sauté until liquid has evaporated.
4. Add potatoes and remaining ingredients. Mix gently.

5. Cover, cook slowly until tender, about 20 minutes. Stir frequently, adding more sour cream or water, if necessary to prevent sticking.
6. Correct seasonings. Serve.

JABLKOVÝ ZÁVIN (Czech Republic)

Apple Strudel

Number of Servings: 11
Serving Size: 3-inch slice
Total Yield: 2 each 17-inch strudels

Cooking Method: Bake

INGREDIENTS	WEIGHT	VOLUME
DOUGH:		
flour	13¼ oz	2⅔ cups
salt		⅛ teaspoon
egg	1¾ oz	1 each
water, lukewarm	4 oz	½ cup
vinegar		½ teaspoon
lard or butter, melted	½ oz	1 tablespoon
FILLING:		
bread crumbs	2¼ oz	¾ cup
butter, unsalted, melted	5½ oz	½ cup + 3 tablespoons
apples, peeled, pared, sliced	2 lbs	about 6
walnuts, chopped	1¾ oz	⅓ cup
raisins	1¾ oz	⅓ cup
sugar	3¾ oz	½ cup
cinnamon	¼ oz	2 teaspoons
confectioners' sugar	to dust	

> Author's note: Although typical of strudel dough found in many countries of Eastern Europe, this dough is quite tough. It lacks the large amount of butter or fat used in many doughs. Personally, I prefer strudel wrapped with phyllo dough. For instructions on working with phyllo dough, see the recipe for spanikopita in Chapter 9 on the Middle East.

DOUGH:

1. Sift flour and salt into bowl, form a well.
2. Add egg, water, vinegar, and lard or butter into well, stir with fork until moistened.
3. Knead dough until smooth and elastic.
4. Shape into ball, cover, let rest about 30 minutes.
5. Cover table with clean cloth, sprinkle with flour. Place dough in center, roll out ⅛-inch thick.
6. Slide hands under dough, stretch dough with backs of clenched fists, working from center in all directions until dough is paper thin.

FILLING:

1. Make filling while dough rests. Preheat oven to 375 degrees. Brown bread crumbs in 1½ oz (3 tablespoons) butter. Set aside.
2. Combine apples, nuts, raisins, sugar, and cinnamon, mix gently.
3. Lightly brush stretched dough with some of remaining 4 oz (½ cup) melted butter.
4. Sprinkle with bread crumbs.
5. Spread apples in a log about 5-inches from the top of the dough.

6. Bring top of dough over apples to begin roll, then grasp cloth and use it as guide to roll dough like a jellyroll.
7. Roll dough, brushing underside with butter as you roll. Pinch ends when finished.
8. Transfer to greased or parchment-lined sheet pan. Brush top with melted butter. Slit top of dough in several places so steam can escape.
9. Bake for 35 to 45 minutes, until golden.
10. Cool slightly, dust with sifted confectioners' sugar. Slice and serve while warm or at room temperature.

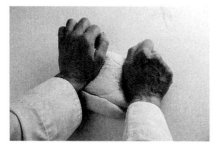

Kneading strudel dough

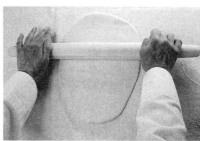

Rolling strudel dough on table

Stretching strudel dough until thin

Filling placed at top of dough; lifting dough to roll over filling

Lifting cloth to help roll dough over filling

Sifting confectioners' sugar over baked strudel

Slice of Jablkový Závin (Apple Strudel) on plate decorated with caramelized sugar

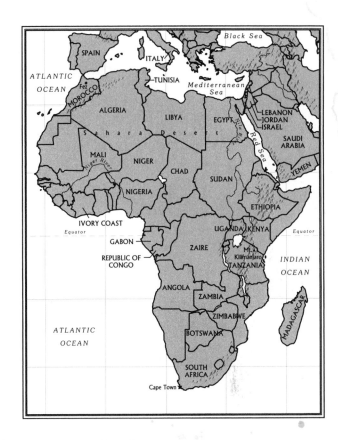

CHAPTER 8
The Countries of Africa

By the end of this chapter, you will be able to

- Identify various areas of Africa and the types of foods consumed in those areas
- Understand why the cuisine of northern Africa differs so greatly from the area lying south of the Sahara Desert
- Explain why soups and stews dominate the diet in Africa
- Understand the role of starches and fat in the African diet
- Explain how the weather conditions impact the cuisine of Africa
- Prepare a variety of dishes from different African countries

HISTORY

Archeologists believe people inhabited eastern Africa two million years ago, and those early Africans were the first humans to roam the earth and the beginning of civilization. Evidence shows that Stone Age people later lived in Africa and that cereals, grains, and tubers played a major role in the diet of these early inhabitants.

In the quest for spices, Phoenicians rounded the Cape of Good Hope as early as 600 B.C. Situated in the Pacific Ocean between Europe and the Spice Islands, Africa became an important part of the trade route that ran between Asia and Europe about 1,000 years ago. Like several port cities in Italy, port cities in Africa developed into major trading centers during this time. The heavy Middle Eastern influence that arrived then is still apparent in the cuisine and culture of northern Africa.

Although Arabic heritage dominated the areas north of the Sahara Desert, inhabitants south of the Sahara consisted of blacks from more than 800 different ethnic tribes. Because each tribe possessed its own culture, religion, language, and cuisine, great diversity developed and still exists throughout Africa.

During the late 1400s and the 1500s, Europeans came to Africa in search of gold and slaves. The slave trade resulted in many Africans being forced to live in distant lands, including the Caribbean, South America, and North America. Although Europeans left their mark on the cuisines of Africa, the African cuisine entered other cultures when, as slaves, Africans arrived at their new homelands with their recipes. Because of the similarity of the climates found in many of these new lands and their native Africa, these slaves were able to plant crops and prepare the recipes from their homeland. This facilitated the transference of the African culinary traits to these foreign lands.

The Dutch arrived in Cape Town, South Africa, in 1652. Before too long, they imported slaves from Malaysia to work on the plantations. Like the African slaves transported to foreign lands, these slaves arrived with their native recipes, spices, and cooking techniques. As a result, significant culinary influence in South Africa comes from the Dutch and the Malaysians. When the French came to South Africa, they brought vine cuttings to grow grapes for wine. A legacy to those French settlers, today the wine industry in South Africa flourishes.

Colonization in Africa occurred rapidly in the late 1800s and early 1900s with the governments of France, Britain, Germany, Italy, Spain, Belgium, and Portugal each controlling some areas of Africa. The French and British dominated most of the western coast while the British governed much of the eastern and southern sections of the continent. The country in power exerted heavy influence over the customs and cuisine of each nation it controlled. By the second half of the 1900s, much strife and resistance toward the ruling Europeans appeared because the people of Africa wanted independence from the European control.

Throughout history and into the present, two factors are responsible for widespread hunger and starvation in many areas of Africa. First, a number of the countries experience poverty and poor living conditions as a result of poor soil and unfavorable growing conditions. Second, numerous natural disasters routinely plague the continent, including droughts, floods, and insect infestations. These create huge crop loses and the ensuing devastation of land and life.

TOPOGRAPHY

Desert covers two-fifths of Africa; another two-fifths consists of grasslands; forests and other land types occupy the remaining one-fifth. The equator runs through central Africa, so a tropical, hot, and humid climate predominates. In fact, 90 percent of the country lies in the tropics. Although some of the areas are situated near the equator, high elevations cause a temperate rather than a tropical climate, for example, parts of Ethiopia and Tanzania.

Africa contains about 20,000 miles of coast with borders on the Mediterranean Sea in the north, the Atlantic Ocean in the west, the Indian Ocean in the east, and the Red Sea on the northeastern side. This yields ample seafood for the areas with coastline. Two large rivers, the Nile and the Congo, provide freshwater fish. The longest known river in the world, the Nile flows for more than 4,000 miles! In addition, several large lakes in eastern Africa, Lake Victoria, Lake Tanganyika, and Lake Malawi, provide abundant fish. In areas with access to the waters, fish and seafood provide the main source of protein for the inhabitants.

Lying in the northwest corner of Africa, Morocco borders the Atlantic Ocean on the west and the Mediterranean Sea on the north. Only eight miles and the Strait of Gibraltar separate Spain (and the continent of Europe) from

Morocco. The Atlas Mountains run through the center of the country in the north; the southern section contains the Sahara Desert. Diverse topography, including five mountain ranges, coastline, fertile agricultural land, and desert, makes up the land in Morocco.

The largest desert in the world, the Sahara lies across northern Africa forming a barrier separating the northern and southern portions of Africa. The resulting isolation led to very limited mixing of the cultures and cuisines on either side of this arid divider.

The western part of Africa contains rain forests, lots of palm trees, and generally tropical conditions. The Niger River runs from east to west across Nigeria. The southern side of Nigeria borders the Atlantic Ocean. With so many water sources, seafood remains the mainstay here.

High plateau and some lush, fertile areas make up the central portion of Africa lying south of the Sahara. Some rain forests exist in this section, too. Hot, dry summers and rainy winters form the climate. Depending on location within the region, very windy conditions or cold winters might prevail.

Eastern Africa has the most spectacular scenery in Africa, containing huge plains with spots of grass and trees, dramatic mountains like Mount Kilimanjaro, incredible rock formations, vistas, and varied wildlife. The large lakes lying in this area furnish fish.

On the south side of South Africa, Cape Town is situated on the Atlantic Ocean. With an elevation of 3,500 feet, Table Mountain lies at the Cape of Good Hope. The interior of South Africa consists of vast, semiarid plains surrounded by mountains that lead to green, fertile land along the coast.

Ingredients and Foods Commonly Used Throughout the Cuisine of Africa Include:

- beans
- fish and seafood
- rice, millet, and corn
- cassava
- bananas and plantains
- okra
- peanuts
- tomatoes
- yams
- greens
- peppers and chilies
- cilantro and cumin
- palm oil
- coconuts and tropical fruits

COOKING METHODS

The most frequently used cooking methods remain braising, frying, and grilling. One-pot cookery is prevalent throughout Africa, a remnant of cooking over an open fire. Benefits of braising (one-pot cookery) are twofold: It extends the small amount of available meat and tenderizes tough meat through the slow cooking process. As a result, the African mainstay remains stews and soups.

With plenty of oil available, frying continues as an often-used cooking technique. Besides providing a frying medium, the oil also functions as a significant source of calories in a land that often yields too little food for the inhabitants.

Like one-pot cookery, grilling is another carryover from cooking over an open fire. Baking and roasting occur infrequently.

With unpredictable growing conditions due to the amount of rainfall (either too much or not enough), salt drying and pickling continue as two methods of preserving foods in many African countries. These preservation techniques remain important because the condition of the next crop is always an unknown.

REGIONS

Nomads still herd livestock in the dry and desert areas of Africa. Dates grow in the oases found in the Sahara Desert, but not much else thrives there. The northern area contains the most fertile regions on the continent of Africa. Wheat, barley, fruits, and vegetables grow in this region. The eastern and southern areas produce peanuts, corn, millet, and sorghum. The wetter areas of the west and center yield bananas, plantains, rice, cassava, and yams. People living in the east eat lots of yams and cassava, while in the southeast, choice foods include seafood and yam stews. Cassava, okra, and spinach in soups and stews appear regularly in the southwest. In fact, most of the world's cassava, yams, cashews, cocoa beans, vanilla beans, and cashews come from Africa.

The countries north of the Sahara Desert bear more resemblance to the countries of the Middle East and Mediterranean than to the rest of Africa. Most inhabitants claim Middle Eastern ancestry; in fact, Arabic is spoken in much of this area, and the Islamic religion dominates. With more crops available, the cuisine in the north is richer and contains more gastronomic possibilities than the cuisines found in the regions south of the Sahara. Although north Africans use many spices and herbs, they lean toward the aromatic rather than the spicy, hot flavorings preferred in much of the south. Favored spices in the north include cumin, caraway, garlic, coriander, pepper, cinnamon, saffron, ginger, and hot red peppers. Because abundant fresh fruits thrive in northern Africa, dishes from those areas often include fresh and dried fruits cooked in the savory dishes.

The cuisine of Morocco shows a long history combining the influences of different people and their civilizations and reflecting the cultures of Africa, Europe, and the Middle East. The Arabs invaded in 683 leaving their indelible mark on the Moroccan culture and cuisine. The famous, ancient walled city of Fez was founded in 808 A.D. Influences from the Middle East and France are particularly strong throughout Morocco.

Although bordering the Atlantic and the Mediterranean, Moroccans consume surprisingly little seafood. Commonly seen in the areas north of the Sahara, sweet components combined with sour ones like vinegar or lemon often

CASSAVA

Cassava is an edible root widely consumed as a starch; it is cooked whole or as pulp, but most often used in powder form. In granulated, powder form, it is called *manioc* in Brazil, tapioca in America, and *gari* in Africa. Although not high in nutritional value, cassava is an important, filling staple in the diets of many countries in Africa, Brazil, and the Caribbean.

Tagine; photo courtesy of Dorling Kindersley

flavor savory dishes. Preserved lemons and many types of olives appear in numerous dishes both in Morocco and throughout northern Africa. *Tagine*, a type of meat stew often containing fruit, is associated with Moroccan cookery. Named after the cooking pot, the *tagine* has a cone-shaped lid with a hole in the top so some steam can escape during cooking.

Moroccans consume ample amounts of wheat products, including flatbreads and *couscous*. A well-known Moroccan dish, *couscous* is actually tiny pasta made from durum wheat semolina. Regional variations of *couscous* abound. Some prefer *couscous* plain, some like it sweet, and others combine it with meat or vegetables.

With high regard for fragrances in both the food and dining experience, orange flower water or rose water are often incorporated into desserts, coffee, and even sprinkled on the table. Like the Middle East, the people of northern Africa favor very sweet desserts. Tea remains the beverage of choice.

Quite different from the cuisines found in the rest of Africa where a pot of soup or stew functions as the entire meal, a North African meal includes multiple courses. Unlike most African countries, Moroccans serve their guests generous amounts of food, as well as a variety of different dishes. Guests encounter tables laden with more food than could possibly be consumed. Like the Asian cuisines, great care is taken to juxtapose sweet, salty, bitter, and spicy tastes within dishes, courses, and/or the entire meal. North African cooks devote considerable effort to creating culinary interest and excitement with a meal.

Moroccans prefer to eat with their hands rather than with silverware. To facilitate eating without forks, knives, and spoons, meats are cut into cubes before cooking and thick sauces prevail. Bread is used to pick up the remaining sauces and bits of food left in the bowl.

Although the hot, humid climate prevailing in western Africa is conducive to the production of abundant agriculture, most of the land consists of poor soil, resulting in meager crops. A profusion of tropical fruits thrive here, in spite of the poor soil. Stews appear most often. They have the advantage of using any available foods, as well as extending the limited food supplies. Generous use of chili peppers leads to the hot, spicy food served in much of this area. Besides their use as a seasoning, peppers are highly valued for medicinal purposes.

THE ART OF EATING WITH ONE'S HANDS

In several African countries, including Ethiopia and Morocco, it is customary to eat with one's hands. The right hand replaces the silverware. Do not think this way of eating lacks manners. Quite the contrary, there exists a different set of "rules" and etiquette for eating with hands.

Before the meal begins, everyone washes his/her hands. Often, bowls of water are brought to the table and everyone partakes in the washing ritual.

The food for the entire table is served on one platter. Each guest eats the portion directly in front of him/her. Only the right hand is used to pick up food—never the left hand. In Morocco, diners use only the first three fingers of the right hand for handling food. Licking fingers is considered very poor manners. Moroccans use bread to scoop the food and clean the plate at the end of the meal. In Ethiopia, *injera*, a spongy flatbread much like a pancake, is used to scoop the food and soak up the last bits of sauce remaining on the platter.

The most common foods found in Nigeria include beans, plantains, bananas, yams, okra, and cassava. Primarily Muslim, the diet in northern Nigeria centers on beans.

Countries on the western coast take advantage of their proximity to the ocean and the inhabitants consume much seafood. These people often use salted and dried fish. An astounding amount of hot chilies are eaten here, often too much for the American palate. Okra stew appears frequently in this part of Africa.

Located in the Sahara Desert yet with the Niger River running through it, Mali became the most important center of trading for the Islamic people in medieval times. Situated on the trade route across the Sahara, Mali served as the seat for the ancient empires that traveled the trade route. Founded in the eleventh century, the city of Timbuktu lies on the Niger River in central Mali. Although Mali is a landlocked country, the people eat lots of freshwater fish from the river. A rapid-growing fish that thrives in warm waters, tilapia remains a popular variety.

The central part of Africa lying south of the Sahara consists of poor soil, high plateau, some rain forests, and occasional fertile growth regions. Poor growing conditions and poor soil result in sparse food supplies and a narrow range of available ingredients. The people of this region subsist on any available food, and, as a result, they eat a repetitive diet, consuming the same foods over and over. The primary staple, corn appears everywhere in this area. Combined with any obtainable vegetables or meat, corn functions as the major portion of the diet in the poorer areas of the central region. Much like cornmeal mush, *samp* is prepared alone or combined with other ingredients such as peanuts or beans. With the exception of Congo and Gabon, the dishes in central Africa are not spicy hot. In those countries, abundant chilies regularly appear, and the heat level even surpasses that of western Africa.

The famous safaris and Mount Kilimanjaro hail from the eastern section of Africa. Parts of this area experience temperate rather than tropical climate due to the high elevations. As is true in several other areas of Africa, the lack of rainfall in some years creates severe droughts that severely limit food supplies.

The influence of Britain and India remains apparent in most of eastern Africa. Having been under British rule, bland, not spicy cooking prevails in Kenya, Uganda, and Tanzania; however, hot chili peppers often are passed separately as a condiment to accompany the food. Curry powder appears frequently, a remnant of the Indian influence. Ethiopia, which was never under

Britain's control, uses generous amounts of spicy hot flavoring. The basis of the diet consists of stews and soups accompanied by starch, usually rice, corn, and/or banana.

The cuisine of Ethiopia developed without the addition of sugar. When the Italian Fascists came to Ethiopia in 1935, they introduced sugar. Before that time, salt or spices were added to coffee as we use sugar. The Ethiopians developed a spicy seasoning called *berbere,* which contains cumin, coriander, ginger, cardamom, nutmeg, cinnamon, allspice, paprika, fenugreek, salt, pepper, and cayenne. *Berbere* flavors many Ethiopian dishes. A similar seasoning mixture, *piripiri,* is commonplace in Mozambique. Hot, spicy food remains the norm in both of these countries. *Wot,* the Ethiopian term for stew, is served regularly, eaten with hands, and scooped with the flatbread, *injera.* All meats except pork are eaten here; pork consumption violates Islamic religious laws.

The land in Tanzania yields a wide variety of fruits, and many of the recipes here incorporate fruit into them. The exotic cuisine of Tanzania includes curries and other foods exhibiting the influence of people from India, Portugal, and Iraq who came there to trade.

Situated in the southeast of Africa, Zimbabwe also has experienced a number of droughts. In an attempt to ensure food through the winter, the people dry any excess foods remaining after the wet, summer season. Having no ocean borders and no major rivers running through it, the cuisine of Rhodesia features much more meat.

The South African cuisine shows influence from Britain, Malaysia, Holland, and northern Europe. Because of significant British, Indian, and Malaysian influences, curries remain widely consumed in South Africa. A stew containing lamb or mutton, onion, and other vegetables, *bredie* appears often in South Africa. With coasts on the Indian and Atlantic Oceans, seafood is plentiful. Great diversity in the food exists based on a person's wealth. Poor people consume lots of *mealies,* a porridge made from corn. *Bourewors,* a sausage dish, is a popular national Afrikaner dish. The wealthy have access to a large quantity and variety of foods.

CUISINE

Africa's economy remains poor for a number of reasons. Much of the soil is poor and yields meager crops. Unpredictable weather conditions lead to droughts and floods. Insect infestations often destroy crops. Many farmers produce only enough food to feed their families. Starvation remains a reality in Africa and accounts for numerous deaths.

An incredibly diverse continent, the climates of Africa range from tropical to arid to temperate. The terrain includes coasts, rain forests, snow-capped mountains, grasslands, and desert. With so many topographical and climatic variations, it is no wonder that the cuisines differ greatly. The countries with borders on the oceans and seas consume much seafood; however, inland countries rely on hunting and herding for meat. Most Africans' diets consist primarily of fruits, vegetables, legumes, and grains.

Corn, beans, okra, cassava, plantains, yams, greens, and *dendê* (palm oil) remain staple ingredients in many of the African countries. Whether mixed with coconut milk, combined with meats, mixed into cornmeal mush, or added to one of the many other preparations, Africans consume large quantities of greens. Similarities exist between the cuisines of Africa and those of Central America, South America, and the Caribbean because of the similarity of the available ingredients and the influences from the people of these countries on each other. Depending on the area, hot chilies appear in many recipes.

Like many countries in Latin America, the Middle East, and Asia, meat is not plentiful enough to be served alone as an entrée. As a result, particularly in the countries south of the Sahara, any available food ingredients—meats, seafood, and/or vegetables—are combined in a pot and cooked into soup or stew. Meat becomes one of several ingredients making up the entrée or perhaps served alone as a condiment. The difference between soup and stew is the amount of liquid incorporated; both preparations contain the same ingredients and flavorings.

Starches and grains play a crucial role in the African diet. Perhaps consumed three times a day, generous portions of starch accompany the soup or stew and function as a filling staple. Whether served alone or combined with other foods, bland grains and starches compliment the spicy entrées consumed in many areas. The variety of starches available depends on the geographic location on the continent. Choices include rice, corn, millet, teff (a grain grown at high elevations), plantains or green varieties of bananas, yams, cassava, wheat, and others. Semolina, the primary ingredient in *couscous*, grows in the north of Africa. Yams and cassava root grow in the west, cornmeal in the south and central areas, and bananas and plantains in the very wet areas. From each of these products comes the starch for that region, usually prepared as a stiff porridge resembling cornmeal mush.

Some of the one-pot dishes commonly served throughout Africa include tagines from the north, groundnut stews (containing ground nuts, often peanuts) from the west, and curries from the east and south. Accompanied by appropriate grains or bread from the region, these one-pot dishes function as the complete meal. The cuisines of the countries in the western portion of Africa use more seafood, while meat consumption is higher in eastern Africa. Legumes, however, are widely consumed in all of Africa.

Many of the African cuisines include a lot of fat by American standards. Sometimes the fat is added at the beginning of cooking to sauté the meats and vegetables before adding liquid. Africans, however, often incorporate fat into the dish near the end of cooking to create a sauce based on fat. Although food supplies remain sparse in many of these countries, oil from palms, peanuts, and other vegetables are abundant throughout tropical Africa. By weight, fats contain a higher amount of calories than other foods, and those extra calories are needed to augment the meager calories obtained from the normal diet.

An abundance of tropical fruits and palm trees grow in this hot, humid climate. All sorts of foods and objects are made from parts of the palm tree. Heavy and strongly flavored palm oil remains the major cooking fat. Valued for both its meat and milk, the fruit of the palm tree, coconuts, appears in all areas of the menu. Among the myriad other uses of the precious palm tree, palm sap becomes wine while materials from the palm tree are used in clothing and for building. The major cash crop for this area, peanuts, appears in many dishes both in paste form (peanut butter) or coarsely ground adding texture as well as flavor to the dish.

Because of limited food, inhabitants in many areas south of the Sahara consume only one meal a day with snacks at other times. Meals usually consist of one-pot dishes except in the extreme north and south of Africa. Breakfast is a robust meal consisting of beans and rice or other foods that we normally think of as entrées. Africans believe that people need to consume a hearty breakfast containing ample calories before departing for work. If available, both the afternoon and the evening meals typically consist of soup or stew served with a starch. In northern Africa, guests receive feastlike meals; however, families still consume the one-pot dish and a starch.

REGION	AREA	WEATHER	TOPOGRAPHY	FOODS
Morocco	Northwest	Rainy from September or October until April or May, dry rest of year	Coast, desert, mountains, fertile plains	Seafood, sugar, beans, barley, corn, wheat, tomatoes, onions, citrus fruits, potatoes, vegetables, olives, figs, almonds, dates
Mali	West	Tropical, hot	Sahara Desert, semiarid, grasslands	Seafood, fish, peanuts, corn, millet, rice, vegetables, cassava, yams, fruits
Ivory Coast	West	Tropical, temperate on coast with ocean currents	Coast, savanna, tropical rain forest	Cocoa, coffee, corn, rice, cassava, yams, plantains, bananas, pineapple, sweet potatoes
Ghana	West	Tropical, temperate on coast with ocean currents	Forests, plateaus, savanna, grasslands	Seafood, poultry, millet, rice, plantains, corn, cassava, yams, tropical fruits, cocoa, coffee
Nigeria	West	Tropical	Niger River, swamps, plains, plateaus, forests, mountains	Livestock, corn, peanuts, rice, millet, wheat, cassava, yams, bananas, plantains, tropical fruits, coffee, cocoa
Central Africa	Central	Hot, dry summers, wet, cool winters	High plateaus, isolated lush areas, rain forests, mountains	Freshwater fish, poultry, corn, rice, cassava, yams, bananas, plantains, honey
Ethiopia	East	Temperate in high elevations, very hot in lowlands, rainy summers, subject to droughts	Highlands, mountains, deserts	Cattle, sheep, goats, grains, corn, teff, vegetables, onions, sugar, coffee
Kenya	East	Tropical, hot and dry	Rift Valley, some arid land, grasslands	Cattle, sheep, goats, seafood, beans, fruits, vegetables, corn, sugar, coffee, tea
Tanzania	East	Varies from hot and rainy coasts to temperate mountains	Plateaus, mountains (Mount Kilimanjaro), Great Rift Valley	Seafood, cattle, poultry, peanuts, rice, corn, grains, vegetables, plantains, yams, coconuts, bananas, sugar, coffee, spices, cashews, tea
South Africa	South	Mostly temperate, mild and sunny	Coasts, plateaus, mountains, desert	Beef, game, seafood, sheep, corn, peanuts, soy, wheat, apples, grapes, coffee, wine

Review Questions

1. Explain the differences in cuisine between the north, south, east, west, and central portions of Africa.
2. What factors created the differences between these regions?
3. What historical and geographic influences contributed to the contrasting cuisines of northern Africa and the rest of the continent?
4. Discuss the spices used in the foods in various parts of Africa.
5. How does the weather influence the foods and cuisine of Africa?
6. Explain the role and importance of starches and fats in the African diet.
7. What is one-pot cookery and why is it so prevalent in Africa?

Glossary

berbere Spicy seasoning mixture used in Ethiopia containing cumin, coriander, ginger, cardamom, nutmeg, cinnamon, allspice, paprika, fenugreek, salt, pepper, and cayenne

bourewors A popular Afrikaner sausage dish

bredie A stew served in South Africa containing lamb or mutton, onions, and other vegetables

couscous A tiny pasta shaped like a grain made from semolina

dendê Palm oil

injera A spongy flatbread served in Ethiopia, used to scoop food

mealies A porridge made from corn

millet A grain

piripiri Spicy seasoning mixture used in Mozambique

samp A cornmeal mush

tagine A type of stew containing meat and often fruit served in Morocco; a pot used for cooking a *tagine* with a cone-shaped lid containing a hole on the top so some steam can escape

teff A grain grown at high elevations

tilapia A rapid-growing freshwater fish that thrives in warm waters

wot Ethiopian term for stew

Author's note: Preparation of many African dishes includes a lot of oil or fat by American standards. The reason for this is that several varieties of fat are available, whereas other food supplies are often quite limited. As a result, fat functions as a significant source of calories for many Africans.

To maintain authenticity, I was not going to reduce the fat in the recipes. After much pondering, I decided to cut much of the excess fat from the recipes because I think the average American customer would want less fat. If that is not what your clientele wants, add extra fat to the recipes.

MOROCCAN OLIVES (Morocco)

Total Yield: 1 lb

Food Balance: Spicy and salt/acid
Wine Style: Medium-bodied fruity—White Zinfandel, Riesling, fruity Chardonnay or Shiraz
Example: Beringer Vineyards Founders Estate Chardonnay or Shiraz

INGREDIENTS	WEIGHT	VOLUME
black or green olives	1 lb	
parsley, minced	1 oz	6 tablespoons
cilantro, fresh, minced	1¼ oz	6 tablespoons
garlic, minced		3 cloves or 1½ teaspoons
red pepper flakes		1 teaspoon
cumin, ground		½ teaspoon

Moroccan Olives; photo courtesy of Dorling Kindersley

INGREDIENTS	WEIGHT	VOLUME
lemon juice, fresh	½ oz	2 tablespoons
lemon zest, grated		½ teaspoon

1. Rinse olives, crack them with a mallet or flat side of knife, cover with cold water and refrigerate overnight.
2. Drain well.
3. Combine remaining ingredients, mix into olives.
4. Refrigerate at least 2 or 3 days before serving.

HARIRA (Morocco)

Vegetable and Meat Soup

Number of Servings: 8 Cooking Method: Boil, braise, sauté
Serving Size: 8 oz
Total Yield: 4 lbs, 6 oz

Food Balance: Sweetness and protein taste
Wine Style: Soft- to medium-bodied Gewürztraminer, Pinot Noir to lighter Merlots or Cabernet Sauvignon
Example: Château Souverain Merlot

INGREDIENTS	WEIGHT	VOLUME
butter	½ oz	1 tablespoon
onion, diced	5 oz	1 cup or 1 medium
parsley, minced	1½ oz	1 cup
black pepper		1 teaspoon
turmeric		1 teaspoon
cinnamon		½ teaspoon
lamb shoulder, trimmed, cut into ½-inch cubes	8 oz	

> Ramadan, a holy month in the Muslim religion, includes fasting throughout the day. Harira is the traditional food served at the end of the day to break the fast.

INGREDIENTS	WEIGHT	VOLUME
wings and back of 1 chicken		
lentils, dried	3¾ oz	½ cup
cilantro, minced	½ oz	2 tablespoons
tomatoes, ripe, peeled and seeded or canned plum tomatoes	2 lbs	
water	3 lb	1½ qts or 6 cups
soup noodles, fine	1 oz (dry)	½ cup
semolina or substitute flour, all-purpose	1¼ oz	3 tablespoons
water	4 oz	½ cup
salt	¼ oz	1 teaspoon

GARNISH:

lemon wedges

1. Melt butter in large pot. Sauté onion, parsley, black pepper, and turmeric for 3 to 4 minutes, then add cinnamon, lamb and chicken.
2. Cook slowly until golden brown, about 15 minutes.
3. Wash lentils. Purée tomatoes.
4. Add lentils and cilantro to meat mixture. Cook 15 minutes over low heat.
5. Add 3 lbs (1½ quarts) water to pot. Cook until lentils are soft, about 45 minutes to one hour.
6. Cook noodles separately. Mix semolina and 4 oz (½ cup) water thoroughly.
7. Just before service, add noodles and salt to soup. Boil for two minutes.
8. Stir semolina into soup. Cook 3 minutes, stirring constantly. Correct seasonings.
9. Serve with lemon wedges.

Harira (Vegetable and Meat Soup); photo courtesy of Dorling Kindersley

COOKED CARROT SALAD (Morocco) ━

Number of Servings: 9
Serving Size: 4 oz
Total Yield: 2 lbs, 6 oz

Cooking Method: Boil

INGREDIENTS	WEIGHT	VOLUME
water	1 lb	2 cups
carrots, washed, peeled, cut into ¼-inch rounds	2 lbs, 13 oz	16 medium
garlic, minced, mashed	¼ oz	2 cloves
paprika		½ teaspoon
cumin, ground		½ teaspoon
olive oil	½ oz	1 tablespoon
red wine vinegar	1 oz	2 tablespoons
black pepper		¼ teaspoon
salt		½ teaspoon
parsley, minced		1 tablespoon

1. Bring 1 lb (2 cups) water to boil. Add carrots and garlic, cook until just tender, about 10 minutes.
2. Drain carrots, rinse with cold water to stop cooking. Place them in bowl.
3. Mix remaining ingredients in small bowl, pour over salad, mix well.
4. Cover with plastic wrap, leave at room temperature for at least 30 minutes to allow the flavors to mix. Correct seasonings.
5. Serve at room temperature.

MAFE (Senegal) ━

Chicken Peanut Stew

Number of Servings: 8
Serving Size: 13 oz
Total Yield: 6 lbs, 12 oz

Cooking Method: Braise

Food Balance: Sweet and spicy
Wine Style: Soft and fruity Blush wines, Gewürztraminer, Pinot Noir
Example: Meridian Vineyards Pinot Noir

INGREDIENTS	WEIGHT	VOLUME
chicken, whole *or*	3 to 3½ lbs	1 each
bone-in chicken breasts	2½ lbs	2 whole
oil	1 oz	2 tablespoons
onions, diced	7 oz	1 large
tomatoes, canned plum	4 oz	½ cup
tomato paste	1½ oz	2 tablespoons
water, boiling	1 lb, 12 oz	3½ cups
salt		½ teaspoon
peanut butter	4¾ oz	½ cup
sweet potatoes, peeled, cut into 1-inch cubes	14 oz	1 large
carrots, peeled, cut into 1-inch pieces	5 oz	2 each

> Any variety of vegetables may be used in this dish. Africans do not eat as much meat as Americans, so the portion size does not reflect serving a quarter chicken as is usual in America. Each portion contains some meat and a lot of vegetables.

Mafe (Chicken Peanut Stew)

INGREDIENTS	WEIGHT	VOLUME
turnips, cut into 1-inch cubes	8 oz	2 each
cabbage, chopped into 1½- to 2-inch pieces	14 oz	½ small head
green pepper, diced	8½ oz	1 large
okra, sliced	4 oz	1 cup
chili pepper, serano or cayenne, minced	¼ oz or to taste	1 each or to taste

1. Cut chicken into small pieces. If using only breasts, cut each half breast in half. Wash chicken well.
2. Heat oil in pot, brown chicken. Add half the onion, stir until golden brown. Drain fat.
3. Chop tomatoes into chunks, add to chicken. Thin tomato paste in boiling water, add to pot.
4. Add salt. Thin peanut butter with some of liquid from pot, stir it in gradually, reduce heat, simmer for half an hour.
5. Add sweet potatoes, let cook 5 minutes.
6. Add turnips, let cook another 5 minutes.
7. Add carrots, let cook another 5 minutes.
8. Add cabbage, let cook another 5 minutes.
9. Add green pepper, let cook another 5 minutes.
10. Grind remaining onion and hot pepper in processor. Add to pot.
11. Add okra, let cook 5 to 10 minutes, until chicken and all the vegetables are tender.
12. Correct seasonings. Serve over rice or other grain.

CHICKEN AND APRICOT TAGINE (Morocco)

Number of Servings: 8   Cooking Method: Braise
Serving Size: ¼ chicken
Total Yield: 6 lbs, 14 oz

Food Balance: Spicy and sweet
Wine Style: Soft and fruity Chenin Blanc or Semillon, fruity Beaujo-
    lais, low tannin/oak Reds
Example: Beringer Vineyards Gamay Beaujolais

INGREDIENTS	WEIGHT	VOLUME
apricots, dried	12 oz	2 cups
olive oil	½ oz	1 tablespoon
chicken, cut into quarters or bone-in breasts or leg quarters	4 to 5 lbs	2 each whole or 8 pieces
garlic, minced, pulverized	½ oz	4 cloves
turmeric or saffron		1 teaspoon
coriander, ground		1 teaspoon
cumin, ground		1 teaspoon
ginger, ground		½ teaspoon
salt	¼ oz	1 teaspoon
black pepper		1 teaspoon
cayenne or hot chili peppers		½ to 2 teaspoons or 2 to 4 peppers, to taste
onions, finely sliced	1 lb, 4 oz	4 large
lemon juice, fresh	3 oz	2 lemons or 6 tablespoons

The smaller amount of cayenne is fairly hot; add more after tasting the dish. This dish may be prepared with lamb, chicken, or a combination. Lamb requires a longer cooking time by about 45 minutes to 1 hour.

Chicken and Apricot Tagine; photo courtesy of the New Zealand Beef and Lamb Marketing Bureau

1. Soak apricots in water for several hours or overnight.
2. Heat oil in heavy pan, add chicken, sauté until brown.
3. Stir in garlic and spices, cook for 2 to 3 minutes.
4. Add onion, soaking water from apricots (not apricots), and water to just cover meat, if necessary.
5. Bring to boil, reduce heat to low, cover, simmer for 30 minutes.
6. Add apricots and lemon juice, cook 30 minutes or until done.
7. Correct seasonings. Serve chicken and sauce on top of rice or *couscous*.

KERRIEBOONTJIES BREDIE (South Africa)

Curried Lamb and Beans

Number of Servings: 13   Cooking Method: Braise
Serving Size: 6 oz
Total Yield: 4 lb, 15 oz

Food Balance: Protein, spicy
Wine Style: Fruity, low oak/tannins, Zinfandel, Chateauneuf-du-Pape, Viognier, Gewürztraminer, Rosé, or soft Merlot
Example: Château Souverain Zinfandel

INGREDIENTS	WEIGHT	VOLUME
onions, thinly sliced	1 lb, 12 oz	6 medium
oil	1½ oz	3 tablespoons
lamb, ribs or shoulder, trimmed of fat, cut into pieces	4 lbs	
salt	¼ oz	1 teaspoon

Kerrieboontjies Bredie (Curried Lamb and Beans)

INGREDIENTS	WEIGHT	VOLUME
pepper		½ teaspoon
curry powder	¼ oz	2 teaspoons
jalapeño pepper, minced	¼ oz	½ each or to taste
garlic, smashed	½ oz	4 cloves
black-eyed peas, cooked, drained	4 lbs	four 1 lb cans

lemon juice, fresh

1. Brown onion in oil until golden.
2. Add meat, salt, and pepper. Sauté until meat begins to lose red color.
3. Cover and simmer until meat is about half-cooked, about 45 minutes to 1 hour. (Add a little water if necessary.)
4. Add curry powder, garlic, and jalapeño. Cook until meat is almost tender, about 30 to 45 minutes.
5. Add beans and simmer until meat is tender and flavors are blended. Correct seasonings.
6. Drizzle with lemon juice before serving. Accompany with rice.

TANZANIAN CHICKEN STEW (Tanzania—East Africa)

Number of Servings: 12
Serving Size: 14 oz
Total Yield: 5 lbs, 8 oz

Cooking Method: Braise

Food Balance: Sweet and spicy
Wine Style: Soft and fruity Gewürztraminer or Fume Blanc
Example: Château St. Jean Gewürztraminer

INGREDIENTS	WEIGHT	VOLUME
chicken, cut into pieces	6 to 7 lbs	2 each
onions, sliced	14 oz	2 large
chicken stock	1 lb	2 cups
oil	2 oz	¼ cup
tomatoes, canned, chopped	1 lb, 1 oz	2 cups
garlic, minced or pulverized	½ oz	4 cloves
chili peppers		2 or 3 each
curry powder	½ oz	4 teaspoons
cloves, whole		6 each
green peppers, seeded, cut into strips	1 lb, 14 oz	4 each
coconut milk	15½ oz	2 cups
potatoes, peeled, sliced very thin	1 lb, 12 oz	4 each
salt	to taste	

> Because this recipe does not contain so many vegetables, I recommend that each diner receive a piece of chicken. This recipe can be very hot, so adjust the hot peppers to your guests' palates. Peppers that are not seeded make this dish quite spicy. Consider removing seeds and ribs from peppers to reduce heat and/or use one pepper.

1. Sauté onion in hot oil until soft, add tomatoes, garlic, chili peppers, cloves, curry powder, and green peppers. Sauté about 5 minutes.
2. Add chicken, sauté about 5 minutes. Add chicken stock, half the coconut milk (7¾ oz or 1 cup), and potatoes.
3. Simmer 30 minutes, uncovered, stirring occasionally.
4. Add remaining coconut milk, simmer until all is tender, about 20 minutes.

5. Remove chicken pieces to serving platter. Stir stew to break up and slightly mash potatoes. Correct seasonings.
6. Serve chicken on a bed of rice topped with sauce.

PEIXE A LUMBO (Mozambique)

Fish and Shrimp Stew

Number of Servings: 9   Cooking Method: Sauté, braise
Serving Size: 7 oz
Total Yield: 4 lbs

Food Balance: Protein, sweet, spicy
Wine Style: Soft and fruity Chenin Blanc or Pinot Gris, Beaujolais
Example: Beringer Chenin Blanc

INGREDIENTS	WEIGHT	VOLUME
shrimp, uncooked medium-size	1 lb	
sea bass, red snapper, or other white fish, about 1-inch thick	2 lbs	
olive oil	½ oz	1 tablespoon
onions, finely diced	12 oz	2 large
red bell peppers, seeded, deribbed, finely diced	14 oz	2 large
tomatoes, peeled, chopped or drained canned plum tomatoes, chopped	7 oz	2 medium or ⅔ cup
cilantro, fresh, minced	½ oz	2 tablespoons
salt	¼ oz	1 teaspoon
hot chilies		1 teaspoon, or to taste
COCONUT MILK:		
coconut, unsweetened	1½ oz	½ cup
water, boiling	8 oz	1 cup

1. Pour boiling water over coconut, let sit for at least 15 minutes.
2. Strain through fine mesh strainer or cheesecloth, pressing coconut to extract all liquid. Discard solid coconut, reserve coconut milk.
3. Peel and devein shrimp. Wash in cold, running water. Wash fish. Drain seafood well. Refrigerate until ready to use.
4. Heat oil in skillet, sauté onions and peppers until soft, stirring frequently about 5 minutes.
5. Add tomatoes, stirring frequently, cook until most of liquid evaporates.
6. Remove pan from heat, add cilantro, salt, and chilies. Correct seasonings.
7. Place half of fish in bottom of pan, top with half shrimp, then half sautéed vegetables. Repeat layers with remaining ingredients.
8. Pour in coconut milk, partially cover pan, and bring to simmer over moderate heat, then reduce heat to low and cook until done, about 10 to 15 minutes. Alternately, bake in 325-degree oven until done. Correct seasonings.
9. Serve over bed of rice.

COUSCOUS IN THE FEZ MANNER (Morocco)

Couscous *with Lamb and Vegetables*

Number of Servings: 9   Cooking Method: Braise
Serving Size: 10 oz
Total Yield: 6 lbs, 3 oz

Food Balance: Spicy and sweet
Wine Style: Light to medium-bodied Viognier, fruity Chardonnay,
   Cote-du-Rhone, or Zinfandel
Example: Beringer Vineyards North Coast Zinfandel

INGREDIENTS	WEIGHT	VOLUME
raisins	3 oz	¾ cup
water, boiling	as needed	
lamb shoulder, trimmed,	1 lb	
cut into 1½-inch cubes		
onions, diced	10 oz	2 medium
olive oil	½ oz	1 tablespoon
cilantro, minced	½ oz	2 tablespoons
saffron or turmeric		½ teaspoon
ginger, ground	¼ oz	1 teaspoon
black pepper	¼ oz	1½ teaspoon
salt [omit if using stock]	¼ oz	1 teaspoon
water or stock	as needed	
eggplant, peeled, cut into	11 oz	1 small to
1-inch cubes		medium
couscous	1 lb	2½ cups
water, cold	1 lb	2 cups
carrots, peeled, 1½-inch strips	12 oz	4 medium
turnips, peeled and quartered	12 oz	3 medium
zucchini, cut into quarters	13 oz	2 medium
hot pepper, minced	¼ oz or	½ jalapeño or
	to taste	to taste
chickpeas, cooked	1 lb	one 1 lb can
pine nuts	1½ oz	4 tablespoons
olive oil	½ oz	1 tablespoon
harissa sauce, optional		

> *This couscous recipe may be changed to include any available vegetables, meat, or poultry. Just be sure to alter the cooking times and to add each ingredient at the appropriate time so none of the ingredients is overcooked and mushy.*

> *Appearing frequently as an accompaniment to Moroccan and Tunisian dishes, harissa is a hot sauce made from hot chilies, garlic, caraway, cumin, olive oil, and sometimes other ingredients. Purchase it in a store selling Middle Eastern foods or prepare it from scratch.*

1. Place raisins in bowl. Cover with boiling water and let sit.
2. Place lamb, onions, oil, spices, salt, and herbs in pan (in which colander can fit snugly in top of pan). Gently cook, while stirring, for 10 minutes.
3. Add enough water or stock to cover meat. If using uncooked chickpeas, add the presoaked beans to pan now. If using canned, they will be added later.
4. Bring to boil, reduce heat, cover, and simmer for 1 hour. Meanwhile, place eggplant cubes in colander and salt. Let drain, to remove excess moisture and bitterness.
5. While meat is cooking, place *couscous* in large bowl, gently stir in 1 lb (2 cups) cold water. Immediately drain and allow grains to stand for 10 to 15 minutes. Fluff with fingers to remove any lumps. Place *couscous* into colander or *couscousier*. Steam colander on top of stew in pot for the last 30 minutes before serv-

ing. (Place steamer in pan 5 minutes after carrots and turnips have been cooking.)

6. Correct seasonings, add carrots and turnips. Continue cooking for 10 minutes.
7. Add eggplant, cook another 15 minutes.
8. Add zucchini, hot pepper, and cooked chickpeas, cook another 10 minutes. Meat and vegetables should be tender.
9. Meanwhile, sauté pine nuts in ½ ounce (1 tablespoon) oil. When lightly browned, add drained raisins to pan and heat through.
10. Correct seasonings in stew.
11. To serve, place *couscous* in mound on platter. Remove meat and vegetables with slotted spoon and put over *couscous*. Pour half of liquid over *couscous*. Garnish with pine nuts and raisins.
12. Serve with bowl of remaining broth and harissa sauce.

Sautéing meat and spices

Fluffing soaked *couscous*

Adding carrots and turnips

Colander of *couscous* fitted into pot, ready to cover and steam

Sautéing pine nuts and raisins

Couscous in the Fez Manner (*Couscous* with Lamb and Vegetables)

SPINACH STEW (Central Africa)

Number of Servings: 11
Serving Size: 7 oz
Total Yield: 5 lbs, 3 oz

Cooking Method: Braise

Food Balance: Sweet, spicy
Wine Style: Soft and fruity Chenin Blanc, Blush wines, ripe Shiraz
Example: Black Opal Shiraz

INGREDIENTS	WEIGHT	VOLUME
onions, diced	1 lb, 2 oz	4 medium
oil	1 oz	2 tablespoons
tomatoes, peeled, chopped	1 lb, 8 oz	4 each
green pepper, diced	12 oz	2 each
spinach, fresh, washed, cut into pieces	4 lb	
salt	½ oz	2 teaspoons
hot chili peppers or red pepper flakes, crushed		1 to 4 fresh or 1 to 2 tablespoons or dried, to taste
peanut butter	9½ oz	1 cup
water	½ to 1 oz	1 to 2 tablespoons

1. Heat oil in pan, add onions and sauté until tender but not brown.
2. Add tomatoes and green peppers, sauté 1 or 2 minutes.
3. Add spinach, salt, and chili peppers or red pepper flakes. Cover and simmer about 5 minutes.

Spinach Stew

4. Mix peanut butter with one or two tablespoons of water to make smooth paste. Add to spinach, stir well.
5. Stirring frequently, continue cooking on low heat for about 10 minutes.
6. Correct seasonings. Serve with rice or another starch.

CURRIED CORN (Kenya)

Number of Servings: 9   Cooking Method: Boil
Serving Size: 4 oz
Total Yield: 2 lbs, 7 oz

INGREDIENTS	WEIGHT	VOLUME
oil	½ oz	1 tablespoon
onion, medium dice	5 oz	1 medium
garlic, smashed		1 clove
curry powder, hot Madras		½ to 1 teaspoon, to taste
corn, fresh or frozen, cut from cob	1 lb, 7½ oz	5 cups
coconut milk	7¾ oz	1 cup
cornstarch		½ teaspoon
tomatoes, peeled, seeded, diced	7 oz	2 medium
salt		½ teaspoon
black pepper		¼ teaspoon

1. Heat oil in pan until hot, add onion and garlic, cook, stirring occasionally, until lightly browned.
2. Add curry powder, stirring to coat well.
3. Add corn, continue cooking a few minutes. Meanwhile, combine cornstarch and coconut milk.
4. Add coconut milk–cornstarch combination and remaining ingredients to corn, stir well.
5. Lower heat and cook, stirring occasionally, for 7 minutes, or until most of coconut milk is absorbed and corn is tender.
6. Correct seasonings. Serve.

BEIGNETS DE BANANES (West Africa)

Banana Fritters

Number of Servings: 8   Cooking Method: Deep-fry
Total Yield: 9½ oz batter

> **Start the batter the day before using.** Other fruits also work well in this recipe.

INGREDIENTS	WEIGHT	VOLUME
BATTER:		
eggs	3½ oz	2 each
water	1 oz	2 tablespoons
milk	1 oz	2 tablespoons
lemon zest, grated		¼ teaspoon
nutmeg		few gratings
flour, sifted	3 oz	¾ cup

Beignets de Bananes (Banana Fritters)

INGREDIENTS	WEIGHT	VOLUME
sugar	1 oz	2 tablespoons
salt	dash	
peanut oil for deep frying		
bananas, firm, ripe	1 lb, 8 oz	4 large
confectioners' sugar for dusting		

BATTER:

1. Sift flour, sugar, and salt in bowl. Set aside.
2. Mix eggs, water, milk, lemon zest, and nutmeg in another bowl. Mix thoroughly.
3. Add dry ingredients to wet ingredients. Whisk well.
4. Cover bowl and refrigerate for one day.

TO PREPARE FRITTERS:

1. Heat 1½ inches of oil to 375 degrees in pan or deep fryer.
2. Peel bananas and cut crosswise into 1-inch pieces.
3. Dip pieces into batter, fry until golden brown on each side.
4. Drain on absorbent paper.
5. Serve warm, sprinkled with sifted confectioners' sugar.

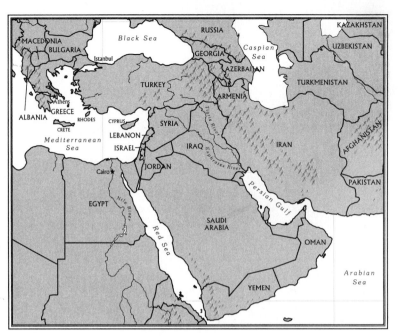

CHAPTER 9

Lebanon, Jordan, Iraq, Saudia Arabia, Syria, Iran, Greece, & Egypt

By the end of this chapter, you will be able to

- Identify food ingredients and dishes frequently served in the Middle Eastern countries
- Explain how the spice route in the 1400s impacted the cuisine of the Middle East
- Explain how religions influenced the cuisine of the Middle East
- Describe the significance of the desert on the Middle Eastern cuisine
- Prepare a variety of Middle Eastern dishes

This section on the Middle East includes the countries of Iran, Iraq, Syria, Lebanon, Saudi Arabia, and Jordan, which are traditionally thought of as the Middle East, as well as Greece, Turkey, and Egypt. Although Greece lies in Europe and Egypt is in Africa, their cuisines contain so many similarities to those of the Middle East that they are discussed in this chapter. In fact, the similarities and differences between the cuisines of these countries are more like the variations between provinces or regions within many countries. Israel, however, will be covered in a separate chapter as the culinary history and culinary traits of that country differ in many ways.

HISTORY

Evidence indicates that around 100,000 B.C. Stone Age man lived near the Jordan River. About 9,000 years ago, man first learned to farm and raise livestock in Mesopotamia, which lies in the area we call the Middle East. Olive trees were cultivated in this area by 4000 B.C. Obviously, a very long culinary history exists in this part of the world. Because of extensive travel throughout the Middle Eastern countries, the nations influenced each other's cuisines greatly, and the differences between these countries are more like the regional differences found within other countries.

Two very early civilizations, Sumeria and Egypt, developed around rivers in this area around 3500 to 3000 B.C. The Sumers settled in Mesopotamia on the fertile plain between the Euphrates and Tigris rivers in what is now Iraq; the Egyptians lived in Egypt on the Nile River. These civilizations made a number of contributions to the world, including inventing the first writing system and the calendar, and building cities.

In the 1400s, the Middle East was situated on the "spice route" between Europe, the Far East, and central Africa. This location affected their culinary history in two ways: the introduction of many foods from other areas and the opportunity to obtain a variety of foods from Asia, including citrus fruits, almonds, rice, new fruits and vegetables, sugar, and many spices. From India, they adopted rice, eggplant, and numerous spices, including saffron. Although the New World provided tomatoes and sweet peppers, they learned about *couscous* from Morocco.

Because the land was so arid, nomads roamed the area moving their herds of sheep and goats in search of the sparse grasses. This greatly influenced the types of foods eaten as well as the cooking techniques; any available food ingredients were primarily cooked over an open fire in the desert.

Three major religions, Islam, Christianity, and Judaism, began in the Middle East. Although 90 percent of the inhabitants in this area are Muslim (Islamic), much religious strife continues here. Religion created a significant influence on the cuisines in this part of the world. Forbidden in both the religions of Islam and Judaism, pork is rarely served in most of the Middle Eastern countries. Lamb remains the most often consumed meat in this part of the world, both because sheep adapt to nomadic herding, and they survive better than cattle in the barren, arid areas that exist here. In addition, Muslims are forbidden the consumption of alcohol, so drinking and cooking with alcohol are uncommon.

Historians say western civilization began in Greece 2,500 years ago. Even though Greece lies in Europe, their foods and methods of preparation were so influenced by the cuisines to the east that many consider the cuisine of Greece to be a part of the Middle East. About 7000 B.C., inhabitants from the east entered Greece, bringing with them sheep and the introduction of new foods such as lamb, peas, and beans. Later, people from the north moved into Greece. Unlike the rest of the Middle East, Christianity is the most prevalent religion in Greece where Catholicism and the Greek Orthodox religion reign. As a result, pork and alcoholic beverages are consumed here, which is not true in most of the Middle East.

The tradition of chefs wearing a tall white hat comes from the Greeks in the Middle Ages. Many of the fine cooks of that time were scholars who decided to cook in the Orthodox monasteries. To distinguish themselves from the scholars who wore tall black hats, the cooks donned a tall white hat, a tradition that still exists today.

TOPOGRAPHY

The arid Middle East is composed of huge areas of sand, rocky mountains, sparsely vegetated hills, and high plateaus. Water was and is the key to existence throughout these countries. Although the majority of the land remains expansive desert, the areas that have sufficient rainfall, border rivers or the sea, or have installed irrigation systems produce large, flavorful fruits and vegetables.

The Lebanese Mountains dominate Lebanon. In Syria, the area around Damascus and the Barada River in the southwest contains very fertile land. The rest of the country consists of desert.

Two major rivers, the Tigris and the Euphrates, run from Turkey through Syria and Iran to the Persian Gulf. Land around these rivers as well as other small rivers in Syria, Iran, and Lebanon is very lush and contains rich soil, leading to calling these areas the "Fertile Crescent." The Persian Gulf borders Iran, Iraq, and Saudi Arabia. The Caspian Sea lies on the northern border of Iran. Greece, Turkey, Syria, Lebanon, Israel, and Egypt border the Mediterranean Sea. Other than where the rivers flow, desert, mountains, salt lakes, and high plateaus comprise most of Iran.

Turkey is a mountainous peninsula with the Mediterranean lying to the south and west and the Black Sea to the north. A fertile plain runs along the northwestern coast.

Thick forests make up the northern part of Greece while the south is arid and quite dry. Hundreds of Greek islands dot the Mediterranean Sea. In fact, no land in Greece lies more than eighty-five miles from a sea.

The Nile River runs from north to south through Egypt. Although the majority of Egypt was too arid to farm, rich, productive farmland describes the soil in the Nile River Valley, particularly at the delta. Now, irrigation from the Nile has transformed much of this once barren land into fertile farmland.

Ingredients Commonly Used Throughout the Cuisines of the Middle East Include:

- lamb and mutton
- yogurt
- chickpeas and lentils
- bread, wheat, and wheat products
- rice
- eggplant, spinach, and okra
- olives and olive oil
- garlic
- lemon
- mint
- many herbs and spices, including mint, dill, flat-leaf parsley, cilantro, garlic, ground red pepper, cinnamon, paprika, cumin, coriander, ginger, allspice, and saffron
- figs and dates
- honey
- pine nuts

COOKING METHODS

Basically, the most common cooking methods carryover from the time when the nomads roamed the deserts, cooking over an open fire. Meats are often roasted or cooked on a spit over fire as they were in ancient times. Larger, tender meats such as a whole young lamb appear grilled or cooked over fire in this manner. Smaller cubes of meat are often placed on a skewer, *shish kebob*, and grilled over fire. Credit for inventing *shish kebob* goes to Turkish warriors who skewered chunks of mutton on their swords and held it over the campfire.

Stewing or braising the smaller cuts of meat is prevalent throughout the Middle East. Placing any available ingredients in a pot and cooking that over the fire also hails from the days of the nomads traveling the desert with their herds of sheep and/or goats.

REGIONS

Throughout the Middle East, nuts appear frequently in both sweet and savory recipes. Walnuts are the choice in Turkey, almonds in Iran, and pine nuts in Syria, Egypt, and the Mediterranean regions. Pistachios remain popular throughout all of these countries.

Lemon and egg often show up in Greek cookery, exemplified by the famous egg and lemon soup, *avgolemono. Ouzo*, an anise-flavored alcoholic beverage that turns cloudy when mixed with water, remains a popular Greek beverage. *Retsina*, a sharp-tasting Greek wine, is another drink frequently consumed with *mazza*, appetizers much like Spanish *tapas*.

African influence on the cuisine of Egypt is apparent by the use of *couscous*, tiny, grainlike semolina pasta that is commonly prepared in the countries of northern Africa. *Couscous* appears as part of the main dish or sweetened and served for dessert.

CUISINE

Throughout the Middle East, countless varieties of *mazza* (appetizers) are served. People enjoy these small portions in the evening with alcoholic drinks in Greece and throughout the rest of the Middle East in eating establishments accompanied by alcoholic and nonalcoholic beverages. Some examples of *mazza* include small portions of any of the myriad of salads, marinated meats or cheeses, olives, raw vegetables, or *kibbe*, a ground lamb and grain patty that is served either raw or cooked.

Grains and legumes form the foundation of the Middle Eastern diet. With the earliest leavened bread traced back to ancient Egypt, bread is truly the staff of life in the Middle East. From *pita* bread (pocket bread) to flat breads to crackers and yeast breads, every Middle Eastern meal includes some type of bread. It is said that an adult in Egypt eats three pounds of bread daily!

Besides being ground into flour for bread, wheat appears in other forms in the Middle Eastern diet. Cracked wheat is boiled and dried to become *bulgur*, a grain that rehydrates quickly and appears in salads, in stuffings, and as a side dish.

Rice runs a close second to wheat in popularity. In some areas of the Middle East, almost all entrées incorporate rice, and it often appears as a side dish, too. *Chelo kebah*, a dish consisting of rice, marinated lamb, spices, and yogurt, is the national dish of Iran. *Chelo kebah* comes in countless variations, depending on where it is prepared. These variations involve the type of meat used and whether vegetables are included. *Chelo*, steamed rice, and *polo*, a steamed rice casserole containing combinations of fruits, vegetables, nuts, and meats, remain two Iranian favorites. In one form or another, rice is included with meals in Egypt, Iran, and Turkey. Middle Eastern cooks prepare

---

THE BEGINNINGS OF WHEAT

Archeologists discovered evidence of wheat farming in the Middle East 8,000 to 10,000 years ago. This wheat eventually became the foundation for bread and pasta. Evidence proves that the Arabs actually dried pasta. The Etruscans made pasta and from there it spread east to the Chinese around 3000 B.C. and then west to the Romans and Greeks. In terms of the introduction of pasta to Italy, the country known for pasta, the Arabs introduced pasta in Sicily when they ruled there. In addition, Marco Polo returned to Italy from China in the 1200s and brought pasta with him.

dry, fluffy, well-separated grains of rice; none of the sticky rice as is preferred in the Orient.

Combined with other legumes or grains, legumes (beans) function as a significant source of protein throughout the Middle East. A typical Egyptian breakfast includes fava beans. Lentils and chickpeas appear often in a variety of dishes. Chickpeas form the basis for *hummus*, a spread combining chickpeas with garlic, lemon juice, and *tahini* (sesame seed paste). Another chickpea product, *falafel*, is a spicy fritter sold by street vendors. Tucked in pita bread, the popularity of *falafel* in the Middle East rivals that of the hot dog in the United States. A well-liked dish, *mujaddarah* is a mixture of lentils and rice.

Whether prepared as a whole piece of meat, cubed and marinated, or ground, lamb remains the meat of choice throughout the Middle East and shows up cooked in many ways. Ground meat in a variety of forms appears on the Middle Eastern table. Extremely popular in Syria and Lebanon, *kibbe neyya* consists of a mixture of raw ground lamb or sometimes beef mixed with onions, *bulgur*, and seasonings. As stated earlier, it is served both raw and cooked. Greece is known for *gyros*, lamb cooked on a rotisserie that is sliced in thin shavings and served plain or in pita bread. Because no part of the animal is wasted, organ meats, including tripe, heart, lungs, liver, brains, and sweetbreads, are widely consumed.

People in the Middle East enjoy a myriad of salads. Salad dressings usually consist of lemon juice and sometimes vinegar mixed with oil or a yogurt-based dressing. Ample mint and parsley in salads create the flavoring associated with the Middle East. All sorts of vegetables and grains become salads. *Tabbohleh* is a well-known salad composed of *bulgur*, mint, parsley, lemon juice, olive oil, chopped tomato, and sometimes chickpeas.

High-quality fruits and vegetables thrive in this part of the world, and main dishes often combine meat with fruits. Figs, dates, pomegranates, quince, and citrus fruits are widely consumed. Except on special occasions, fresh fruit or fruit compote normally ends the meal.

Brought to the Middle East from India about 1,500 years ago, the eggplant appears often and in many guises. It functions as an appetizer, vegetable, and entrée. Served sautéed, stewed, or mashed, "westerners" know it best as part of the Middle Eastern and Greek dish, *moussaka*, which consists of alternating layers of ground lamb, fried eggplant, and sauce.

Preparation of the eggplant usually begins with one of the following two methods. The first method of preparation involves slicing or dicing the eggplant, then sprinkling it with salt and allowing it to sit at least one-half hour to remove excess water and bitterness from the eggplant. The second method is to char the eggplant over an open flame (or gas burner, electric burner, or under broiler) until the skin is blistered and black. At that point, the peel of the eggplant removes easily and the eggplant flesh can be cooked with other ingredients or used in a myriad of other preparations. Another frequent vegetable appearing in these cuisines, sweet peppers are usually peeled with a similar but different procedure. Peeling peppers requires charring in the same manner as eggplant, immediately placing them in an enclosed container (like a bag) to steam, then peeling under cool water.

Middle Eastern people consume all sorts of *dolma*, a filling enclosed in an edible wrapper. Fillings include a ground lamb and pine nut filling, rice and mint, or anything imaginable. The wrappers are often grape leaves or cabbage leaves. Aromatic spices and herbs are an important ingredient in *dolma* fillings, as well as most other dishes served in the Middle East. Stuffed vegetables remain popular in many forms, including such classics as stuffed eggplant, zucchini, or peppers. The stuffings contain ground meats with grain or may be vegetarian consisting of grains and vegetables.

Abundant spices and herbs flavor the foods throughout the Middle East. Some of these include mint, dill, flat-leaf parsley, cilantro, garlic, ground red pepper, cinnamon, paprika, cumin, coriander, ginger, allspice, and saffron. Sesame seeds are widely used, both in their natural state as the whole seed and ground into paste form, *tahini*.

Although most of the land is desert, the lands by the many seas and rivers have access to ample seafood. Caviar, roe, shellfish, and fish are prevalent in these areas. The Caspian Sea, which borders Iran on the north, produces sturgeon and the prized Beluga caviar. Where the rivers transect the land, the ground is transformed into fertile farmland yielding very high-quality fruits and vegetables. Through irrigation, areas that once were barren desert now produce abundant crops.

Feta, a goat's milk cheese, is served as an appetizer with drinks, as a salad, or combined with other ingredients in a main course such as *spanakopita*, a spinach and *feta* mixture layered with phyllo dough. Several other strongly flavored cheeses made from goat or sheep's milk flavor many dishes.

Another important food in the Middle East, yogurt is a fermented, cultured milk product. Used in a myriad of ways, yogurt appears in soups, beverages, marinades, side dishes, snacks, and desserts. Extremely important in the cuisine of Iran, many say no meal is complete without some form of yogurt. Some people attribute health benefits including long life to this food.

Water or a yogurt drink such as *aryan*, a frothy, salty yogurt beverage, accompanies meals in the Middle East. Tea is the national drink of Iran, while strong, sweet Turkish coffee remains an important part of Middle Eastern life. A demitasse (small cup) of Turkish coffee begins all business transactions and is offered at all visits.

Used throughout the Middle East, phyllo dough is a paper-thin dough made from flour and water. It appears in a wide range of preparations of both sweet and savory dishes, from *spanakopita* to *baklava*. Phyllo and *kadayif*, a shredded variety of phyllo dough that resembles shredded wheat, often form the base of the cloyingly sweet desserts preferred in these countries. Honey and dried fruits in the fillings enhance the sweetness. Whether the meal ends with fresh fruit or a confection, a demitasse of very strong, sweetened coffee often flavored with rose water is served.

The harder the cheese, the healthier the cheese.

CHEESES OF THE MIDDLE EAST

Feta Usually made from sheep's milk but sometimes made from goat's milk; fresh cheese stored in brine; salty flavor, crumbly soft texture, used in cooking as well as eaten as an appetizer

Haloumi Made from sheep's milk; mild flavor; often contains fresh mint which lends a mint flavor to this mild cheese; a stretched curd cheese, which refers to the process of handling the curds when making the cheese, resulting in cheese with a springy texture resembling that of cooked chicken

Kasseri Made from sheep's milk or a combination of goat's and sheep's milk; pungent salty flavor; firm yet rubbery and stringy texture; a stretched curd cheese

Labneh Made from sheep's or goat's milk; fresh cheese made by draining soured milk or yogurt; tangy flavor; soft texture; also called Lebbene, Lebney, and Gibne

Manori Made from sheep's milk; mild nutty flavor; soft, buttery, slightly crumbly texture

Myzithra Made from sheep's milk; a fresh cheese produced from the whey remaining after making feta cheese; also called Anthotiro; nutty flavor; flavor and texture similar to ricotta cheese; used in cooking sweet and savory foods and eaten plain

In the Middle East and much of Africa, food is scooped up and eaten with the fingers or pieces of flat bread instead of forks and knives. Traditionally, the hands are washed at the beginning and end of the meal at the table. Only the thumb and the first two fingers on the right hand pick up the food. Dining while sitting on the floor is customary.

Because of the hot days, the main meal is served in the afternoon followed by a *siesta*. The evening meal occurs late in the evening. This light meal often consists of *mazza* followed by a salad.

REGION	AREA	WEATHER	TOPOGRAPHY	FOODS
Syria	Western Middle East	Southwest: hot	Coast, plains, Barada River, fertile farmland	Livestock, wheat, legumes, vegetables, fruits
		Northeast: hot	Euphrates River	Sheep, fruits
		Remaining: hot	Plateaus, desert	Sheep, goats
Lebanon	Western Middle East	Hot	Coastal plains, mountains, Mediterranean Sea	Sheep, vegetables, fruits
Jordan	Western Middle East	West: mild	Mountains, valleys, plains	Wheat, barley, olives, cabbage, eggplant, cucumbers, tomatoes, nuts, citrus fruits, melons
		Remaining: hot	Desert	Sheep, goats
Iraq	Central Middle East	Northwest: cool, moderate	Hilly, Tigris and Euphrates rivers	Sheep, goats, seafood, legumes, wheat, figs, dates, olives
		Remaining: hot	Desert, plains, mountains	
Iran	Eastern Middle East	Hot desert and plateaus, cold in mountains	Caspian Sea, rivers, desert, mountains, salt lakes, plateaus	Sheep, goats, cattle, seafood, wheat, rice, barley, dates, lentils
Saudi Arabia	Southwest and central Middle East	East: hot West: hot	Desert, plateaus plains, mountains	Sheep, goats, cattle, dates, wheat, melons, tomatoes
Turkey	Northwestern Middle East	Southeast and interior: hot summers and cold winters, northeast: cold winters and mild summers, south and west: mild winters and hot summers	Fertile plains, hills, valleys, mountains	Sheep, goats, livestock, wheat, barley, corn, beets, olives, nuts, fruits, vegetables
Greece	Eastern Europe	Mild, wet winters, hot, dry summers	Mountains, rocky terrain, coasts, pastures	Sheep, cattle, poultry, wheat, corn, olives, beets, grapes, raisins, fruits
Egypt	Northwest Africa	North and east: hot	Coastal, Nile valley	Fruits, wheat, rice, legumes, vegetables, sugar
		West and central: hot	Desert	Sheep, goats, camels

WORKING WITH PHYLLO DOUGH

Don't let working with phyllo dough intimidate you! It is really quite simple, as long as a few rules are followed.

1. Always keep unused phyllo covered with a *damp* towel. Uncovered dough becomes dry and brittle, and breaks very easily. If the towel is too wet, the dough will pick up too much moisture and become soggy, causing the layers to stick together. Too dry or too wet results in dough that cannot be worked.
2. Using a pastry brush, apply some liquid fat to the dough. Depending on the use, oil or melted butter is used. To reduce the amount of fat, some apply pan spray to the dough instead of brushing it with fat.
3. After applying fat, stack dough as required for recipe. Some recipes call for a light sprinkling of bread crumbs or cake crumbs on the fat before adding next sheet of dough. The fat separates the layers of dough while baking, achieving the crisp, flaky finished product.

Review Questions

1. Discuss influences that molded the cuisine of the Middle East, including the weather, the topography, and religion.
2. What cooking methods are most prevalent in the Middle East and why?
3. What role do grains and legumes play in this cuisine? Give examples of dishes using these foods.
4. What is phyllo dough? How is it used?
5. What is *mazza*? Give examples.
6. Which meat is most widely consumed and why?
7. Name and describe five dishes associated with the Middle East.

Glossary

bulgur Cracked wheat that is boiled and then dried (dehydrated)

chelo Steamed rice

chelo kebah A dish consisting of rice, marinated lamb, spices, and yogurt; the national dish of Iran

couscous A tiny, grainlike semolina pasta

dolma A filling usually of meat and/or rice enclosed in an edible wrapper such as grape leaves or cabbage leaves

falafel A spicy chickpea fritter

feta A sheep's milk cheese with a salty flavor and crumbly texture; quite popular throughout the Middle East

gyros Lamb cooked on a rotisserie, which is sliced in thin shavings and served in pita bread or plain

hummus A spread combining chickpeas with garlic, lemon juice, *tahini*, and other ingredients

kadayif A shredded variety of phyllo dough that looks like shredded wheat

kibbe A ground lamb and grain patty that is served either raw or cooked

mazza Appetizers

moussaka A dish consisting of alternating layers of ground lamb, fried eggplant, and sauce

ouzo An anise-flavored alcoholic beverage that turns opaque when mixed with water; a popular drink in Greece

pita bread Also called pocket bread; a yeast bread dough formed into a disk then baked in a very hot oven, a pocket forms in the bread during baking

polo An Iranian favorite dish consisting of steamed rice containing combinations of fruits, vegetables, nuts, and meats

retsina A Greek sharp wine

✹ *shish kebob* Smaller cubes of meat and sometimes vegetables placed on a skewer, then grilled over fire

✹ *spanakopita* A dish consisting of phyllo dough layered with a spinach and feta mixture

✹ *tahini* Sesame seed paste, like peanut butter made from sesame seeds

DOLMADES (Greece)

Meat Stuffed Grape Leaves

Serving Size: 2½ to 3 inch roll   Cooking Method: Boil, sauté
Total Yield: 40 to 50

Food Balance: Protein/acid balanced
Wine Style: Wide variety—Pinot Grigio, Pinot Blanc, Sauvignon Blanc, Grenache, Zinfandel
Example: Château Souverain Zinfandel

INGREDIENTS	WEIGHT	VOLUME
FILLING:		
olive oil	½ oz	1 tablespoon
onion, minced	6 oz	1 medium
ground lamb or beef, lean	1½ lb	
rice	3½ oz	½ cup
mint, fresh, minced*	½ oz	2 tablespoons
dill, fresh, minced*	½ oz	2 tablespoons
salt	to taste	
pepper	to taste	
water	6 oz	¾ cup
lemon juice	1 oz	½ lemon or 2 tablespoons
preserved grape leaves	50–60	1 jar
lemons, thinly sliced		2 each
boiling water		
lemon juice	to taste	
GARNISH:		
lemon		
mint		

*If fresh is unavailable, substitute ½ oz or 2 teaspoons of the dried herb.

FILLING:

1. Heat olive oil in large skillet, add onion and sauté until tender, but not brown.
2. Add meat, sauté over medium heat until crumbly and browned. Drain excess oil.
3. Add rice, mint, dill, salt, and pepper, stir until rice is glazed. Add 6 oz (¾ cup) water, simmer and cook, uncovered for five minutes, until liquid is absorbed.
4. Stir in lemon juice, set aside to cool. Correct seasonings.

TO ASSEMBLE:

1. Cut stems from grape leaves. Place leaves in bowl, pour boiling water over leaves to cover. Drain and rinse. Set aside to cool.
2. Line bottom of large saucepan with 2 or 3 large leaves.
3. Place each leaf shiny side down. Place one tablespoon of filling in center of leaf. Fold sides in just to cover the edge of the filling (burrito style), then roll from the top.
4. Stack rolls, seam side down, in an even layer in prepared saucepan. Place 3 lemon slices over rolls, repeat layering rolls and lemon slices. Place inverted plate on top of rolls to prevent their moving while cooking. Pour boiling water to within 1 inch of saucepan rim. Cover and simmer over low heat until rice is tender, about 40 minutes. Leaves should be tender yet slightly chewy.
5. Cool slightly. Arrange on platter. Sprinkle with lemon juice to taste. If desired, garnish with lemon and mint.

Placing filling on leaf; photo courtesy of Dorling Kindersley

Folding leaf around filling; photo courtesy of Dorling Kindersley

Rolling leaf; photo courtesy of Dorling Kindersley

Placing dolmades in pan; photo courtesy of Dorling Kindersley

Dolmades (Meat Stuffed Grape Leaves); photo courtesy of Dorling Kindersley

Baba Ghannouj (Eggplant Sesame Dip); photo courtesy of Dorling Kindersley

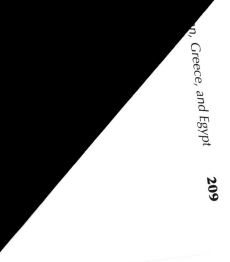

slice, heavily salt w/ Kosher, water

roast for 30-35 min.

❋ BABA GHANNOUJ (Arabic)

Eggplant Sesame Dip

Total Yield: 1 lb, 4½ oz   Cooking Method: Bake

INGREDIENTS	WEIGHT	VOLUME
eggplant	1 lb, 5 oz	1 large
garlic, pulverized	¼ oz	2 cloves or 1 teaspoon
tahini	4½ oz	½ cup
lemon juice, fresh	2 oz	¼ cup
salt		½ teaspoon
pepper		¼ teaspoon
parsley, finely chopped	¼ oz	1 tablespoon

1. Preheat oven to 400 degrees. With fork, pierce eggplant in several places.
2. Place eggplant in oven on rack and bake until soft, about 45 minutes. Cool enough to handle.
3. Peel. Cut eggplant into pieces and place in bowl of food processor.
4. Add remaining ingredients except parsley. Pulse to mix thoroughly. Eggplant does not need to be completely smooth.
5. Add parsley and pulse a few more times. Correct seasonings.
6. Place in serving bowl or in mound on platter. Garnish with more chopped parsley, if desired. Serve with raw vegetables or pieces of pita bread to scoop the dip.

Hummus (Chickpea Sesame Dip); photo courtesy of the Bean Education & Awareness Network (B.E.A.N.)

HUMMUS (Arabic)

Chickpea Sesame Dip

Total Yield: 1 lb, 3½ oz

INGREDIENTS	WEIGHT	VOLUME
chickpeas (garbanzo beans), cooked	11½ oz	2 cups
garlic, pulverized		3 cloves
tahini	6¾ oz	¾ cup
lemon juice, fresh	2 oz	¼ cup
salt	¼ oz	1 teaspoon
pepper		¼ teaspoon
cayenne pepper, ground		dash
parsley, finely minced	¼ oz	1 tablespoon

1. Place chickpeas in bowl of food processor. Process until smooth.
2. Add remaining ingredients except parsley. Process until well blended.
3. Add parsley and pulse a few times. Correct seasonings.
4. Place in serving bowl or in mound on platter. Garnish with more chopped parsley, if desired. Serve with raw vegetables or pieces of pita bread to scoop the dip.

DUGH KHIAR (Iran)

Chilled Cucumber Yogurt Soup

Number of Servings: 9
Serving Size: 6 oz
Total Yield: 3 lbs, 8 oz

Food Balance: Protein/acid balance
Wine Style: Light- to medium-bodied Chenin Blanc, Pinot Blanc, White Merlot, soft Chardonnay, Grenache
Example: Stone Cellars Chardonnay

INGREDIENTS	WEIGHT	VOLUME
cucumbers, peeled, coarsely shredded	1 lb, 6½ oz	2 large
garlic, crushed	¼ oz	2 cloves
yogurt, plain	1 lb, 1 oz	2 cups
buttermilk	1 lb	2 cups
mint, chopped fresh	½ oz	2 tablespoons
salt	¼ oz or to taste	1 teaspoon or to taste
raisins	1¼ oz	¼ cup
green onions, chopped	¼ oz	1 tablespoon

1. Combine cucumber, garlic, mint, and yogurt in large bowl. Stir gently to mix well.
2. Stir in remaining ingredients.
3. Chill at least 2 hours. Correct seasonings. Serve.

SOUPA AVGOLEMONO (Greece)

Egg and Lemon Soup

Number of Servings: 13   Cooking Method: Boil, sauté
Serving Size: 6 oz
Total Yield: 5 lbs, 3 oz

Food Balance: Protein/acid
Wine Style: Light- to medium-bodied Johannisberg Riesling, Pinot Blanc, White Zinfandel, light Pinot Noir
Example: Château St. Jean Pinot Blanc

INGREDIENTS	WEIGHT	VOLUME
chicken stock	3 lbs	6 cups
olive oil	1 oz	2 tablespoons
onion, finely diced	5 oz	1 medium
rice	2¾ oz	⅓ cup
lemon juice	2 oz	2 large or ¼ cup
eggs	6¾ oz	4 each
pepper		¼ teaspoon

GARNISH:

mint, finely chopped

1. Bring chicken stock to boil in large saucepan.
2. Sauté onion in olive oil until soft. Add rice and sauté until starting to brown.
3. Add rice, onions, and pepper to stock, bring to boil, reduce heat to low and simmer, partially uncovered, about 15 minutes, until rice is *al dente*. Reduce heat to low.
4. Beat eggs with whisk, add lemon juice.

5. Whisking constantly, slowly add about one cup hot chicken stock to eggs to temper.
6. Over low heat, slowly pour egg mixture into stock, whisking constantly.
7. Cook over low heat for a few minutes, until soup thickens enough to coat back of spoon lightly. Do not boil; eggs might curdle. Correct seasonings.
8. Garnish with mint, if desired.

TABOULI

Bulghur Salad

Number of Servings: 8
Serving Size: 4 oz
Total Yield: 2 lbs, 3 oz

INGREDIENTS	WEIGHT	VOLUME
bulghur	7½ oz	1 cup
water, boiling	12 oz	1½ cups
mint, finely minced	1 oz	¼ cup
parsley, finely minced	2 oz	1 cup
lemon juice, fresh	4 oz	½ cup
onion, finely minced	3 oz	1 small
garlic, pulverized	¼ oz	2 cloves
salt		1¼ teaspoons
pepper		⅛ teaspoon
olive oil	2 oz	¼ cup
tomatoes, diced	9 oz	2 medium
chickpeas, cooked, optional (garbanzo beans)	3 to 6 oz	½ to 1 cup

Can add diff things to this

Tabouli (Bulghur Salad); photo courtesy of Dorling Kindersley

1. Place bulghur in bowl, cover with boiling water. Let sit until cool, at least 15 to 20 minutes.
2. Add remaining ingredients, except tomatoes. Refrigerate at least 2 hours.
3. Correct seasonings. Add tomatoes and serve.

MOUSSAKA (Greece)

Baked Eggplant, Lamb, and Béchamel Sauce

Number of Servings: 9   Cooking Method: Bake, boil, broil
Serving Size: 8 oz
Total Yield: 4 lbs, 11 oz

Food Balance: Protein
Wine Style: Soft and fruity Chenin Blanc, Rosé, or Merlot
Example: Beringer Chenin Blanc or Stone Cellars Merlot

INGREDIENTS	WEIGHT	VOLUME
FILLING:		
eggplant, peeled, cut into ½-inch slices	3 to 3¾ lbs	3 medium
salt	as needed	
olive oil	1½ oz	3 tablespoons
onions, diced	7½ oz	1½ cups
ground lamb, lean	1½ lb	
tomatoes, plum, canned, chopped	13 oz	1½ cups
tomato purée	6 oz	¾ cup
garlic, minced or pulverized		1½ teaspoons or 3 cloves
oregano, dried leaf		1½ teaspoons
cinnamon, ground	¼ oz	1 teaspoon
salt		1½ teaspoons
black pepper, ground	to taste	
Parmesan or kefalotiri cheese, grated	2¼ oz	9 tablespoons
BÉCHAMEL SAUCE:		
butter	1½ oz	3 tablespoons
flour	1½ oz	3½ table-spoons
milk	1 lb, 12 oz	3½ cups
onion, finely diced	4 to 5 oz	1 medium
cloves, whole		2 each
bay leaf		1 large
salt	¼ oz	1 teaspoon
nutmeg	few gratings, to taste	

SAUCE:

1. Simmer milk, onion, cloves, bay leaf, and salt in pan for 20 minutes.
2. Melt butter in pan, whisk in flour, and cook until it is a white roux.

3. Whisk milk mixture into roux. Add few gratings of nutmeg. Let cook slowly for 20 to 25 minutes. Correct seasonings. Strain.

FILLING:

1. Sprinkle eggplant slices lightly with salt, place in colander in sink or another bowl to catch liquid that will drip. Place weight on top and let sit at least 30 minutes.

2. Place onions and lamb in skillet over medium heat, stir frequently to break up any lumps, cook until no traces of pink remain and onions are soft, about 8 minutes. Drain excess fat from pan.

3. Add tomatoes, tomato purée, garlic, oregano, cinnamon, salt, and black pepper. Bring to boil over high heat, stir frequently, cook until most of liquid evaporates. Correct seasonings.

4. Preheat broiler. Press eggplant slices in colander to eliminate moisture. Lay slices on sheet pan, brush lightly with oil.

5. Broil until lightly brown. Turn slices over, brush with oil, broil other side.

TO ASSEMBLE:

1. Preheat oven to 325 degrees.

2. Spread half of eggplant slices in overlapping rows in bottom of ½-pan steam table insert. Sprinkle ⅓ of grated cheese over eggplant, pour lamb mixture on top, spreading evenly in pan. Arrange remaining eggplant on top, sprinkle with half of remaining cheese. Pour Béchamel sauce over eggplant, sprinkle with remaining cheese.

3. Bake in middle of oven for 30 minutes, increase heat to 400 degrees and bake for 15 minutes longer, or until top is golden brown.

4. Remove the dish from the oven, let it rest at room temperature for 5 or 10 minutes before serving.

Moussaka (Baked Eggplant, Lamb, and Béchamel Sauce); photo courtesy of Dorling Kindersley

KIBBEYET (Syria and Lebanon)

Stuffed Ground Lamb and Bulgur Mixture

Number of Servings: 11   Cooking Method: Bake, sauté
Serving Size: 6 oz
Total Yield: 4 lbs, 6 oz

Food Balance: Protein
Wine Style: Light- to medium-bodied Gewürztraminer, White Merlot,
   soft Merlot or rich Shiraz/Zinfandel
Example: Beringer Vineyards Gewürztraminer or Zinfandel

INGREDIENTS	WEIGHT	VOLUME
RAW MEAT MIXTURE:		
bulgur wheat, fine	9 oz	1½ cups
onions, minced	1 lb, 3 oz	4 medium or 4 cups
salt	½ oz	2 teaspoons
cinnamon		½ teaspoon
allspice		½ teaspoon
black pepper		½ teaspoon
lamb, ground	1 lb, 8 oz	
FILLING:		
butter	1 oz	2 tablespoons
pine nuts	3 oz	8 tablespoons or ⅔ cup
onion, finely diced	9 oz	2 medium or 2 cups
lamb, ground	1 lb	
cinnamon		½ teaspoon
allspice		½ teaspoon
salt	to taste	
black pepper	to taste	
mint, minced	1 oz	¼ cup
ASSEMBLY:		
butter, melted	1 oz	2 tablespoons

RAW MEAT:

1. Place bulgur wheat in bowl, cover with cold water, let soak 10 minutes. Drain well, squeezing gently to eliminate water.
2. Place onions, salt, and spices in food processor with a little iced water (about ½ to 1 oz or 1 to 2 tablespoons), blend to thick paste.
3. Add meat, process until very smooth. Scrape bowl of food processor several times.
4. Add bulgur, process until smooth.

FILLING:

1. Sauté nuts in butter until beginning to brown. Add onions and sauté until softened.
2. Add meat and seasonings, stir so meat does not clump, sauté until lightly browned.

Kibbeyet (Stuffed Ground Lamb and Bulgur Mixture); photo courtesy of Dorling Kindersley

TO ASSEMBLE:

1. Spray steam table pan insert with pan spray. Preheat oven to 375 degrees.
2. Spread half of raw kibbi mixture in pan, top with filling mixture.
3. Spread remaining raw kibbi mix on top.
4. Brush with melted butter, cut diamond pattern into top of kibbi, using diagonal knife strokes.
5. Bake for about 30 to 35 minutes, until done, browned and crisp.

ALTERNATIVE COOKING:

Form 2½- to 3-oz of raw meat into oval shape. Make hollow ridge along the length of top of meat with index finger. Place about ¾ oz filling into ridge. Seal top to enclose filling. If necessary, dip finger into cold water to smooth meat. Place kibbe ovals on greased baking sheet. Brush with melted butter and bake for about 20 to 25 minutes, until browned. Kibbe ovals are often deep-fried instead of baked.

GARÍTHES ME FÉTTA (Greece)

Shrimp with Feta Cheese and Tomatoes

Number of Servings: 8
Serving Size: 8 oz
Total Yield: 4 lbs, 2 oz

Cooking Method: Sauté, bake

Food Balance: Acid/salt balanced
Wine Style: Wide variety—the dish is very balanced so enjoy the wine of your choice.

Example: Beringer Vineyards Sauvignon Blanc, Napa Valley Chardonnay, Knight Valley Cabernet Sauvignon

INGREDIENTS	WEIGHT	VOLUME
TOMATO SAUCE:		
olive oil	¾ oz	1½ tablespoons
onions, minced	10 oz	2 each medium
tomatoes, peeled, diced, canned or fresh	1 lb, 10 oz	3 cups
white wine, dry	8 oz	1 cup
garlic, minced, smashed		3 cloves
oregano, dried	¼ oz	1 tablespoon
parsley, fresh, flat-leaf, minced	2 oz	⅔ cup
salt		½ teaspoon
pepper		¼ teaspoon
shrimp, peeled and deveined	2 lb, 2 oz	
olive oil	¾ oz	1½ tablespoons
lemon juice, fresh	2 oz	¼ cup
tomatoes, peeled, thinly sliced	8 oz	2 each
feta cheese, crumbled	8 oz	1½ cups

TO PREPARE SAUCE:

1. Heat olive oil in skillet over medium heat, add onion, sauté until translucent.
2. Add tomatoes, then remaining sauce ingredients, stir occasionally, cook uncovered for about 20 minutes, until sauce thickens. Correct seasonings.
3. Remove from heat.

ASSEMBLY:

1. Preheat oven to 450 degrees.
2. Heat olive oil in large skillet until hot, add shrimp and sauté until just pink, about 1 minute.
3. With slotted spoon, remove shrimp from skillet, place in bowl, pour on lemon juice and toss gently.
4. Spread tomato sauce evenly in bottom of ovenproof pan, top with shrimp, then tomato slices, and sprinkle feta cheese on last.
5. Bake 10 to 15 minutes, until cheese begins to melt. Serve immediately with or over rice.

SPANAKOPITA (Greece)

Spinach-Feta Cheese Pie

Number of Servings: 8 entrée portions
            17 appetizer portions
Serving Size: 8 oz—entrée
            4 oz—appetizer
Total Yield: 4 lbs, 5 oz

Cooking Method: Bake, sauté

Food Balance: Salted protein
Wine Style: Wide variety—Graves (Sauvignon Blanc), Shiraz, and Cabernet Sauvignon
Example: Meridian Vineyards Cabernet Sauvignon

INGREDIENTS	WEIGHT	VOLUME
spinach fresh, washed, stems removed, chopped	2 lb	
olive oil	2 oz	¼ cup
onions, minced	4 oz	1 medium
dill leaves, fresh, minced (may substitute ¼ oz or 2 tablespoons dried dill)	¾ oz	¼ cup
parsley, minced	¾ oz	¼ cup
salt		½ teaspoon
black pepper		¼ teaspoon
feta cheese, finely crumbled	8 oz	
eggs, lightly beaten	10 oz	6 each
milk	2 oz	¼ cup
phyllo pastry dough	1 lb	l package
olive oil or melted butter	2¾ oz	⅓ cup or 5½ tablespoons

Placing buttered sheet in baking pan so corners fan out

1. In skillet or braiser, heat 2 oz (¼ cup) olive oil over moderate heat until hot. Add onions, stirring frequently, sauté until soft and transparent but not brown.
2. Stir in spinach, cook a few minutes, until wilted.
3. Add dill, parsley, salt, and black pepper. Cook, stirring constantly, until most of liquid has evaporated.
4. Cool to room temperature, then add milk, cheese, and eggs. Correct seasonings.
5. Preheat oven to 375 degrees. Grease 9- by 13-inch pan.
6. Lay stack of phyllo sheets on counter. Keep unused phyllo dough covered with damp towel to prevent drying out. Move one sheet of dough to work surface. With pastry brush, brush with oil or melted butter. Move brushed sheet into pan, dough will hang over sides.
7. Remove next sheet of dough, brush with fat, move into pan as above. Fit into pan with phyllo sheet slightly turned so corners of dough fan out around pan.
8. Continue until all but three phyllo sheets are in pan. Pour in filling, smoothing to form even layer.
9. Fold excess dough from sides to cover filling, brush top with butter or oil.

Pouring filling into phyllo lined pan

Folding dough over filling

Cutting baked Spanakopita

Spanakopita (Spinach-Feta Cheese Pie)

10. Brush remaining sheets and place on top of pan. Fold excess dough into pan. Brush top with butter or oil.
11. Make three cuts in top down to filling so steam may escape.
12. Bake for about 45 to 50 minutes, until golden. Let cool a few minutes before slicing.
13. Cut into squares and serve hot or at room temperature.

MUJADDARAH (Arabic)

Lentil and Rice Pilaf

Number of Servings: 10 for entrée   Cooking Method: Boil
                    20 for side dish
Serving Size: 9 oz for entrée
            4½ oz for side dish
Total Yield: 5 lbs, 14 oz

Food Balance: Protein
Wine Style: Light- to medium-bodied Pinot Grigio or Fume Blanc, Blush, Grenache
Example: Wolf Blass Grenache

INGREDIENTS	WEIGHT	VOLUME
brown lentils, rinsed	10½ oz	2 cups
onion, finely diced	10 oz	2 medium
olive oil	1 oz	2 tablespoons
rice, long-grain	11½ oz	2 cups
salt	¼ oz	1 teaspoon
black pepper		½ teaspoon
cumin, ground		1 teaspoon
allspice, ground		½ teaspoon
TOPPING (OPTIONAL):		
olive oil	1 oz	2 tablespoons
garlic, smashed	½ oz	4 cloves
onions, finely sliced	1 lb, 4 oz	4 medium

1. Cover lentils with water and soak for at least 2 hours.
2. Drain and cover with at least 5 cups water, cover, and boil gently for 20 minutes.
3. Fry diced onion until golden brown in 1 oz (2 tablespoons) oil.
4. Add fried onion, rice, and seasonings to lentils. Stir well, bring to boil, reduce heat to simmer, cover pot, cook for 20 minutes or until rice and lentils are tender and water is absorbed. Check toward end of cooking period to see that there is enough water to keep the contents moist, add water, if needed.
5. Correct seasonings.

FOR TOPPING:

Fry garlic and sliced onions in remaining oil until brown in color.

TO SERVE:

Place in mound on serving dish or on individual plates. Garnish with fried onions and garlic.

STUFFED RED PEPPERS (Arabic)

Number of Servings: 12   Cooking Method: Bake, sauté
Serving Size: 1 stuffed pepper
Total Yield: 12 stuffed peppers

Food Balance: Sweet/protein
Wine Style: Soft and fruity Chenin Blanc, Pinot Blanc, soft Sauvignon
   Blanc, Blush, Rosé, Grenache
Example: Beringer Vineyards Rosé de Saignee or LVS White Zinfandel

INGREDIENTS	WEIGHT	VOLUME
red peppers, medium	about 4½ lb	12 each
olive oil	1 oz	2 tablespoons
water or tomato sauce	about 2 lbs	about 4 cups or 1 qt
FILLING:		
raisins	3½ oz	½ cup
onions, finely diced	1 lb, 2 oz	4 medium
olive oil	1 oz	2 tablespoons
rice, long-grain, cooked	3 lb, 1 oz	10 cups
tomatoes, peeled, chopped	12½ oz	4 medium
cilantro, minced	1 oz	¼ cup
mint, minced	1 oz	¼ cup
pine nuts	2 oz	6 tablespoons
cinnamon		1 teaspoon
allspice		1 teaspoon
black pepper		1 teaspoon
salt	¾ oz	1 tablespoon

> *This recipe calls for cooking the stuffed peppers in water or tomato sauce. If the peppers will be served with sauce, use the tomato sauce instead of water for cooking.*

> *Note: This aromatic rice used as the filling for the following stuffed peppers also may be served hot, as a side dish, or cold, as a salad.*

1. Place raisins in bowl, pour boiling water over them. Let sit until ready to use, then drain.
2. Cut tops off peppers, remove seeds and pith, reserve tops. Preheat oven to 350 degrees.
3. Heat oil in frying pan, lightly sauté peppers and tops all over until they soften but still retain their shape.

FILLING:
1. Heat oil in frying pan. Add onions, sauté until softened.
2. Mix all filling ingredients together in bowl.

TO ASSEMBLE:
1. Stuff peppers with filling, place in ovenproof pan.
2. Put tops on peppers. Pour water or tomato sauce in dish. (It should come about one-third to halfway up peppers.)
3. Bake until peppers are tender for about 30 minutes.

BAKLAVA (Greece)

Layered Nut Pastry

Number of Servings: 12   Cooking Method: Bake
Serving Size: 3- by 3¾-inches
Total Yield: 9- by 13-inch pan

Food Balance: Very sweet
Wine Style: Very sweet
Example: Château St. Jean Late Harvest Johannisberg Riesling

INGREDIENTS	WEIGHT	VOLUME
SYRUP:		
sugar	15 oz	2 cups
water	8 oz	1 cup
lemon juice	1 oz	2 tablespoons
orange blossom water	1 oz	2 tablespoons
BAR:		
phyllo dough	1 lb	1 package
butter, unsalted, melted	6 oz, as needed	¾ cup or 1½ sticks, as needed
nuts, coarsely chopped (pistachios, walnuts, or almonds)	10 oz	2½ cups
sugar	1 oz	2 tablespoons

FOR SYRUP:

1. Combine sugar, water, and lemon juice in saucepan. Simmer until thick enough to coat back of spoon.
2. Add orange blossom water and simmer another 2 minutes.
3. Cool, chill thoroughly.

FOR BAR:

1. With pastry brush, coat 9- by 13-inch pan with butter. Preheat oven to 350 degrees.
2. Lay stack of phyllo sheets on counter. Keep unused phyllo dough covered with damp towel to prevent drying out. Move one sheet of dough to work surface. With pastry brush, brush with oil or melted butter. Move into prepared pan, folding sides or overlapping sheets to make it fit.
3. Repeat using half of phyllo sheets.

Baklava (Layered Nut Pastry); photo courtesy of Dorling Kindersley

4. Mix nuts with sugar. Spread evenly over dough in pan.
5. Repeat stacking remaining buttered phyllo sheets in pan.
6. Brush top with butter. Using sharp knife, score pastry into diagonals, forming diamonds.
7. Bake for 30 minutes at 350, raise temperature to between 400 and 425, bake another 15 minutes, until puffy and light golden.
8. Remove from oven, pour chilled syrup evenly over baklava. Cool to room temperature.
9. Following cut marks, cut into diamonds. Arrange baklava on platter and serve.

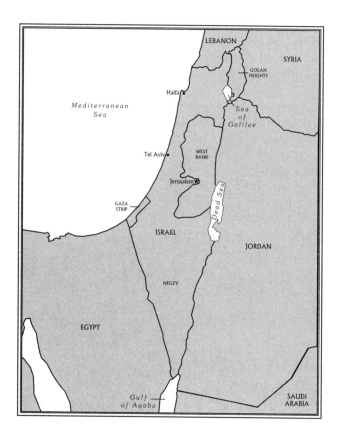

CHAPTER 10
Israel

By the end of this chapter, you will be able to

- Understand the diversity of cooking methods and dishes prepared in Israel
- Explain the transformation of barren land to farmland in Israel
- Describe the growing conditions that exist in Israel and why a bounty of crops are produced there
- Identify some of the kosher dietary laws
- Prepare a variety of Israeli dishes

HISTORY

On May 14, 1948, the nation of Israel was formed in spite of intense hostility from its Arab neighbors. That hostility still exists today, and the borders of this tiny nation frequently change as the conflict continues. Designated as a home for the Jewish people who had been persecuted throughout history, Jewish people from around the world immigrated to this new land. A new country, Israel is a culinary melting pot in every way.

The area that became Israel in 1948 primarily consisted of barren land containing mountains, canyons, swamp, and arid desert. The Israelis studied, experimented, and transformed that poor soil into fertile and productive farmland. They drained the land that was swamp and irrigated the desert with massive irrigation networks. Through the use of breeding, pesticides, fertilizers, and irrigation, Israelis increased production of livestock and crops. In the first twenty years after becoming a nation, Israel raised the production of dates by thirty-eight times, increased banana production by sixteen, and citrus fruits by almost four. In addition to producing plenty of food for the residents, Israelis export a huge amount of very high-quality produce all over the world.

Almost one-third of Israel's agricultural production occurs on a *kibbutz*, a commune or agricultural collective. These collectives actually began in the late nineteenth century. Those who live and work on a particular *kibbutz* own the entire business of that *kibbutz*, including the crops, the equipment, the housing and buildings, and so on. This has been a successful venture in Israel where about 100,000 people living in *kibbutzes* produce the agricultural needs and export for a country of over several million.

Kashrut, the ancient kosher dietary laws of Judaism, forbids the consumption of pork and shellfish. To be considered kosher, an animal must have cloven hooves and chew their cud. Permitted seafood needs a backbone, fins, and scales. Therefore, pork and shellfish including shrimp, lobster, scallops, mussels, oysters, and clams are among the forbidden foods under *kashrut*. In addition, special butchering procedures must be followed when processing the meat. Because eating blood is not allowed, meat in Israel typically is prepared and served well done. Also, the mixing of milk and meat at the same meal is forbidden, so one either eats a meat meal or a dairy meal.

TOPOGRAPHY

From north to south, Israel is less than 300 miles long. Just a little larger than the state of Massachusetts, the country of Israel spans only sixty-three miles across its widest point. Despite its small size, Israel experiences an incredible diversity of temperatures and terrain, ranging from desert to mountains to subtropical farmland. Arid desert comprises half of the land in Israel.

The Judean Desert lies in the mideastern part of the country next to the Dead Sea. In the south, the Negev highlands contain three huge erosion craters unlike any in the world. To the extreme south lies still more desert. The northern and western parts of Israel experience very hot and dry summers, but the winter brings rains to this area that consists of Mediterranean beaches, orchards, extensive fields of fertile irrigated farmland, and lush forests.

Although the western coast of Israel borders the Mediterranean Sea, the terrain through much of the central portion of the country contains mountains, valleys, and deserts. The Sea of Galilee and the Dead Sea are on Israel's eastern border; the Red Sea lies to the south.

Ingredients and Foods Commonly Used Throughout the Cuisine of Israel Include:

- seafood and fish
- lamb

KASHRUT (KOSHER DIETARY LAWS)

- Dairy and meat may not be eaten together, so a meal is either dairy or meat; however, a number of foods are classified *parve,* meaning they can accompany either meat or dairy (eggs, vegetable oils and margarine, vegetables, and fruits are a few of the *parve* foods).
- Separate dishes, silverware, cooking pans, and utensils must be used for meat and dairy preparation and eating.
- Meat must be from animals with cloven hooves and who chew their cud, which eliminates pork.
- Seafood must have a backbone as well as scales and fins, which eliminates all shellfish.
- Special slaughtering procedures must be followed for all animals consumed.
- Only approved facilities may process meat and package kosher foods.
- No blood may be consumed so meat must be cooked until no pink shows.

- falafel
- hummus
- pita bread and challah
- citrus fruits
- all sorts of fruits and vegetables
- olives and olive oil

COOKING METHODS

Truly a melting pot of cuisines, the Israelis have adapted cooking techniques and methods from their many, diverse ancestors. Virtually all cooking methods are found in Israel. The grilling of meats and popularity of shish kebobs reflects the Middle Eastern influence, which was a natural extension of cooking over an open fire in the desert. From their European heritage, Israelis adopted the cooking techniques of baking, braising, and poaching. With an abundance of fresh fish flourishing here, poaching, grilling, and baking are all frequently used cooking methods.

REGIONS

In Israel, rain falls during the winter months, with the only possibility of snowfall occurring in the northern and central hills. Hot, dry summers exist throughout most of the land, particularly in the desert areas.

The capital of Israel, Jerusalem, lies in the center of the country and enjoys fairly moderate temperatures. Built on a series of hills, it is located near Israel's central mountain range, which runs north to south. These mountains create a "watershed" effect that provides Jerusalem with rainfall, although, the Dead Sea area to the east remains hot and dry. A profusion of kosher restaurants as well as dairy (serving no meat products) and vegetarian (serving no meat or seafood) restaurants exist in Jerusalem.

The coastal cities of Tel Aviv and Haifa lie on the Mediterranean Sea on the western side of the country. Tempered by the sea, this area experiences moderate temperatures. Tel Aviv, now the center of Israel's commerce, consisted of sand dunes less than a century ago.

The mountainous Golan Heights and the Sea of Galilee are situated on the northern side. Actually a freshwater lake, the Sea of Galilee is fed by the Jordan River, which enters it from the north, exits from the south, and continues flowing to the Dead Sea. The area around the Sea of Galilee lies 700 feet below sea level, and the warm climate found here supports the growth of subtropical vegetation.

The Negev Desert is in the south. Eilat, the major city in this area, lies at the southern border. Although this region experiences hot days, the nights in the areas with high elevations cool off drastically.

CUISINE

People from more than eighty nationalities immigrated to Israel, bringing their native cuisine with them. When the *Sephardic* Jews from Greece, Turkey, Spain, and Northern Africa moved to Israel, they arrived bearing the foods from their homelands. The same is true for the *Ashkenazi* Jews from Eastern Europe who brought *borscht* (beet soup), *gefilte* fish (a fish dumpling served cold), *knishes* (dumplings consisting of dough surrounding one of several fillings), *challah* (braided egg bread), and *kugel* (noodle pudding). The Jews from

Northern Europe contributed bagels and pretzels to the foods of Israel. So the cuisine of Israel is composed of a culinary melting pot with representation from almost every ethnic cuisine added to the Middle Eastern cuisine which, of course, is native to the area. Currently, Israeli culinary professionals are developing a cuisine of their own, one that uses the incredible bounty of available fresh ingredients and is based on the weather conditions in their country, instead of centering around foods from the colder climates of Europe.

Foods sold by street vendors are widely available in many areas in Israel, particularly in the larger cities. Middle Eastern specialties, including *hummus* (*tahini* and chickpea spread served with torn pieces or wedges of pita bread); *falafel* (referred to as Israeli hot dogs, these fried chickpea patties are served in pita bread and topped with salad); *shwarma* (grilled slices of meat served in a pita with salad); *borekas* (turnovers of phyllo dough filled with spinach or potato); and *kibbe* (fried patties of seasoned ground meat and bulgur), appear at vendors' stands on many streets.

Mezze, small appetizers, are consumed in Israel as they are throughout the Middle East. Green and red chilies spice much of the Israeli food; chili-based relishes often accompany meals. Borrowed from the North African cuisine, *harissa*, a hot pepper paste is commonly used in Israel. The Yemenites and Moroccans are particularly fond of chilies and hot, spicy foods.

Seafood abounds, particularly along the Mediterranean, the northern coast, and in the Galilee regions. Many types of fish, including grouper, red and gray mullet, red snapper, talapia, and sea bream, thrive here. Fish stews or soups similar to *bouillabaisse* are common in Jaffa. Prepared with a variety of cooking methods, Israelis bake, fry, braise, poach, and grill seafood. Because of the very fresh quality of the fish, it is often simply grilled or baked and served with a sauce.

A staggering abundance of fruits grows in Israel today. Some of the available fruits include watermelon, figs, dates, prickly pears, all sorts of citrus fruits, apples, grapes, mangoes, kiwi, and every variety of exotic fruit. As a result, Israelis consume lots of fruit. Much of this high-quality fruit is exported.

Bread accompanies meals. *Challah*, a rich egg bread, is formed in a braid and served every Friday night as part of the Sabbath meal. A part of every wedding and holiday, *challah* is baked in a symbolic circle for *Rosh Hashanah*, the Jewish New Year, to symbolize the never-ending circle of life. Used as a pocket for holding sandwiches or as a scoop for hummus or other *mezze*, *pita* bread appears frequently.

Like their Middle Eastern neighbors, Israelis like very sweet desserts. The most common confections include fruit compotes, *baklava*, and other typical Middle Eastern pastries combining phyllo dough and nuts. *Malabi*, a popular flan-type custard, is served in a cup and topped with a sweet, syrupy fruit topping. Another well-liked confection is *halvah*, a sesame candy that comes in several flavors—plain, chocolate, or marbled with chocolate. It is packaged as a candy bar or sold by the slice when cut from a large loaf.

Breakfast is an important meal in Israel, especially on the *kibbutz* where manual labor produces hungry workers. A whole range of foods may be served, among them *labaneh*, a cheese made from curdled yogurt.

With the exception of the Friday night Sabbath meal, the evening meal in Israel follows the late dining pattern customary in Mediterranean and Middle Eastern countries. The Friday night meal is served at sundown in celebration of the beginning of the Sabbath, the day of rest. *Cholent*, a dish with a long culinary history, consists of a slowly cooked meat casserole containing rice or barley, beans, meat, and potatoes. This Eastern European dish met North African and Middle Eastern influences in Israel. Because no work is performed on the Sabbath, preparation for the dish begins on Friday before

REGION	AREA	WEATHER	TOPOGRAPHY	FOODS
Jordan Valley	East	Hot	Fertile farmland	Winter vegetables, fruits, avocados, bananas, guava, mangos, citrus
Jezreel Valley	North	Hot summers, wet winters	Valley between mountains	Cereals
Hulah Valley	Northeast	Hot	Marsh until irrigated, fertile farmland	Corn
Golan	Northeast	Temperate	Mountains	Grapes, apples, fruits
Galilee	North	Hot summers, wet winters	Dan and Banias rivers flow from Mount Hermon into Sea of Galilee	Fish, trout, tilapia
Negev Desert	South	Hot	Desert until irrigated, three erosion craters, shore on south	Cereals, wheat
Judean Desert	Mideast	Hot	Canyons, desert, Dead Sea	Salad vegetables, tomatoes
West	West	Hot summers, wet winters	Mediterranean coast	Fish, seafood
Jerusalem area	Central to east	Hot summers, moderate winters	Hills, mountains, forests, Dead Sea	Sheep, goats dates, oranges, bananas, papayas

sundown when the Jewish Sabbath begins. Traditionally, the prepared *cholent* is taken to a commercial bakery where it is baked in the oven at a very low temperature throughout the night. After services on Saturday, the *cholent* is picked up at the bakery, taken home, and consumed.

Review Questions

1. Discuss the different ethnic groups making up the population of Israel and their contributions to the cuisine.
2. What was the land in Israel like in 1948 and how has it changed?
3. Name four of the laws of *kashrut*.
4. Name and describe four Israeli dishes.

Glossary

Ashkenazi **Jews** Jewish people with Eastern European heritage

borekas Turnovers of phyllo dough filled with spinach or potato

borscht Beet soup

challah Braided egg bread that is served traditionally on the Sabbath and all holidays

cholent Known as Sabbath stew; a slowly cooked casserole containing rice or barley, beans, meat, and potatoes; traditionally cooked at a low temperature in an oven in a commercial bakery all Friday night then eaten Saturday, as no work may be performed on the Sabbath

falafel Fried chickpea patties served in pita bread topped with salad and a *tahini* sauce; known as Israeli hot dogs

---

SOME OF THE TRADITIONAL JEWISH HOLIDAYS

Rosh Hashanah Jewish New Year, in the fall, sweet foods are served to represent a coming sweet year

Yom Kippur Day of Atonement, ten days after *Rosh Hashanah*

Chanukah Festival of Lights, in December, potato *latkes* traditionally served

Purim Festival of Esther, in the spring

Pesach Passover, in the spring celebrating the escape of the Jewish people from the bondage of the Egyptians, *matzo* replaces bread, no bread products consumed during the week of Passover

All holidays, including the Sabbath, begin and end at sundown.

---

gefilte **fish** A fish dumpling that is served cold and usually accompanied by horseradish

harissa Hot pepper paste used in Morocco

hummus Chickpea and *tahini* spread served with pita bread

kashrut The rules governing kosher diet and preparation

kibbe Seasoned ground meat and bulgur that is fried

kibbutz A farm collective where the people who live and work on the farm actually own the entire business

knish A dumpling consisting of dough surrounding one of several fillings

kugel Often called noodle pudding, a casserole usually consisting of noodles, cottage cheese, sour cream, raisins, and cinnamon; other vegetables can form a kugel

labaneh A cheese made from curdled yogurt

latkes Potato pancakes, traditionally served at Chanukah

mezze Appetizers

parve Foods that can accompany either meat or dairy products

Sephardic **Jews** Jewish people from Greece, Turkey, Spain, and Northern Africa

shwarma Grilled slices of meat served in a pita with salad

tahini Sesame seed paste

CHOPPED LIVER

Number of Servings: 18 canapés   Cooking Method: Sauté
Serving Size: 1-oz canapé
Total Yield: 1 lb, 3 oz

Food Balance: Protein
Wine Style: Soft and fruity Riesling, White Zinfandel, Viognier, Rosé, Beaujolais
Example: Château St. Jean Johannisberg Riesling or Viognier

INGREDIENTS	WEIGHT	VOLUME
chicken livers	1 lb	
onions, diced	4½ oz	1 medium
butter, melted or chicken fat	1½ oz	3 tablespoons

Chopped liver is easily molded into shapes. Since chopped liver is brown, garnish with red peppers, radishes, or other colorful items to brighten the platter.

Chopped Liver

INGREDIENTS	WEIGHT	VOLUME
salt	¼ oz	1 teaspoon
pepper		¼ teaspoon
eggs, hard cooked, diced	6¾ oz	4 each

party rye or crackers

1. Wash liver, let drain thoroughly.
2. Sauté liver with onions in melted butter or chicken fat until liver is done, no longer pink.
3. Cool liver and onions about 5 minutes, place in bowl of food processor. Pulse a couple of times.
4. Add remaining ingredients, pulse until fine, but not too smooth. Do not let it become fine paste.
5. Correct seasonings. Refrigerate until serving time.
6. Place on platter and garnish. Serve with party rye bread or crackers.

CHICKEN SOUP WITH CHICKEN KREPLACH

Chicken Soup with Chicken-Filled Dumplings

Number of Servings: 12   Cooking Method: Boil
Serving Size: 4 per serving
Total Yield: 50 kreplach

Food Balance: Protein/neutral
Wine Style: Wide variety—Chenin Blanc, Chardonnay, soft Reds, Merlot
Example: Stone Cellars Chardonnay or Merlot

INGREDIENTS	WEIGHT	VOLUME
chicken soup	5 lb	2½ qt
DOUGH:		
flour, all purpose	8½ oz	1¾ cups plus 2 tablespoons
salt		¾ teaspoon
eggs	5 oz	3 each
FILLING:		
oil	½ oz	1 tablespoon
onion, finely diced	4 oz	1 medium
chicken, cooked	8 oz	2 cups
egg	1¾ oz	1 each
salt		½ teaspoon
pepper		¼ teaspoon
nutmeg		few gratings, to taste

GARNISH:

parsley, minced

> Called Jewish wontons or Jewish tortellini, kreplach are usually filled with meat, chicken, or cheese. Although most often served in chicken soup, kreplach may be sautéed with onions and served as an appetizer or side dish.

DOUGH:

1. Place 6¾ oz (1½ cups) flour in bowl of food processor, add eggs and salt.
2. Pulse until dough begins to form ball.
3. Add remaining flour by the tablespoon, process a few seconds after each addition. Process until dough forms ball, about 30 seconds.
4. On lightly floured surface, knead briefly by hand until very smooth.
5. Cover dough and let rest for 30 minutes at room temperature.

FILLING:

1. Heat oil in skillet, add onion, sauté until soft and just beginning to brown, about 10 minutes.
2. Chop chicken in food processor until fine.
3. Add egg and seasonings, process until smooth.
4. Refrigerate filling until ready to use.

ASSEMBLY:

1. Cut dough into 2 or 3 pieces. Keep unused dough covered.
2. Flatten or roll out one piece dough. If necessary, flour lightly.
3. Put dough through pasta machine with rollers at widest setting. Continue putting dough through at this setting until smooth.
4. Reduce width setting by one notch and put dough through machine.
5. Continue reducing setting size and feeding dough until the smallest setting.
6. Lay dough on lightly floured surface.
7. Place ¾-teaspoon mounds of filling about 1½ inches apart on dough, cut dough into about 2½-inch squares.
8. Brush 2 adjacent sides of square with water, fold dough over filling to form triangle, pressing moistened sides against dry sides to make tight seal. Some people join opposite ends of triangle together to form ring. *See photograph of preparing wontons in Chapter 11—China.*

9. Place finished triangle on floured sheet of parchment paper. Repeat rolling and shaping with remaining dough and filling. (Finished kreplach may be refrigerated, well wrapped, for 1 day.)

SERVE:

1. To cook, add kreplach to large pot of boiling salted water. Bring to boil, reduce heat to simmer, cover, and cook over low heat 15 minutes.
2. Remove with slotted spoon, drain well. (Cooked kreplach can be refrigerated for 2 days or frozen.)
3. To serve, simmer kreplach in hot chicken soup for 10 to 15 minutes. Garnish with minced parsley.

ORANGE AND OLIVE SALAD

Number of Servings: 8 or 16
Serving Size: 1 orange per person if segmented without membrane
        1 orange per 2 people if just sliced and cut
Yield: 1 lb, 7 oz (8 oranges segmented without membrane)

INGREDIENTS	WEIGHT	VOLUME
oranges	4 lb	8 each
VINAIGRETTE:		
lemon juice, fresh	4 oz	2 lemons or ½ cup
olive oil	4 oz	½ cup
garlic cloves, crushed	1 oz	5 cloves
salt		½ teaspoon
cumin		1 teaspoon
paprika		1½ teaspoons
cayenne		up to ⅛ teaspoon or to taste
GARNISH:		
black olives		as desired, 3 to 5 per serving

1. Combine ingredients for vinaigrette. Mix well, refrigerate. (May be prepared ahead.)
2. Peel oranges removing pith with sharp paring knife. To remove membrane, cut on each side of membrane to the middle, staying as close to membrane as possible. To cut with membrane, slice oranges across grain, then cut into pieces.
3. Mix oranges with enough vinaigrette to coat well.
4. Serve alone or place on bed of lettuce drizzled with vinaigrette. Garnish with olives.

Removing pith and skin from orange; photo courtesy of Dorling Kindersley

Cutting orange sections away from membrane; photo courtesy of Dorling Kindersley

Orange and Olive Salad

CHEESE BLINTZES

Cheese Filled Crêpes

Yield: 13—5 to 5½ inch   Cooking Method: Sauté
       30—3½ to 4 inch

Food Balance: Very sweet and protein
Wine Style: Sweet and fruity late harvest wines, Rieslings, Sauternes, sweet Sherry
Example: Château St. Jean Late Harvest Riesling

The wrapper prepared for blintzes is very similar to a crêpe. The smaller size blintzes require about 1/3 less filling than the larger ones, so either reduce the filling amount or increase the number of wrappers.

INGREDIENTS	WEIGHT	VOLUME
WRAPPER:		
flour, all purpose	4½ oz	1 cup
salt		¼ teaspoon
eggs	6¾ oz	4 each
milk	8 oz	1 cup
butter, melted	¼ oz	½ tablespoon
butter, for frying		
FILLING:		
cottage cheese	13 oz	1½ cups
cream cheese	1 lb	
sugar	3 oz	⅓ cup
eggs, well beaten	3½ oz	2 each
salt		¼ teaspoon
lemon peel, grated	¼ oz	2 teaspoons
butter, melted	1 oz	2 tablespoons
vanilla		1 teaspoon

ACCOMPANIMENTS:

sour cream
applesauce

FOR WRAPPER:

1. Place all ingredients in bowl of food processor, pulse to mix well.
2. Chill for 10 minutes.
3. Lightly butter skillet, heat over medium heat. Pour just enough batter into skillet to cover bottom of pan with thin, even layer when pan is tilted (about 1½ ounces or 3 tablespoons for a 7½-inch skillet, about 1 ounce or 2 tablespoons for a 5-inch skillet).

Ladling batter into pan while tilting pan; photo courtesy of Dorling Kindersley

Releasing pancake from pan; photo courtesy of Dorling Kindersley

Cheese Blintzes (Cheese Filled Crêpes)

4. Cook until lightly brown on one side, then remove from pan and stack on plate with cooked side up.

FOR FILLING:

1. Blend cream cheese and sugar in mixer with paddle attachment until creamy.
2. Add remaining ingredients and mix well.

TO ASSEMBLE:

1. Place crêpe on flat surface with browned side up.
2. Spoon filling across center of crêpe (larger blintzes need about 3 tablespoons of filling, smaller size need about 1 tablespoon).
3. Fold edges on sides to cover some of filling, then roll crêpe.
4. Refrigerate until needed or sauté in buttered pan until lightly brown and warmed through.
5. Serve with sour cream and applesauce.

FALAFEL

Deep-fried Chickpea Balls

Number of Servings: 7   Cooking Method: Deep-fry
Serving Size: Three 1-oz patties or balls per pita half
     Twenty-two 1-oz patties or balls for appetizers
Total Yield: 1 lb, 6 oz

Food Balance: Protein/balanced
Wine Style: Soft and fruity Gewürztraminer, Sauvignon Blanc, Pinot Noir
Example: Château St. Jean Gewürztraminer or Pinot Noir

INGREDIENTS	WEIGHT	VOLUME
chickpeas (garbanzo beans), cooked or canned, drained	11½ oz	2 cups
garlic, pulverized		3 cloves
celery, finely minced	2¼ oz	½ cup
scallions, finely minced	2 oz	½ cup
eggs	3½ oz	2 each
tahini	2 oz	3 tablespoons
cumin		½ teaspoon
tumeric		¼ teaspoon
cayenne		¼ teaspoon
salt		1½ teaspoons
flour	¾ oz	3 tablespoons
flour for coating, optional		
oil, for frying		

1. In food processor, purée chickpeas. Transfer to bowl.
2. Add other ingredients to chickpeas, mix well to blend.
3. Chill thoroughly.
4. Heat fat in skillet for deep-frying.
5. Form mixture into 1-inch balls or patties, 1 oz or about 1 tablespoon. If desired, coat with flour.

Felafel (Deep-fried Chickpea Balls); photo courtesy of Dorling Kindersley

6. Fry until golden brown, about 2 or 3 minutes. Drain on paper towels.
7. Serve in pita bread half topped with tahini sauce *(recipe follows)* and diced tomatoes and cucumbers.

YOGURT–TAHINI SAUCE

Yogurt and Sesame Paste Sauce

Number of Servings: 12
Serving Size: 2 oz
Total Yield: 1 lb, 9 oz

INGREDIENTS	WEIGHT	VOLUME
tahini	10 oz	1⅓ cups
yogurt, unflavored	10 oz	1⅓ cups
garlic, pulverized	¼ oz	2 cloves
lemon juice, fresh	2½ oz	5 tablespoons
parsley, finely minced	1 oz	¼ cup
scallions, finely minced	1 oz	¼ cup
salt		to taste
cayenne		couple of shakes
paprika		couple of shakes
cumin		¼ teaspoon

1. Mix all ingredients together. Blend well.
2. Refrigerate until needed. Correct seasonings.
3. Serve at room temperature with falafel in pita (3 tablespoons equals 2 oz, enough for half pita with falafel).

GRILLED FISH WITH CAPER VINAIGRETTE

Number of Servings: 12   Cooking Method: Grill
Serving Size: 4 to 5 oz cooked fish with
                1½ oz vinaigrette
Total Yield: 9 oz vinaigrette
                3 to 3¾ lb fish

Food Balance: Acid balanced
Wine Style: Wide variety—Pinot Grigio, Sauvignon Blanc, Pinot
    Blanc, soft Reds, Grenache
Example: Campanile Pinot Grigio or Wolf Blass Grenache

INGREDIENTS	WEIGHT	VOLUME
VINAIGRETTE:		
lemon juice, fresh	2 oz	¼ cup
salt		½ teaspoon
pepper, ground		¼ teaspoon
cayenne pepper, ground		couple of shakes, to taste
capers, drained, chopped	1½ oz	2 tablespoons
parsley, fresh, minced	½ oz	2 tablespoons
olive oil	5½ oz	¾ cup
sea bass, halibut fillets, or other white fish, 1-inch thick	4½ lb	
vegetable or olive oil	½ oz	1 tablespoon

1. Combine lemon juice, salt, pepper, and cayenne pepper in small bowl.
2. Whisk in olive oil, capers, and parsley. Refrigerate.
3. Preheat grill or broiler.
4. Brush fish lightly with oil on both sides.
5. Cook fish until opaque and tender, about 4 or 5 minutes per side.

Grilled Fish with Caper Vinaigrette; photo courtesy of The Norwegian Seafood Export Council—www. seafood.no. Photography by Kjell Ove Storvik

6. Whisk vinaigrette. Correct seasonings.
7. Serve fish hot, napped with vinaigrette. Four to 5 ounce portion needs about 1½ ounces (2 tablespoons) vinaigrette.

✗ BEEF, CARROT, AND SWEET POTATO TZIMMES

Beef Stew

Number of Servings: 11   Cooking Method: Braise
Serving Size: 8 oz
Total Yield: 5 lb, 11 oz

Food Balance: Sweet/protein
Wine Style: Soft and fruity Johannisberg Riesling, soft Chardonnay, Grenache, White Merlot, Shiraz
Example: Beringer Founders' Estate or Stone Cellars Shiraz

> Many prepare tzimmes as a vegetable stew consisting of carrots, prunes, and perhaps other vegetables without meat. Others cook tzimmes with a brisket instead of stew meat. After cooking, the brisket is removed, sliced, and served with the remaining vegetables as a side dish. To symbolically usher in a sweet New Year, this sweet dish graces many tables at Rosh Hashanah.

INGREDIENTS	WEIGHT	VOLUME
oil	½ oz	1 tablespoon
boneless chuck or stew meat, trimmed, cut into 1½-inch cubes	2 lb	
onions, diced	12 oz	2 large
carrots, peeled, cut into 1-inch chunks	1 lb, 4 oz	6 each
salt		½ teaspoon
water	about 32 oz, to cover	about 1 qt, to cover
potatoes, peeled, large dice	14 oz	2 large
sweet potatoes, peeled, large dice	1 lb, 6 oz	2 large
honey	3 oz	¼ cup
cinnamon		½ teaspoon
pepper		½ teaspoon
prunes, pitted	8 oz	1⅓ cups

GARNISH:

parsley, minced

1. Heat oil in pan, add meat, brown well on all sides. Remove meat from pan.
2. Add onions to pan, sauté until lightly brown.
3. Return meat to pan, add carrots, salt, and enough water to just cover.
4. Bring to boil, then cover and simmer over low heat, skimming once or twice, for 1 hour.
5. Add potatoes, honey, and seasonings to meat. Mix gently.
6. Bring to boil, partly cover, simmer 30 minutes. Meanwhile, cover prunes with hot water, soak about 30 minutes.
7. Gently stir stew once. Remove prunes from liquid, reserving liquid for later thinning if necessary. Add prunes to pan.
8. Uncover, simmer 30 minutes or until meat is very tender. To prevent sticking, shake pan occasionally, but do not stir or the vegetables may break.

9. Stew should be moist but not soupy. If too much liquid, let it stand for an hour to absorb excess. Use reserved prune water if more liquid is needed.
10. Serve, garnished with minced parsley, if desired.

CHOLENT

Sabbath Stew

Number of Servings: 8   Cooking Method: Braise
Serving Size: 4 oz meat
        9 oz vegetable and sauce
Total Yield: 10 lbs, 8 oz
        2 lbs, 1 oz meat
        8 lbs, 7 oz vegetable and sauce

Food Balance: Protein
Wine Style: Light- to medium-bodied, rich fruity Pinot Blanc or Chardonnay, White Zinfandel, Grenache, soft Zinfandel, Shiraz
Example: Greg Norman Chardonnay

INGREDIENTS	WEIGHT	VOLUME
dried beans, lima, great northern, or chickpeas, or as desired	8 oz	1⅓ cups
beef brisket	3 lbs, 9 oz	
flour	½ oz	2 tablespoons
oil	½ oz	1 tablespoon
onions, diced	1 lb	3 medium
garlic, smashed	¼ oz	2 cloves
salt	½ oz	2 teaspoons
pepper		½ teaspoons
paprika	¼ oz	1 tablespoon
cinnamon		¼ teaspoon
ginger		¼ teaspoon
barley	7½ oz	1 cup
turnips	8 oz	2 small to medium

INGREDIENTS	WEIGHT	VOLUME
carrots, peeled	7 oz	4 each
potatoes, peeled	2 lb	8 medium
boiling water		

1. Soak dried beans in water overnight.
2. Preheat oven to 325 degrees.
3. Dredge meat in flour. Heat oil in heavy pan, brown meat on all sides.
4. Place meat in roasting pan. Top with seasonings, onion, garlic, and barley. Surround with drained beans, turnips, carrots, and potatoes.
5. Cover with boiling water and bake for 3 to 4 hours, until meat is tender and beans are soft.
6. Remove meat, slice across grain and serve with bean and vegetable sauce.

Carrot Tzimmes (Honey Glazed Carrots); photo courtesy of Dorling Kindersley

CARROT TZIMMES

Honey Glazed Carrots

Number of Servings: 10
Serving Size: 4 oz
Total Yield: 2 lbs, 10 oz

Cooking Method: Boil

INGREDIENTS	WEIGHT	VOLUME
carrots, peeled, sliced, ½- to ¾-inch thick	3 lbs	
butter	2 oz	4 tablespoons
orange juice	5 oz	⅔ cup
salt		pinch
ginger, powdered		¾ teaspoon
honey	3 oz	4 tablespoons or ¼ cup

GARNISH:
parsley, fresh, minced

1. Heat butter in pan.
2. Add carrots, sauté a few minutes.
3. Add remaining ingredients, cover, simmer until ¾ tender, about 10 to 15 minutes.
4. Uncover, cook another 10 to 15 minutes, until carrots are tender and much of liquid evaporates.
5. Serve immediately, sprinkled with parsley.

POTATO LATKES

Potato Pancakes

Yield: Twenty-five 2-oz patties
Seventeen 3-oz patties
Total Yield: 3 lbs, 3 oz

Cooking Method: Sauté

INGREDIENTS	WEIGHT	VOLUME
baking potatoes, peeled (Idaho)	2½ lb	6 to 7 medium
onion, quartered	7 oz	1 large
eggs, lightly beaten	3½ oz	2 each
matzo meal	1¼ oz	¼ cup
salt	¼ oz	1 teaspoon
black pepper		¼ teaspoon
oil	8 oz, as needed	1 cup, as needed

SERVING SUGGESTIONS:

unsweetened applesauce
sour cream

1. Place onion in food processor, pulse a few times, until onion is diced. Transfer onion bits into small bowl.
2. Grate potatoes in food processor using medium-coarse shredding disk.
3. Place shredded potatoes in colander over large bowl, add onion and mix with hands, squeezing out potato liquid as much as possible.
4. Let mixture drip for a few minutes.
5. Pour out potato liquid from bowl under colander, but leave starch that clings to bowl.
6. Combine potato mixture, eggs, matzo meal, salt, and black pepper in bowl with potato starch, stir well.
7. Let mixture rest for about 10 minutes. Form potato mixture into desired size of patty.
8. Heat ¼-inch oil in skillet until hot. Add latkes, reduce heat to medium. Cook about 5 minutes per side, until golden brown. Drain on paper towels.
9. Serve with applesauce and/or sour cream.

Potato Latkes (Potato Pancakes); photo courtesy of the Idaho Potato Commission

NOODLE KUGEL

Noodle Pudding

Number of Servings: 19   Cooking Method: Bake
Serving Size: 4 oz
Total Yield: 4 lbs, 15 oz

INGREDIENTS	WEIGHT	VOLUME
noodles, wide or medium	12 oz	
apples, grated	1 lb, 2 oz	3 medium
sour cream	11 oz	1¼ cup
cottage cheese	12 oz	1½ cups
eggs	5 oz	3 each
sugar	2 oz	4 tablespoons
cinnamon		1 teaspoon
nutmeg		⅛ teaspoon
salt		¼ teaspoon
butter, melted	2 oz	4 tablespoons or ½ stick
orange juice	8 oz	1 cup

1. Cook noodles until *al dente*, done but still firm, drain, rinse with cold water.
2. Preheat oven to 350 degrees.
3. Pour melted butter into 9- by 12-inch pan, coating bottom and sides of pan.
4. Mix remaining ingredients in bowl. Correct seasonings.
5. Pour mixture into prepared pan, turn gently to mix in remaining butter.
6. Bake, uncovered, for about 50 minutes.

DRIED FRUIT COMPOTE

Number of Servings: 14   Cooking Method: Braise
Serving Size: 4 oz
Total Yield: 3 lbs, 11 oz

A single dried fruit or any combination of fruits can form the compote. Use red or white wine according to personal preference.

INGREDIENTS	WEIGHT	VOLUME
apricots, dried	12 oz	2 cups
dates, dried	10 oz	2 cups
prunes, dried	14 oz	2 cups
water	1 lb	2 cups
dry red or white wine	1 lb	2 cups
cinnamon stick		2 each
cloves, tied in cheesecloth		4 each
sugar	1¾ to 3½ oz, to taste	¼ to ½ cup, to taste

GARNISH:
almond slices, toasted
whipped cream, slightly sweetened

Dried Fruit Compote; photo courtesy of Dorling Kindersley

1. Combine all ingredients except sugar in nonreactive bowl or pan. Soak a couple of hours or overnight.
2. Place fruit and soaking liquid in saucepan, add sugar. Add more water, if necessary, so fruit is just covered.
3. Bring just to boil, reduce heat and simmer for 15 to 20 minutes, until tender.
4. Let cool to room temperature, then remove cinnamon stick and cloves. Refrigerate.
5. Serve cold, garnished with toasted almond slices and a dollop of whipped cream.

CHAPTER 11
China

By the end of this chapter, you will be able to

- Understand how Chinese philosophy is reflected in the cuisine
- Identify several provinces of China and explain characteristics of the cuisines found there
- Identify which grain predominates in the north and in the south and explain why
- Discuss various cooking techniques used in China and the advantages of those techniques
- Prepare a variety of Chinese dishes

HISTORY

Prehistoric people inhabited northern China more than 250,000 years ago. Written records document Chinese history from as early as the middle 1700s B.C. Having existed for more than 3,500 years, historians claim the world's oldest living civilization comes from China.

Proven by the discovery of ornate eating and drinking vessels dating from 3,500 years ago, archeologists know that formalized culinary practices took place at that time. Throughout history and into the present, China has exhibited high culinary awareness, and the culinary traits found in this country strongly reflect its culture.

Tenets of Chinese philosophy affected the food and cuisine as early as 1100 B.C. Foods were identified with two cosmic concepts, Yin-Yang and the Five Elements. Today, these two philosophies continue to influence the choice of foods that are combined to make both an individual dish and an entire meal. The Chinese believe proper food combinations are important to achieve balance and harmony in the body and spirit.

Briefly, yin represents the feminine, dark, and cool, while yang stands for the masculine, light, and hot. Every food is labeled either yin or yang. Although yin and yang are opposites, the important issue in food, art, and numerous areas of Chinese life remains the successful combining of these two opposite forces. The proper union of yin and yang elements creates harmony and balance. As a result, the Chinese possess a strong sense of balancing opposites. For example, sweet taste sensations are juxtaposed with sour tastes, and soft textures enhance crunchy ones. Careful consideration also extends to the colors of the foods composing a dish, the color of the foods in relation to the plate, as well as many other aspects of balance within each dish and the entire meal. All this leads to the Chinese meal structure, which consists of placing all of the dishes on the table at one time. This enables the diner to chose from an assortment of flavors, textures, and taste sensations among foods that combine to provide balance and harmony within the meal.

A second and similar type of philosophy leading to balance and harmony is found in the Five Elements. Those elements are water, wood, fire, earth, and metal. Considered the building blocks of life, these five elements or energy forces move constantly, changing continually as life itself. The Chinese believe putting them together in the proper combination creates the natural order of things, again leading to balance and harmony. Like other Chinese philosophies, the five elements extend to include many issues as diverse as medicine, martial arts, and food. Each of the five elements relates to one of the five taste sensations: water represents salt, wood represents sour, fire represents bitter, earth represents sweet, and metal represents spicy or pungent. Every food is assigned an element, and the goal is the proper combination of the foods (with their corresponding flavor sensations) to reach balance within each dish and the entire meal.

This theory of balance also exhibits itself with another philosophy, *tsai-fan*. *Tsai* refers to any cooked dish of protein or vegetable, and *fan* translates to "cooked rice" or grain. In *tsai-fan* as with the Five Elements and Yin-Yang, the proper balance is the goal. In order to achieve that balance, a meal must include grain with another food.

In the past as today, the Chinese strongly believe that eating should be pleasurable as well as healthful with the end-result in both cosmic principles and health reflecting the harmony and balance within the foods. Creating that harmony and balance in the foods leads to harmony and balance within the body and spirit.

During the period from 600 to 900 A.D., Chinese physicians began attributing many culinary principles to health. They recommended eating whole grains and sparse amounts of meat. Throughout history and now, many Chinese believe that foods cure diseases, as well as contain the key to good health and longevity.

Not arriving in China until the eighteenth century, sweet potatoes, corn, red chilies, and peanuts came to China from the New World. All these foods became well integrated into the Chinese cuisine with peanuts achieving particular importance as a source of oil. Because it possesses a high smoking point, peanut oil ranks as excellent oil for stir-frying over high heat, which is a frequently used cooking technique in China.

Various dynasties ruled from 1766 B.C. until 1911. In 221 B.C., the Qin dynasty united the many small states of China into an empire with a strong central government. Revolution occurred in 1911, ending thousands of years of rule by the dynasties. Turmoil ensued until 1949 when the Communists took control.

Although numerous invaders conquered parts of China throughout history, they left relatively little influence. Explorers and invaders tended to take more contributions from China home with them than they left behind. Generally, the Chinese chose to adopt little from foreigners.

TOPOGRAPHY

China occupies most of the eastern part of Asia. The third largest country in the world, only Russia and Canada have more landmass.

A land of many contrasts, some of the driest deserts and highest mountains as well as very fertile farmland exist in China. This country consists of a vast amount of land, containing diverse topography, climates, and terrains. Subartic regions prevail in the north, and tropical lowlands comprise the south. The east contains fertile plains, but extensive desert makes up much of the west. Forests and fertile farmland cover a large portion of the northeast. Mountains lie in the east central region; the west has dry, rocky plateaus and mountains; the Himalaya Mountains loom on the southwestern border; and the northwest is desert.

Wild differences in climatic conditions follow the varying terrain. The north and west endure long, hard, cold winters, while the central and southern areas experience mild to warm winters. Hot, humid summers reign in southern Manchuria, but the arid northwest has hot, dry summers. Tibet and the Himalayas lie in the southwestern section, which experiences harsh winters and windy conditions prevailing throughout the year due to the high elevation.

Lakes dot the landscape, and many rivers including the Yangtze and the Yellow Rivers run through China. The Pacific Ocean borders on the eastern side. As a result of this wealth of bodies of water, freshwater fish and seafood are available in many areas.

Ingredients and Foods Commonly Used Throughout the Cuisine of China Include:

- rice
- wheat and millet
- peanuts
- cabbages, greens, and bok choy
- carrots
- sweet potatoes
- water chestnuts, bamboo shoots, and bean sprouts
- mushrooms and fungi
- tofu and soybeans
- seafood—both fresh and dried
- pork and poultry
- onions, garlic, and spring onions
- ginger
- soy sauce
- rice wine and rice vinegar
- tea

COOKING METHODS

The most well-known Chinese cooking method, *chao* or stir-frying, developed as a way to save scarce cooking fuel. Cutting the food into small pieces and cooking rapidly over high heat required the least amount of cooking time and, therefore, used less fuel. Besides cooking quickly, this method has two other distinct advantages: stir-frying preserves the texture of the food, and it retains valuable nutrients.

Wok; photo courtesy of Dorling Kindersley

Wok; photo courtesy of Dorling Kindersley

Used for stir-frying, a *wok* is a pan with sloping sides and a rounded bottom. The rounded bottom eliminates corners where food might stick. Stir-frying involves heating oil in the wok until very hot, adding the foods in the order of their cooking time (beginning with the items requiring the most time to cook), meanwhile constantly stirring the food while it cooks quickly over high heat. Vegetables are cooked until done, but still crisp.

Another frying technique, deep-frying appears often. Again, this method conserves fuel as foods submerged in hot fat cook quickly. Sometimes, deep-frying is combined with another method; for example, an item might be deep-fried to produce a crisp crust before steaming.

Poaching, parboiling, and steaming are used for the cooking of soups, stews, rice, and many other items. Steaming appears as a method for cooking whole duck, chicken, or fish, as well as individual items such as steamed buns or dumplings. Bamboo steamers, which hold the foods during the steaming process, can be stacked on top of each other in a wok. This facilitates steaming several foods at one time, another way of conserving the limited heating fuel.

Sand-pot or clay-pot cooking is actually braising. The traditional pot used for this method resembles a squat, earthenware pot with a lid. Commonly seen throughout China, this, like all the cooking methods, is often combined using more than one cooking technique with a food item to alter the texture and taste.

THE UBIQUITOUS WOK

Because of the limited amount of available fuel for cooking, the wok was developed. The design of this bowl-shaped, metal pan allows food to cook quickly yet evenly. The pan's round shape eliminates corners where food can become stuck, overcook, or burn. Stirring the food in a wok causes the food to sweep the sides of the pan in a circular motion, almost a type of centrifugal force movement. Furthermore, the wok can accommodate a stack of steamers or fit a whole fish, which gently curls conforming to the curves of the wok. Although the burners on Oriental stoves resemble deep wells that steadily hold the round-bottomed pan, the wok sits in a ring over the burner on western stoves.

Bamboo Steamer; photo courtesy of Dorling Kindersley

Pickling, smoking, and wind drying became popular during the T'ang Dynasty (618 to 906 A.D.) as methods of preserving food for use during the long winter. Preserved, smoked, and pickled foods are still widely used.

REGIONS

Most of the population resides in the eastern third of China. The majority of large cities are found in that region.

With different climates, terrain, and growing conditions, wheat grows well in the north of China while rice thrives in the south. As a result, wheat in the form of noodles, dumplings, and sometimes bread functions as the grain staple in the north. A symbol of longevity, many think noodles were actually invented in China. People in the south eat rice instead, consuming at least one pound of rice each day. Evidence exists of rice growing in China 5,000 years ago. The symbol of life and fertility, many western cultures have embraced this philosophy and throw rice at the bride and groom after a wedding.

Great differences exist among the regional cuisines of China. Overwhelmingly, the cuisine of each region depends on the food that grows or is raised there. Generally, favorable growing conditions result in more crops flourishing in the areas south of the Yangtze River. Lots of shrimp, crab, and fish are consumed in the eastern and southeastern coastal areas. The provinces of Sichuan and Hunan prepare spicy foods, whereas many other areas prefer mild or even bland dishes. The cooking method of choice throughout the southern regions remains stir-frying.

The northern regions are hampered by long, cold winters and dry, arid conditions, resulting in limited crops; however, the summer yields abundant produce including tomatoes, cucumbers, eggplant, pears, grapes, and persimmons. The cuisine of the north tends to be lighter than the other areas of China. Simple yet elegant describes this food, as opposed to the cooking of the south. Steaming and poaching are often preferred cooking methods, preserving the natural flavors of the food.

In the northern region, meat is usually marinated, then barbecued, boiled, or roasted rather than fried. Lamb, a carryover from the nomadic Mongolian tribes of central Asia, remains popular in this region. Duck and chicken also appear frequently. Peking (or Beijing) duck hails from the north and consists of crisp duck slices accompanied by rolled pancakes and a sweet sauce. Sweet and sour dishes are a favorite here.

Due to the climate, wheat and millet grow in the north, not rice. So noodles, steamed buns, and egg rolls predominate. Hot peppers do not appear here; garlic, onions, soy sauce, and ginger are the flavorings of choice. Soy sauce appears everywhere, in cooking and as a dipping sauce. A variety of dipping sauces accompanies the plainly cooked foods.

The eastern coastal regions enjoy the best weather in China with mild weather defining each season. The combination of fertile farmland, abundant rainfall, and a good climate produces a profusion of crops. Ample coastline, lakes, and rivers provide abundant seafood and freshwater fish with shrimp, crab, and duck appearing frequently. More sugar is used in the cooking of this area than any other, and soy sauce appears less. The provinces lying in this region generate diverse cuisines including rich stocks, gravies and sauces, soups, and stews. With such a bounty of foods available, the emphasis lies on very fresh tasting foods. Preferred flavorings include ginger, green onions, and soy sauce. Cooking in this region often includes rice wine or rice vinegar. Rice thrives in the eastern region, particularly near the Yangtze River.

Dishes of the central region (Szechwan) exhibit use of red chilies as well as garlic, spring onions, and ginger. Other flavorings used in this highly spiced cuisine include rice vinegar and peanuts, as well as sesame oil, seeds, and paste. Hot and sour soup exemplifies the flavors found in the cooking of this region. Many foods are marinated before cooking. Foods preserved by smoking, salting, drying, and pickling appear frequently. When planning meals, cooks from this region think about featuring the five elements or taste sensations—sweet, sour, salty, pungent or spicy, and bitter. With the exclusion of pungent, the remaining four taste sensations are currently defined by scientists as those discerned by the human palate.

Located in the south-southwest, Yunnan experiences much isolation as a result of the mountainous terrain. With ample open land, game abounds. Known for their ham, many consider it the finest in China. All sorts of nuts, including peanuts, walnuts, pine nuts, and chestnuts, are incorporated into dishes from this region.

Dim sum, snack foods eaten for lunch or any time throughout the day, originated in the southern region of Canton. Available in a whole range of forms and flavors, *dim sum* includes soups, steamed buns, stuffed dumplings, sweet and savory pastries, and much more. *Dim sum* resembles Spanish *tapas* or Middle Eastern *mezze*.

Rice vinegar, ginger, and spring onions flavor many foods in the south, where the natural flavors of the food are emphasized. Chefs and cooks give a lot of consideration to the visuals of a dish as well as its texture. Crisp vegetables pair with tender meats or fish to produce a variety of textures within each dish. Cooking from the southern region features many sauces. Garnishes adorn plates and platters, and the colors of the food command much attention.

With several rivers and close proximity to the sea, seafood appears in many dishes, often mixed with meats or vegetables. Oyster sauce and shrimp paste flavor lots of dishes.

Most agree the cuisine of the south serves the fanciest, most sophisticated dishes of all the regional cuisines. Certainly, the widest range of recipes comes from this area. Some compare the Cantonese cuisine with that of France.

AREAS OF CHINA

North—Inner Mongolia
Northeast—Manchuria, Peking (Beijing)
Northwest—Xinjiang
Central—Szechwan, Hunan
East—Shanghai, Fukien
Southwest—Tibet
South—Canton, Yunnan

CUISINE

Many claim the Chinese diet is the most nutritionally balanced diet in the world. Certainly, throughout their history, medicine and food have been linked closely. The Chinese believe diet and food directly influence health and disease, so one's diet determines one's health.

Preparation and cooking remain two distinctly different aspects of food production here. Differing from western cookery, the time required to prepare the food for Chinese cooking usually is more than the actual time needed to cook the food. Both meat and vegetables are meticulously chopped into small, uniform pieces to ensure quick and even cooking. The importance of evenly sized pieces cannot be overstated because a variety of sizes results in overcooked and undercooked ingredients. In addition, all ingredients must be prepared before the cooking begins because the actual cooking process happens very rapidly.

Nothing is wasted in the Chinese kitchen. Literally all parts of the animal are consumed, from the beak to the feet. Seafood shells and heads go into the stockpot, even if the pot contains chicken stock. Leftover dishes are transformed into new creations with no resemblance to their former identity.

The most important type of food remains grains followed by vegetables. As stated before, the grain of choice depends on the region, with wheat preferred in the north and rice in the south. Besides grains, the most prevalent foods in the diet include soybeans, cabbages, all sorts of greens, onions, and garlic.

Small amounts of meat and seafood are added to vegetables. Consumed at every meal throughout the south, rice is eaten with vegetables and/or available protein, but not alone. Generally, bites of rice alternate with bites of the other food items. Although diners might put some of the sauce from a dish on the rice, the Chinese do not mix their food directly with the rice. Incidentally, the Chinese prefer a long grain variety of rice as opposed to short grain.

Widely consumed, tofu or soybean curd functions as a major source of protein. Pork and poultry remain the most popular meats. As a result of the huge fishing industry, fish and shellfish play a significant role in the Chinese diet.

Vegetables are never boiled, rather their cooking includes stir-frying and then perhaps braising. Crisp, *al dente* vegetables prevail, not the limp vegetables commonly served in many western cuisines.

China produces more rice, wheat, and pears than any other country in the world. Many other foods grow well, including sweet potatoes, cabbage, carrots, corn, potatoes, beets, tomatoes, apples, sugar cane, peanuts, soybeans, millet, and tea. The Chinese diet is rich in fruits and vegetables.

Dairy products play an almost nonexistent role in this cuisine. A number of ingredients not used in the western cuisines, including shark's fins, tiger lily buds, snake, bear paws, and sea cucumbers, appear in Chinese dishes.

The Chinese cuisine provides ample vegetarian dishes for Buddhists, a religious sect that forbids meat consumption. Chinese Moslems' diet resembles the kosher foods of Israel. Pork and seafood without scales or backbone are not allowed.

Cornstarch is the most often used thickening agent in China as opposed to the flour used in the majority of western dishes. This eliminates the *roux* used so frequently in the west and replaces it with a mixture of cornstarch and water combined with other flavorings.

Common flavorings and condiments used in Chinese cookery include soy sauce, rice wine, rice vinegar, bean paste, plum sauce, oyster sauce, sugar, salt, ginger, garlic, and sesame oil. The basis of several products, soybeans make soy sauce, fermented beans, bean paste, and *hoisin*. Seasonings and condiments are used to enhance the natural flavors of the foods, not to change them. Some of the frequently used spices include star anise, a licorice-flavored spice; ginger; Szechwan pepper; and five-spice powder composed of fennel, cloves, anise seed, Szechwan pepper, and cinnamon. Ginger comes in several forms, including the fresh root, crystallized, and powder. Marinades appear frequently, both to impart flavor and tenderize before the quick cooking.

Throughout China, cooks pay a lot of attention to the balance of flavors, colors, aromas, and textures in food. The contrast between soft and smooth foods, hard and crunchy, salty and sweet, and so on creates that highly prized balance and harmony, as well as making the food more interesting and appealing for the diner.

When courses are served, their order differs greatly from those found in western meals. Soups may appear more than once throughout the meal, functioning as a palate cleanser between courses in a formal dinner. Dessert might be served in the middle of the meal and hors d'oeuvres appear where those flavors fit. Again, the balance of flavors and textures throughout the meal rather than a certain course in a specific order remains the important concept.

The aesthetics of food has always been very important to the Chinese. Both simple and intricate fruit and vegetable carvings often garnish plates and buffet tables.

Depending on the region, a typical Chinese breakfast consists of rice porridge (*congee*), chicken noodle soup, or a doughnutlike fried pastry. Egg rolls or dumplings filled with meat or shrimp are served for lunch. The main meal includes vegetables with small amounts of meat or seafood, soup, and rice or noodles (depending on the region).

A typical dinner includes several dishes and often more than one type of soup. Normally, all dishes are placed in the center of the table, and diners take as much as desired from each dish. A festive dinner will feature ten or twelve dishes. Eating utensils include chopsticks and soup spoons.

The most popular beverage throughout China remains tea. Besides being an important part of daily life and ceremonies, numerous varieties of tea have medicinal uses. Rice wine also becomes incorporated into ceremonies and rituals. In fact, brides and grooms drink rice wine during a Chinese wedding.

Review Questions

1. Which grain predominates in the north and south? Why? How is it prepared (what form does it take)?
2. Name four provinces or regions and explain the differences in the flavorings and cooking of each.

REGION	AREA	WEATHER	TOPOGRAPHY	FOODS
North	Beijing, Shantung, Honan	Long, cold winters; dry, arid, summers; windy	Desert, mountains	Duck, lamb, chicken, seafood, wheat, corn, millet, peanuts, sorghum, cabbage, greens, fruits
East	Shanghai, Fukien	Mild to semitropical	Coast, plains, fertile farmland, Yangtze River, rolling hills, lakes	Seafood, freshwater fish, pork, poultry, rice, soy sauce, vegetables, fruits
West	Tibet	Long, cold winters; cool summers; windy, dry	Mountains, rocky plateaus, desert	Yak, barley
Central	Szechwan	Semitropical, hot, humid summers; mild winters	Mountains, valleys, fertile farmland, Yangtze River	Game, pork, poultry, seafood, soybeans, rice, wheat, corn, hot peppers, legumes, fungus, herbs, fruits
	Hunan	Hot, humid summers; mild winters	Fertile farmland, lakes	Meat, fish, poultry, rice, vegetables
South	Canton	Hot, humid summers; mild winters	Mountains, valleys, fertile land, coast, rivers	Seafood, fish, poultry, game, pork, rice, dim sum, vegetables, sweet potatoes, fruits, tea
	Yunnan	Mild	Mountains, rivers, lakes	Freshwater fish, ham, game, nuts, vegetables

3. Explain yin and yang and its affect on the cuisine of China.
4. Describe stir-frying, including the preparation of the food and the actual cooking process.
5. What are the advantages of stir-frying as a cooking method?

Glossary

chao Cooking technique known as stir-frying

congee Rice (or millet or barley) porridge served for breakfast, to babies, and to ill people

dim sum Snack foods eaten for lunch or any time throughout the day; originated in the southern region of Canton, can include soups, steamed buns, stuffed dumplings, sweet and savory pastries, and much more

hoisin A sweet and spicy sauce made from soybeans used in cooking, marinades, and dips

tofu Soybean curd; a cheeselike substance made from soybeans; a complete protein

tsai-fan Protein or vegetable served with rice

wok A pan with sloping sides and a rounded bottom used for stir-frying and other cooking methods

Yin-Yang Complex philosophy that affects food, art, and other aspects of Chinese life; deals with combining opposites to achieve balance and harmony;

yin represents the feminine or dark while yang stands for the masculine or light; the important issue remains the successful combining of these two forces to achieve the harmony and balance in the food, art, or any medium which leads to balance and harmony in the body and spirit

CH 'UN-CHÜAN

Spring Rolls

Number of Servings: 14 spring rolls
Serving Size: 1¼ oz filling per spring roll
Total Yield: 1 lbs, 1½ oz filling

Cooking Method: Deep-fry, sauté (stir-fry)

Food Balance: Protein
Wine Suggestion: Light- to medium-bodied Sauvignon Blanc, Chardonnay, Pinot Noir, Merlot
Example: Beringer Founders' Estate Chardonnay

INGREDIENTS	WEIGHT	VOLUME
FILLING:		
mushrooms, forest or any variety, dried	¼ oz	4 each
cornstarch	½ oz	1 tablespoon
water	1 oz	2 tablespoons
oil	1 oz	2 tablespoons
pork, ground	8 oz	
rice wine or dry sherry	½ oz	1 tablespoon
soy sauce	1 oz	2 tablespoons
sugar		½ teaspoon
shrimp, shelled, deveined, finely diced	6¾ oz (8 oz in shells)	
Chinese cabbage	7½ oz	2 cups
celery, finely diced	9½ oz	2 cups or 5 stalks
bean sprouts, fresh	8 oz	
sesame oil		¼ teaspoon
salt	¼ oz	1 teaspoon
spring roll wrappers		
oil, peanut, or other	for deep-frying	

FILLING:

1. Place mushrooms in bowl, cover with warm water. Let soak for 30 minutes. Drain mushrooms, dice.
2. Mix cornstarch with 1 oz (2 tablespoons) cold water. Set aside.
3. Heat ½ oz (1 tablespoon) oil in wok until hot.
4. Add pork, stir-fry about 2 minutes, until no longer pink.
5. Add rice wine, ½ oz (1 tablespoon) soy sauce, sugar, shrimp, and mushrooms, stir-fry for another minute, until shrimp turns pink.
6. Remove to bowl and set aside.
7. Heat remaining ½ oz (1 tablespoon) oil in wok until hot.
8. Add cabbage and celery, stir-fry 4 or 5 minutes, add bean sprouts and salt. Mix well.
9. Add pork mixture to pan, stir to mix well.
10. Cook over medium heat, stirring constantly, until liquid starts to boil.

Ch 'Un-Chüan (Spring Rolls); photo courtesy of Dorling Kindersley

11. Add cornstarch mixture and sesame oil, stir constantly until slightly thickened and mixture has glaze.
12. Transfer to bowl, cool to room temperature. Refrigerate if not using immediately.

ASSEMBLY:

1. Place wrapper on table with point up. Place about 1¼ oz (¼ cup) filling diagonally across center of wrapper.
2. Fold lower end of wrapper over filling, tucking point under filling.
3. Using finger or pastry brush, wet exposed edges of wrapper with cold water.
4. Fold side flaps over filling, press gently to seal.
5. Roll wrapper into cylinder, gently pressing edges to seal.
6. Place filled spring rolls on sheet pan and cover well. Refrigerate until ready to fry.
7. Heat oil in wok for deep-frying (375 degrees).
8. Place 5 or 6 spring rolls in hot oil, fry for about 3 or 4 minutes, until crisp and golden brown.
9. Drain well. Repeat with remaining rolls.
10. Serve accompanied by hot mustard sauce and duck sauce or hot chili sauce and soy sauce.

CELERY IN GARLIC VINAIGRETTE (Hunan)

Total Yield: 1 lb

Food Balance: Sweet, sour, and spicy
Wine Style: Soft and fruity Riesling, Chenin Blanc, Gewürztraminer, Blush wines
Example: Beringer White Zinfandel or Gewürztraminer

INGREDIENTS	WEIGHT	VOLUME
celery, fresh, inner stalks, cut into 2½- by ½-inch sticks, strings removed	1 lb	5 cups
kosher salt	¼ oz	1 teaspoon
sugar		½ teaspoon
VINAIGRETTE:		
soy sauce		1 tablespoon plus 2 tea-spoons
sugar	1 oz	2 tablespoons
sesame oil	1¼ oz	2 tablespoons
rice vinegar		1½ teaspoons
hot chili oil		½ teaspoon
garlic, minced	¼ oz	1½ teaspoons or 2 cloves

> Almost like a pickle, this celery accompanies other dishes, becomes part of a salad, or is served with drinks.

1. Mix celery with salt and sugar in bowl. Let stand at room temperature for 40 minutes, tossing occasionally.
2. Whisk ingredients for vinaigrette in bowl until slightly thickened. Let rest 10 minutes.
3. Drain celery, rinse with cool water, drain on paper towels to dry.
4. Place celery in bowl, pour on vinaigrette. Mix well.
5. Refrigerate for 3 to 4 hours, mixing often.
6. Serve slightly chilled, as an accompaniment to other dishes.

SUAN-LA-T'ANG (Szechuan)

Hot and Sour Soup

Number of Servings: 11
Serving Size: 8 oz
Total Yield: 5 lbs, 13 oz

Cooking Method: Boil, braise

Food Balance: Acidic
Wine Style: Dry, crisp acidity, Pinot Grigio, Sauvignon Blanc, Chablis, Pinot Noir, cool climate Reds
Example: Meridian Vineyards Pinot Noir

INGREDIENTS	WEIGHT	VOLUME
mushrooms, dried Chinese	½ oz	8 each
cornstarch	2 oz	¼ cup
water, cold	4 oz	½ cup
chicken stock	4 lbs	2 qts or 8 cups
soy sauce	2 oz	¼ cup
bamboo shoots, canned, julienne	4 oz	1 cup
pork, boneless, trimmed, julienne	8 oz	
tofu (bean curd), firm, ½-inch dice	1 lb, 4 oz	
pepper		½ teaspoon
vinegar, rice or white	2 oz	¼ cup
egg, lightly beaten	3½ oz	2 each
sesame seed oil		4 teaspoons
hot oil, *optional*	to taste	

> Add chili oil for a spicy soup.

Suan-La-T'ang (Hot and Sour Soup)

INGREDIENTS	WEIGHT	VOLUME
GARNISH:		
scallion, including green, finely sliced	1 oz	2 each

1. Place mushrooms in bowl, cover with 1 cup warm water. Let soak for 30 minutes.
2. Mix cornstarch with 4 oz (½ cup) cold water. Set aside.
3. Drain mushrooms, julienne.
4. Combine stock, soy sauce, mushrooms, bamboo shoots, and pork in large pot.
5. Bring to boil, reduce heat, cover pan and simmer for 3 minutes.
6. Add bean curd, vinegar, and pepper. Bring to boil.
7. Stir cornstarch mixture, pour into soup. Stir until soup thickens.
8. Slowly pour in egg, stirring gently.
9. Stir in sesame seed oil.
10. Taste to balance flavors, correct seasonings. For more spice, add hot oil. To make it more sour, add vinegar.
11. Serve, garnished with scallions.

SU-MI-T'ANG

Velvet Corn Soup

Number of Servings: 9   Cooking Method: Boil, braise
Serving Size: 8 oz
Total Yield: 4 lbs, 8 oz

Food Balance: Sweet and protein
Wine Style: Soft and fruity Viognier, Pinot Blanc, Riesling, White
   Zinfandel
Example: Château St. Jean Pinot Blanc

INGREDIENTS	WEIGHT	VOLUME
cornstarch	½ to ¾ oz	1 to 1½ table-spoons
oil	½ oz	1 tablespoon
cold water	1 to 1½ oz	2 to 3 table-spoons
scallions, chopped, green and white	¾ oz	3 tablespoons, 1 each
ginger, fresh, peeled, finely minced		1 teaspoon
ham, cured, finely chopped	1½ oz	¼ cup
Chinese rice wine or dry sherry	1 oz	2 tablespoons
chicken stock	2 lbs, 8 oz	5 cups
cream-style corn	1 lb, 14 oz	2 each 15-oz cans
salt		to taste
egg whites	2 oz	2 each

GARNISH:

cilantro, fresh, minced

1. Mix cornstarch with 1 to 1½ oz (2 to 3 tablespoons) cold water in
   small bowl. Set aside.
2. Heat oil in pot until hot.
3. Over medium high heat, add scallion and ginger, stir for 15 seconds, add ham, stir another 15 seconds, add rice wine.
4. Add stock, stir, add corn, stirring often, heat until almost boiling.
5. Over medium heat, stir cornstarch mixture into soup, cook over
   low heat for several minutes to thicken slightly. Add salt, if
   needed, correct seasonings.
6. Beat egg whites until frothy.
7. Pour egg whites in thin, steady stream into soup, pouring from
   about 6 inches above pot.
8. Stir once gently, halfway through adding, then again at end.
9. Serve in bowls, garnish with cilantro.

HÜN-T'UN-T'ANG

Wonton Soup

Number of Servings: 11 to 13 servings   Cooking Method: Boil
Serving Size: 5 to 6 wontons
Total Yield: at least 67 wontons
           16¼ oz filling,
           ¼ oz filling in each wonton

Food Balance: Protein
Wine Style: Light- to medium-bodied, fruity Gewürztraminer, Char-
   donnay, Pinot Noir, Beaujolais
Example: Meridian Vineyards Chardonnay or Pinot Noir

> *There are a number of different ways to fold wontons; two are described here. Also, wonton wrappers vary in size. The amount of filling will depend on the size of the wrapper. Each wonton needs only a little filling.*

INGREDIENTS	WEIGHT	VOLUME
wonton wrappers		
water, cold		
FILLING:		
ground pork	12 oz	
soy sauce	½ oz	1 tablespoon
ginger, fresh, peeled, minced		¾ teaspoon
scallions, sliced ³⁄₁₆-inch thick	½ oz	1 each
spinach, cooked, chopped, squeezed dry or use chopped frozen	4 oz	1 each 10 oz frozen or 6 tablespoons

chicken soup (depending on serving size, prepare 8 oz per person)

GARNISH:
spinach, fresh, chiffonade

FILLING:
1. Combine all ingredients except spinach, mix well.
2. Mix in spinach.
3. Refrigerate until ready to use.

ASSEMBLY:
1. Place wonton wrapper on table, moisten edges with cold water.
2. Place about ¼ oz (¾ to 1 teaspoon) filling just below center of wrapper.
3. Fold one side over filling, tucking edge under filling.
4. Roll into cylinder, leaving ½-inch point of wrapper unrolled.
5. Moisten ends with cold water.
6. Using both hands, grasp two ends of the cylinder and pull them behind roll until ends overlap slightly.
7. Pinch ends firmly together.
8. Place formed wonton on sheet pan and cover.

OR

1. Place wonton wrapper on table, moisten edges with cold water.
2. Place about ¼ oz (¾ to 1 teaspoon) filling just below center of wrapper.
3. Fold one side over filling to form triangle. Press to seal seams well.
4. Moisten two corners across from each other with cold water.
5. Using both hands, grasp those two corners, twist to bring them behind wonton.
6. Pinch firmly together to seal.
7. Place formed wonton on sheet pan and cover.

COOK:
1. Bring large pot of water to boil.
2. Add wontons, return to boil.
3. Reduce to medium heat, cook uncovered for about 5 minutes, until tender but still *al dente*.
4. Drain wontons.
5. Add wontons and spinach to hot chicken soup.
6. Return to boil. Serve.

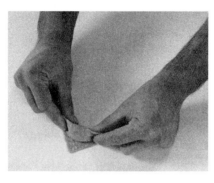

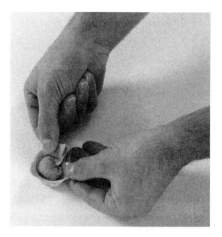

First fold of wrapper over filling; photo courtesy of Dorling Kindersley

Folding the wonton; photo courtesy of Dorling Kindersley

Bending the wonton; photo courtesy of Dorling Kindersley

Boiling the wontons; photo courtesy of Dorling Kindersley

Hün-T'un-T'ang (Wonton Soup); photo courtesy of Dorling Kindersley

PICKLED CABBAGE PEKING STYLE (Peking)

Number of Servings: 15
Serving Size: 2 oz
Total Yield: 1 lb, 14 oz

INGREDIENTS	WEIGHT	VOLUME
white cabbage, cored, shredded finely	2 lbs	1 small head
salt	1¼ oz	2 tablespoons
ginger root, peeled, fine julienne	½ oz	¾-inch slice
sugar	3¼ oz	5 tablespoons
oil, peanut or corn	1¼ oz	2½ tablespoons

Serve this as a spicy condiment to accompany other dishes.

Pickled Cabbage Peking Style

INGREDIENTS	WEIGHT	VOLUME
sesame oil	1¼ oz	2½ table-spoons
red chilies, dried, seeded, minced		3 each
Szechwan peppercorns		1 teaspoon
rice vinegar	2½ oz	5 tablespoons

1. Place cabbage in large bowl, sprinkle with salt, mix well, set aside for 2 or 3 hours.
2. Squeeze excess water from cabbage, place in clean bowl.
3. Sprinkle sugar over cabbage, place ginger in bunch on top of cabbage in center of bowl.
4. Heat both oils until very hot in small saucepan over high heat, remove from heat, add chilies and peppercorns.
5. Pour hot mixture over ginger first and then cabbage in bowl.
6. Pour on vinegar, mix well.
7. Refrigerate for 2 or 3 hours before serving. Correct seasonings.

BEAN CURD AND PORK (Szechwan, West)

Number of Servings: 10   Cooking Method: Deep-fry, sauté (stir-fry)
Serving Size: 8 oz
Total Yield: 5 lbs

Food Balance: Protein, sweet and spicy
Wine Style: Light and fruity Sauvignon Blanc, soft Chardonnay, Gamay—Beaujolais, and soft Cabernet
Example: Stone Cellars Cabernet Sauvignon

INGREDIENTS	WEIGHT	VOLUME
dried mushrooms, black	¾ oz	9 each
tofu, soybean curd, firm, cut into 1-inch cubes	2 lb, 4 oz	
pork, lean, julienne	9 oz	
frying oil, peanut or corn for deep-frying		
green pepper, finely diced	14 oz	3 medium
carrot, peeled, thinly sliced	6¾ oz	3 small
bamboo shoots, thinly sliced	4½ oz	2¼ cups
scallions, diced	3 oz	6 each
ginger, fresh, peeled, minced	¾ oz	9 slices
red chili peppers, minced	¾ oz or to taste	3 to 6 each or to taste

MARINADE:

sugar	½ oz	1 tablespoon
light soy sauce	½ oz	1 tablespoon
rice wine or dry sherry	½ oz	1 tablespoon
cornstarch	1 oz	2 tablespoons
oil, peanut or corn	1 oz	2 tablespoons

SAUCE:

cornstarch	1 oz	2 tablespoons
water, cold	2 oz	4 tablespoons
chicken stock	1 lb, 8 oz	3 cups
dark soy sauce	1½ oz	3 tablespoons
oyster sauce	4½ oz	6 tablespoons
rice vinegar	½ oz	1 tablespoon
sugar	1 oz	2 tablespoons
sesame oil	1½ oz	1 tablespoon

Bean Curd and Pork

1. Soak mushrooms in warm water for 30 minutes. Remove from water and cut into quarters.
2. Place tofu cubes on paper towels to remove moisture.
3. Mix marinade ingredients in bowl, mix well. Add pork, mix well, refrigerate for 15 minutes.
4. Mix cornstarch with 2 oz (4 tablespoons) cold water in bowl. Add remaining sauce ingredients, mix well. Set aside.
5. Deep-fry tofu in hot fat in wok for about 2 minutes, until lightly colored and crisp. Place on paper towels to drain.
6. Remove all but 1 oz (2 tablespoons) oil from wok. Stir-fry pork until pink color is gone. Remove from wok.
7. Stir-fry green peppers and carrots about 1 minute.
8. Add bamboo shoots, remaining vegetables, ginger, and chili peppers, stir-fry 1 to 1½ minutes.
9. Add tofu, meat, and sauce mixture. Bring to boil, stirring constantly.
10. Lower heat, simmer for 5 minutes, until tofu and meat are tender. Correct seasonings.
11. Serve with rice.

KUNG PAO CHICKEN (Szechwan)

Spicy Chicken with Peanuts

Number of Servings: 10   Cooking Method: Sauté (stir-fry)
Serving Size: 8 oz
Total Yield: 5 lbs, 5 oz

Food Balance: Spicy, protein
Wine Style: Soft and fruity Gewürztraminer, White Zinfandel, soft Chardonnay
Example: Stone Cellars Chardonnay

INGREDIENTS	WEIGHT	VOLUME
MARINADE:		
soy sauce	3 oz	6 tablespoons
rice wine or dry sherry	3 oz	6 tablespoons
sugar	½ oz	1 tablespoon
cornstarch	¾ oz	1½ tablespoons
scallion, finely chopped	¾ oz	3 tablespoons
ginger, fresh, peeled, minced	¾ oz	1½ tablespoons
chicken, trimmed, boneless cut into bite-sized pieces	2 lb, 13 oz	
oil, peanut or other high temperature	6 oz	¾ cup
chili peppers, red, fresh, quartered, seeds removed		12 each
peanuts, shelled, skinned	10½ oz	2 cups
scallions, sliced ¾-inch	3¾ oz	12 each
garlic, peeled, sliced	2¼ oz	18 cloves
rice vinegar	1 oz	2 tablespoons
SAUCE:		
chicken stock	1 lb	2 cups
soy sauce	3 oz	6 tablespoons

Kung Pao Chicken (Spicy Chicken with Peanuts); photo
courtesy of Dorling Kindersley

INGREDIENTS	WEIGHT	VOLUME
rice wine or dry sherry	1½ oz	3 tablespoons
sugar	¾ oz	1½ table- spoons
cornstarch	¾ oz	1½ table- spoons

1. Combine all ingredients for marinade in bowl, add chicken, mix well, refrigerate for 20 minutes.
2. Combine all ingredients for sauce, mix and set aside.
3. Heat oil until hot. Fry chili peppers until dark brown. Remove from oil, set aside.
4. Fry peanuts until golden. Remove, drain well.
5. Remove all but thick coating of oil (about 2 oz or 4 tablespoons).
6. Heat oil, sauté chicken for 2 minutes.
7. Add scallions and garlic, sauté for 30 seconds, add chili peppers and sauce mixture.
8. Cover, simmer until chicken is tender, about 2 minutes.
9. Stir in vinegar. Correct seasonings.
10. Stir in peanuts. Serve with rice.

HOT BEAN THREAD NOODLES WITH SHREDDED PORK

Number of Servings: 9
Serving Size: 8 oz
Total Yield: 4 lbs, 13 oz

Cooking Method: Sauté (stir-fry)

Food Balance: Spicy protein
Wine Style: Soft and fruity Pinot Gris, Pinot Blanc, White Zinfandel, Rosé
Example: Beringer Rosé de Saignee

INGREDIENTS	WEIGHT	VOLUME
bean thread vermicelli	7½ oz	
mushrooms, dried black	¾ oz	9 each
pork, boneless, shredded	7½ oz	
oil, peanut or corn	3 oz	6 tablespoons
green pepper, seeded, cut into narrow strips	1 lb, 2 oz	3 each
onion, peeled, cut into narrow strips from root to top end, separated	15 oz	3 medium
chili peppers, fresh, red, seeds and ribs removed, cut into narrow strips	½ to ¾ oz	3 to 5 each
ginger, fresh, minced	¾ oz	6 slices
garlic, peeled, minced	¾ oz	3 teaspoons or 6 cloves
cilantro, fresh, minced	½ to ¾ oz	2 to 3 tablespoons
MARINADE:		
rice wine or dry sherry	½ oz	1 tablespoon
cornstarch	½ oz	1 tablespoon
SAUCE:		
chicken stock	1 lb, 8 oz	3 cups
dark soy sauce	1½ oz	3 tablespoons
rice vinegar	½ oz	1 tablespoon
sugar		1½ teaspoons
sesame oil	½ oz	1 tablespoon
chili oil	¼ to ½ oz, to taste	2 to 3 teaspoons, to taste

1. Soak vermicelli in warm water until softened. Drain and cut into 2-inch lengths.
2. Soak mushrooms for 25 minutes. Dice finely.
3. Combine pork with marinade ingredients, mix well. Refrigerate for 20 minutes.
4. Combine sauce ingredients in bowl, set aside.
5. Heat oil in wok, stir-fry onion and both peppers for 2 minutes.
6. Push to side of pan, add ginger and garlic. Stir-fry about 30 seconds.
7. Add pork, stir-fry until white, about 45 seconds.
8. Add drained bean threads, stir-fry briefly.
9. Pour in sauce, simmer until liquid is absorbed and noodles are tender. Correct seasonings.
10. Stir in cilantro, mix.
11. Serve, accompanied by rice.

SHRIMPS WITH PEAS AND CASHEW NUTS (South)

Number of Servings: 9
Cooking Method: Sauté (stir-fry)
Serving Size: 8 oz
Total Yield: 4 lbs, 9 oz

Food Balance: Protein
Wine Style: Light- to medium-bodied Chenin Blanc, Chardonnay, soft Reds
Example: Meridian Vineyards Santa Barbara Chardonnay

INGREDIENTS	WEIGHT	VOLUME
shrimp, peeled, deveined	2 lb, 4 oz	
cashew nuts, raw	9 oz	2 cups
frying oil	5 oz	10 tablespoons
peas, fresh or frozen	12 oz	3 cups
MARINADE:		
egg white, beaten	5 oz	5 each
rice wine or dry sherry	2 oz	¼ cup
ginger, fresh, peeled, minced	¾ oz	1½ tablespoons
cornstarch	1½ oz	3 tablespoons
SAUCE:		
cornstarch	½ oz	1 tablespoon
soy sauce	3 oz	6 tablespoons
rice wine or dry sherry	1½ oz	3 tablespoons
sugar	½ oz	1 tablespoon
black pepper		1½ teaspoons
chicken stock	12 oz	1½ cups

1. Mix marinade ingredients in bowl, add shrimp. Refrigerate for 15 minutes.
2. Mix sauce ingredients together mixing cornstarch with wine and soy sauce first. Set aside.
3. Heat oil to moderately hot, fry cashews about 2 minutes, until golden.
4. Remove, drain well.
5. Add shrimps, sauté until pink, stirring frequently.
6. Add peas and sauce mixture, bring to boil. Correct seasonings.
7. Simmer, stirring constantly for 45 seconds, stir in cashews. Serve with rice.

HUNAN CRISPY DUCK (Hunan)

Number of Servings: 8
Cooking Method: Steam, deep-fry
Serving Size: ¼ duck
Total Yield: 2 ducks

Food Balance: Sweet/protein sauce
Wine Style: Soft and fruity Gewürztraminer, rich nontannic Reds, Amarone, Shiraz, Zinfandel
Example: Château Souverain Zinfandel

Hunan Crispy Duck; photo courtesy of Dorling Kindersley

INGREDIENTS	WEIGHT	VOLUME
duck	8 to 10 lbs	2 each
frying oil for deep-frying		
SEASONING:		
star anise, crushed	½ oz	8 each
fennel seeds, crushed	½ oz	2 tablespoons
Chinese brown peppercorns, crushed	¼ oz	2 tablespoons
salt	1 oz	4 teaspoons
ginger, fresh, peeled, minced	1½ oz	4 tablespoons
scallions, finely diced	1 oz	4 tablespoons
rice wine or dry sherry	1 oz	2 tablespoons

CONDIMENTS:

duck sauce
hoisin
plum sauce

1. Combine seasoning ingredients.
2. Wash and clean duck, rub inside and out with seasoning. Refrigerate until ready to cook.
3. Using bamboo steamer in wok or rack in pot, cover and steam duck over rapidly boiling water for 2½ hours. Add more water, as necessary, while steaming.
4. Remove duck, wipe off seasonings on inside and outside.
5. Heat deep-frying oil in wok until hot, lower duck into oil and fry until completely crisp.
6. Serve whole, to be torn into strips. Serve with rice and accompaniments of duck sauce, hoisin, and/or plum sauce.

BROWNED NOODLES WITH PORK

Number of Servings: 8
Serving Size: 10 oz
Total Yield: 5 lbs, 6 oz

Cooking Method: Sauté (stir-fry)

Food Balance: Protein sauce
Wine Style: Soft and fruity Riesling, White Zinfandel, Beaujolais-
  Villages, Pinot Noir
Example: Château St. Jean Pinot Noir

INGREDIENTS	WEIGHT	VOLUME
Chinese egg noodles, dried	1 lb	
mushrooms, forest or any variety, dried	½ oz	12 each
pork, lean, julienne	1 lb	
frying oil, peanut or corn	5 oz	10 table-spoons
garlic, minced	1 oz	6 cloves
scallions, cut into 1-inch sections, white and green parts separated	5 oz	12 each
rice wine or dry sherry	1 oz	2 tablespoons
bean sprouts	1 lb	
Chinese red vinegar (optional)		to taste

MARINADE:		
cornstarch	¼ oz	1½ teaspoons
water, cold	1 oz	2 tablespoons
sugar		1 teaspoon
thin soy sauce (regular)		2 teaspoons
thick soy sauce	½ oz	2 teaspoons
pepper		½ teaspoon
rice wine or dry sherry		2 teaspoons

SAUCE:		
cornstarch		5 teaspoons
mushroom water and stock, cool	1 lb	2 cups
thin soy sauce		4 teaspoons
thick soy sauce	1½ oz	2 tablespoons
oyster sauce	2½ oz	3 tablespoons

1. Add noodles to boiling water, boil for about 4 minutes, until *al dente*.
2. Drain in colander, rinse under cold running water. Let dry for 1 hour, turning occasionally to ensure even drying.
3. Meanwhile, soak mushrooms in warm water for 30 minutes. Reserve soaking liquid (for sauce), julienne mushrooms.
4. For marinade, mix cornstarch and water in bowl. Add remaining marinade ingredients, add pork and mix well. Refrigerate for 30 minutes.
5. For sauce, mix cornstarch with some stock in bowl. Add remaining ingredients. Set aside.
6. Heat 3 oz (6 tablespoons) oil in large frying pan over high heat until hot.
7. Add noodles, arranging them evenly to edges.
8. Fry about 1 minute, until golden brown but not burned.
9. Turn noodle cake over with spatula or toss. Fry other side until golden brown.
10. Remove to warm serving plate, keep warm in oven.
11. Heat wok with 1 oz (2 tablespoons) oil over high heat.
12. Add garlic, then add ⅔ of white scallion, stir a few times.
13. Add pork, stir until it loses pink color.

Browned Noodles with Pork; photo courtesy of Dorling Kindersley

14. Pour in wine, stir.

15. Add mushrooms and ⅔ of green scallions, stir constantly. Remove to warm plate.

16. Wash wok. Heat with 1 oz (2 tablespoons) oil.

17. Add remaining white scallions and bean sprouts. Stir until cooked but still crunchy, about 2 minutes.

18. Add remaining green scallions. Transfer to plate with other cooked ingredients.

19. Lower heat, stir sauce and pour into wok. Bring to boil, stirring constantly.

20. Return cooked meat and vegetables to sauce. Heat thoroughly. Correct seasonings.

21. Pour over noodle cake. Serve by cutting noodles and serving a wedge. Accompany with red Chinese vinegar, if desired.

TSAO-NI-HÜN-TÜN

Date Wontons

Number of Servings: 9   Cooking Method: Deep-fry
Serving Size: 3 each
Total Yield: 29 wontons
             1 lb, 5 oz filling

INGREDIENTS	WEIGHT	VOLUME
dates, pitted, finely chopped	1 lb	2¾ cups
walnuts, finely chopped	4½ oz	1 cup
orange rind, finely grated	¼ oz	2 tablespoons

INGREDIENTS	WEIGHT	VOLUME
5 spice powder		¼ teaspoon
water	as needed	
wonton wrappers		1 package

oil for deep-frying

confectioners' sugar

1. Combine dates, walnuts, orange rind, and 5 spice powder in bowl, knead until mixture can form ball. Add water (very little) if necessary.
2. Place wonton wrapper on work surface with point at top, moisten edge of wonton with finger dipped in water.
3. Form about ¾ oz (1 tablespoon) filling into cylinder about 1¼-inch long. Place across wonton just below center.
4. Roll top edge of wonton tightly over filling and tuck under filling, then roll wonton forward until dough forms cylinder. Press edge to seal well.
5. Stick finger into open ends of wonton, press filling gently, twist to seal ends.
6. Heat oil to 375 degrees.
7. Fry wontons, a few at a time to maintain temperature, until golden brown.
8. Remove, place on absorbent paper to drain.
9. To serve, dust wontons with confectioners' sugar.

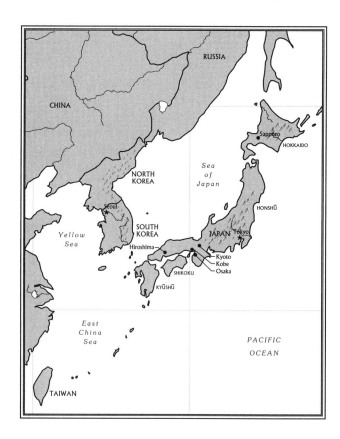

CHAPTER 12
Japan and Korea

By the end of this chapter, you will be able to

- Explain how the cuisines of Japan and Korea differ from each other and from the other Asian cuisines
- Describe the differences in sauces and flavorings used in Japan and Korea
- Understand how the geography and topography of these countries influence their cuisines
- Discuss the Japanese idea of aesthetics surrounding the food, presentation of food, the meal, and table setting
- Prepare a variety of Japanese and Korean dishes

HISTORY

Early descendants of Japan migrated from Asia, primarily from China and Korea. These inhabitants were hunters and gatherers, living off the animals and plants native to the islands. Around 300 B.C., an agricultural society developed, and the Japanese began growing rice and irrigating the farmland. The strongest influence on Japan, however, came from the Chinese between 400 and 800 A.D.

In the late thirteenth century, Marco Polo discovered Japan, but larger numbers of Europeans did not arrive until the middle 1500s. At that time, the Portuguese introduced the technique of battering and deep-frying foods to the Japanese. True to their light, simple style of cookery and emphasis on the natural flavors of the food, the Japanese adopted this cooking technique and developed *tempura*. Well known throughout the world, *tempura* consists of an incredibly light batter that delicately coats vegetables, seafood and/or meat for deep-frying. This is a sharp contrast to the heavy crust of batter that masks the flavor of the coated food which is used in the deep-frying found in most other countries.

With a large Buddhist population, vegetarian dishes abound in Japan. In fact, until one hundred years ago, the Japanese diet contained no meat. The protein basis of the diet revolved around seafood and soybeans, particularly the versatile soybean curd called *tofu*.

Today, Japan's economy remains very strong, and the people enjoy a high standard of living. Although with the times changing, fast food and chain restaurants now flourish in the cities of Japan. The traditional diet and style of eating that is/was so indicative of Japan's past culinary heritage has changed for many of the younger generation. Some feel the increased protein consumption (particularly red meat) might be responsible for the rise in heart disease and certain types of cancer that were almost nonexistent in Japan in the past.

The first people to settle in Korea came from areas to the north and northwest about 5,000 years ago. In 2333 B.C., the first Korean state was established. The Chinese moved into the northern part of Korea in 108 B.C. and seized control. Exerting profound influence on this new land, the Chinese introduced Buddhism and Confucianism in the eighth century, which the Koreans adopted. Today, these remain the two major religions found in Korea. Mongol tribes conquered the land in 1259, Manchu armies took control in the 1600s, and the Japanese invaded Korea several times throughout their history. All these intruders left some effect, but the strongest influence came from the Chinese.

From 1392 until 1910, the Yi dynasty ruled Korea while sustaining numerous invasions from the Chinese and Japanese. During that time, a stringent class system developed. With four distinct classes of people, great differences existed between the cooking of the royalty and that of the common people. The aristocracy enjoyed refined cookery, using a large number of ingredients, many spices, complex cooking procedures, and elaborate table settings. On the other hand, the common people ate simple foods with simple preparations.

The Portuguese introduced hot chili peppers to Korea in the 1500s, and the cuisine changed dramatically. During the period from the seventeenth to the nineteenth centuries, no foreigners were allowed into Korea, and the country remained free from intruders for a couple of hundred years. Korea continued as an agricultural-based society until the Japanese took control in 1910, when Korea became a Japanese colony. Japan's rule lasted thirty-five years, until the end of World War II in 1945. At that time, the country was divided into two countries, North and South Korea. The North was set up as a Communist society under the control of the Soviet Union, and the South was established as a democracy.

TOPOGRAPHY

Four large islands and thousands of small ones comprise the country of Japan. A small country in area, Japan ranks as one of the densest countries in the world in terms of population. Mountains run through most of the interior of the islands, but flatlands containing the cities and farmland make up the coastal areas. Most of Japan's people live in large cities along the coasts.

Situated east of Asia, Japan lies in the northern Pacific Ocean. The Pacific Ocean borders on the east and south; the Sea of Japan is to the west separating it from Korea. Many rivers transect Japan, providing water for irrigating available farmland. In addition to the threat of volcanic eruption from the numerous volcanoes rising with the mountains, the country is prone to earthquakes.

Ocean currents exert a great effect on the weather in Japan, creating large diversity in the climates found in this small country. Cold winters reign in the north, whereas subtropical conditions exist in the south, producing favorable environments for a wide variety of crops.

Lying in eastern Asia, the peninsula of Korea juts out from the northeastern side of China with the Soviet Union and China bordering on the north. Korea contains over 1,400 miles of coastline and more than 3,000 islands. The Sea of Japan lies between Korea and Japan; the Yellow Sea is on Korea's western side.

Korea is divided into two countries, North and South Korea. The majority of the population resides in the coastal areas because, like Japan, mountains, hills, and valleys comprise most of the interior portion of the country. Fertile plains make up the coasts lying to the west, northeast, and south. *Monsoons*, seasonal winds, blow in the summer and winter, molding the climate. In the winter, the cold *monsoon* causes cold winters except on the eastern side of the mountains because they form a barrier that block the winds. The summer *monsoons* produce hot, humid summers. In July and August, the *monsoons* bring heavy rains.

Ingredients and Foods Commonly Used Throughout the Cuisines of Japan and Korea Include:

- many varieties of seaweed
- seafood, including all sorts of shellfish, squid, crab, tuna, bonito, mackerel, trout, and sardines
- beef (Korea)
- tofu
- rice
- cabbage, Chinese cabbage, and radishes
- pickled vegetables
- *kimch'i* (Korea)
- mandarin oranges, apples, oranges, pears, and strawberries
- soy sauce and soybean paste—*miso* (Japan) and *dhwen-jang* (Korea)
- ginger, scallions, and garlic
- rice wine (*sake* and *mirin*) and rice vinegar
- tea

COOKING METHODS

The Japanese use a number of cooking methods. Steaming, boiling, grilling, stir-frying (sautéing), and deep-frying appear frequently. Steaming emphasizes the natural flavors of the foods, a goal of Japanese cookery. *Tempura*, an example of deep-frying, remains one of the most widely known Japanese dishes. Pickling excess seafood and vegetables preserves these food items for times when they are less plentiful.

One-pot cookery called *nabémono* is common, particularly in the winter. Preparation of the food occurs beforehand. Platters containing raw, cut foods are placed before the diners, and they actually cook the food at the table in a communal pot of broth placed over a heat source. The diners place the food ingredients in the boiling broth, adding the ingredients requiring the longest cooking time first. They remove and eat the ingredients as soon as they are cooked, ensuring that the food maintains its fresh quality, texture, and flavor. The cooking happens rapidly; some refer to this cookery as "quick stew." At the end, noodles or rice are added to the flavorful broth to absorb it, then the noodles or rice are eaten.

NABÉMONO

Sometimes called a quick cooking stew, *nabémono* comes in countless varieties depending on the diners' preference and the available ingredients. Any assortment of ingredients can be used, including all types of seafood, meats, tofu, and vegetables. One particularly filling type of *nabémono* that is popular with *sumo* wrestlers, *chanko-nabe*, contains many types of seafood, chicken, potatoes, and a variety of vegetables. The well-known *sukiyaki*, another *nabémono*, consists of thin slices of beef and vegetables cooked in the broth. Regardless of the type of *nabémono,* each diner receives a small bowl of *ponzu,* a dipping sauce to accompany it.

Like the Japanese, Koreans use a variety of cooking methods, including grilling, boiling, steaming, stir-frying, and deep-frying. Before cooking, Koreans cut, chop, and slice the foods finely. Beef preparation usually includes tenderizing the meat by pounding, slicing it thinly, and then marinating it before cooking. As in Japan, one-pot cookery remains quite popular in Korea.

Preservation by pickling occurs regularly. *Kimch'i*, a pickled cabbage (or other vegetable) mixture, is served with every meal. Many other varieties of pickled vegetables and legumes accompany meals.

REGIONS

The most northern of the four large islands that comprise Japan, Hokkaidō, has coastal plains with the interior section containing mountains, hills, and forests. Long, cold winters and cool summers exist here. Fishing and dairy farming are the main agricultural industries on this island.

Situated south of Hokkaidō, Honshū comprises the central part of Japan. Mountains and valleys make up the interior while the coastal areas are plains. Warm, humid summers and average winters reign here.

To the south lie two islands, Skikoku and Kyūshū. Both experience hot summers and mild winters, so rice grows very well. Mountains and hills comprise much of Skikoku, and many fruits and vegetables thrive on this island. Kyūshū contains mountains in the interior surrounded by hills, forests, and plains.

Only 15 percent of the land in Japan is suitable for farming. As a result, the Japanese terrace the hills, irrigate, and fertilize to maximize the crop production. With their reverence for rice, every small tract of land that might support agriculture becomes a rice paddy.

With such limited land resources, pastures for cattle grazing are scarce. As a result, the meager cattle spend their lives confined to barns except in northern Japan, home of the famous Kōbe beef. Some of the most prized and expensive beef in the world, Kōbe cattle enjoy pampered lives filled with beer and massages to create well-marbled, tender beef.

Farming in North Korea occurs on collective farms that are run by the government. Primarily situated on the plains in the northwest, major crops include rice, vegetables, fruits, corn, and potatoes. The western and southern coasts of South Korea contain the majority of the farms. The most prevalent crops include rice, barley, wheat, and vegetables.

Although Korea is divided into two countries, the cooking in both countries remains quite similar. North and South Koreans prepare many of the same dishes. One of the few differences is that the people of North Korea prefer pork while those in the south eat more beef, but, basically, seafood and *tofu* form the foundation of the protein consumed in both countries. The fishing industry continues to flourish for both North and South Korea.

CUISINE

In both Japan and Korea, the basis of the diet is seafood accompanied by rice and pickled vegetables. The Japanese and Koreans traditionally eat rice with every meal, both preferring the more glutinous short-grained varieties of rice. Although various types of pasta sometimes replace rice at a Japanese meal, bowls of hot, plain rice accompanied by pickled vegetables usually conclude the meal, whether or not noodles were served.

The cuisine of Japan differs from other Asian cuisines in several ways. First, although portions are small, the aesthetics of each dish or plate take on epic proportions. Great importance lies on the appearance and presentation of the food. The goal is to capture the diner's attention with the freshness and natural flavors of the food, the beauty of each dish, the atmosphere, and the whole meal. Second, although all the foods for a meal are served at once like most of the other Asian cuisines, diners in Japan receive their own portions on individual plates and bowls instead of serving family style from large bowls in the middle of the table. Third, the complexity of flavors found in the sauces of other Asian countries is absent here. Japanese chefs do not want to shroud the natural flavors of the food with multiflavored sauces. In addition, the Japanese use less oil than other Asian cuisines in their cookery, which further emphasizes the light, natural flavors of the foods.

Great care is taken to place the food beautifully and artistically in every way. Consideration of all aspects of appearance, including the color in both the food and the plate or bowl, the arrangement of the food on the plate, the flowers on the table, the setting of the table, and even the placement of the table in the dining room, assume paramount importance and consideration in Japan. Some describe the Japanese food on the plate as minimalist, actually referring to it as a work of art. The creation of an aesthetically pleasing plate and dining experience remains the goal of the Japanese chef.

With the focus on simplicity as well as the natural flavors of each of the foods, only absolutely fresh food products are acceptable. Menus in homes and restaurants truly change with the seasons and what is available and fresh at the market that day. The emphasis remains on the texture, taste, smell, and appearance of the individual ingredients, the completed dish, and the entire meal. These principles become apparent in foods associated with the Japanese cuisine such as *sushi* and *sashimi*, raw fish preparations; *tempura*, individual food items coated with a very light batter and deep-fried; and the many soups consisting of a *miso* (fermented soybean paste) flavored broth containing one or just a few ingredients.

Seafood, tofu, soup, a variety of other dishes, fresh and pickled vegetables, and steamed rice form a typical Japanese meal. Prolific vegetable dishes include salads, pickled, raw, and cooked preparations. Like most Asians, the diet includes smaller amounts of protein with lots of vegetables and ample amounts of rice.

Some type of soup appears at most meals. There are two popular types of Japanese soups: clear broth and a thick soup flavored with *miso*. Breakfast in Japan often consists of the thick, *miso*-based soup.

Surrounded by oceans, seaweed plays a significant role in the cuisines of both Japan and Korea. Many varieties of seaweed, both fresh and dried, appear in myriad dishes. A significant source of minerals, seaweed is used as a flavoring, a frequent soup ingredient, and combined with all sorts of vegetables and seafood in salads. Depending on the type of seaweed, the flavor can seem quite foreign to many "western" palates, sometimes requiring repeated exposure to the seaweed until acquiring a taste for it. *Dashi*, Japanese stock made from dried bonito (fish) and dried kelp (seaweed), forms the foundation for much Japanese cookery, including soups, braised dishes, and sauces.

Appearing in many guises, the soybean plays a major role in the Japanese diet. Two seasonings derived from soybeans, *miso* (fermented soybean paste) and *shōyu* (soy sauce), show up everywhere. Protein-rich *tofu*, soybean curd, appears regularly in the cuisines of both Japan and Korea, often consumed at all meals in Japan. Like China, cooks in these two countries use few, if any, dairy products.

Seasonings used in Japanese cookery reflect simplicity and allow the natural, delicate flavors of the food to dominate. Primary flavoring ingredients include *shōyu*, *miso*, various seaweeds, and two rice wines, *sake* and *mirin*. *Wasabi*, a sinus-opening, spicy hot horseradish condiment used as a dipping sauce enhances the flavors and textures of *sushi* and *sashimi*.

Many restaurants in Japan specialize so narrowly that they prepare only one type of food or one method of preparation in the restaurant. Noodle houses serve only noodle dishes; *tempura* restaurants feature only deep-fried *tempura*; *sushi* bars provide vinegar-flavored rice wrapped around vegetables and/or raw fish. Some restaurants specialize with such a restricted focus that they prepare only one type of fish.

Almost like the Japanese version of fast food, noodles remain popular throughout Japan. Noodle houses, restaurants serving all types of noodle dishes, flourish. Two types of noodles are served often: *soba*, a buckwheat noodle, and *udon*, which is made from wheat.

Like the rest of Asia, all dishes arrive at the Japanese table at the same time. Dishes might be served piping hot, but room temperature foods remain perfectly acceptable. In fact, the Japanese believe the natural flavors of the food come through better at room temperature. Meals end with steamed rice and pickled vegetables and perhaps fresh fruit. When served, dessert appears at tea ceremonies.

THE JAPANESE TEA CEREMONY

During the fourteenth and fifteenth centuries, the Zen Buddhists developed the tea ceremony, which remains one of the traditional arts today. This ancient ritual involves the preparation and service of powdered green tea to guests. The very simple and deliberate tea ceremony as well as its goals reflect several aspects of Zen philosophy and bring enjoyment to the guest on all levels, including the physical and intellectual. True to Zen philosophy, the guest achieves this inner peace by intently concentrating on the beauty of nature and the simplicity of the ceremony. The sound of the water (used to make the tea), the glow of the fire (on which the water is heated for tea), and the beauty of the objects used in the tea ceremony heighten the senses. All conversation focuses on these subjects and simplicity. The guests experience a spiritual awakening through the Zen approach of appreciating and living each moment.

Although not many attend or have tea ceremonies today, many Japanese study the art of the tea ceremony for years. Only the very rich or Buddhist monks actually have tea ceremonies.

KIMCH'I

Kimch'i remains a well-known staple on the Korean table. Although outside of Korea many think *kimch'i* is fermented cabbage, it is also prepared from radishes, cucumbers, and other vegetables. Different types of *kimch'i* are prepared in the various regions in Korea. *Kimch'i* recipes differ based on the main vegetable making up the *kimch'i*, other ingredients that contribute to the flavoring, and the method of preparation and/or fermentation. Although most varieties of *kimch'i* are highly spiced, some Koreans prefer quite mild *kimch'i*. Again, the amount of spiciness varies from region to region. In addition, *kimch'i* preparation changes with the season, with different types prevalent in each season. A fermented food like yogurt, Koreans believe *kimch'i* contains all sorts of medicinal and healthful benefits. Besides aiding in digestion, its high lactic acid content helps *kimch'i* maintain the proper balance of flora in the intestines. Also, some believe *kimch'i* has anti-carcinogenic effects.

Combinations of the five flavor elements—sweet, sour, salty, bitter, and hot or pungent—create the tastes associated with Korean cookery. Common flavorings used in Korea include ginger, garlic, soy sauce, vinegar, sesame oil, sesame seeds, hot peppers, black pepper, and scallions. Whether consumed raw, pickled, or grilled, garlic appears with all foods at all meals. Koreans prefer spicy foods and use a variety of hot peppers in the form of chili pastes and finely sliced hot peppers. A well-known Korean condiment, *kimch'i*, a spicy fermented mixture of cabbage, radish, or other vegetable, appears with rice at every meal, including breakfast. Several condiments, pickles, and salads known as *panch'an* usually accompany meals. Vegetables, beans, or seaweed often become *panch'an*.

Koreans prefer a meal of beef, pork, seafood, or tofu, accompanied by *kimch'i*, a variety of vegetables, pickled vegetables, soup, and rice. A popular South Korean beef dish, *bulgogi* consists of marinated strips of beef grilled at the table. Unlike the typical western approach to protein foods, Koreans often mix seafood with pork, beef, and/or chicken within a dish, depending on what is available. Like other Asian countries, limited quantities of high-protein foods accompany large amounts of rice, other grains, and vegetables. Koreans consume barley and several types of beans, often combining them with the omnipresent rice. Whether made from rice, grains, or legumes, noodles play a significant role in Korean cookery.

Like the Chinese, Koreans believe food prevents and cures disease, as well as promotes good health. Good taste and healthful eating remain priorities in the cooking of Korea. Well-seasoned foods dominate the cuisine with most foods marinated or seasoned before cooking and then seasoned again after cooking.

Koreans place all dishes in large bowls on the table at once. Rice, soup, and at least one variety of *kimch'i* are always included. Diners use bowls, not plates, for their food. Although a variety of dishes are prepared, Koreans consume the same foods for breakfast, lunch, and/or dinner.

SOME KOREAN CUSTOMS AND MANNERS

- Everyone at the table begins eating when the oldest person present at the table takes the first bite.
- No one leaves the table until the oldest person has finished eating.
- Leaving chopsticks standing in the rice is a ceremonial custom that only occurs at a memorial service for the dead.

REGION	AREA	WEATHER	TOPOGRAPHY	FOODS
Japan:				
Hokkaidō	North	Long, cold winters, cool summers	Mountains, hills, forests, coastal plains	Seafood, Kōbe beef, dairy, seaweed
Honshū	Central	Mild winters, hot summers	Mountains, valleys, plains on coast	Seafood, seaweed, rice
Skikoku	South	Mild winters, hot summers	Mountains, hills, coastal plains	Seafood, tuna, bonito, mackerel, sardines, trout, crabs, shellfish, squid, seaweed, rice, vegetables, fruits
Kyūshū	South	Mild winters, hot summers	Mountains, hills, coastal plains, forests	Seafood, tuna, bonito, mackerel, sardines, trout, crabs, shellfish, squid, seaweed, rice, vegetables, fruits
Korea:				
North Korea	North	Cold winters, hot, humid summers, *monsoons,* moderate climate in east	North: plains, hills, coast, farmland; center: mountains, forests; east: coast, hills, lowlands, farmland; south: mountains, forests, valleys, hills	Seafood, shellfish, squid, pollock, sardines, hogs, rice, barley, wheat, soybeans, corn, potatoes, vegetables, fruits
South Korea	South	Cold winters, hot, humid summers, *monsoons,* moderate climate in east	North: mountains, forests, valleys, hills, coasts; center and east: hills, forests, mountains, valleys, coasts; south: hills, plains, coast	Seafood, filefish, pollock, oysters, hogs, cattle, chicken, rice, barley, soybeans, wheat, potatoes, sweet potatoes, Chinese cabbage, vegetables, melons, apples

In many Korean homes, the heartiest meal of the day is served in the morning. They believe ingesting the main meal in the morning provides the most nutrients for the full day ahead. Therefore, lunch and the evening meal are both light meals.

The beverage of choice in Japan and Korea remains tea. The Japanese prefer green tea, and Koreans often drink tea made from barley or rice. Two rice wines, *sake*, served warm in the winter, and *mirin*, a sweeter wine used only for cooking, appear often in Japan. Rice wine, beer, and *soju*, a distilled grain liquor, remain the most popular alcoholic beverages in Korea.

Review Questions

1. Explain similarities and differences between the Japanese cuisine and other Asian cuisines.
2. Describe the Japanese philosophy on food and dining, including the goal of chefs cooking this cuisine.

3. Discuss the seasonings used commonly in the cookery of Japan and those used in the cookery of Korea.
4. Discuss food ingredients that are prevalent in both Japan and Korea because of the topography and geography of these two countries.
5. Which foods appear at all Japanese and Korean meals?
6. Describe the differences in service and presentation between a Korean and a Japanese meal.
7. What is *kimch'i* and what is its role in the Korean diet?

Glossary

bulgogi Marinated strips of beef grilled at the table, a popular Korean dish

dashi Japanese stock made from dried bonito and dried kelp, forms the foundation for much Japanese cookery, including soups and braised dishes

dhwen-jang Bean paste, Korean

katsuo Dried bonito shavings, bonito is a fish in the mackerel family

kimch'i A spicy, fermented cabbage or vegetable mixture popular in Korea; served at every meal

kombu Dried kelp, a seaweed

mirin Japanese sweet rice wine used for cooking

miso Fermented bean paste, used as a flavoring for soups or sauces, Japanese

monsoons Seasonal winds that affect the weather

nabémono One-pot cookery common in Japan; similar to fondue, diners cook their own food in a pot of stock heating on the dining table

panch'an Condiments, pickles, and salads, served with Korean meals

ponzu A dipping sauce

sake Japanese rice wine, served warm in the winter

sashimi Raw fish sliced thinly, accompanied by *wasabi*

soba A noodle made from buckwheat

soju Korean distilled grain liquor

sushi Raw fish, vinegared rice, and often vegetable(s) rolled in a wrapper like *nori* seaweed; accompanied by *wasabi*

tempura Individual food items coated with a very light batter and deep-fried, well-known Japanese dish

tofu Soybean curd, a protein food

udon A noodle made from wheat

wasabi Very pungent, spicy hot green horseradish dipping sauce served as a condiment with raw fish in Japan

DASHI (Japan)

Fish and Seaweed Stock

Total Yield: 1 qt or 2 lbs   Cooking Method: Boil

> Dashi forms the basis for many Japanese soups and sauces.

INGREDIENTS	WEIGHT	VOLUME
water	2 lbs	1 qt
kombu (kelp), dried	½ oz	2- by 4-inch piece
katsuo (dried bonito shavings)	½ oz	1 cup

1. Wipe *kombu* lightly with damp cloth, place in saucepan, cover with water.
2. Bring to simmer over medium low heat, simmer for 10 minutes.
3. Remove kelp, add *katsuo*, remove pan from heat, let sit few minutes until *katsuo* settles to bottom of pan.
4. Strain stock, cool, and refrigerate until needed (freeze if longer than 3 days).

MISO SHIRU (Japan)

Bean Paste Soup with Tofu

Number of Servings: 8   Cooking Method: Boil
Serving Size: 8 oz
Total Yield: 4 lbs, 9 oz

Food Balance: Protein
Wine Style: Light- to medium-bodied Chenin Blanc, Viognier, Chardonnay, Rosé
Example: Beringer Vineyards Chenin Blanc or Founders' Estate Chardonnay

INGREDIENTS	WEIGHT	VOLUME
dashi (*recipe above*)	4 lb	2 qts
aka miso (reddish brown miso)	5½ oz	½ cup
tofu (soybean curd), rinsed, cut into ½-inch cubes	8 oz	
scallions, sliced thinly, with green	1½ oz	2 each
mushrooms, button or any variety, sliced	1½ oz	4 each

1. Heat dashi in saucepan until hot.
2. In small bowl, add some of hot dashi to miso, mix well.

Miso Shiru (Bean Paste Soup with Tofu); photo courtesy of Kikkoman Corporation

3. Add miso mixture to saucepan of dashi, mix well, strain if lumps remain.
4. Add tofu and scallions, heat over medium heat until just simmering.
5. Add mushroom slices, serve.

AONA NO GOMA-AE (Japan)

Leafy Greens with Sesame Dressing

Number of Servings: 12
Serving Size: 3 oz
Total Yield: 2 lbs, 5 oz

Cooking Method: Boil

INGREDIENTS	WEIGHT	VOLUME
leafy greens like watercress, spinach, komatsuna, or combination, washed, cut into 2-inch pieces	3 lbs, 8 oz	
sesame seeds	2 oz	6 tablespoons
sugar	1½ oz	3 tablespoons
soy sauce (*shoyu*)	1½ to 2 oz	3 to 4 tablespoons

GARNISH:

sesame seeds, toasted

1. Place greens in pan, making sure stems are on bottom, cook until wilted, about 2 minutes.
2. Rinse with cold water in colander, drain well, squeezing to remove excess water.
3. Toast sesame seeds in dry skillet, being careful not to burn. Cool, grind with mortar and pestle or in food processor.
4. Mix sesame seeds, sugar, and soy sauce. Set aside until ready to serve.
5. Combine sesame seed dressing with greens, serve small portion in separate bowl to accompany other dishes and rice. Garnish with sprinkling of toasted sesame seeds, if desired.

KIMCH'I (Korea)

Pickled Cabbage

Number of Servings: 45
Serving Size: 2 oz
Total Yield: 5 lbs, 11 oz

INGREDIENTS	WEIGHT	VOLUME
Chinese cabbage	2 lb, 4 oz	¾ head
kosher salt	1¾ oz	3 tablespoons
water	3 lbs	1½ quarts

INGREDIENTS	WEIGHT	VOLUME
STUFFING:		
daikon radish, peeled, cut into ⅛-inch julienne	1 lb, 1 oz	1 each
ginger, fresh, peeled	1½ oz	2 each 3-inch cubes
garlic, peeled	2 oz	20 cloves
water	3 oz	6 tablespoons
scallions, finely sliced	6 oz	16 each
cayenne, ground	¼ oz	4 teaspoons
sugar		2 teaspoons
anchovy fillets, drained, patted dry, minced	2 oz	1 each 2 oz can
kosher salt	1 oz	2 tablespoons
flour, all purpose	½ oz	2 tablespoons
water	1 lb, 8 oz	3 cups

1. Trim bottom of the cabbage, keeping leaves attached. Quarter head lengthwise.
2. Wash carefully, removing all dirt from between leaves.
3. Combine 3 lbs (1½ quarts) water and 1¾ oz (3 tablespoons) salt in bowl, add cabbage, place plate and weight on top to prevent floating. Soak 4 hours.
4. Place ginger and garlic in food processor or blender, add 1½ oz (3 tablespoons) water, process until smooth.
5. Mix radish, ginger-garlic paste, scallions, cayenne, sugar, and anchovies; add 1 oz (2 tablespoons) salt; mix.
6. Place flour in small pan, whisk in 1 lb, 8 oz (3 cups) water, bring to simmer, cook gently until slightly thickened.

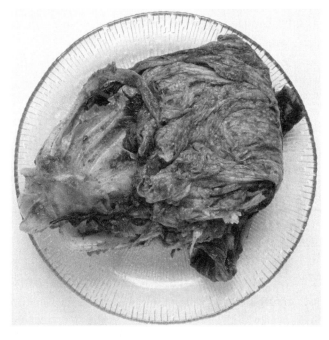

Kimch'i (Pickled Cabbage); photo courtesy of Dorling Kindersley

7. Remove cabbage from salt water, rinse several times, drain.
8. Place some stuffing between each cabbage leaf, place stuffed cabbage quarters in nonreactive bowl or other container, pour flour water over cabbage.
9. Cover, leave at room temperature for 2 days, until fermented, then refrigerate until needed. Less fermenting time is required in hot weather.
10. To serve, slice crossways and serve in bowl with a little fermenting liquid.

MU SAINGCHAI (Korea)

Radish Salad

Number of Servings: 10
Serving Size: 2 oz
Total Yield: 1 lb, 4 oz

INGREDIENTS	WEIGHT	VOLUME
DRESSING:		
soy sauce	1 oz	2 tablespoons
sesame oil		2 teaspoons
rice vinegar	½ oz	1 tablespoon
sugar		2 teaspoons
sesame seeds, toasted, ground	¼ oz	1 tablespoon
hot red chili, seeded, minced		½ each or to taste
daikon radish, peeled, julienne	12 oz	1 each
apple, peeled, cored, julienne	4½ oz	1 each
scallions, thinly sliced	2 oz	2 each

1. Combine all dressing ingredients in small bowl.
2. Combine radish, apple, and scallions in bowl, pour in dressing, toss to mix.
3. Cover, chill before serving.

SUKJU NAMUL (Korea)

Bean Sprout Salad

Number of Servings: 15   Cooking Method: Boil
Serving Size: 2 oz
Total Yield: 1 lb, 14 oz

INGREDIENTS	WEIGHT	VOLUME
bean sprouts, mung bean or other	1 lb, 6 oz	6 cups
soy sauce	3 oz	6 tablespoons
sesame oil		4 teaspoons
rice vinegar	1 oz	2 tablespoons
garlic	¼ oz	2 cloves
sugar		4 teaspoons

Sukju Namul (Bean Sprout Salad); photo courtesy of Dorling Kindersley

INGREDIENTS	WEIGHT	VOLUME
black pepper		¼ teaspoon
cayenne pepper		¼ to ½ tea-spoon, to taste
scallions, finely chopped	4 oz	4 each

1. Bring saucepan of water to boil over high heat, add bean sprouts, cook 1 minute.
2. Pour bean sprouts into colander, rinse with cold water, drain well, place in bowl.
3. In small bowl, combine remaining ingredients, stir well to dissolve sugar, pour over sprouts.
4. Mix well, chill, then serve.

OI NAMUL (Korea)

Cucumber Salad

Number of Servings: 8
Serving Size: 2 oz
Total Yield: 1 lb, 1 oz

INGREDIENTS	WEIGHT	VOLUME
cucumbers, peeled, seeded, thinly sliced	1 lb, 11 oz	2 large
salt, kosher	½ oz	1 tablespoon
water	8 oz	1 cup

INGREDIENTS	WEIGHT	VOLUME
rice vinegar	1 oz	2 tablespoons
sugar		1 teaspoon
cayenne		¼ teaspoon
garlic, minced		1 clove
scallion, minced		1 each
sesame seeds, toasted, ground	¼ oz	1 tablespoon

1. Place cucumbers in bowl, sprinkle with salt, add water.
2. Soak for 15 minutes, drain well.
3. Combine remaining ingredients, pour over cucumbers, mix well.
4. Chill well, serve.

TEMPURA (Japan)

Deep-fried, Battered Vegetables, Seafood, Poultry, and/or Meat

Number of Servings: 8   Cooking Method: Boil, deep-fry
Total Yield: batter—1 lb, 14 oz

Food Balance: Protein
Wine Style: Light- to medium-bodied Riesling, mild Whites, Pinot Gris, Pinot Blanc, Blush, Beaujolais, Grenache
Example: Château St. Jean Pinot Blanc

> Any variety of vegetables, seafood, or meat becomes tempura. Do not prepare tempura batter very far in advance, and keep it very cold.

INGREDIENTS	WEIGHT	VOLUME
DIPPING SAUCE:		
dashi broth	1 lb	2 cups
soy sauce (*shoyu*)	3 oz	6 tablespoons
sake	3 oz	6 tablespoons
sugar		4 teaspoons
daikon radish, grated	6 oz	
BATTER:		
flour, all purpose, sifted	7½ oz	1½ cups
cornstarch	3 oz	½ cup
eggs	3½ oz	2 each
water, cold	1 lb	2 cups

oil for deep frying
flour for dredging

assorted vegetables cut into slices or strips, for example, peppers, broccoli, pea pods, green beans, carrots, potatoes, sweet potatoes, onion, or mushrooms
shrimp, peeled, deveined
chicken, boneless, skinless, cut into strips
flour, for dipping

SAUCE:
1. Combine all sauce ingredients except daikon in pan, bring to boil, reduce heat and simmer 1 minute.
2. Remove from heat.
3. Pour into individual bowls with ¾-oz daikon mound in each bowl.

Tempura (Deep-fried, Battered Vegetables, Seafood, Poultry, and/or Meat); photo courtesy of Dorling Kindersley

BATTER:
1. Mix eggs and water in bowl.
2. Sift together flour and cornstarch, add to egg mixture.
3. Stir a few times with fork, mix only until combined, some lumps should remain.

FRYING:
1. Heat oil in wok or deep skillet until 350 degrees.
2. Lightly coat food items with flour, then coat with batter.
3. Place a few items in fat, do not add many items at once or temperature of fat lowers too much.
4. Fry until golden and food item is properly cooked (vegetables still crisp and meat cooked to proper temperature). Remove loose pieces of batter from wok.
5. Serve immediately, accompanied by dipping sauce.

SALMON TERIYAKI (Japan)

Number of Servings: 8
Serving Size: about 4 oz fish,
   1 salmon steak
Total Yield: about 2 lbs

Cooking Method: Boil, broil, or grill

Food Balance: Sweet/protein
Wine Style: Soft and fruity Gewürztraminer, Johannisberg Riesling, Blush, mild Reds, Grenache, Pinot Noir
Example: Wolf Blass Riesling or Grenache

Salmon Teriyaki; photo courtesy of Kikkoman Corporation

> Teriyaki sauce can be used with any desired fish (although fatty fish varieties work best), chicken, or meat. Basically, it entails marinating in the sauce, broiling, and brushing with more of the sauce while broiling.

INGREDIENTS	WEIGHT	VOLUME
salmon steaks	about 3 lbs	8 each, small
SAUCE:		
sake	6 oz	¾ cup
soy sauce (*shoyu*)	6 oz	¾ cup
sugar	3½ oz	7 tablespoons
ginger		2 each ½-inch slices
garlic, minced		1 clove

1. Mix all ingredients for sauce in saucepan, bring to boil, lower heat, simmer for 5 minutes.
2. Remove from heat, cool to room temperature.
3. Cover fish with marinade, refrigerate for 30 minutes.
4. Preheat grill or broiler.
5. Cook fish for 5 or 10 minutes on each side, depending on thickness of fish, meanwhile, brushing with marinade 3 or 4 times while cooking. Fish will develop rich brown glaze.
6. Serve immediately with rice and extra sauce, if desired.

CHAP CHAE (Korea)

Cellophane Noodles with Beef and Vegetables

Number of Servings: 11   Cooking Method: Stir-fry (sauté)
Serving Size: 7 oz
Total Yield: 5 lbs

Food Balance: Protein/sweet
Wine Style: Soft and fruity Riesling, Blush, Shiraz
Example: Beringer Founders' Estate Shiraz

INGREDIENTS	WEIGHT	VOLUME
MARINADE:		
sugar	1 oz	2 tablespoons
soy sauce	2 oz	¼ cup
scallions	½ oz	2 tablespoons
garlic, minced	¼ oz	2 cloves
sesame oil	1 oz	2 tablespoons
black pepper, ground		½ teaspoon
cellophane noodles (mung bean threads)	4 oz	
beef steak or fillet, sliced ⅛-inch thick across the grain	1 lb	
mushrooms, dried, Chinese	½ oz	12 each
spinach, fresh, thick stems removed	10 oz	1 package
onions, sliced thinly	8 oz	2 medium
carrots, julienne, 3-inch long	8 oz	4 each
garlic, minced	¼ oz	2 cloves
bamboo shoots, julienne	8 oz	1½ cups
Chinese cabbage, julienne	8 oz	6 leaves
FRYING:		
sesame oil	1 oz	2 tablespoons
SAUCE:		
soy sauce	4 oz	½ cup
sugar	1 oz	2 tablespoons
sesame oil	1 to 2 oz	2 to 4 table-spoons

Chap Chae (Cellophane Noodles with Beef and Vegetables); photo courtesy of Dorling Kindersley

INGREDIENTS	WEIGHT	VOLUME
sesame seeds, roasted, ground	1 oz	3 tablespoons
water	4 to 8 oz	½ to 1 cup

1. To roast sesame seeds, toast in pan over medium high heat until popping and beginning to smell, then grind in processor or mortar and pestle.
2. Place cellophane noodles in bowl, cover with warm water, soak for 30 to 45 minutes, until soft. Drain, cut into 3-inch lengths.
3. Mix marinade ingredients in bowl, add meat, mix, refrigerate for 30 minutes.
4. Cover mushrooms with warm water, soak for 30 minutes, remove from water, slice thinly.
5. Cook spinach about 1 or 2 minutes, until soft. Remove from pan, rinse with cold water, squeeze to remove excess water, cut into strips.
6. Heat sesame oil in wok or skillet over high heat, add onion, one minute later add carrot and garlic, two or three minutes later, add bamboo shoots, cabbage, and spinach.
7. Remove vegetables to bowl, add beef and mushrooms to pan, cook until meat is just done, about 1 or 2 minutes.
8. Remove meat to bowl with vegetables, turn heat to medium low.
9. Add sauce ingredients to wok, mix well, turn heat to medium, add cellophane noodles, then ingredients from bowl.
10. Correct seasonings, and serve with rice.

SAENGSUN CHIGAE (Korea)

Fish, Shellfish, and Tofu Stew

Number of Servings: 9   Cooking Method: Braise, stir-fry (sauté)
Serving Size: 9 oz
Total Yield: 5 lbs, 5 oz

Food Balance: Spicy/protein
Wine Style: Soft and fruity Gewürztraminer, Riesling, Blush, Rosé
Example: Beringer Vineyards Gewürztraminer or Rosé de Saignee

INGREDIENTS	WEIGHT	VOLUME
mushrooms, dried Chinese	½ oz	10 each
beef, tender, sliced very thinly	4 oz	
zucchini or yellow squash, cut into ⅓-inch rounds	5 oz	1 small
garlic, peeled, minced	¼ oz	2 cloves
soy sauce	½ oz	1 tablespoon
sesame oil		1 teaspoon
hot bean paste*	2¾ oz	4 tablespoons
scallions, cut into 2-inch pieces	1½ oz	4 each

*If hot bean paste is unavailable, add paprika (½ oz or 1½ tablespoons), cayenne (1 teaspoon), and sugar (½ oz or 1 tablespoon) to bean paste (2¾ oz or 4 tablespoons).

INGREDIENTS	WEIGHT	VOLUME
green bell pepper, cut into ½-inch squares	2 oz	¼ each
red bell pepper, cut into ½-inch squares	2 oz	¼ each
clams		6 to 8 small
tofu, cut into 1-inch cubes	1 lb, 2 oz	1 package
fish fillets, haddock, cod, or scrod, cut across grain into 3 or 4 pieces	1 lb	
water	1 lb, 14 oz	3¾ cups
oil		1 teaspoon

1. Soak mushrooms in warm water for 30 minutes, drain, cut into quarters.
2. Combine mushrooms, beef, zucchini, garlic, soy sauce, sesame oil, and bean paste in bowl. Refrigerate until needed.
3. Place fish, scallions, and peppers in bowl, refrigerate until needed.
4. Scrub clams well under cold running water, place in bowl with tofu, refrigerate until needed.
5. In wide pot that can be brought to table, heat oil over medium high heat until hot, add meat mixture, stir-fry for 2 minutes.
6. Add water, bring to simmer, add ingredients from fish bowl.
7. Bring to simmer, cover, simmer 5 minutes.
8. Add clams and tofu, make sure clams are submerged in liquid.
9. Cover, cook on medium low about 5 minutes, until clams open.
10. Serve over rice.

BULGOGI (Korea)

Fiery Beef

Number of Servings: 8   Cooking Method: Grill
Serving Size: 4 oz meat
            1¼ oz sauce
Total Yield: 2 lbs, 3 oz meat
            11 oz sauce

Food Balance: Spicy/protein
Wine Style: Soft and fruity Riesling, Gewürztraminer, Blush, Grenache, rich Zinfandel or Shiraz
Example: Beringer Founders' Estate Zinfandel or Shiraz

INGREDIENTS	WEIGHT	VOLUME
beef, rump, top round, or fillet, sliced ⅛-inch thick on diagonal	2 lbs	
soy sauce	3 oz	6 tablespoons
rice vinegar	2 oz	4 tablespoons
sesame oil	2 oz	4 tablespoons
sesame seeds, toasted, ground	½ oz	2 tablespoons
sugar		1½ teaspoons

INGREDIENTS	WEIGHT	VOLUME
scallions, minced	1½ oz	4 each
garlic, minced	1 oz	2 tablespoons or 8 to 10 cloves
black pepper, ground		¾ teaspoon
sesame seeds	1 oz	3 tablespoons
SAUCE:		
soy sauce	3 oz	6 tablespoons
sesame oil		4 teaspoons
water	2 oz	¼ cup
rice wine	2 oz	¼ cup
sesame seeds, toasted, ground	½ oz	2 tablespoons
scallions, minced		1 each
garlic, minced	¼ oz	2 cloves
sugar		4 teaspoons

1. Place meat in stainless steel or nonreactive bowl, add remaining ingredients, mixing well into meat.
2. Marinate in refrigerator overnight or 24 hours, mix occasionally.

SAUCE:

1. Mix all ingredients together in small bowl.
2. Serve from small bowls.

ASSEMBLY:

1. Preheat broiler or grill.
2. Drain meat, grill meat in broiler or over coals for 25 to 40 seconds on each side, until done.
3. Serve with rice and sauce.

Marinating beef; photo courtesy of Dorling Kindersley

Grilling beef; photo courtesy of Dorling Kindersley

Bulgogi (Fiery Beef); photo courtesy of Dorling Kindersley

KARINTO (Japan)

Deep-fried Cookies

Number of Servings: 9   Cooking Method: Deep-fry
Serving Size: 1¼ oz
Total Yield: 12 oz

INGREDIENTS	WEIGHT	VOLUME
flour, all purpose	5¼ oz	1 cup
baking powder		1 teaspoon
salt		dash
sugar, white	¾ oz	1½ table-spoons
egg	1¼ oz	1 each
milk	1½ oz	3 tablespoons
oil for frying		
ICING:		
brown sugar	5 oz	¾ cup
water	1¼ oz	3½ table-spoons

> You may want to accompany these cookies with some ice cream or sorbet.

1. Sift flour, baking powder, salt, and sugar together in bowl.
2. Add egg and milk, mix just until well blended and smooth.
3. Lightly flour table, roll out dough ¹⁄₁₆- to ⅛-inch thick, cut into strips ½ by 2½ inches.
4. Heat oil for deep-frying in wok or frying pan, add strips of cookie dough, a few at a time so oil temperature does not lower too much.
5. Fry until golden on both sides, remove and drain on absorbent paper.
6. Mix icing ingredients in saucepan, heat without stirring until thickened and 242 degrees on candy thermometer.
7. Add cookies (in batches) to sugar, turn over with tongs, remove to parchment-lined or oiled pan.
8. Repeat until all cookies are coated. Serve with ice cream or sorbet, if desired.

CHAPTER 13
Vietnam, Thailand, and Indonesia

By the end of this chapter, you will be able to

- Explain how the cuisines of Vietnam, Thailand, and Indonesia differ from other Asian cuisines

- Identify nations that influenced the cuisines of Vietnam, Thailand, and Indonesia, and discuss the effects of each nation on the cuisine

- Understand how the geography and topography influenced the cuisines of these countries

- Name prevalent food and flavoring ingredients used in the cuisines of Vietnam, Thailand, and Indonesia

- Prepare a variety of dishes from Vietnam, Thailand, and Indonesia

HISTORY

Chinese from the north and islanders from the south first settled Vietnam. As a result, the most common heritage found in Vietnam remains Malaysian and Chinese ancestry. China ruled this land for about a thousand years, from 100 B.C. until 900 A.D. After that time, Vietnam became an independent country.

In the ensuing years, people from India arrived seeking spices to trade, while people from countries in the west came looking for trade as well as lands to colonize. Vietnam's independence lasted until France gained control in the late sixteenth century. Prior to the French occupation, Vietnam functioned as an agricultural society; however, the French introduced industry to this country. France's rule lasted until World War II, when Japan invaded Vietnam.

With Japan's defeat in World War II, they lost control of Vietnam. France tried to regain command, but they ended up ruling the southern part while Russia ruled the northern portion of the country. What began as a civil war between the north and south of Vietnam in 1957 escalated into a war involving a number of countries that lasted until the 1970s. As a result of ongoing heavy bombing and fighting, Vietnam and the Vietnamese people changed greatly, both physically and emotionally. Many rural residents moved to the cities seeking jobs and/or shelter. Shelling, bombing, and defoliation destroyed much land and property. Even today, many years after the fighting ended, significant impact from the Soviet Union and United States still remains strong in Vietnam.

Although influence from the Chinese is quite apparent in the north, the south exhibits remnants of the Indian and French presence. From the Chinese, the Vietnamese adopted chopsticks, stir-fries, bean curd, and a fondness for noodles. Curries came from the Indian influence, and the French culinary traditions introduced pâtés, French bread, sauces, and butter to the cuisine of Vietnam.

People from southeastern Asia migrated to Thailand around 4,500 years ago. Most Thai descendants are of Malaysian descent with some Chinese and Arabic ancestry. Today, Thailand remains a predominately Buddhist country with beautiful Buddhist temples called *wat* in every village.

The Europeans entered Thailand in the 1500s; however, they never gained control of this country. In fact, Thailand remains one of the few countries in Asia that was never ruled by a western nation, and other Asian countries rarely conquered it.

Much of the culinary influences that exist in Thailand today resulted from its geographic location. Situated less than 100 miles from Vietnam and China, Thailand shares borders with Cambodia, Laos, Burma, and Malaysia. Evidence of culinary traits from these countries appears throughout Thailand.

Known as the Spice Islands, Indonesia attracted traders from India, Arabia, and Holland seeking spices. The Indonesians learned of kebabs from the Arabs. Applying their own culinary slant, the kebabs became *satay*, skewered marinated meats that are grilled and served with a peanut dipping sauce.

At various times in their history, the Chinese, Indians, Portuguese, Dutch, and English ruled Indonesia. The Portuguese gained control in the 1500s, the Dutch conquered in the 1670s, and Indonesia finally achieved independence in 1945. Each of these ruling countries left culinary and other influences behind. The well-known *rijsttafel*, literally rice table, was developed by the Dutch settlers. This opulent display of rice and many different dishes required numerous servants to prepare and serve. No longer existing in the same profusion, the *rijsttafel* of today is more like a buffet.

TOPOGRAPHY

Vietnam lies in Southeast Asia, to the south of China. With the South China Sea bordering on its eastern side and the Gulf of Tonkin to the north, Vietnam contains more than 1,400 miles of coastline providing access to ample amounts of seafood.

Although mountains, forests, and jungles make up much of the north, the land around the Red River Delta and the coastal plains provides fertile

---

SOUTHEAST ASIA

Southeast Asia includes the countries lying south of China, east of India, and north of Australia. About the size of Europe, this area spans three time zones. All the countries within Southeast Asia share a similar climate due to the *monsoons*, seasonal winds. Each experiences a tropical climate with pronounced rainy and dry seasons. More than 1,000 languages are spoken throughout Southeast Asia. The major religions found in this area include Hinduism, Buddhism, Islam, and some Christianity.

farmland where crops flourish in the northern region. The central portion contains mountains. Lowlands and fertile land for crops along the coast and the Mekong Delta comprise the southern region. All of Vietnam experiences tropical weather with hot, humid, rainy summers and drier, warm winters. The *monsoons* control the climate.

Also situated in Southeast Asia, Thailand is bordered by Burma, Laos, and Cambodia on its west, north, and east. A narrow strip of land surrounded by the Andaman Sea to the west and the Gulf of Thailand to the east connects Thailand to Malaysia on the south. Rivers crisscross the country and provide the main transportation. Until recent times, canals functioned as roads throughout much of Thailand. With miles of coastline and many rivers, seafood and fish are abundant and comprise a major portion of the diet.

Mountains, forests, dry plateau, and some fertile river valleys compose much of the northern section of Thailand. The central area contains plains, rivers, and fertile farmland, and the south is made up of jungle, mountains, plains, and coastline. Like Vietnam and Indonesia, Thailand's climate is tropical and strongly affected by the *monsoons*. Hot, dry springs; cool, dry winters; and hot, wet summers prevail throughout most of the country with more moderate temperatures found in the mountains.

Lying between Australia and Southeast Asia, more than 13,000 islands comprise the country of Indonesia. About half of these islands remain uninhabited. Surrounded by the Indian and Pacific oceans, the islands of Indonesia stretch over a distance of 3,000 miles with the equator running through them. As a result, a hot, humid, tropical climate supporting abundant plant growth prevails, except at the high altitudes of the mountains. Some of the diverse land on these islands consists of mountains, volcanoes, and uninhabited, dense jungle.

Ingredients and Foods Commonly Used Throughout the Cuisines of Vietnam, Thailand, and Indonesia Include:

- seafood and fish
- rice and rice noodles
- coconut, coconut milk, and coconut oil
- fish sauce
- shrimp paste
- curry pastes
- scallions, garlic, and ginger
- lemongrass
- aromatic herbs, including cilantro, basil, and mint
- hot chili peppers and hot sauce
- fresh fruits and vegetables
- peanuts

COOKING METHODS

Steaming, boiling, simmering or braising, grilling or broiling, stir-frying, and deep-frying are cooking methods commonly used in these three countries. Baking is not seen often.

Grilling meats, fish, and bean curd remains popular. Meats are often cut into strips, marinated, then placed on a skewer before grilling. A variety of foods are prepared by steaming, including whole fish, vegetables, custards, and rice. Like Japan's *nabémono*, people in both the north and south of Vietnam frequently cook foods in a pot of boiling broth at the table, adding various food items to the boiling liquid with chopsticks.

The Vietnamese, Thai, and Indonesians use less oil for stir-frying foods than is customary in China. Of course, stir-frying is sautéing over high heat in a round-bottomed wok or other pan.

REGIONS

The diet of the Vietnamese consists mainly of seafood, rice, and vegetables. With its close proximity to rivers and the sea, fish and seafood remain the primary animal protein consumed in both North and South Vietnam. Squid, shrimp, lobster, and many varieties of fish abound. Fish sauce, *nu'ó'c mắm*, is consumed at every meal.

Because of a lack of land for grazing, chicken and pork appear more often than beef. Poultry follows seafood in availability, and small amounts of pork appear in many dishes. Beef is reserved for special occasions except in the north where there are some pasturelands and plains. Lamb and mutton remain unknown. Various game meats and fowl thrive in the mountainous regions, as well as the jungles and forests. As with other Asian countries, small amounts of meat are extended with larger quantities of vegetables and rice.

The Chinese coveted Vietnam because of the fertile rice growing areas in the Mekong and Red River deltas. The Chinese influence on the cuisine of Vietnam is most apparent in the northern region with the use of bean curd, star anise, spring rolls, and soups. Like the Chinese, the Vietnamese prepare stir-fried dishes, and they eat rice separately from the other dishes, rather than mixing them together like people from areas to the south.

A foundation of the cuisine, rice accompanies all dishes like in the other Southeast Asian cuisines. The Vietnamese prefer fluffy, separate grains of rice rather than the sticky rice favored in Japan and Korea.

Rice and noodles dominate the Vietnamese diet, although French bread adopted during the French occupation remains quite popular. French influence on the cuisine is apparent, particularly with the use of garlic, sauces, and butter.

Generally, Vietnamese recipes contain a wide variety and ample amounts of fresh herbs; however, the use of spices varies from region to region. With fewer spices available in the north, the dishes tend to be less spicy than those eaten in the south. Influence from the Indian cuisine prevails in southern Vietnam and shows up with the curries and various rice pancakes.

The Vietnamese use little oil in their cookery; the simmering of foods appears more often than stir-frying. Thickening agents are rarely used; rather food is presented in a simpler, more natural state.

Soup, another staple in this cuisine, is consumed regularly. Breakfast in Vietnam often consists of *phó'*, a North Vietnamese rice noodle soup in a beef broth strongly flavored with cilantro, garlic, and *nu'ó'c mắm* (fish sauce). Paper-thin slices of raw beef and rice noodles are placed in a bowl, then covered with boiling broth that cooks the meat. A popular soup served at any meal, many consider *phó'* the national dish of Vietnam.

Like most Asian countries, all foods comprising the Vietnamese meal are served at once. Typically, various hot dishes accompany salads and lots of rice. To compose a salad, any variety of vegetables (and perhaps meat or seafood) are wrapped in a lettuce leaf, then enclosed in a rice paper wrapper, dipped in *nu'ó'c mắm* sauce, and eaten. The Vietnamese table setting includes a saucer at each place setting for holding *nu'ó'c mắm* dipping sauce.

In Thailand, the revered rice actually represents life itself. Like most of the countries in Southeast Asia, the foundation of the diet revolves around rice, which accompanies every meal. In fact, each Thai inhabitant consumes about one pound of rice every day! A prolific rice-growing region, this nation exports huge quantities of rice. A very important principle in the cookery of Thailand, *kaeng* means liquid. This refers to the amount of liquid in a dish, which determines whether rice can be mixed directly into the dish. The Thai cook plans the menu for a meal to create a balance of dishes with and without abundant sauce or *kaeng*.

Hearty curries featuring large chunks of pork are served in the north of Thailand, whereas lighter curries flavored with coconut milk and small pieces of meat, poultry, or seafood distinguish curries from the south. The curries of Thailand contain a mixture of aromatics, peppers, spices, and coconut milk; they differ greatly from Indian curries. Three distinct types of Thai curries exist—yellow, red, and green. The ingredients that make up the sauce determine the color of the curry. The mildest of the curries, yellow, obtains its characteristic color from turmeric. The red ones contain red chili peppers, and the hottest variety, green, is made with green chili peppers.

Many characterize food of Thailand as hot; however, the food is much more complex than that single word. Aromatic herbs and coconut milk combine with the fiery chilies to produce complicated flavors that dominate the dishes found in Thailand. Thai food is described as many layers of different flavors that marry together to create an interesting and multileveled taste sensation. Basil, mint, cilantro, lemongrass, ginger, garlic, shallots, coriander, and fish sauce are just a few of the commonly used flavorings. To further heighten the appeal of the dishes, the Thai cook pays attention to the color, texture, and taste of each of the various ingredients used to create a dish so the final dish attracts the diner with a variety of flavors, textures, and colors.

Fruits and vegetables play a major role in the cuisine of Thailand with one or more salads served at each meal. All sorts of food items make their way into salads, providing healthy additions to meals. Piles of bean sprouts, lettuce, beans, and herbs accompany the spicy hot dishes and function to cool the spiciness. Fresh fruits normally end the Thai meal, but, when desserts are served, they tend to be less sweet than those consumed in the other Southeast Asian countries.

Most of the population of Indonesia resides in the Greater Sunda Islands to the west, which includes Borneo, Java, and Sumatra. Java ranks as the most populated island. With miles of coastline and many rivers, seafood and fish abound throughout Indonesia.

As with Vietnam and Thailand, rice forms the foundation of the Indonesian meal. In fact, Indonesians eat rice daily at all three meals. Although people from many other Southeast Asian countries eat rice separately from the other dishes, Indonesians mix rice with their other foods. Combining the fiery, hot Indonesian dishes with ample amounts of rice makes them taste less spicy.

Typically, the Indonesian cook juxtaposes sweet, sour, salty, and spicy taste sensations. Fiery *sambal*, Indonesian hot sauce, and coconut milk combine to form sweet and spicy flavorings. An important part of the Indonesian table, *sambal* accompanies the rice served at every meal.

Although most Indonesians practice the Islamic religion, the island of Bali remains a stronghold for the Hindu residents. Religion determines many culinary preferences, particularly regarding dietary restrictions with meat. Muslims do not eat pork, so other meats prevail in the Islamic areas. Although rare in much of Southeastern Asia, lamb appears frequently in Indonesia.

Each sect prepares ceremonial foods that continue as an important facet of the Indonesian cuisine. *Selametan*, a ceremonial feast, marks important events in Indonesia. Many foods in Indonesia represent spiritual issues, and the foods served at *selametan* include special foods such as *tumpeng*. Originating in Java, *tumpeng*, which means rice cone, graces the table at every important festival, including weddings and parties for newborn children. Traditionally, a variety of foods decorate this ceremonial pyramid of rice.

Significant differences exist between the cuisines of the various regions of Indonesia. The foods served in Sumatra are quite spicy, whereas inhabitants of Java prefer sweeter tastes. Many flavor similarities are apparent, however, throughout Indonesia. True for many countries with tropical climates, coconut milk and coconut oil appear everywhere. Also, sweet soy sauce (*kecap*), peanuts, and fermented shrimp paste (*trassi*) flavor a wide range of dishes throughout these islands.

Gado-gado, a salad consisting of a variety of vegetables topped with a peanut sauce dressing, remains popular in most areas of Indonesia. Other well-known dishes include *satay*, grilled meat accompanied by a spicy peanut sauce, and *soto*, a chicken and coconut milk soup.

Isolation caused by the distance between islands has resulted in great variation in the preparations and methods of cooking the same ingredients and dishes throughout the country. With tropical growing conditions, many crops thrive. Corn, rice, coffee, tea, a variety of spices, peanuts, cassava, bananas, sweet potatoes, and many other fruits and vegetables flourish here.

Seventy percent of the world's nutmeg grows in Indonesia; cinnamon, cloves, and peppers also thrive on these islands. Interestingly, the Indonesians do not cook with nutmeg or cloves, but they cook with all sorts of peppers, including hot chili peppers and peppercorns of various colors.

Unlike most inhabitants of Southeast Asia, Indonesians eat with their fingers, not chopsticks. The food is rolled into a ball with the fingers on the right hand, then picked up and eaten with the same hand. The left hand is used only for passing food.

CUISINE

The coconut holds an esteemed place in the cooking of each of these countries. With a lack of dairy cattle, the abundant palm trees provide coconuts, coconut oil, and coconut milk that forms the basis for many sauces. An ingredient used in curries throughout this part of the world, coconut pairs well with hot chilies by providing a sweet taste sensation to counteract the spicy hot. Grated or shredded, coconut meat appears in a myriad of dishes, both sweet and savory. Each of these countries feature a dish of seafood, chicken, or beef rolled in a taro or banana leaf then steamed in coconut milk. Coconuts touch every part of the menu, from appetizers to beverages and desserts.

RICE

Rice plays a major role in both the diet and the culture throughout Southeast Asia, as well as the rest of Asia. First, it functions as a staple food in the Asian countries. As a result, rice ranks supreme in importance as a food crop. Also, its significance is reflected in its constant appearance and importance in festivals, many of which surround the planting or harvesting of rice. Finally, rice assumes a prominent role in cultural events. Rice wine is often drunk as part of the wedding ceremony, and newlyweds are showered with rice as a symbol of good luck and hope for fertility and prosperity in their lives together.

Many varieties of bananas grow in these three countries, and, like the coconut, this fruit appears in numerous forms and dishes. Sautéed, salted, underripe bananas often accompany the main meal. Ripe bananas are grilled, sautéed, cooked in custards, or coated with rice and/or coconut and eaten as a snack or dessert. As stated earlier, even the banana leaves are used. Like the cornhusks used to wrap *tamales* in Mexico and Central America, banana leaves function as a wrapper to enclose fillings for cooking (usually steaming).

Peanuts play a major role in these cuisines. Whether chopped peanuts are sprinkled over a finished dish or ground peanuts flavor the sauces, peanuts add flavor and texture to dishes throughout these three countries.

Probably more than any other ingredient, fish flavorings contribute the characteristic tastes associated with each of these countries. Called *nám pla* in Thailand and *nu'ó'c mắm* in Vietnam, fish sauce replaces the soy sauce used in other Asian countries. Fish sauce is made from fermented anchovies and salt. Paired with meat, poultry, seafood, tofu, and/or vegetables, the flavor of fish sauce permeates the dishes and functions as the major flavoring ingredient in both Vietnam and Thailand. Frequently used in Indonesia, shrimp paste (*trassi*) lends a fishlike taste to Indonesian dishes.

REGION	AREA	WEATHER	TOPOGRAPHY	FOODS
Vietnam	North	Tropical, hot, humid, rainy summers, dry warm winters, *monsoons*	Mountains, forests, jungles, Red River Delta, coastal plains, fertile farmland	Seafood, rice
	Central and south	Tropical, hot, humid, rainy summers, dry warm winters, *monsoons*	Lowlands, mountains, Me Kong Delta, coastal plains, fertile farmland	Seafood, rice, corn, soybeans, peanuts, vegetables, fruits, sweet potatoes, coconuts, sugar
Thailand	North	Tropical, hot, humid, rainy summers, dry warm winters, *monsoons*	Mountains, forests, rivers, plateau, fertile river valleys	Fish, shellfish, tuna, herring, shrimp, rice, cassava, corn, pineapples, coconuts, sugar
	Central	Tropical, hot, humid, rainy summers, dry warm winters, *monsoons*	Plains, rivers, fertile farmland	Fish, shellfish, tuna, herring, shrimp, rice, corn, cassava, pineapples, sugar
	South	Tropical, hot, humid, rainy summers, dry warm winters, *monsoons*	Coasts, jungle, plains, mountains	Seafood, fish, shrimp, rice, cassava, corn, coconuts, pineapples, tropical fruits, sugar
Indonesia	West: Greater Sunda Islands, Borneo, Java, Sumatra	Hot, humid, wet and dry seasons, *monsoons*	Coasts, rain forest, mountains, rivers, volcanoes, valleys, forests, plains	Fish, seafood, rice, peanuts, spices, sweet potatoes, tropical fruits, bananas, coconuts, sugar
	South: Bali, Timor	Hot, humid, wet and dry seasons, *monsoons*	Coast, mountains, rivers	Seafood, fish, corn, spices
	East: Moluccas	Hot, humid, wet and dry seasons, *monsoons*	Coast, mountains, equator	Seafood, fish, rice, spices

Kerrieboontjies Bredie (Curried Lamb and Beans)

Spinach Stew

Dolmades (Meat Stuffed Grape Leaves); photo
courtesy of Dorling Kindersley

Beignets de Bananes (Banana Fritters)

Couscous in the Fez Manner (*Couscous* with Lamb
and Vegetables)

Baba Ghannouj (Eggplant Sesame Dip); photo courtesy of Dorling Kindersley

Moussaka (Baked Eggplant, Lamb, and Béchamel Sauce); photo courtesy of Dorling Kindersley

Tabouli (Bulghur Salad); photo courtesy of Dorling Kindersley

Hummus (Chickpea Sesame Dip); photo courtesy of the Bean Education & Awareness Network (B.E.A.N.)

Kibbeyet (Stuffed Ground Lamb and Bulgur Mixture); photo courtesy of Dorling Kindersley

Spanakopita (Spinach-Feta Cheese Pie)

Baklava (Layered Nut Pastry); photo courtesy of Dorling Kindersley

Chopped Liver

Felafel (Deep-fried Chickpea Balls); photo courtesy of Dorling Kindersley

Cheese Blintzes (Cheese Filled Crepes)

Orange and Olive Salad

Grilled Fish with Caper Vinaigrette; photo courtesy of The Norwegian Seafood Export Council—www.seafood.no. Photography by Kjell Ove Storvik

Carrot Tzimmes (Honey Glazed Carrots); photo courtesy of Dorling Kindersley

Potato Latkes (Potato Pancakes); photo courtesy of the Idaho Potato Commission

Dried Fruit Compote; photo courtesy of Dorling Kindersley

Ch 'Un-Chüan (Spring Rolls); photo courtesy of Dorling Kindersley

Suan-La-T'ang (Hot and Sour Soup)

Hün-T'un-T'ang (Wonton Soup); photo courtesy of Dorling Kindersley

Pickled Cabbage Peking Style

Bean Curd and Pork

Kung Pao Chicken (Spicy Chicken with Peanuts); photo courtesy of Dorling Kindersley

Hunan Crispy Duck; photo courtesy of Dorling Kindersley

Browned Noodles with Pork; photo courtesy of Dorling Kindersley

Sukju Namul (Bean Sprout Salad); photo courtesy of Dorling Kindersley

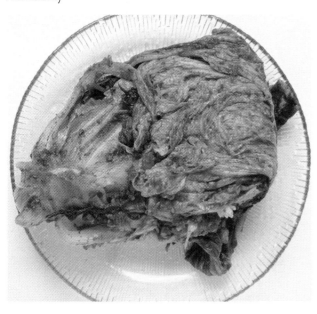

Kimch'i (Pickled Cabbage); photo courtesy of Dorling Kindersley

Tempura (Deep-fried, Battered Vegetables, Seafood, Poultry, and/or Meat); photo courtesy of Dorling Kindersley

Miso Shiru (Bean Paste Soup with Tofu); photo courtesy of Dorling Kindersley

Salmon Teriyaki; photo courtesy of Kikkoman Corporation

Bulgogi (Fiery Beef); photo courtesy of Dorling Kindersley

Phở' (Beef and Noodle Soup); photo courtesy of Dorling Kindersley

Satay Atam (Chicken Kebabs with a Peanut Sauce); photo courtesy of Dorling Kindersley

Chap Chae (Cellophane Noodles with Beef and Vegetables); photo courtesy of Dorling Kindersley

Tôm Yam Kûng (Hot and Sour Shrimp Soup);
photo courtesy of Dorling Kindersley

Dau Chua (Pickled Carrot and Daikon Salad); photo
courtesy of Dorling Kindersley

Gado-Gado (Mixed Vegetable Salad); photo courtesy
of Dorling Kindersley

Pad Thai (Noodles with Shrimp and Pork); photo courtesy of Dorling Kindersley

Mee Krob (Crisp Rice Noodles with Shrimp and Pork)

Kaeng Pet Kai Normai On (Chicken and Bamboo Shoots in Red Curry)

Shah Jahani Biryani (Lamb and Saffron Rice Casserole)

Tandoori Murghi (Chicken Baked in Tandoor Oven); photo courtesy of the American Spice Trade Association

Kheera Raita (Cucumber and Yogurt Salad); photo courtesy of Dorling Kindersley

Dahi Machi (Fish in Yogurt Sauce); photo courtesy of Dorling Kindersley

Masoor Dal (Spiced Lentil Purée); photo courtesy of Dorling Kindersley

Sabzi Molee (Mixed Vegetable Curry); photo courtesy of Dorling Kindersley

Kheer (Rice Pudding); photo courtesy of Dorling Kindersley

Matar Pullao (Green Pea Pilaf)

Masaledar Sem (Spicy Green Beans); photo courtesy of Dorling Kindersley

Cream of Crab Soup; photo courtesy of Dorling Kindersley

Salad with Avocado and Mango

Shearer's Stew (Lamb Stew with Dumplings); photo courtesy of Dorling Kindersley

Deep-fried Fish; photo courtesy of Dorling Kindersley

Sautéed Trout with Macadamia Nuts; photo courtesy of Dorling Kindersley

Spinach with Currants

Salsa Cruda (Uncooked Spicy Tomato Sauce); photo courtesy of Dorling Kindersley

Guacamole (Avocado Dip); photo courtesy of Dorling Kindersley

Mole de Guajolote (Turkey in Mole Sauce); photo courtesy of Dorling Kindersley

Sopa de Elote (Corn Soup); photo courtesy of Dorling Kindersley

Pavlova (Meringue Shell Filled with Whipped Cream and Fruit); photo courtesy of Dorling Kindersley

Huachinango a la Veracruzana (Red Snapper, Veracruz Style); photo courtesy of the American Spice Trade Association

Empanadas de Horno (Meat Filled Turnovers); photo courtesy of Dorling Kindersley

Frijoles (Beans); photo courtesy of the Bean Education & Awareness Network (B.E.A.N.)

Chili Rellenos (Stuffed Chili Peppers)

Frijoles Refritos (Refried Beans); photo courtesy of Dorling Kindersley

Escabeche de Pescado (Fish Escabeche)

Sopa de Feijão (Brazilian Bean Soup); photo courtesy of Dorling Kindersley

Chupe de Camarones (Shrimp Chowder)

Cebiche de Hongos (Mushroom Ceviche)

Arroz con Pato (Braised Duck with Cilantro Rice)

Pabellon Criollo (Beef in Tomato Sauce with Black Beans, Rice, and Plantains)

Locro (Squash Stew)

Flan (Caramel Custard); photo courtesy of Dorling Kindersley

Pepper Pot

Stamp and Go (Salt Cod Fritters); photo courtesy of The Norwegian Seafood Export Council—www.seafood.no. Photography by Alf Börjessen

Mixed Bean Salad; photo courtesy of Dorling Kindersley

Shrimp and Mango Curry; photo courtesy of Dorling Kindersley

Ropa Vieja (Shredded Beef)

Jerk Pork (Pork with Spicy Rub); photo courtesy of Dorling Kindersley

Moros y Cristianos (Black Beans and Rice); photo courtesy of Dorling Kindersley

Caribbean Bananas

Many Muslims live in these areas, which means no pork or alcohol consumption. These dietary restrictions do not apply to Hindus or Christians, however.

Dessert in each of these countries usually consists of fresh fruits. Prepared desserts are reserved for special occasions.

Review Questions

1. Name flavorings and ingredients commonly used in the cuisines of Vietnam, Thailand, and Indonesia.
2. How do the cuisines of these three countries differ from other Asian cuisines?
3. Name at least one major difference between the cooking of North and South Vietnam.
4. Describe cooking methods often used in these three countries.
5. Discuss which animal proteins are consumed in each of these countries and why.
6. Discuss how water and the equator have affected the cuisines of these countries.
7. Which countries influenced the cuisines of Vietnam, Thailand, and Indonesia? Discuss those influences.

Glossary

gado-gado An Indonesian salad consisting of a variety of vegetables accompanied by peanut sauce dressing

kaeng Thai word for liquid, refers to amount of liquid in a dish

kecap Sweet soy sauce used in Indonesia

monsoons Seasonal winds that affect the climate

nám pla Fish sauce used extensively in Thailand

nu'ó'c mắm Fish sauce used extensively in Vietnam

phó' Rice noodle soup in a meat broth strongly flavored with cilantro, garlic, and *nu'ó'c mắm;* commonly eaten for breakfast in Vietnam but served at any meal; considered the national dish of Vietnam

rijsttafel Literally meaning rice table, opulent display of many different dishes accompanied by rice, requiring many servants for preparation and service, developed by the Dutch settlers

satay Grilled meat accompanied by a spicy peanut sauce commonly served in Indonesia

selametan Ceremonial feast that marks important events in Indonesia

soto Indonesian chicken and coconut milk soup

tumpeng An Indonesian ceremonial rice dish consisting of a cone of rice decorated with a variety of foods, served at all important events

CHẢ GIÒ (Vietnam)

Spring Rolls

Number of Servings: 9   Cooking Method: Deep-fry
Serving Size: 3 each 3-inch rolls
Total Yield: 28 each 3-inch rolls

Food Balance: Protein
Wine Style: Light- to medium-bodied Chenin Blanc, Pinot Blanc, mild
  Chardonnay, Blush, Beaujolais, Grenache
Example: Beringer Chenin Blanc, Greg Norman Chardonnay

Accompany with Nu'ố'c Mắm Cham (recipe follows).

INGREDIENTS	WEIGHT	VOLUME
FILLING:		
cellophane noodles	1 oz	
mushrooms, dried Chinese	½ oz	8 each
mushrooms, dried, tree ears		2 tablespoons
scallion, minced	½ oz	1 each
onion, minced	2 oz	1 small
pork, ground	4 oz	
white crab meat, cooked, shredded	4 oz	
egg	1¾ oz	1 each
salt		¼ teaspoon
black pepper		⅛ teaspoon

Vietnamese rice papers
oil for deep-frying

GARNISH:		
soft lettuce like Boston, washed, leaves separated	about 10 oz	1 large head

mint leaves, fresh, washed
Nu'ố'c Mắm Cham (dipping sauce), *recipe follows*

FILLING:

1. Soak dried mushrooms and tree ears in hot water for 30 minutes. Remove and chop finely.
2. Soak cellophane noodles in hot water for 20 to 30 minutes. Drain, cut into ½-inch lengths.
3. Combine all filling ingredients, mix well, refrigerate until needed.

TO ASSEMBLE:

If using 4-inch rice paper, use whole. If 9-inch rice paper, cut in half or quarters (depending on desired size of spring roll) after soaking.

1. Soak rice paper in warm water just until barely softened and pliable, remove from water. Cut in half or quarters if necessary.
2. Place desired amount of filling (about ¾ oz or 1 tablespoon for half 9-inch) in log shape on lower third of rice paper.
3. Fold bottom edge (closest to you) over filling, fold in both sides. Brush top inside edge with water, then roll filling toward top of rice paper, encasing filling completely.
4. Place finished spring roll on parchment-lined pan, folded side down.
5. Continue making remaining rolls.
6. Refrigerate until frying.

TO FRY:

1. Heat frying oil until 350 degrees.
2. Add spring rolls, a few at a time (so temperature is not lowered too much), fry until golden, about 5 minutes.
3. Drain on absorbent paper.

TO SERVE:

1. Place bowl of Nu'ó'c Mắm Cham at each diner's place.
2. Place lettuce leaves and mint on platter, place spring rolls on separate platter (for individual service, place these three ingredients on one platter).
3. Take spring roll, place on lettuce leaf (or part of one if leaf too large), place few mint leaves on top, roll lettuce around spring roll, dip in Nu'ó'c Mắm Cham and enjoy.

NU'Ó'C MẮM CHAM (Vietnam)

Fish Sauce Seasoned with Lime Juice

Number of Servings: 8
Serving Size: 2 oz (¼ cup)
Total Yield: 1 lb

INGREDIENTS	WEIGHT	VOLUME
sugar	3 oz	6 tablespoons
water, warm	4 oz	½ cup
hot red or green chilies, fresh, minced	up to 2 oz	2 to 4 each
garlic, minced, mashed	¼ oz	2 cloves
lime juice	4 oz	½ cup
fish sauce	4 oz	½ cup

> *Purchase fish sauce from Asian grocery.*

1. Mix sugar and water in jar or bowl, shake or whisk until sugar dissolves.
2. Add remaining ingredients, mix well to combine.
3. Refrigerate until needed.
4. Pour into individual bowls for each diner.

SATAY ATAM (Indonesia)

Chicken Kebabs with a Peanut Sauce

Number of Servings: 8   Cooking Method: Broil
Serving Size: 3 oz meat with
        ¾ oz peanut sauce
Total Yield: 1 lb, 8 oz meat

Food Balance: Protein/sweet
Wine Suggestion: Soft and fruity Chenin Blanc, Johannisberg Riesling, White Zinfandel, Grenache
Example: Beringer Chenin Blanc or Johannisberg Riesling, Wolf Blass Grenache

INGREDIENTS	WEIGHT	VOLUME
chicken, boneless, skinless, cut into 1-inch cubes	2 lbs	2 whole breasts

> *Serve with warm Peanut Sauce (recipe follows).*

Satay Atam (Chicken Kebabs with a Peanut Sauce); photo courtesy of Dorling Kindersley

INGREDIENTS	WEIGHT	VOLUME
MARINADE:		
garlic, minced, mashed	½ oz	4 cloves
ginger, peeled, minced	1 oz	2-inch cube
kecap manis (sweet soy sauce)	1 oz	2 tablespoons
soy sauce	1 oz	2 tablespoons
lime juice	1 oz	2 tablespoons
coriander, ground		2 teaspoons
sugar	¼ oz	2 teaspoons
cayenne pepper		½ teaspoon

bamboo or metal skewers

1. Combine all marinade ingredients in bowl, mix well.
2. Add chicken to marinade, mix well, cover and refrigerate for 2 to 24 hours.
3. Soak bamboo skewers in water for at least 30 minutes before using to prevent them from burning while grilling.
4. Thread about three chicken pieces on skewer.
5. Preheat broiler or grill, grill skewers about 4-inches from heat source for 5 minutes on each side, until done.
6. Serve with warm peanut sauce (*recipe follows*).

SAMBAL KACANG (Indonesia)

Peanut Sauce

Number of Servings: 11 Cooking Method: Boil
Serving Size: 1 oz
Total Yield: 11 oz or 1¼ cups

INGREDIENTS	WEIGHT	VOLUME
peanut butter, smooth or crunchy	3¼ oz	⅓ cup

INGREDIENTS	WEIGHT	VOLUME
garlic, minced, mashed		1 clove
cayenne pepper		½ teaspoon
brown sugar	½ oz	1 tablespoon
lime juice	1 oz	2 tablespoons
coconut milk	1 oz	2 tablespoons
kecap manis (sweet soy sauce)	½ oz	1 tablespoon
water	4 oz	½ cup

1. Mix all ingredients in saucepan, stir often, bring to boil.
2. Turn heat to medium low, stirring occasionally, cook until thickened, about 15 to 20 minutes.
3. Correct seasonings, remove from heat, refrigerate for storage.

PHÓ' (Vietnam)

Beef and Noodle Soup

Number of Servings: 9   Cooking Method: Boil
Serving Size: 6 oz soup containing
          ¾ oz cooked meat, 2 oz noodles,
          ¼ oz bean sprouts, 1 oz raw steak
Total Yield: 3 lbs, 8 oz soup

Food Balance: Protein/spicy
Wine Style: Light- to medium-bodied Gewürztraminer, Pinot Blanc, Viognier, Blush, Rosé
Example: Château St. Jean Gewürztraminer or Viognier

INGREDIENTS	WEIGHT	VOLUME
beef stock	4 lbs	2 qts
beef chuck, in one piece	1 lb	
onion, sliced ¼-inch thick	6½ oz	1 large
carrot, peeled, sliced	3 oz	1 each
ginger, peeled, cut in half	1 oz	2-inch piece
stick cinnamon		2-inch stick
star anise		2 each
peppercorns, whole		1 teaspoon
fish sauce	2 oz or to taste	¼ cup or to taste

CONDIMENTS:

rice stick noodles	8 oz	
beef, steak, tender, sliced paper thin	10 oz	
bean sprouts, blanched for 5 seconds, rinsed in cold water	2¾ oz	1 cup
scallions, thinly sliced, green included	2 oz	2 each
chilies, hot, sliced thinly		to taste
cilantro, minced	¾ oz	¼ cup
lime wedges		
fish sauce		

> The paper-thin sliced raw beef cooks in the bowl from the heat of the boiling stock placed over it. Typically, this soup is served for breakfast in many Vietnamese households, but it also appears on lunch and dinner menus.

Phở' (Beef and Noodle Soup); photo courtesy of Dorling Kindersley

1. Place stock, beef chuck, onion, carrot, ginger, cinnamon stick, star anise, and peppercorns in large pot. Simmer for 2 or 3 hours, until meat is tender.
2. Meanwhile, soak rice noodles in water for at least 30 minutes.
3. Prepare condiments, placing bean sprouts, scallions, chilies, cilantro, and lime wedges on platter or separate bowls for table.
4. Strain stock, add water to make 3 lbs, 8 oz (7 cups), remove beef chuck, cut into thin slices.
5. Drain rice stick noodles, add to boiling water for 1 or 2 minutes, until tender.
6. Drain in colander, rinse with cold water, place noodles in bowl of cold water until needed.
7. Heat soup, add fish sauce, taste to correct seasonings. Bring to boil.
8. Heat noodles by dipping briefly in boiling water.
9. Place some noodles, raw beef, and cooked beef in bowl, cover with boiling soup.
10. Serve immediately, let each diner add condiments, as desired.

TÔM YAM KÛNG (Thailand)

Hot and Sour Shrimp Soup

Number of Servings: 8   Cooking Method: Boil
Serving Size: 8 oz
Total Yield: 4 lbs, 5 oz

Food Balance: Spicy/acid
Wine Style: Light- to medium-bodied Johannisberg Riesling, Gewürztraminer, Viognier, Blush, Grenache, Beaujolais
Example: Beringer Johannisberg Riesling, Viognier, or White Zinfandel

INGREDIENTS	WEIGHT	VOLUME
shrimp, medium, peeled and deveined, reserve shells	1 lb	
lemongrass, fresh	½ oz	2 each
lime rind, finely grated	¼ oz	1 tablespoon
fish sauce	1 oz	2 tablespoons
chicken stock	3 lb	1½ quarts
lime juice	2 oz	¼ cup
chili paste	¾ oz	1 tablespoon
sugar	1 oz	2 tablespoons
mushrooms, button or other variety, fresh, quartered, parboiled for 1 minute	8 oz	3 cups

GARNISH:

green chilies, hot, fresh, finely cut into rounds	½ oz	2 each
cilantro, minced	½ oz	3 tablespoons

1. Discard dry outer leaves and dry top from lemongrass, cut remainder into 3-inch pieces, crush using flat part of knife.
2. Place stock, shells, lemongrass, and lime rind into pan, bring to
   boil, lower heat and simmer for 20 minutes.
3. Strain stock, add fish sauce, lime juice, chili paste, and sugar,
   mix, correct seasonings.
4. Add mushrooms, bring to boil, add shrimp.

Tôm Yam Kûng (Hot and Sour Shrimp Soup); photo
courtesy of Dorling Kindersley

5. Cook over medium heat for 2 minutes, until shrimp become opaque.
6. Serve immediately, accompanied by garnishes.

DAU CHUA (Vietnam)

Pickled Carrot and Daikon Salad

Number of Servings: 10
Serving Size: 3 oz
Total Yield: 1 lb, 15 oz

Cooking Method: Boil

INGREDIENTS	WEIGHT	VOLUME
carrots, peeled, julienne	1 lb	4 to 5 large
daikon radish, peeled, julienne	1 lb	4 cups
salt, kosher	¼ oz	1 teaspoon
water	11 oz	1⅓ cups
rice vinegar	5½ oz	⅔ cups
sugar	2 oz	¼ cup

1. Place carrots and daikon in strainer in sink or over bowl. Sprinkle with salt, mix well. Let stand 30 minutes.
2. Combine water, rice vinegar, and sugar in pan, bring to boil, remove from heat, cool to room temperature.
3. After 30 minutes, rinse carrots and daikon with cold water, squeeze dry, place in bowl.
4. Pour vinegar mixture over carrots and daikon, mix gently. Refrigerate 1 hour before serving.
5. Remove carrots and daikon from liquid for serving as accompaniment to other dishes.

Dau Chua (Pickled Carrot and Daikon Salad); photo courtesy of Dorling Kindersley

GADO-GADO (Indonesia)

Mixed Vegetable Salad

Number of Servings: 11   Cooking Method: Boil
Serving Size: 4 oz vegetables,
                     1 oz peanut dressing
Total Yield: 2 lbs, 12 oz

INGREDIENTS	WEIGHT	VOLUME
potatoes, cooked, peeled, sliced, ¼-inch thick	10 oz	2 each
eggs, hard-boiled, peeled, quartered	5 oz	3 each
green beans, trimmed, blanched	5 oz	
carrot, peeled, cut into ⅜-inch matchsticks	2½ oz	1 each
cauliflower, flowerets, blanched	7 oz	2 cups
cabbage, sliced thinly, blanched	6 oz	2 cups
bean sprouts, blanched	4 oz	1 cup
cucumber, peeled, sliced, ¼-inch thick	5 oz	½ each

> Accompany with Peanut Sauce (recipe included earlier).

> Use any vegetables desired, just be sure to blanch each vegetable until still crunchy, then rinse under cold water to stop the cooking. Bean sprouts require about 15 seconds, carrots and cauliflower about 3 minutes, green beans about 2 minutes, and so on. Keep each vegetable separate for arranging on the plate.

1. Blanch each vegetable in boiling water until barely tender yet crisp, rinse with cold water, drain well.
2. Set aside, keeping each vegetable separate.
3. Arrange vegetables on platter or individual plates, being mindful of color and texture of vegetables.
4. Serve, dressed with Peanut Sauce drizzled over vegetables.

Gado-Gado (Mixed Vegetable Salad); photo courtesy of Dorling Kindersley

BÁNH XẾO (Vietnam)

Happy Pancakes

Number of Servings: 13   Cooking Method: Sauté
Serving Size: 10- to 12-inch pancake
Total Yield: 3 lbs, 15 oz pancake batter

Food Balance: Protein
Wine Style: Light- to medium-bodied Chenin Blanc, Sauvignon Blanc,
    Blush, fruity Chardonnay, Beaujolais
Example: Château Souverain Sauvignon Blanc or Beringer Gamay
    Beaujolais

> These pancakes make an excellent luncheon item, appetizer, or addition to an assortment of dishes. The Nư'ớc Mắm dipping sauce is a necessity with them!

INGREDIENTS	WEIGHT	VOLUME
BATTER:		
rice flour	1 lb, 5 oz	3½ cups
water	2 lbs	1 qt
turmeric		½ teaspoon
scallion, thinly sliced	1 oz	2 each
FILLING:		
ground pork	8 oz	
shrimp, peeled and deveined	8 oz	
garlic, minced, mashed	¼ oz	2 cloves
scallions, minced	1 oz	2 each
black pepper		as needed
fish sauce		2 teaspoons
onion, thinly sliced	4 oz	1 medium
mushrooms, button or any variety, sliced	6¼ oz	10 each
mung bean sprouts	10 oz	3¼ cups

oil, for frying

Nư'ớc Mắm Cham (dipping sauce)

1. Whisk rice flour and water together, add turmeric and scallion, mix well. Refrigerate until needed.
2. In bowl, mix pork with sprinkling of pepper and half the minced scallions, garlic, and fish sauce, refrigerate until needed.
3. In another bowl, mix shrimp with sprinkling of pepper and other half of scallions, garlic, and fish sauce, refrigerate until needed.
4. Heat about ½ oz (1 tablespoon) oil in large nonstick skillet over high heat.
5. Place about ¾ oz pork, ¾ oz shrimp, few slices of onion and mushrooms in skillet, cook about 1 minute over high heat.
6. Stir batter well, add just enough batter to coat pan, about 3¾ oz (3-oz ladle). Tilt pan to spread in thin even layer.
7. Cover, cook until edges of pancake turn brown, about 3 to 4 minutes.
8. Place ¾ oz (¼ cup) beans sprouts on half of pancake, fold other half over it (like an omelet).
9. Serve immediately, accompanied by Nư'ớc Mắm Cham.

BO VIÊN (Vietnam)

Beef Balls

Number of Servings: 10   Cooking Method: Boil
Serving Size: Four 1-oz beef balls, 3 oz broth
Total Yield: 2 lbs, 8 oz raw meat
             Forty 1-oz beef balls
             4 lbs (2 quarts) broth

Food Balance: Protein
Wine Style: Light- to medium-bodied Chenin Blanc, Pinot Grigio, light Pinot Noir
Example: Campanile Pinot Grigio or Beringer North Coast Pinot Noir

INGREDIENTS	WEIGHT	VOLUME
BEEF BALLS:		
fish sauce	4 oz	½ cup
water	4 oz	½ cup
potato starch	½ oz	4 teaspoons
sugar		1 teaspoon
baking powder	½ oz	2 teaspoons
black pepper		¼ teaspoon
beef, round, boneless, trimmed of fat, sliced thin across grain	2 lbs	
sesame oil	¾ oz	1½ tablespoons
BROTH:		
water	3 lbs	1½ qts
fish sauce		1½ teaspoons
salt		¼ to ½ teaspoon
GARNISHES:		
scallions, sliced thinly		
black pepper		
chili paste		

1. Mix fish sauce, water, potato starch, sugar, baking powder, and black pepper in bowl.
2. Add meat slices to bowl, mix well, cover and refrigerate for 5 hours.
3. Process meat to paste in food processor.
4. Place some sesame oil on palms, form 1-oz (1 tablespoon) meatballs.
5. Bring water to boil over high heat, add balls, boil 5 minutes until they float to surface, remove from water.
6. Add fish sauce and salt to water, boil broth, add beef balls to reheat.
7. Serve 4 beef balls with 3 oz (⅓ cup) of broth, garnish with scallions, a sprinkling of black pepper, and chili paste.

PEPES IKAN (Indonesia)

Spicy Fish

Number of Servings: 8   Cooking Method: Broil
Serving Size: 5 oz
Total Yield: 2 lbs, 4 oz

Food Balance: Sweet/sour/spicy
Wine Style: Soft and fruity Gewürztraminer, White Merlot, or Zinfandel, Grenache, soft Shiraz
Example: Beringer White Zinfandel or Gewürztraminer, Stone Cellars Shiraz

INGREDIENTS	WEIGHT	VOLUME
onion, diced	4½ oz	1 medium
garlic, minced		3 cloves
chili flakes, dried, chopped		1½ teaspoons
shrimp paste		¾ teaspoon
salt	½ oz	2 teaspoons
sugar	¼ oz	1½ teaspoons
tamarind paste, dissolved in 1½ oz (3 tablespoons) water	¾ oz	1 tablespoon
tomato, chopped, ripe or canned	3¾ oz	¾ cup
fish fillets, haddock, flounder, sole	3 lbs	

3 sheets aluminum foil

1. Place onion, garlic, chili flakes, shrimp paste, salt, sugar, tamarind paste, and tomato in bowl of food processor or blender, blend until coarse paste.
2. Preheat broiler.
3. Cover both sides of fish with paste, place ⅓ of fish on each piece of foil, wrap tightly.
4. Place foil packet under broiler for ten minutes, turn, cook another ten minutes.
5. Open packet, turning back edges, and broil 5 minutes, to brown fish.
6. Serve hot, accompanied by rice.

PAD THAI (Thailand)

Noodles with Shrimp and Pork

Number of Servings: 8   Cooking Method: Stir-fry (sauté)
Serving Size: 9 oz
Total Yield: 4 lbs, 15 oz

Food Balance: Acid/spicy
Wine Style: Light- to medium-bodied Gewürztraminer, Viognier, mild Chardonnay, mild Reds, Shiraz, Zinfandel, Merlot
Example: Meridian Gewürztraminer, Beringer Founders' Chardonnay or Shiraz

INGREDIENTS	WEIGHT	VOLUME
noodles, dried, rice-stick, about ⅛-inch wide	1 lb	1 package
fish sauce	4 oz	½ cup
rice vinegar	4 oz	½ cup
sugar	2½ oz	6 tablespoons
catsup	1½ oz	2 tablespoons
oil	½ oz	1 tablespoon
garlic, minced, mashed	2 oz	14 cloves

INGREDIENTS	WEIGHT	VOLUME
shrimp, medium, peeled, deveined	8 oz	
pork tenderloin, cut into bite-size strips	8 oz	
eggs, slightly beaten	3½ oz	2 each
Thai chili powder or cayenne		2 teaspoons or to taste
scallions, angle-cut into 1½-inch pieces, include greens	4 oz	8 each
peanuts, unsalted, shelled, finely chopped	4 oz	⅔ cup
bean sprouts	8½ oz	3 cups
cilantro, minced	¾ oz	¼ cup

CONDIMENTS:

bean sprouts
peanuts, unsalted, finely chopped
lime wedges
Thai chilies, finely sliced
cilantro, minced

1. Soak rice sticks in bowl of warm water until they are soft, about 15 minutes.
2. Combine fish sauce, rice vinegar, sugar, and catsup in small bowl, stir to dissolve sugar.
3. Drain noodles, set aside until needed.
4. Heat oil in wok over medium high heat, add garlic, shrimp, and pork, stir-fry until shrimp and pork lose raw color, about 1 minute.
5. Add sauce mixture, bring to boil, add noodles, gently toss in sauce.
6. Stir-fry until noodles absorb sauce, about 2 minutes.
7. Pour eggs into pan, mix eggs down under noodle mixture, cook without stirring for 15 seconds.

Pad Thai (Noodles with Shrimp and Pork); photo courtesy of Dorling Kindersley

8. Add chili powder or cayenne and scallions, stir-fry until the scallions are cooked, about 1 to 2 minutes.
9. Stir in peanuts and bean sprouts until well mixed.
10. Transfer to serving platter, sprinkle with cilantro, serve accompanied by condiments.

MEE KROB (Thailand)

Crisp Rice Noodles with Shrimp and Pork

Number of Servings: 10
Serving Size: 5 oz
Total Yield: 3 lbs, 6 oz

Cooking Method: Sauté (stir-fry),
   deep-fry

Food Balance: Spicy/ sweet and sour
Wine Style: Fruity, light- to medium-bodied blush wines, fruity Whites—
   Pinot Gris to Riesling; soft rich Reds—Shiraz to Zinfandel
Example: Château Souverain Zinfandel

> This dish may be prepared with any combination of meats or vegetables desired.

INGREDIENTS	WEIGHT	VOLUME
dried mushrooms, forest or other type	¼ oz	6 each
oil for deep-frying		
eggs, lightly beaten	3½ oz	2 each
rice stick noodles	8 oz	
pork, boneless, lean, ¼-inch strips	8 oz	
onions, diced	2¼ oz	½ medium
garlic, minced	¾ oz	5 large cloves
shrimp, peeled and deveined	1 lb	
red chilies, hot, seeded, minced		2 each
sugar	3¾ oz	½ cup
tomato paste	¾ oz	2 tablespoons
fish sauce	2 oz	¼ cup
lime juice, fresh	2 oz	¼ cup
lime zest	¼ oz	1 tablespoon
green beans, julienne	3½ oz	20 each
sambal	¾ oz or to taste	1 tablespoon or to taste
bean sprouts	10 oz	4 cups
cilantro, minced	½ oz	¼ cup

GARNISH:

scallion brushes
chili pepper strips
deep-fried eggs, see recipe below

1. Soak mushrooms in ¼ cup water for 20 minutes, slice mushrooms, reserve soaking water.
2. Heat oil for deep-frying in wok or deep-fryer until 350 degrees.
3. Dribble about ½ oz (1 tablespoon) egg from gloved fingers into hot oil, moving hand in circular motion so egg falls into strands.
4. Fry for 30 seconds, turn lacelike egg gently, fry another 30 seconds, until golden brown, drain on paper toweling.
5. Dip hand in cold water, repeat process with remaining eggs.

6. Divide rice noodles into 3 or 4 pieces, fry one piece at a time. Fry for 1 minute, turn gently with tongs, fry another 30 seconds, until light brown. Drain on paper toweling.

7. Remove all oil except 1 oz (2 tablespoons) from wok, heat over high heat.

8. Add pork, stir-fry 1 minute, add onions and garlic, fry another minute, add shrimp and chili peppers, fry another minute.

9. Add sugar, bring to boil, then add tomato paste, mushrooms, soaking water, cook for a few minutes over medium high heat to thicken sauce.

10. Add fish sauce, lime juice and zest, cook a few minutes.

11. Add green beans and *sambal*, cook about two minutes, until beans are *al dente*.

12. Add bean sprouts, cook 30 seconds to 1 minute, correct seasonings.

13. Place ⅓ crisp noodles in large bowl, top with ⅓ of stir-fry mixture.

14. Mix gently with tongs, repeat with remaining 2 portions.

15. Top with cilantro, garnish with deep-fried egg, scallion brushes, and chili strips. Serve immediately.

Placing rice noodles in hot fat

Removing rice noodles from hot fat

Dripping egg from hand into hot fat

Mixing Mee Krob ingredients together in bowl

Mee Krob (Crisp Rice Noodles with Shrimp and Pork)

KAENG PET KAI NORMAI ON (Thailand)

Chicken and Bamboo Shoots in Red Curry

Number of Servings: 10   Cooking Method: Boil
Serving Size: 6 oz
Total Yield: 4 lbs

Food Balance: Sweet and protein
Wine Style: Soft and fruity Chenin Blanc, light to medium Chardonnay, Rosé, Gamay Beaujolais
Example: Beringer Vineyards Founders Estate Chardonnay

INGREDIENTS	WEIGHT	VOLUME
coconut milk, unsweetened	2 lbs, 10 oz	5¼ cups, 3 cans
chicken, boneless, skinless, cut into 1-inch cubes	2 lbs, 4 oz	
red curry paste, purchased or homemade, *recipe follows*	7½ oz	¾ cup
lime zest, julienne	¾ oz	2 tablespoons
bamboo shoots, julienne	1 lb, 8 oz	3 each 8-oz cans
fish sauce	2¼ oz	4½ tablespoons
brown sugar	1½ oz	3 tablespoons
basil leaves, fresh	2¼ oz	3 cups

1. Break or cut basil leaves into small pieces, set aside until needed.
2. Reserve 8 oz (1 cup) thick coconut milk, place remainder in pan with chicken, bring to boil.
3. Cook on medium high heat about 10 minutes, add curry paste, lime zest, and bamboo shoots, cook 5 minutes.
4. Lower heat, add fish sauce and brown sugar, mix well.

Kaeng Pet Kai Normai On (Chicken and Bamboo Shoots in Red Curry)

5. Add remaining coconut milk, bring to boil.
6. Quickly stir in basil leaves, correct seasonings, serve immediately with rice.

NAM PRÍK KAENG DANG (Thailand)

Red Curry Paste

Total Yield: 1 lb or 1½ cups

INGREDIENTS	WEIGHT	VOLUME
hot red chilies, whole, dried, seeded	½ oz	16 each
ginger, peeled, minced	2 oz	4-inch piece
lime zest	½ oz	2 small limes
lemongrass, fresh, peel outer dried leaves, use 6 inches from root, sliced	½ oz	2 each
onion, diced	5 oz	1 medium
garlic, minced	1½ oz	8 large cloves
cilantro stems	½ oz	12 to 16 each
shrimp paste	1½ oz	2 tablespoons
paprika	½ oz	4 teaspoons
coriander, ground	¼ oz	1 teaspoon
cumin, ground	¼ oz	1 teaspoon
cinnamon		¼ teaspoon
turmeric		½ teaspoon
cardamom, ground		¼ teaspoon
salt	¼ oz	1 teaspoon

> *Refrigerate or freeze extra curry paste.*

1. Chop chilies into pieces, cover with water, let soak about 45 minutes.
2. Place all ingredients except chilies in blender, pour chilies and soaking water into blender.
3. Process until fine paste, store in jar, and refrigerate until needed.

GULAI DAUN BAYEM (Indonesia)

Spinach in Coconut Milk

Number of Servings: 9   Cooking Method: Boil
Serving Size: 4 oz
Total Yield: 2 lbs, 6 oz

INGREDIENTS	WEIGHT	VOLUME
coconut milk	14 oz	2 cups
green chilies, fresh, minced	¾ oz	3 each
garlic, minced	½ oz	3 large cloves
onion or shallots, thinly sliced	4 oz	1 medium onion or 8 shallots

INGREDIENTS	WEIGHT	VOLUME
spinach, tough stems removed, washed, sliced 1-inch wide	1 lb, 10 oz	2 bags
salt	¼ oz or to taste	1 teaspoon or to taste

1. Place coconut milk, chilies, garlic, and onions in pan, bring to boil for 3 minutes.
2. Add spinach, cook a few minutes, until tender, add salt.
3. Correct seasonings, serve immediately.

SALA LOBAK (Indonesia)

Cabbage with Red Pepper Sauce

Number of Servings: 9
Serving Size: 4 oz
Total Yield: 2 lbs, 6 oz

Cooking Method: Stir-fry (sauté)

INGREDIENTS	WEIGHT	VOLUME
red bell pepper, diced	8 oz	1 large
hot chili pepper, minced	1 to 1½ oz or to taste	2 each or to taste
onion, diced	4 oz	2 small
garlic, minced	½ oz	4 cloves
shrimp paste	¼ oz	1 teaspoon
tamarind paste dissolved in 3 oz (6 tablespoons) water	½ oz	2 teaspoons
oil	2½ oz	5 tablespoons
cabbage leaves, outer leaves, then inner leaves for required weight, shredded	2 lbs	1 small head
salt	¼ oz	1 teaspoon

1. Combine red and chili peppers, onion, garlic, shrimp paste, and tamarind paste in blender or food processor, blend until coarse paste.
2. Heat oil in wok until hot, add paste, stirring constantly, cook 4 or 5 minutes, until dark red.
3. Add cabbage and salt, stir for 30 seconds, lower heat to medium low and cook for about 8 minutes, until cabbage is done. Correct seasonings.
4. Serve accompanied by rice and other dishes that contain sauces.

SANGKHAYA (Thailand)

Steamed Coconut Custard

> Instead of steaming this custard in small cups, it may be steamed in coconut halves or small pumpkins. If steaming in a pumpkin, serve some of the meat of the pumpkin with the custard.

Number of Servings: 8
Serving Size: 8 small cups containing 2 oz each
Total Yield: 1 lb, 1 oz

INGREDIENTS	WEIGHT	VOLUME
eggs	6¾ oz	4 each

INGREDIENTS	WEIGHT	VOLUME
coconut milk, unsweetened	1 lb, 2 oz	2 cups
brown sugar	5½ oz	¾ cup
rose water (optional)		⅛ teaspoon

1. Beat eggs lightly, stir coconut milk well, whisk into eggs.
2. Whisk brown sugar into egg mixture.
3. Place mixture in double boiler over simmering water, whisking constantly, cook until mixture thickens into custard. *Be careful to keep heat low so eggs do not curdle.*
4. Strain custard into small bowls or cups, cover with foil, steam over simmering water for 15 to 20 minutes, until custard is barely set and knife inserted into custard comes out almost clean. (If steaming in larger container, custard may require an hour to steam.)
5. Cool, and then refrigerate until serving.

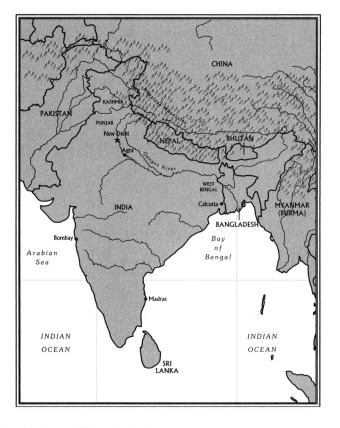

CHAPTER 14
India

By the end of this chapter, you will be able to

- Discuss the major religions found in India and their role in molding India's cuisine
- Explain similarities and differences between the cuisines found in the north and south of India
- Discuss the importance and uses of spices in the cookery of India
- Define *thali* and describe the Indian method of eating a meal
- Prepare a variety of Indian dishes

HISTORY

Evidence shows people inhabited India 200,000 years ago. The first documented civilization in India occurred about 2500 B.C. in the area that is now western India.

Religion was and still remains an important part of both India's history and its culinary makeup. Many Muslims and Hindus lived in India, as they do today. Throughout the history of India, there have been periods of violence and times of peaceful coexistence between these two religious groups, as well as other religious sects. Offshoots of the Hindu religion, Buddhism and Jainism developed in the 500s and 400s B.C. in India. Besides Hindus, Muslims, Buddhists, and Jains, India is home to Sikhs, Zoroastrians, Christians, and Jews. Many religious sects flourish in India, each following their own dietary laws.

India has endured a seemingly endless stream of invaders throughout their history, including the Greeks in the 300s B.C., the Arabs, the Huns, and many more. India's Golden Age occurred between 320 and 500 A.D. when the Gupta Dynasty ruled. The arts, mathematics, science, and literature thrived during this time; however, after this period, a series of invasions from more aggressive Asians and Middle Eastern people ensued. This time of fighting and strife lasted until the sixteenth century when the Moghul Empire invaded and conquered.

These Muslim Moghuls entered India from Persia in the Middle East. The Moghuls left a significant mark on the Indian cuisine, which remains most pronounced in the north of India. They introduced lamb and grilled kebobs in addition to preparing many of their native dishes, including rice pilafs, *biriyani* (a baked rice and meat dish), and meats marinated and cooked with yogurt. The Indians adopted many of the Moghul dishes as well as the use of yogurt for marinating meats and making sauces. They quickly learned a preference for smooth, delicate sauces from these invaders. Besides culinary influence, the Moghuls left their impact on many other aspects of Indian life. They built magnificent mosques and palaces such as the Taj Mahal, developed cities, and introduced an extravagant and opulent lifestyle. Their rule lasted until the latter part of the 1700s when the British gained control.

Throughout history, many explorers, including the Romans, Phoenicians, Portuguese, and Dutch, came to India in search of spices. Indeed, they found a bounty of spices in this land. These explorers returned to their homelands bearing spices, but they left remnants of their own culinary culture behind with the people of India.

In 1498, Portuguese explorers arrived in India in search of spices, gold, silk, and other treasures. They introduced chili peppers from the New World, and these hot peppers immediately became an important part of the Indian cuisine. In addition, these explorers brought cashews, potatoes, and tomatoes. The Portuguese ruled the western part of India for 400 years.

The British arrived in the 1600s. In the late eighteenth century, India became a British colony and remained under the rule of Britain until 1947 when they became an independent nation. As a result of the long British rule of India, the Indians made a lasting impact on the cuisine of Britain, and the British strongly influenced the cuisine of India.

An important man in India's history, Mohandas Ghandi became the leader of the Indian National Congress in 1920 and led the movement to gain independence from Britain. Ghandi believed in nonviolence and promoted nonviolent tactics against the British, which proved to be very effective. Under Ghandi's direction, the Indians refused to pay taxes and boycotted all things that were British, including schools, government, and the purchase of goods. Ironically, this leader who stood for nonviolence was assassinated in 1948, one year after India received their independence.

In 1940, Pakistan was carved out of India and established as a primarily Muslim country. As a result, today about 80 percent of the inhabitants of India are Hindus and 15 percent are Muslims. Densely populated India uses fourteen languages and at least 240 dialects.

India remains a country of extreme wealth and extreme poverty. Most Indians still follow the *caste* system which divides people into four *castes* or social classes with four distinct levels from the very poor to the privileged. Although the *castes* are not as strong today as in the past, little intermarriage or mingling takes place between people of different *castes*. As a result, people marry within their *caste*, and the children of that marriage belong to the same *caste*. In this way, the *caste* system continues, and inhabitants of India have little chance to change their social position.

TOPOGRAPHY

A peninsula jutting into the Indian Ocean, India is located in southern Asia. Pakistan and the Arabian Sea lie to its west; Bangladesh and the Bay of Bengal are to the east; China, Nepal, and Bhutan are found to the north.

Basically, distinct regions based on the topography comprise India. Lying at India's northern border with China and Nepal, the Himalayan Mountains, the world's highest mountain range runs through the extreme northern section of India. The climate in these snow-capped mountains consists of cold winters and cool summers, conducive to growing many crops, including fruits and walnuts. Abundant mushrooms grow wild in this terrain.

South of the mountains, the land changes to plains, valleys, and rivers. The Ganges and Indus rivers run through this area, providing rich soil for fertile farmland and a bounty of fish for consumption. Most of the people of India reside in this region.

The east consists of fertile plains and coastline. Abundant seafood and fish are available here, and ample crops include rice, coconuts, and many vegetables. Eastern India receives abundant rainfall; in fact, some of the highest measured rainfall found anywhere occurs here.

Contrarily, hot, arid land with desert conditions describes the land in the west. Seafood from the coasts dominates the diet of those living in this region as significantly fewer crops grow here.

The central-southern portion of the Indian peninsula, called Deccan, contains plateau in the center, surrounded by mountains on the east and west, with coastal plains lying between the mountains and the coast. Tropical conditions and jungles predominate in the south. Much of this land is fertile farmland, yielding all sorts of grains including the famous *basmati* rice, wheat, corn, millet, and barley. Legumes and many vegetables flourish in this region.

Lying near the equator, the extreme south experiences hot, humid, tropical weather with seasonal *monsoons*, seasonal rains. Seafood, fish, coconuts, bananas, and a myriad of tropical fruits and vegetables flourish in this hot climate.

The climate in India includes three seasons: the cool season of the fall and winter, the hot season existing in the spring, and the rainy season found in the summer. The cool season means cold weather in the mountainous areas, but temperate, warm, or hot weather in the other regions. In particular, the southern regions experience extremely hot conditions during the hot season. The *monsoons* have an enormous effect on the crops making India susceptible to both flooding and droughts, which often leads to crop failures and starvation.

Ingredients and Foods Commonly Used Throughout the Cuisine of India Include:

- rice and wheat
- legumes including lentils, split peas, mung beans, and chickpeas
- goat and lamb
- seafood and fish
- vegetables, including spinach, cauliflower, potatoes, peas, pumpkin, and sweet potatoes
- fruits including bananas, plantains, mangoes, oranges, and coconuts
- chutneys and pickled fruits and vegetables
- garlic

- cilantro
- coriander, cumin, ginger, turmeric, cardamom, fenugreek, hot chilies, mustard, fennel, cloves, and cinnamon
- *ghee* (clarified butter)

COOKING METHODS

In the early days, much of the food was either grilled over an open fire or cooked in a pot placed in the embers of the fire. Of course, this one-pot cookery resulted in stewlike curries and was perfect for the long, slow cooking needed for legumes. To extend the available meat, the tender cuts of meat joined vegetables on a skewer for grilling, and the tougher cuts entered the pot for braising—the slow cooking method necessary to make them tender.

Baking in a *tandoor* oven occurs most frequently in the north. This clay oven becomes very hot from fuel of wood or charcoal, and it is used for cooking meat, poultry, seafood, fish, or vegetables on skewers, as well as for baking flatbreads. Skewered foods are marinated in a yogurt and spice mixture before cooking, then the skewers are lowered into the vat-shaped oven. Flatbreads are slapped against the inside walls of the hot oven where they adhere and quickly cook.

Stir-frying remains a popular cooking technique in India, particularly with the large number of vegetable dishes served throughout this country. Like the Oriental wok, Indians use a deep pan with a rounded bottom and handles on each side called a *karahi*. Another pan found in Indian kitchens, the *tava* is a slightly concave griddle made of cast iron. Frequently used for sautéing, several varieties of flatbreads are cooked on an ungreased *tava*. Deep-frying also appears regularly in this cuisine.

Steaming remains the most frequently used cooking technique in the south. Often, banana leaves enclose the foods to be steamed. Like the tamale of Mexico, leaf-wrapped foods were placed in the embers of the fire for steaming in the past. Today, large and small steaming pots are standard equipment in most southern Indian kitchens.

With many rivers and lots of ocean surrounding this peninsula, fresh seafood and fish abound. Seafood preparations include frying, baking, poaching, grilling, or steaming.

The preservation of fruits and vegetables is commonplace throughout India. Pickles and chutneys (intensely flavored, spicy relishes) function as an important part of the Indian meal, as well as preserving the bounty of fruits and vegetables for meager times. Drying foods occurs in the mountainous north where harsh winters limit the growing season. Another preservation technique, salting, is frequently employed to extend available food supplies for times when less is available. Like Africa, parts of India are susceptible to flooding and droughts, and the condition of the next crops remains an unknown.

REGIONS

India is a densely populated nation with the second largest population of any country in the world. The diverse topography and climate that exists here created strong regional culinary differences. In addition, dietary laws from the various religious groups in India caused pronounced effects on the cuisine. These three issues—topography, climate, and religion—molded the cuisine of each region. As a result, great differences exist between the cuisines found in the various regions. These differences are particularly apparent between the north and south of India.

Flatbreads made from wheat function as the predominate starch in the north, but inhabitants of the southern regions eat rice with their meals. The food prepared in the north tends to be subtler in seasoning, while hot curries and highly spiced dishes dominate southern dishes. With ample coastline on three sides, much seafood is consumed in the east, west, and south. Although the arid regions of the west yield fewer crops, they produce peas and beans (legumes). Accompanied by bread, these legumes form a major portion of the diet in this region.

Baked flatbreads and skewers of meats, poultry, seafood, and vegetables roasted in the famous *tandoori* oven hail from the north. Usually marinated in a yogurt mixture, these meats are often seasoned with *garam masala*, a mixture of spices. The traditional orange color of the meats cooked in the *tandoor* usually comes from food coloring, not spices. Although the northerners bake their foods, the people of the south prefer to steam many of their dishes.

Although high meat consumption reigns in the north, the diet of people in western, eastern, and southern India includes lots of fish and seafood and much less meat. Myriad vegetarian dishes come from the south, where many Hindu vegetarians reside. Typical of inhabitants in many hot climates throughout the world, the people of the tropical south prefer hot, spicy dishes and use lots of coconut and coconut milk. In addition, tamarind and mustard seeds flavor many of their dishes.

Although many of the same spices are used in both the north and south, their treatment makes them taste differently. In the north, spices are cooked or roasted in a dry pan, then ground and added to the foods. People in the south prefer to mix the spices into a wet paste and then combine the spice paste with the dish.

All Indians drink cold water with the meal, but coffee or tea generally follows the meal. Northerners prefer tea, and often serve spiced tea after the meal. The people of the south choose coffee flavored with milk and sugar instead of tea.

CUISINE

Hindus, Muslims, and people of numerous other religious sects live in India, each possessing their own philosophies and dietary laws. Muslims do not eat pork. Hindus consider the cow a sacred animal, so they consume no beef. In addition, Hindus believe in reincarnation, so many abstain from eating any meat. Jains, members of another eastern religion that developed from Hinduism, believe strongly in reincarnation. As a result, followers of that religion eat no meat, fish, poultry, or eggs because that animal could have been a person in another lifetime. Many also refrain from eating root vegetables because digging them might injure a worm or other underground creature. They abstain from red foods such as tomatoes and beets because the color is reminiscent of blood. As a result of the numerous religious restrictions on meat, the Indian cuisine is rich in vegetarian dishes.

With religious dietary laws forbidding consumption of pork and beef, the most popular meats remain lamb and goat. More meat is eaten in the north than the south of India, and lamb became a favorite as a result of the Moghul influence. The Moghuls ate lots of meat in their native Persia, but abstained from pork because of their Muslim faith. When they entered India, they found a country where the cow was sacred, so that left lamb, goat, and chicken for their consumption. Reminiscent of the Middle Eastern ground lamb dish, *kibbe*, northern Indians prepare *kofta*, a ground lamb and hard-boiled egg dish.

Chicken appears often in India, where preparation involves removing the skin to facilitate the absorption of spices and marinades. In addition, cooks make shallow cuts in the meat so more of the marinade penetrates into it. Chicken is cut into smaller pieces than is customary in many western cultures for two reasons. First, like many other Asian cuisines, less meat accompanies greater amounts of vegetables and grains in the Indian diet. Second, smaller pieces expose more surface area to absorb the spices and marinade.

Ample seafood and fish are available along the coasts and near rivers, so inhabitants in those areas consume lots of seafood and fish. Similar to Dover sole, pomfret is one of the most prevalent and popular fish from the coasts of India. Other frequently consumed fish include mackerel and sardines. Fish preparation in the coastal areas often involves flavoring with *masala*, a blend of spices, as well as coconut or coconut oil. Shellfish also abounds, and many dishes containing shrimp, clams, crabs, and other shellfish are served.

Rice, wheat, grains, and beans form the basis of the Indian diet. In fact, an Indian meal is incomplete if not accompanied by either bread (wheat) or rice. As stated before, rice is the staple grain in the south, whereas some form of wheat accompanies meals in the north. Inhabitants of southern India eat rice three times a day. It is not unusual for a family to have twenty-five different recipes for rice in their repertoire. Several types of unleavened flatbreads are served in India. Usually made from whole grain flours such as chapati, a finely ground whole wheat flour, these breads are cooked by deep-frying, sautéing on a dry griddle, or baking. Grown in the foothills of the Himalayas, *basmati* rice is a nutty-flavored, long grain variety of rice used throughout India, but especially in the north. The flavor of this rice improves with aging, so high-quality *basmati* rice is aged a minimum of six months. The aromatic *basmati* rice is preferred for *biriyani*, pilafs, and other dishes; but, depending on the use, Indians choose other types of rice. In fact, over 1,000 varieties of rice flourish in India. Like wheat, rice appears in a number of forms, including puffed rice and rice flour. Indians prepare an endless variety of rice pancakes, which function as breakfast through much of southern India.

INDIAN FLATBREADS

chapati Cooked on an ungreased *tava;* made from *chapti* flour
parathas Cooked on an ungreased *tava*
naan Baked in a tandoori oven
poori Deep-fried

Legumes play a huge role in the Indian cuisine, functioning as a major source of protein for the many vegetarians and people who cannot afford meat. *Dal* refers to any split legume, including lentils and split mung beans. One of the most popular legumes, lentils appear in many recipes throughout the country. *Dal* also refers to a mild purée of lentils or beans that is commonly served in the north. Southerners prefer a spicy lentil dish called *sambar*.

Although pronounced regional differences in the cuisine exist, yogurt as well as ample amounts of fresh fruits, chutneys, and pickles accompany meals throughout India. Two condiments, chutneys and pickles, are made

---

DAL AND LEGUMES COMMONLY USED IN INDIA

- red lentils—*masoor dal*
- yellow lentils—*thoor dal*
- yellow split peas—*chana dal*
- black-eyed peas—*lobbia*
- split mung beans—*moong dal*
- red kidney beans—*rajma*
- aduki beans—*ma*
- black gram beans—*ural dal*
- chickpeas—*chhole*

---

from all sorts of fruits and vegetables. Originating in India, the intensely flavored, spicy chutney joins a myriad of foods to heighten the flavor sensations by adding a whole range of flavor components to the Indian meal. Chutneys and pickles can be spicy, aromatic, hot, mild, sweet, tart, and/or salty. Another frequently served item, yogurt relishes contain any vegetable or fruit combined with yogurt. *Raita*, a yogurt salad, frequently accompanies plain roasted or grilled meats, as well as highly spiced foods. The best known variety is probably cucumber *raita*. Yogurt functions as a cooling component after spicy foods.

Vegetable cookery reaches new heights in India. Abundant varieties of vegetables grow in this country of diverse climate and topography ranging from snow capped mountains to tropical jungles. With so many vegetarians and the year-round availability of vegetables, they function as a major component of the diet. Vegetables appear in numerous guises cooked in combinations and with an extensive range of herbs and spices. Many types of vegetable curries abound. Potatoes, spinach, cauliflower, pumpkins, peas, and sweet potatoes rank high in popularity.

With a bounty of fruits available throughout the year, Indians also consume ample amounts of fresh fruit. Like the African and Latin American countries, bananas and plantains show up often. Curries frequently incorporate fruit, which counters the spiciness of the dish. Fresh fruit or fruit pastes accompany many meals, and fruit juices or fruit and yogurt beverages remain popular.

Instead of thickening sauces with flour or cornstarch like the western cuisines, Indians use spices, spice pastes, yogurt, or other vegetables to thicken their sauces. Unlike flour or cornstarch, these thickening items actually contribute to the flavor of the dish. Indian dishes are classified "wet" or "dry," depending upon how much liquid their sauce contains. Obviously, loose or liquid sauces are called "wet," and they are eaten with flatbread or rice formed into a ball. "Dry" foods contain spices and herbs but no actual sauce. Indian chefs carefully plan a meal so that it includes both wet and dry dishes to offer variety to the diner.

Many say spices distinguish the Indian cuisine from all others. Indian cookery incorporates abundant spices and herbs, both fresh and dried, into dishes. In the past, spices were prized for their flavor, medicinal properties, and ability to act as a preservative for the food; today, spices are chosen for a particular dish primarily based on their flavor and the color they impart to the finished dish. They still are valued, however, for their medicinal and health properties. Myriad spices are stocked in the Indian kitchen. Common spices found in this cuisine include cumin, coriander, turmeric, ginger, garlic, cardamom, mustard seeds, and cayenne pepper. Whether sautéed in a dry pan or cooked in oil, which further enhances the flavor when added to the dish, the aromatic spices preferred throughout India are cooked to intensify their flavor before incorporating them into the dish. In order to obtain the maximum taste, many spices are purchased whole, cooked, or toasted just before using, then ground and added to the dish. In the end, it is the combination of spices as well as the method of handling that makes each dish unique.

FREQUENTLY USED SPICE BLENDS

- Curry Powder—contains varying amounts of coriander, cumin, fennel, fenugreek, mustard, pepper, cloves, turmeric, and cayenne pepper, used throughout India
- *Garam Masala*—contains varying amounts of black pepper, cinnamon, cloves, and nutmeg and sometimes cumin, cardamom, coriander; frequently used in northern India
- *Panch Phoron*—contains varying amounts of cumin, fennel, fenugreek, mustard, and nigella; frequently used in eastern India

---

Lots of spices grow in India, including peppercorns, turmeric, ginger, nutmeg, cardamom, cloves, and chili peppers. Three well-known *masalas*, spice blends, are associated with the Indian cuisine: curry powder blends, *garam masala*, and *panch phoron*. Although used throughout India, curry powder blends vary greatly from region to region, with each family preparing the combination of herbs and spices they like the best. The blends are prepared in small quantities at home and stored for short periods of time to ensure freshness; they are not purchased already blended. *Garam masala* is found mostly in the north, and *panch phoron* appears in the east. Throughout India, curry refers to any richly spiced dish with a careful blend of spices to achieve the desired flavor.

Ghee, clarified butter, remains the preferred cooking fat in India although vegetable oils are used also. Several types of oils are used, each imparting their own flavor to the dish. Mustard oil appears frequently in dishes from the eastern part of India.

GHEE

To prepare *ghee*, melt butter in saucepan. When completely melted, the clear fat of the butter floats on top and the milk solids, water, and other impurities sink. Carefully pour or ladle the clear fat into another dish—this is the *ghee*. Discard remaining milk solids and water at bottom of pan.

Typical throughout most of Asia, Indian meals conclude with fresh fruit rather than dessert; however, desserts are served for special occasions. Indian desserts tend to be quite sweet and are often based on milk, grains, fruit, or nuts.

Indians celebrate a myriad of festivals, and food is always part of the celebration. Sometimes a particular food or dish is served, other times the celebration involves a feast. From harvest and religious days to weddings and births, rich and poor Indians mark important occasions with a festival.

Lassi, yogurt beverages, appear either as fruit and yogurt combinations or as a salty yogurt drink. Both varieties remain popular beverages, with the yogurt functioning to counter the heat of spicy foods. Beer or nonalcoholic beer frequently accompanies the meal, but the most common beverage with meals remains water. Muslims consume no alcohol.

Typically, Indians dine more like the Asians and Middle Eastern people than those from the western cultures. Rather than serving the foods from bowls and platters placed in the middle of the table, every diner receives a small portion of each food served on a *thali*, a platter containing small bowls of the various foods being served at the meal. Instead of serving courses, all the foods are presented at once, even dessert. Like Moroccans, Indians eat with their hands; flatbreads in the north and rice rolled into balls in the south are used to scoop their food. Only the right hand handles the food, and, as part of the dining ritual, diners wash their hands before the meal begins and again at its conclusion. Then the *paan*, an assortment of aromatic spices and herbs, is served. Indians chew these spices and herbs after the meal to clear the palate, aid digestion, and leave the diner with a pleasant flavor sensation.

Generally, breakfast is light, consisting of tea or coffee and a pastry, potato curry, rice pancake, or whatever item is customary in that region. For example, in the south, a legume and rice or a rice pancake accompanies coffee for breakfast. The main meal of the day is served midday, and the evening meal is light. A typical main meal includes a meat dish, a starch (rice or bread, depending on the region), a legume, vegetable, yogurt, fresh fruit, pickles and/or chutney, and perhaps a salad. Both the midday and evening meals are presented on a *thali*. Like the Asians, much care is taken to balance the textures, flavors, and colors of the foods and dishes. From the British influence, many

Thali; photo courtesy of Dorling Kindersley

REGION	AREA	WEATHER	TOPOGRAPHY	FOODS
Himalayas	North	Cold winters, cool summers	Mountains	Goat, lamb, milk, cheese, wheat, rice, flatbreads, walnuts, fruits, mushrooms, saffron
Plains	North central, Delhi	Cold winters, hot summers	Plains, valleys, Ganges River, fertile farmland	Fish, goat, chicken, lamb, milk, cheese, wheat, rice, *basmati*, millet, corn, barley, legumes, flatbreads, walnuts, mushrooms, fruits
Bengal	East, Calcutta	Tropical, hot and humid	Coast, rain forest, fertile plains	Seafood, fish, rice, legumes, coconuts, vegetables
West	West	Hot	Desert, coast	Seafood, fish, legumes, peas
Deccan	Central	Hot, tropical	Coasts, plateaus, coastal plains, mountains, hills	Seafood, fish, grains, rice, *basmati*, wheat, corn, millet, barley, legumes, vegetables, coconuts, cinnamon, ginger, black pepper, turmeric
South	South	Tropical, hot and humid, *monsoons*	Coasts, plains	Fish, seafood, rice, tropical fruits and vegetables, coconuts, bananas, spices

Indians partake in tea in the afternoon. In India, tea or coffee accompanies a variety of snack-type foods, as opposed to the British custom of serving lots of sweets and some savory foods.

Review Questions

1. Name the two most prevalent religions found in India and discuss the impact of each on the cuisine.
2. Discuss the differences between the cuisines of the north and south, including differences in spicing, ingredients, and foods.
3. What is the role of herbs and spices in the cookery of India?
4. What is a *thali* and how is it used?
5. Describe the Indian method of eating, including eating utensils, courses, and typical foods consumed at the main meal.
6. Name five herbs and spices commonly used in the cuisine of India.

Glossary

basmati An aromatic type of long grain rice preferred in India, grown in the foothills of the Himalayas

biriyani A baked rice dish that usually contains *basmati* rice flavored with saffron and meat

Paneer, India's premier cheese, is prepared by curdling cow's milk, then pressing the curds. The mildly flavored cheese is ready to eat in a few days. Appearing in myriad guises, this cheese is served deep-fried, marinated, baked in a *tandoori* oven, and incorporated into all sorts of dishes. Paneer is a stretched curd cheese, which refers to the process of handling the curds when making the cheese, resulting in cheese with a springy texture resembling that of cooked chicken.

caste One's social class; four distinct *castes* or social levels exist in Indian society and relatively little intermingling occurs between these *castes*

chapti flour A finely ground whole wheat flour

chutney Spicy relish made from fruit or vegetable used as a condiment to accompany many foods

dal Actually means split legumes; also refers to a dish of mildly spiced lentil purée widely consumed in the north

ghee Clarified butter, cooking fat of choice throughout India

karahi A wok-type deep pan with a rounded bottom and handles on each side used for frying

lassi A yogurt drink

masala A mixture of spices, also called a spice blend

paan An assortment of aromatic spices and herbs to clear the palate and aid digestion that is served at the end of the meal

raita Yogurt salad

sambar Spicy lentil dish widely consumed in the south

tandoori oven A clay oven used to roast skewers of meats, poultry, seafood, or vegetables as well as bake flatbreads over very high heat, used in the north of India

tava A concave griddle made of cast iron

thali Actually means the platter or tray holding the small bowls, but known as the Indian method for eating meals where each diner receives a platter containing small bowls of the various foods being served

GOBHI PAKODE

Cauliflower Fritters

Number of Servings: 8   Cooking Method: Boil, deep-fry
Serving Size: 3 to 4 fritters, 5 to 6½ oz
Total Yield: about 16 fritters per
   head of cauliflower
   batter: 1 lb, 4 oz

Food Balance: Balanced protein
Wine Style: Soft and fruity Riesling, Pinot Blanc, Beaujolais, Grenache
Example: Château St. Jean Pinot Blanc

Many varieties of fritters are served in India both as snacks and with the meal. If reheating fritters, bake in a 375-degree oven or fry them again.

INGREDIENTS	WEIGHT	VOLUME
cauliflower, trimmed, flowerets	2 lbs, 6 oz	2 small to medium heads

INGREDIENTS	WEIGHT	VOLUME
BATTER:		
chick pea flour, *besan*	9 oz	2 cups
coriander, ground	½ oz	2 tablespoons
black pepper		½ teaspoon
cayenne		¼ teaspoon
salt	½ oz	2 teaspoons
oil	1 oz	2 tablespoons
cold water	12 oz	1½ cups

oil for deep-frying

1. Parboil or steam cauliflower until half cooked, rinse with cold water to stop cooking. Set aside until ready to fry.
2. Place flour and spices in bowl of food processor, pulse to mix well, add oil and pulse to mix.
3. With processor running, add water through feed tube, mix well, transfer to bowl, mix, add a little water to batter if too thick.
4. Cover, let rest at least 30 minutes. Refrigerate if holding overnight.
5. Heat oil in pan until 375 degrees. Coat cauliflower with batter.
6. Fry until golden brown, a few pieces at a time so oil temperature remains fairly constant.
7. Remove fritters to absorbent toweling to drain, keep warm in low oven.
8. Serve hot.

RASAM

Spicy Lentil Broth

Number of Servings: 10   Cooking Method: Sauté, boil
Serving Size: 7 oz
Total Yield: 4 lbs, 12 oz (not strained)

Food Balance: Spicy, protein
Wine Style: Soft and fruity Gewürztraminer, Viognier, Pinot Blanc, Beaujolais, soft Merlot, Zinfandel
Example: Beringer Vineyards Viognier or Gamay Beaujolais

INGREDIENTS	WEIGHT	VOLUME
thoor dal (yellow lentils)	7¾ oz	1 cup
turmeric		1 teaspoon
water	to cover, 1 lb	2 cups
ghee	½ oz	1 tablespoon
black mustard seeds		¾ teaspoon
cumin seeds	¼ oz	1 teaspoon
fenugreek seeds		¼ teaspoon
coriander seeds	¼ oz	2 teaspoons
garlic, minced	¼ oz	2 cloves
jalapeño or other chili, seeded, ribs removed, minced, *optional*	¾ oz or to taste	1 each or to taste
tomatoes, chopped, fresh or canned	1 lb	2 cups
tamarind paste	¾ oz	1 tablespoon

Originating in the south, this spicy soup is served as a broth throughout India. The soup is either strained to remove the lentil pulp or it is allowed to settle (the broth rises and the pulp sinks) and the broth at the top is served. Some refer to this soup as the Indian version of consomme.

INGREDIENTS	WEIGHT	VOLUME
salt	½ oz	2 teaspoons
sugar		1 teaspoon
water	1 lb, 8 oz	3 cups
cilantro, leaves, fresh, minced	½ oz	2 tablespoons

1. Place *thoor dal*, turmeric, and 1 lb (2 cups) water in pan. Bring to boil, turn heat to low and simmer, partially covered, for 30 minutes until soft.
2. Heat *ghee* in sauté pan, cook all seeds in covered pan until beginning to pop. Add garlic and chili pepper, sauté to soften. Add tomatoes, salt, and sugar, cook a few minutes.
3. Transfer tomato mixture to bowl of food processor, process until smooth.
4. Add dal to processor, process until smooth, return to pan.
5. Add 1 lb, 8 oz (3 cups) water to pan, bring to boil. Reduce heat and simmer, partially covered, for 30 minutes.
6. Correct seasonings, serve garnished with cilantro.

KHEERA RAITA

Cucumber and Yogurt Salad

Number of Servings: 8
Serving Size: 4 oz
Total Yield: 2 lbs

> Raita is a "cooling" salad to counter spicy foods.

INGREDIENTS	WEIGHT	VOLUME
yogurt, plain	1 lb, 2 oz	2 cups
salt	¼ oz	1 teaspoon

Kheera Raita (Cucumber and Yogurt Salad); photo courtesy of Dorling Kindersley

INGREDIENTS	WEIGHT	VOLUME
cumin, roasted, ground		½ teaspoon
cayenne		¼ teaspoon
cilantro or mint leaves, minced	½ oz	2 tablespoons
cucumber, peeled, grated	1 lb, 5 oz	2 large

GARNISH:

paprika

1. Combine yogurt, salt, cumin, cayenne, and cilantro or mint in bowl, refrigerate until needed.
2. Place cucumber in colander to drain, place colander in bowl to catch liquid, refrigerate until needed.
3. At serving time, mix cucumber into yogurt. Sprinkle with paprika. Serve.

TANDOORI MURGHI

Chicken Baked in Tandoor Oven

Number of Servings: 8   Cooking Method: Bake
Serving Size: ¼ chicken
Total Yield: 2 chickens, 8 pieces

Food Balance: Spicy and protein
Wine Style: Soft and fruity Gewürztraminer, Viognier, Pinot Noir, Shiraz, Merlot
Example: Château St. Jean Gewürztraminer or Pinot Noir

INGREDIENTS	WEIGHT	VOLUME
chickens, quartered or desired pieces	5 to 7 lbs	2 whole or 8 pieces

> Marinate this chicken up to 24 hours before baking.

MARINADE:

yogurt, plain	13½ oz	1½ cups
garlic, minced		3 cloves
ginger, peeled, minced	¼ oz	1 tablespoon
paprika	¼ oz	1 tablespoon
fennel, ground		¾ teaspoon
coriander, ground	¼ oz	1½ tablespoons
cumin, ground	¼ oz	1½ teaspoon
cardamom, ground	¼ oz	2 teaspoons
cayenne pepper		¼ teaspoon
black pepper		¼ teaspoon
cinnamon		¼ teaspoon
cloves, ground		⅛ teaspoon
lemon juice, fresh	¾ oz	1½ tablespoons

ghee, for basting, if desired

1. Remove skin from chicken, make cuts into meat halfway to the bone about 1-inch apart.
2. Mix marinade ingredients in bowl of food processor, process until smooth.

Tandoori Murghi (Chicken Baked in Tandoor Oven); photo courtesy of the American Spice Trade Association

3. Coat chicken pieces with marinade, making sure marinade goes into slits.
4. Cover and refrigerate for up to 24 hours, turning at least once while marinating.
5. Preheat oven to 500 degrees.
6. Remove excess marinade from chicken. Bake until done, about 20 to 25 minutes, turning pieces once during baking. Baste with *ghee*, if desired.
7. Serve immediately.

SHAH JAHANI BIRYANI

Lamb and Saffron Rice Casserole

Number of Servings: 9   Cooking Method: Sauté, boil, braise
Serving Size: 8 oz
Total Yield: 4 lbs, 13 oz

Food Balance: Protein and sweet
Wine Style: Soft and fruity Pinot Blanc, Chardonnay, rich, softer Merlots and Shiraz
Example: Château St. Jean Pinot Blanc or Sonoma Chardonnay

> This dish hails from the Mohgul influence and appears at many festivals. Although the preparation seems quite involved, the meat for this dish can be prepared ahead of time and refrigerated until needed.

INGREDIENTS	WEIGHT	VOLUME
basmati rice	14 oz	2 cups
water	2 lbs	4 cups
saffron threads		½ teaspoon
milk, warm	1 oz	2 tablespoons
onions, peeled	1 lb	3 medium
garlic, peeled, minced	½ oz	4 cloves
ginger, fresh, peeled, minced	¼ oz	2 teaspoons
almonds	¾ oz	2 tablespoons

INGREDIENTS	WEIGHT	VOLUME
water	1 oz	2 tablespoons
ghee	3 oz	6 tablespoons
almonds, blanched, slivered	1½ oz	¼ cup
cashews	1½ oz	¼ cup
raisins, golden	1½ oz	¼ cup
lamb, boneless, lean, cut into 1-inch cubes	1 lb, 8 oz	
yogurt, plain	9 oz	1 cup
water	4 oz	½ cup
cinnamon stick		1-inch piece
cardamom seeds		½ teaspoon
cumin seeds	¼ oz	1 teaspoon
coriander seeds	¼ oz	1 teaspoon
cayenne pepper		¼ teaspoon
cloves		4 each
peppercorns	¼ oz	1 teaspoon
nutmeg		½ teaspoon or ⅙ whole
salt	¼ oz	1 teaspoon

TO FINISH RICE:

water	2 lbs	4 cups
salt	¾ oz	1 tablespoon

GARNISH:

eggs, hard-boiled, peeled, quartered		3 each

1. Rinse rice thoroughly, drain, place in bowl or pan with 2 lbs (4 cups) water. Soak at least 3 hours.
2. Place saffron threads in warm milk, soak at least 3 hours.
3. Cut 11 oz (2 each) onions in half through root end, cut into thin slices (half rings). Dice remaining 5 oz (1 each) onion.
4. Place diced onion, garlic, ginger, ¾ oz (2 tablespoons) almonds, and 1 oz (2 tablespoons) water in bowl of food processor. Process until smooth paste.
5. Heat 3 oz (6 tablespoons) *ghee* in pan over medium high heat, sauté onion slices until brown, about 5 to 10 minutes. Remove with slotted spoon, drain on absorbent paper. Place golden raisins in same pan, sauté until plump, about 45 seconds, remove to absorbent paper. Place 1½ oz (¼ cup) slivered almonds and cashews in pan, sauté until golden, remove to absorbent paper.
6. Sauté lamb in same pan until browned, remove to bowl.
7. Stirring constantly, sauté onion paste in same pan until beginning to brown, add a few tablespoons water if sticking. Add meat and juices from bowl to pan.
8. Add yogurt, one tablespoon at a time, stirring constantly. Add 4 oz (½ cup) water, mix well, bring to simmer, turn heat to low, cover, simmer for 30 minutes.
9. Meanwhile, finely grind cinnamon, cardamom, cumin, coriander, cayenne, cloves, peppercorns, and nutmeg in coffee or spice grinder.
10. Add ground spices and salt to meat. Cover and simmer another 30 minutes. Meat should be tender and sauce thick. If sauce is not thick, remove cover and reduce until thick.

Shah Jahani Biryani (Lamb and Saffron Rice Casserole)

11. Meanwhile, preheat oven to 325 degrees. Drain and rinse rice. Boil 2 lbs (4 cups) water and ¾ oz (1 tablespoon) salt in saucepan, sprinkle rice into boiling water, return to boil, boil rapidly for 6 minutes, drain rice.

12. Place cooked meat in bottom of ovenproof dish, top with rice, mounding rice at center to form hill, make well into center of mound, drizzle saffron milk along sides of well. Scatter ½ oz (2 tablespoons) fried onions on top of rice.

13. Cover tightly with aluminum foil, then lid. Place in oven, bake 40 minutes.

14. Remove from oven, mix lamb and rice, if desired. Top with remaining onions, raisins, cashews, and almonds. Cover, allow to sit a few minutes to heat toppings.

15. Garnish with hard-boiled eggs, serve immediately.

DAHI MACHI

Fish in Yogurt Sauce

Number of Servings: 10 Cooking Method: Sauté, poach (boil)
Serving Size: 6 oz
Total Yield: 3 lbs, 14 oz

Food Balance: Spicy protein
Wine Style: Light- to medium-bodied Chenin Blanc, Pinot Blanc, light Chardonnay, White Zinfandel
Example: Beringer Chenin Blanc

INGREDIENTS	WEIGHT	VOLUME
dry mustard		1½ teaspoons
water	1 oz	2 tablespoons
fish fillets, skinless, boneless, cod, haddock, or any firm fish, rinsed, cut into 2-inch pieces	2 lbs, 8 oz	
flour	2 oz	¾ cup
oil or *ghee*	6 oz	¾ cup or 12 tablespoons
onion, diced	1 lb, 4 oz	4 cups or 4 each
ginger, fresh, peeled	½ oz	2-inch piece
garlic, peeled, minced	¼ oz	2 cloves
turmeric		½ teaspoon
cayenne		½ teaspoon
cumin		¼ teaspoon
cinnamon		¼ teaspoon
cloves		⅛ teaspoon
cardamom		¼ teaspoon
salt		1½ teaspoons
yogurt, plain	15 oz	1½ cups
GARNISH:		
cilantro, fresh, minced	1½ oz	6 tablespoons
green chilies, seeded, minced	1 oz	2 to 4 each

> Frequently served in Bengal, this fish has a thick sauce for eating with rice and fingers.

1. Mix mustard with 1 oz (2 tablespoons) water.
2. Lightly dredge fish with flour.
3. Heat enough oil in pan to cover bottom with ¼-inch, sauté fish until seared and lightly browned, about 1 minute per side, remove to plate when done. Add oil to pan, as needed.
4. Heat remaining oil in pan, add onions, stir constantly and sauté until golden, about 10 minutes.

Dahi Machi (Fish in Yogurt Sauce); photo courtesy of Dorling Kindersley

5. Add ginger and garlic, sauté another minute. Add all spices except mustard, sauté for 15 seconds.
6. Remove from heat, add yogurt and mustard.
7. Transfer onion-spice mixture to bowl of food processor, process until smooth paste, return to pan.
8. Bring sauce to simmer, add fish and any juices to sauce, cover, simmer until fish is done, 3 to 4 minutes. Be careful not to overcook fish.
9. Correct seasonings, serve garnished with cilantro and green chilies.

MASOOR DAL

Spiced Lentil Purée

Number of Servings: 8
Serving Size: 4 oz
Total Yield: 2 lbs, 3 oz

Cooking Method: Braise, sauté

> *Dal is served with most Indian meals. It functions as a sauce to moisten any dry food, including grilled meat or rice. Dal may be prepared with any number of legumes. The red lentils used in this recipe turn yellow when cooked.*

INGREDIENTS	WEIGHT	VOLUME
red split lentils, *masoor*, washed	10 oz	1¼ cups
water	1 lb, 8 oz	3 cups
ginger, peeled	¼ oz	½-inch piece
turmeric		½ teaspoon
salt	¼ oz or to taste	1 teaspoon or to taste
ghee	1½ oz	3 tablespoons
cumin seeds	¼ oz	1 teaspoon
garlic, minced	½ oz	4 cloves
coriander, ground		1 teaspoon
cayenne		¼ teaspoon

Masoor Dal (Spiced Lentil Purée); photo courtesy of Dorling Kindersley

INGREDIENTS	WEIGHT	VOLUME
GARNISH:		
cilantro, fresh, minced	½ oz	3 tablespoons

1. Place lentils, water, ginger, and turmeric in pan, bring to boil.
2. Reduce heat, partially cover and simmer for 20 minutes, until tender. If necessary to prevent sticking, add more water. Remove from heat, add salt.
3. Heat *ghee* in small frying pan, add cumin seeds, sauté until darkened, a few seconds.
4. Add garlic, coriander, and cayenne, sauté about 45 seconds, pour into lentils and mix well. Remove ginger. Correct seasonings.
5. Serve, sprinkled with cilantro. Accompany with rice and/or flatbread.

SABZI MOLEE

Mixed Vegetable Curry

Number of Servings: 8   Cooking Method: Sauté, boil
Serving Size: 10 oz
Total Yield: 5 lbs

Food Balance: Spicy, sweet
Wine Style: Soft and fruity Viognier, Gewürztraminer, Chenin Blanc, White Zinfandel
Example: Beringer Vineyards Gewürztraminer or Viognier

INGREDIENTS	WEIGHT	VOLUME
ginger, peeled, minced	¾ oz	1½-inch piece or 2 tablespoons
onion, diced	7 oz	1 large
garlic, peeled, minced	1 oz	8 cloves
green chilies, seeded, minced	1¼ oz or to taste	2 each or to taste
water	1 oz	2 tablespoons
ghee or vegetable oil	1½ oz	3 tablespoons
black mustard seeds	¼ oz	1 teaspoon
cumin seeds	¼ oz	1½ teaspoons
coriander, ground	¼ oz	1 tablespoon
cumin, ground	¼ oz	1½ teaspoons
turmeric		½ teaspoon
potato, cut into 1-inch dice	7 oz	1 medium
sweet potato, cut into 1-inch dice	7½ oz	1 medium
carrots, peeled, cut into ½-inch slices	7 oz	2 each
eggplant, cut into 1-inch dice	14 oz	1 small
green beans, trimmed, cut into 1½-inch lengths	8 oz	
green peppers, seeded, large dice	1 lb, 1 oz	2 each
salt	½ oz	2 teaspoons
sugar		½ teaspoon

Use any desired vegetables in this dish.

Sabzi Molee (Mixed Vegetable Curry); photo courtesy of Dorling Kindersley

INGREDIENTS	WEIGHT	VOLUME
coconut milk, unsweetened	14 oz	
cilantro, minced	½ oz	3 tablespoons
paprika		¼ teaspoon

1. Place ginger, onion, garlic, green chilies, and water in bowl of food processor, purée until paste, scrapping down sides of bowl as needed.
2. Heat *ghee* in pan, add mustard seeds and cumin, sauté until mustard seeds begin to pop.
3. Add onion paste, sauté about 3 minutes, add coriander, ground cumin, and turmeric. Sauté another 30 seconds.
4. Add potato, sweet potato, carrots, and eggplant. Stir constantly and cook for 5 minutes.
5. Add green beans, green peppers, salt, sugar, and coconut milk. Cover and simmer for 12 minutes.
6. Add cilantro and paprika, simmer for 5 to 10 minutes, until vegetables are tender. Correct seasonings.
7. Serve immediately with rice.

SAAG ALOO

Spinach and Potatoes

Number of Servings: 10   Cooking Method: Sauté, braise
Serving Size: 4 oz
Total Yield: 2 lbs, 11 oz

INGREDIENTS	WEIGHT	VOLUME
ghee	1½ oz	3 tablespoons
black mustard seeds	½ oz	1 tablespoon
onion, peeled, cut in half through root, then into thin rings	5 oz	1 medium
garlic, peeled, minced	¼ oz	2 cloves
potatoes, peeled, 1-inch dice	1 lb, 3 oz	5 small to medium
cayenne		¼ teaspoon
salt	¼ oz	1 teaspoon
spinach, fresh, washed, stems removed, sliced	1 lb	Two 10-oz packages

> This is a mild dish, so it accompanies spicy dishes quite well.

1. Heat *ghee* in pan, add mustard seeds, sauté until they begin to pop, add onions, sauté 2 minutes.
2. Add garlic, sauté another minute or two.
3. Add potatoes, cayenne, salt, and spinach. Enough water will cling to spinach to cook, but if it becomes dry, add 1 tablespoon water.
4. Cover tightly, simmer for about 35 minutes, stirring occasionally, until potatoes are done.
5. Correct seasonings. Serve.

MASALEDAR SEM

Spicy Green Beans

Number of Servings: 12
Serving Size: 4 oz
Total Yield: 3 lbs, 3 oz

Cooking Method: Sauté, boil

INGREDIENTS	WEIGHT	VOLUME
ginger, fresh, peeled, minced	1 oz	3-inch piece
garlic, peeled	2½ oz	20 cloves
water	4 oz	½ cup
oil, vegetable or *ghee*	2½ oz	5 tablespoons
cumin seeds	½ oz	1 tablespoon + 1 teaspoon
chili pepper, dried, hot, minced	¼ oz	2 each
coriander, ground		1 tablespoon + 1 teaspoon
tomatoes, peeled, fresh or canned, finely chopped	1 lb	2 cups
tamarind paste	1¼ oz	1½ tablespoons
water	8 oz	1 cup
green beans, fresh, washed, stems removed, cut into ½-inch length	2 lbs, 4 oz	
salt	½ oz	2 teaspoons
black pepper, ground		¼ teaspoon
cumin, ground, roasted	¼ oz	2½ teaspoons

> These beans get an acidic kick from the tamarind. Serve them with milder dishes.

1. Place ginger in bowl of food processor, turn processor on, drop garlic into bowl through feed tube.

Masaledar Sem (Spicy Green Beans); photo courtesy of Dorling Kindersley

2. Scrape down sides of bowl, add 4 oz (½ cup) water and process until smooth paste.
3. Heat oil in pan over medium heat, add cumin seeds, then chili peppers. Sauté until peppers darken.
4. Add garlic paste, sauté, stirring constantly, for about 1 minute. Add coriander, stir for 30 seconds.
5. Add tomatoes, stir and cook for 2 minutes, crushing tomato pieces against side of pan.
6. Add beans, tamarind paste, salt, black pepper, and 8 oz (1 cup) water, bring to simmer, cover and simmer for about 8 minutes, until beans are tender.
7. Remove cover. If necessary, raise heat to high and reduce liquid.
8. Correct seasonings, add ground cumin. Serve.

MATAR PULLAO

Green Pea Pilaf

Number of Servings: 13   Cooking Method: Sauté, boil
Serving Size: 4 oz
Total Yield: 3 lbs, 5 oz

> To facilitate removal of the whole spices from the finished dish, enclose spices in cheesecloth after sautéing, then add them to the rice with the water.

INGREDIENTS	WEIGHT	VOLUME
basmati rice, washed or subsititute long grain	14 oz	2 cups
water, cold, for soaking	2 lbs	4 cups
ghee	1 oz	2 tablespoons

Matar Pullao (Green Pea Pilaf)

INGREDIENTS	WEIGHT	VOLUME
onion, small dice	5 oz	1 medium
ginger, peeled	¼ oz	½-inch piece
garlic, minced	¼ oz	2 cloves
cumin seeds	¼ oz	1 teaspoon
cinnamon stick		3-inch piece
cardamom pods, green		6 each
cloves, whole		6 each
bay leaf		2 each
salt	½ oz	2 teaspoons
green peas	10 oz	2 cups

1. Place rice and water in bowl, soak for 30 minutes to 2 hours, drain, reserving soaking water.
2. Heat *ghee* in heavy pan over medium high heat, add cumin, cinnamon, cardamom, cloves, and bay leaf. Sauté until cumin darkens.
3. Add onion and ginger. Sauté until the onion begins to brown at edges, about 4 minutes.
4. Add garlic and rice. Sauté a few minutes, until rice begins to brown.
5. Add salt and 1 lb, 8 oz (3 cups) reserved water (adding more water if necessary to make amount), bring to boil, reduce heat, partially cover, simmer for 8 minutes.
6. Cover pan, reduce heat to low, simmer another 10 minutes, remove from heat.
7. Stir in peas, cover pan, let sit 5 to 10 minutes.
8. Remove whole spices and ginger, fluff rice with fork, serve immediately.

CHAPATI

Whole Wheat Flatbread

Serving Size: 1 oz for each
    chapati
Total Yield: 14 oz dough

Cooking Method: Sauté

> *Chapati accompanies all Indian dishes well. Chapati flour is finely ground whole wheat flour containing both the bran and wheat germ.*

INGREDIENTS	WEIGHT	VOLUME
chapati flour	8¾ oz	2 cups
water, warm	5½ oz	⅔ cup
chapati flour, as needed for rolling		
ghee, as needed for brushing		

1. Place flour in bowl of food processor or in large bowl if mixing by hand.
2. With processor running, slowly pour water through feed tube, pulse until dough comes together into ball, process another minute until smooth.
3. Remove from processor, if not pliable knead until smooth and pliable. If mixing by hand, combine flour and water, then knead until smooth and pliable.
4. Cover and let rest 1 to 8 hours at room temperature. If longer, refrigerate dough and bring to room temperature before using.
5. Scale dough into 1-oz pieces, form piece into smooth ball, pat into disk, roll into thin circle with rolling pin using flour as needed to prevent sticking. Cover disks with moist towel after rolling, do not stack disks.
6. Heat griddle or heavy skillet over medium high heat, place disk on hot griddle. Cook for about 1½ minutes, until brown spots appear on underside. Turn disk with tongs, cook other side for another minute, until brown spots appear.
7. Remove from heat, stack on plate or eat immediately, brushed with *ghee*, if desired. May be kept warm, covered in low oven.

KHEER

Rice Pudding

Number of Servings: 15
Serving Size: 5 oz
Total Yield: 4 lbs, 13 oz

Cooking Method: Boil

INGREDIENTS	WEIGHT	VOLUME
half and half	4 lbs	2 qts
milk	1 lb	2 cups
basmati rice	6 oz	½ cup
sugar	5½ oz	⅔ cup
cardamom, ground		2 teaspoons
raisins	2 oz	¼ cup
GARNISH:		
almonds, sliced, toasted	3 oz	½ cup
pistachios, chopped	1½ oz	¼ cup

Kheer (Rice Pudding); photo courtesy of Dorling Kindersley

1. Combine half and half and milk in pan, bring to boil over low heat.
2. Meanwhile, wash rice, let drain. Add rice to milk, simmer for 1 to 2 hours, until rice is cooked and milk thickens.
3. Add raisins, sugar, and cardamom, and cook a few more minutes.
4. Serve warm or chilled, garnished with almonds and pistachios.

CHAPTER 15
Australia

By the end of this chapter, you will be able to

- Discuss the influence of the Aborigines on the cuisine of Australia
- Explain how the climate, geography, and topography influenced Australia's cuisine
- Discuss the role of the British Isles on the cuisine of Australia
- Prepare a variety of Australian dishes

HISTORY

Historians believe the Aborigines migrated from Indonesia and inhabited Australia more than 40,000 years before white settlers arrived. Living as nomads, the Aborigines hunted and gathered food but planted no crops. They dried some fruits, vegetables, and meats to last them through the droughts and lean times, but, basically, they subsisted on the foods they found.

In the time before the arrival of the Europeans, more than 500 different tribes inhabited Australia, hunting animals and foraging for plants, seeds, and berries. These people occupied the coastal areas, as well as the outback. The outback refers to the large areas of "bush country" in the interior sections of the country. Because of sparse population, people could roam the outback for days, weeks, or months without seeing another human.

Dutch explorers arrived in Australia in the early part of the seventeenth century, but they did not stay to settle this desolate-looking land. Many Dutch returned to Australia after World War II, along with significant numbers of immigrants from many other countries. At that time, instead of introducing their native Dutch foods to Australians, they brought foods from Indonesia, their colony to the north.

In 1788, the British discovered Australia and established a penal colony there. With the United States having recently won their freedom from Britain in the Revolutionary War, the British needed a new place to ship prisoners to relieve their overcrowded jails. So, Australia became both the new home for

---

DREAMTIME

Dreamtime, the Aborigines' belief and story of creation, celebrates the time when powerful spirits created the land and the people who inhabit it. Although the Aborigines kept no written history, knowledge of Dreamtime comes from pictures found painted on rocks and walls.

---

many British and Irish prisoners, as well as a colony of the British Commonwealth. As a result, most Australians trace their ancestry to the British and Irish, and many of their customs and culinary traditions exhibit strong influence from these two heritages.

As the Aborigines planted no crops, farming in Australia began with the British settlers in the late eighteenth century. At first, the British disregarded the tropical fruits and vegetables that flourished here and planted the "cool weather" crops that grew in their homeland. The settlers arrived bearing seeds from their former home and introduced plants indigenous to the British Isles into the very different climate of Australia. Of course, those crops did not thrive in the warmer, drier climate of Australia. As a result, lack of food was a serious problem for these early settlers. Eventually, they learned from the Aborigines and used the many different native plants and animals that prospered in Australia.

Lutherans from Germany seeking religious freedom settled in southern Australia in the 1800s. They made several contributions to the Australian culinary scene, particularly in the areas of farming, growing fruits, and making wines. In the middle of the 1800s, many Irish immigrated to Australia to escape starvation during the potato famine. Then with the discovery of gold in 1851, lots of immigrants flocked to Australia seeking their fortunes. The Chinese population rose dramatically at this time, leaving a significant Chinese influence on the Australian cuisine.

Since the end of World War II, more than 2 million immigrants from Greece, Italy, other European countries, and Southeast Asia have settled in Australia. Each group of people arrived bringing the culinary traditions of their homeland. As a result, Australia has become a melting pot and the cuisine reflects that diversity.

TOPOGRAPHY

Lying southeast of Asia between the Pacific and Indian oceans, the country of Australia is both a continent and a very large island. The entire country lies in the Southern Hemisphere, which means the seasons are the reverse of those found in the Northern Hemisphere, for example, January falls in the summer.

Australia consists primarily of flat land with the exception of the Great Dividing Range and a few small mountainous areas. The Great Dividing Range lies in the east, running the entire length of the country from north to south. Plains and plateaus make up most of the Australian countryside. The interior section consists of flat, dry land, much actually desert. In fact, one-third of the land in Australia classifies as desert. Grasslands flourish in the areas that receive enough rain, and those grasslands provide grazing for lots of livestock.

Lying close to the equator, the northern third of Australia has a tropical climate with wet summers and dry winters as a result of the *monsoons*, tropical winds. The rest of the country experiences mild to cool winters and warm summers. Pronounced rainy seasons exist throughout Australia; droughts occur between the rainy seasons. Many rivers and lakes contain water only during the rainy season, but underground water supplies provide much of the needed water for livestock and inhabitants throughout the year.

Ingredients and Foods Commonly Used Throughout the Cuisine of Australia Include:

- beef and veal
- lamb
- seafood and fish
- potatoes
- kiwi, apples, pears, grapes, tropical fruits, and other fruits
- sugar and sweet foods
- beer and wine

COOKING METHODS

The Aborigines created an oven by digging a pit, lining it with stones, and then building a fire in the pit. When the fire burned down, the hot stones and glowing embers remained, creating a hot, smoldering pit. Using this heat source, the Aborigines used two cooking methods that are still popular today, steaming and grilling. Steaming was accomplished by wrapping vegetables, seafood, or other items in taro or banana leaves, then placing them in the pit of glowing embers to steam. To grill, foods were cooked directly over the fire or embers.

A continuation of the grilling over an open fire so often used by the Aborigines, barbecuing has become a ritual in Australia. All sorts of foods, including meats, seafood, sausages, kebobs, and vegetables, are grilled. With infrequent rainfall and the Australians' love of the outdoors, the barbecue, known as the "barbie" in Australia, remains the cooking method of choice for many occasions, particularly when entertaining.

Grilling and roasting continue as the most common methods for cooking meats. Roasted meats originate from the British influence. Another carryover from the British, boiling continues as the usual method of vegetable cookery.

REGIONS

The coastal areas receive more rainfall than the interior, so most of the crops grow near the coasts. Most Australians live at or near the coasts with the largest population found in the southeastern coastal region. In fact, 80 percent of the population resides in Australia's five largest cities, which are located near the coasts.

Cattle and sheep thrive in the vast interior lands of Australia. Land that receives more rainfall than desert supports vast amounts of grasslands suitable for grazing livestock. Huge ranches where cattle and sheep are raised exist throughout Australia, providing bountiful meat. As a result, meat consumption in this country remains very high. Australians prepare large pieces of meat like roasts, steaks, and chops as opposed to the Asian and African countries where small amounts of meat are extended with vegetables and starches.

Diverse wildlife lives in Australia with several animal species thriving here that are not seen in most of the rest of the world. Kangaroos, platypus, emu, wallabies, snakes, and lizards are just a sample of the varied wildlife. Native tribes regularly consumed many of these animals, particularly in the outback regions where rainfall was limited and food was sparse.

Abundant crops and animals thrive in the different areas of Australia, producing a bounty of fruits, vegetables, seafood, fish, and meats. Because of the diversity of climates and land conditions existing here, most types of produce, fish, seafood, and animals for meat flourish somewhere on this continent. Tropical fruits, vegetables, and fish abound in the tropical northern sections while the southern part of the country yields produce and seafood requiring a temperate climate. Apples and pears grow throughout Australia, as do the grapes that become wine. Although the passion fruit proliferates there and some varieties of apples and other fruits were developed in Australia, the fruit that many associate with Australia and New Zealand is the kiwi.

The eastern section of Australia contains forests, fertile farmland, coasts, plains, and low mountains. This area receives more rainfall than any other region in Australia, which accounts for the fertile farmland and prolific crops. Shrimp and tuna come from the coast here; cattle, sheep, wheat, oats, rice, sugar, peanuts, vegetables, bananas, pineapple, and other fruits thrive in the east.

Grasslands, desert, and some coastline make up the central portion. Much of the land here endures very dry conditions. The coasts yield shrimp and tuna, sheep and cattle thrive in the grasslands, and wheat, barley, and grapes come from this central section of Australia.

The west is composed of plateaus, grasslands, desert, and coastal plains. Sheep, cattle, lobster, wheat, oats, vegetables, and fruits are produced in this region. Most of the crops come from the northern and southwestern parts of the western region.

CUISINE

The Australian cuisine continues to blossom. The typical diet consists of lots of meat, and many British and Irish dishes reflect the strong British/Irish heritage. Some of the favorite British dishes include roasted lamb, meat pies (pasties), shepherd's pie, fish and chips, and various puddings. Today, the chefs of Australia focus on two things. First, they capitalize on the bounty and incredible variety of meat, seafood, fish, fruits, and vegetables available in their country. Second, the chefs combine aspects from the many cuisines represented by immigrants from around the world. In the years since World War II, Australia has developed into a melting pot, and the cuisine reflects influences from around the globe, including many of the Asian and Polynesian countries lying nearby. In essence, Australian chefs are developing a new Australian cuisine, using their native food products combined with a fusion of the cuisines from the many immigrants.

Because of the limited amount of rainfall, Australians enjoy many days of sunshine. As a result, life revolves around outdoor activities, including all sorts of sports, hiking, and picnics. This love for the outdoors leads to a national fondness for the barbecue, when foods both are cooked and eaten outside. Favorite grilling items for the barbie include steaks, chops, and sausages.

Meat is abundant throughout the country, and Australians consume ample quantities of it, particularly beef, veal, and lamb. Beef ranks as the favorite meat followed by lamb, then pork, game, and poultry. Traditionally, Australians eat steaks, chops, meat pies, or sausages for the entrée at the main meal of the day accompanied by potatoes and vegetables. Many consume meat three times a day—at breakfast, tea, and the main meal. A well-liked dish, Shearer's stew, consists of lamb stew with dumplings. Rabbits used to be widely consumed, and chickens were seldom eaten, but now that has switched and chicken appears frequently. All sorts of game show up on menus, including kangaroo, crocodile, emu, venison, buffalo, and more.

Another popular dish borrowed from their British heritage, meat pies rank as the favorite snack. They take the place of the American hot dog at a ball game. This well-liked snack is only one of a proliferation of sweet and savory snacks consumed by the Australians who are known for their fondness for snacks.

Ample coastline, lakes, and rivers coupled with this country's diverse climates yield a wide assortment of seafood and fish. With the cool waters of the south and the tropical waters in the north, countless varieties of fish thrive here. In fact, it seems that most types of fish flourish somewhere in Australia. Oysters, scallops, shrimp, crayfish, clams, abalone, and other shellfish abound. Although much is exported, Australians have access to ample amounts of fresh seafood. The favorite method of preparing fish still remains deep-frying, and deep-fried potatoes usually accompany the fish, producing the traditional English fish and chips. Carpetbagger steak, another popular Australian dish, combines two favorite food items in an unusual way. Oysters fill a pocket cut into the side of a beefsteak, then the steak is grilled.

With the bounty of fruits, vegetables, and nuts growing on this continent, it is not surprising that they appear in many dishes in all areas of the menu. Indigenous to Australia, the macadamia nut was exported to Hawaii where a huge trade market developed. Kiwi and passion fruit appear frequently. Fruits are often combined with meats or seafood. A variation on carpetbagger steak, the pocket cut in the steak is filled with fruit rather than oysters. Fish recipes sometimes incorporate nuts in the breading, and salads in Australia frequently combine both vegetables and fruits. Olive trees thrive in the south, and olive oil production has developed into a large market. Like the British, the Australians prefer to cook their meat and vegetables until well done. Traditional Australian cooking does not feature *al dente* vegetables or pink beef and lamb.

Beginning about thirty years ago, the dairy farmers and cheesemakers started producing cheese in Australia. Now hundreds of varieties of cheeses made from the milk of cows, sheep, and goats come from here.

Consumption of sugar remains very high with all sorts of desserts and ice cream available. Desserts commonly follow the evening meal, and many sweet snacks are consumed. *Pavlova*, a large meringue shell filled with whipped cream and fresh fruits, is an Australian dessert named for the famous Russian ballerina, Anna Pavlova.

Australians eat three meals per day, often partake in tea in the afternoon, and are known to snack frequently. Following the British pattern, breakfast

---

AUSTRALIAN CHEESES

With an abundance of available milk from sheep, cows, and goats, the Australians produce many cheeses that are known in other countries, including Brie, Cheddar, Gruyère, feta, mozzarella, Neufchâtel, and many varieties of blue cheese. They also produce some that are not so widely recognized:

King River Gold Made from cow's milk, slightly sharp flavor, semi-soft texture
Polkolbin Made from cow's milk, sharp spicy flavor, semi-soft texture
Washed Rind Cheese Sweet mild flavor, soft creamy texture

REGION	AREA	WEATHER	TOPOGRAPHY	FOODS
Australia	East	North: tropical; rest: warm summers, mild to cool winters	Low mountains, plains, plateaus, coast, forests, Great Dividing Range, fertile farmland	Cattle, sheep, seafood, shrimp, oysters, tuna, fish, dairy, wheat, oats, rice, corn, sugar, peanuts, potatoes, vegetables, bananas, pineapple, apples, pears, citrus, grapes, other fruits
	Central	North: tropical; rest: warm summers, mild to cool winters	Flat, grasslands, desert	Cattle, sheep, shrimp, tuna, wheat, barley, grapes, apples, pears
	West	North: tropical; rest: warm summers, mild to cool winters	Flat, grasslands, plateaus, desert, coastal plains	Cattle, sheep, lobster, wheat, oats, potatoes, rice, apples, pears, grapes, fruits, vegetables

tends to be a large meal. It may consist of porridge or cereal, eggs, bacon or a thin steak, and toast. The substantial evening meal includes a first course followed by an entrée and two or three side dishes. Salad either accompanies the entrée or follows it. The meal concludes with dessert.

Another tradition from their British ancestors, tea remains the most popular hot drink. Beer consumption remains high, but, with the proliferation of the vineyards and the wine industry in Australia, wine has joined beer as a popular and much consumed beverage. The growing wine industry continues to flourish, and much wine is exported to countries around the world. In fact, many rank Australia as one of the finest wine-producing regions in the world.

Review Questions

1. Describe the type of oven built by the Aborigines, and discuss two cooking methods used with that oven.
2. Why did the British settle in Australia?
3. Explain the British influence on the cuisine of Australia.
4. Explain why Australia produces such a wide range of food products.
5. Discuss how the climate, geography, and topography have affected the cuisine of Australia.

Glossary

barbie The barbecue grill

monsoons Tropical winds

outback The large areas of bush country in the interior sections of Australia

Pavlova An Australian dessert consisting of a large meringue shell filled with whipped cream and fresh fruits; named for the famous ballerina, Anna Pavlova

shearer's stew Lamb stew with dumplings

SAUSAGE ROLLS

Number of Servings: 14
Serving Size: 1 sausage roll
Total Yield: 14 rolls
              1 lb, 2 oz dough

Cooking Method: Bake

Food Balance: Protein to balanced/neutral
Wine Style: Wide variety from Pinot Grigio to Chardonnay and from Blush to Cabernet
Example: Château Souverain Chardonnay or Cabernet Sauvignon

INGREDIENTS	WEIGHT	VOLUME
PASTRY:		
flour, all purpose	8½ oz	2 cups
salt		¼ teaspoon
baking powder		½ teaspoon
butter, unsalted, cold, cut into about 12 pieces	6 oz	1½ sticks
water, cold	2½ oz	⅓ cup
sausage, lean, finely ground	14 oz	
flour	¾ oz	2 tablespoons
egg, beaten	1¾ oz	1 each

PASTRY

1. Place flour, salt, and baking powder in bowl of food processor, pulse to blend.
2. Place butter over flour, pulse to mix until size of peas.
3. With machine running, pour water through feed tube, pulse until dough forms ball.
4. Remove from processor, wrap in plastic wrap, refrigerate until needed.

ASSEMBLY:

1. Preheat oven to 375 degrees.
2. Roll about 1 oz pastry dough into square about ⅛-inch thick, brush edges with water.
3. Form 1 oz sausage into sausage link shape, roll in flour, place just below center of pastry.
4. Fold pastry over sausage to join two opposite sides, press edge to seal, crimp with fork or crimper (do not seal the two end sides).
5. Brush with egg.
6. Bake in center of oven for about 30 minutes, until golden brown. Serve immediately.

CREAM OF CRAB SOUP

Number of Servings: 10
Serving Size: 7 oz
Total Yield: 4 lbs, 8 oz

Cooking Method: Boil

Cream of Crab Soup; photo courtesy of Dorling Kindersley

Food Balance: Sweet/protein to balanced
Wine Style: Rich/medium-bodied Viognier, Chenin Blanc, Chardonnay, light Rosé and Reds
Example: Beringer Viognier

INGREDIENTS	WEIGHT	VOLUME
butter	1½ oz	3 tablespoons
onions, diced small	12 oz	2 large or 2 cups
celery, diced small	4 oz	2 stalks or 1 cup
flour	2 oz	6 tablespoons
milk, hot	3 lb	6 cups or 1½ quart
white pepper		¼ teaspoon
salt		1¾ teaspoons
hot red pepper, ground		⅛ teaspoon or to taste
crabmeat, drained, fresh, frozen or canned, all shell and cartilage removed	1 lb, 8 oz	
heavy cream	12 oz	1½ cups
sherry, pale dry	2 oz	¼ cup
lemon juice		2 teaspoons
nutmeg		⅛ teaspoon

GARNISH:

paprika

1. Melt butter over medium heat, add onions and celery, sauté until vegetables are soft, about 5 minutes.
2. Add flour, mix well.

3. Slowly whisk milk into pan in thin stream, add salt and both peppers, stirring constantly, cook until mixture comes to boil and thickens.
4. Strain soup through sieve, pressing on vegetables to extract all liquid, then discard vegetables.
5. Return soup to pan, add crabmeat and cream, stir over medium heat until heated, about 3 minutes.
6. Add sherry, lemon juice, and nutmeg, correct seasonings.
7. Serve, topped with sprinkling of paprika.

SALAD WITH AVOCADO AND MANGO

Number of Servings: 8
Serving Size: 6 oz
Total Yield: 3 lbs

INGREDIENTS	WEIGHT	VOLUME
DRESSING:		
olive oil	5 oz	⅔ cup
lemon juice	2 oz	4 tablespoons
salt		¼ teaspoon
mustard, dry		½ teaspoon
pepper, ground		⅛ teaspoon
mustard, prepared	½ oz	2 teaspoons
SALAD:		
bacon slices, cooked, drained, chopped	½ oz	2 slices

Salad with Avocado and Mango

INGREDIENTS	WEIGHT	VOLUME
mangoes, peeled, sliced	14 oz	2 each
avocados, peeled, sliced	11½ oz	2 each
nuts, toasted, chopped	4 oz	⅔ cup
lettuce, Boston or any type, washed, torn into bite-sized pieces	14 oz	2 heads

DRESSING:

1. Mix all ingredients together in container.
2. Shake well for 45 seconds, until well combined. Correct seasonings.

SALAD:

1. Combine all ingredients in large bowl.
2. Just before serving, pour dressing over salad, using just enough to lightly coat ingredients.
3. Serve immediately, arranging slices of avocado and mango decoratively on top.

SALAD WITH TOMATO, CHEDDAR, AND PINEAPPLE

Number of Servings: 11
Serving Size: 5 oz
Total Yield: 3 lbs, 8 oz

INGREDIENTS	WEIGHT	VOLUME
VINAIGRETTE:		
red wine vinegar	1½ oz	3 tablespoons
orange or pineapple juice	3 oz	6 tablespoons
olive oil	3 oz	6 tablespoons
salt		½ teaspoon
pepper		¼ teaspoon
SALAD:		
lettuce, torn into bite-sized pieces	14 oz	9 cups
tomatoes, fresh, cut into bite-size pieces or cherry tomatoes halved	1 lb, 2 oz	6 small
pineapple, fresh, diced	12 oz	1½ cups
cheddar cheese, grated	3 oz	1 cup
nuts, toasted, chopped	2¼ oz	6 tablespoons
scallions, minced	¾ oz	2 tablespoons

1. Mix all ingredients for vinaigrette in jar or processor, shake until well mixed and slightly thickened. Correct seasonings.
2. Mix all salad ingredients in bowl.
3. At serving time, pour vinaigrette over salad, toss gently to coat thoroughly. Correct seasonings. Serve.

SHEARER'S STEW

Lamb Stew with Dumplings

Number of Servings: 10 Cooking Method: Braise
Serving Size: 11 oz
Total Yield: 7 lbs, 8 oz

Food Balance: Protein/balanced
Wine Style: Medium to strong wines—Sauvignon Blanc, rich fruity
  Reds, Merlot, Shiraz
Example: Beringer Alluvium (Merlot)

INGREDIENTS	WEIGHT	VOLUME
STEW:		
oil	2 oz	¼ cup
lamb, boneless shoulder, cut into 1½- to 2-inch cubes	2 lbs, 4 oz	
flour	2 oz	½ cup
onions, sliced ¼-inch thick	9 oz	2 each
carrots, sliced ¾-inch thick	5 oz	3 each
parsnips, sliced ¾-inch thick	6½ oz	2 each
celery, diced	5½ oz	2 stalks
green pepper, cut in half, sliced ¼-inch thick	4½ oz	1 small
garlic, minced	¼ oz	2 cloves
lamb or meat stock, hot	2 lbs	1 qt
Worcestershire sauce	½ oz	1 tablespoon
black pepper		½ teaspoon
cucumbers, peeled, seeded, grated	1 lb, 3 oz	2 each
DUMPLINGS:		
flour, all purpose, sifted	6 oz	1½ cups
baking powder	¼ oz	2 teaspoons
salt	¼ oz	1 teaspoon
black pepper		½ teaspoon
milk	6 oz	¾ cup

FOR STEW:

1. Wash meat, dry, dredge meat with flour.
2. Heat 1½ oz (3 tablespoons) oil in pot until hot, brown meat cubes on all sides, then remove from pan. Sauté meat in batches so the pan is not crowded.
3. Add remaining oil, sauté onions, carrots, celery, parsnip, and garlic over medium heat until soft.
4. Sprinkle any remaining flour over vegetables, stir well, slowly whisk stock into vegetables, add pepper and Worcestershire sauce.
5. Add lamb, cover and simmer on low heat until lamb is tender, about 1½ to 2 hours. Correct seasonings.

FOR DUMPLINGS:

1. Sift flour, baking powder, salt, and pepper into bowl, add milk, stirring just to blend.
2. Drop by teaspoon into stew, cover and simmer about 10 minutes, then turn dumplings.

Shearer's Stew (Lamb Stew with Dumplings); photo courtesy of Dorling Kindersley

TO FINISH:

1. Cook another 5 minutes, add cucumbers.
2. Cook about 5 minutes, serve immediately. Top each serving with at least one dumpling.

SAUTÉED TROUT WITH MACADAMIA NUTS

Number of Servings: 8   Cooking Method: Sauté
Serving Size: 1 trout

Food Balance: Balanced/neutral
Wine Style: Light- to medium-bodied Riesling, Chardonnay, Rosé, Merlot, Cabernet Sauvignon
Example: Château Souverain Chardonnay

INGREDIENTS	WEIGHT	VOLUME
trout, bones removed	3 lb (without heads)	8 each
flour, for coating	6 oz	1½ cups
salt	¼ oz	1 teaspoon
black pepper		¼ teaspoon
eggs	6¾ oz	4 each
macadamia nuts, ground	8 oz	1½ cups
butter	2 oz	4 tablespoons
oil	2 oz	4 tablespoons
lemons	2 oz	2 each

GARNISH:

lemons, quartered		2 to 4 each
macadamia nuts, sautéed in butter		

Sautéed Trout with Macadamia Nuts; photo courtesy of
Dorling Kindersley

1. For breading fish, mix flour with salt and black pepper and place
   on plate or piece of parchment paper. Beat eggs in shallow bowl.
   Place nuts on separate plate or piece of parchment.
2. Wash trout, dry, one at a time coat trout with flour, shake to remove excess flour, dip in egg, then coat with nuts, and place
   breaded fish on plate or rack. Refrigerate until service.
3. Heat oil and butter in skillet, using enough for ¼-inch coating in
   pan.
4. Add fish, sauté for 3 to 5 minutes, squeeze some lemon juice over
   fish, turn fish over with spatula, squeeze lemon juice over fish,
   sauté another 3 to 5 minutes, until crisp and done.
5. Remove from pan, drain on paper toweling, serve immediately
   garnished with lemon wedges and sautéed macadamia nuts.

DEEP-FRIED FISH

Number of Servings: 8   Cooking Method: Deep-fry
Serving Size: about 6 oz fillet raw
  weight before breading
Total Yield: 1 lb, 14 oz batter

Food Balance: Protein to neutral
Wine Style: Fruity, light-bodied Pinot Grigio, Sauvignon Blanc, Pinot
  Noir
Example: Campanile Pinot Grigio

INGREDIENTS	WEIGHT	VOLUME
fish fillets, white, mild, washed	3 lbs	
BEER BATTER:		
flour, all purpose	14 oz	3 cups

Deep-fried Fish; photo courtesy of Dorling Kindersley

INGREDIENTS	WEIGHT	VOLUME
salt		1½ teaspoons
pepper		½ teaspoon
eggs	6¾ oz	4 each
beer	9 oz	1 cup plus 2 tablespoons

flour, for dredging fish
vegetable oil for frying

ACCOMPANIMENTS:

malt vinegar
tartar sauce
catsup

BATTER:

1. Sift dry ingredients into bowl, form a well in center.
2. Place eggs in well, whisk while pouring in beer, whisk until smooth.
3. Cover and refrigerate at least one hour.

ASSEMBLY:

1. Heat about 2-inches oil in pan for deep-frying.
2. Dip fish into flour for light coating, then dip into batter to coat.
3. Place fish into hot oil, adding 2 or 3 pieces at a time, then let oil temperature rise again before frying next batch.
4. Fry until golden, then drain on absorbent paper.
5. Serve immediately, accompanied by French fries (chips), malt vinegar, tartar sauce, and/or catsup.

STEAK WITH BANANA

Number of Servings: 1   Cooking Method: Grill
Serving Size: 1 steak

Food Balance: Sweet and protein
Wine Style: Soft to rich Reds, fruity Chardonnay, soft Merlot, or fruity Shiraz
Example: Meridian Santa Barbara Chardonnay

INGREDIENTS	WEIGHT	VOLUME
steak, Delmonico or tenderloin	8 oz or desired size	
banana, sliced	3½ oz	1 small
sherry, dry	2 oz	¼ cup
pepper	sprinkling	
pineapple, fresh, sliced	3 oz	1 slice

1. Cut deep pocket into side of steak, pour one or two teaspoons dry sherry inside pocket.
2. Insert banana in pocket, close with wooden toothpicks, sprinkle both sides of steak with pepper.
3. Place steak in bowl, pour remaining sherry over it, cover and marinate 4 hours or overnight in refrigerator.
4. Preheat grill or broiler.
5. Grill or broil steak to desired temperature, grill pineapple slice.
6. Remove toothpicks, serve immediately, topped with grilled pineapple.

PORK CHOPS OR CHICKEN WITH APRICOT MARINADE

Number of Servings: 8
Serving Size: 2 pork chops, 1 chicken
    breast, or 1 pork chop
    and ½ chicken breast
Total Yield: 1 lb, 4 oz or 2¼ cups marinade

Cooking Method: Boil, grill

Food Balance: Sweet and sour/balanced
Wine Style: Fruity/medium-bodied Viognier, Gewürztraminer, Shiraz, Zinfandel
Example: Beringer Founders' Estate Shiraz

INGREDIENTS	WEIGHT	VOLUME
MARINADE:		
apricots, dried	4¼ oz	½ cup
water	8 oz	1 cup
onion, minced	2¼ oz	½ medium
white vinegar	4 oz	½ cup
catsup	2½ oz	¼ cup
honey	3¾ oz	⅓ cup
soy sauce		1 teaspoon
oil	½ oz	1 tablespoon

pork chops or chicken breasts

MARINADE:
1. Place apricots and water in pan, bring to boil, lower heat and simmer for 15 minutes, until tender.
2. Purée mixture in food processor until smooth, return to pan.
3. Add remaining marinade ingredients to pan, bring to boil, reduce heat, simmer for 5 minutes.
4. Cool, refrigerate until needed, keeps for several weeks refrigerated.

ASSEMBLY:
1. Preheat grill. Place pork chops or chicken breasts on grill.
2. Brush meat with marinade whenever turned.
3. Serve meat immediately when done, accompanied by extra marinade, if desired.

SPINACH WITH CURRANTS

Number of Servings: 9
Serving Size: 4 oz
Total Yield: 2 lbs, 6 oz

Cooking Method: Sauté

INGREDIENTS	WEIGHT	VOLUME
butter	2 oz	4 tablespoons
currants, dried	2½ oz	1 cup
spinach, washed, stems removed, cut into 1½-inch slices	2 lbs, 13 oz	
salt	¼ oz	1 teaspoon
pepper		1 teaspoon

1. Melt butter in large pan over low heat, add currants and cook slowly until plumped (currants soften and swell).
2. Add spinach, salt, and pepper to pan, stir well.
3. Cover pan, cook over medium heat until spinach is wilted, about 3 to 5 minutes.
4. Stir well, correct seasonings, serve immediately.

Spinach with Currants

ROASTED POTATOES AND GARLIC

Number of Servings: 9   Cooking Method: Sauté, bake
Serving Size: 5 oz
Total Yield: 2 lbs, 14 oz

INGREDIENTS	WEIGHT	VOLUME
potatoes, red or small white, peeled	2 lbs, 14 oz	18 each
olive oil	1½ oz	3 tablespoons
garlic, peeled	3¼ oz	18 large cloves
salt		½ teaspoon
black pepper		¼ teaspoon

1. Wash and dry potatoes, preheat oven to 375 degrees.
2. Heat oil in skillet, add potatoes, sauté until browned on all sides.
3. Place potatoes and garlic in ovenproof dish, sprinkle with salt and pepper, mix gently.
4. Pour remaining oil from sautéing over potatoes.
5. Cover and bake until potatoes and garlic are tender, about 40 minutes.

PAVLOVA

Meringue Shell Filled with Whipped Cream and Fruit

Number of Servings: 8 to 10   Cooking Method: Bake
Total Yield: One 9-inch dessert

INGREDIENTS	WEIGHT	VOLUME
MERINGUE:		
egg whites	4 oz	½ cup
cream of tartar		¼ teaspoon
sugar	7½ oz	1 cup
cornstarch	½ oz	2 tablespoons
vinegar, white		½ teaspoon
vanilla		1 teaspoon
TOPPING:		
heavy whipping cream	12 oz	1½ cups
confectioners' sugar		2 teaspoons
vanilla		1 teaspoon
kiwi, peeled, sliced ¼-inch thick	about 12 oz	4 each

apricot glaze, optional

> *Any fruit or mixture of fruits can top this dessert. This confection is best served the day it is made so the meringue stays crisp. Many prepare the meringue shell without piping a wall to hold the filling by using a flat disk of meringue topped with whipped cream and fruit.*

MERINGUE:

1. Remove 1 oz (2 tablespoons) sugar, set aside. Sift remaining sugar with cornstarch, set aside.
2. Trace 8-inch circle on sheet of parchment paper, place on sheet pan, preheat oven to 275 degrees.
3. Beat egg whites and cream of tartar at high speed until half stiff, slowly add reserved 1 oz (2 tablespoons) sugar.
4. Beat until stiff peaks, fold in sifted ingredients, then add vinegar and vanilla.

Pavlova (Meringue Shell Filled with Whipped Cream and Fruit); photo courtesy of Dorling Kindersley

5. Spread meringue on circle about ⅜-inch thick, place meringue in piping bag fitted with ⅜- or ½-inch round tip, pipe border around perimeter (to form wall of shell), pipe another line on top of border.
6. Place in middle of oven for 10 minutes to set meringue, remove, pipe another line on top of border, return to oven.
7. Bake for a total of 30 minutes at 275 degrees, reduce temperature to 250 and bake another hour, until firm but not brown.
8. Remove from oven, cool completely before filling.

FILLING:
1. Whip cream on high speed until soft peaks, scrape down sides of bowl, add sugar.
2. Continue beating until medium-firm peaks, then add vanilla.
3. Spread cream evenly over meringue shell.
4. Starting at outer edge, lay kiwi slices overlapping slightly on top, changing directions with each row (one row clockwise, the next row counterclockwise). If desired, coat with apricot glaze.
5. Refrigerate, covered tightly, until service.
6. To serve, cut into pie-shaped wedges.

CHAPTER 16
Mexico

By the end of this chapter, you will be able to

- Describe the impact of the Mayans and Aztecs on the Mexican cuisine
- Discuss the influence of the Spanish on the cookery of Mexico
- Explain how the topography of Mexico affected the cuisine
- Name foods that the European explorers found in Mexico and then introduced to their countries
- Name foods that the Europeans introduced to Mexico
- Name foods and flavorings prevalent in the cuisine of Mexico
- Prepare a variety of Mexican dishes

HISTORY

The first known inhabitants of Mexico lived there before 8000 B.C. Although the Mayans and Aztecs remain the most recognized of the Indians who inhabited this land, many different Indian tribes dwelled in the area that now comprises Mexico. During the classic period from 250 to 900 A.D., Indians constructed impressive structures such as pyramids and temples, some of which still stand today. In addition, they built cities, and the population increased dramatically during this time.

Thousands of years before the European explorers discovered Mexico, the Indians of the Maya and Aztec civilizations developed sophisticated cuisines. Both Mayan and Aztec leaders indulged in huge feasts. In fact, historians claim that anywhere from sixty to 500 dishes were served at these feasts! After landing in Mexico, the explorers from Europe learned of many new foods, including beans, corn, tomatoes, peppers, squash, pumpkins, chocolate, bananas, avocados, cashews, exotic fruits, and new varieties of fish. The explorers took these new foods back to their native countries where many were readily adopted into the cuisines.

Considering how early in history they lived, the Mayans and Aztecs were involved in sophisticated studies and research in a number of areas. As a result, these remarkable people developed an advanced culture and invented a calendar, a written language, an accounting system, as well as making significant discoveries in the fields of medicine and astronomy. The Mayans and Aztecs experimented with plants to develop better strains of their native vegetables. From these two Indian cultures, the Europeans learned new procedures for cultivation that they applied to their crops when they returned to their homelands.

Although many different Indian tribes inhabited this country, the rugged terrain prevented them from associating with each other. This isolation led to pronounced regional variations that developed throughout Mexico.

In 1521, the Spanish and Portuguese discovered Mexico and introduced almonds, citrus fruits, onions, garlic, rice, cinnamon, wheat, hogs, and dairy products to the Mexicans. The Aztecs, the last Indian tribe to rule Mexico, lost control of their country to the Spanish, who ruled Mexico for the next 300 years. During that time, the foods and cooking methods of Mexico fused with those of Spain, and a great marriage occurred between these two cuisines.

Flavorings used in Mexico changed as onions and garlic were added to many of the native dishes. The introduction of hogs provided both meat and lard, pig fat. The lard was particularly important as Mexicans had no source of fat available until the Spanish arrived and brought both lard and butter. This opened the world of frying to the Mexicans who wholeheartedly embraced this cooking technique. Today, the influence of the Indians and the Spanish remains the most prominent on the cuisine of Mexico.

In the 1860s, the French conquered Mexico and introduced the Mexicans to pasta. The French rule only lasted a few years, and by 1867, Mexico became an independent country. A number of revolutions occurred in Mexico in the late 1800s and early 1900s. Although the economic picture improved during World War II, the country remains quite poor.

TOPOGRAPHY

Located just south of the western United States, Mexico lies at the northern end of Central America. To the southeast, Guatemala and Belize link Mexico to the rest of Central America. The Pacific Ocean is situated on the west and south; the Gulf of Mexico and Caribbean Ocean lie to the east. The Rio Grande River forms over half of Mexico's 2,000-mile border with the United States.

Diverse climate and terrain make up the land of Mexico, which includes tropical rain forests, mountains, valleys, very arid land, and grasslands. Accounting for the intense isolation that existed between the regions, two-thirds of the land in Mexico consists of high, rugged mountains and rolling plateaus.

Two volcanic mountain ranges with peaks as high as 17,000 feet run through Mexico. The mountains of the Western Sierra Madre run from the north to the south along the Pacific coast; the Eastern Sierra Madre lies parallel to that range along the Atlantic Ocean. Mountainous areas and plateaus form the land between these two mountain ranges. In some areas, the mountains yield to coastal plains where crops are planted, but arid land surrounds the mountains in the northern and north-central areas. A wide variety of crops grow throughout these areas because the great fluctuations in the elevations causes diverse climatic conditions.

The central region primarily consists of dry land with temperatures determined by the altitude. The southern regions receive more rainfall, and, as a result, many types of crops flourish here. Dense forests comprise the southwestern coastal area.

Composed of tropical rain forest and grasslands, the Yucatan peninsula is located in southeastern Mexico. Tropical climate dominates the Yucatan Peninsula, as well as all of the coasts of Mexico.

Ingredients and Foods Commonly Used Throughout the Cuisine of Mexico Include:

- beans
- corn
- chili peppers—dried and fresh
- tortillas
- rice
- lard
- pork
- onions and garlic
- tropical fruits and vegetables
- tomatoes and tomatillos
- squash, sweet potatoes, and pumpkins
- avocados
- bananas and plantains
- prickly pear and cactus
- pumpkin seeds, sesame seeds, and numerous varieties of nuts
- cilantro and cumin
- cinnamon and cloves
- chocolate
- coffee

COOKING METHODS

Prior to the Spaniards' arrival in Mexico in the sixteenth century, the Aztecs, Mayans, and other native Indians boiled, stewed, steamed, baked, broiled, or ate their food raw. Like many countries with meager amounts of meat, stewing and braising were common both to tenderize the tough meat and to extend it.

The Spanish introduced lard and butter in 1521, which made fat available to the Mexicans. After that, both sautéing and deep-frying became popular and often used cooking techniques. Even today, Mexicans fry lots of foods. Most kitchens in Mexico are equipped with a griddle, *comal*, for frying a variety of food items. Many sauces are prepared by grinding or puréeing the ingredients together, sautéing the paste, adding liquid to the paste, then placing the food item(s) into the sauce.

A precursor to the New England clam bake, the Indians dug a pit, made a fire in the pit, let it burn down, and then cooked over the smoldering embers. Sometimes, a whole animal was cooked slowly in the pit. Other times, pots of food were placed in the pit, covered with mud and/or leaves, and left to simmer. This oven/pit functioned to bake or steam foods. Today most Mexicans steam tamales and other foods in a steamer over simmering water.

REGIONS

Two factors account for the extensive differences found among the regional cuisines of Mexico. As mentioned before, the first cause came from the isolation that resulted from the rugged terrain. The mountains, steep valleys,

TO PEEL FRESH PEPPERS

Roast peppers over open flame of grill or gas burner or place in broiler until charred and blackened. Place charred peppers in bag for a few minutes to soften skin, then remove from bag and peel under cool running water.

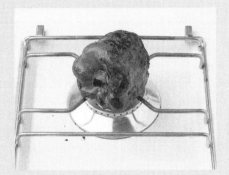

Charring pepper over flame; photo courtesy of Dorling Kindersley

Placing charred pepper in bag to steam; photo courtesy of Dorling Kindersley

Peeling pepper under running water; photo courtesy of Dorling Kindersley

canyons, and desert areas created difficult travel between regions. This led to the formation of about thirty-two distinct states and territories, and each developed and still retains its own regional cuisine.

The second factor rose from the wide range of climates existing in Mexico. Although the mountainous regions experience cool weather, the arid lands remain very dry and hot (except those in the mountains), and the tropical areas are hot and humid. These diverse weather conditions resulted in different crops and animals flourishing in the various regions, which led to the necessity of adapting recipes. For example, *tamales* are prepared throughout Mexico, but cornhusks wrap the filling in the cooler climates, while cooks in tropical areas surround the *tamale* filling with banana leaves.

The varied climates of Mexico fall into three distinct zones that are determined by the altitude. Areas with elevation up to 3,000 feet experience tropical conditions characterized by long, hot summers and mild winters. Temperate climate exists in land with altitudes from 3,000 to 6,000 feet, and these areas are the most conducive to raising crops. The cold zone includes terrain above 6,000 feet.

Because of insufficient rainfall and mountainous terrain, only 12 percent of the land in Mexico is suitable for use as farmland. Basically, the northern part of Mexico is dry, while the southern area receives more rainfall and contains much of the farmland. Some of the crops grown in the south include corn, beans, sugar, coffee, vanilla, cacao, potatoes, avocados, chili peppers, tomatoes, coconuts, oranges, bananas, grapes, lemons, mangoes, and pineapples.

The north of Mexico consists of rather arid land, providing grasslands for the grazing of cattle and farmland for growing varieties of wheat adapted to require less moisture. As a result, inhabitants of the north consume a lot of cheese and, unlike the rest of Mexico, prefer beef instead of pork. Due to the dry climate and availability of beef, *cecina*, dried beef, remains a staple here. In addition, milder, less spicy dishes prevail in the north. With high wheat production, tortillas made from wheat are more common here, while residents of the south favor corn tortillas.

The coasts experience tropical weather, yielding a myriad of wonderful fruits and vegetables that thrive in the hot and humid conditions. Many tropical fruits and vegetables including bananas, plantains, avocados, coconuts, and papayas flourish throughout the year in these areas.

Mexico is divided into six regions. The peninsula lying south of California, the Pacific Northwest, consists of dry, desertlike mountains with rolling hills in the interior. The coastal areas contain fertile farmland producing crops including grapes and dates, as well as abundant cattle and seafood. With the bounty of fresh seafood, *ceviche*, seafood "cooked" or marinated in lime juice until it turns opaque, hails from this region.

The largest region, the Plateau of Mexico encompasses the central portion. This varied land contains volcanoes, lakes, plateaus, flatlands, and mountains. The Sierra Madre Mountains and Mexico City lie within this region. In addition to ample seafood, corn, beans, wheat, and barley grow here.

The Gulf Coastal Plain lies in the east and consists of dry land, forests, tropical rain forest, and rich farmland. The Rio Grande River flows through this region. Forests and dry land make up the north, while the south contains rich farmland and tropical rain forests. With rivers and coastline, ample fish and seafood are available here. In addition to consuming lots of seafood, inhabitants of this region like spicy foods and coconut.

Lying in the south, the resort city of Acapulco lies in the region called the Southern Uplands. The steep ridges and deep gorges that comprise much of the landscape in this region make growing crops difficult, but plenty of seafood remains available here. The state of Oaxaca in the south was a center of Aztec culture, and the cooking strongly reflects that Aztec heritage.

In the southeast of Mexico, east of the Southern Uplands, lies the Chiapas Highlands. Consisting of flat-topped mountains, coffee and fruits thrive in this region.

Finally, the Yucatan Peninsula lies to the far southeast, dividing the Gulf of Mexico from the Caribbean Sea. This hot, humid area contains lots of plateaus. An isolated region, the Yucatan peninsula was once cut off from the mainland by thick jungles and swamps. The cooking of this region exemplifies the cuisine of the Mayans with hot and spicy foods predominating. Ample seafood, cacao, coffee, corn, and sugar come from the Yucatan.

CUISINE

From the time of the Mayans and Aztecs to the present, beans and corn formed the foundation of the Mexican cuisine. Both foods appear in numerous guises and are served at almost every meal.

When served separately, legumes (beans) and grains (corn, wheat, rice, etc.) do not contain the necessary amino acids to form complete protein; however, combining a legume with grain creates a complete protein. Although meat and dairy products provide complete protein by themselves, both these products were scarce in Mexico before the Spanish arrived in the sixteenth century. Like people in many countries with limited food resources, the early Mexicans developed mainstays in their diet that formed protein-rich combinations of foods that we now call complementary proteins. The foods most closely associated with Mexico, including beans in a corn or wheat tortilla or beans and rice, exemplify this combining of legumes with grain to create a complete protein. These foods formed the basis of the Mexican diet and contained the various amino acids necessary to create the complete protein needed by humans.

For an explanation of complementary protein, see the sidebar on page 397 in Chapter 17—South America.

A staple in the Mexican diet, beans combined with a grain still provide the majority of protein consumption throughout Mexico. Many types of beans are available, and they show up prepared in a countless variety of ways including boiled, mashed, and fried, as well as in stews and soups. In addition to appearing at the breakfast table, beans are served as a separate course after the entrée at the main meal of the day, *comida*.

Corn, a sacred plant in the religion of the Aztecs, joins beans to form the foundation of most meals. Although soups, appetizers, entrées, and vegetables contain whole corn, ground corn, *masa*, replaces grains such as wheat or rye, which are used so widely in breads, dumplings, and pasta throughout Europe and the Middle East. To make *masa*, dried corn is processed with lime (the chemical, not the fruit) and water to soften it before grinding. Using all parts of the corn plant, even the husks are used as the outer wrapper in *tamales* to hold the inside ingredients together and protect them from the ashes of the fire. After cooking, the husks are removed and discarded, leaving the steamed filling to eat.

Tortillas; photo courtesy of Dorling Kindersley

Consumed at every meal, the tortilla is a flat, unleavened disk of bread made from *masa* or wheat flour, and cooked on a *comal*. Before the Spanish arrived and introduced wheat to Mexico, all tortillas were made from corn. Today, most wheat tortillas appear in the north because much wheat grows there. Whether made from corn or wheat, the tortilla encases all varieties of fillings and functions as bread in the Mexican version of a sandwich. The versatile tortilla becomes a wrapper for many dishes (burrito, tostado, taco, enchilada), a scoop for dips (cut and served plain or deep-fried as chips), a replacement for noodles in soup (julienne tortilla), or a substitute for croutons on a salad (deep-fried pieces). Served plain or fried, as a whole round or in pieces, tortillas remain an intrinsic part of the Mexican cuisine.

Another staple grain introduced by the Spaniards in the sixteenth century, rice appears with great frequency. Often cooked with tomatoes and/or chilies, it accompanies most entrées. Preparation of Mexican rice usually begins by frying the rice like a pilaf. This causes the grains to remain separate instead of the sticky rice favored in many Asian countries.

Pork remains the favorite meat throughout most of Mexico, except in the north where beef is preferred. Because meat is both not abundant and tough, Mexicans tend to cook it a long time and then shred it. Available meat is extended by using it in soups, stews, or as a filling mixed with the ubiquitous beans. A small amount goes a long way in the typical meat taco where a little meat is placed down the middle of a soft corn tortilla, topped with sauce, then the tortilla is rolled to encase the filling. Myriad fillings include beans, cheese, vegetables, meats, or any combination of these ingredients. Only the American version of the taco is served in a deep-fried corn tortilla shell. In Mexico, burritos are tacos prepared with a wheat tortilla. When deep-fried, the burrito is called a *chimichanga*.

Another popular method of extending meager meat supplies, sausages use the less desirable parts of the animal. They play a substantial role in the cuisine of Mexico because a small amount of sausage cooked in a dish adds a lot of flavor. *Chorizo*, a well-known Mexican (and Spanish) pork sausage, appears often.

With miles and miles of coastline and many rivers, seafood and fish abound and comprise much of the diet in the areas where they are available. Seafood soups similar to the French *bouillabaisse* appear with significant regional variations. Difficult travel caused by the mountains in the interior regions prohibited transporting the seafood in its fresh state, but drying or salting seafood made it possible to transport it into the interiors of the country. Dried shrimp is a flavoring used throughout Mexico. Like many countries, including Spain, Italy, and Scandinavia, salted cod remains popular and is part of the traditional Christmas Eve dinner.

First produced after the Spanish introduced dairy cattle, cheese still plays an important role in the Mexican cuisine. Numerous types of *queso* (cheeses) are available, many possessing unique melting properties. Mexican cheeses fall into three categories: fresh, melting, and hard cheeses. Fresh cheeses become soft and hot when heated, but do not melt. These cheeses appear as fillings for meats and vegetables. *Chili rellenos*, a mild chili pepper that is stuffed and deep-fried, often features a filling of fresh cheese.

Melting cheeses melt into a smooth consistency and do not separate or become stringy. *Quesadillas*, one example of the many dishes that utilize melting cheeses, consists of a tortilla topped with cheese and strips of roasted, peeled peppers or any other desired ingredients, folded in half and fried until the cheese melts.

The third category, hard cheeses are usually full-flavored cheeses. They are most often served in two ways: grated or crumbled and sprinkled over dishes or added to fillings to create a more complex taste. Mexicans also cook and garnish with thick, cultured cream similar to the French crème frâiche. To prepare this cream, heavy whipping cream is cultured with yogurt or buttermilk.

Fresh Cheeses

blanco fresco Made from cow's milk, mild flavor, firm texture, sometimes called *para freir*

fresco Made from combination of cow's and goat's milk, mild flavor, soft, crumbly, somewhat grainy texture

panela Salty mild flavor, spongy, soft texture

requeson Mild flavor, spreads easily

Melting Cheeses

asadero Made from cow's milk, slightly tangy, stretched curd cheese, prevalent in northern Mexico

oaxaca Made from cow's milk, slightly tangy, stretched curd cheese, braided cheese with soft texture

chihuahua Spongy

quesillo Known as string cheese, from Oaxaca

queso quesadila Mild flavor, soft texture

Hard Cheeses

añejo Made from cow or goat's milk, salty flavor, crumbly hard texture, similar to Parmesan cheese, aged, sometimes called *queso Cotija*

The many sauces used in Mexican cookery differ greatly from those found in Europe. Appearing on most dishes, both spicy and mildly spiced sauces enliven dry fillings, beans, and meat. Mexicans prefer to mix the foods into thick sauces to form a stewlike consistency rather than serving thinner sauces, which are traditionally poured over the food or used to nap the food item. Adding a minimum of liquid during preparation and sautéing of the sauce produces the concentrated, intensely flavored, thick sauce favored in Mexico. The foods mixed with the thick sauce often are scooped with a tortilla, rather than eaten with a fork.

Mexicans grind or crush many ingredients, including whole spices, herbs, seeds, peppers, onions, garlic, and other flavorings into a paste before incorporating them into the sauce or dish. To facilitate this, most Mexican kitchens are equipped with a *metate*, a type of vessel used for grinding ingredients. Also, a mortar and pestle is found in most kitchens. Today, the food processor expedites this grinding or puréeing procedure.

Using indigenous ingredients, many sauces are tomato based and flavored with chilies and cilantro. Salsas provide an excellent example of these flavor combinations. Another ingredient long used in Mexico, pumpkin seeds were first grown by the Mayans. A frequent addition to Mexican sauces, ground pumpkin seeds thicken the sauce, as well as enhance its flavor. In Mexican cookery, *roux*, flour, or cornstarch is not used to thicken sauces. Rather, ground seeds, nuts, tortillas, and/or bread are used to thicken sauces while adding flavor and texture.

A well-known Mexican sauce dating from the Aztecs, *mole* actually contains unsweetened chocolate in addition to chilies, tomatoes, and a variety of spices, herbs, and ground seeds and nuts. Every region makes its own version of *mole*, and any meat, poultry, seafood, or vegetable can be prepared in a *mole* sauce. Depending on the ingredients used, *moles* come in green, red, and black variations. *Mole poblano*, turkey in a *mole* sauce, dates back to pre-Columbian times and remains a favorite holiday dish. Indigenous to Mexico, the turkey appears in *mole*, as well as many other preparations.

Salsa, the major condiment of Mexico, plays an important role in the cuisine. Made from an endless assortment of ingredients, salsa is usually prepared with a base of tomatoes or tomatillos. Often referred to as green tomatoes, *tomatillos* actually are not tomatoes at all. Sometimes replacing tomatoes in salsas and sauces, *tomatillos* lack the sweetness of tomatoes, thereby creating a base with a tangier flavor. Although some salsa is quite *picante* or hot, others contain milder peppers, resulting in a less spicy condiment. A dish of salsa sits on every dining table where diners use it as a dip for strips of tortillas or deep-fried tortilla chips, and they add salsa to any prepared dishes, including eggs, tacos or burritos, entrées, beans, and vegetables.

One of the identifying characteristics of Mexican cooking remains the extensive use of chili peppers. In varying degrees of heat ranging from mild to fiery, more than 100 types of peppers appear in all sorts of dishes. Beans and rice rise to new heights with the addition of chili peppers. The ribs and seeds of the chili pepper contain the most heat, so removing them greatly reduces the spiciness. Chilies appear in many preparations, including meats, salsas, sauces, and *adobo*, a seasoning paste containing ground chili peppers, herbs, spices, and vinegar. Fresh and dried peppers are used raw, cooked, roasted and pickled. *Chipotles*, jalepeño peppers that are smoked and then dried, lend a distinctive, smoky flavor to dishes. Known as *escabeche*, pickled peppers and vegetables appear often as condiments.

Information about the heat of peppers on the Scoville scale is on page 425 in Chapter 18—The Caribbean.

SOME OF THE AVAILABLE CHILI PEPPERS

Fresh Chili Peppers

cayenne Hot to very hot

habañero Very, very hot

jalapeño Hot

poblano Mild to medium

Scotch bonnet Extremely hot, rated the hottest chili pepper

serrano Hot to very hot

tabasco Very hot

Dried Chili Peppers

ancho Dried poblaño peppers, mild heat

chipotle Dried, smoked jalapeño peppers, hot to very hot heat

guajillo Dried mirasole peppers, somewhat hot heat

pasilla Dried chilaca peppers, medium to hot heat

Ancho Chili; photo courtesy of Dorling Kindersley

Chipotle Chili; photo courtesy of Dorling Kindersley

Pasilla Chili; photo courtesy of Dorling Kindersley

HANDLING CHILI PEPPERS

- Wearing gloves when handling peppers keeps the spicy oils found in the peppers off your hands. Those volatile oils remaining on hands can cause stinging in the eyes or any open or sensitive areas when rubbed.
- The seeds and veins (or ribs) of the pepper contain the most heat, so removing them from the peppers definitely tones down the spiciness and heat.

Other herbs and spices prevalent in Mexican cookery include cilantro, *epazote*, oregano, cinnamon, cumin, anise, bay leaf, and allspice. Cilantro flavors many dishes found in all parts of the menu. *Epazote* is added to tortilla dishes and beans, particularly black beans. *Achiote*, annatto seeds, give a yellow color to the dish and appear frequently in the Mexican cuisine.

Imparting a definite flavor to dishes, the most commonly used cooking fat remains lard. Other cooking oils and fats are sometimes used, depending on the desired taste of the dish.

Soups claim an important place in the Mexican diet. Prepared in myriad varieties, soups precede the entrée at the main meal of the day. Served both cold and hot, the many types include those with a base of chicken broth, cream soups, and some almost as thick as stews. *Pozole*, a thick stewlike soup containing pork and hominy, remains a favorite throughout the country.

Local open-air markets selling fresh fruits, vegetables, and often meats, seafood, beans, herbs, spices, and even crafts exist in all but the smallest towns. With the limited meat supply and the profusion of vegetables flourishing throughout the country; zucchini, greens, and *chayote*, sometimes called green pear, are just a few of the available vegetables that are eaten alone or as filling for a tortilla.

TO PEEL FRESH TOMATOES

Place whole tomato in pot of boiling water deep enough to cover the tomato for 15 to 20 seconds. Remove tomato from water and place in cold water or allow to cool at room temperature. When cool enough to handle, peel skin with knife.

Placing tomatoes in boiling water; photo courtesy of Dorling Kindersley

Placing tomatoes in cold water; photo courtesy of Dorling Kindersley

Peeling cooled tomato; photo courtesy of Dorling Kindersley

As found in the Caribbean and other countries in the tropics, both sweet and savory bananas play a significant role in this cuisine. Plantains function as a vegetable and accompany many entrées, banana leaves wrap foods for steaming, and sweet bananas show up fried, boiled, grilled, or eaten raw.

Another favorite throughout Mexico, the indigenous avocado appears often. Incorporated into all sorts of dishes, it is served raw, as well as used in soups, stews, and other dishes. Its best-known preparation remains *guacamole*, a spread made of mashed avocado, onion, tomato, and chilies. Recipes for *guacamole* vary greatly from region to region.

Tomatoes show up constantly as an ingredient in all sorts of sauces, salsas, and dishes prepared throughout Mexico. Used roasted, cooked, and raw, they lend color, as well as various flavors and textures to a myriad of dishes.

With ample arid land, the flourishing cactus plants enter into Mexico's culinary world. Cacti appear in salads, sauces, juices, and either stewed or fried as a vegetable. The popular prickly pear is the fruit of the *nopales* cactus. Tequila is made from the *agave* cactus.

Chocolate originated in this part of the world. Frequently served as a beverage, it is usually paired with cinnamon. Another nonalcoholic drink consumed in huge quantities, coffee functions as a flavoring as well as a beverage. The Mexicans prepare very strong coffee and flavor it with plenty of sugar. With abundant fresh fruits available, fruit juices continue as popular drinks. Favorite alcoholic beverages remain beer, rum, and tequila.

Like their Spanish ancestors who were influenced by the Arabs, Mexicans prefer very sweet desserts. A typical dessert plate served in Mexico even includes candy. Often incorporating fruit in fresh, candied, or paste form, desserts frequently include nuts and lots of eggs in their preparation. Many desserts contain nuts, including pine nuts, peanuts, almonds, pecans, or walnuts. Flans and other custardlike confections remain very popular.

The day begins with a breakfast of fruit, tortillas or sweet rolls, and coffee or hot chocolate; but some people also eat meat, eggs, and/or beans with breakfast. Many consume a midmorning snack to hold them until the main meal of the day, which is eaten around two o'clock in the afternoon. Consisting of several courses, *comida* is the largest meal of the day. Soup precedes the entrée that is accompanied by a vegetable or salad. A bowl of beans follows the entrée, then comes a dessert usually consisting of fresh or stewed fruit. Tortillas and salsa are included on the table for *comida*. Much like the traditional English tea, *merienda* features pastries with coffee or hot chocolate served around six in the evening. Eaten at nine or ten o'clock, the light, late evening meal, *cena*, might consist of one or two appetizers and a bowl of soup.

Review Questions

1. Name at least four foods commonly consumed by the Indians in Mexico before the European explorers arrived.
2. Name at least five foods introduced to Mexico by the Spaniards.
3. Describe the topography and climate found in Mexico. Explain how they influenced the regional cuisines.
4. What is salsa and how is it used in Mexico?
5. Name and describe several Mexican dishes including *mole*, burrito, and taco.
6. Which flavorings are most prevalent in Mexican cookery?
7. Describe the daily meal pattern for inhabitants of Mexico.

		WEATHER	TOPOGRAPHY	FOODS
		Hot	Interior: arid, mountains; coast: fertile farmland	Cattle, seafood, cheese, wheat, dates, peppers, grapes, prickly pears
		Some temperate, some hot	Mountains, lakes, forests, volcanoes, flatlands, plateaus	Seafood, game, goat, barley, wheat, corn, beans, vegetables, squash, pumpkin, chili peppers, mushrooms, fruits, chocolate
Gulf Coastal Plain	East includes Veracruz	North: arid; south: hot, humid	North: coast, forests; south: tropical coast, rain forest, rich farmland	Seafood, black beans, sugar, corn, tropical fruits and vegetables
Southern Uplands	South includes Oaxaca	Hot, humid	Coast, plateaus, forests, grasslands	Seafood, beans, corn, avocado, plantains, squash, tomatoes, chili peppers, pumpkins, bananas
Chiapas Highlands	Southeast	Hot, humid	Coast, valleys, flat-topped mountains, farmland	Seafood, game, beans, mushrooms, jalapeños, fruits, coffee, cacao
Yucatan	Southeast	Tropical, hot, humid	Coast, grasslands, swamps, plateaus, forest, jungle, rain forest	Seafood, beans, corn, chili peppers, sugar, tropical fruits and vegetables, plantains, bananas, avocado, papaya, mango, vanilla, cacao, coffee

Glossary

achiote Ground annatto seeds used in cooking that give a yellow color to the dish

adobo A seasoning paste containing ground chili peppers, herbs, spices, and vinegar used in many preparations, including meats and salsas

burrito A taco prepared with a wheat tortilla

cecina Dried beef popular in northern Mexico

cena Light evening meal served around nine or ten o'clock

ceviche Seafood "cooked" or marinated in lime juice until it becomes opaque

chayote A common vegetable in Mexico sometimes called a green pear

chili relleno A chili pepper stuffed with cheese, meat, or another filling, then dipped in batter and deep-fried

chimichanga A deep-fried burrito

chorizo A well-known Mexican (and Spanish) pork sausage

comida The main meal of the day, eaten around two o'clock in the afternoon

escabeche Pickled peppers or vegetables

guacamole A spread consisting of mashed avocado, onion, tomato, and usually chili peppers, ingredients vary from region to region

masa Ground corn used for making tortillas and other foods

merienda Similar to the English tea, pastries and coffee or hot chocolate are served around six in the evening

mole Savory Mexican sauce containing unsweetened chocolate, chilies, tomatoes, and spices

picante Hot, spicy

quesadillas A tortilla topped with cheese and roasted, peeled peppers or other ingredients, if desired, folded in half and fried until the cheese melts

queso The Mexican word for cheese

taco Meat, beans, cheese, vegetables, or any combination of filling possibilities placed down the middle of a soft corn tortilla, topped with sauce, then the tortilla is rolled to encase the filling

tamales Entrée consisting of corn husks or banana leaves encasing filling ingredients which are steamed, then the husks or leaves are discarded and the filling is eaten

tortilla A flat, unleavened disk made from wheat or corn and cooked on a dry griddle; eaten at every meal; Mexican bread

GUACAMOLE

Avocado Dip

Number of Servings: 10
Serving Size: 2 oz or ¼ cup
Total Yield: 1 lb, 4 oz or 2½ cups

Food Balance: Protein
Wine Style: Soft and fruity Johannisberg Riesling, Chenin Blanc, Viognier, Blush, Grenache
Example: Beringer Chenin Blanc

Guacamole (Avocado Dip); photo courtesy of Dorling Kindersley

> *Guacamole can function in many areas of the menu. Traditionally, a dip served with warm tortillas or tortilla chips, it is delicious as part of a salad or as a condiment or side dish. The buttery texture of avocado adds a smooth texture to any plate. Guacamole darkens with exposure to air, so if not serving immediately, cover tightly to avoid oxidation. Many insert the avocado pit into the dip saying it helps prevent the guacamole from darkening.*

INGREDIENTS	WEIGHT	VOLUME
onion, white, minced	¾ oz	2 tablespoons
chilies, serrano, seeded if desired, minced	½ oz or to taste	1 or 2 each or to taste
cilantro, leaves, fresh, minced	½ oz	2 tablespoons
lime juice, fresh		2 teaspoons
tomato, peeled, seeded, chopped	6 oz	1 medium
avocado, peeled, seeded	12½ oz	2 medium
salt		½ teaspoon

1. Place avocado in bowl, mash with fork against side of bowl until chunky paste.
2. Add remaining ingredients, mix well.
3. Serve immediately, accompanied by tortilla chips or warm tortillas, as part of a salad, or as a condiment with another dish. If not serving immediately, place avocado pit into dip and cover tightly with plastic wrap to prevent it from turning brown (oxidation).

SALSA CRUDA

Uncooked Spicy Tomato Sauce

Number of Servings: 8
Serving Size: 2 oz or ¼ cup
Total Yield: 1 lb, 2 oz or 2 cups

Salsa Cruda (Uncooked Spicy Tomato Sauce); photo courtesy of Dorling Kindersley

Food Balance: Sweet, spicy, protein
Wine Style: Soft and fruity Gewürztraminer, Sauvignon Blanc, Pinot
  Blanc, Beaujolais
Example: Stone Cellars Shiraz

INGREDIENTS	WEIGHT	VOLUME
tomatoes, peeled, diced	1 lb	2 large
chilies, serrano, minced, seeded if desired	¼ oz or to taste	1 or 2 each or to taste
cilantro, leaves, fresh, minced	¼ oz	1 tablespoon
onion, white, minced	2 oz	⅓ cup or ½ small
lime juice, fresh		2 teaspoons
salt		½ teaspoon

> A bowl of salsa sits on the dining table in Mexico as Americans and Europeans have salt and pepper on the table.

1. Mix all ingredients in bowl.
2. Correct seasonings. Serve with tortilla chips or as a condiment with any dish.

SOPA DE ELOTE

Corn Soup

Number of Servings: 12   Cooking Method: Sauté, boil
Serving Size: 8 oz
Total Yield: 6 lbs, 6 oz

Food Balance: Sweet, protein
Wine Style: Soft and fruity Johannisberg Riesling, Chenin Blanc, mild
  Chardonnay, White Zinfandel, Grenache
Example: Meridian Santa Barbara Chardonnay

INGREDIENTS	WEIGHT	VOLUME
poblano chilies, fresh, charred, peeled, or canned	fresh 1 lb, 7 oz, canned 9 oz	4 each or 2 small cans
tomato, fresh, peeled, chopped, or canned	12 oz	2 medium or 1⅓ cup
onion, white, diced	6 oz	1 medium
butter	1½ oz	3 tablespoons
corn, cut from cob or frozen	2 lb, 4 oz	about 9 ears or 6 cups
chicken stock	4 lbs	2 qt or 8 cups
cream, heavy	8 oz	1 cup
salt		to taste

GARNISH:

sour cream

1. If using fresh corn, cook chicken stock with corn cobs for at least 30 minutes.
2. Remove seeds and veins from chilies, place in bowl of food processor with tomatoes, onions, and 12 oz (2 cups) corn. Pulse until reduced to paste.
3. Melt butter in pan, add paste and simmer for 10 minutes.

Sopa de Elote (Corn Soup); photo courtesy of Dorling Kindersley

4. Remove cobs from stock (if cobs were used), add paste and remaining corn to stock, simmer until corn is tender, about 25 minutes.
5. Add cream and cook just until warm. Be careful not to curdle the soup. Add salt, if needed. Correct seasonings.
6. Serve immediately, garnished with a dollop of sour cream.

SOPA DE TORTILLAS

Tortilla Soup

Number of Servings: 10   Cooking Method: Sauté, boil
Serving Size: 8 oz
Total Yield: 5 lbs

Food Balance: Sweet/sour, spicy
Wine Style: Soft, fruity Chenin Blanc, White Zinfandel, Grenache, Beaujolais
Example: Beringer LVS White Zinfandel (blend of Chardonnay and White Zinfandel)

INGREDIENTS	WEIGHT	VOLUME
chicken stock	4 lbs	2 qts or 8 cups
oil or lard	1 oz	2 tablespoons
onion, white, diced small	5 oz	1 medium
garlic, peeled, minced	¼ oz	2 cloves
jalapeño, seeded, deveined, minced	¼ oz	½ whole
tomato, fresh, peeled, seeded, diced	12 oz	2 each
chicken breasts, cooked, diced	7½ oz	2 cups or 2 breasts
lime juice, fresh	1 oz	2 tablespoons
pepper		¼ teaspoon
oregano		½ teaspoon

Cutting Tortilla Strips; photo courtesy of Dorling Kindersley

GARNISH:

tortilla, cut into strips
oil or lard for frying
jalapeño or serrano peppers, minced

OPTIONAL GARNISH:

Monterey Jack cheese, grated
avocado, diced
lime juice, fresh

1. Heat chicken stock to simmering.
2. Heat oil in skillet, sauté onion about 3 or 4 minutes, add garlic and jalapeño, sauté another couple of minutes, until softened.
3. Add tomato to skillet, sauté another 3 or 4 minutes.
4. Add sautéed vegetables to chicken broth, add chicken, lime juice, pepper, and oregano. Simmer about 15 minutes.
5. Correct seasonings.

GARNISH:

1. Fry tortilla strips slowly in oil or lard until golden brown.
2. Drain well on absorbent paper.

ASSEMBLY:

1. Place hot soup in bowl.
2. Top with tortilla strips.
3. Serve accompanied by peppers and bowls of optional garnishes, if desired.

ENSALADA DE NOCHE BUENA

Christmas Eve Salad

Number of Servings: 9
Serving Size: 6 oz
Total Yield: 3 lbs, 9 oz

INGREDIENTS	WEIGHT	VOLUME
sugar	3¾ oz	½ cup
wine vinegar	2 oz	¼ cup
beets, cooked, chopped, fresh or canned	6 oz	3 medium
oranges, peeled, sectioned, membrane removed	8 oz	3 each
jicama, peeled, sliced	15 oz	1 each
apple, tart, peeled, cored, sliced	8 oz	1 each
bananas, peeled, sliced	11½ oz	3 each
lettuce		
peanuts, chopped	3 oz	½ cup

1. Mix sugar and vinegar together until sugar dissolves, set aside.
2. Mix beets, oranges, jicama, apples, and bananas in bowl. Add vinegar mixture and mix gently. Refrigerate until needed.
3. To serve, place fruit mixture on bed of lettuce, sprinkle with peanuts.

Note: See pages 232–233 in Chapter 10—Israel—recipe for Orange and Olive Salad which contains instructions for and photographs of removing rind and cutting orange into segments.

MOLE DE GUAJOLOTE

Turkey in Mole Sauce

Number of Servings: 22 to 25   Cooking Method: Sauté, braise

Serving Size: 6 to 7 oz
Total Yield: 4 lbs, 10 oz sauce (8½ cups)
            about 10 lbs total

Food Balance: Spicy/protein/sweet
Wine Style: Soft/rich and fruity Johannisberg Riesling, White Merlot, Grenache, soft Reds, Shiraz, Merlot, Zinfandel
Example: Wolf Blass or Black Opal Shiraz

This dish dates back to the Aztecs. Besides the traditional turkey, mole sauce compliments a variety of dishes including pork, chicken, duck, enchiladas, and more. The list of ingredients looks intimidating, but the recipe is not that difficult. Basically, ingredients are sautéed, then puréed. The sauce can be prepared in advance and refrigerated or frozen. Use only the amount of sauce needed to accompany the turkey, save any remaining sauce for other dishes or freeze it for later use.

INGREDIENTS	WEIGHT	VOLUME
CHILIES:		
pasilla chilies	1¼ oz	4 each
mulato chilies	2 oz	5 each
ancho chilies	2¾ oz	6 each
chipotle chilies	¼ oz	1 each
oil or lard	½ oz	1 tablespoon
water, boiling	as needed	
TURKEY:		
turkey, cut into serving pieces	10 to 12 lbs	1 each
oil or lard	1½ oz	3 tablespoons
SEASONING PASTE:		
almonds	2½ oz	⅓ cup
peanuts, shelled	2 oz	⅓ cup
pumpkin seeds, hulled	2 oz	⅓ cup

INGREDIENTS	WEIGHT	VOLUME
sesame seeds	2 oz	⅓ cup
raisins	1¾ oz	¼ cup
peppercorns		6 each
stick cinnamon		¾-inch piece
coriander seeds		⅛ teaspoon
aniseed		⅛ teaspoon
bay leaf		1 each
cloves		4 each
onion, white, diced	7 oz	1 large
garlic cloves, unpeeled	¾ oz	3 to 4 large
corn tortilla, stale	1 oz	1 each
French bread, stale	1 oz	2 each ¾-inch slices
tomatoes, peeled, chopped	10 oz	1 cup
tomatillos, fresh, husks removed, chopped or canned	7 oz	2 each or 1 cup
turkey or chicken broth	2 lb	1 qt or 4 cups
chocolate, unsweetened, cut into small pieces	1½ oz	
turkey or chicken broth		as needed for thinning

GARNISH:

tortillas, corn or wheat
sesame seeds, toasted

CHILIES:

1. Cut chilies open, remove seeds and veins, save ¾ oz (3 tablespoons) seeds. Tear peppers into pieces.
2. Heat ½ oz (1 tablespoon) oil in skillet, sauté chilies quickly, stir constantly being careful not to burn them.
3. Place chilies in bowl, cover with boiling water, set aside for at least one hour.
4. Drain when ready to use, reserve soaking liquid.

SEASONING PASTE:

1. Heat frying pan, add almonds and peanuts, shake pan to keep them moving, toast until lightly browned, pour into bowl of food processor fitted with knife attachment.
2. Add pumpkin seeds to pan, cover (because they pop and jump from pan), shake pan to keep them moving, toast until lightly browned, pour into bowl of food processor.
3. Add sesame seeds to pan, cover (because they pop and jump from pan), shake pan to keep them moving, toast until lightly browned, pour into bowl of food processor.
4. Add raisins to pan, shake pan to keep them moving, toast lightly, transfer to bowl of food processor.
5. Add reserved chili seeds, peppercorns, cinnamon, coriander, aniseed, bay leaf, and cloves to pan, shake pan to keep them moving, toast lightly, pour into bowl of food processor.
6. Add soaked chilies and 4 oz (½ cup) soaking liquid from chilies to processor bowl. Pulse until consistency of thick paste, scraping down sides of processor several times, as needed.

Adding turkey to mole sauce; photo courtesy of Dorling Kindersley

Mole de Guajolote (Turkey in Mole Sauce); photo courtesy of Dorling Kindersley

7. Add tortilla and bread to pan, toast lightly just to dry, tear into pieces, add to processor bowl.
8. Place garlic cloves in pan, toast on all sides until skin darkens, one or two minutes, peel garlic, mince, add to processor bowl.
9. Add onion to processor bowl, pulse to process until thick paste, scraping down sides of processor several times. Refrigerate until needed.

TOMATO—TOMATILLO PASTE:

1. If using fresh tomatillos, peel husks, place tomatillos in pan of water, bring to boil, reduce heat and simmer for 10 minutes. Remove from water, cool slightly, chop coarsely.
2. Place tomatillos and tomatoes in bowl of food processor, pulse until reduced to paste. Reserve until ready to use.

TURKEY:

1. Preheat oven to 350 degrees.
2. Heat 1 oz (2 tablespoons) oil in pan, sauté turkey pieces until browned. Do not wash pan, reserve for sautéing seasoning paste.
3. Place turkey in ovenproof pan, cover, bake for about 1¼ hours, until done.
4. Cool slightly, cut into slices or small pieces, as desired.
5. Skim fat from pan drippings, deglaze pan by adding stock to make 2 lbs (1 qt).

FINAL ASSEMBLY:

1. Heat pan used to sauté turkey, add tomato and tomatillo mixture, simmer for 10 minutes, stirring often.
2. Add 8 oz (1 cup) stock, simmer for 10 minutes, stirring often.
3. Add seasoning paste, remaining stock, and chocolate. Simmer for 40 minutes, stirring occasionally. (May be prepared to this point and refrigerated.)

4. Place turkey in pan, cover with mole sauce, simmer for about 20 minutes. If necessary, thin sauce with more stock, sauce should be thick enough to coat spoon. Correct seasonings.

5. Serve accompanied by tortillas. If desired, sprinkle with toasted sesame seeds.

HUACHINANGO A LA VERACRUZANA

Red Snapper, Veracruz Style

Number of Servings: 8   Cooking Method: Sauté, bake
Serving Size: 7 oz
Total Yield: 3 lbs, 10 oz

Food Balance: Protein/acid balanced
Wine Style: Wide variety Pinot Grigio, Sauvignon Blanc, Grenache, medium-bodied Reds, Merlot
Example: Château Souverain Sauvignon Blanc

INGREDIENTS	WEIGHT	VOLUME
red snapper or other ocean fish, fillets or (traditionally) fish with head and tail left on	1 lb, 13 oz	
lime juice, fresh	1½ oz	3 tablespoons
TOMATO SAUCE:		
olive oil	1 oz	2 tablespoons
onion, white, diced	6 oz	1 large
garlic, peeled, minced	¼ oz	2 cloves
tomatoes, peeled, seeded, chopped, fresh or canned	2 lbs	3¾ cups
bay leaf		1 each
oregano		¾ teaspoon

> This dish makes a great first course. Reduce the amount of jalapeño if a less spicy dish is desired. Some recipes for this dish dredge the red snapper in flour, fry it, then cover it with the tomato sauce and serve it. Some add parboiled potatoes to the tomato sauce.

Huachinango a la Veracruzana (Red Snapper, Veracruz Style); photo courtesy of the American Spice Trade Association

INGREDIENTS	WEIGHT	VOLUME
cinnamon		⅛ teaspoon
cloves		⅛ teaspoon
sugar		½ teaspoon
jalapeños or escabeche (pickled jalapeños), cut into strips	½ oz or to taste	2 each or to taste
green olives, pitted, cut in half	1½ oz	¼ cup
capers	1 oz	2 tablespoons

1. Place fish in ovenproof dish, pour lime juice over fish, cover and refrigerate at least 2 hours.
2. Preheat oven to 350 degrees.
3. Heat oil in skillet, add onion, sauté, stirring often for a couple of minutes, add garlic and sauté until softened.
4. Add tomatoes, spices, olives, capers, and jalapeños or escabeche. Cook for 10 minutes over medium high flame, stirring constantly.
5. Pour sauce over fish, bake for about 30 minutes, until done.
6. Serve immediately, accompanied by rice or potatoes.

MANCHA MANTELES

Tablecloth Strainer (Chicken and Pork Braised with Fruits)

Number of Servings: 8
Serving Size: ¼ chicken
Total Yield: 11 lbs, 8 oz

Cooking Method: Sauté, braise

Food Balance: Spicy, sweet, protein
Wine Style: Soft and fruity Gewürztraminer, White Merlot, Grenache, soft Shiraz or Zinfandel
Example: Beringer Founders' Estate Shiraz or Zinfandel

INGREDIENTS	WEIGHT	VOLUME
pork, lean, cut into 1-inch cubes	1 lb, 8 oz	
chicken stock	3 lbs	6 cups
chicken, cut into serving pieces	about 6 lbs	2 each
oil or lard	2½ oz	5 tablespoons
almonds, unskinned	8½ oz	1½ cups
sesame seeds	1½ oz	¼ cup
ancho chilies, seeds, veins, and stem removed	2 oz	6 each
pasilla chilies, seeds, veins, and stem removed	¾ oz	4 each
tomatoes, peeled, seeded, chopped	1 lb, 8 oz	4 each
cinnamon	¼ oz	2 teaspoons
salt	½ teaspoon	2 teaspoons
plantain, peeled, cut into ¼-inch slices	9 oz	2 small
pineapple, cubes, fresh or canned	14½ oz	2 cups
apple, peeled, cored, large dice	1 lb	2 large

1. Place pork in pan with stock, simmer for 25 minutes, drain pork, reserve stock.

2. Heat oil in large pan, sauté chicken pieces until lightly browned, remove from pan, set aside.
3. In same oil, sauté almonds until lightly browned, drain and place in bowl of food processor.
4. In same oil, sauté sesame seeds until lightly browned (use lid because they will pop out of pan), drain, and place in bowl of food processor.
5. In same oil, sauté chilies about 2 minutes, drain, and place in bowl of food processor.
6. Add tomatoes and 1 lb (2 cups) reserved stock to food processor. Process until thick, smooth paste.
7. Reheat same pan. Stirring constantly, sauté paste, cinnamon, and salt about 4 minutes.
8. Add 1 lb, 12 oz (3½ cups) stock to paste, stir well.
9. Add meats and fruits to sauce, cover and simmer for 1 to 1¼ hours, until meats are tender. Add more stock if needed.
10. Correct seasonings. Serve with tortillas and/or rice.

CHILI RELLENOS

Stuffed Chili Peppers

Number of Servings: 10
Serving Size: 6 oz (1 filled pepper) with 3 oz sauce
Total Yield: 1 lb, 14 oz picadillo
　　　　1 lb, 14 oz sauce

Cooking Method: Braise, sauté, deep-fry

Food Balance: Protein, sweet, spicy
Wine Style: Soft and fruity Chenin Blanc, Sauvignon Blanc, Pinot Blanc, Zinfandel, Merlot
Example: Meridian Sauvignon Blanc

INGREDIENTS	WEIGHT	VOLUME
poblano peppers	3 lbs, 10 oz	10 each
PICADILLO:		
pork, boneless, cut into large cubes	2 lbs	
onion, white, sliced	2 oz	½ small
garlic, peeled, sliced	¼ oz	2 cloves
oil or lard	1½ oz	3 tablespoons
tomatoes, peeled, seeded, chopped, fresh or canned	1 lb	2 large or 1¾ cups
onions, white, diced	4 oz	1 small
garlic, peeled, minced	¼ oz	2 cloves
cinnamon		¾ teaspoon
cloves		¾ teaspoon
salt	¼ oz	1 teaspoon
pepper		1 teaspoon
raisins	3½ oz	½ cup
SAUCE:		
tomatoes, peeled, chopped, fresh or canned	1 lb	2 large or 1¾ cups

> Cheese makes a wonderful alternative to the pork filling, picadillo. If available, use queso Oaxaca, otherwise substitute Muenster cheese. For preparation of cheese rellenos, fill peppers with about 2 oz cheese cut into 3 pieces by ½-inch strips. Flour and batter, then fry. Any extra picadillo makes a wonderful filling for tortillas.

INGREDIENTS	WEIGHT	VOLUME
onions, white, diced	2 oz	½ small
garlic, peeled, minced	¼ oz	2 cloves
cinnamon		½ teaspoon
cloves		¼ teaspoon
pepper		¾ teaspoon
bay leaves		2 each
thyme		¼ teaspoon
almonds	1 oz	2 tablespoons
oil or lard	1 oz	2 tablespoons
stock, pork or chicken	1 lb, 8 oz	3 cups

BATTER:

flour	as needed, for dusting	
eggs	5 oz	3 each
salt		¼ teaspoon
oil for deep-frying		

PEPPERS:

1. Char peppers on grill or over flame of burner until blackened and blistered, but not soft.
2. Place in plastic bag, seal and wait about 15 minutes.
3. Remove from bag, peel skin from peppers. Be careful not to cut peppers.
4. Make slit on one side of pepper just large enough to remove seeds and ribs, rinse with cold water, set aside until needed.

PICADILLO:

1. Place meat, sliced onion, and sliced garlic in pan, cover with cold water, bring to boil, lower heat and simmer until tender, about 45 to 50 minutes.
2. Drain meat, reserve stock. Remove fat from stock when cold. Shred meat, refrigerate if not using right away.
3. Heat oil in pan, add meat, cook a few minutes, add spices, cook another minute or two.
4. Add tomatoes, cook over high heat stirring constantly, about 10 minutes, until almost dry.
5. Correct seasonings. Set aside or refrigerate until needed.

SAUCE:

1. Purée tomatoes, onion, garlic, almonds, and spices.
2. Heat oil in pan, add purée, stirring constantly, sauté over high heat for about 5 minutes.
3. Add stock, cook over medium heat for 15 minutes. Correct seasonings.

CHILI PREPARATION:

1. Stuff pepper with 3 oz (⅓ cup) picadillo. Close using toothpicks to fasten.
2. Place flour on plate, dredge peppers in flour, set aside.

BATTER:

1. Whip egg whites until stiff peaks.
2. Add salt and yolks, one at a time, until mixed.

ASSEMBLY:

1. Heat about 1-inch oil in pan for deep-frying or use deep-fryer.
2. Place pepper in batter, turn to coat.
3. Gently place pepper into hot oil, fry until golden brown.

4. Remove from oil, drain well on paper toweling. Remove toothpicks.
5. Place tomato sauce on plate, top with chili relleno *or* place peppers in pan of sauce, heat over low flame, then serve.

Note: See photographs for charring and peeling peppers on page 365 in chapter.

Removing seeds and veins from peeled pepper

Filling pepper with picadillo

Coating rellenos (stuffed peppers) with batter

Chili Rellenos (Stuffed Chili Peppers)

FRIJOLES

Beans

Number of Servings: 10   Cooking Method: Braise
Serving Size: 6 oz
Total Yield: 3 lbs, 13 oz

INGREDIENTS	WEIGHT	VOLUME
beans, pinto, black or any type	1 lb	2½ cups
onion, white, diced	7 oz	1 large
oil or lard	½ oz	1 tablespoon
salt	¼ oz or to taste	1 teaspoon or to taste

Traditionally, a bowl of not spicy beans (with some of the cooking liquid) is served after the entrée. Salsa, which sits on every dining table, or peppers are added to the beans, if desired.

Frijoles (Beans); photo courtesy of the Bean Education & Awareness Network (B.E.A.N.)

ACCOMPANIMENTS:

salsa
chili pepper slices, fresh or pickled

1. Rinse beans well, place in pot, cover with cold water, refrigerate to soak overnight.
2. Add onion and oil, bring to boil, simmer until done, about 1½ to 2 hours, depending on type of bean.
3. Season with salt to taste. If desired, mash some of the beans to slightly thicken the sauce.
4. Serve beans and some of the bean liquid in a small bowl. If desired, the diner adds chili peppers or salsa to beans.

FRIJOLES REFRITOS

Refried Beans

Number of Servings: 9
Serving Size: 4 oz
Total Yield: 2 lbs, 5 oz

Cooking Method: Sauté

Appearing very frequently throughout Mexico, these beans accompany almost any food. Although they are rather bland, refried beans are served with the ever-present bowl of salsa.

INGREDIENTS	WEIGHT	VOLUME
oil or lard	2½ oz	5 tablespoons
onion, white, small dice	12 oz	2 each
beans, any kind, cooked, with some broth	2 lbs, 6 oz	6 cups

1. Heat oil in heavy pan, sauté onion until soft, a few minutes.
2. Add 12 oz (about 2 cups) beans to pan, mash well with spoon or spatula.
3. Continue adding beans, mashing until coarse purée.
4. Sauté until purée starts to dry out.
5. Serve, accompanied by salsa.

Frijoles Refritos (Refried Beans); photo courtesy of Dorling Kindersley

COLIFLOR EN ADOBO ROJO

Cauliflower in Red Adobo Sauce

Number of Servings: 9   Cooking Method: Sauté, boil
Serving Size: 4 oz
Total Yield: 2 lbs, 7 oz
            Sauce: 9 oz or 1 cup

Food Balance: Spicy/protein
Wine Style: Soft and fruity Johannisberg Riesling, White Zinfandel, Beaujolais
Example: Beringer Gamay Beaujolais

INGREDIENTS	WEIGHT	VOLUME
ADOBO SAUCE:		
ancho chilies, seeded, veins removed	1½ oz	5 each
water, boiling	8 oz	1 cup
garlic, unpeeled	¾ oz	4 large
cumin		¼ teaspoon
black peppercorns		4 each
cloves		2 each
oregano		1 teaspoon
stock or water	8 oz or as needed	1 cup or as needed
oil or lard	½ oz	1 tablespoon
cauliflower, flowerets	2 lbs, 3 oz	2 heads

> Although traditionally used with pork, adobo sauce accompanies all sorts of meats, poultry, and vegetables.

1. Heat skillet, sauté chilies briefly until just beginning to color, do not burn. Flatten them with spatula for even cooking, and remove from pan.

2. Place garlic in pan over medium heat, cook until light brown spot appears on each side, remove from pan. When cool, peel garlic and mince.
3. Tear chilies into pieces, place in bowl, cover with boiling water, set aside for 30 minutes.
4. Place garlic, oregano, cumin, cloves, black peppercorns, and 4 oz (½ cup) stock or water in bowl of food processor, pulse to break spices.
5. Add chilies to processor, process until paste.
6. Heat oil in pan, add paste and sauté for 5 minutes, stirring constantly.
7. Steam or boil cauliflower until three-quarters done, pour off water.
8. Add adobo paste and 4 oz (½ cup) stock or water to pan with cauliflower, heat over medium low heat until cauliflower is done, about 5 minutes. Add more stock or water, if needed.
9. Serve immediately.

CALABACITAS CON CREMA

Creamed Zucchini

Number of Servings: 8   Cooking Method: Boil
Serving Size: 4 oz
Total Yield: 2 lbs, 4 oz

INGREDIENTS	WEIGHT	VOLUME
zucchini, diced	1½ lbs	2 medium
tomatoes, peeled, chopped	12 oz	2 each or 1½ cups
mint, fresh, minced	¼ oz	2 tablespoons
cilantro, fresh, minced	¾ oz	3 tablespoons
jalapeño, fresh, seeds and veins removed, minced	¼ oz	½ each
pepper		¼ teaspoon
cinnamon		½ teaspoon
cloves		¼ teaspoon
salt		½ teaspoon or to taste
heavy cream	2 oz	¼ cup
stock or water	as needed	

1. Place all ingredients in pan.
2. Stirring occasionally, simmer until zucchini is tender, about 10 to 15 minutes. Add stock or water if too dry. Almost no liquid should remain at end of cooking.
3. Correct seasonings. Serve.

ARROZ A LA MEXICANA

Mexican Rice

Number of Servings: 11   Cooking Method: Sauté, boil
Serving Size: 4 oz
Total Yield: 2 lbs, 15 oz

INGREDIENTS	WEIGHT	VOLUME
rice, long-grain	10½ oz	1½ cups
tomatoes, peeled, fresh or canned, chopped	8 oz	1 large or 1 cup
onion, white, small dice	2 oz	½ small
garlic, peeled, minced		1 clove
oil or lard	1½ oz	3 tablespoons
chicken stock, hot	1 lb, 12 oz	3½ cups

peas, optional

> To prepare more spicy Mexican rice, add one or two serrano peppers to the tomato mixture. Do not overdo it; this rice should not be too picante.

1. Purée tomatoes, onion, and garlic in food processor.
2. Heat oil in pan over high heat, add rice, and sauté until lightly browned.
3. Add tomato purée, sauté, stirring constantly until liquid is absorbed.
4. Add stock, bring to boil, lower heat, cover and simmer until most of liquid is absorbed, about 18 to 20 minutes. If desired, add peas to pan for last few minutes of cooking.
5. Remove pan from heat, let rest still covered, about 10 minutes.
6. Serve.

POLVORONES

Shortbread Cookies

Total Yield: 15 oz raw dough,   Cooking Method: Bake
    40 each, 2-inch cookies

INGREDIENTS	WEIGHT	VOLUME
almonds, unskinned	3 oz	½ cup
flour, all purpose	8 oz	1½ cups
sugar	1½ oz	3 tablespoons
baking powder		1 teaspoon
salt		⅛ teaspoon
butter, unsalted or half butter and half shortening, cold, cut into pieces	5 oz	1 stick + 2 tablespoons or 10 tablespoons

confectioners' sugar, for sifting on
    baked cookies

> These fragile cookies resemble "Mexican wedding cookies" with their soft, crumbly texture and coating of confectioners' sugar; however, they are rolled out and cut into rounds rather than baked as balls of dough to produce a mound. Traditionally, these cookies are wrapped in tissue paper like a bonbon.

1. Preheat oven to 350 degrees.
2. On separate pans, bake almonds and flour until lightly browned, about 14 to 18 minutes, Remove from oven, cool.
3. Place almonds and sugar in bowl of food processor, pulse until almonds are finely ground.
4. Add flour, baking powder, and salt to processor bowl, pulse to mix well.
5. Place butter pieces in processor, pulse to mix well until dough comes together.
6. Wrap in plastic wrap, refrigerate several hours or overnight.
7. Preheat oven to 350 degrees, position oven rack in top of oven.

8. Remove dough from refrigerator. If using all butter, hit dough with rolling pin to flatten a bit. Place dough on parchment paper or plastic wrap, top with piece of plastic wrap and roll dough to ¼-inch thickness.

9. Cut out 2-inch cookies, reroll scraps, continue cutting cookies until dough is used.

10. Bake on parchment-lined pans in top of oven for 12 to 15 minutes, until lightly browned.

11. Immediately after removing from oven, sift thick layer of confectioners' sugar over cookies. Leave on pans until completely cooled.

12. Transfer to airtight storage container with spatula—these cookies are fragile and break easily.

CHAPTER 17
South America

By the end of this chapter, you will be able to

- Discuss contributions made by the Inca Indians that impacted South America and the world
- Discuss the influences of other countries on the cuisines of South America
- Identify differences and similarities in the cuisines of South American countries
- Name food products prevalent in various areas of South America
- Prepare a variety of South American dishes

HISTORY

By 6000 B.C., various Indian tribes roamed throughout the continent of South America. It is believed that these people were Asians who traveled through Alaska to North America, then continued their migration from North America through Central America to South America.

The cuisines found in many South American countries reflect heavy influence from the Indians who inhabited the area long before the Europeans discovered this part of the world. In particular, the Inca Indians exerted a profound effect that is still widely felt. The heart of the Incan civilization flourished in the area that is now Peru, Ecuador, Bolivia, and Chile. As a result, these countries exhibit very strong remnants of the Incan cuisine.

When the Spanish arrived in South America at the beginning of the sixteenth century, they introduced pigs, cows, lamb, chickens, goats, wheat, dairy products, and almonds to these new lands. In exchange, the European explorers learned of corn, beans, potatoes, tomatoes, chili peppers, chocolate, tobacco, avocados, squash, sweet potatoes, pineapples, and vanilla from the New World. Because several of these products play such a significant role in the cuisines of Europe, it is astounding to realize that the Europeans knew nothing of these foods until the sixteenth century.

Around 1500, the Spanish arrived in Venezuela and Colombia, discovering a land with almost impassable terrain inhabited by just a few Indians. Only the quest for gold made them continue on and explore these two countries.

In 1531, the Spanish came to Peru, a land ruled by Inca Indians. As was true of the Aztecs in Mexico, the Incan ruler indulged in huge feasts with many, many dishes (some accounts say up to 500!) prepared for him. The Spanish discovered a land where only a little meat was available to royalty, and the common people had almost none. A diet of beans and grains replaced meat, except for those who lived near the coasts, rivers, and lakes where seafood and fish were plentiful.

The Spanish introduced the Peruvians to butter, cheese, and milk, which they quickly incorporated into their cooking. Just like when the Spanish brought lard and butter to the Mexicans who had no source of fat in their cuisine, the introduction of butter allowed the Peruvians to fry foods because prior to that time they had no source of fat. The cuisine of Peru developed into a melding of Incan and Spanish foods, now known as Creole cooking.

The inventive Inca Indians worked extensively with plant breeding to improve their crops, and the European conquerors learned much about agriculture and horticulture from them. Besides adapting existing produce to withstand the climate in the mountains, they developed many new varieties of vegetables, particularly corn, potatoes, and hot peppers. Realizing the effect of altitude on the plants, they experimented with growing crops at different altitudes to take advantage of the variations that occurred in the vegetables.

In addition, the Incans terraced the slopes of the Andes in Peru, producing bountiful crops on the steep inclines. Then they devised an intricate system of canals to irrigate all areas of the mountains. By utilizing the force of water going downhill, they even irrigated up the sides of the mountains! The Incans transformed once barren land into some of the best farmland in the world.

Another of their significant culinary contributions was in the area of food preservation. The Inca Indians figured out methods to air-dry, salt, dehydrate, and freeze-dry foods.

Lying east of the Incan settlements, relatively few Indians inhabited the area that is now Brazil. As a result, when the Portuguese arrived in 1533, they had a strong impact on the cuisine. Because they needed lots of laborers to work on the sugar plantations, the Portuguese imported slaves from western Africa. Realizing that the climate was similar to their home in Africa, the slaves planted yams, okra, greens, and other foods from western Africa and then prepared their native recipes. The Brazilians adopted the use of strong seasonings, *dendê* (palm oil), smoked and dried fish, and the vegetables from these African slaves. Soon, the African foods and recipes became part of the cuisine of Brazil. Although this cuisine shows some of the Indian influence, the Portuguese and the Africans left the most pronounced effects on the cookery of Brazil.

TOPOGRAPHY

With the exception of two interior countries, Bolivia and Paraguay; all countries in South America border an ocean or sea. The Pacific Ocean lies to the west, the Atlantic Ocean is situated on the east, and the Caribbean Sea borders on the north. In the south, the Drake Passage separates South America from Antarctica.

The high mountains of the Andes span 4,500 miles and run parallel to the coast through Venezuela, Colombia, Ecuador, Peru, Bolivia, Paraguay, Chile, and Argentina. With peaks above 20,000 feet, the Andes is the longest chain and second highest group of mountains in the world. Even though some of these mountains lie near the equator, the high altitudes result in cool temperatures throughout the year. Although the Incans terraced the mountains in Peru allowing them to grow crops, the mountains in Chile were too steep to terrace. As a result, significantly fewer vegetables were produced in Chile.

Venezuela and Colombia lie in northern South America. Dense jungles line the coasts and the Andes Mountains loom in the distance. The valleys in the Andes provide fertile farmland and a temperate climate for growing crops.

Three neighboring countries, Peru, Ecuador, and Chile, lie along the western coast of South America. All these countries border the Pacific Ocean and contain mountains from the Andes running parallel to the coast.

Besides mountains, Peru's diverse topography includes desert and rain forest. The desert lying in the narrow strip of land between the ocean and the Andes is almost void of vegetation except in a spot where more than fifty tiny rivers run in a path from the mountains to the ocean. Irrigation from these many rivers provides fertile land for crops. The world's largest rain forest occurs in Peru at the Amazon River; rain forest also covers much land in Ecuador.

Forests, arid lands, and grasslands comprise Chile's coastal area. Lying in the north of Chile, the Atacama Desert has had no recorded rainfall throughout history.

Brazil remains a huge country with varied topography. Although the north of Brazil contains jungles, savannas, and dry brush country, temperate highlands with fertile farmland exist in the south. The second longest river in the world, the Amazon River cuts through Brazil, Bolivia, and Peru, creating dense, tropical forests.

Lying south of Brazil, Uruguay and Argentina have very fertile farmland and a temperate climate. The *pampa* consists of humid grasslands that is ideal for raising livestock. Most of the high-quality meat produced in South America comes from the *pampa* in these two countries.

Ingredients Foods Commonly Used Throughout the Cuisines of South America Include:

- beef
- game
- guinea pig (Peru)
- corn
- all sorts of beans
- rice
- potatoes, yams, and sweet potatoes
- squash
- chili peppers
- cassava
- tropical fruits and vegetables
- bananas and plantains
- peanuts
- coconuts, coconut milk, and coconut oil
- sugar

COOKING METHODS

Because almost no fats existed in South America prior to the arrival of the Spanish in the sixteenth century, foods were boiled, steamed, broiled over an open fire, stewed, or toasted in a dry pan. Frying was not an option. Hearty soups and stews were prepared by braising which served both to tenderize the tough meat and extend the meager supply.

Traditional ovens did not exist here, but, like Mexico, baking and steaming were done by digging a pit, lining it with stones, burning wood or charcoal in the pit, then baking or steaming the food from the heat radiating from the stones and embers after the fire burned down. A precursor of the New England "clambake," this outdoor barbecue still occurs in the mountainous and coastal areas where its use marks any festive occasion.

As mentioned before, the Incans preserved foods by air-drying, salting, dehydrating, and freeze-drying. This provided food through the cold winters in the mountains and times of poor crops throughout the rest of the land.

REGIONS

South America contains very diverse conditions in terms of both terrain and climate. Mountains, dense jungles, tropical rain forests, rivers, arid land, and desert made travel extremely difficult. Isolation played a significant role in the development of cuisines in the different regions.

Although the climate in the Andes Mountains remains temperate with seasons, the rest of Peru has no distinct seasons. As a result, crops mature throughout the year. Arid, hot, desertlike conditions prevail in the area west of the mountains by the coast, whereas the land east of the mountains is tropical, hot, and humid. Peru and Ecuador share similar topography, so the climates and cuisines have much in common. The cuisine in the mountains varied greatly from those in other areas due to two factors: differences in the available foods produced in each area and the isolation created by the difficult terrain. This isolation made the sharing of foods and recipes close to impossible both in the mountains and on either side of them.

On the southwestern side of South America lies Chile, a narrow country containing more diverse topography and climate. The northern third consists of desert with almost no rainfall and nothing growing. Lying near Antarctica, the southern third is cold, mountainous country with thick forests and tremendous rainfall. The third in the middle features fertile valleys of rich, sandy soil and a Mediterranean climate consisting of hot, dry summers and cool, wet winters. Ideal for growing grapes, large vineyards yielding some high-quality wines cover the countryside in this part of Chile.

Several different regions comprise the large country of Brazil. The hot, humid, and tropical central portion is transected by the Amazon River and contains dense tropical rain forest. Tropical fruits and vegetables thrive in the hot and humid areas. The southern section consists of mostly grasslands with a few rivers. Directly on the coasts, the land becomes forest. Most of the major cities lie in the coastal areas.

In the southern portion of South America, Uruguay and most of Argentina contain humid grasslands. Called the *pampa*, the richest farmland in South America is located here. This area boasts ideal amounts of rainfall and a temperate climate. Both countries produce a profusion of crops and lots of animals for meat. Uruguay raises both cattle and sheep, whereas Argentina primarily produces beef.

CUISINE

Generally, culinary traits from the Indians as well as from Portugal and Spain appear in all of the South American cuisines. European cooking methods and ingredients combined with the indigenous foods of South America to create the cuisines of the various countries.

Except in the *pampa* of Argentina and Uruguay, meat is not plentiful throughout South America. Because much of the available meat was tough, the slow braising of shredded or chopped meats in various sauces became the cooking method of choice. This produced stews and hearty soups, which still remain popular throughout both Central and South America. Although plentiful seafood and fish exist along the coasts, rivers, and lakes, beans and grains continue as the most important staples throughout South America. The combination of legumes and grains forms complete protein, which is the foundation of the diet in much of South America as well as Central America. Abundant fruits and vegetables grow in the tropical areas. Bananas, plantains, and coconuts remain mainstays in the cuisines found in the tropics.

COMPLEMENTARY PROTEIN

Amino acids make up the structure we call protein. There are nine *essential* amino acids that the human body cannot produce, so these nine must be obtained from foods. Although meat, dairy, and soy products contain all the necessary amino acids to form complete protein, grains, seeds, and legumes contain only some of the essential amino acids needed to make complete protein. Seeds and grains are low in one group of the essential amino acids and high in another group, but legumes reverse that. Although legumes are high in the group of amino acids that are low in grains, grains are high in the amino acids that are low in legumes. So, when these foods are eaten together, they combine and provide all the essential amino acids necessary to form complete protein. In essence, the amino acids in these foods complement each other and create complete protein.

Peru has a rich culinary history based on both the Incan civilization and the difficult terrain. As a result, two distinct Creole cuisines exist—one in the mountains and the other on the coast. Meats included fish, game, llamas, and guinea pigs. In the valleys of the Andes Mountains, the Indians raised many types of potatoes, *quinoa* (a type of grain), beans, pumpkins, squash, and other crops that could withstand the cool weather in the mountains. First cultivated around 200 B.C., potatoes rank supreme in the mountainous portions of Peru. Peruvians also produce and consume a staggering number of varieties of corn, another favorite food. In fact, the Incans developed more varieties of corn here than anywhere in the world. A staple, the various types of corn were raised for usage with differing culinary purposes. Some kernels remain soft for grinding into meal or flour; other strains produce huge kernels.

Although Peru is situated near the equator, ocean currents temper the weather. Cooking in the coastal area includes abundant seafood, fruits, and vegetables in the areas where irrigation transformed some of the desert into fertile farmland. A stark contrast from the Andes region, the dishes of the coastal region reflect a richer and more elaborate cuisine than that of its mountainous neighbor.

The Peruvian chili seasoning, *aji*, shows up in many dishes, including appetizers, soups, stews, entrées, and vegetables. The ubiquitous *aji* appears as commonly in the cuisine of Peru as chilies appear in Mexican cooking. Served throughout Latin America, *ceviche* originated in Peru. To prepare *ceviche*, raw fish is marinated in lemon and lime juices flavored with onion, garlic, and other spices. The acid from the citrus juices essentially "cooks" the fish, and the appearance of the fish changes from raw to opaque. In Peru, *ceviche* is typically served with a garnish of sweet potatoes and small pieces of corn on the cob.

People in the tropical northern coastal regions of Peru and coastal Ecuador consume lots of bananas, plantains, and peanuts. Bananas permeate all parts of the menu and are prepared in a variety of ways, including boiled, fried, and even ground into flour for use in breads and pastries. A reflection on the European influence, many dishes from the areas where the Incans once lived incorporate cheese and cream.

Rice continues as an important staple throughout Brazil. Rather than steamed and served dry as in many Asian cuisines, rice preparation involves first sautéing in the style of pilaf and then mixing in other vegetables and seasonings. Layered with meat, seafood, vegetables, and/or sauce, rice becomes the basis for the Brazilian version of casseroles. Like most of Latin America, beans form the foundation of the diet in Brazil. Black beans remain the most popular legume and appear in a myriad of dishes. *Feijoada completa,* a dish combining beans with several smoked and cured meats and seasonings, is considered the national dish of Brazil.

Crops raised in the hot, humid jungles and the hot, dry grasslands of Brazil include peanuts, bananas, coconuts, yams, and *manioc,* a starchy root vegetable also called cassava. The jungles yield a profusion of tropical fruits, including mangos, papayas, breadfruit, oranges, bananas, coconuts, and more. Coconut and coconut milk appear in all sorts of dishes from soups and stews to desserts. Brazilians also use abundant ginger and lemon juice. The region of Bahia in eastern Brazil exhibits the strongest African influence and is reputed to have the finest cuisine in the country. Seafood abounds while coconut milk and hot chilies flavor most dishes in Bahia. Fish stews remain standard fare in northeastern Brazil.

Beans accompanied by starchy mashes or rice dominate the diet in the central region. When meat is available in this region, pork including sausage and bacon ranks as first choice. Many types of chili peppers are used in all sorts of dishes and condiments. Some of the best cheeses produced in Brazil come from the central regions.

The south of Brazil enjoys a temperate climate and actually contains *pampa*s like Argentina. Plentiful beef comes from this area, and wine is produced here.

A type of cornbread, *arepa,* is the staff of life in Venezuela and Colombia. Filled with meat, stuffed *arepa* appears fried or boiled as a dumpling in soup. In the mountainous regions, people consume great quantities of potatoes. The tropical or semitropical regions feature soups and stews with the starchy root, cassava, replacing the potato that is so favored in the higher elevations. Again, in these warmer areas, bananas and plantains appear as a staple used in soups and stews, as a side dish, or dessert. Bananas and plantains are served grilled, fried, or boiled. Wasting no part of the plant, banana leaves are wrapped around fillings to hold them together while cooking in the coals or steaming. As in Brazil, coconuts and coconut milk appear in many dishes, both sweet and savory.

Venezuela and Colombia produce cattle, but the meat is tough compared with American standards. As a result, stewing or braising remain popular cooking techniques, as the meat becomes tender by cutting it into small pieces and cooking it slowly.

The cattle from Argentina are a different story. The very high-quality beef that is the norm here functions as a staple in the Argentine diet. Served as often as three times a day, beef often appears in several courses within a meal. A popular appetizer served as a first course, picnic fare, or a snack, the *empanada* is a small turnover or pie filled with any combination of meats and seasonings. Uruguay raises more sheep than beef, so lots of lamb and mutton are consumed in addition to beef. The presence of pumpkin and squash in soups, stews, and desserts shows the Indian influence on the cuisine of these two countries.

Most cattle raised in the *pampa* feed on the grass rather than being fed grain in a feed lot. Often compared with free range chickens, many feel this produces meat containing less fat. Some describe Argentine beef as having a more gamelike flavor and a more grainy texture than beef from the United States.

With miles of coastline, seafood replaces scarce meat in Chile. More seafood is consumed in Chile than in any other Latin American country, but the ubiquitous bean still ranks supreme here. In fact, the national dish of Chile consists of a mixture of beans, corn, and squash called *porotos granados*. Two seasonings are associated with Chile: *color*, an orange-red flavoring that combines garlic, paprika, and melted fat and *pebre*, a sauce made of onions, garlic, chili peppers, coriander, vinegar, and olive oil.

Coffee, the beverage of choice through most of South America, is served at all meals and between meals, too. Over half of the world's coffee comes from Latin America. Colombia produces very high quality coffee, but Brazil's coffee is usually blended with another coffee of higher quality.

Sweets play a large role in the cuisines of South America where sugar is plentiful and used generously. All fruits and several vegetables, including sweet potatoes and squash, are served candied. Also intensely sweet, pastes are prepared from many fruits. These are used as a filling for pastries or eaten plain. By North American standards, South American desserts are cloyingly sweet. Probably the best known of the South American desserts remains flan, a molded custard. Nuts are plentiful and incorporated into many confections. Another popular dessert in Central and South America as well as the Caribbean is sautéed bananas and sugar drizzled with rum or brandy.

The main meal of the day occurs in the afternoon. Consisting of several courses, this large meal is traditionally followed by a *siesta*, nap. Meals follow the same pattern as those of Mexico: breakfast is comprised of fruit, tortillas or sweet rolls, coffee or hot chocolate, and perhaps meat, eggs, and/or beans. Midmorning snacks hold the diner until the main meal in the afternoon. Around six o'clock in the evening, pastries and coffee or hot chocolate are consumed. Then a light evening meal is served at nine or ten o'clock.

Review Questions

1. Discuss the effect of the Andes Mountains on the cuisines of South America.
2. What did the Inca Indians contribute to the cuisines of South America?
3. Name five foods that the Europeans learned about when they discovered South America.
4. Name four food products and flavorings that are prevalent in South America.
5. Discuss which animal proteins are consumed in various areas of South America and why.

REGION	AREA	WEATHER	TOPOGRAPHY	FOODS
Venezuela	West	Cool	Mountains	Cattle, potatoes
	North	Hot	Coast, forest	Seafood, bananas, plantains, coconuts, cassava
Colombia	Central, west central	Cool	Mountains	Cattle, potatoes, coffee
	West	Hot	Coast, rain forest	Seafood, bananas, plantains, coconuts, cassava
Ecuador	West, coastal	Hot	Coast, rain forest	Seafood, plantains, bananas, peanuts, corn, chilies, fruits, vegetables
	East, Andes	Cool	Mountains, steep valleys	Llama, beans, quinoa, potatoes, squash, corn, pumpkin
Peru	West, coast	Arid, hot	Coast, desert, small rivers for irrigation	Seafood, plantains, bananas, peanuts, corn, chili peppers, fruits, vegetables
	East, Andes	Cool	Mountains, steep valleys	Llama, beans, corn, quinoa, potatoes, squash, pumpkin
Brazil	Northern two-thirds	Hot	Tropical rain forest, savannas, dry brush land	Seafood, game, nuts, peanuts, manioc, corn, sweet potatoes, yams, okra, plantains, coconut, oranges, papaya, mangos, breadfruit, bananas, dates, coffee, sugar, cocoa
	Lower third	Temperate	Grasslands, fertile farmland	Cattle, many fruits and vegetables
Chile	Northern third	Hot, arid	Desert, little or no rainfall	Seafood
	Middle third	Hot, dry summers; cool, wet winters	Fertile valleys	Seafood, grapes, wine
	Southern third	Cold	Mountains, forest	Seafood
Uruguay	*Pampa*	Temperate	Humid grasslands	Sheep, beef, many crops
Argentina	*Pampa*	Temperate	Humid grasslands, fertile farmland	Beef, wine, many crops

Glossary

aji Spicy chili seasoning frequently used in the cooking of Peru

arepa Type of cornbread

ceviche Dish consisting of raw fish marinated in citrus juices with other seasonings; the citrus juice "cooks" the fish, changing its appearance from raw to opaque; originally from Peru, *ceviche* is served throughout Latin America

color An orange-red flavoring that combines garlic, paprika, and melted fat; used in Chile

creole Style of cooking melding Incan and Spanish culinary components

dendê An orange-colored oil made from palm; brought to Brazil by slaves from western Africa where it is used extensively

empanada Small turnover or pie filled with any combination of meats and seasonings

feijoada completa Dish combining beans with a variety of smoked and cured meats and seasonings, the national dish of Brazil

manioc A starchy root vegetable which is sometimes called cassava

pampa Humid grasslands that are found in Argentina and Uruguay, ideal lands for raising livestock

pebre A sauce made of onions, garlic, chili, coriander, vinegar, and olive oil, used as a seasoning in Chile

porotos granados Dish containing a mixture of beans, corn, and squash; the national dish of Chile

quinoa A grain that thrives in the mountains, originally raised by the Inca Indians and still consumed today

---

SOUTH AMERICAN CHEESES

Argentina and Uruguay produce cheeses that are much like the Italian hard grating cheeses, parmesan and romano. Argentina also produces reggianito, which is made from cow's milk and tastes similar to parmesan. It is a firm cheese that is often grated. Sardo is made from cow's milk, tastes similar to romano; it is firm and often grated.

EMPANADAS DE HORNO (Argentina)

Meat Filled Turnovers

Serving Size: 4-inch turnover   Cooking Method: Bake
Total Yield: 18 to 20 turnovers

Food Balance: Sweet/spicy/protein
Wine Style: Soft and fruity Gewürztraminer, Blush, Beaujolais, Grenache, soft Shiraz
Example: Beringer Founders' Estate Shiraz, Black Opal Shiraz

INGREDIENTS	WEIGHT	VOLUME
DOUGH:		
flour, all purpose	9 oz	2 cups
salt	¼ oz	1 teaspoon
butter, cold, cut into 5 pieces	5 oz	½ cup plus 2 tablespoons
water, cold	2½ oz	⅓ cup
FILLING:		
raisins	2 oz	4 tablespoons
onions, finely chopped	3 oz	½ cup or 1 small
olive oil	½ oz	1 tablespoon
water	4 oz	½ cup

INGREDIENTS	WEIGHT	VOLUME
sirloin steak, boneless, cut into ¼-inch cubes	8 oz	
hot pepper, dried, crushed		1 teaspoon
cumin, ground		¼ teaspoon
paprika		½ teaspoon
salt		½ teaspoon
black pepper		few grindings

TO ASSEMBLE:

eggs, hard boiled, each cut into 10 slices		2 each
green olives, pitted, quartered	2 oz	20 each

FOR DOUGH:

1. Place flour and salt in bowl of food processor. Pulse a couple of times.
2. Place butter on top. Pulse a few times to cut into dough, until mixture forms pea-sized pieces.
3. With machine running, add water through feed tube. Pulse a few times until dough forms a ball.
4. Remove dough from bowl, wrap in plastic wrap. Store in refrigerator while preparing filling.

FOR FILLING:

1. Soak raisins in 8 oz (1 cup) boiling water for 10 minutes, drain thoroughly. Set aside.
2. Combine onions, olive oil, and water in skillet. Boil over high heat until water is evaporated.
3. Add meat, cook, stirring constantly, until browned. Stir in remaining ingredients. Set filling aside.

TO ASSEMBLE:

1. Preheat oven to 400 degrees.

Empanadas de Horno (Meat Filled Turnovers); photo courtesy of Dorling Kindersley

2. Roll dough on lightly floured surface about ⅛-inch thick. Cut out 4-inch rounds. Only roll scraps once again or it may become too tough.
3. Place ¾ ounce (about 1 tablespoon) filling in center of each round. Top filling with piece of egg and 4 pieces of olive.
4. Using pastry brush, moisten perimeter of dough with water. Fold dough in half, press edges firmly together, and curve to form crescent. Flute joined edges of dough as a pie crust.
5. Bake on ungreased baking sheet in middle of oven for 15 to 20 minutes, until golden.

ESCABECHE DE PESCADO
(Throughout South America)

Fish Escabeche

Number of Servings: 6 to 8 appetizers
Serving Size: 3 to 4 oz fish plus
   vegetables for appetizer, double
   for entrée
Total Yield: 2 lbs, 10 oz

Cooking Method: Deep-fry,
  boil

Food Balance: Spicy/acid
Wine Style: Light- to medium-bodied Johannisberg Riesling, Pinot Grigio, Sauvignon Blanc, Chablis, Blush, Rosé, Grenache, light Reds
Example: Campanile or Meridian Vineyards Pinot Grigio, Wolf Blass Grenache

INGREDIENTS	WEIGHT	VOLUME
fish fillet, boneless, cod, haddock, whitefish, cut into 6 or 8 pieces, or use whole fish	1 lb, 8 oz	
flour	2 oz	½ cup
kosher salt	¼ oz	1 teaspoon
paprika	¼ oz	2 teaspoons
cayenne		⅛ teaspoon
oil for deep-frying		
onion, sliced ⅜-inch slices	7 oz	1 large
carrot, sliced on diagonal ½-inch	3½ oz	1 each
garlic, peeled	1 oz	6 cloves
jalapeño peppers	3¾ oz	4 each
paprika	¼ oz	2 teaspoons
bay leaves		2 each
red wine vinegar	8 oz	1 cup
red wine	8 oz	1 cup
thyme		1 teaspoon
stock, chicken or fish	8 oz	1 cup

> Actually fried, marinated fish, this dish is served as an appetizer or entrée throughout Latin America. Each country prepares their own variation of this popular dish, which features many types of fish, shrimp, or chicken. Traditionally, escabeche is served at room temperature.

1. Combine flour, salt, ¼ oz (2 teaspoons) paprika, and cayenne on plate, mix well. Dredge fish in flour mixture.
2. Heat oil for deep-frying in heavy pan, fry fish, a few pieces at a time, to maintain temperature of oil. Fry fish until golden, about 5 minutes.

Escabeche de Pescado (Fish Escabeche)

3. Drain well on absorbent paper, then place in nonreactive bowl in single layer. Refrigerate until needed.
4. Pour off all but about ¼-inch oil, heat oil, add onions, carrots, and garlic, sauté until golden.
5. Add jalapeños, remaining ¼ oz (2 teaspoons) paprika, and bay leaves. Sauté another minute or two.
6. Add vinegar, bring to boil, reduce heat and simmer 5 minutes.
7. Add red wine, bring to boil, reduce heat and simmer 5 minutes.
8. Add thyme and stock, bring to boil, reduce heat and simmer 15 minutes.
9. Pour hot liquid over fish, let cool, serve immediately or cover and refrigerate until ready to serve. Serve fish accompanied by some of the pickled vegetables and marinating liquid.

SOPA DE FEIJÃO (Brazil)

Brazilian Bean Soup

Number of Servings: 10   Cooking Method: Sauté, boil
Serving Size: 8 oz
Total Yield: 5 lbs, 2 oz

Food Balance: Salt balanced
Wine Style: Wide variety Pinot Blanc, full-bodied Chardonnay, strong Reds, Cabernet Sauvignon
Example: Beringer Vineyards Private Reserve Chardonnay or Cabernet Sauvignon

INGREDIENTS	WEIGHT	VOLUME
dried black beans	1 lb	2½ cups
ham hock, optional		1 each
olive oil	½ oz	1 tablespoon
onion, diced	10 oz	2 medium
garlic, peeled, minced	½ oz	4 cloves
jalapeño peppers, seeded, deribbed, minced	1½ oz	2 each
cumin, ground		1 teaspoon
cloves, ground		½ teaspoon
salt	¾ oz or to taste	1 tablespoon or to taste

> *Use less salt if preparing soup with ham hock.*

GARNISH:

sour cream
lemon or lime slices

1. Wash beans thoroughly, cover with water, and soak overnight in refrigerator or place in boiling water. Turn off heat and soak for 2 or 3 hours.
2. If using ham hock, boil in water for 15 minutes, then drain and discard water.
3. Heat olive oil over medium heat, add onions and sauté about 4 minutes.
4. Add garlic and peppers, sauté another 2 or 3 minutes, until softened.

Sopa de Feijão (Brazilian Bean Soup); photo courtesy of Dorling Kindersley

5. Add sautéed onions, garlic, peppers and ham hock, if desired, to beans. Bring to boil, reduce heat and simmer until beans are soft, about 1 hour 15 minutes.

6. Remove ham hock if used, cut meat from bone into bite-sized pieces, refrigerate until needed.

7. Purée soup in food processor until smooth. If too thick, add liquid. Add salt and ham, if used. Correct seasonings.

8. Serve hot, topped with sour cream and lemon or lime slice, if desired.

CHUPE DE CAMARONES (Peru)

Shrimp Chowder

Number of Servings: 15
Serving Size: 8 oz
Total Yield: 7 lbs, 10 oz

Food Balance: Protein, spicy
Wine Style: Soft, fruity, and light Pinot Grigio, Chardonnay, light Pinot Noir or Chianti
Example: Campanile Pinot Grigio, Beringer Vineyards Founders Estate Pinot Noir

INGREDIENTS	WEIGHT	VOLUME
shrimp, unpeeled	1 lb, 8 oz	
crayfish	1 lb	
bay leaves		2 each
water	1 lb	2 cups
olive oil	1 oz	2 tablespoons
garlic, minced	½ oz	4 cloves
onion, diced	6 oz	1 large
celery, diced	4½ oz	1 cup
salt		½ teaspoon
pepper		½ teaspoon
cumin, ground		½ teaspoon
oregano, dried		½ teaspoon
hot pepper flakes or cayenne (which will be hotter)		½ teaspoon
tomato purée	12 oz	12-oz can
fish stock	2 lb	4 cups or 1 qt
potatoes, peeled, diced, ½-inch	1 lb	3 large
rice	4¾ oz	½ cup
corn	4½ oz	1 cup
milk, whole	1 lb	2 cups
queso fresco or feta cheese	8 oz	

GARNISH:

parsley, finely chopped
yellow pepper, hot, roasted
crayfish (optional)

Chupe de Camarones (Shrimp Chowder)

1. Peel and devein shrimp, reserving shells. Rinse shrimp, slice on the diagonal into 2 or 3 pieces (depending on size of shrimp). Refrigerate until needed. If desired, reserve one crayfish to garnish each serving. Peel and chop remaining crayfish into shrimp-sized pieces.
2. Boil shells with water and bay leaves for 10 minutes, strain broth and set aside.
3. Heat ½ oz (1 tablespoon) oil in large pot over medium heat.
4. Sauté onions, garlic, and celery for 1 or 2 minutes. Add salt, pepper, cumin, oregano, hot pepper flakes or cayenne, stirring until onions are wilted but not browned.
5. Add tomato purée, reserved stock, and fish stock. Bring to boil.
6. Add rice and potatoes. Lower heat and simmer. If using fresh corn, add when potatoes are halfway done. If using frozen corn, add when potatoes are almost tender.
7. When potatoes are cooked, add milk and grated or crumbled cheese.
8. Heat remaining oil in sauté pan. Sauté shrimp and crayfish for one minute, then add to chowder. Correct seasonings.
9. To serve, sprinkle with parsley and garnish with whole crayfish and a piece of roasted pepper, if desired.

CEBICHE DE HONGOS (Peru)

Mushroom Ceviche

Number of Servings: 8
Serving Size: 3½ oz
Total Yield: 1 lb, 12 oz

INGREDIENTS	WEIGHT	VOLUME
mushrooms, washed, cut into quarters	1 lb	
olive oil	2 oz	¼ cup or 4 tablespoons
red onion, julienne	6 oz	1 large
green onion, thinly sliced	1 oz	¼ cup
lemon juice, fresh	8 oz	1 cup
garlic, minced	¼ oz	2 cloves
hot red pepper, finely chopped	¼ oz	1 each
salt	to taste	
pepper	to taste	
celery, diced	1½ oz	¼ cup
oregano	¼ oz	1 teaspoon
cilantro, minced	¼ oz	1 tablespoon

GARNISH:

cilantro, minced
sweet potato, cooked, cut into 1-inch slices
corn on the cob, cooked, cut into 1- or 1½-inch pieces

1. Mix mushrooms and olive oil in bowl, set aside.
2. Soak both onions in salted water, set aside.
3. Combine lemon juice, garlic, hot red pepper, salt, and pepper. Add mushrooms and marinate for 30 minutes at room temperature.
4. Add celery, oregano, drained onions, and cilantro. Toss well and marinate 30 minutes. Correct seasonings.
5. To serve, place ceviche on leaf of lettuce, sprinkle with more finely chopped cilantro and hot pepper, if desired. Garnish with piece of sweet potato and corn on the cob.

Cebiche de Hongos (Mushroom Ceviche)

VATAPA (Brazil)

Fish Stew

Number of Servings: 8   Cooking Method: Braise
Serving Size: 7 oz
Total Yield: 3 lbs, 10 oz

Food Balance: Sweet/spicy
Wine Style: Soft and fruity Gewürztraminer, Johannisberg Riesling, Blush, Grenache
Example: Beringer Vineyards, Château St. Jean, or Wolf Blass Gold Label Riesling

INGREDIENTS	WEIGHT	VOLUME
coconut, unsweetened	9 oz	3 cups
milk	12 oz	1½ cups
water	12 oz	1½ cups
fish, any white, firm fleshed variety	2½ lbs	
shrimp, peeled and deveined	1 lb	
olive oil	2 oz	¼ cup
garlic, crushed	¼ oz	2 cloves
onion, diced	7 oz	1 large
tomatoes, chopped, canned plum	8 oz	1 cup
hot chili pepper, finely chopped	¼ oz	1 each
peanuts, unsalted, ground	3¼ oz	½ cup
ginger, minced	¼ oz	1 tablespoon
cilantro, finely chopped	¼ oz	1 tablespoon
salt	½ oz	2 teaspoons
water	1 lb	2 cups
cornmeal	2 oz	6 tablespoons

1. Grind peanuts in food processor using pulse. Cut fish across grain into pieces about 2 inches wide.
2. Place coconut, milk, and 12 oz (1½ cups) water into saucepan and simmer for 30 minutes. Strain and reserve liquid. Discard coconut.
3. Heat oil in skillet or braising pan over medium heat. Sauté fish and shrimp lightly, do not overcook. Remove fish and seafood to plate, and refrigerate until needed.
4. Sauté onions in same skillet until soft. Add garlic and sauté another minute. Add tomatoes, ginger, hot chili pepper, cilantro, salt, and 1 lb (2 cups) water. Bring to boil, cover skillet and simmer 15 minutes. Strain, pushing on vegetables to remove all juices. Reserve broth.
5. Meanwhile simmer coconut milk, peanuts, and cornmeal for about 10 minutes, until thickened. Stir often to prevent lumping.
6. Return fish broth to skillet. Whisk cornmeal mixture into broth. Heat thoroughly and add seafood. Cook until heated through. Correct seasonings.
7. Serve over rice.

ARROZ CON PATO (Peru)

Braised Duck with Cilantro Rice

Number of Servings: 12   Cooking Method: Braise
Serving Size: ¼ duck or 2 pieces

Food Balance: Balanced protein
Wine Style: Wide variety Sauvignon Blancs to Chardonnays, Chilean
   Merlot to Zinfandel
Example: Tarapaca Merlot or Château Souverain Cabernet Sauvignon

> *This recipe includes a large amount of rice to accompany the duck. Like much of South America, dishes in Peru contain large quantities of grains and/or vegetables with smaller portions of meat or seafood.*

INGREDIENTS	WEIGHT	VOLUME
lemon juice, fresh	4 oz	½ cup
cumin, ground		1½ teaspoons
salt		1½ teaspoons
black pepper, ground		¾ teaspoon
duck	12 to 15 lbs	3 each
light beer	3 lb	4 each 12-oz bottles
dark beer (Guinness or bock)	1 lb	2 cups
rice, long grain	2 lb, 7 oz	6 cups
cilantro, minced	4½ oz	1½ cups
green peas, fresh or frozen	1 lb	3 cups
salt		1½ teaspoons
pepper	¼ oz	¾ teaspoon

1. Wash duck thoroughly. Cut each duck into 8 serving pieces, trim all visible fat.
2. Mix lemon juice, cumin, 1½ teaspoons salt, and ¾ teaspoon pepper in stainless steel bowl. Add duck pieces, turn to coat, marinate, refrigerate for at least several hours.
3. In heavy pan, sear duck on all sides until browned. Render as much fat from ducks as possible, drain.
4. Add beers, bring to boil over high heat, scraping drippings from bottom and sides of pan. Reduce heat to low, cover and cook for 45 minutes, or until leg is tender when pierced with knife. Transfer duck to heated plate, cover to keep warm.

Arroz con Pato (Braised Duck with Cilantro Rice)

5. Strain cooking liquid, saving 5 lbs, 4 oz (2 qts, 20 oz or 10½ cups). If there is not enough, add water.

6. Bring to boil over high heat, stir in rice and return to boil. Reduce heat to low, cover pan, and simmer undisturbed for 20 minutes, or until the rice has absorbed all liquid. Stir in cilantro, peas, 1½ teaspoons salt, and ¾ teaspoon pepper. Correct seasonings.

7. Place duck pieces on rice, cover and return to low heat for a few minutes to heat the duck through.

8. To serve, mound rice and peas, top with duck pieces.

PABELLON CRIOLLO (Venezuela, Columbia)

Beef in Tomato Sauce with Black Beans, Rice, and Plantains

Number of Servings: 12
Serving Size: 5 oz meat, 4½ oz beans
Total Yield: 3 lbs, 12 oz meat
          3 lbs, 6 oz beans

Cooking Method: Broil

Food Balance: Sweet/protein
Wine Style: Light- to medium-bodied Johannisberg Riesling, Pinot Blanc, soft Chardonnay, soft/rich Reds, Grenache, Shiraz, Merlot
Example: Beringer Founders Estate Shiraz or Merlot

INGREDIENTS	WEIGHT	VOLUME
BLACK BEANS:		
black beans, dried	1lb, 4 oz	3 cups
olive oil	1½ oz	3 tablespoons
green pepper, finely diced	7 oz	1½ cups
onions, finely diced	3 oz	¼ cup or 1 small
garlic, minced or pulverized	½ oz	2 teaspoons or 4 cloves
salt	½ oz	2 teaspoons
cilantro, fresh sprigs		6 each
MEAT:		
sirloin of beef, lean top or boneless steak, ½-inch thick	4 lbs	
olive oil	4 oz	½ cup
onions, coarsely chopped	10 oz	2 cups
garlic, minced or pulverized	½ oz	2 teaspoons or 4 cloves
tomatoes, canned plum drained, chopped	1 lb, 14 oz	4 cups
cumin, ground	¼ oz	2 teaspoons
salt	½ oz	2 teaspoons
RICE:		
olive oil	2 oz	¼ cup
onion, whole, peeled	6 oz	1 large
green pepper, seeds and ribs removed	8 oz	1 large

INGREDIENTS	WEIGHT	VOLUME
rice, long grain	1 lb, 10 oz	4 cups
water, boiling	4 lbs	8 cups or 2 qts
salt	1 oz	4 teaspoons

PLANTAINS:

vegetable oil	3 oz	⅓ cup
plantains, ripe, peeled		4 large

BLACK BEANS:

1. Rinse black beans well. Cover with water and soak overnight or put into a pot of boiling water, turn off heat, and let soak several hours.
2. Bring to boil over high heat, reduce heat to low and simmer, uncovered, for 2 hours until almost tender.
3. In skillet, heat oil over moderate heat. Add green pepper, onions, garlic, and salt. Cook for 3 minutes, stirring constantly, then add to beans. Add cilantro and cook for 15 minutes, or until beans are tender. Discard cilantro. Cover and set aside.

MEAT:

1. Grill or broil steak 4-inches below heat source for about 5 minutes on each side, until medium rare.
2. Cut meat into strips ¼-inch wide and 1½-inches long.
3. In skillet, heat oil over moderate heat. Add onions and garlic, cook about 5 minutes, stirring occasionally until onions are soft and transparent but not brown. Add tomatoes, cumin, and salt. Reduce heat to low and cook, uncovered, for 30 minutes, stirring

Pabellon Criollo (Beef in Tomato Sauce with Black Beans, Rice, and Plantains)

frequently, until tomato juices evaporate and sauce becomes a thick purée.

4. Add strips of beef, mix well, cover skillet, and put it aside.

RICE:

1. Preheat oven to 250 degrees.
2. In heavy pan, heat oil over moderate heat until hot. Add onion and pepper, sauté for 5 minutes turning frequently. Add rice and stir constantly for 2 or 3 minutes to coat rice with oil.
3. Pour boiling water over rice, add salt, and bring to boil. Stir once or twice, cover pan, reduce heat to low. Simmer undisturbed for 20 minutes, until rice is tender and has absorbed all liquid.
4. Discard onion and pepper. Keep rice warm in oven.

PLANTAINS:

1. Cut crosswise in half and lengthwise into 6 or 8 slices.
2. Heat oil in skillet over moderate heat. Sauté plantain pieces for 2 or 3 minutes on each side until tender and golden brown.

TO ASSEMBLE:

1. Return beans and beef to low heat and cook to heat them through.
2. Spoon beef into center of heated platter or plate. Surround with alternating mounds of rice and black beans. Decorate with plantain slices and serve.

LOCRO (Many South American Countries)

Squash Stew

Number of Servings: 9 Cooking Method: Sauté, braise
Serving Size: 4 oz side dish
Total Yield: 2 lbs, 5 oz

Food Balance: Sweet and protein
Wine Style: Soft and fruity Gewürztraminer to Viognier, Blush or Rosé to Pinotage
Example: Château St. Jean Viognier

INGREDIENTS	WEIGHT	VOLUME
olive oil	1 oz	2 tablespoons
butternut squash, peeled, seeded, cut into 1-inch cubes	1 lb, 9½ oz	1 each, 4 cups
onion, small, diced	6 oz	1 large
garlic, peeled, minced		1 clove
oregano		½ teaspoon
turmeric		1 teaspoon
cumin		½ teaspoon
cayenne		¼ teaspoon
pepper		¼ teaspoon
chicken stock	4 oz	½ cup
corn, fresh or frozen	5 oz	1 cup
half and half	4 oz	½ cup
queso fresco or feta	3 oz	½ cup

GARNISH:

parsley, minced

> This dish varies from country to country. Some omit the cheese and half and half; others add a piece of fish; some recipes include other vegetables. Rice usually accompanies locro, which functions as an entrée or side dish.

Locro (Squash Stew)

1. Heat oil over medium heat, add onion, sauté for 2 or 3 minutes.
2. Add garlic and spices, sauté 1 minute.
3. Add squash and stock, simmer for 10 minutes if using fresh corn, 20 minutes if using frozen corn. Add water, as needed, to keep from burning.
4. Add corn, cook another 15 minutes for fresh corn, 5 minutes for frozen corn. The squash will cook a total of 25 minutes.
5. Add half and half and cheese, stir gently, remove from heat. Correct seasonings.
6. Serve immediately, garnished with parsley.

PAPAS A LA HUANCAINA (Peru)

Potatoes with Cheese and Chili Sauce

Number of Servings: 8
Serving Size: 1 potato

INGREDIENTS	WEIGHT	VOLUME
fresh lemon juice	2 oz	¼ cup
dried hot pepper, seeded, crumbled	⅛ to ¼ oz	1½ teaspoon
salt		½ teaspoon
black pepper	few grindings	
onion, peeled, thinly sliced, separated into rings	6 oz	1 large
boiling potatoes, peeled	2 lbs, 3 oz	8 medium
queso blanco, fresh, mozzarella, or Muenster cheese, grated	3 oz	1 cup

INGREDIENTS	WEIGHT	VOLUME
heavy cream	5½ oz	⅔ cup
turmeric	¼ oz	1 teaspoon
black pepper	few grindings	
red or green hot chili, fresh, seeded, minced	¼ oz	1 fresh
olive oil	2½ oz	⅓ cup

GARNISH:

red or green hot chili, fresh, seeded, cut lengthwise into ½-inch strips		1 each
eggs, hard-cooked, cut lengthwise into halves		4 each
black olives		8 each

1. Combine lemon juice, dried pepper, salt, and black pepper in large bowl. Add onion rings, turning to coat evenly. Cover the bowl and set aside to marinate at room temperature.
2. Boil potatoes until tender but not falling apart.
3. Combine cheese, cream, turmeric, fresh pepper, salt, and black pepper in food processor, process for 30 seconds, until smooth and creamy.
4. Heat olive oil in heavy skillet over moderate heat. Add cheese mixture, reduce heat to low, and cook, stirring constantly for 5 to 8 minutes, until sauce thickens.
5. To assemble, arrange potatoes on heated platter or plate and pour sauce over them. Place drained onion rings and fresh pepper strips over the potatoes. Garnish with eggs and black olives.

COUVE A MINEIRA (Brazil)

Greens

Number of Servings: 9   Cooking Method: Sauté
Serving Size: 4 oz
Total Yield: 2 lbs, 4 oz

INGREDIENTS	WEIGHT	VOLUME
kale, fresh, stems removed, washed, sliced thinly	1 lb, 14 oz	
olive oil	1½ oz	3 tablespoons
onion, minced	1 lb	3 medium
garlic, minced	¾ oz	6 cloves
salt	¼ oz	1 teaspoon
pepper		1 teaspoon
coriander, ground		¾ teaspoon
mace, ground		⅛ teaspoon

> This recipe works with almost any green vegetable.

1. Heat oil in large pan over medium heat, add onion, sauté about 3 minutes, until soft.
2. Add garlic, sauté another 1 or 2 minutes.
3. Add kale and seasonings, cook about 8 to 10 minutes until done.
4. Correct seasonings. Serve.

FLAN

Caramel Custard

Number of Servings: 6 to 8
Total Yield: One 7- to 8-inch round

INGREDIENTS	WEIGHT	VOLUME
sugar	2 oz	¼ cup
water	½ oz	1 tablespoon
eggs	6¾ oz	4 each
sweetened condensed milk	14 oz	
water	8 oz	1 cup
vanilla		1 teaspoon

GARNISH:

fresh fruit

1. Preheat oven to 350 degrees.
2. Place sugar and ½ ounce (1 tablespoon) water in small heavy saucepan, mix just to moisten sugar. Cook over medium high heat, brush any sugar crystals from side of pan with pastry brush dipped in cold water. Do not stir.
3. Cook until light golden brown in color. Immediately pour into glass ovenproof dish (1-quart soufflé pan), and roll pan to cover bottom and sides evenly with caramelized sugar.

Flan (Caramel Custard); photo courtesy of Dorling Kindersley

4. Beat eggs until frothy. Combine condensed milk, 8 oz (1 cup) water, and vanilla. Pour into eggs and mix.
5. Pour mixture into prepared pan. Bake in bain marie (hot water bath—place soufflé dish in larger pan and add hot water to come halfway up sides of soufflé dish) for about 1 hour, until knife inserted in center of custard comes out clean.
6. Refrigerate for several hours or overnight.
7. Unmold on serving platter. Firm custard will be surrounded by thin caramel from caramelized sugar in pan.
8. To serve, slice like a pie. Spoon some caramel sauce on each piece. Garnish with fresh fruit.

CHAPTER 18
Caribbean Islands

By the end of this chapter, you will be able to

- Explain the role of the Arawaks and Caribs in the history of the Caribbean Islands
- Name the European countries that ruled islands of the Caribbean
- Explain the culinary influences from various nationalities on the cuisines of the Caribbean Islands
- Discuss factors that limited crops on the islands of the Caribbean
- Name foods that are prevalent on the Caribbean Islands
- Prepare a variety of dishes from the Caribbean Islands

HISTORY

Originally, two tribes from South America, the peace-loving Arawaks and the more aggressive Caribs, migrated to the islands scattered throughout the Caribbean Sea. The Arawaks arrived around 600 A.D., and they survived on the foods they found on the islands. Fish, including snapper, grouper, and shrimp; native animals like wild hogs; and abundant tropical fruits and vegetables growing there formed the basis of the Arawaks' diet. Guava, pineapple, cashews, sweet potatoes, pumpkin, papaya, and cassava flourished on the Caribbean Islands. In addition, the Arawaks discovered the hot pepper growing in these tropical islands, and this spicy addition quickly became an ingredient in most of their dishes. A lasting influence from the Arawaks, hot peppers still flavor many dishes found throughout the islands of the Caribbean.

The Arawaks and Caribs who inhabited these Caribbean islands endured intrusions and invasions from European countries looking for two things: the food products that grow in a tropical climate and lands to possess. They found both in the islands of the Caribbean. Besides discovering herbs, spices, and other native foods in the Caribbean Islands, the Europeans found the tropical lands to plant the crops they desired. While the island inhabitants learned of new foods from the Europeans, the natives taught the Europeans much about surviving in the Caribbean Islands.

Sailing the seas in search of spices, Christopher Columbus discovered islands in the Caribbean around 1490 and claimed them for Spain. Within seventy years of the Spanish landing, the Arawaks lost all control of their homeland and became slaves to their European rulers. Better fighters, the Caribs held off the Europeans for much longer, but they eventually could not keep them from ruling their lands.

The Spanish introduced pigs, cattle, and goats to these islands. Obtained from the pigs, lard became the favored cooking fat. Soon salted and dried meats entered the cuisine of the Caribbean. In addition, the Spaniards brought and planted many fruits and herbs on the islands, including bananas, plantains, coconuts, ginger, sugar cane, mangoes, citrus fruits, oregano, and cumin. With the introduction of sugar cane, the Spanish established large sugar plantations that required lots of labor. Soon, native people were enslaved to work on the plantations, but many of the Arawaks died from diseases and being overworked. More slaves were needed, so they imported Africans to the Caribbean Islands to work the land.

In 1498, Christopher Columbus landed in Trinidad at the southern end of the islands near South America. The Spanish ruled that island for 300 years, during which time the Dutch and French periodically exchanged control. After three centuries of Spanish control, Trinidad came under the rule of Britain. This exchange of power between Spain, Britain, France, Denmark, and the Netherlands occurred repeatedly on many islands from the time of the arrival of the first European settlers. As a result of the intense power struggles that raged, European countries actually exchanged control of St. Lucia six different times during a twenty-year span.

Christopher Columbus landed on Cuba in 1492. A typical story throughout the islands, in less than twenty years, the Spanish ruled Cuba and the native Arawaks became slaves. Strong Spanish influence still predominates in Cuba affecting the language, cuisine, and culture. Fidel Castro became the first Communist premier in 1959. In 1962, the United States restricted travel to Cuba and prohibited trade.

In their quest for places to produce coffee and sugar, the French took control of Martinique, Haiti, and Guadeloupe. The French influence remains apparent in the cooking, language, and culture on these islands.

The Dutch ruled Bonaire, Curacao, and Aruba. Remnants of the Dutch cuisine are exhibited with the fondness for Edam cheese and split pea soup, which are served frequently on these islands. In addition, the Dutch introduced many spices from their colony, Indonesia on islands they ruled.

With this continual exchange of power on the islands, the English controlled many islands, including Jamaica, Grenada, Trinidad, and Tobago. They introduced rum, breadfruit, and the mango to the Caribbean culinary world. Islands with British heritage serve many foods adopted from the British. For example, the Jamaican beef patty is a direct descendant of the Cornish pasties served throughout the British Isles.

When slavery was banned in the nineteenth century, cheap laborers from around the world were imported to the islands to work on the sugar plantations and other large farms. Many immigrants came from India and Southeast Asia. Of course, these workers brought their native cuisines with them to their new land, and those cuisines fused with the cuisines of the Caribbean. The Indian influence remains quite prominent with the islanders adopting curries, pilafs, rice, chutneys, and the spices used to flavor Indian dishes. Chop suey, stir-fries, and sweet and sour dishes entered the Caribbean cuisines from the Chinese.

RULE OVER SOME OF THE ISLANDS

British
Anguilla
Barbados
British Virgin Islands
Cayman Islands
Grenada
Jamaica
Nevis
Tobago
Trinidad

Dutch
Aruba
Bonaire
Curacao

French
Guadeloupe
Haiti
Martinique

Spanish
Cuba
Dominican Republic
Puerto Rico

The U.S. Virgin Islands consists of three islands, St. Croix, St. John, and St. Thomas. Settled by the Arawaks and Caribs as early as 300 B.C., these islands attracted the Spanish, British, French, Danish, and Dutch. After being governed by several European countries, the United States purchased these islands from the Danish in 1917.

TOPOGRAPHY

Often called the West Indies, the Caribbean Islands are strewn throughout the Caribbean Sea. They form a wide arc of islands stretching from the United States to South America. The Caribbean Islands are divided into two large regions. The Greater Antilles in the north is comprised of Cuba, Haiti, Dominican Republic, Jamaica, and Puerto Rico. Lying in the eastern Caribbean, the Lesser Antilles includes numerous islands situated from the Virgin Islands south to Trinidad and west to Aruba.

These islands contain diverse terrain and climates. Some of the climatic differences result from ocean breezes known as trade winds. Besides affecting the climate, trade winds impact the amount of rainfall an area receives which, of course, affects the terrain and the growing conditions. As a result, some islands are almost barren with cacti and small scruffy trees and bushes, whereas other islands support lush vegetation and some even contain rain forests.

Great topographical differences exist among the islands. Some of the islands are perfectly flat; many others contain a mountainous terrain. Of course, cooler temperatures prevail in the mountainous regions, which affects the crops that grow there. The famous Blue Mountain coffee grows in the Blue Mountains of Jamaica. Volcanic eruptions created many of the islands, and active volcanoes still exist on some.

Curacao contains arid vistas with desert vegetation and cacti growing. Contrarily, the island of Dominica is quite lush with volcanoes and mountains making up much of the landscape. Cuba, the largest of the Caribbean islands lies just south of Florida. Many believe that landmass was once joined to the United States. Situated at the southern end of the Caribbean Islands just north of Trinidad and Tobago, Curacao, Aruba, and Bonaire form the Netherlands Antilles. These islands lie close to the coast of Venezuela.

Ingredients and Foods Commonly Used Throughout the Cuisines of the Caribbean Islands Include:

- seafood—fresh and salted
- pork and lard
- beans and rice
- bananas and plantains
- coconut
- sweet potatoes, yams, taro, and cassava
- corn
- callaloo and greens
- pumpkins
- tropical fruits including mango, papaya, breadfruit, and pineapple
- hot peppers
- herbs and spices including thyme, allspice, peppers, cinnamon, nutmeg, cloves, and oregano

COOKING METHODS

Grilling and spit roasting are seen commonly throughout the Caribbean, a remnant from the Arawaks who brought the cooking method, grilling, with them from South America. With the well-known Jamaican meat preparation called jerk, pork, poultry, other meats, or fish is coated with a highly spiced seasoning paste, marinated, then grilled. When the West African preference for cooking in earthen pits joined the Arawaks' affinity for flavoring meats by rubbing them with hot pepper seasoning, the birth of jerk resulted. Jerk dishes now appear on menus throughout the islands and the United States.

Introduced to the islands by the Spanish, frying quickly became a popular and frequently used cooking technique. Abundant vegetable oil and lard provided the necessary medium for both deep-frying and sautéing. Prevalent in Africa, deep-frying was adopted by the Caribbeans for use with a myriad of foods including seafood, meat, vegetables, fruits, and fritters made with all sorts of ingredients.

Like so many other countries with a limited supply of meat, one-pot cookery prevails as a method of extending the small amount of meat while the long, slow braising tenderizes the tough cuts of meat. This method has the added advantage of using any available meats and vegetables.

The native Indians smoked meat to preserve it in the hot climate. Salted fish and meat also extended the protein supply, particularly for the slaves who were allowed only meager amounts of fresh meat.

REGIONS

The cookery differs on each island because of a number of factors. First, the Spanish, English, French, and Dutch controlled various islands of the Caribbean from the 1500s to the twentieth century. Each island exhibits culinary traits adopted from the ruling countries, and, in many cases, islands had several ruling nations in their history. Further culinary influences came from the immigrants brought to the islands from Africa, India, and China to work as slaves or cheap labor. These people prepared their native dishes and fused their native cookery with the cuisine of their new land. Second, the varying topography and climate existing on each of the islands resulted in different crops growing and animals being raised there.

Although the climate throughout the Caribbean is conducive to growing abundant crops, many of the islanders live in poverty. Poor soil, crop devastation by insects, hurricanes, lack of rain, and old agricultural machinery and techniques are some of the problems that plague farmers in the Caribbean. As a result, the islanders must import at least part of their food supplies, leading to expensive food.

As is true with different regions in other countries, a number of the same dishes are prepared on many islands. Variations on the dish distinguish it on each island. Countless renditions of bean fritters, fish fritters, blood sausage, stuffed crabs, fried corn bread, pepper pot (vegetable soup prepared with any available meat and vegetables), curries, beans and rice, and callaloo (a soup made of greens and other ingredients depending on where it is prepared) appear in homes and on menus throughout the islands.

CUISINE

The African slaves exerted a profound effect on the Caribbean cuisine that still prevails throughout the islands. Because both Africa and the Caribbean Islands experience a tropical climate, similar crops grow in both these areas. As a result, the African immigrants could plant the foods that grew in their homeland, cook their native recipes, and produce their familiar dishes of African origin. They introduced plantains, beans, cornmeal dishes, okra, and yams into the cuisine of the islanders, and these foods quickly became a part of the Caribbean cuisine.

Creole cooking, a fusion of French, Spanish, and African influences, appears throughout the Caribbean, Latin America, and parts of the United States. The vegetables and seafood of Africa join Spanish herbs and spices and the wonderful French sauces resulting in a unique cookery. Although many think Creole cookery contains spicy, hot flavorings, it does not. The spicy chilies so prevalent in the African cuisines are absent from Creole cookery.

All sorts of seafood abound in these islands. Large, meaty fish such as swordfish, tuna, dolphin, and marlin; smaller fish including grouper, snapper, and mackerel; and a myriad of shellfish such as lobster, conch, shrimp, and crab provide a constant source of protein-rich foods. Many associate conch with the Caribbean, because it appears on menus in fritters, chowder, and salads. Although surrounded by ocean and an abundance of seafood, slaves in the Caribbean had no time to fish. Because salting and drying preserved the fish even in the heat of the tropical islands, this became a mainstay in their diet. Salted fish still plays an important role in the native Caribbean cuisine, appearing in many traditional dishes.

The Arawaks hunted wild hogs before the Spanish introduced the pig. Pork remains the most popular meat. Chicken, duck, turkey, goat, and beef also are consumed.

A bounty of vegetables thrives in the tropical climate of the Caribbean. With a year-round growing season, the abundant vegetables fill the gaps left by the limited meat supplies. As a result, many meat dishes contain lots of vegetables. The Arawaks ate corn, and today it appears often, both as a vegetable or ground into cornmeal and cooked into porridge or bread. Years ago as well as today, root vegetables formed a substantial part of the diet of the Caribbean native. Taro, cassava, and yams appear in many preparations. Fruits, plantains and bananas are cooked in a number of ways and often accompany meals. Depending on their ripeness, plantains regularly appear sautéed, boiled, or baked and function as a starch. Even the plantain leaves are used as a wrapper to hold other foods when steaming.

All sorts of dried beans, as well as rice, form the foundation of the Caribbean diet. Beans, often called peas in the islands, appear as salads, a side dish, or combined with rice and served as an entrée. Different versions of beans and rice are prepared on each island. When the Asian immigrants moved to the Caribbean, they introduced rice into the diet, where it was quickly adopted as a mainstay in the cuisine.

Fruits flourish here and claim a significant place in the cuisine and diet of the islanders. Numerous varieties of fruits grow, including citrus fruits, mango, papaya, pineapple, avocado, coconuts, and more. The grapefruit, guava, and pineapple are indigenous to the islands. Coconut appears in all sorts of dishes from appetizers to desserts. Islanders use all parts of the coconut, including the milk, meat, and oil.

A bounty of herbs, spices, and hot peppers flavor dishes in Caribbean cookery. The favorite herb remains thyme. A profusion of spices thrive in the tropical conditions here. Jamaica produces lots of allspice, which comes from the pimento tree and appears in many dishes on that island. Cinnamon, ginger, peppercorns, and nutmeg grow well throughout the islands. Forty percent of the world's nutmeg and mace comes from Grenada. A myriad of sweet and hot peppers thrive here. Numerous peppers, including the hottest variety, the Scotch bonnet, flavor many of the dishes prepared throughout the islands. Although many islanders season liberally with chili peppers, several islands, including Cuba and Puerto Rico, do not prepare many spicy dishes.

Mace and nutmeg come from the same plant, the tropical nutmeg tree. The spice nutmeg is the kernel of the seed, and the outer shell or membrane covering the nutmeg is the mace. Both spices are ground for use in sweet and savory dishes.

Caribbean curries evolved from the Indian influence. Although prevalent in many places with tropical climates, curries differ greatly by containing the spices preferred in each area. Curries usually are seasoned with turmeric, mustard, ginger, cloves, garlic, and cumin in the Caribbean; however, variations on curries are found from island to island.

Islanders like cloyingly sweet desserts, and they are served often. Evaporated, condensed milk replaces fresh milk in many confections. Numerous desserts contain bananas, coconut, other fruits, and/or rum. British desserts such as puddings, buns, and trifle often appear on the islands with a history of British rule.

With the abundance of fruit growing in the Islands, fruit juices are popular and frequently served. Beer and rum remain the preferred alcoholic beverages. Made from sugar cane, rum was first made in the seventeenth century by the British on the island of Barbados. The many varieties of rum include dry, dark, light, and heavy. Although many islands produce their own brands, each island's beer and rum has its own characteristics. Rum appears in numerous recipes for food and drinks, and countless recipes for rum drinks are served throughout the islands.

Review Questions

1. Discuss how history has influenced the cuisines of the Caribbean Islands.
2. Explain the exchange of power that occurred between European nations occupying the islands in the Caribbean and how that impacted the cuisine.
3. Discuss how the climate/weather affects the cuisines in the Caribbean Islands.
4. Name five foods that are common ingredients throughout the Caribbean Islands.
5. Name and describe at least three dishes frequently served throughout the islands of the Caribbean.

REGION	AREA	WEATHER	TOPOGRAPHY	FOODS
Greater Antilles: Cuba	South of Florida	Semitropical; dry, mild winters; wet summers	Mountains, rolling hills, grasslands, farmland, coast	Seafood, pork, rice, cassava, sugar, sweet potatoes, corn, peas, beans, okra, chilies, vegetables, fruits, citrus fruits, rum
Jamaica	South of Cuba	Tropical, hot and humid, rainy spring and fall	Rolling hills, mountains, plains, plateaus, coast	Seafood, livestock, poultry, rice, yams, plantains, sugar, vegetables, fruits, bananas, coconuts, ginger, allspice, coffee, cocao beans, rum
Lesser Antilles: Virgin Islands St. Thomas, St. Croix, and St. John	East of Puerto Rico	Tropical, moderated by trade winds	Hills, fertile land, coast	Seafood, beef, eggs, chickens, vegetables, fruits, nuts
Martinique and Guadeloupe	South Caribbean, north of Trinidad and Tobago	Tropical, hot and humid summer and fall, milder winter and spring, trade winds	Hills, mountains, volcanoes, coast	Seafood, livestock, sugar, rice, fruits, vegetables, bananas, pineapple, cocoa, coffee, rum
Trinidad and Tobago	South Caribbean, just north of Venezuela	Tropical, hot and humid	Forests, flatlands, farmland, hills, mountains, coast	Seafood, beans, sugar, vegetables, coconuts, sweet potatoes, fruits, cocoa, coffee, rum

Scoville units measure the level of capsaicin in the pepper. Capsaicin contains the heat. Heat levels found in individual peppers fluctuate greatly because the heat level varies from plant to plant.

Pepper	Scoville Units
Bell	0
Pepperoncini	100–500
Poblaño	500–1000
Ancho, Pasilla	1,000–1,500
Cascabel	1,500–2,500
Jalapeño, Chipolte	2,500–10,000
Serrano	5,000–20,000
Cayenne, Piquin, Tabasco, Aji	30,000–50,000
Thai	50,000–100,000
Habañero, Scotch Bonnet	80,000–300,000

For information on handling chili peppers, refer to page 371 in Chapter 16, Mexico.

Glossary

callaloo Greens obtained from the taro plant; also the name of a soup made of greens and other ingredients, including salt pork, crab, and/or coconut milk

pepper pot Vegetable soup prepared with any available meat and vegetables

CHEESES OF THE CARIBBEAN ISLANDS

Crema Mexicana Thick rich soft cream, flavor similar to whipping cream
Duroblando Strong flavor, firm texture
Queso fresco Made from cow's and goat's milk, mild flavor, soft crumbly texture, does not melt
Queso media luna Mild taste, semifirm texture, favorite in Puerto Rico, sometimes called *queso de papa*
Queso para freír Mild flavor, firm texture, does not melt

STAMP AND GO (Jamaica)

Salt Cod Fritters

Number of Servings: 8   Cooking Method: Deep-fry
Serving Size: 3 patties
Total Yield: 1 lb, 8 oz raw batter
         24 patties

Stamp and Go (Salt Cod Fritters); photo courtesy of The Norwegian Seafood Export Council—www.seafood.no. Photography by Alf Börjessen

Food Balance: Protein/ spicy
Wine Style: Wide variety—light- to medium-bodied Pinot Gris or Grigio, Sauvignon Blanc, Chardonnay, Rosé, Chianti
Example: Meridian Pinot Grigio/Sauvignon Blanc or Santa Barbara Chardonnay

INGREDIENTS	WEIGHT	VOLUME
salt cod	8 oz	
flour	4¾ oz	1 cup
baking powder		1 teaspoon
salt		½ teaspoon
thyme		¼ teaspoon
water, cold	6 oz	¾ cup
egg	1¾ oz	1 each
onion, minced	4 oz	1 small
garlic, minced		1 clove
hot pepper, seeded and deribbed, minced	¼ oz	½ each
vegetable oil, for frying		

1. Place salt cod in bowl, cover with cold water, refrigerate at least 12 hours, changing water at least once or twice.
2. Drain fish, place in pan, cover with fresh water, bring to boil, continue boiling about 10 minutes.
3. Drain, shred finely, discarding any skin or bones.
4. Place flour, baking powder, salt, and thyme in bowl, stir in water and egg.
5. Add onions, garlic, hot pepper, and fish, stir to blend.
6. Heat about ½-inch oil in frying pan until hot, drop in fish mixture by tablespoonful, fry until golden brown on both sides, about 2 to 3 minutes.
7. Drain on absorbent paper, serve hot.

CALLALOO (Eastern Caribbean)

Soup with Greens and Crab

Number of Servings: 14   Cooking Method: Braise
Serving Size: 8 oz
Total Yield: 7 lbs, 4 oz

Food Balance: Spicy sweet
Wine Style: Soft and fruity Johannisberg Riesling, Gewürztraminer,
   Viognier, Beaujolais, Grenache
Example: Beringer Vineyards Johannisberg Riesling or Viognier

INGREDIENTS	WEIGHT	VOLUME
butter	1 oz	2 tablespoons
onion, finely chopped	10 oz	2 large or 2 cups
garlic, minced	½ oz	4 cloves
callaloo greens or spinach, washed, stems removed, cut into ½-inch strips	1 lb, 11 oz	
hot pepper, minced or ground cayenne pepper, optional	to taste	
chicken stock	4 lbs	8 cups or 2 qts
coconut milk, unsweetened	13 oz	1½ cups
crabmeat, fresh, canned, or frozen, all shell and cartilage removed	12 oz	
black pepper		1 teaspoon

1. Melt butter in large pan over medium heat, add onions, sauté gently for about 3 minutes.
2. Add garlic, sauté another 3 minutes.
3. Add greens and optional hot pepper, mix well, cook until soft, about 5 minutes.
4. Add stock, coconut milk, and black pepper, bring to boil, then reduce heat and simmer uncovered until greens are tender, about 10 minutes.
5. Add crabmeat, simmer another five minutes.
6. Correct seasonings, serve.

PEPPER POT (Western Caribbean)

Number of Servings: 9   Cooking Method: Braise
Serving Size: 10 oz
Total Yield: 5 lbs, 11 oz

Food Balance: Spicy protein
Wine Style: Light and fruity, rich Gewürztraminer, Blush wines,
   Grenache, and rich Zinfandel
Example: Beringer Vineyards Gewürztraminer, North Coast Zinfandel, or Wolf Blass Grenache

INGREDIENTS	WEIGHT	VOLUME
bacon, diced or salt pork, cut into thin strips	3 oz	3 slices

A cross between soup and stew, this dish hails from the time of the Arawaks. Any available ingredients went in the pot and soon a meal emerged. Every island prepares a different version of this dish.

Pepper Pot

INGREDIENTS	WEIGHT	VOLUME
pork, lean, cubed	8 oz	
onion, thinly sliced	13½ oz	2 large
chicken stock	3 lbs	6 cups
habenero or jalapeño chili, seeds removed, minced	¼ oz (habenero) or ¾ oz (jalapeño)	1 each
callaloo or spinach, washed, stems removed, cut roughly	10 oz	
kale, washed, stems removed, cut roughly	1 lb, 5 oz	
okra, sliced	5 oz	12 each or 1½ cups
yam, peeled, sliced, cut into quarters	8 oz	1 small to medium
thyme, dried	¼ oz	2 teaspoons
black pepper, ground		½ teaspoon
salt	to taste	

1. Place bacon or salt pork in large pot, sauté over medium heat to render fat, about 10 minutes.
2. Add pork and onions, sauté about 5 minutes, until pork browns and onions soften.
3. Add stock, bring to boil, reduce heat, cover, simmer 1½ hours.
4. Add remaining ingredients and simmer another 1 hour.
5. Correct seasonings, remove salt pork (if used), serve.

RICE SALAD

Number of Servings: 8
Serving Size: 4 oz
Total Yield: 2 lbs

Cooking Method: Boil (rice)

INGREDIENTS	WEIGHT	VOLUME
curry powder	¼ oz	2 teaspoons
turmeric		¼ teaspoon
salt		½ teaspoon
black pepper, ground		¼ teaspoon
water	1 oz	2 tablespoons
yogurt, plain	6 oz	⅔ cup
raisins	1½ oz	3 tablespoons
onion, minced	1 oz	1 tablespoon
vinegar, cider	2 oz	¼ cup
rice, cooked, cooled	15 oz	2 cups
green bell pepper, diced	3½ oz	½ cup
red bell pepper, diced	3½ oz	½ cup

GARNISH:

lettuce leaves

1. Mix spices and water in bowl, add yogurt, raisins, and onion. Mix well.
2. Add peppers and rice, stir gently.
3. Cover and refrigerate several hours or overnight.
4. Correct seasonings, serve on base of lettuce leaves.

MIXED BEAN SALAD

Number of Servings: 15
Serving Size: 4 oz
Total Yield: 3 lbs, 13 oz

Cooking Method: Boil (individual ingredients)

INGREDIENTS	WEIGHT	VOLUME
SALAD INGREDIENTS:		
black-eyed peas, cooked	9½ oz	1 cup
kidney beans, cooked	9½ oz	1 cup
chickpeas, cooked	7½ oz	1 cup
green beans, cooked *al dente*	6 oz	36 each
avocado, firm, ripe, peeled, cubed	11 oz	2 each
onion, sliced thinly	6 oz	2 small
red pepper, cut into strips	7 oz	1 each
chives, minced	¼ oz	6 each
DRESSING:		
garlic, minced, smashed	½ oz	4 cloves
hot red pepper, seeded, minced	¼ to ½ oz	1 small
salt	¼ oz	1 teaspoon
black pepper, ground		¼ teaspoon
allspice, ground		1 teaspoon
vinegar, cider	3 oz	6 tablespoons
lemon juice, fresh	¾ oz	1½ tablespoons
olive oil	5 oz	⅔ cup

lettuce leaves

1. Combine all salad ingredients in bowl.
2. Whisk all dressing ingredients together in another bowl, jar, or processor, whisk or process until dressing thickens.

Mixed Bean Salad; photo courtesy of Dorling Kindersley

3. Pour dressing over salad, mix gently.
4. Cover and refrigerate a few hours or overnight, correct seasonings.
5. Serve on lettuce leaves.

JERK PORK (Jamaica)

Pork with Spicy Rub

Number of Servings: 8   Cooking Method: Grill
Serving Size: 5 to 6 oz
Total Yield: 3 lbs

Food Balance: Spicy/protein
Wine Style: Soft and fruity Gewürztraminer, Viognier, Rosé, Dolcetto, Beaujolais, Grenache
Example: Beringer Gewürztraminer, Rosé De Saignee, or Gamay Beaujolais

> *Adjust the heat of the marinade with the choice of pepper and/or by removing the seeds and ribs of the pepper to make it milder.*

INGREDIENTS	WEIGHT	VOLUME
pork fillets or chops	3 lbs, 8 oz	
MARINADE:		
onion, diced	6 oz	1 large
garlic, minced	¼ oz	2 cloves

Jerk Pork (Pork with Spicy Rub); photo courtesy of Dorling Kindersley

INGREDIENTS	WEIGHT	VOLUME
hot chilies, jalapeño or habanero, seeded and deribbed if desired, minced	1¾ oz	3 each
ginger, fresh, peeled, minced	¼ oz	¼-inch thick piece
soy sauce	½ oz	1 tablespoon
allspice		1 teaspoon
thyme		1 teaspoon
cinnamon		½ teaspoon

1. Combine all marinade ingredients in bowl of processor.
2. Process until mixture becomes thick paste, scraping down sides of bowl as needed.
3. Rub mixture over pork, cover and refrigerate several hours or overnight.
4. Preheat grill, place pork on grill without removing marinade, cook pork until done.
5. Serve immediately.

CARIBBEAN BAKED CHICKEN

Number of Servings: 8
Serving Size: ¼ chicken
Total Yield: 7 lbs, 2 oz

Cooking Method: Bake

Food Balance: Acidic/spicy
Wine Style: Light- to medium-bodied Chenin Blanc, Pinot Blanc, Pinot Grigio, Blush, rich Shiraz or Syrah
Example: Château St. Jean Pinot Blanc, Black Opal Shiraz, Meridian Vineyards Syrah

INGREDIENTS	WEIGHT	VOLUME
chicken, cut into quarters, skin removed, if desired	about 6 lbs	2 each
dark rum	6 oz	¾ cup
soy sauce	6 oz	¾ cup
lime juice	2¾ oz	⅓ cup
onion, finely diced	14 oz	2 large
garlic, minced	1 oz	8 cloves
ginger, minced	1½ oz	¼ cup
hot pepper, seeds and ribs removed, minced	3 oz or to taste	4 each or to taste
thyme, dried	1 oz	¼ cup
mustard, dry, ground		1 teaspoon
cornstarch	½ oz	1 tablespoon
water, cold	1 oz	2 tablespoons

1. Wash chicken, place in ovenproof pan.
2. Place rum, soy sauce, lime juice, onion, garlic, ginger, pepper, thyme, and mustard in food processor, pulse until paste, scraping down sides of bowl, about 30 seconds.
3. Pour paste over chicken pieces, refrigerate at least 4 hours.
4. Preheat oven to 350 degrees.
5. Place chicken in oven, bake about 1 hour, until chicken is done. Turn chicken once or twice, baste with pan juices two or three times.
6. Meanwhile, combine cornstarch with water, mix well, set aside.
7. Remove chicken from oven, and remove chicken from roasting pan.
8. Stirring constantly, add cornstarch mixture to pan, cook over medium heat until slightly thickened. Correct seasonings.
9. Add chicken to pan and stir to coat.
10. Serve immediately, accompanied by rice.

ROPA VIEJA (Cuba and Puerto Rico)

Shredded Beef

Number of Servings: 14
Serving Size: 6 oz
Total Yield: 5 lbs, 4 oz

Cooking Method: Braise

Food Balance: Protein and spice
Wine Style: Fruity light- to medium-rich Blush, fruity Chardonnay, Syrah, and rich Merlot
Example: Meridian Vineyards Syrah

This dish is served in the islands of the Caribbean with Spanish heritage. Ropa vieja literally means "old clothes," and the dish is prepared with leftover or tough cuts of meat. If leftover meat is unavailable, simmer about 4½ lbs meat with bay leaves and diced onion in water until tender, about 2 hours.

INGREDIENTS	WEIGHT	VOLUME
beef, cooked, flank or brisket	2 lbs, 8 oz	
oil	1½ oz	3 tablespoons
onion, diced	1 lb, 2 oz	2 large
garlic, minced	½ oz	4 cloves
green pepper, seeded, diced	8 oz	1 large

Ropa Vieja (Shredded Beef)

INGREDIENTS	WEIGHT	VOLUME
jalapeño pepper, seeds and ribs removed, minced	1½ oz	2 each
tomatoes, canned, plum, diced	2 lbs, 1 oz	4 cups or 1 qt
oregano, dried		1 teaspoon
allspice		½ teaspoon
salt	¼ oz	1 teaspoon
capers, drained	1 oz	2 tablespoons

1. Shred meat by cutting into ¼-inch strips with the grain, then cut those strips into 2-inch lengths. Refrigerate until needed.
2. Heat oil in large pan over medium high heat, add onion, garlic, green pepper, and jalapeño, sauté about 5 minutes.
3. Add tomatoes, oregano, allspice, salt, capers, and meat, cook about 10 minutes, stirring frequently.
4. Correct seasonings, serve immediately accompanied by rice.

SHRIMP AND MANGO CURRY

Number of Servings: 10
Serving Size: 8 oz
Total Yield: 5 lbs

Cooking Method: Sauté

Food Balance: Sweet and spicy
Wine Style: Soft and fruity Riesling, Gewürztraminer, Viognier, Blush wines, Amarone, Grenache
Example: Château St. Jean Johannisberg Riesling, Gewürztraminer, or Viognier

Shrimp and Mango Curry; photo courtesy of Dorling Kindersley

If ripe mangoes are unavailable, try substituting ripe pineapple for the mango.

INGREDIENTS	WEIGHT	VOLUME
butter	1 oz	2 tablespoons
onion, small dice	8 oz	2 small
garlic, minced	½ oz	4 cloves
ginger, fresh, peeled, minced	1 oz	2 tablespoons
jalapeño, seeds and ribs removed, minced	½ oz	1 each
curry powder	¾ oz	3 tablespoons
salt		¾ teaspoon
sweet potato, peeled, large dice	1 lb, 2 oz	2 large
water	1 lb, 8 oz	3 cups
shrimp, peeled and deveined	2 lbs	
mango, peeled, diced	about 1 lb	2 each

1. Melt butter in saucepan over medium heat, add onions, garlic, ginger, and jalapeño. Sauté until soft, about 3 minutes.
2. Add curry powder and salt, stir to mix.
3. Add water and sweet potato, continue to cook, uncovered, until almost soft, about 12 to 15 minutes.
4. Add shrimp and mango, stir occasionally, cook until shrimp is done, about 5 to 7 minutes. Correct seasonings.
5. Serve immediately over rice.

MOROS Y CRISTIANOS (Cuba)

Black Beans and Rice

Number of Servings: 14

Serving Size: 4 oz side dish

Total Yield: 3 lbs, 8 oz

Cooking Method: Boil

Food Balance: Protein/balanced

Wine Style: Wide variety Pinot Blanc, Sauvignon Blanc, Merlot, Shiraz, or Zinfandel

Example: Château Souverain Sauvignon Blanc, Merlot, or Zinfandel

INGREDIENTS	WEIGHT	VOLUME
black beans, dried	7½ oz	1 cup
vegetable oil	½ oz	1 tablespoon
onion, diced	6 oz	1 large
garlic, minced	¼ oz	2 cloves
rice	10½ oz	1½ cups
water	1 lb, 8 oz	3 cups
salt	½ oz	2 teaspoons
black pepper		1 teaspoon

> *This dish may be served as a side dish to accompany an entrée (particularly a spicy one) or it may be served as an entrée.*

1. Wash beans, place in pot, cover with water, soak in refrigerator overnight.
2. Bring beans (covered with water) to boil, reduce heat and simmer until almost tender, about 45 minutes to 1 hour. Add more water, if necessary to prevent burning.
3. Heat oil in pan, add onion and garlic, and sauté until soft, about 4 minutes.
4. Add rice, sauté until rice begins to brown.
5. Add water, salt, black pepper, beans, and remaining bean liquid. Bring to boil, reduce heat, cover, simmer 20 minutes, and remove from heat. All liquid should be absorbed.
6. Let sit 10 minutes still covered.
7. Correct seasonings, serve.

Moros y Cristianos (Black Beans and Rice); photo courtesy of Dorling Kindersley

COU-COU (Barbados)

Cornmeal Mush with Okra

Number of Servings: 13   Cooking Method: Boil
Serving Size: 4 oz
Total Yield: 3 lbs, 4 oz

> Refrigerate leftover cou-cou. When firm, slice and sauté (like polenta).

INGREDIENTS	WEIGHT	VOLUME
cornmeal	7½ oz	2 cups
water, cold	2 lbs, 8 oz	5 cups
okra, cut into ¼-inch rounds	12 oz	3½ cups
salt	½ oz	2 teaspoons
hot sauce		1 teaspoon or to taste
butter	1 oz	2 tablespoons

1. Combine cornmeal and 1 pound (2 cups) water in bowl, set aside.
2. Bring remaining water to boil, add okra, and boil until tender, about 4 to 5 minutes.
3. Reduce heat to low, add salt, gradually add cornmeal, stirring constantly with wooden spoon.
4. Cook, stirring constantly, until mixture becomes very thick and begins to leave sides of pan.
5. Transfer to bowl, place butter on top to melt, serve immediately.

CARIBBEAN BANANAS

Number of Servings: 10   Cooking Method: Sauté
Serving Size: 1 banana

INGREDIENTS	WEIGHT	VOLUME
butter	5 oz	10 tablespoons or 1 stick + 2 tablespoons

Cooked sugar mixture just before adding bananas

Caribbean Bananas

INGREDIENTS	WEIGHT	VOLUME
brown sugar	10½ oz	1½ cups
lime juice, fresh	2 oz	¼ cup
dark rum	8 oz	1 cup
allspice, ground	¼ oz	2 teaspoons
cinnamon, ground		1 teaspoon
bananas, peeled, quartered (sliced in half through width and length) or sliced diagonally into slices about 2½- to 3-inches long	3 lbs, 2 oz	10 each

ice cream, if desired

1. Melt butter in skillet, add brown sugar, stirring constantly. Cook over medium heat until thick and syruplike, about 2 to 3 minutes.
2. Add lime juice, rum, allspice, and cinnamon. Cook until thick, about 2 to 3 minutes. Light rum to burn off alcohol, if desired.*
3. Add banana pieces, turn gently to coat them thoroughly with syrup, cook until slightly softened, about 1 or 2 minutes.
4. Serve immediately, alone or over ice cream.

*Be very careful! If burning rum, carefully hold match to liquid in skillet. Immediately move hand out of the way. Gently shake pan until flame subsides, then proceed.

Glossary

achiote Ground annatto seeds used in cooking that give a yellow color to the dish, used frequently in Mexico

adobo A seasoning paste containing ground chili peppers, herbs, spices, and vinegar used in many preparations, including meats and salsas in Mexico

aioli Mayonnaise flavored with garlic

aji Spicy chili seasoning frequently used in the cooking of Peru

al dente Literally "to the tooth," meaning cooked until done but still crisp, Italian term

antipasto An assorted appetizer platter usually containing salami, cheese, olives, and grilled vegetables, popular in Italy

aquavit Literally "water of life" in Swedish, a strong liquor made from potatoes or grains, its flavoring comes from caraway, anise, fennel, coriander, star anise, or any combination of these herbs, first made in the 1400s

arepa Type of cornbread commonly eaten in Venezuela and Colombia

***Ashkenazi* Jews** Jewish people with Eastern European heritage

bacala Salted cod fish prepared in Italy

Backerei German bakeries that sell all sorts of breads and rolls

bangers and mash Sausages and mashed potatoes served in pubs throughout the British Isles

barbie The Australian term for a barbecue grill

basmati An aromatic type of long grain rice preferred in India, grown in the foothills of the Himalayas

beef *stroganoff* A stewlike dish consisting of pieces of beef cooked with mushrooms, onions, and sour cream, originated in Russia

berbere Spicy seasoning mixture used in Ethiopia containing cumin, coriander, ginger, cardamom, nutmeg, cinnamon, allspice, paprika, fenugreek, salt, pepper, and cayenne

beurre blanc Butter sauce often used in France

bigos The national dish of Poland, consists of sauerkraut cooked with a variety of meats and sausages

biriyani   A baked rice dish that usually contains *basmati* rice flavored with saffron and meat, popular in India

biscuits   British word for cookies

blinis   Small, buckwheat pancakes traditionally topped with sour cream, smoked salmon, caviar, or other toppings, originated in Russia

borekas   Turnovers of phyllo dough filled with spinach or potato, popular in Israel

borscht   Soup made from beets and other ingredients, popular in Eastern Europe

bourewors   A popular Afrikaner sausage dish

Braunschweiger   Liverwurst or liver sausage that originated in the town of Braunschweig in northern Germany

bredie   A stew served in South Africa containing lamb or mutton, onions, and other vegetables

brigades   Teams of people working in the kitchen who prepare food items according to the type of cooking techniques involved in the preparation

brodetto   Italian fish soup resembling the French soup, *bouillabaise*

bulgogi   Marinated strips of beef grilled at the table, a popular Korean dish

bulgur   Cracked wheat that is boiled and then dried (dehydrated)

burrito   A taco prepared with a wheat tortilla, popular in Mexico

café au lait   Strong coffee mixed with warmed milk served throughout France

callaloo   Greens obtained from the taro plant; also the name of a soup served in the Caribbean Islands made with greens and other ingredients, including salt pork, crab, and/or coconut milk

calvados   Apple brandy made in Normandy in the northwest of France

Campari   Bitter, red liquor served as an aperitif from the region of Lombard (in Italy)

cannellini   White kidney beans frequently consumed in Italy

cassoulet   A one-pot dish containing various meats, white beans, and herbs; originated in Languedoc (in France)

caste   One's social class; four distinct *castes* or social levels exist in Indian society and relatively little intermingling occurs between these *castes*

cawl   Clear broth containing vegetables served in Wales (British Isles)

cecina   Dried beef popular in northern Mexico

cena   Light evening meal served around nine or ten o'clock in Mexico

ceviche   Dish consisting of raw fish marinated in citrus juices with other seasonings; the citrus juice "cooks" the fish, changing its appearance from raw to opaque; originally from Peru, *ceviche* is served throughout Latin America

challah   Braided egg bread that is served traditionally on the Sabbath and all holidays in Israel and in Jewish homes throughout the world

chao   Cooking technique known as stir-frying; Chinese term

chapti **flour**   A finely ground whole wheat flour

charcuterie   French word that refers to all sorts of sausages and cured meats

charlotte russe   A molded dessert consisting of a core of Bavarian cream folded with whipped cream surrounded by ladyfinger biscuits, a French confection

chartreuse   A molded dish with a decorative outside of colorful vegetables and an inside containing vegetables, game, and/or poultry *chayote* A common vegetable in Mexico sometimes called a green pear

chelo Steamed rice popular in the Middle East

chelo kebah A dish consisting of rice, marinated lamb, spices, and yogurt; the national dish of Iran

chili relleno A chili pepper stuffed with cheese, meat, or another filling, then dipped in batter and deep-fried, served in Mexico

chimichanga A deep-fried burrito, popular in Mexico

chips Thickly cut French fries served throughout the British Isles

cholent Known as Sabbath stew; a slowly cooked casserole containing rice or barley, beans, meat, and potatoes; traditionally cooked at a low temperature in an oven in a commercial bakery all Friday night then eaten Saturday, as no work may be performed on the Sabbath; served in Israel and Eastern Europe

chorizo A pork sausage flavored with garlic and paprika popular in Spain and Mexico

choucroute Popular casserole containing sauerkraut, various meats, and sausage, usually accompanied by boiled potatoes, served in Alsace-Lorraine (in France)

churros *Choux* pastry dough deep-fried in olive oil and eaten at breakfast; sold by street vendors in Spain

chutney Spicy relish made from fruit or vegetable used as a condiment to accompany many foods, popular in India

cockaleekie A thick chicken soup containing leeks and barley from Scotland

colcannon An Irish dish containing potatoes mixed with kale or cabbage

color An orange-red flavoring that combines garlic, paprika, and melted fat; used in Chile

comida The main meal of the day in Mexico, eaten around two o'clock in the afternoon

confit A method of slow cooking goose or duck in fat, popular in France

congee Rice (or millet or barley) porridge served in China for breakfast, to babies, and to ill people

couscous A tiny pasta shaped like a grain, made from semolina, popular in the northern part of Africa

creole Style of cooking melding Incan and Spanish culinary components

crêpes Thin, delicate pancakes, served rolled around a savory or sweet filling; originated in Brittany (in France)

dal Actually means split legumes; also refers to a dish of mildly spiced lentil purée widely consumed in the north of India

dashi Japanese stock made from dried bonito and dried kelp, forms the foundation for much Japanese cookery, including soups and braised dishes

dendê An orange-colored oil derived from the palm; brought to Brazil by slaves from western Africa where it is used extensively

dhwen-jang Bean paste, Korean

dim sum Snack foods eaten for lunch or any time throughout the day; originated in the southern region of Canton (in China), can include soups, steamed buns, stuffed dumplings, sweet and savory pastries, and much more

dolma A filling usually of meat and/or rice enclosed in an edible wrapper such as grape leaves or cabbage leaves, popular throughout the Middle East

Emmentaler   Type of Swiss cheese from Bavaria

empanada   Small turnover or pie filled with any combination of meats and seasonings wrapped in a soft, flaky crust, popular in South America and Spain

escabeche   Pickled peppers or vegetables served in Mexico

falafel   Fried chickpea patties served in pita bread topped with salad and a *tahini* sauce; known as Israeli hot dogs; served throughout the Middle East

feijoada completa   Dish combining beans with a variety of smoked and cured meats and seasonings, the national dish of Brazil

feta   A sheep's milk cheese with a salty flavor and crumbly texture, quite popular throughout the Middle East

fish and chips   Deep-fried fish and thickly cut French fries, served with malt vinegar; popular throughout the British Isles

fjords   Inlets in Scandinavia

foie gras   The highly prized goose liver prominent in France, produced by force-feeding geese so they develop large livers for this delicacy

Forellen blau   Literally meaning "blue trout" in German, this fish is prepared by dropping a live trout in boiling water containing a little vinegar; the vinegar causes the skin of the fish to take on a blue cast, therefore the name

frikadeller   Ground meat mixture that is made into meatballs, patties, or used as forcemeat; popular in Denmark

frito misto di Mare   Assorted deep-fried fish and seafood; Italian term

gado-gado   An Indonesian salad consisting of a variety of vegetables accompanied by peanut sauce dressing

garde manger   Preparation of cold foods and garnishes

gazpacho   Cold tomato vegetable soup; originated in Andalusia (in Spain)

gefilte **fish**   A fish dumpling that is served cold and usually accompanied by horseradish; originated in Eastern Europe, served in Israel

ghee   Clarified butter, cooking fat of choice throughout India

golabki   Polish stuffed cabbage roll cooked in a tomato-based sweet and sour sauce

golubtsi   Russian stuffed cabbage roll surrounded by a sour cream sauce

goulash   Hungarian beef stew containing onions, tomatoes, and potatoes

grappa   Clear-colored, sharp-tasting brandy made in Italy

gravlax   Salmon cured with salt, sugar, and dill, popular in Scandinavia

gremolada   Aromatic ingredients, including lemon zest, parsley, rosemary, sage, and garlic that are added to braised veal shanks (*ossobuco*) a few minutes before serving; Italian term

guacamole   A spread consisting of mashed avocado, onion, tomato, and usually chili peppers; ingredients vary from region to region, popular throughout Mexico

gyros   Lamb cooked on a rotisserie, then sliced in thin shavings and served in pita bread or plain; served in Greece

haggis   Scottish dish consisting of sheep's heart, liver, and lung mixed with oatmeal, stuffed in a sheep's stomach and boiled

haricots   Thin, tender green beans; French word

harissa   Hot pepper paste used in Morocco

hoisin   A sweet and spicy sauce made from soybeans used in cooking, marinades, and dips in China

holubtsi   Ukrainian stuffed cabbage rolls filled with meat, kasha, and rice *hummus*　A spread combining chickpeas with garlic, lemon juice, *tahini*, and other ingredients; served throughout the Middle East

injera　A spongy flatbread served in Ethiopia, used to scoop food

jambon Serrano　Spanish cured ham with a sweet-salty taste similar to the *prosciutto* of Italy

kadayif　A shredded variety of phyllo dough that looks like shredded wheat

kaeng　Thai word for liquid, refers to amount of liquid in a dish

Kaffeestunde　Literally translated "coffee hour" in German, a late afternoon snack consisting of pastry and coffee or other beverage

karahi　A wok-type deep pan with a rounded bottom and handles on each side used for frying in India

kasha　Buckwheat groats, which is a grain

kashrut　The rules governing kosher diet and preparation

katsuo　Dried bonito shavings; bonito is a fish in the mackerel family, frequently used in Japanese cookery

kecap　Sweet soy sauce used in Indonesia

kibbe　Ground lamb and grain patty that is served either raw or cooked, popular throughout the Middle East

kibbutz　A farm collective in Israel where the people who live and work on the farm actually own the entire business

kimch'i　Spicy, fermented cabbage or vegetable mixture popular in Korea; served at every meal

kippers　Smoked herring, frequently served at breakfast or tea in the British Isles

Kirschwasser　Strong cherry liqueur produced in the Black Forest (in Germany)

klippfisk　Popular dish containing salted cod; served in Norway

knedlíky　Dumplings served frequently in the Czech Republic

knish　A dumpling consisting of dough surrounding one of several fillings; popular in Israel

kombu　Dried kelp, a seaweed often used in Japanese cookery

Konditorei　Bakeries that sell pastries found in Germany; they usually contain tables and chairs where customers can sit and order a slice of pastry or ice cream with coffee or other beverages

kugel　Often called noodle pudding, a casserole usually consisting of noodles, cottage cheese, sour cream, raisins, and cinnamon; other vegetables can form a kugel, popular in Israel

labaneh　A cheese made from curdled yogurt, served in the Middle East

lassi　A yogurt drink popular in India

latkes　Potato pancakes, traditionally served at Chanukah

Lebkuchen　Spiced honey cookie eaten alone or baked in large pieces and used as the base for gingerbread houses; popular in Germany

mamaliga　Cornmeal mush served in Romania, resembles the Italian polenta

manioc　A starchy root vegetable sometimes called cassava

marinara　A tomato-based sauce containing no meat; served often in Italy

masa　Ground corn used for making tortillas and other foods in Mexico

masala　A mixture of spices frequently used in India, also called a spice blend *mazza*   Appetizers served throughout the Middle East

mealies   A porridge made from corn, often consumed by poor people in South Africa

merienda   Similar to the English tea, pastries and coffee or hot chocolate are served around six in the evening in Mexico

meseta   High, dry plateaus in Spain

Metzgerie   Shops carrying cold cuts and sausages in Germany

mezze   Appetizers served throughout the Middle East

millet   A grain

minestrone   Italian vegetable soup

mirin   Japanese sweet rice wine used for cooking

miso   Fermented bean paste, used as a flavoring for soups or sauces, Japanese

mititei   Garlic-infused meat balls from Romania

Mittagessen   The main meal of the day in Germany, served in the afternoon around twelve or one o'clock

mole   Savory Mexican sauce containing unsweetened chocolate, chilies, tomatoes, and spices

Molkerien   Shops selling milk, cheeses, and other dairy products in Germany

monsoons   Seasonal winds that affect the weather

moussaka   A dish consisting of alternating layers of ground lamb, fried eggplant, and sauce from Greece

mutton   Old lamb, which contains a stronger flavor and tougher texture than younger lamb

nabémono   One-pot cookery common in Japan; similar to fondue, diners cook their own food in a pot of stock heating on the dining table

nám pla   Fish sauce used extensively in Thailand

nu'ó'c mǎm   Fish sauce used extensively in Vietnam

olla podrida   A casserole containing almost anything that can be stewed; literally translated "rotten pot"; originated in central Spain

ossobuco   Braised veal shanks popular in Italy

outback   The large areas of bush country in the interior sections of Australia

ouzo   An anise-flavored alcoholic beverage that turns transparent when mixed with water; a popular drink in Greece

paan   An assortment of aromatic spices and herbs to clear the palate and aid digestion that is served at the end of the meal in India

paella   A casserole of saffron rice with a variety of meats, chicken, seafood, and vegetables named for the pot in which it is cooked; originated in Valencia (Spain); every region has its own variation of this national dish

pampa   Humid grasslands found in Argentina and Uruguay; ideal lands for raising livestock

pancetta   Unsmoked pork used for flavoring in Italy

panchan   Condiments, pickles and salads, served with Korean meals

paprikash   Hungarian stew–type dish containing plenty of paprika

parve   Kosher foods that can accompany either meat or dairy products

pasta e fagioli   Tomato-based soup containing pasta and beans; popular in Italy

pasty   A turnover usually filled with meat, potatoes, and vegetables served in the British Isles

Pavlova An Australian dessert consisting of a large meringue shell filled with whipped cream and fresh fruits; named for the famous ballerina, Anna Pavlova

pebre A sauce made of onions, garlic, chili peppers, coriander, vinegar, and olive oil; used as a seasoning in Chile

pepper pot Vegetable soup prepared with any available meat and vegetables; popular in the Caribbean Islands

pesto Basil garlic sauce served with pasta and other dishes, originated in the city of Genoa (in Italy)

Pfefferpotthast A stew of beef short ribs containing lots of pepper; served in Germany

phó' Rice noodle soup in a meat broth strongly flavored with cilantro, garlic, and *nu'ó'c mӑm;* commonly eaten for breakfast in Vietnam but served at any meal; considered the national dish of Vietnam

picante Mexican word for hot and spicy

piripiri Spicy seasoning mixture used in Mozambique

piroshki Baked or fried dumplings filled with meat and cabbage popular in Russia

***pita* bread** Also called pocket bread; a yeast bread dough formed into a disk then baked in a very hot oven, a pocket forms in the bread during baking; popular throughout the Middle East

polenta Starch made of cornmeal that sometimes replaces pasta in the north of Italy

polo An Iranian favorite dish, consisting of steamed rice containing combinations of fruits, vegetables, nuts, and meats

ponzu A dipping sauce; used in Japan

porotos granados Dish containing a mixture of beans, corn, and squash; the national dish of Chile

porridge Cooked cereal, usually oatmeal; British term

potato crisps British for the American version of potato chips

prawns Large shrimp

primo piatto Literally first course in Italy, this usually consists of soup, pasta, rice, or polenta and is followed by the meat course

prosciutto Salted, air-cured ham from Italy

quesadillas A tortilla topped with cheese and roasted, peeled peppers or other ingredients; if desired, folded in half and fried until the cheese melts; served in Mexico

queso The Mexican word for cheese

quinoa A grain that thrives in the mountains; originally raised by the Inca Indians and still consumed today

ragu Italian tomato-based sauce containing meat

raita Yogurt salad, popular in India

retsina A Greek sharp wine

rijsttafel Literally meaning rice table, opulent display of many different dishes accompanied by rice, requiring many servants for preparation and service, developed by the Dutch settlers in Indonesia

risotto Creamy rice dish popular in the north of Italy

rømmegrøt Porridge made with sour cream that is popular in Norway

rôtisseur Person in kitchen responsible for foods that require roasting; French word *sake*   Japanese rice wine, served warm in the winter

saltimbocca   Dish consisting of pounded veal with a thin slice of *prosciutto*, seasoned and braised in white wine (Italian)

sambar   Spicy lentil dish widely consumed in the south of India

Sambuca   Clear, anise-flavored liqueur served as an afterdinner cordial; originated in Italy

samp   Cornmeal mush widely consumed in central Africa

sarma   Spicy stuffed cabbage roll, containing cayenne and garlic; prepared in Yugoslavia

sarmale   Romanian stuffed cabbage roll

sashimi   Raw fish sliced thinly, accompanied by *wasabi;* served in Japan

satay   Grilled meat accompanied by a spicy peanut sauce; commonly served in Indonesia

saucier   Person in kitchen responsible for preparation of sauces; French word

Sauerbraten   Beef marinated in an acidic liquid (often vinegar, but it depends on the region), then braised; served throughout Germany

Schnitzel   Veal cutlets that are pounded thin, sometimes breaded, and then pan-fried, popular in Germany

Schwartzwälder Kirschtorte   Black Forest cherry cake, a torte featuring cake layers flavored with *Kirschwasser,* a cherry liquor, filled with whipped cream and a cherry filling; originated in the Black Forest region (in Germany)

scone   A slightly sweetened bread product (like an American biscuit) containing dried currants; popular in the British Isles

selametan   Ceremonial feast that marks important events in Indonesia

Sephardic **Jews**   Jewish people from Greece, Turkey, Spain, and Northern Africa

shearer's stew   Lamb stew with dumplings served in Australia

shepherd's pie   A dish containing cooked beef topped with mashed potatoes; served throughout the British Isles

shish kebob   Smaller cubes of meat and sometimes vegetables placed on a skewer, then grilled over fire; widely consumed in the Middle East

shwarma   Grilled slices of meat served in a pita with salad, served in the Middle East

smörgåsbord   A buffet laden with all sorts of meats, seafood, vegetables, salads, cheeses, and breads; contains as many as sixty food items; popular in Sweden

smørrebrød   Literally "buttered bread," an opened-faced sandwich with a base of thin bread or cracker that is spread with butter, then topped with meat, seafood, or cheese and crowned with an eye-catching garnish; the Danes are known for these sandwiches, which resemble a canapé

soba   Oriental noodle made from buckwheat

soju   Korean distilled grain liquor

soto   Indonesian chicken and coconut milk soup

spaetzel   A starch that is a cross between a dumpling and a noodle; popular in Germany and areas in France near the German border

spanakopita   A dish consisting of phyllo dough layered with a spinach and feta mixture from Greece

steak and kidney pie   A stewlike combination of kidneys and steak topped with a pastry crust popular in the British Isles

Stollen Traditional Christmas bread that originated in Dresden (in Germany)

sushi Raw fish, vinegared rice, and often vegetable(s) rolled in a wrapper like *nori* seaweed; accompanied by *wasabi;* popular in Japan

taco Meat, beans, cheese, vegetables, or any combination of filling possibilities placed down the middle of a soft corn tortilla, topped with sauce, then the tortilla is rolled to encase the filling; popular in Mexico

tagine A type of stew containing meat and often fruit served in Morocco; a pot used for cooking a *tagine* (stew) with a cone-shaped lid containing a hole on the top so some steam can escape

tahini Sesame seed paste, like peanut butter made from sesame seeds; used throughout the Middle East

tamales Mexican entrée consisting of corn husks or banana leaves encasing filling ingredients that are steamed, then the husks or leaves are discarded and the filling is eaten

tandoori **oven** A clay oven used to roast skewers of meats, poultry, seafood, or vegetables, as well as bake flatbreads over very high heat; used in the north of India

tapas Small snacks or appetizers served throughout Iberia

tarte **Tatin** An upside-down apple pie; apples, butter, and sugar are caramelized, then topped with pie dough and baked; the cooked tart is inverted on a plate after baking; a French confection

tava Concave griddle made of cast iron used in Indian cookery

teff A grain grown at high elevations

tempura Individual food items coated with a very light batter and deep-fried; well-known Japanese dish

thali Actually refers to the platter or tray that holds the small bowls during a meal, but known as the Indian method for eating meals where each diner receives a platter containing small bowls of the various foods being served

tilapia A rapid-growing freshwater fish that thrives in warm waters

tofu Soybean curd; a cheeselike substance made from soybeans; a complete protein

töltött kaposzta Hungarian stuffed cabbage roll

tortilla A flat, unleavened disk made from wheat or corn and cooked on a dry griddle; eaten at every meal; Mexican bread

treacle A sweet syrup such as maple syrup or molasses; popular in the British Isles

tsai-fan Protein or vegetable served with rice

tumpeng An Indonesian ceremonial rice dish consisting of a cone of rice decorated with a variety of foods, which is served at all important events

udon Oriental noodle made from wheat

varenyky Boiled dumplings with potatoes, sauerkraut, cheese, or fruits, garnished with sour cream, fried onions, or bacon bits; served in the Ukraine

wasabi Very pungent, spicy hot, green horseradish dipping sauce served as a condiment with raw fish in Japan

Westphalian ham A delicate, smoked ham similar to Italian *prosciutto* prepared in Westphalia (in Germany), served sliced very thinly on buttered rye or pumpernickel bread

wok A pan with sloping sides and a rounded bottom used for stir-frying

wot Ethiopian term for stew

Wurst   Any of the countless varieties of sausages served in Germany

Yin-Yang   Complex philosophy that affects food, art, and other aspects of Chinese life; deals with combining opposites to achieve balance and harmony; yin represents the feminine or dark while yang stands for the masculine or light; the important issue remains the successful combining of these two forces to achieve the harmony and balance in the food, art, or any medium which leads to balance and harmony in the body and spirit

Yorkshire pudding   A savory battercake cooked in meat fat, usually served with roast beef in the British Isles

zabaglione   Dessert sauce containing eggs, sugar, and Marsala wine; popular in Italy

zakuska   Assorted hors d'oeuvres or bite-size morsels of food

Zwiebelkuchen   Quichelike pie consisting of a pastry shell with a filling of bacon, eggs, cream, and onions; popular in Germany

Bibliography

Aaron, Jan, and Salom, Georgine Sachs. *The Art of Mexican Cooking*. New York: Doubleday, 1965.

Alford, Jeffrey and Duguid, Naomi. *Hot, Sour, Salty, Sweet: A Culinary Journey through Southeast Asia*. New York: Artisan, 2000.

Bailey, Adrian, and the Editors of Time-Life Books. *The Cooking of the British Isles*. New York: Time-Life Books, 1969.

Bailey, Adrian, and the Editors of Time-Life Books. *Recipes: The Cooking of the British Isles*. New York: Time-Life Books, 1969.

Bannerman, Colin. *Acquired Tastes Celebrating Australia's Culinary History*. Canberra, Australia: National Library of Australia, 1998.

Bar-David, Molly Lyons. *The Israeli Cookbook*. New York: Crown Publishers, 1964.

Bates, Margaret. *The Belfast Cookery Book*. London: Pergamon Press Ltd., 1967.

Beck, Simone. *Food & Friends*. New York: Viking Penguin, 1991.

Bonekamp, Gunnevi. *Scandinavian Cooking*. New York: Garland Books, 1973.

Břizová, Joza, et al. *The Czechoslovak Cookbook*. New York: Crown Publishers, Inc., 1965.

Brown, Dale, and Editors of Time-Life Books. *The Cooking of Scandinavia*. New York: Time-Life Books, 1968.

Bugialli, Giuliano. *Foods of Tuscany*. New York: Stewart, Tabori & Chang, 1992.

Casas, Penelope. *The Foods and Wine of Spain*. New York: Alfred A. Knopf, 1982.

Casas, Penelope. *Tapas, The Little Dishes of Spain*. New York: Alfred A. Knopf, 1989.

Chamberlain, Lesley. *The Food and Cooking of Eastern Europe*. London: Penguin Books, 1989.

Chamberlain, Samuel. *British Bouquet: An Epicurean Tour of Britain*. New York: Gourmet Distributing Company, 1963.

Child, Julia, Bertholle, Louisette, and Beck, Simone. *Mastering the Art of French Cooking*, Volume I. New York: Alfred A. Knopf, 1961.

Claiborne, Craig, Franey, Pierre, and the Editors of Time-Life Books. *Classic French Cooking*. New York: Time-Life Books, 1970.

Condon, Richard, and Bennett, Wendy. *The Mexican Stove.* New York: Double-day, 1973.

Craig, Elizabeth. *The Scottish Cookery Book.* London: Andre Deutsch, 1956.

Cullen, Nuala. *Savoring Ireland.* New York: Quadrillion Publishing Ltd., 1998.

DeMers, John. *Caribbean Cooking.* New York: HPBooks, 1997.

Dosti, Rose. *Middle Eastern Cooking.* Tuscon, AZ: HP Books, 1982.

Dosti, Rose. *Mideast & Mediterranean Cuisines.* Tuscon, AZ: Fisher Books, 1993.

Downer, Lesley. *At the Japanese Table: New and Traditional Recipes.* San Francisco: Chronical Books, 1993.

Duong, Binh, and Kiesel, Marcia. *Simple Art of Vietnamese Cooking.* New York: Prentice Hall, 1991.

Dutt, Monica. *The Art of Indian Cooking.* New York: Bantam Books, Inc., 1972.

Ellmer, Bruno H. *Classical and Contemporary Italian Cooking for Professionals.* New York: Van Nostrand Reinhold, 1990.

Feibleman, Peter S., and the Editors of Time-Life Books. *The Cooking of Spain and Portugal.* New York: Time-Life Books, 1969.

Feibleman, Peter S., and the Editors of Time-Life Books. *Recipes: The Cooking of Spain and Portugal.* New York: Time-Life Books, 1969.

Fisher, M.F.K., and the Editors of Time-Life Books. *The Cooking of Provincial France.* New York: Time-Life Books, 1968.

Fitzgibbon, Theodora. *A Taste of Ireland.* London: Weidenfeld and Nicolson, 1968.

Freson, Robert. *The Taste of France.* New York: Stewart, Tabori & Chang, 1983.

Ganor, Avi, and Maiberg, Ron. *Taste of Israel.* New York: Rizzoli International Publications, 1990.

Germaine, Elizabeth, and Burckhardt, Ann L. *Cooking the Australian Way.* Minneapolis, MN: Lerner Publications Company, 1990.

Gopal, Sharda. *Step by Step Indian Cooking.* New York: Barron's Educational Series, 1987.

Guermont, Claude, and Frumkin, Paul. *The Norman Table.* New York: Charles Scribner's Sons, 1985.

Gupta, Pranati Sen. *The Art of Indian Cuisine.* New York: Hawthorn Books, Inc., 1974.

Hachten, Harva. *Best of Regional African Cooking.* New York: Hippocrene Books, 1970.

Hafner, Dorinda. *A Taste of Africa.* Berkley, CA: Ten Speed Press, 1993.

Hahn, Emily, and the Editors of Time-Life Books. *The Cooking of China.* New York: Time-Life Books, 1968.

Hahn, Emily, and the Editors of Time-Life Books. *Recipes: The Cooking of China.* New York: Time-Life Books, 1968.

Harbutt, Juliet. *Cheese.* Minocqua, WI: Willow Creek Press, 1999.

Harris, Dunstan A. *Island Cooking: Recipes from the Caribbean.* Freedom, CA: Crossing Press, 1988.

Harris, Jessica. *The Africa Cookbook: Tastes of a Continent.* New York: Simon & Schuster, 1998.

Harris, Jessica B. *Tasting Brazil.* New York: Maxmillan Publishing Company, 1992.

Hayes, Babetta. *Two Hundred Years of Australian Cooking.* Melbourne, Australia: Thomas Nelson, Ltd., 1970.

Hazelton, Nika Standen. *The Cooking of Germany.* New York: Time-Life Books, 1969.

Hazelton, Nika Standen. *Classical Scandinavian Cooking.* New York: Charles Scribner's Sons, 1987.

Hazen, Marcella. *More Classic Italian Cooking*. New York: Alfred A. Knopf, 1978.

Hazen, Marcella. *Marcella Cucina*. New York: Harper Collins Publishers, 1997.

Hillman, Howard. *Great Peasant Dishes of the World*. Boston, MA: Houghton Mifflin Company, 1983.

Jacobs, Lauraine. *New Taste New Zealand*. North Shore City, New Zealand: Tandem Press, 1996.

Jaffrey, Madhur. *Madhur Jaffrey's Indian Cooking*. New York: Barron's Educational Series, 1983.

Jaffrey, Madhur. *A Taste of India*. New York: Atheneum, 1986.

Jaffrey, Madhur. *Far Eastern Cookery*. New York: Harper & Row, 1989.

Jenkins, Steven. *Cheese Primer*. New York: Workman Publishing, 1996.

Kasper, Lynne Rossetto. *The Italian Country Table*. New York: Scribner, 1999.

Katzen, Mollie. *Moosewood Cookbook*. Berkeley, CA: Ten Speed Press, 1977.

Kennedy, Diana. *The Cuisines of Mexico*. New York: Harper & Row, Publishers, 1972.

Kennedy, Diana. *Recipes from the Regional Cooks of Mexico*. New York: Harper and Row, 1978.

Kennedy, Diana. *My Mexico*. New York: Clarkson Potter, 1998.

Koplan, Steven, Smith, Brian H., and Weiss, Michael A. *Exploring Wine*. New York: Van Nostrand Reinhold, 1996.

Lalbachan, Pamela. *The Complete Caribbean Cookbook*. Boston, MA: Charles E. Tuttle Co., Inc., 1994.

Laurd, Elisabeth. *The Old World Kitchen*. New York: Bantam Books, 1987.

Law, Ruth. *The Southeast Asia Cookbook*. New York: Donald I. Fine, Inc., 1990.

Lenôtre, Gaston. *Lenôtre's Desserts and Pastries*. New York: Barron's, 1975.

Leonard, Jonathan Norton, and the Editors of Time-Life Books. *Latin American Cooking*. New York: Time-Life Books, 1968.

Leonard, Jonathan Norton, and the Editors of Time-Life Books. *Recipes: Latin American Cooking*. New York: Time-Life Books, 1976.

Leung Mai. *The Chinese People's Cookbook*. New York: Harper & Row, 1979.

Levy, Faye. *Faye Levy's International Jewish Cookbook*. New York: Warner Books, Inc., 1991.

Lo, Kenneth. *Regional Chinese Cookbook*. New York: Larousse and Co., 1981.

MacMillan, Maya Kaimal. *Curried Flavors*. New York: Abbeville Press Publishers, 1996.

Mark, Theonie. *Greek Islands Cooking*. Boston, MA: Little, Brown and Company, 1974.

Marks, Copeland. *The Indonesian Kitchen*. New York: Atheneum, 1981.

Martin, Yan Kit. *Chinese Cooking: Step-by-Step Techniques*. New York: Crescent Books, 1984.

Morris, Sally. *British and Irish Cooking*. New York: Garland Books, 1972.

Nelson, Kay Shaw. *The Eastern European Cookbook*. New York: Dover Publications, 1973.

Newman, Graeme. *The Down Under Cookbook*. New York: Harrow and Heston, 1987.

Newman, Graeme, and Newman, Betsy. *Good Food from Australia*. New York: Hippocrene Books, 1997.

Ngô, Bach, and Zimmerman, Gloria. *The Classic Cuisine of Vietnam*. New York: Barron's, 1979.

Nickles, Harry, and the Editors of Time-Life Books. *Middle Eastern Cooking*. New York: Time-Life Books, 1969.

Ojakangas, Beatrice. *Scandinavian Cooking*. Tucson, AZ: HP Books, 1983.

Ortiz, Elisabeth Lambert. *The Complete Book of Mexican Cooking.* New York: J. B. Lippincott, 1965.

Osborne, Christine. *Australian and New Zealand Food and Drink.* New York: Bookwright Press, 1989.

Papashvily, Helen, Papashvily, George, and the Editors of Time-Life Books. *Recipes: Russian Cooking.* New York: Time-Life Books, 1969.

Passmore, Jacki, and Reid, Daniel. *The Complete Chinese Cookbook.* New York: Exeter Books, 1982.

Rau, Santha Rama, and the Editors of Time-Life Books. *The Cooking of India.* New York: Time-Life Books, 1969.

Reekie, Jennie. *Traditional French Cooking.* New York: St. Martin's Press, 1975.

Roden, Claudia. *The Good Food of Italy Region by Region.* New York: Alfred A. Knopf, 1990.

Roden, Claudia. *The Book of Jewish Food.* New York: Alfred A. Knopf, Inc., 1996.

Rojas-Lombardi, Felipe. *The Art of South American Cooking.* New York: HarperCollins Publishers, 1991.

Romagnoli, Margaret, and Romagnoli, G. Franco. *The Romagnolis' Table.* Boston, MA: Little, Brown and Company, 1975.

Ruggieri, Luisa de. *Italian Cooking.* New York: 'Round the World Cooking Library, 1972.

Sahni, Julie. *Classic Indian Cooking.* New York: William Morrow and Company, Inc., 1980.

Sahni, Julie. *Julie Sahni's Introduction to Indian Cooking.* Berkeley, CA: Ten Speed Press, 1998.

Scharfenberg, Horst. *The Cuisines of Germany.* New York: Poseidon Press, 1980.

Scott, David. *Recipes for an Arabian Night.* New York: Pantheon Books, 1983.

Seranne, Ann, and Gaden, Eileen. *The Best of Near Eastern Cookery.* New York: Doubleday, 1964.

Sheffer, Nelli, and Sheraton, Mimi. *Food Markets of the World.* New York: Harry N. Abrams, Inc., 1997.

Singh, Balbir. *Mrs. Balbir Singh's Indian Cookery.* London: Mills & Boon Limited, 1971.

Sodsook, Victor. *True Thai, The Modern Art of Thai Cooking.* New York: William Morrow and Company, Inc., 1995.

Solomon, Charmaine. *The Complete Asian Cookbook.* New York: McGraw-Hill Book Company, 1976.

Solomon, Jay. *A Taste of the Tropics.* Freedom, CA: Crossing Press, 1991.

Steinberg, Rafael, and the Editors of Time-Life Books. *Pacific and Southeast Asian Cooking.* New York: Time-Life Books, 1970.

Steinberg, Rafael, and the Editors of Time-Life Books. *Recipes: Pacific and Southeast Asian Cooking.* New York: Time-Life Books, 1972.

Tropp, Barbara. *The Modern Art of Chinese Cooking.* New York: William Morrow and Company, 1982.

Urakami, Hiroko. *Japanese Family-Style Recipes.* New York: Kodansha America, Inc., 1992.

Van der Post, Laurens, and the Editors of Time-Life Books. *African Cooking.* New York: Time-Life Books, 1970.

Volokh, Anne. *The Art of Russian Cuisine.* New York: Macmillan Company, 1983.

Von Bremzen, Anya, and Welchman, John. *Please to the Table: The Russian Cookbook.* New York: Workman Publishing Company, 1990.

Wason, Betty. *The Art of German Cooking.* New York: Doubleday & Company, Inc., 1967.

Wilde, Mary Poulos. *The Best of Ethnic Home Cooking.* Los Angeles, CA: J. P. Tarcher, Inc., 1981.

Willan, Anne. *French Regional Cooking.* New York: William Morrow and Company, Inc., 1981.

Wolfe, Linda, and the Editors of Time-Life Books. *The Cooking of the Caribbean Islands.* New York: Time-Life Books, 1970.

Wolfe, Linda, and the Editors of Time-Life Books. *Recipes: The Cooking of the Caribbean Islands.* New York: Time-Life Books, 1970.

World Book Encyclopedia. Chicago: World Book Inc., 1999.

Zane, Eva. *Middle Eastern Cookery.* New York: Charles Scribner's Sons, 1974.

SUBJECT INDEX

RECIPE INDEX

Recipes in Native Language

Recipes by Course in Native Language